Ecological Inference

Ecological Inference: New Methodological Strategies brings together a diverse group of scholars to survey the latest strategies for solving ecological inference problems in various fields. The last half decade has witnessed an explosion of research in ecological inference – the attempt to infer individual behavior from aggregate data. The uncertainties and the information lost in aggregation make ecological inference one of the most difficult areas of statistical inference, but such inferences are required in many academic fields, as well as by legislatures and the courts in redistricting, by businesses in marketing research, and by governments in policy analysis.

Gary King is the David Florence Professor of Government at Harvard University. He also serves as the director of the Harvard–MIT Data Center and as a member of the steering committee of Harvard's Center for Basic Research in the Social Sciences. He was elected president of the Society for Political Methodology and Fellow of the American Academy of Arts and Sciences. Professor King received his Ph.D. from the University of Wisconsin. He has won numerous awards for his work, including the Gosnell Prize for his book *A Solution to the Ecological Inference Problem* (1997), on which the research in this book builds. His home page can be found at http:// GKing.Harvard.edu.

Ori Rosen is Assistant Professor of Statistics at the University of Pittsburgh. His research includes work on semiparametric regression models, applications of mixtures-of-experts neural network models in regression, and applications of Markov chain Monte Carlo methods. Professor Rosen was educated at the Technion, and he later served as Mellon Postdoctoral Fellow at Northwestern University.

Martin A. Tanner is Professor of Statistics at Northwestern University. He has authored and coauthored nearly 100 research articles on wide-ranging topics in theoretical and applied statistics. His previous books include *Investigations for a Course in Statistics* (1990), *Tools for Statistical Inference* (1996), and *Statistics for the 21st Century* (2001). Professor Tanner is a Fellow of the American Statistical Association and the Royal Statistical Society, and he has been honored with the 1993 Mortimer Spiegelman Award as well as the American Statistical Association's Continuing Education Excellence Award. He has served as editor of the *Journal of the American Statistical Association (Theory and Methods)*. Professor Tanner received his Ph.D. from the University of Chicago.

Analytical Methods for Social Research

Series Editors

R. Michael Alvarez, California Institute of Technology
Nathaniel L. Beck, New York University
Lawrence L. Wu, New York University

Analytical Methods for Social Research presents texts on empirical and formal methods for the social sciences. Some series volumes are broad in scope, addressing multiple disciplines; others focus mainly on techniques applied within specific fields, such as political science, sociology, and demography.

Previously published:

Event History Modeling: A Guide for Social Scientists, Janet M. Box-Steffensmeier and Bradford S. Jones

Ecological Inference

New Methodological Strategies

Edited by

Gary King
Harvard University

Ori Rosen
University of Pittsburgh

Martin A. Tanner
Northwestern University

PUBLISHED BY THE PRESS SYNDICATE OF THE UNIVERSITY OF CAMBRIDGE
The Pitt Building, Trumpington Street, Cambridge, United Kingdom

CAMBRIDGE UNIVERSITY PRESS
The Edinburgh Building, Cambridge CB2 2RU, UK
40 West 20th Street, New York, NY 10011-4211, USA
477 Williamstown Road, Port Melbourne, VIC 3207, Australia
Ruiz de Alarcón 13, 28014 Madrid, Spain
Dock House, The Waterfront, Cape Town 8001, South Africa

http://www.cambridge.org

First published 2004

Printed in the United States of America

Typefaces Minion 10/12 pt., Helvetica Neue Condensed, and Lucida Typewriter
System LATEX 2_ε [TB]

A catalog record for this book is available from the British Library.

Library of Congress Cataloging in Publication Data

Ecological inference : new methodological strategies / edited by Gary King, Matrin A.
    Tanner, Ori Rosen.
      p.   cm.
    Includes bibliographical references (p.).
    ISBN 0-521-83513-5 – ISBN 0-521-54280-4 (pbk.)
      1. Social sciences – Statistical methods.   2. Political statistics.   3. Inference.   I. King, Gary.
    II. Tanner, Martin Abba, 1957–   III. Rosen, Ori.
    HA29.E27   2004
    330′.72′7 – dc22   2004045500

ISBN 0 521 83513 5 hardback
ISBN 0 521 54280 4 paperback

Contents

Contributors

Micah Altman Harvard-MIT Data Center (HMDC), Harvard University, Cambridge, Massachusetts

Eric J. Beh School of Quantitative Methods and Mathematical Sciences, University of Western Sydney, Sydney, Australia

Kenneth Benoit Department of Political Science, Trinity College, Dublin, Ireland

Ernesto Calvo Department of Political Science, University of Houston, Houston, Texas

Ray L. Chambers Southampton Statistical Sciences Research Institute, University of Southampton, Southampton, United Kingdom

Wendy K. Tam Cho Departments of Political Science and Statistics, University of Illinois at Urbana-Champaign, Urbana, Illinois

J. Kevin Corder Department of Political Science, Western Michigan University, Kalamazoo, Michigan

Carol A. Gotway Crawford National Center for Environmental Health, Centers for Disease Control and Prevention, Atlanta, Georgia

Rob Eisinga Department of Social Science Research Methods, University of Nijmegen, Nijmegen, The Netherlands

Marcelo Escolar Department of Geography, Universidad de Buenos Aires, Buenos Aires, Argentina

Philip Hans Franses Econometric Institute, Erasmus University, Rotterdam, The Netherlands

Daniela Giannetti Department of Political Science, University of Bologna, Bologna, Italy

Jeff Gill Department of Political Science, University of California, Davis, California

Bernard Grofman Department of Political Science, University of California, Irvine, California

Sebastien Haneuse Department of Biostatistics, University of Washington, Seattle, Washington

George G. Judge Department of Agricultural and Resource Economics, University of California, Berkeley, California

Gary King Center for Basic Research in the Social Sciences, Harvard University, Cambridge, Massachusetts

Michael Laver Department of Political Science, Trinity College, Dublin, Ireland

Jeffrey B. Lewis Department of Political Science, University of California, Los Angeles, California

Rogério Silva de Mattos Department of Economic Analysis, Federal University of Juiz de Fora, Minas Gerais, Brazil

Michael P. McDonald Department of Public & International Affairs, George Mason University, Fairfax, Virginia

Samuel Merrill Department of Mathematics and Computer Science, Wilkes University, Wilkes-Barre, Pennsylvania

Douglas J. Miller Department of Agricultural Economics, Purdue University, West Lafayette, Indiana

Ben Pelzer Department of Social Sciences Research Methods, University of Nijmegen, Nijmegen, The Netherlands

Kevin M. Quinn Center for Basic Research in the Social Sciences, Harvard University, Cambridge, Massachusetts

Ori Rosen Department of Statistics, University of Pittsburgh, Pittsburgh, Pennsylvania

Ruth Salway Department of Mathematical Sciences, University of Bath, Bath, United Kingdom

David G. Steel School of Mathematics and Applied Statistics, University of Wollongong, Wollongong, Australia

Martin A. Tanner Department of Statistics, Northwestern University, Evanston, Illinois

Álvaro Veiga Department of Electrical Engineering, Pontifical Catholic University of Rio de Janeiro (PUC-Rio), Rio de Janeiro, Brazil

D. Stephen Voss Department of Political Science, University of Kentucky, Lexington, Kentucky

Jonathan Wakefield Departments of Statistics and Biostatistics, University of Washington, Seattle, Washington

Christina Wolbrecht Department of Political Science, University of Notre Dame, Notre Dame, Indiana

Linda J. Young Department of Statistics, College of Medicine, University of Florida, Gainesville, Florida

Preface

The authors of the chapters in this volume hail from academic disciplines with markedly different substantive concerns. Indeed, we suspect that not many books have been written with contributions from political scientists, electrical engineers, economists, agricultural economists, geographers, statisticians, applied statisticians, mathematicians, public health researchers, biostatisticians, and computer scientists. Yet, while the substantive problems pursued by the diverse disciplinary origins of these researchers vary enormously, they all have a deep, if not widely recognized, methodological common ground. Although the style and terminology often obscure this fact, they all use roughly the same theories of inference and many of the same statistical methods. The subject of this book is *ecological inference*, the problem of reconstructing individual behavior from group-level data, which indeed turns out to be a key problem in all these fields, as well as a variety of others, which we were not able to include. Not only is ecological inference required in a growing number of applications, it has a large number of scholars working on the methods of ecological inference – now larger than at any time in history.

Because our work seems to have had a particularly visible role in the renewed interest in ecological inference, we found ourselves in a unique position of getting to know many otherwise unconnected scholars from this vast array of scholarly fields. So that our new scholarly acquaintances could get to know each other, begin to build on each other's work, and start to create a more densely connected scholarly network that spans everyone's traditional discipline, substantive concerns, and methodological commonalities, we held an intensive conference at Harvard University in June of 2002. The early version of the chapters herein were first presented during lively discussions at that conference. We hope the publication of this book enables methodologists whom we were not able to invite to the conference, or who find themselves working on similar issues, to now be able to join in the discussion. Others interested in different statistical problems may also find this work of some interest. The limited information available means that ecological inference is an especially difficult area of statistical inference, and so we have found that studying it illuminates fundamental problems that do not surface as clearly when learning statistics in the context of other applications.

We thank Kim Schader and Jaronica Fuller for their help in organizing a superb conference, and we appreciate the outstanding help of Kim, Colleen McMahon, Cindy Munroe, and Alison Ney in preparing this volume. Special thanks go to the Center for Basic Research in the Social Sciences for providing financial and logistical support for the conference. Our appreciation goes to the anonymous reviewers from Cambridge University Press for their insightful comments on the project. We especially appreciate the patience and efforts of our authors on whom we inflicted proposals, travel, presentations, discussants, and revisions and then called on them for subsequent rounds of review to provide written comments on each other's chapters. Finally, we are indebted to the crew at Cambridge University Press, including Ed Parsons and Eleanor Umali, for everything they have done to facilitate the entire publication process.

Gary King
Ori Rosen
Martin Tanner

INTRODUCTION

Information in Ecological Inference: An Introduction

Gary King, Ori Rosen, and Martin A. Tanner

Researchers in a diverse variety of fields often need to know about individual-level behavior and are not able to collect it directly. In these situations, where survey research or other means of individual-level data collection are infeasible, ecological inference is the best and often the only hope of making progress. Ecological inference is the process of extracting clues about individual behavior from information reported at the group or aggregate level.

For example, sociologists and historians try to learn who voted for the Nazi party in Weimar Germany, where thoughts of survey research are seven decades too late. Marketing researchers study the effects of advertising on the purchasing behavior of individuals, where only zip-code-level purchasing and demographic information are available. Political scientists and politicians study precinct-level electoral data and U.S. Census demographic data to learn about the success of candidate appeals with different voter groups in numerous small areal units where surveys have been infeasible (for cost or confidentiality reasons). To determine whether the U.S. Voting Rights Act can be applied in redistricting cases, expert witnesses, attorneys, judges, and government officials must infer whether African Americans and other minority groups vote differently from whites, even though the secret ballot hinders the process and surveys in racially polarized contexts are known to be of little value.

In these and numerous other fields of inquiry, scholars have no choice but to make ecological inferences. Fortunately for them, we have witnessed an explosion of statistical research into this problem in the last five years – both in substantive applications and in methodological innovations. In applications, the methods introduced by Duncan and Davis (1953) and by Goodman (1953) accounted for almost every use of ecological inference in any field for fifty years, but this stasis changed when King (1997) offered a model that combined and extended the approaches taken in these earlier works. His method now seems to dominate substantive research in academia, in private industry, and in voting rights litigation, where it was used in most American states in the redistricting period that followed the 2000 Census. The number and diversity of substantive application areas of ecological inference has soared recently as well. The speed of development of statistical research on ecological inference has paralleled the progress in applications, too, and in the last five years we have seen numerous new models, innovative methods, and novel computation schemes. This book offers a snapshot of some of the research at the cutting edge of this field in the hope of spurring statistical researchers to push out the frontiers and applied researchers to choose from a wider range of approaches.

Ecological inference is an especially difficult special case of statistical inference. The difficulty comes because some information is generally lost in the process of aggregation, and that information is sometimes systematically related to the quantities of interest. Thus, progress in this field has usually come from discovering new sources of information or inventing better ways of harvesting existing information and using it to improve our inferences about individual-level behavior. This book is organized around these sources of information and methods for their extraction. We begin this overview chapter in Section 0.1 by very briefly summarizing some relevant prior research, on which the authors in this volume build. This section also serves to introduce the notation used, when convenient, in the rest of the book. Section 0.2 then summarizes the subsequent chapters.

0.1 NOTATION AND BACKGROUND

0.1.1 The Ecological Inference Problem

For expository purposes, we discuss only an important but simple special case of ecological inference, and adopt the running example and notation from King (1997: Chapter 2). The basic problem has two observed variables (T_i and X_i) and two unobserved quantities of interest (β_i^b and β_i^w) for each of p observations. Observations represent aggregate units, such as geographical areas, and each individual-level variable within these units is dichotomous.

To be more specific, in Table 0.1, we observe for each electoral precinct i ($i = 1, \ldots, p$) the fractions of voting age people who turn out to vote (T_i) and who are black (X_i), along with the number of voting age people (N_i). The quantities of interest, which remain unobserved because of the secret ballot, are the proportions of blacks who vote (β_i^b) and whites who vote (β_i^w). The proportions β_i^b and β_i^w are not observed because T_i and X_i are from different data sources (electoral results and census data, respectively) and record linkage is impossible (and illegal), and so the cross-tabulation cannot be computed.

Also of interest are the district-wide fractions of blacks and whites who vote, which are respectively

$$B^b = \frac{\sum_{i=1}^p N_i X_i \beta_i^b}{\sum_{i=1}^p N_i X_i} \tag{0.1}$$

and

$$B^w = \frac{\sum_{i=1}^p N_i (1 - X_i) \beta_i^w}{\sum_{i=1}^p N_i (1 - X_i)}. \tag{0.2}$$

These are weighted averages of the corresponding precinct-level quantities. Some methods aim to estimate only B^b and B^w without giving estimates of β_i^b and β_i^w for all i.

0.1.2 Deterministic and Statistical Approaches

The ecological inference literature before King (1997) was bifurcated between supporters of the method of bounds, originally proposed by Duncan and Davis (1953), and supporters of statistical approaches, proposed even before Ogburn and Goltra (1919), but first formalized into a coherent statistical model by Goodman (1953, 1959).[1] Although Goodman and

---

[1] For the historians of science among us: despite the fact that these two monumental articles were written by two colleagues and friends in the same year and in the same department and university (the Department of Sociology at the University of Chicago), the principals did not discuss their work prior to completion. Even judging by today's standards, nearly a half-century after their publication, the articles are models of clarity and creativity.

Table 0.1 Notation for precinct i

Race of voting age person	Voting decision		
	Vote	No vote	
Black	β_i^b	$1 - \beta_i^b$	X_i
White	β_i^w	$1 - \beta_i^w$	$1 - X_i$
	T_i	$1 - T_i$	

Note: The goal is to estimate the quantities of interest, β_i^b (the fraction of blacks who vote) and β_i^w (the fraction of whites who vote), from the aggregate variables X_i (the fraction of voting age people who are black) and T_i (the fraction of people who vote), along with N_i (the known number of voting age people).

Duncan and Davis moved on to other interests following their seminal contributions, most of the ecological inference literature in the five decades since 1953 was an ongoing war between supporters of these two key approaches, often without the usual academic decorum.

0.1.2.1 Extracting Deterministic Information: The Method of Bounds

The purpose of the method of bounds and its generalizations is to extract deterministic information, known with certainty, about the quantities of interest.

The intuition behind these quantities is simple. For example, if a precinct contained 150 African-Americans and 87 people in the precinct voted, then how many of the 150 African-Americans actually cast their ballot? We do not know exactly, but bounds on the answer are easy to obtain: in this case, the answer must lie between 0 and 87. Indeed, conditional only on the data being correct, $[0, 87]$ is a 100% confidence interval. Intervals like this are sometimes narrow enough to provide meaningful inferences, and sometimes they are too wide, but the ability to provide (nontrivial) 100% confidence intervals in even some situations is quite rare in any statistical field.

In general, before seeing any data, the unknown parameters β_i^b and β_i^w are each bounded on the unit interval. Once we observe T_i and X_i, they are bounded more narrowly, as

$$\beta_i^b \in \left[\max\left(0, \frac{T_i - (1 - X_i)}{X_i} \right), \ \min\left(\frac{T_i}{X_i}, 1 \right) \right],$$

$$\beta_i^w \in \left[\max\left(0, \frac{T_i - X_i}{1 - X_i} \right), \ \min\left(\frac{T_i}{1 - X_i}, 1 \right) \right]. \tag{0.3}$$

Deterministic bounds on the district-level quantities B^b and B^w are weighted averages of these precinct-level bounds.

These expressions indicate that the parameters in each case fall within these deterministic bounds with certainty, and in practice they are almost always narrower than $[0, 1]$. Whether they are narrow enough in any one application depends on the nature of the data.

0.1.2.2 Extracting Statistical Information: Goodman's Regression

Leo Goodman's (1953, 1959) approach is very different from Duncan and Davis's. He looked at the same data and focused on the statistical information. His approach examines variation in the marginals (X_i and T_i) over the precincts to attempt to reason back to the district-wide fractions of blacks and whites who vote, B^b and B^w. The outlines of this approach, and the problems with it, have been known at least since Ogburn and Goltra (1919). For example, if in precincts with large proportions of black citizens we observe that many people do not vote, then it may seem reasonable to infer that blacks turn out at rates lower than whites. Indeed it often is reasonable, but not always. The problem is that it could instead be the case that the whites who happen to live in heavily black precincts are the ones who vote less frequently, yielding the opposite ecological inference with respect to the individual-level truth.

What Goodman accomplished was to formalize the logic of the approach in a simple regression model, and to give the conditions under which estimates from such a model are unbiased. To see this, note first that the accounting identity

$$T_i = X_i \beta_i^b + (1 - X_i) \beta_i^w \tag{0.4}$$

holds exactly. Goodman showed that a regression of T_i on X_i and $1 - X_i$ with no constant term could be used to estimate B^b and B^w, respectively. The key assumption necessary for unbiasedness that Goodman identified is that the parameters and X_i are uncorrelated: $\text{Cov}(\beta_i^b, X_i) = \text{Cov}(\beta_i^w, X_i) = 0$. In the example, the assumption is that blacks vote in the same proportions in homogeneously black areas as in more integrated areas.[2] Obviously, this is true sometimes and it is false at other times.

As Goodman recognized, when this key assumption does not hold, estimates from the model will be biased. Indeed, they can be very biased, outside the deterministic bounds, and even outside the unit interval. Goodman's technique has been used extensively in the last half-century, and impossible estimates occur with considerable frequency (some say in a majority of real applications; see Achen and Shively, 1995).

0.1.3 Extracting Both Deterministic and Statistical Information: King's EI Approach

From 1953 until 1997, the only two approaches used widely in practice were the method of bounds and Goodman's regression. King's (1997) idea was that the insights from these two conflicting literatures in fact do not conflict with each other; the sources of information are largely distinct and can be combined to improve inference overall and synergistically. The idea is to combine the information from the bounds, applied to both quantities of interest for each and every precinct, with a statistical approach for extracting information within the bounds. The amount of information in the bounds depends on the data set, but for many data sets it can be considerable. For example, if precincts are spread uniformly over a scatterplot of X_i by T_i, the average bounds on β_i^b and β_i^w are narrowed from [0, 1] to less than half of that range – hence eliminating half of the ecological inference problem with certainty. This additional information also helps make the statistical portion of the model far less sensitive to assumptions than previous statistical methods that exclude the information from the bounds.

To illustrate these points, we first present all the information available without making any assumptions, thus extending the bounds approach as far as possible. As a starting point, the

---

[2] King (1997: Chapter 3) showed that Goodman's assumption was necessary but not sufficient. To have unbiasedness, it must also be true that the parameters and N_i are uncorrelated.

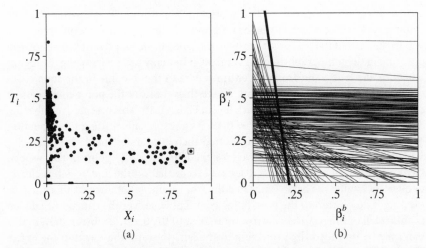

Figure 0.1. Two views of the same data: (a) a scatterplot of the observables, X_i by T_i; (b) this same information as a tomography plot of the quantities of interest, β_i^b by β_i^w. Each precinct i that appears as a point in (a) appears instead as a line (because of information lost due to aggregation) in (b). For example, precinct 52 appears as the dot with a little square around it in (a), and as the dark line in (b). The data are from King (1997: Figures 5.1, 5.5).

graph in Figure 0.1a provides a scatterplot of a sample data set as observed, X_i horizontally by T_i vertically. Each point in this plot corresponds to one precinct, for which we would like to estimate the two unknowns. We display the unknowns in part (b) of the same figure; any point in that graph portrays values of the two unknowns, β_i^b (plotted horizontally) and β_i^w (vertically). Ecological inference involves locating, for each precinct, the one point in this unit square corresponding to the true values of β_i^b and β_i^w, since values outside the square are logically impossible.

To map the knowns onto the unknowns, King began with Goodman's accounting identity from Equation 0.4. From this equation, which holds exactly, we solve for one unknown in terms of the other:

$$\beta_i^w = \left(\frac{T_i}{1 - X_i} \right) - \left(\frac{X_i}{1 - X_i} \right) \beta_i^b, \tag{0.5}$$

which shows that β_i^w is a *linear* function of β_i^b, where the intercept and slope are known (since they are functions of the data, X_i and T_i).

King then maps the knowns from Figure 0.1a onto Figure 0.1b by using the linear relationship in Equation 0.5. A key point is that each dot in (a) can be expressed, without assumptions or loss of information, as what King called a "tomography" line within the unit square in (b).[3] It is precisely the information lost due to aggregation that causes us to have to plot an entire line (on which the true point must fall) rather than the goal of one point for each precinct in Figure 0.1b. In fact, the information lost is equivalent to having a graph of the (β_i^b, β_i^w) points but having the ink smear, making the points into lines and partly but not entirely obscuring the correct positions of the points.

---

[3] King also showed that the ecological inference problem is mathematically equivalent to the ill-posed "tomography" problem of many medical imaging procedures (such as CAT and PET scans), where one attempts to reconstruct the inside of an object by passing X-rays through it and gathering information only from the outside. Because the line sketched out by an X-ray is closely analogous to Equation 0.5, King called the latter a *tomography line* and the corresponding graph a *tomography graph*.

What does a tomography line tell us? Before we know anything, we know that the true (β_i^b, β_i^w) point must lie somewhere within the unit square. After X_i and T_i are observed for a precinct, we also know that the true point must fall on a specific line represented by Equation 0.5 and appearing in the tomography plot in Figure 0.1. In many cases narrowing the region to be searched for the true point from the entire square to the one line in the square can provide a significant amount of information. To see this, consider the point enclosed in a box in Figure 0.1a, and the corresponding dark line in Figure 0.1b. This precinct, number 52, has observed values of $X_{52} = 0.88$ and $T_{52} = 0.19$. As a result, substituting into Equation 0.5 gives $\beta_i^w = 1.58 - 7.33\beta_i^b$, which when plotted then appears as the dark line in (b). This particular line tells us that in our search for the true $(\beta_{52}^b, \beta_{52}^w)$ point in (b), we can eliminate with certainty all area in the unit square except that on the line, which is clearly an advance over not having the data. Translated into the quantities of interest, this line tells us (by projecting it downward to the horizontal axis) that wherever the true point falls on the line, β_{52}^b must fall in the relatively narrow bounds of $[0.07, 0.21]$. Unfortunately, in this case, β_i^w can only be bounded (by projecting to the left) to somewhere within the entire unit interval. More generally, lines that are relatively steep, like this one, tell us a great deal about β_i^b and little about β_i^w. Tomography lines that are relatively flat give narrow bounds on β_i^w and wide bounds on β_i^b. Lines that cut off the bottom left (or top right) of the figure give narrow bounds on both quantities of interest.

If the only information available to learn about the unknowns in precinct i is X_i and T_i, a tomography line like that in Figure 0.1 exhausts all this available information. This line immediately tells us the known bounds on each of the parameters, along with the precise relationship between the two unknowns, but it is not sufficient to narrow in on the right answer any further. Fortunately, additional information exists in the other observations in the same data set (X_j and T_j for all $i \neq j$), which, under the right assumptions, can be used to learn more about β_i^b and β_i^w in our precinct of interest.

In order to borrow statistical strength from all the precincts to learn about β_i^b and β_i^w in precinct i, some assumptions are necessary. The simplest version (i.e., the one most useful for expository purposes) of King's model requires three assumptions, each of which can be relaxed in different ways.

First, the set of (β_i^b, β_i^w) points must fall in a single cluster within the unit square. The cluster can fall anywhere within the square; it can be widely or narrowly dispersed or highly variable in one unknown and narrow in the other; and the two unknowns can be positively, negatively, or not at all correlated over i. An example that would violate this assumption would be two or more distinct clusters of (β_i^b, β_i^w) points, as might result from subsets of observations with fundamentally different data generation processes (such as from markedly different regions). The specific mathematical version of this one-cluster assumption is that β_i^b and β_i^w follow a truncated bivariate normal density

$$\mathrm{TN}(\beta_i^b, \beta_i^w | \breve{\mathcal{B}}, \breve{\Sigma}) = \mathrm{N}(\beta_i^b, \beta_i^w | \breve{\mathcal{B}}, \breve{\Sigma}) \frac{\mathbf{1}(\beta_i^b, \beta_i^w)}{R(\breve{\mathcal{B}}, \breve{\Sigma})}, \tag{0.6}$$

where the kernel is the untruncated bivariate normal,

$$\mathrm{N}(\beta_i^b, \beta_i^w | \breve{\mathcal{B}}, \breve{\Sigma}) = (2\pi)^{-1} |\breve{\Sigma}|^{-1/2} \exp\left[-\frac{1}{2}(\beta_i - \breve{\mathcal{B}})' \breve{\Sigma}^{-1} (\beta_i - \breve{\mathcal{B}}) \right], \tag{0.7}$$

and $\mathbf{1}(\beta_i^b, \beta_i^w)$ is an indicator function that equals one if $\beta_i^b \in [0, 1]$ and $\beta_i^w \in [0, 1]$ and zero otherwise. The normalization factor in the denominator, $R(\breve{\mathcal{B}}, \breve{\Sigma})$, is the volume under the untruncated normal distribution above the unit square:

$$R(\check{\mathfrak{B}}, \check{\Sigma}) = \int_0^1 \int_0^1 N(\beta^b, \beta^w | \check{\mathfrak{B}}, \check{\Sigma}) \, d\beta^b \, d\beta^w. \tag{0.8}$$

When divided into the untruncated normal, this factor keeps the volume under the truncated distribution equal to one. The parameters of the truncated density, which we summarize as

$$\check{\psi} = \{\check{\mathfrak{B}}^b, \check{\mathfrak{B}}^w, \check{\sigma}_b, \check{\sigma}_w, \check{\rho}\} = \{\check{\mathfrak{B}}, \check{\Sigma}\}, \tag{0.9}$$

are on the scale of the untruncated normal (and so, for example, $\check{\mathfrak{B}}^b$ and $\check{\mathfrak{B}}^w$ need not be constrained to the unit interval even though β_i^b and β_i^w are constrained by this density).

The second assumption, which is necessary to form the likelihood function, is the absence of spatial autocorrelation: conditional on X_i, T_i and T_j are mean-independent. Violations of this assumption in empirically reasonable (and even some unreasonable) ways do not seem to induce much bias.

The final, and by far the most critical, assumption is that X_i is independent of β_i^b and β_i^w. The three assumptions together produce what has come to be known as the *basic* EI model.[4] King also generalizes this assumption, in what has come to be known as the *extended* EI model, by allowing the truncated normal parameters to vary as functions of measured covariates, Z_i^b and Z_i^w, giving

$$\begin{aligned}
\check{\mathfrak{B}}_i^b &= \left[\phi_1(\check{\sigma}_b^2 + 0.25) + 0.5\right] + (Z_i^b - \bar{Z}^b)\alpha^b, \\
\check{\mathfrak{B}}_i^w &= \left[\phi_2(\check{\sigma}_w^2 + 0.25) + 0.5\right] + (Z_i^w - \bar{Z}^w)\alpha^w,
\end{aligned} \tag{0.10}$$

where α^b and α^w are parameter vectors to be estimated along with the original model parameters and that have as many elements as Z_i^b and Z_i^w have columns. This relaxes the mean independence assumptions to

$$E(\beta_i^b | X_i, Z_i) = E(\beta_i^b | Z_i),$$
$$E(\beta_i^w | X_i, Z_i) = E(\beta_i^w | Z_i).$$

Note that this extended model also relaxes the assumptions of truncated bivariate normality, since there is now a separate density being assumed for each observation. Because the bounds, which differ in width and information content for each i, generally provide substantial information, even X_i can be used as a covariate in Z_i. (The recommended default setting in EI includes X_i as a covariate with a prior on its coefficient.) In contrast, under Goodman's regression, which does not include information in the bounds, including X_i leads to an unidentified model (King, 1997: Section 3.2).

These three assumptions – one cluster, no spatial autocorrelation, and mean independence between the regressor and the unknowns conditional on X_i and Z_i – enable one to compute a posterior (or sampling) distribution of the two unknowns in each precinct. A fundamentally important component of EI is that the quantities of interest are not the parameters of the likelihood, but instead come from conditioning on T_i and producing a posterior for β_i^b and β_i^w in each precinct. Failing to condition on T_i and examining the parameters of the truncated bivariate normal only makes sense if the model holds exactly and so is much more

---

[4] The use of EI to name this method comes from the name of his software, available at http://GKing.Harvard.edu.

model-dependent than King's approach. Since the most important problem in ecological inference modeling is precisely model misspecification, failing to condition on T assumes away the problem without justification. This point is widely regarded as a critical step in applying the EI model (Adolph and King, with Herron and Shotts, 2003).

When bounds are narrow, EI model assumptions do not matter much. But for precincts with wide bounds on a quantity of interest, inferences can become model-dependent. This is especially the case in ecological inference problems, precisely because of the loss of information due to aggregation. In fact, this loss of information can be expressed by noting that the joint distribution of β_i^b and β_i^w cannot be fully identified from the data without some untestable assumptions. To be precise, distributions with positive mass over *any* curve or combination of curves that connects the bottom left point ($\beta_i^b = 0$, $\beta_i^w = 0$) to the top right point ($\beta_i^b = 1$, $\beta_i^w = 1$) of a tomography plot cannot be rejected by the data (King, 1997: 191). Other features of the distribution are estimable. This fundamental indeterminacy is of course a problem, because it prevents pinning down the quantities of interest with certainty; but it can also be something of an opportunity, because different distributional assumptions can lead to the same estimates, especially in that only those pieces of the distributions above the tomography lines are used in the final analysis.

0.1.4 King, Rosen, and Tanner's Hierarchical Model

In the continuing search for more information to bring to bear on ecological inferences, King, Rosen, and Tanner (1999) extend King's (1997) model another step. They incorporate King's main advance of combining deterministic and statistical information, but begin modeling a step earlier, at the individuals who make up the counts. They also build a hierarchical Bayesian model, using easily generalizable Markov chain Monte Carlo (MCMC) technology (Tanner, 1996).

To define the model formally, let T_i' denote the *number* of voting age people who turn out to vote. At the top level of the hierarchy they assume that T_i' follows a binomial distribution with probability equal to $\theta_i = X_i \beta_i^b + (1 - X_i)\beta_i^w$ and count N_i. Note that at this level it is assumed that the *expectation* of T_i', rather than T_i' itself, is equal to $X_i \beta_i^b + (1 - X_i)\beta_i^w$. In other words, King (1997) models T_i as a continuous proportion, whereas King, Rosen, and Tanner (1996) recognize the inherently discrete nature of the counts of voters that go into computing this proportion. The two models are connected, of course, since T_i'/N_i approaches θ_i as N_i gets large.

The connection with King's tomography line can be seen in the contribution of the data from precinct i to the likelihood, which is

$$\left(X_i \beta_i^b + (1 - X_i)\beta_i^w\right)^{T_i'} \left(1 - X_i \beta_i^b - (1 - X_i)\beta_i^w\right)^{N_i - T_i'}. \tag{0.11}$$

By taking the logarithm of this contribution to the likelihood and differentiating with respect to β_i^b and β_i^w, King, Rosen, and Tanner show that the maximum of Equation 0.11 is not a unique point, but rather a line whose equation is given by the tomography line in Equation 0.5. Thus, the log likelihood for precinct i looks like two playing cards leaning against each other. As long as T_i is fixed and bounded away from 0.5 (and X_i is a fixed known value between 0 and 1), the derivative at this point is seen to increase with N_i, i.e., the pitch of the playing cards increases with the sample size. In other words, for large N_i, the log likelihood for precinct i degenerates from a surface defined over the unit square into a single playing card standing perpendicular to the unit square and oriented along the corresponding tomography line.

At the second level of the hierarchical model, β_i^b is distributed as a beta density with parameters c_b and d_b, and β_i^w follows an independent beta with parameters c_w and d_w. While β_i^b and β_i^w are assumed *a priori* independent, they are *a posteriori* dependent. At the third and final level of the hierarchical model, the unknown parameters c_b, d_b, c_w, and d_w follow an exponential distribution with a large mean.

A key advantage of this model is that it generalizes immediately to arbitrarily large $R \times C$ tables. This approach was pursued by Rosen, Jiang, King, and Tanner (2001), who also provided a much faster method-of-moments-based estimator. For an application, see King, Rosen, Tanner, and Wagner (2003).

0.2 NEW SOURCES OF INFORMATION IN ECOLOGICAL INFERENCE

We did not attempt to impose an *ex ante* structure on the authors as they were writing, and do not pretend that all the chapters fit into neatly delineated categories. This book is only intended to be a snapshot of a fast-growing field. If you are looking for a textbook, check back in a few years when we have learned more!

Nevertheless, we did need to order the chapters in some way. Our choice was to sort them according to the new sources of information they bring to bear on the ecological inference problem. Thus, Part One offers some alternative baselines that help indicate how much information is lost due to aggregation, and precisely what information is left. For example, in Chapter 1, Jon Wakefield offers a "baseline model," which attempts to make minimal assumptions about individuals and then aggregate up. Remarkably, the likelihood for this model is not flat over the tomography line, even without priors. Similarly, in Chapter 2, Steel, Beh, and Chambers provide a means of formally quantifying the information lost in the aggregation process and thus precisely how much information is left in the aggregate data. They do this through parametric models and hypothesis tests, such as a test for the homogeneity of β_i^b and β_i^w across tables. The authors also show how the increase of even a small amount of information in a standard ecological inference model can greatly improve inferences, even if survey respondents cannot be grouped into precincts or relevant geographic areas. They illustrate their ideas with data from the 1996 Australian census. And finally, in Chapter 3, Stephen Voss shows how the most commonly used method, King's ecological inference model, provides a baseline for understanding and parsing out contextual and compositional effects intertwined in aggregate data.

Part Two of this book is devoted to including sources of information through new models and methods. In Chapter 4, Jeff Lewis finds information where no one had looked before, by including two or more parallel and correlated ecological inference models in the same analysis. His approach, which can be thought of as analogous to a Bayesian version of a "seemingly unrelated regression model," extends King's model by incorporating a key feature of numerous data sources.

In Chapter 5, Bernard Grofman and Samuel Merrill propose three relatively simple methods for ecological inference where the data consist of 2×2 tables. All three introduce new assumptions justified by the authors in terms similar to local smoothing algorithms. The idea is that precincts similar to other precincts on the basis of observables are likely to be similar on unobservables too. The argument introduces a form of information that the authors use to identify where on the tomography lines the point estimates probably lie. The first method is based on minimizing the squared distances from the overall tomography line to each of the precinct-level tomography lines. The other two methods are constrained variants of Goodman regression. Specifically, the second method uses analogous distances to those used in the first method, but on transformed coordinates rather than the (β_i^b, β_i^w) coordinates. The last method combines Goodman regression with the Duncan–Davis method of bounds. The proposed methods are shown to give answers similar to King's model in several real data sets.

Kevin Corder and Christina Wolbrecht, in Chapter 6, are concerned with estimating newly enfranchised women's turnout in the 1920 U.S. elections in three states. They use the hierarchical Bayesian binomial–normal model proposed by Wakefield but employ informative priors based on prior elections and census data. Their central contribution is to recognize new forms of information in terms of detailed prior, nonsample knowledge of the problem. For example, we know almost for certain that in this period, when women had just gotten the vote, they cast their ballots less frequently than men. In statistical terms, we are essentially certain that $\beta_i^b > \beta_i^w$ for all i and so we can sample from only the portion of the tomography line satisfying the constraint. This greatly increases the information content in their analyses.

In Chapter 7, George Judge, Douglas Miller, and Wendy Tam Cho model the ecological inference problem as an ill-posed inverse problem with a solution selected from the set of feasible solutions – either via maximizing entropy, which implies one set of assumptions, or using the Cressie–Read statistic, which allows for the choice among a variety of others. This approach enables the authors to bring new information to the ecological inference problem in the form of assumptions about individual behavior, often learned from prior survey and other work. The model can be fitted to $R \times C$ tables and allows for explanatory variables reflecting individual spatial or temporal heterogeneity.

In Chapter 8, Ben Pelzer, Rob Eisinga, and Philip Hans Franses propose a model for estimating individual-level binary transitions based on repeated cross-sectional data. The basic problem is equivalent to the classic ecological inference problem with 2×2 tables, where the unknown transition probabilities play the role of the unknown cell probabilities. They introduce assumptions in order to model important information available as lags of some exogenous variables. Inference is performed via maximum likelihood, parametric bootstrap and MCMC methods. The methodology is illustrated with data on personal computer ownership in Dutch households.

Part Three is devoted to methods that attempt to include geographic or time series information in models of ecological inference. In Chapter 10, Kevin Quinn develops Bayesian hierarchical models for ecological inference in the presence of temporal dependence. He builds on Wakefield's approximation to a convolution of binomials and puts priors on the approximate likelihood's parameters reflecting temporal dependence. This class of models may also be useful in some situations for spatial or simultaneous spatiotemporal dependence. Inference is performed via MCMC methods. Quinn studies the methodology via simulated data, as well as by analyzing real data on voting registration by race in Louisiana counties over a 14-year period. Carol Gotway Crawford and Linda Young, in Chapter 10, give an overview of the ecological inference problem from a spatial statistics perspective. These authors point out that ecological inference is a special case of the change-of-support problem in geostatistics, which refers to the geometric size, shape, and spatial orientation of the regions associated with the observed measurements. Changing the support of a variable thus creates a new variable. The problem of how the spatial variation in one variable relates to that in the other is the change-of-support problem, a possible solution being spatial smoothing. The authors illustrate these issues with a case study on low-birth-weight babies.

In Chapter 11, Ernesto Calvo and Marcelo Escolar consider ecological inference in the presence of spatial heterogeneity, which may lead to underestimated standard errors or new forms of bias on top of the aggregation bias inherent in ecological inference. In this chapter the authors allow for spatial heterogeneity by using geographically weighted regression in the context of Goodman's and King's ecological inference models. Their idea is to incorporate a nonparametric term reflecting spatial effects into these models, resulting in semiparametric models. These models are explored via simulation and with Peronist voting data.

Chapter 12 introduces methods of ecological inference that draw on the extensive spatial epidemiology literature. Therein Sebastien Haneuse and Jon Wakefield show how to model spatial and nonspatial heterogeneity. They incorporate important new information into ecological inference by modeling the fact that multiple diseases share common risk factors, and these risk factors often exhibit spatial clustering. Modeling this clustering, they show, can greatly improve ecological inferences.

Finally, in Part Four, we include comparisons of some existing ecological inference methods. Ruth Salway and Jon Wakefield contrast ecological inference in political science, which tends to focus on descriptive quantities such as the fraction of African Americans voting for the Democrats, and in epidemiology, in which interest is primarily in causal inferences (Chapter 13). Of course, political scientists and most others are also interested in causal inferences, and so the work here should be of general interest. The key problem in making causal inference is confounding, and so Salway and Wakefield analyze the combined effects of confounding bias along with aggregation bias. They show how sources of information about confounding can help improve ecological inferences.

Kenneth Benoit, Michael Laver, and Daniela Giannetti in Chapter 14 discuss the use of King's model in the context of an extensive split-ticket voting application. In Chapter 15, Rogério Silva de Mattos and Alvaro Veiga compare Goodman's regression, King's model, and the hierarchical beta-binomial model (King, Rosen, and Tanner, 1999). To facilitate the simulation-based comparison, the authors use their own version of the beta–binomial model where estimation is performed via the ECM algorithm. The authors' main conclusion is that King's model is superior to the other methods in predictive ability.

In Chapter 16, Micah Altman, Jeff Gill, and Michael McDonald compare the numerical properties of implementations of Goodman regression, King's model, and McCue's method. They look at sources of numerical inaccuracy such as floating point arithmetic, nonlinear optimization, and pseudorandom numbers. The stability and accuracy of the algorithms are tested by introducing random perturbations into the data. The authors' recommendation is to use data perturbations as a diagnostic test in addition to any other diagnostic tools associated with these ecological inference methods.

REFERENCES

Achen, Christopher H. and W. P. Phillips Shively. 1995. *Cross-Level Inference*. Chicago: University of Chicago Press.

Adolph, Christopher and Gary King, with Michael C. Herron and Kenneth W. Shotts. 2003. "A Consensus Position on Second Stage Ecological Inference Models," *Political Analysis*, 11: 86–94.

Duncan, Otis Dudley and Beverly Davis. 1953. "An Alternative to Ecological Correlation," *American Sociological Review*, 18: 665–666.

Goodman, Leo. 1953. "Ecological Regressions and the Behavior of Individuals," *American Sociological Review*, 18: 663–666.

Goodman, Leo. 1959. "Some Alternatives to Ecological Correlation," *American Journal of Sociology*, 64: 610–624.

King, Gary. 1997. *A Solution to the Ecological Inference Problem: Reconstructing Individual Behavior from Aggregate Data*. Princeton: Princeton University Press.

King, Gary, Ori Rosen, and Martin A. Tanner, 1999. "Binomial–Beta Hierarchical Models for Ecological Inference," *Sociological Methods and Research*, 28: 61–90.

King, Gary, Ori Rosen, Martin A. Tanner, and Alexander Wagner. 2003. "The Ordinary Election of Adolf Hitler: A Modern Voting Behavior Approach," http://gking.harvard.edu/files/abs/making-abs.shtml.

Ogburn, William F. and Inez Goltra. 1919. "How Women Vote: A Study of an Election in Portland, Oregon," *Political Science Quarterly*, 3, XXXIV: 413–433.

Rosen, Ori, Wenxin Jiang, Gary King, and Martin A. Tanner. 2001. "Bayesian and Frequentist Inference for Ecological Inference: The $R \times C$ Case," *Statistica Neerlandica*, 55, 2: 134–156.

Tanner, M. A. 1996. *Tools for Statistical Inference: Methods for the Exploration of Posterior Distributions and Likelihood Functions*, 3rd ed., New York: Springer-Verlag.

1 Prior and Likelihood Choices in the Analysis of Ecological Data

Jonathan Wakefield

ABSTRACT

A general statistical framework for ecological inference is presented, and a number of previously proposed approaches are described and critiqued within this framework. In particular, the assumptions that all approaches require to overcome the fundamental nonidentifiability problem of ecological inference are clarified. We describe a number of three-stage Bayesian hierarchical models that are flexible enough to incorporate substantive prior knowledge and additional data. We illustrate that great care must be taken when specifying prior distributions, however. The choice of the likelihood function for aggregate data is discussed, and it is argued that in the case of aggregate 2×2 data, a choice that is consistent with a realistic sampling scheme is a convolution of binomial distributions, which naturally incorporate the bounds on the unobserved cells of the constituent 2×2 tables. For large marginal counts this choice is computationally daunting, and a simple normal approximation previously described by Wakefield (2004) is discussed. Various computational schemes are described, ranging from an auxiliary data scheme for tables with small counts, to Markov chain Monte Carlo algorithms that are efficient for tables with larger marginal counts. We investigate prior, likelihood, and computational choices with respect to simulated data, and also via registration–race data from four southern U.S. states.

1.1 INTRODUCTION

Ecological inference problems, in which aggregate summaries rather than individual data are observed, are common in many disciplines, including political science, sociology, and epidemiology; see Achen and Shively (1995), Cleave, Brown, and Payne (1995), King (1997), and other chapters in this volume for examples and references to specific applications. In this chapter we consider the situation in which the association between two binary variables is to be investigated. In the case in which the study area contains m areas, the data consist of the observed margins in each of the m constituent 2×2 tables.

To motivate our discussion we introduce a specific example. The data concern voter registration and racial background information for individuals from 275 counties in four southern U.S. states: Florida, Louisiana, and North and South Carolina. The data we analyze consist of the total voting age population, the total black population, and the number who were registered to vote, in 1968. These data have previously been analyzed by King (1997) and King, Rosen, and Tanner (1999). Figure 1.1 plots the proportion of registered voters against the proportion black, in each of the 275 counties. Though the data from the three counties in the bottom right (those with the lowest populations registered) appear influential, the general trend is that the proportion registered decreases as the proportion in the county who are black increases, the obvious explanation being that blacks are less likely to register. Alternative explanations exist, however; in particular, the same pattern could be observed

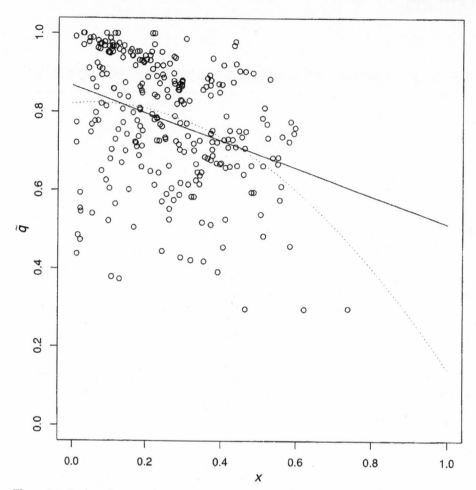

Figure 1.1. Registration–race data from four states: proportion registered, $\tilde{q}_i$, versus proportion black, x_i, $i = 1, \ldots, 275$. The solid line shows the weighted least squares linear fit, and the dotted line the weighted least squares quadratic fit.

if whites are less likely to register if in a predominantly black county, if blacks are more likely to register in a predominantly white county, or if individual race is an unimportant predictor of registration behavior, and instead an individual's behavior, whether black or white, is predicted by the proportion of blacks in the area. In each of these scenarios the proportion black/white in an area is an example of a *contextual* variable, a variable reflecting characteristics of individuals in a shared environment. Hence to infer from Figure 1.1 that blacks are more likely to register than whites could be an example of what Selvin (1958), following the influential article of Robinson (1950), called the *ecological fallacy*, an incorrect inference concerning individual effects gleaned from aggregate data. In an extreme case, the aggregate relationship could be the reverse of the true individual relationship, a phenomenon closely related to Simpson's paradox (Simpson, 1951); see Wakefield (2004) for further discussion.

The outline of this chapter is as follows. In Section 1.2 we describe the fundamental difficulty of ecological inference, and in Section 1.3 we describe a particular likelihood function and compare it with alternatives that have been explicitly or implicitly used previously. In Section 1.4 various prior distributions are considered, including hierarchical approaches.

Table 1.1 Table summarizing data in area i

	$Y = 0$	$Y = 1$	
$x = 0$		Y_{0i}	N_{0i}
$x = 1$		Y_{1i}	N_{1i}
	$N_i - Y_i$	Y_i	N_i

Note: In an ecological study the margins only are observed.

Section 1.5 describes how computation may be carried out for a number of the Bayesian models discussed in the previous sections. A number of simulated examples are considered in Section 1.6, and Section 1.7 provides an analysis of the race–registration data. Section 1.8 contains a concluding discussion. The hierarchical models described in this chapter may be fitted using the freely available `WinBUGS` software (Spiegelhalter, Thomas, and Best, 1998); an appendix gives sample code.

1.2 THE FUNDAMENTAL DIFFICULTY OF ECOLOGICAL INFERENCE

For a generic individual, $Y = 0$ [1] will denote the event that an individual is unregistered [registered] (the response), and $X = 0$ [1] the event that an individual is of black [white] race (the predictor). Table 1.1 describes the notation that we will use throughout the paper. In an aggregate situation we do not observe the internal counts Y_{0i}, Y_{1i}; the fundamental difficulty of ecological inference is that we are interested in these two quantities, but it is their sum Y_i only that we observe.

In the ecological inference literature the inference problem has often been treated as the imputation of the missing data, Y_{0i}, Y_{1i}, and due to this perspective approaches have often implicitly adopted a finite sampling view. In contrast to this approach, in this paper we consider a hypothetical infinite population of exchangeable blacks and whites within each area, and define the parameter p_{ji} to be the fraction of race j in this hypothetically infinite population of area i that register. Hence, as we illustrate below, p_{ji} also represents the probability that a randomly selected individual of race j in area i registers. Under this viewpoint an estimate of this probability, $\hat{p}_{ji}$, is not in general equal to the true (but unobserved) fraction registered, Y_{ji}/N_{ji}, which we denote by $\bar{p}_{ji}$. In a finite sample view we may simply consider the N_{ji} individuals as consisting of Y_{ji} who register, and $N_{ji} - Y_{ji}$ who are unregistered, without consideration of an infinite population. In this latter view, if Y_{ji} were observed then inference is complete since the population has been observed. In contrast, in the infinite population view, even if Y_{ji} is observed, uncertainty concerning p_{ji} will remain (though may be small if N_{ji} is large). To draw a link between the two views suppose there are $N_{ji}^* \geq N_{ji}$ hypothetical individuals of race j in area i, and Y_{ji}^* of these are registered. We now draw a random sample of size N_{ji} of these individuals; the number registered, Y_{ji}, is then a central hypergeometric random variable with parameters N_{ji}, N_{ji}^*, Y_{ji}^*, that is

$$
\Pr(Y_{ji} = y \mid N_{ji}, N_{ji}^*, Y_{ji}^*) = \frac{\dbinom{Y_{ji}^*}{y} \dbinom{N_{ji}^* - Y_{ji}^*}{N_{ji} - y}}{\dbinom{N_{ji}^*}{N_{ji}}},
$$

for $y = \max(0, N_{ji} - N_{ji}^* + Y_{ji}^*), \ldots, \min(Y_{ji}^*, N_{ji})$ (see McCullagh and Nelder, 1989, p. 256, for more details). Now suppose Y_{ji}^* and N_{ji}^* approach infinity in such a way that $Y_{ji}^*/N_{ji}^* \to p_{ji}$. Then the number registered is a binomial random variable

$$\Pr(Y_{ji} = y \mid p_{ji}, N_{ji}) = \binom{N_{ji}}{y} p_{ji}^y (1 - p_{ji})^{N_{ji}-y},$$

for $y = 0, \ldots, N_{ji}$, and this is the probability generating mechanism that we will assume for the unobserved individual-level data, Y_{ji}, in the hierarchical models we suggest later in the paper.

To see the indeterminacy of ecological inference more clearly we write, for area i,

$$\frac{Y_i}{N_i} = \frac{Y_{0i} + Y_{1i}}{N_i} = \frac{Y_{0i}}{N_{0i}} \times \frac{N_{0i}}{N_i} + \frac{Y_{1i}}{N_{1i}} \times \frac{N_{1i}}{N_i}$$

which may be rewritten as

$$\tilde{q}_i = \tilde{p}_{0i} \times x_i + \tilde{p}_{1i} \times (1 - x_i), \tag{1.1}$$

where $\tilde{q}_i$ is the fraction registered, $\tilde{p}_{0i}$ and $\tilde{p}_{1i}$ are the black and white fractions registered, and x_i and $1 - x_i$ are the proportions black and white respectively; the latter are observed while the registration fractions for blacks and whites are unobserved. From Equation 1.1 we see that many competing explanations are possible for the observed $\tilde{q}_i$; that is there are many true fractions $\tilde{p}_{0i}$, $\tilde{p}_{1i}$, that may lead to the observed $\tilde{q}_i$. Another way of expressing this unidentifiability is that the overall fraction is a convex combination of $\tilde{p}_{0i}$ and $\tilde{p}_{1i}$. In terms of the underlying probabilities p_{ji}, there is no constraint beyond $0 < p_{ji} < 1$. This is a crucial difference between the finite sample and infinite sampling views.

We now describe two extreme explanations that are consistent with Equation 1.1. First, following Goodman (1953, 1959), we may assume that $\tilde{p}_{0i}$ and $\tilde{p}_{1i}$ are such that

$$E[\tilde{p}_{ji} \mid x_i] = p_j, \tag{1.2}$$

$j = 0, 1$, so that the fractions are uncorrelated with x_i. The expectation here is with respect to repeated sampling in areas with proportion of blacks x_i. We then have

$$E[\tilde{q}_i \mid x_i] = p_0 \times x_i + p_1 \times (1 - x_i) = a + bx_i, \tag{1.3}$$

where $a = p_1$ and $b = p_0 - p_1$. Although it is only the expectations of the fractions that are considered constant in Equation 1.2, the usual way of imputing the internal fractions is to simply take

$$\tilde{p}_{ji} = p_j,$$

which is equivalent to a model in which the fractions themselves are constant. This model has sometimes been described as *Goodman regression*, but we prefer the name *ecological regression*, as Goodman did not encourage general use of the approach, and in particular was aware that the "constancy assumption" (1.2) would often not be appropriate. The assumption of constancy allows the mean to be derived, but to formulate an estimation method it would be desirable to derive the variance and covariance of $Y_i = N_i \tilde{q}_i$. In general it has been assumed that counts in different areas are independent (see Chapter 12 of this book for details of a hierarchical model that incorporates spatial dependence), and various forms for the variance have been considered. As we will describe in detail in Section 1.3, a plausible likelihood leads to Y_i following a convolution distribution with variance that depends on p_{0i} and p_{1i}. Here for illustration we consider estimation under the assumption that the variance is proportional to N_i and use weighted least squares for estimation. In Figure 1.1 the ecological regression line under weighted least squares, with weights proportional to N_i, is superimposed; the size of the residual variability about the line is evident.

A very simple model, termed the *nonlinear neighborhood model* (Freedman et al., 1991), is to assume that $p_{0i} = p_{1i} = q_i$, i.e. to assume that registration and individual race are independent. This allows the table to be collapsed, and inference is straightforward. Freedman (2001) states that in this model, "... behavior is determined by geography not demography." The model acknowledges that the probabilities are heterogeneous across areas, but does not appear reasonable in many instances, since it does not allow an individual effect due to race. A specific version of the nonlinear neighborhood model, the *linear neighborhood model*, was also described by Freedman et al. (1991) and makes the assumption that $E[p_{0i}|x_i]$ and $E[p_{1i}|x_i]$ are identical but depend on the proportion black via the linear form

$$E[p_{0i}|x_i] = E[p_{1i}|x_i] = E[q_i|x_i] = a + b_i, \tag{1.4}$$

which is identical to Equation 1.3 though the interpretation and imputed internal cells are drastically different under the two models. This was the reason Freedman et al. (1991) introduced the model, to illustrate the fundamental unidentifiability of ecological inference.

Figure 1.2 gives the estimates of the black and white fractions registered under a variety of models including ecological regression (a), the linear neighborhood model (b), and the nonlinear neighborhood model (c). We see that the estimates under the three approaches are very different (though the neighborhood models give identical population averaged fractions under certain estimation techniques; see Freedman et al., 1991). In model 1.4, x_i is an example of a contextual effect; note that taking $1 - x_i$ as the contextual effect, or assuming that x_i and $1 - x_i$ are both contextual effects, leads to identical imputations. Ecological regression gives estimates for whites that are considerably greater than for blacks.

It seems realistic in political science applications to believe that in many situations the registration of an individual will be associated with both their own race *and* the race of those around them (that is, we believe that registration will be a function of both demography and geography), particularly if we allow race in both cases to be surrogates for other variables such as income, education level, etc. A model that attempts to allow this possibility follows from assuming that

$$E[\tilde{p}_{ji}|x_i] = a_j + b_j x_i,$$

so that an individual's registration probability depends both on their own race (through the a_j terms) and on the context (through a strength of association b_j). This model leads to

$$E[\tilde{q}_i|x_i] = (a_0 + b_0 x_i)x_i + (a_1 + b_1 x_i)(1 - x_i) = \alpha + \beta x_i + \gamma x_i^2,$$

where $\alpha = a_1$, $\beta = a_0 + b_1 - a_1$, and $\gamma = b_0 - b_1$. Hence we have four unknowns to estimate from just three parameters. This unidentifiability has typically been resolved by assuming that one of b_0, b_1 is zero (preferably based on substantive background knowledge; see for example Achen and Shively, 1995: Chapter 5). Hence two possible quadratic models are produced, though there are an infinite number of possibilities, depending on how we resolve the unidentifiability; for example, we could fix the ratio $r = b_0/b_1$ to give $b_1 = \gamma/(r - 1)$.

The quadratic curve is drawn in Figure 1.1, and we see there is noticeable curvature; the quadratic coefficient is -0.77 with standard error 0.34 (with the three outlying areas

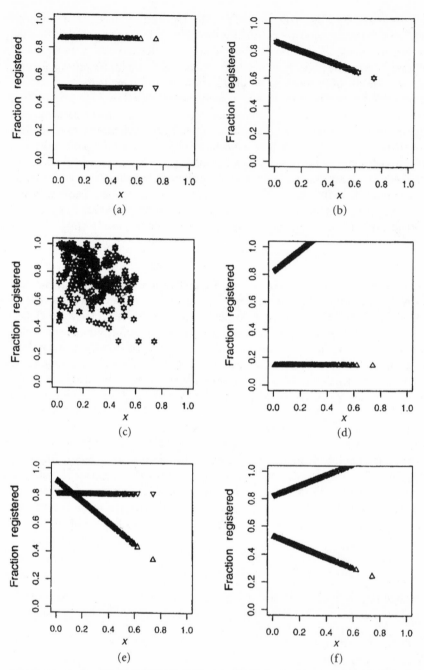

Figure 1.2. Registration–race data: estimates of black and white fractions registered, $\bar{p}_{0i}$ and $\bar{p}_{1i}$, respectively, under various models, $\triangledown$ for blacks and $\triangle$ for whites: (a) ecological regression, (b) linear neighborhood model, (c) nonlinear neighborhood model, (d) quadratic model with contextual effect for blacks only, (e) quadratic model with contextual effect for whites only, (f) quadratic model with equal contextual effects of race for each individual, and the registration probability depending on the contextual effect of the proportion in the same race.

influencing this curvature). The two interpretations of the quadratic model with $b_0 = 0$ and $b_1 = 0$ were taken with the registration–race data, and Figures 1.2d and e give the estimates under these two scenarios; the predicted fractions registered for blacks and whites are very different from the ecological regression estimates under each of the quadratic models. We see in panel (d) that a contextual effect for blacks only gives black fractions greater than white fractions and inadmissible values beyond approximately 0.3, casting considerable doubt on this model. In panel (e), the assumption of contextual effects for whites only gives white registration estimates below black ones for the majority of the x range (in contrast to ecological regression).

We note that if we were to believe that the fraction registered for both blacks and whites had the same contextual effect, i.e. $b_0 = b_1$ (in the spirit of the linear neighborhood model), then this term would not be estimable under the quadratic model described above, since it results in $\gamma = 0$. However, we note in passing that an identifiable model is obtained if we take $b_0 = -b_1$, which is equivalent to

$$E[\tilde{p}_{0i}|x_i] = a_0 + b_0 x_i$$

and

$$E[\tilde{p}_{1i}|x_i] = a_1 - b_0 + (1 - x_i)b_0,$$

so that the proportions registered depend on the contextual effect of the proportions in the *same* race in area i, with the effect sizes being equal. Under this model we obtain the imputations

$$\tilde{p}_{0i} = \hat{\alpha} + \hat{\beta} + \frac{\hat{\gamma}}{2} + \frac{\hat{\gamma}}{2}x_i$$

and

$$\tilde{p}_{1i} = \hat{\alpha} - \frac{\hat{\gamma}}{2}x_i.$$

For illustration we fitted this model, and it resulted in the imputed fractions displayed in Figure 1.2f. We see that inadmissible estimates arise for the blacks for x greater than approximately 0.5 (and the white fractions are lower than the black fractions for all areas).

Other regression-type approaches, with a nonparametric flavor, are described by Chambers and Steel (2001). Gelman et al. (2001) describe diagnostics that may be used to assess the assumptions underlying ecological regression.

As we will see, although the assumption that $\tilde{q}_i$ is uncorrelated with x_i may be a major problem in some applications (examples are given by Freedman et al., 1998, 1999, and Freedman, 2001), a further problem with ecological regression is the assumption that the *estimated* fractions are not allowed to vary across areas, so that the between-area variability is not acknowledged. Least squares procedures are known to provide consistent estimates of regression parameters under a range of distributions of the errors, but are also known to be very poor at providing *predictions* of observable quantities; for this, some knowledge of the distribution of the error terms is required. The great benefit of the hierarchical approach that was popularized by King (1997) is that between-area differences in fractions are assigned a distribution, so allowing variability in the estimates of race-specific fractions across areas. Lindley and Smith (1972) show that hierarchical models can show great benefits, in terms of mean squared error, of unit-specific (in this case area-specific) estimates, by borrowing strength across units.

To conclude, in this section we have reviewed how two competing explanations with vastly different interpretations and inferential implications lead to an identical mean function, and shown that an extended quadratic model has unidentifiability problems of its own. To overcome this unidentifiability and estimate $2m$ quantities from m observables, it is clear that any approach that is considered must make assumptions (or incorporate additional individual-level data). It is not immediately apparent, but also true, that the totality of assumptions from any approach will be uncheckable from the aggregate data alone. In all observational studies untestable assumptions such as "no unmeasured confounding" are required for causal interpretations, but ecological studies provide a particularly vulnerable study design in that the amount of information concerning quantities of interest is much smaller than in typical individual-level observational studies.

1.3 LIKELIHOOD FUNCTION

In the previous section we simply derived the form of the marginal fraction registered under various assumptions. In this section we derive a likelihood function under a plausible sampling scheme, and compare this with various (often implicit) likelihoods that have been used in the ecological literature. Recall that

$$p_{0i} = \Pr(Y = 1 | x = 0, i) \quad \text{and} \quad p_{1i} = \Pr(Y = 1 | x = 1, i) \tag{1.5}$$

are the population probabilities. Returning to Table 1.1, we first note that if Y_{0i} and Y_{1i} were observed, then if we were to assume that each of the N_{0i} black individuals in area i have independent Bernoulli responses with probability p_{0i}, and each of the N_{1i} white individuals in area i have independent Bernoulli response with probability p_{1i} (and the black and white responses are independent), then

$$Y_{ji} | p_{ji} \sim \text{Binomial}(N_{ji}, p_{ji}),$$

$j = 0, 1, i = 1, \ldots, m$. Under this sampling scheme, if Y_{0i} and Y_{1i} are unobserved, then the sum Y_i follows a convolution of these binomial distributions:

$$P(Y_i | p_{0i}, p_{1i}) = \sum_{y_{0i}=l_i}^{u_i} \binom{N_{0i}}{y_{0i}} \binom{N_{1i}}{Y_i - y_{0i}} p_{0i}^{y_{0i}} (1 - p_{0i})^{N_{0i}-y_{0i}} p_{1i}^{Y_i - y_{0i}} (1 - p_{1i})^{N_{1i}-Y_i+y_{0i}},$$

$$\tag{1.6}$$

where

$$l_i = \max(0, Y_i - N_{1i}), \qquad u_i = \min(N_{0i}, Y_i). \tag{1.7}$$

These values correspond to the admissible values that Y_i can take, given the margins in Table 1.1. McCullagh and Nelder (1989) consider this likelihood under the assumption that $p_{0i} = p_0$ and $p_{1i} = p_1$; see also Achen and Shively (1995: 46).

For large tables this form is computationally intractable, but, as discussed by Wakefield (2004), when each of the binomial distributions in each row of Table 1.1 is approximated by a normal, the resultant convolution is normal and is given by

$$P(Y_i = y_i | p_{0i}, p_{1i}) \propto (2\pi V_i)^{-1} \exp\left\{-\frac{1}{2V_i}(y_i - \mu_i)^2\right\}, \tag{1.8}$$

where

$$\mu_i = \mu_i(p_{0i}, p_{1i}) = N_i \times q_i = N_i\{p_{0i}x_i + p_{1i}(1 - x_i)\}$$

and

$$V_i = V_i(p_{0i}, p_{1i}) = N_i\{p_{0i}(1 - p_{0i})x_i + p_{1i}(1 - p_{1i})(1 - x_i)\}.$$

In the ecological regression method described in the last section, with weighted least squares used for estimation, the implicit likelihood is Equation 1.8 with $\mu_i = a + bx_i$ and $\sigma_i^2 = N_i\sigma^2$. Similar equivalences hold for the quadratic models. Hence maximum likelihood estimation with the ecological regression model would use Equation 1.8, though (since the weights depend on p_0, p_1) an iterative procedure would be required to obtain estimates of a and b. Such an approach is likely to provide little improvement over the simpler weighted least squares procedure, since the major inaccuracies in ecological regression arise from assuming no contextual effects and no between-area variability in the fractions. Brown and Payne (1986) use similar approximations to Equation 1.8 in the context of their aggregated compound multinomial model; see also Hawkes (1969). This normal approximation is likely to be adequate in most situations in which the marginal counts are large and the probabilities p_{0i}, p_{1i} are not very close to zero or one (in this case the normal approximation to the binomial for one of the races may be poor), but other similar approximations may be beneficial in some cases (see Barndorff-Neilsen and Cox, 1989: 97, for alternative normal-type approximations to the binomial). We advocate the use of this approximation in the context of hierarchical modeling, and so require an accurate approximation in those regions of p_{0i}, p_{1i} space that are supported by the second-stage prior. We finally note that if we are in a situation where all of the probabilities are close to zero – as in epidemiological applications – or close to one, then a better approximation, which is computationally convenient, is to use the Poisson approximation to the binomial (for details, see Wakefield, 2004).

We now describe a baseline model that allows direct examination of the information in the data in the margin for each table alone, without assuming any commonality of parameters across tables or reducing the dimensionality. Via this model we may examine the likelihood in Equation 1.6 for each table with the assumption of a pair of distinct probabilities in each table. Placing a fixed (that is, nonhierarchical) prior on (p_{0i}, p_{1i}) allows the posterior surface to be examined. We stress that this model is not intended to be used for formal analysis, but rather as a means to provide insight into the hazards of ecological inference. In the limit as $N_i \to \infty$ with $\bar{q}_i$ and x_i remaining constant, examination of the normal approximation to the convolution reveals that the likelihood tends to a line given by $\bar{q}_i = p_{0i}x_i + p_{1i}(1 - x_i)$ (and not a point, which would occur in a regular estimation problem). The likelihood, though, is not flat along this line, but is a curved function in p_{0i} and p_{1i} (due to the curved form of $V(p_{0i}, p_{1i})$), with the maximum lying at one endpoint, and the minimum at the point $p_{0i} = p_{1i}$, which is, independence of race and registration; see Wakefield (2004) and Chapter 2 for more discussion. Again, this makes it clear that if we wish to retain $2m$ parameters in our model, we have to make further assumptions; hierarchical models, such as that described by King (1997) and refined by King, Rosen, and Tanner (1999) and Wakefield (2004), are in this spirit.

King, Rosen, and Tanner (1999) are among the few authors to explicitly state a likelihood and use the binomial sampling model

$$Y_i \mid p_{0i}, \ p_{1i} \sim \text{Binomial}\{N_i, \ p_{0i}x_i + p_{1i}(1 - x_i)\} \tag{1.9}$$

in the context of a hierarchical model (which we will describe fully in Section 1.4). This model may be motivated from the formulation of Section 1.2 by supposing that rather than having sampling without replacement from a population of N_{0i} blacks and N_{1i} whites, we instead have sampling with replacement, so that we have N_i independent Bernoulli trials, each with probability $p_{0i}x_i + p_{1i}(1 - x_i)$. This model is difficult to justify in the current context, but its use rather than the convolution will usually make little difference in tables with large margins (at least, given all of the other problems posed by ecological inference), since in the limit it provides a likelihood that concentrates upon the same line upon which the convolution likelihood concentrates, but is flat (as opposed to curved). Examples of this likelihood for particular tables, along with the convolution and the normal approximation, are provided in Section 1.6.

Duncan and Davis (1953) noted that the bounds

$$\hat{p}_{ji} \in \left(\max\left\{ 0, \ \frac{y_i + N_{ji} - N_i}{N_{ji}} \right\}, \dots, \min\left\{ 1, \ \frac{y_i}{N_{ji}} \right\} \right),$$

$j = 0, 1, i = 1, \dots, m$, could be placed on the fractions. The bounds for p_{0i} follow directly from dividing the bounds on Y_{0i} in Equation 1.7 by N_{0i}; those for p_{1i} follow analogously. These bounds may be written in terms of $\tilde{q}_i$ and x_i; specifically we have

$$\max\left\{ 0, \ \frac{\tilde{q}_i - (1 - x_i)}{x_i} \right\} \le \tilde{p}_{0i} \le \min\left\{ 1, \ \frac{\tilde{q}_i}{x_i} \right\}, \tag{1.10}$$

and similarly, for Y_{1i}/N_{1i},

$$\max\left\{ 0, \ \frac{\tilde{q}_i - x_i}{1 - x_i} \right\} \le \tilde{p}_{1i} \le \min\left\{ 1, \ \frac{\tilde{q}_i}{1 - x_i} \right\}. \tag{1.11}$$

The resulting four distinct cases allow an informal examination of the amount of information in each table. The four cases in Figure 1.3 are as follows: case 1: non-unity upper bounds on p_{0i} and p_{1i}; case 2: nonzero lower bound and non-unity upper bound on p_{0i}, and $(0, 1)$ bound for p_{1i}; case 3: $(0, 1)$ bound for p_{0i}, and nonzero lower bound and non-unity upper bound on p_{1i}; case 4: nonzero lower bounds on p_{0i} and p_{1i}. See Wakefield (2004) for more details.

Figure 1.3 shows the bounds on the fractions for the registration–race data. In panel (a) we see that $\tilde{q}_i$ is greater than x_i in almost all areas, and so we are in cases 3 and 4. Case 3 leads to bounds on $\tilde{p}_{0i}$ of $(0, 1)$ (because registration is close to 1 and the fractions black are small, and so we cannot rule out the possibility that none or all of the blacks are registered). A larger number of areas fall into case 4, since usually $x_i < 0.5$ and so the lower bounds for p_{1i} are substantially above 0 for many areas, the latter because it would not be possible to obtain the total number registered unless at least a fraction of the whites were registered. The average width of the bounds is 0.67 for $\tilde{p}_{0i}$ and 0.26 for $\tilde{p}_{1i}$. The plots in panels (b) and (c) are routinely used in the examples of King (1997). Figure 1.3c shows that the bounds on $\tilde{p}_{1i}$ become wider with increasing x_i, as expected. Figure 1.3d gives the bounds on the difference, and we see that these differences become more centered on zero as x_i increases. The method of bounds of Duncan and Davis (1953) has no explicit likelihood, though the

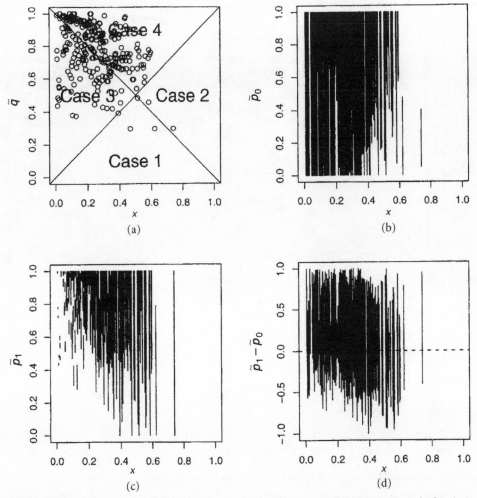

Figure 1.3. (a) Information in bounds as a function of x_i and $\tilde{q}_i$. Deterministic bounds on the fractions registered (MLEs) of: (b) $\tilde{p}_{0i}$, (c) $\tilde{p}_{1i}$, (d) $\tilde{p}_{1i} - \tilde{p}_{0i}$, $i = 1, \ldots, 275$, for the registration–race data.

baseline model described earlier in this section can be thought of as a stochastic version of this method, and also reveals why examining the bounds alone can be deceptive. (See also Wakefield, 2004, in which it is shown that with a flat prior and the convolution likelihood, the predictive distribution of $\tilde{p}_{0i}$, $\tilde{p}_{1i}$ is flat along the homography line.) A difficulty with interpretation is that the width of the bounds depends explicitly on x_i, and so examining any plot of the bounds is difficult because there is an informative selection mechanism at work in the construction of the plot. A very important observation is that the midpoint of the bounds will not provide an unbiased estimate of the true fraction, even in the absence of contextual effects, because their construction is crucially dependent on the proportion black in the area, x_i.

Whereas the convolution and binomial likelihoods were in terms of table–race-specific probabilities of registration p_{ji}, King (1997) models the *fractions* that register $\tilde{p}_{ji}$ (see also the footnote of Cho, 1998: 155), and implicitly assumes a "likelihood" of

$$L(\tilde{p}_{0i}, \tilde{p}_{1i}) = \begin{cases} 1 & \text{if } \tilde{q}_i = \tilde{p}_{0i} \times x_i + \tilde{p}_{1i} \times (1 - x_i), \\ 0 & \text{otherwise,} \end{cases}$$

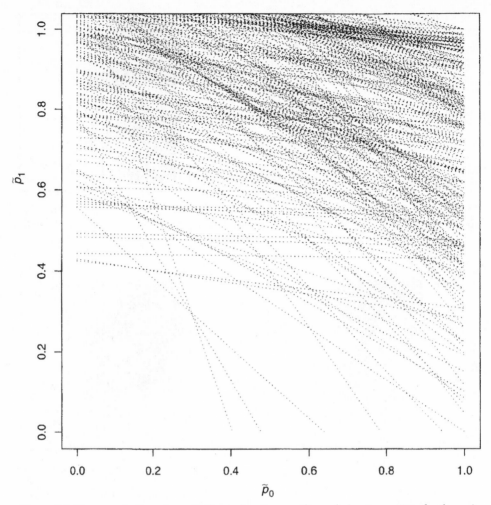

Figure 1.4. Tomography lines $\bar{p}_{1i} = \tilde{q}_i/(1 - x_i) - \bar{p}_{0i} \times x_i/(1 - x_i)$, $i = 1, \ldots, 275$, for the registration–race data.

where $\tilde{q}_i = y_i/N_i$; see King (1997: Equation 7.1). In other words, the only way the data enter into this "likelihood" is via the accounting equation, and the function is flat along this line. We use quotes for "likelihood" here because it is more a statement about missing data than a conventional likelihood function. *Tomography lines*, which are a rearrangement of Equation 1.1 and are given by

$$\bar{p}_{1i} = \frac{\tilde{q}_i}{1 - x_i} - \bar{p}_{0i} \frac{x_i}{1 - x_i},$$

are shown for the registration–race data in Figure 1.4. The bounds for $\bar{p}_{0i}$ and $\bar{p}_{1i}$ are the projections of the tomography lines of Figure 1.4, which was the reason that King constructed the likelihood in his method, and hence the discussion following the description of the bounds is relevant here.

The nonidentifiability of the mean functions in ecological regression and the linear neighborhood model, and the lack of identifiability of all of the parameters in the quadratic model, arise because the contextual effects are assumed linear in x. This model is not natural from a statistical perspective, however, since it allows estimated probabilities to lie outside of their permissible range of $(0, 1)$. As discussed by Wakefield (2004), a general model that allows registration probabilities to depend on both the race of the individual and the contextual effects of race is given by

$$p_{ji} = P(Y = 1 | \text{race } j, \text{ area } i) = g^{-1}(\alpha_{ji} + \beta_j x_i),$$

for a link function $g(\cdot)$. This choice leads to

$$q_i = P(Y = 1 | \text{area } i) = g^{-1}(\alpha_{0i} + \beta_0 x_i) \times x_i + g^{-1}(\alpha_{1i} + \beta_1 x_i) \times (1 - x_i).$$

Ecological regression corresponds to this model with a linear link and with $\alpha_{0i} = \alpha_0, \alpha_{1i} = \alpha_1$, and $\beta_0 = \beta_1 = 0$; the nonlinear neighborhood model has $\alpha_{0i} = \alpha_{1i} = \alpha_i$ and $\beta_0 = \beta_1 = 0$; the linear neighborhood model has $\alpha_{0i} = \alpha_{1i} = \alpha$ and $\beta_0 = \beta_1 = \beta$ with a linear link; and the quadratic model has a linear link with $\alpha_{0i} = \alpha_0$ and $\alpha_{1i} = \alpha_1$. Hence it would appear that it would be profitable to consider the general form with a nonlinear link, logistic and probit forms being the obvious choices. In these cases the model with individual and contextual effects has all parameters identifiable. Unfortunately, assuming nonlinearity theoretically removes the nonidentifiability but in practice is totally dependent on the form chosen, and parameter estimates will in general be highly unstable. This was pointed out by Achen and Shively (1995: 117), who comment that since the contextual effects are not strong and the range of x is often not $(0, 1)$, it would be virtually impossible to discriminate between nonlinear and linear forms (since any function that has a narrow range and does not change greatly may be well approximated with a linear form, via a Taylor series expansion). This is similar to criticisms of Heckman's selection models (Heckman, 1979); see for example Little (1985) and Copas and Li (1997).

1.4 PRIORS

Following King (1997), a number of authors have developed hierarchical approaches in which, rather than reduce the dimensionality of the models as was described in the previous section, the full $2m$ parameters are retained but the probabilities, or some transform, are assumed to arise from a bivariate distribution.

At the second stage of the model, King (1997) assumed that the pair $\tilde{p}_{0i}, \tilde{p}_{1i}$, arise from a truncated bivariate normal distribution, hence imposing identifiability. King (1997) views the truncated bivariate normal distribution as the likelihood, whereas we have referred to the tomography lines as providing the first stage of the model, and the truncated bivariate normal the second stage. Inference is initially carried out via MLE for the five population parameters, using numerical integration, and then simulation is used to make more refined inference. Priors may be placed on the population parameters (which characterize the truncated normal) to give a Bayesian model. In common with the majority of approaches, it is assumed that the fractions form an independent sample from the second stage distribution (here the truncated bivariate normal); see Chapter 12 for a hierarchical model with spatial dependence between the probabilities. The model in its most basic form also assumes that the fractions are uncorrelated with x_i. The latter may be relaxed (see King, 1997: Chapter 9) via the introduction of contextual effects (in the Introduction to this book it is recommended that such effects be included), but reliable estimation of both individual and contextual effects is crucially dependent on the existence of substantive prior information (see the example in Wakefield, 2004, for a further demonstration of this). The freely available EzI software (Benoit and King, 1998) may be used to implement the truncated normal model and its extensions.

At the second stage, King, Rosen, and Tanner (1999) assume that p_{0i} and p_{1i} are independent with

$$p_{ji}|a_j, b_j \sim \text{Beta}(a_j, b_j) \tag{1.12}$$

and with exponential priors $\text{Exp}(\lambda)$ on a_j, b_j, $j = 0, 1$, at the third stage, where λ^{-1} is the mean of the exponential. Specifically, in the example considered it was assumed that these exponential priors had mean 2 ($\lambda = 0.5$), a choice which is in general a poor one in that it does not favor large values of the hyperparameters and (since $a_j + b_j - 2$ is acting like a prior sample size for race j) these are what is needed to add strong information to the sparse marginal data. This choice also produces a prior for each probability which is very strongly U-shaped (since beta priors with $a_j < 1$, $b_j < 1$ are themselves U-shaped, and these values of the hyperparameters are assigned considerable prior weight), which is not desirable in many instances. This is further commented upon in Section 1.7 and discussed more fully in Wakefield (2004); in particular see Figure 7. Choosing much smaller values of λ, for example, $\lambda = 0.01$, produces almost uniform priors on the probabilities, and allows much larger values of the hyperparameters, though we would not universally recommend a particular hyperprior. As the number of tables decreases and the x distribution becomes more asymmetric, this problem becomes more and more acute. The ideal situation is for substantive information to be available for prior specification. The strong dependence on the third stage prior is in stark contrast to the usual generalized mixed model case, for which there is far less dependence (except for priors on variance components, where again care must taken with small numbers of units).

The model given by Equation 1.12 does not allow dependence between the two random effects (note that this is distinct from the independence between pairs of random effects in different areas, which is also assumed), though it is conjugate (giving a marginal distribution for the data that is beta–binomial), which may offer some advantage in computation. The model also allows area-level covariates to be added at the second stage.

Wakefield (2004) proposed as an alternative to the beta model a second stage in which the logits of the registration probabilities arose from a bivariate normal distribution; this model was introduced, for the analysis of a series of 2×2 tables when the internal cells were observed by Skene and Wakefield (1990). Specifically, a reasonably general form is

$$\begin{aligned} \theta_{0i} &= \mu_0 + \beta_0 z_i + \delta_{0i}, \\ \theta_{1i} &= \mu_1 + \beta_1 z_i + \delta_{1i} \end{aligned} \tag{1.13}$$

with

$$\delta_i \sim N_2(0, \Sigma),$$

where

$$\delta_i = \begin{bmatrix} \delta_{0i} \\ \delta_{1i} \end{bmatrix} \quad \text{and} \quad \Sigma = \begin{bmatrix} \Sigma_{00} & \Sigma_{01} \\ \Sigma_{10} & \Sigma_{11} \end{bmatrix}, \tag{1.14}$$

and where θ_{0i} and θ_{1i} denote the logits of the probabilities p_{0i} and p_{1i} in table i, i.e. $p_{ji} = \exp(\theta_{ji})/\{1 + \exp(\theta_{ji})\}$, $j = 0, 1$. In the specification 1.13, z_i represent area-level

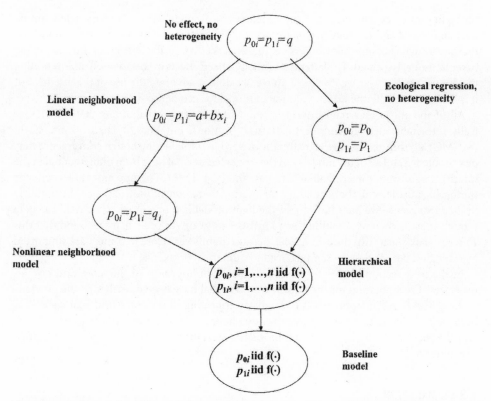

Figure 1.5. Nesting of models. In the baseline model the parameters of $f(\cdot)$ are fixed, while in the hierarchical model the common parameters are estimated from the totality of the data.

characteristics (and may include x_i), and β_0, β_1 are (ecological) log odds ratios associated with these variables. A third-stage hyperprior adds priors on $\mu_0, \mu_1,$ and Σ (and β_0, β_1 if there are covariates). In our limited experience it is difficult to gain information on the covariance term Σ_{01} or on covariate relationships, without strong prior information. The difficulty of estimating contextual effects and the dependence of the area-specific probabilities is a further reinforcement of the lack of information in ecological data. Sensitivity analyses in which Σ_{01} and/or β_0, β_1 are fixed a priori are straightforward under this model, however.

For the case of no covariates and $\Sigma_{01} = 0$, and without substantive information for the registration–race data, we may choose logistic priors with location 0 and scale 1 for μ_0 and μ_1, since these induce uniform priors on $\exp(\mu_j)/\{1 + \exp(\mu_j)\}$ (the median of the registration probability for race j across the population of areas). For the precisions Σ_{00}^{-1}, Σ_{11}^{-1} we specify gamma distributions $Ga(a, b)$ (where the parameterization is such that the mean is given by a/b). In the application here we take $a = 1$ and $b = 0.01$ – these values were chosen via an informal examination of simulations from the prior that it induced for $p_{0i}, p_{1i},$ with different values of a and b. In the `WinBUGS` manual the priors $Ga(0.001, 0.001)$ are often used for precisions within a hierarchical model. This choice is not to be recommended in general (that is, for all applications); here it is a very poor one (and leads to marginal priors for the probabilities that are highly U-shaped).

Figure 1.5 displays the nesting of a number of the models that we have described. The most simplistic model, at the top, is one in which there is a single registration probability for both races and for all areas. Taking the left fork gives the neighborhood models; taking the right fork gives ecological regression. Hierarchical models allow $2m$ parameters but tie the pairs of probabilities together via the assumption of a common distribution from which they are drawn (possibly allowing contextual effects also). At the bottom of the nesting the baseline model is located. The latter is essentially a fixed effects model for each table retaining the $2m$ parameters – as we discussed above, we do not advocate the use of this model, but it is useful to identify the extreme saturated model for ecological data.

All of the above hierarchical models result in posterior distributions that are analytically intractable (as we describe in the next section), but Markov chain Monte Carlo (MCMC) algorithms are relatively straightforward to implement (though convergence may be a problem), and all of the models but the truncated normal have been implemented in the WinBUGS software (Spiegelhalter, Thomas, and Best, 1998). The Appendix gives code for the logistic normal with the normal approximation to the convolution at stage 1. In our fairly limited experience we have found that the logit model is much more stable than the beta model, at least when used within the WinBUGS software. In particular we found that this software may crash with the beta model, because points very close to 0 and 1 are supported by ecological data and when sampled lead to numerical problems.

In the next section we briefly review the Bayesian approach to inference and give an overview of computation for the Bayesian models that have been described in the previous section. The Bayesian approach is particularly appealing in the context of ecological data because for such data modeling assumptions have to be made to enforce identifiability, and the most rigorous way of including such assumptions is via the adoption of a prior distribution.

1.5 COMPUTATION

1.5.1 Derivation of the Posterior Distribution

In the Bayesian approach, all unknown quantities are assigned prior distributions, and the posterior distribution reflects both these distributions and the information in the data that is contained in the likelihood. In the hierarchical models described in Section 1.4, two-stage priors are specified, with the first stage of the prior assuming a common form for the pairs of probabilities, and the second stage assigning *hyperpriors* to the parameters of this form. Letting θ_i represent the pair of table-specific parameters (these may be, for example, probabilities or logits), and ϕ a generic set of hyperparameters upon which the second stage of the prior depends, we have

$$\pi(\theta_1, \ldots, \theta_m, \phi | y_1, \ldots, y_m) \propto p(y_1, \ldots, y_m | \theta_1, \ldots, \theta_m, \phi) \times \pi(\theta_1, \ldots, \theta_m, \phi),$$

and we have

$$p(y_1, \ldots, y_n | \theta_1, \ldots, \theta_m, \phi) = \prod_{i=1}^{m} p(y_i | \theta_i),$$

by conditional independence of counts in different tables, and

$$\pi(\theta_1, \ldots, \theta_m, \phi) = \pi(\theta_1, \ldots, \theta_m | \phi) \times \pi(\phi),$$

to give the two-stage prior. Under the assumption of independence of the table-specific parameters (which would not be true if we assumed spatial dependence between these parameters), we may further write

$$\pi(\theta_1, \ldots, \theta_m|\phi) = \prod_{i=1}^{m} \pi(\theta_i|\phi).$$

Hence, under these assumptions, we have the posterior distribution

$$\pi(\theta_1, \ldots, \theta_m, \phi|y_i, \ldots, y_m) \propto \prod_{i=1}^{m} p(y_i|\theta_i) \times \prod_{i=1}^{m} \pi(\theta_i|\phi) \times \pi(\phi).$$

Inference follows via consideration of marginal posterior distributions and predictive distributions. For example $\pi(\theta_i|y_1, \ldots, y_m)$ is the marginal posterior distribution for the pair of parameters from table i. We may also be interested in imputing the missing counts in table i. This may be carried out via examination of the predictive distribution

$$P(Y_{0i}, Y_{1i}|y_i, \ldots, y_m) = \int P(Y_{0i}, Y_{1i}|\theta_i, N_{0i}, N_{1i}, N_i - y_i, y_i) \times \pi(\theta_i|y_1, \ldots, y_n)\, d\theta_i.$$

If we can simulate from $P(Y_{0i}, Y_{1i}|\theta_i, N_{0i}, N_{1i}, N_i - y_i, y_i)$, then it is straightforward to simulate from the predictive distribution, once samples $\theta_i^{(s)}$ are available from $\pi(\theta_i|N_{0i}, N_{1i}, N_i - y_i, y_i)$, via

$$\frac{1}{S} \sum_{s=1}^{S} P(Y_{0i}, Y_{1i}|\theta_i^{(s)}, N_{0i}, N_{1i}, N_i - y_i, y_i).$$

Each of the distributions within this sum is the distribution of Y_{0i} given the row and column margins and the table probabilities, and is a noncentral (or extended) hypergeometric distribution (e.g. McCullagh and Nelder, 1989). Suppose the odds ratio in the table is given by $\psi_i = p_{0i}(1 - p_{1i})/p_{1i}(1 - p_{0i})$; then Y_{0i} has a noncentral hypergeometric distribution if its distribution is of the form

$$Pr(Y_{0i} = y_{0i}|\psi_i, N_{0i}, N_{1i}, N_i - y_i, y_i)$$

$$= \begin{cases} \dfrac{\dbinom{N_{0i}}{y_{0i}} \dbinom{N_{1i}}{y_i - y_{0i}} \psi_i^{y_{0i}}}{\sum_{u=l_i}^{u_i} \dbinom{N_{0i}}{u} \dbinom{N_{1i}}{y_i - u} \psi_i^{u}} & y_{0i} = l_i, \ldots, u_i, \text{ otherwise,} \\ 0 \end{cases} \tag{1.15}$$

where $l_i = \max(0, y_i - N_{1i})$ and $u_i = \min(N_{0i}, y_i)$. Hence the predictive distribution is an overdispersed noncentral hypergeometric distribution. The distribution of Y_{1i} is obtained as $Y_{1i} = Y_i - Y_{0i}$, and produces $(y_{0i}/N_{0i}, y_{1i}/N_{1i})$ pairs that lie along the tomography line.

1.5.2 Markov Chain Monte Carlo Algorithms

Unfortunately, the integrals required to calculate the posterior and predictive distributions just described are not analytically tractable, and so some form of approximation is required. One such approximation, based on generating samples from the posterior distribution, is particularly well suited to the hierarchical model that we have generically described. This approximation is based on constructing a Markov chain whose stationary distribution is the required posterior distribution. Specifically, we exploit the conditional independences that were used to derive the posterior distribution and simulate repeatedly from the distributions

$$p(\theta_i|\theta_j, \; j \neq i, \; \phi, \; y_1, \ldots, y_m) \propto p(y_i|\theta_i) \times \pi(\theta_i|\phi), \tag{1.16}$$

$i = 1, \ldots, m$, and

$$p(\phi|\theta_1, \ldots, \theta_m, y_1, \ldots, y_m) \propto \prod_{i=1}^{m} \pi(\theta_i|\phi) \times \pi(\phi). \tag{1.17}$$

This MCMC algorithm is used within the `WinBUGS` software; the manual (Spiegelhalter, Thomas, and Best, 1998) gives details of specific algorithms and advice on assessing convergence of the Markov chain. Due to the nonidentifiability of ecological models the Markov chain typically has to be run for a large number of iterations (1–3 million iterations were used for the examples of this paper). The sampled values also typically show extremely high autocorrelations, and so a large number of samples are required for reliable inference. When such samples are retained for all parameters, storage becomes an issue, and so instead the Markov chain may be thinned (that is, samples are only stored every 1000th (say) iteration). Great care must be taken when examination of posterior quantities is carried out to gain some assurance that convergence has been attained – particularly for table-specific parameters, for example, p_{0i}, p_{1i}.

1.5.3 Auxiliary Variables Scheme

An alternative MCMC scheme suggests itself when the event of interest is rare (which is not typical in social science applications). The algorithm is based on introducing the counts Y_{0i} as auxiliary variables. Byers and Besag (2000) describe a Markov chain in such a situation under a rare-event assumption (the latter allows the convolution to be replaced by a Poisson distribution). With the introduction of auxiliary variables Y_{0i} we have a posterior distribution over not only the unknown parameters, but also the missing data:

$$\pi(\theta_1, \ldots, \theta_m, \phi, y_{01}, \ldots, y_{0m}|y_1, \ldots, y_m) = p(y_{01}, \ldots, y_{0m}|y_1, \ldots, y_m, \theta_1, \ldots, \theta_m)$$

$$\times \; p(\theta_1, \ldots, \theta_m, |y_{\phi 1}, \ldots, y_m). \tag{1.18}$$

This introduction seems unhelpful at first, since we have a more complex form than previously, but the benefit is that the conditional distributions for θ_i, which are required for an MCMC algorithm, are now of standard form. Specifically, we may alternate between the conditional distributions given by

$$p(y_{0i}|y_i, \theta_i), \tag{1.19}$$

$i = 1, \ldots, m$, and

$$\pi(\theta_i|N_{0i}, N_{1i}, y_i, y_{0i}), \tag{1.20}$$

$i = 1, \ldots, m$, with $\pi(\phi|\theta_1, \ldots, \theta_m, y_1, \ldots, y_m, y_{01}, \ldots, y_{0m})$ as in Equation 1.17. This algorithm is inefficient for nonrare outcomes; see Section 1.7 for a demonstration.

1.5.4 Rejection Algorithm for Individual Tables

For examination of the likelihood–posterior surface for a single table only via the baseline model, various schemes are possible. The auxiliary scheme just described may be implemented, or we can implement a rejection algorithm. The advantage of the latter is that it provides *independent* samples from the posterior distribution (as opposed to the dependent samples produced by MCMC schemes, including the auxiliary vaiable algorithm).

Since we only have two unknown parameters and a finite range for both, a rejection scheme is straightforward to implement. A generic rejection algorithm for sampling from a density $f(\cdot)$, given a proposal density $g(\cdot)$, proceeds as follows. First find

$$M = \sup \frac{f(z)}{g(z)};$$

then:

1. Sample $Z \sim g(\cdot)$ and, independently, $U \sim U(0, 1)$.
2. Accept Z if

$$U < \frac{f(Z)}{Mg(Z)};$$

otherwise return to 1.

The rejection algorithm depends on M being finite, and the efficiency may be measured through the number of samples that are accepted. The latter is a function of how closely g mimics f. A specific rejection algorithm that is useful in Bayesian inference is to choose g to be the prior distribution $\pi(\cdot)$. In this case M is the maximized likelihood (which we know is finite in the ecological context). Letting $L(\cdot)$ denote the likelihood and $M = L(\hat{Z})$ the maximized likelihood, the algorithm then becomes:

1. Sample $Z \sim \pi(\cdot)$ and, independently, $U \sim U(0, 1)$.
2. Accept Z if

$$U < \frac{L(Z)}{M};$$

otherwise return to 1.

Here $Z = (p_0, p_1)$.

For small tables, the above rejection algorithm of sampling from the prior and rejecting according to the ratio of the convolution at the sampled point to that at the maximum (which is evaluated once only) is feasible. The maximum lies at one of the endpoints of the tomography line; see Wakefield (2004) and Chapter 2 for details.

As the table margins increase in size, the rejection algorithm may become very inefficient, since the likelihood concentrates upon the tomography line and so hardly any points are accepted. The computational expense is greatest for the convolution likelihood, due to the need to evaluate a large number of terms in the summation over the missing data y_{0i}. The normal likelihood is computationally inexpensive, and in our experience provides a very good approximation (examples follow in Sections 1.6 and 1.7).

For table i and for a beta prior, the details of the algorithm are as follows. Let $M_i = L(\hat{p}_{0i}, \hat{p}_{1i})$ denote the supremum of the likelihood for p_{0i}, p_{1i} for either the convolution of binomials or approximating normal likelihood. The rejection algorithm is as follows:

1. Sample $p_{ji} \sim \text{Beta}(a_j, b_j)$, $j = 0, 1$, $U \sim U(0, 1)$, with all generations being independent.
2. Accept p_{0i}, p_{1i} if

$$U < \frac{L(p_{0i}, p_{1i})}{M_i},$$

with $L(p_{0i}, p_{1i})$ given by Equation 1.6 (if the convolution is used); otherwise return to 1.

To address the sensitivity to the prior, the accepted points may be reweighted via the ratio of the new to the original prior, or by thinning the accepted points via another rejection algorithm based on the supremum of the ratio of the priors. See Smith and Gelfand (1992) for details.

Another possibility that we have used as a quick approximation when the size of the table margins is large is to restrict the prior to sampling along the tomography line and then to test using the convolution likelihood. For large margins the likelihood will fall away very quickly to either side of the tomography line.

As we commented in Section 1.3, due to the nonidentifiability, as $N_i \to \infty$ the likelihood tends to a line, and not to a point as in the regular case. For large N_i, with *uniform priors*, the posterior distribution may therefore be approximated by a uniform distribution on the tomography line. In this situation the posterior medians p_{0i}, p_{1i} are therefore approximated by the midpoint of the method of bounds, that is,

$$\hat{p}_{0i} = 0.5 \times \left\{ \min\left(1, \frac{y_i}{N_{0i}}\right) + \max\left(0, \frac{y_i - N_{1i}}{N_{0i}}\right) \right\},$$

$$\hat{p}_{1i} = 0.5 \times \left\{ \min\left(1, \frac{y_i}{N_{1i}}\right) + \max\left(0, \frac{y_i - N_{0i}}{N_{1i}}\right) \right\},$$

since these bounds define the tomography line. We note again that estimates defined in this way will be biased, and the amount of bias depends on x_i. Consequently, examining the midpoints versus x_i (say) will be deceptive. We again stress that examination of the data via the baseline model is an initial exploratory step with inference following from hierarchical modeling.

1.5.5 Discrete Approximation

If we wish to examine the likelihood surface for a single table, then we may simply evaluate the surface over a grid of p_{0i}, p_{1i} values. If we wish to convert to a posterior surface, we may then multiply the likelihood by the prior and then normalize by dividing the product by the sum over all points in the grid. This approach is illustrated in the following sections.

1.6 A SIMPLE EXAMPLE

We begin by examining the data in Table 1.2 in order to illustrate a number of the issues discussed previously, and the use of the baseline model. For these data the bounds on the unobserved fractions are given by $\hat{p}_0 \in (0.2, 0.6)$, $\hat{p}_1 \in (0, 1)$. The MLEs are given by $\hat{p}_0 = 0.2$, $\hat{p}_1 = 1$. We implemented the rejection algorithm described in Section 1.5.4 with the convolution likelihood and independent uniform priors on p_0 and p_1; 2000 samples were generated with acceptance rate 0.41. The posterior means are given by $E[p_0|y] = 0.43$ and $E[p_1|y] = 0.50$. Figure 1.6a displays the posterior for p_0, p_1 (with a uniform prior)

Table 1.2 Simple table to illustrate baseline model

	$Y = 0$	$Y = 1$	
$x = 0$			5
$x = 1$			2
	4	3	7

constructed via the discrete approximation described in Section 1.5.5. The MLE is evident, as is the ridge centered along the tomography line. For such small marginal counts the posterior does not concentrate upon the line, emphasizing the difference between the unobserved fractions $\tilde{p}_0$, $\tilde{p}_1$, which must lie along the tomography line, and the hypothetical probabilities p_0, p_1. Figures 1.6b and c give respectively the normal approximation to the convolution likelihood, which is seen to be relatively accurate even for the small counts of this example, and the binomial likelihood of King, Rosen, and Tanner (1999), which is flat along the tomography line. Figure 1.6d gives King's "likelihood," which is flat along the tomography line and zero elsewhere (the gaps are artifacts of the plotting routine).

Figure 1.7 displays a number of summaries of both the posterior distribution of p_0, p_1 and the predictive distribution of the number of counts under the baseline model using samples obtained from the rejection algorithm. We see that we learn little about p_1, but the posterior distribution for p_0 differs from the prior. Intuitively, the fact that Y_0 cannot take the value 4 or 5 slightly reduces our beliefs in p_0 being close to one. Note that $\Pr(\{p_0 < 0.2\} \cup \{p_0 > 0.6\}|y) = 0.37 \neq 0$, so that values of the hypothetical probabilities outside the bounds are quite likely in this situation in which the margins are small. The sample-based analogue of Figure 1.6a is given in Figure 1.7e, while the marginal distributions are given in Figures 1.7a and c. The predictive distributions for the unobserved cells Y_0 and Y_1 are given in Figures 1.7b and d, and are seen to be flat along the admissible values (as proved in Wakefield, 2004). Finally, the posterior distribution of the difference in the probabilities, $p_1 - p_0$, is given in Figure 1.7f. We obtain $\Pr(p_0 > p_1|y) = 0.48$, so there is a small amount of information to distinguish between p_0 and p_1, but it depends crucially on the prior (particularly on the prior for p_1).

Individual table comparisons such as $\Pr(p_{0i} > p_{1i}|y_i)$ are seen to be extremely hazardous, since only one (and perhaps neither) of the probabilities is well estimated, and so the comparisons are wholly determined by the prior and by x_i and $1 - x_i$, the proportions in the two rows. Examination of those p_{0i} in tables with x_i close to 1, and p_{1i} in tables with x_i close to 0, can be informative, if it is reasonable to assume some commonality across tables. This is the basic assumption of a hierarchical model. If it is possible to obtain an informative prior, then table-specific comparisons are more reasonable.

1.7 REGISTRATION–RACE EXAMPLE

In this section we return to the registration–race data. We first analyze in detail two counties that were considered by King, Rosen, and Tanner (1999). The data from these counties are given in Tables 1.3 and 1.4.

1.7.1 County 150

King, Rosen, and Tanner (1999) considered this county to demonstrate that their approach can detect multimodalities in the posterior distribution. The bounds on the fractions

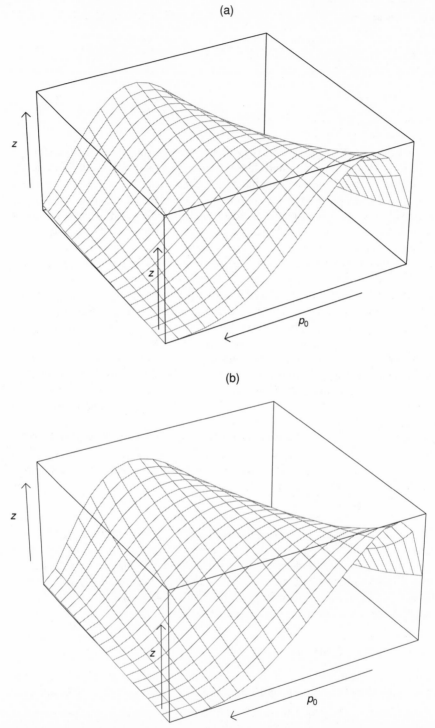

Figure 1.6. Various likelihood surfaces for the data of Table 1.2: (a) convolution likelihood function, (b) normal approximation to the convolution likelihood function, (c) binomial likelihood function of King, Rosen, and Tanner (1999), (d) tomography line "likelihood" of King (1997).

(c)

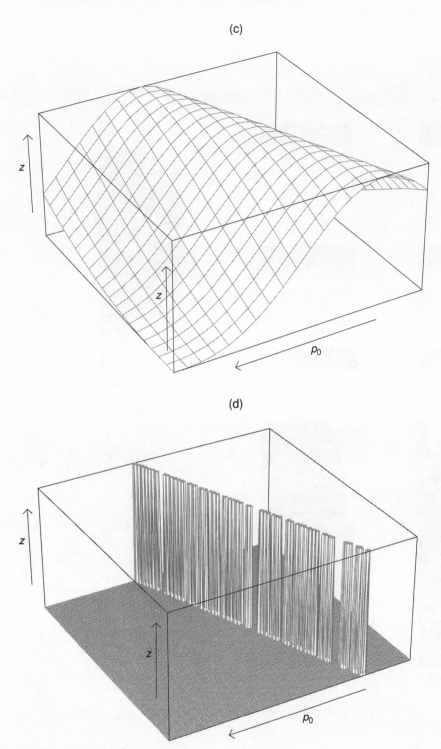

(d)

Figure 1.6. (*continued*)

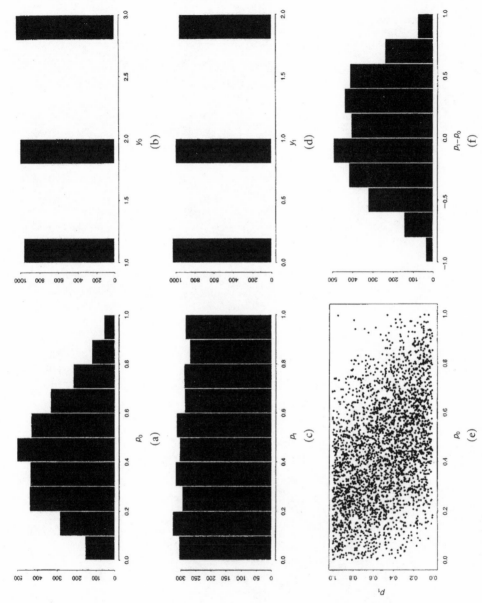

Figure 1.7. Posterior summaries for the data of Table 1.2 under a uniform prior: (a) $\pi(p_0|y)$, (b) $\pi(y_0|y)$, (c) $\pi(p_1|y)$, (d) $\pi(y_1|y)$, (e) $\pi(p_0, p_1|y)$, (f) $\pi(p_1 - p_0|y)$.

Table 1.3 Voter registration–race data for county 150 of King (1997)

		Unregistered $Y = 0$	Registered $Y = 1$	
Black	$x = 0$			4,001
White	$x = 1$			11,199
		6,800	8,400	15,200

registered for blacks and whites are $(0, 1)$ and $(0.39, 0.75)$, respectively, with $\hat{p}_1 - \hat{p}_0 \in (-0.61, 0.75)$. The MLEs for the convolution likelihood in Equation 1.6 are $\hat{p}_0 = 0$, $\hat{p}_1 = 0.75$.

In Figure 1.8a we plot the convolution surface by evaluating the posterior (with independent uniform priors) at a series of grid points as described in Section 1.5.5. For such a large marginal total (15,700) we see that the likelihood is highly concentrated along the tomography line, though the curvature along the line is evident. Figure 1.8b shows the normal approximation, which is very accurate here; Figure 1.8c the binomial likelihood of King, Rosen, and Tanner (1999), which is flat along the tomography line; and Figure 1.8d the implicit "likelihood" of King (1997), which is a flat ridge.

Figure 1.9 shows posterior summaries for the baseline model based on the auxiliary scheme of Section 1.5.3 with two separate chains set off from different points. Panels (a)–(d) clearly show the slow mixing – (a) and (b) show the sample path for p_0, and we see that after 30,000 iterations the chains have not come together. This is due to the nonidentifiability and the fact that the noncentral hypergeometric distribution has nonnegligible probability on a relatively small number of values, hence slowing movement around the space. Recently there has been interest in identifiability in Bayesian models, particularly from an MCMC perspective; see for example Gelfand and Sahu (1999). On the basis of this example and other analyses we have carried out, from this point onward for nonrare outcomes and for individual tables with large counts, we use the rejection algorithm, though we note that investigation of efficient computational schemes, including auxialiary variable schemes, is an important area of future research.

We obtained 1000 independent samples from the posterior $\pi(p_0, p_1 | y)$ using the rejection algorithm and sampling along the tomography line with the convolution likelihood of Equation 1.6; the acceptance rate was 0.80. Using the rejection algorithm and sampling from $U(0, 1) \times U(0, 1)$ with the convolution likelihood was very inefficient, and the accepted points fell almost exactly on the tomography line, as can be seen from Figure 1.9o and p.

Figure 1.10 contains a number of graphical summaries; these may be compared with Figure 4 of King, Rosen, and Tanner (1999). Panels (a), (c), and (e) give representations of the univariate posteriors and bivariate posteriors of $\pi(p_0, p_1 | y)$, while panels (b) and (d) give the predictive distributions for Y_0 and Y_1. The univariate posterior distributions are

Table 1.4 Voter-registration–race data for county 50 of King (1997)

		Unregistered $Y = 0$	Registered $Y = 1$	
Black	$x = 0$			29,494
White	$x = 1$			126,806
		10,800	145,500	156,300

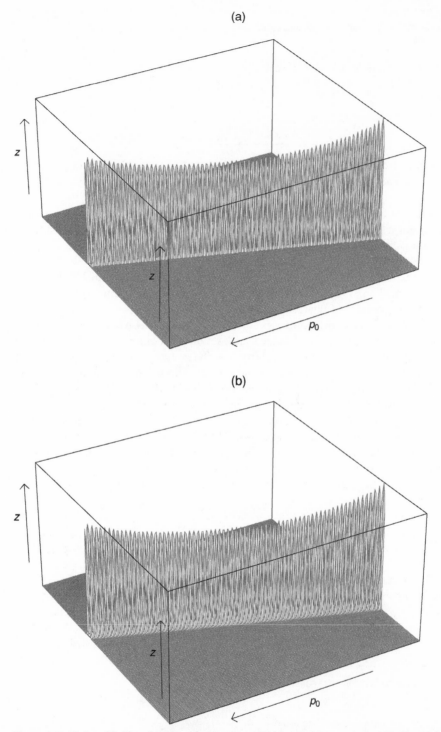

Figure 1.8. Various likelihood surfaces for the data of Table 1.3: (a) convolution likelihood function, (b) normal approximation to the convolution likelihood function, (c) binomial likelihood function of King, Rosen, and Tanner (1999), (d) tomography line "likelihood" of King (1997).

(c)

(d)

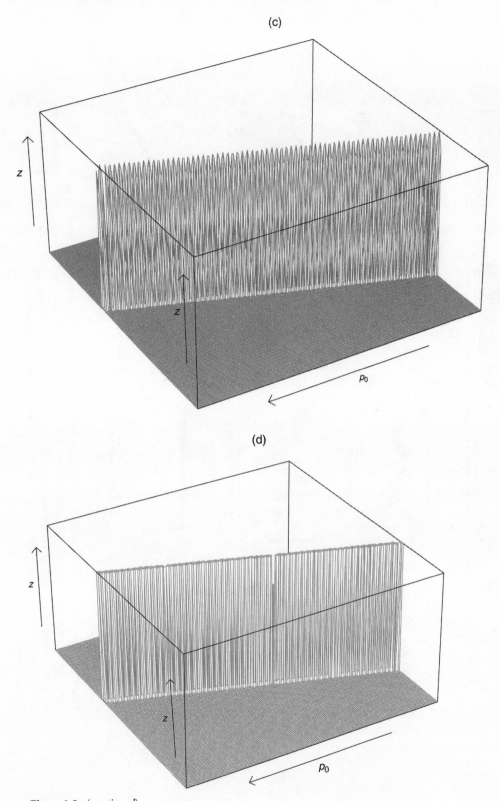

Figure 1.8. (*continued*)

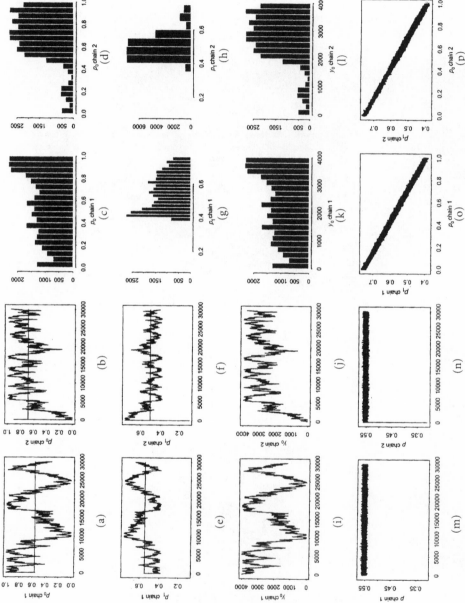

Figure 1.9. Posterior plots from two chains of length 30,000 iterations from an auxiliary variable MCMC algorithm for county 150 of the registration–race data. Panels (a) and (b) give the time series plots for p_0 for chains 1 and 2, respectively; panels (c) and (d) give the resultant histograms. The second and third rows show the equivalent plots for p_1 and y_0, respectively. Panels (m) and (n) give the time series plots for $q = p_0 \times x + p_1 \times (1 - x)$ for the two chains, and panels (o) and (p) the (p_0, p_1) pairs under the two chains.

40

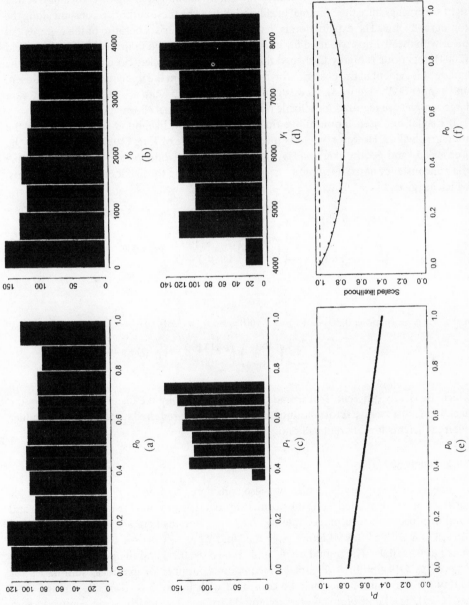

Figure 1.10. Posterior plots for county 150 of the registration–race data: (a) $\pi(p_0|y)$, (b) $\pi(y_0|y)$, (c) $\pi(p_1|y)$, (d) $\pi(y_1|y)$, (e) $\pi(p_0, p_1|y)$, (f) normalized likelihoods along tomography line under convolution and approximating normal likelihood (indistinguishable, solid line), and binomial (dashed line).

close to uniform on the bounds, with the slight U-shape reflecting the shape of the variance V_i in Equation 1.8 along the tomography line. Panel (f) shows the scaled convolution and approximating normal likelihoods along the tomography line, and shows that they are virtually identical; the binomial likelihood is constant along this line and is also included as a dashed line. We note that the bimodality reported for p_0 by King, Rosen, and Tanner (1999) has the same shape as that of the convolution likelihood in Figure 1.10f and is at first sight surprising, since the binomial likelihood utilized by these authors is constant along the tomography line. The explanation is that the bimodality arises because of the exponential prior with mean 2 that was used for a_0, b_0, a_1, b_1. As discussed in more detail by Wakefield (2004), this prior is highly U-shaped for p_0 and p_1, with spikes close to 0 and 1, and the spike at 1 is evident in the posterior for p_1 that is reported in the upper panel of King, Rosen, and Tanner (1999: Figure 4). As we discuss in Section 1.7.3, with an MCMC approach, very large samples are required for reliable reporting of individual county probabilities.

It may at first seem nonintuitive that the convolution likelihood is not flat along the tomography line. However, whereas the tomography line of King (1997) is in terms of the *fractions* $\tilde{p}_{0i}$ and $\tilde{p}_{1i}$, the likelihood is in terms of the *probabilities* p_{0i} and p_{1i}. In this example the nonconstancy of the likelihood is clear from examining the likelihood at the endpoints, which are given by

$$l(p_0 = 0, \ p_1 = 0.75) = P(Y = 8400 | p_0 = 0, \ p_1 = 0.75)$$

$$= \sum_{y_0=0}^{4001} \binom{4001}{y_0} \binom{11199}{8400 - y_0} 0.75^{8400-y_0} 0.25^{2799+y_0}$$

and

$$l(p_0 = 0, \ p_1 = 0.39) = P(Y = 8400 | p_0 = 0, \ p_1 = 0.39)$$

$$= \sum_{y_0=0}^{4001} \binom{4001}{y_0} \binom{11199}{8400 - y_0} 0.39^{8400-y_0} 0.61^{2799+y_0},$$

which are clearly different. Mathematically it is evident why the likelihood is not flat: the likelihood must average across the unobserved cell, and the required summation will produce different heights for different values of p_0, p_1.

1.7.2 County 50

We now examine county 50, which was also considered by King (1997). The rejection algorithm was implemented using the normal approximation along the tomography line and a uniform prior; the acceptance rate was 0.87. The bounds here are (0.63, 1) for $\tilde{p}_0$ and (0.75, 1) for $\tilde{p}_1$, and the MLEs are $\hat{p}_0 = 0.63$ and $\hat{p}_1 = 1$. The posterior means were estimated as 0.81, 0.96. The bound on $\hat{p}_1 - \hat{p}_0$ is $(-0.09, 0.7)$, and the posterior probability $\Pr(p_1 - p_0 > 0 | y) = 0.18$. Figure 1.11 contains a number of graphical summaries for county 50; these summaries may be compared with Figure 3 of King, Rosen, and Tanner (1999). The latter plot shows a large mode around 0.65 which, when compared with Figure 1.11, would appear to be due to the hierarchical prior, showing how strongly inference for a particular table depends on the information from all of the tables. The bimodal nature of the posteriors induced by the poor choice of prior is also evident in Figure 3 of King, Rosen, and Tanner (1999). The normal approximation to the convolution likelihood is again accurate along the tomography line (Figure 1.11d).

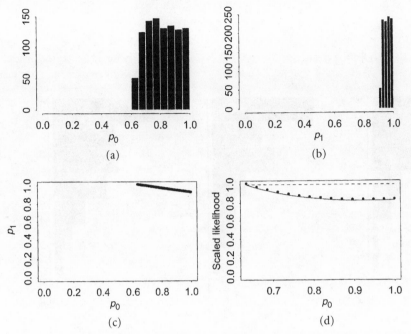

Figure 1.11. Posterior plots for county 50 of the registration–race data: (a) $\pi(p_0|y)$, (b) $\pi(p_1|y)$, (c) $\pi(p_0, p_1|y)$ (d) normalized likelihoods along tomography line under convolution and approximate normal likelihood (indistinguishable, solid line) and binomial likelihood (dashed line).

1.7.3 All Counties

We have already seen from examination of the bounds that there is far more information concerning p_{1i} here, because whites are in the majority in most of the areas. For the registration–race data Figure 1.1 shows the weighted least squares line with weights N_i; we obtain estimates of $\hat{p}_0 = 0.34$, $\hat{p}_1 = 0.89$ from ecological regression. When the three outlying counties are removed, we obtain estimates for $(\hat{p}_0, \hat{p}_1)$ of $(0.41, 0.87)$ with weighted least squares. Hence we see some sensitivity, particularly for p_0.

BASELINE MODELS

We investigated the sensitivity to the prior by assuming Beta(3, 2) and Beta(4, 1) priors in addition to the (uniform) Beta(1, 1) prior. A Beta(3, 2) random variable has 2.5%, 50% and 97.5% points of 0.20, 0.61, 0.93; the equivalent quantities for a Beta(4, 1) random variable are 0.40, 0.84, 0.99. The aim of these analyses is to illustrate the sensitivity of inference to prior assumptions, and we used a very approximate rejection algorithm in which the likelihood was assumed to be constant along the tomography line. The rejection step, as described in Section 1.5.4, then consists in accepting a point based on the ratio of the density of the prior at the point to the density at the supremum of the prior (which is available in closed form).

Figure 1.12 shows the histograms of the empirical distribution of the posterior medians of p_{0i}, p_{1i} under the three beta priors, and Table 1.5 provides numerical summaries. The sensitivity in the distribution of the medians of p_{0i} is evident. Under the Beta(4, 1) prior, 49% of the areas have $\Pr(p_{0i} < p_{1i}|y) > 0.5$, showing that the registration rates for blacks

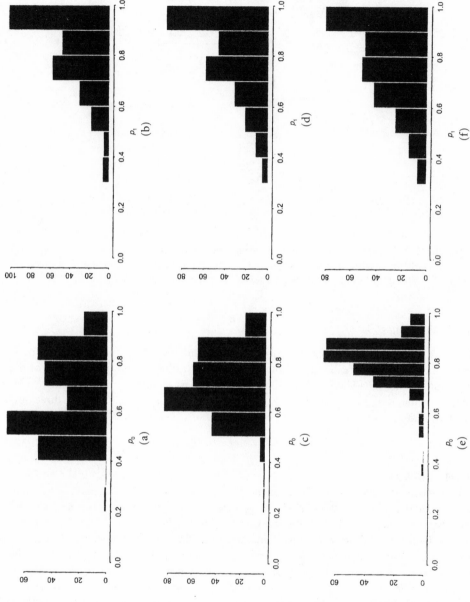

Figure 1.12. Posterior medians for all areas for the registration–race data using the baseline model and independent Beta$(a, b) \times$ Beta(a, b) priors: (a) p_{0i}, $a = 1$, $b = 1$, (b) p_{1i}, $a = 1$, $b = 1$, (c) p_{0i}, $a = 3$, $b = 2$, (d) p_{1i}, $a = 3$, $b = 2$, (e) p_{0i}, $a = 4$, $b = 1$, (f) p_{1i}, $a = 4$, $b = 1$, $i = 1, \ldots, 275$.

Table 1.5 Summaries of distribution of posterior medians of (p_{0i}, p_{1i}) over $i = 1, \ldots, 275$ counties of registration–race data of King (1997) under the baseline model and different prior specifications

Statistic	Beta(1, 1)	Beta(3, 2)	Beta(4, 1)
$\bar{p}_0$	0.66	0.71	0.81
s.d.$\{p_0\}$	0.16	0.13	0.10
2.5%, p_0	0.46	0.47	0.57
50%, p_0	0.63	0.70	0.83
97.5%, p_0	0.98	0.98	0.99
$\bar{p}_1$	0.80	0.79	0.77
s.d.$\{p_1\}$	0.16	0.17	0.17
2.5%, p_1	0.39	0.41	0.37
50%, p_1	0.84	0.82	0.78
97.5%, p_1	1.0	1.0	0.99

and whites are virtually identical. The drop in p_1 in Table 1.5 may be attributed to the negative dependence between p_{0i} and p_{1i} in the likelihood.

For some areas, the rejection rate r was very low under the nonuniform priors, in particular for the outlying areas. This is not surprising when one recognizes that the prior predictive $\Pr(y_i) = r \times M$, where M is the maximized prior in this implementation and is constant for all i (Wakefield, 1996).

HIERARCHICAL MODELS

We first state summaries for the truncated normal model (from King, 1997). The posterior means of the averages of the normal for blacks and whites were 0.62 and 0.83, respectively. For the binomial–beta model of King, Rosen, and Tanner (1999), the means of the beta distributions for blacks and whites were 0.60 and 0.85, respectively (this analysis had exponential priors of mean 2 on the hyperparameters).

At the first stage of the hierarchical model we take the normal approximation to the convolution. At the second stage we assume the model $\theta_{ji} \sim N(\cdot|\mu_j, \Sigma_{jj})$, $j = 0, 1$, with θ_{ji} being the logit of p_{ji}, as in Equations 1.13 and 1.14 with $\Sigma_{01} = 0$ (so that the logits are independent across tables). At the third stage of the model we assumed independent logistic distributions with location 0 and scale 1 (as described in Section 1.4). The variances are more difficult. We report two analyses, one with the naive choice of Ga(0.001, 0.001) priors for Σ_{jj}^{-1}, and the other with Ga(1, 0.01) priors. The models were fitted using the WinBUGS (Spiegelhalter, Thomas, and Best, 1998); the code for the normal approximation to the convolution model is given in the Appendix.

The individual probabilities display very poor mixing in an MCMC approach, and inference for (p_{0i}, p_{1i}) or (Y_{0i}, Y_{1i}) for a particular table would be more accurate using an empirical Bayes approach in which the table of interest was treated as a new table and the prior was taken as the posterior over the population parameters. For example, we could use a rejection algorithm with samples $\theta_i^{(s)}$ from $\pi(\theta_i|\phi^{(s)})$ with $\phi^{(s)} \sim \pi(\phi|y)$, $s = 1, \ldots, S$, being samples from the posterior on the hyperparameters. Given the large margins and large number of tables, this will not be too poor an approximation unless the table has very large margins and/or is outlying.

The population summary parameters in Table 1.6 were obtained from chains that displayed slow convergence. The Markov chain was more stable when the more informative

Table 1.6 Posterior quantiles from hierarchical analyses of the race–registration data of King (1997)

Parameter	Ga(0.001, 0.001)			Ga(1, 0.01)		
	2.5%	50%	97.5%	2.5%	50%	97.5%
$\bar{p}_0$	0.53	0.57	0.62	0.53	0.58	0.63
$\bar{p}_1$	0.84	0.86	0.87	0.83	0.85	0.87
s.d.$\{p_{0i}\}$	0.30	0.32	0.34	0.29	0.32	0.34
s.d.$\{p_{1i}\}$	0.16	0.18	0.20	0.16	0.18	0.20

(and plausible) prior was used for inference. For all analyses we ran the chains for 500,000 iterations of burn-in (to give the chain an opportunity to reach the main mass of the posterior and "forget" its starting position), and then samples from a further 2,500,000 iterations were used for inference (this latter number was greater than was needed but was used for safety). Figure 1.13 shows samples from the Markov chain for four population summary parameters (the names of which are given in the Appendix), and shows strong dependence across iteration.

From Table 1.6 we see that the results for p_1 are relatively robust to the choice of second-stage distribution, as we would expect from Figure 1.12 and the analyses of the previous sections. The number of tables is large here, and so the impact of the prior is not so great.

We attempted to include a correlation parameter in the second-stage distributions, but the resultant Markov chain displayed extremely slow mixing, indicating that there was close to zero information in the data to estimate this parameter. Including x_i as a covariate also produced a poorly mixing chain, corresponding to near-nonidentifiability. This phenomenon is noted by Rosen, Jiang, King, and Tanner (2001: Section 4.2).

In this example we have seen that the white registration probabilities are well estimated in many areas, while there is far more uncertainty associated with the registration probabilities for blacks. We conclude that under the assumption of no contextual effects there is evidence to suggest that, over all, areas the black probabilities are smaller than the white probabilities on average, but the extent of the difference cannot be precisely estimated without an informative prior distribution, or surveys from within a sample of areas. We emphasize that this analysis has not addressed the contextual aspect of the ecological fallacy.

1.8 DISCUSSION

In this chapter we have described and contrasted various models for ecological inference. Examination of the bounds is an important exploratory step, but for inference the use of an appropriate statistical model that naturally incorporates the bounds in a formal manner is required. There is a fundamental indeterminacy that must be acknowledged when ecological data are analyzed; the "solution" to the ecological inference problem is to supplement the aggregate data with accurate individual-level information, or with context-specific prior information, with the former being the preferred source of information. Wakefield (2004) illustrates that such information need only be available on a small subset of individuals. In fact, data on a small subset of the minority group only can provide accurate inference.

The Bayesian hierarchical models described here offer the flexibility to formally accommodate substantive information and/or additional data. An excellent example of the

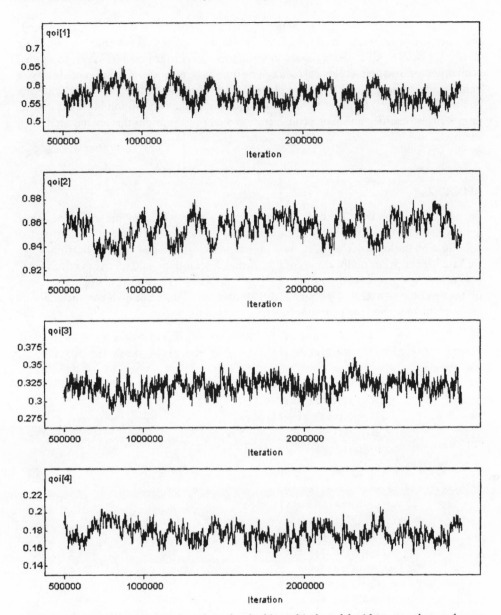

Figure 1.13. Behavior of the Markov chain for the hierarchical model with a normal second-stage distribution with Ga(0.001, 0.001) priors on the precisions. The first 500,000 iterations are treated as a burn-in and are not plotted; the remaining iterations, up to 3,000,000, are plotted. The four parameters qoi[1], qoi[2], qoi[3], qoi[4] are, respectively, p_1, p_2, s.d. (p_0), and s.d. (p_1), and every 1,000th sample is plotted. The dependence in the chain is apparent, showing that large numbers of samples are required for accurate inference. Inferential summaries are given in Table 1.6.

incorporation of both of these aspects, within the hierarchical structure described here, is given in Chapter 6. We recommend that a number of models, reflecting a range of prior assumptions (including the inclusion of contextual effects), be fitted, and the sensitivity to assumptions, in particular contextual effects, be examined. Again the hierarchical models described here provide a flexible class for this comparison.

There are always competing explanations for data in an observational setting, and ecological inference provides an extreme example in that vital influential information is missing due to the design. All analyses should be as context-specific as possible. When combined with other information, ecological data can be used to build a plausible inferential story. A constructive strategy is to start with a plausible individual-level model and then aggregate to find the ecological form (as we did when motivating the convolution likelihood). This approach also clarifies, and allows consideration of, the assumptions that are required by all methods.

APPENDIX

Below we give the WinBUGS code to implement the hierarchical model with the normal approximation to the convolution likelihood at the first stage and independent normal distributions on the logits of the registration probabilities at the second stage. At the third stage we have logistic priors on the means of the normal distributions, and inverse gamma distributions on the variances of the normal distributions. The latter is equivalent to gamma priors on the precisions – note that within WinBUGS the normal distribution is parameterized in terms of the mean and the precision (the reciprocal of the variance).

```
## p[i, 1] = P( Y=1 | X=0, area i ) - Prob of reg given black in area i
## p[i, 2] = P( Y=1 | X=1, area i ) - Prob of reg given white in area i
##   Margins
##              N0[i] - total blacks
##              N1[i] - total whites
##              y[i] - total republicans

model
{
      for (i in 1 : m) {
## Likelihood is the normal approximation to the convolution.
          tildeq[i] ~ dnorm( mu[i], W[i] )
          mu[i] <- x[i] * p[i, 1] + (1 - x[i]) * p[i, 2]
          W[i] <- N[i] /((p[i, 1] * (1 - p[i, 1]) * x[i]) + (p[i, 2]
              * (1 - p[i, 2]) * (1 - x[i])))
          N[i] <- N0[i] + N1[i]
          tildeq[i] <- y[i] / N[i]
          x[i] <- N0[i] / N[i]
## Second stage prior is normal on the logits.
          p[i, 1] <- exp( theta[i, 1] ) / (1 + exp( theta[1, 1] ))
          p[i, 2] <- exp( theta[i, 2] ) / (1 + exp( theta[1, 2] ))
          theta[i, 1] ~ dnorm(mean0, tau0)
          theta[i, 2] ~ dnorm(mean1, tau1)
          temp1[i] <- p[i, 1] * N0[i]
          temp2[i] <- p[i, 2] * (N[i] - N0[i])
    }
        sum1 <- sum(N0[])
        sum2 <- sum(N[]) - sum(N0[])
        t1 <- sum(temp1[]) / sum1
        t2 <- sum(temp2[]) / sum2
```

```
## Third stage priors are logistic and gamma.
      mean0 ~ dlogis(0, 1)
      mean1 ~ dlogis(0, 1)
      tau0 ~ dgamma(1, .01)
      tau1 ~ dgamma(1, .01)
## Quantities of interest to calculate.
      qoi[1] <- exp(mean0) / (1 + exp(mean0)) # Posterior median of p0
      qoi[2] <- exp(mean1) / (1 + exp(mean1)) # Posterior median of p1
      qoi[3] <- t1                  # Population-weighted average for p0
      qoi[4] <- t2                  # Population-weighted average for p1
      qoi[5] <- mean0               # Mean of logit of p0
      qoi[6] <- mean1               # Mean of logit of p1
      qoi[7] <- tau0                # Precision of logit of p0
      qoi[8] <- tau1                # Precision of logit of p1
      qoi[9] <- mean(p[, 1])        # Empirical mean of p0
      qoi[10] <- mean(p[, 2])       # Empirical mean of p1
      qoi[11] <- sd(p[, 1])         # Empirical sd of p0
      qoi[12] <- sd(p[, 2])         # Empirical sd of p1
}
```

REFERENCES

Achen, C. H. and W. P. Shively. 1995. *Cross-Level Inference*. Chicago: University of Chicago Press.

Barndorff-Nielsen, O. E. and D. R. Cox. 1989. *Asymptotic Techniques for Use in Statistics*. London: Chapman and Hall.

Benoit, K. and G. King. 1998. "EzI: An Easy Program for Ecological Inference, Version 2.02." Department of Government, Harvard University, Boston.

Brown, P. J. and C. D. Payne. 1986. "Aggregate Data, Ecological Regression, and Voting Transitions," *Journal of the American Statistical Association*, 81: 452–460.

Byers, S. and J. Besag. 2000. "Inference on a Collapsed Margin in Disease Mapping," *Statistics in Medicine*, 19: 2243–2249.

Chambers, R. L. and D. G. Steel. 2001. "Simple Methods for Ecological Inference in 2 × 2 Tables," *Journal of the Royal Statistical Society, Series A*, 164: 175–192.

Cho, W. K. T. 1998. "If the Assumption Fits . . . : A Comment on the King Ecological Inference Solution," *Political Analysis*, 7: 143–163.

Cleave, N., P. J. Brown, and C. D. Payne. 1995. "Methods for Ecological Inference: An Evaluation," *Journal of the Royal Statistical Society, Series A*, 158: 55–75.

Copas, J. B. and H. G. Li. 1997. "Inference for Non-random Samples (with Discussion)," *Journal of the Royal Statistical Society, Series B*, 59: 55–95.

Duncan, O. D. and B. Davis. 1953. "An Alternative to Ecological Correlation," *American Sociological Reviews*, 18: 665–666.

Freedman, D. A. 2001. "Ecological Inference and the Ecological Fallacy." In N. J. Smelser and P. B. Baltes (eds.), *International Encyclopedia of the Social and Behavioral Sciences*, Volume 6. New York: Elsevier, pp. 4027–4030.

Freedman, D. A., S. P. Klein, J. Sacks, C. A. Smyth, and C. G. Everett. 1991. "Ecological Regression and Voting Rights (and Discussion)," *Evaluation Review*, 15: 673–816.

Freedman, D. A., S. P. Klein, M. Ostland, and M. R. Roberts. 1998. "Review of 'A Solution to the Ecological Inference Problem,' by G. King," *Journal of the American Statistical Association*, 93: 1518–1522.

Freedman, D. A., M. Ostland, M. R. Roberts, and S. P. Klein. 1999. "Reply to G. King (Letter)," *Journal of the American Statistical Association*, 94: 355–357.

Gelfand, A. E. and S. K. Sahu. 1999. "Identifiability, improper priors and Gibbs sampling for generalized linear models," *Journal of the American Statistical Association*, 94, 247–253.

Gelman, A., S. Ansolabehere, P. N. Price, D. K. Park, and L. C. Minnite. 2001. "Models, Assumptions, and Model Checking in Ecological Regressions," *Journal of the Royal Statistical Society, Series A*, 164: 101–118.

Goodman, L. 1953. "Ecological Regressions and the Behavior of Individuals," *American Sociological Review*, 18: 663–666.

Goodman, L. 1959. "Some Alternatives to Ecological Regression," *American Journal of Sociology*, 64: 610–624.

Hawkes, A. G. 1969. "An Approach to the Analysis of Electoral Swing," *Journal of the Royal Statistical Society, Series A*, 132: 68–79.

Heckman, J. J. 1979. "Sample Selection Bias as a Specification Error," *Econometrica*, 47: 153–161.

King, G. 1997. *A Solution to the Ecological Inference Problem.* Princeton, NJ: Princeton University Press.

King, G., O. Rosen, and M. A. Tanner. 1999. "Binomial–Beta Hierarchical Models for Ecological Inference," *Sociological Methods and Research*, 28: 61–90.

Lindley, D. V. and A. F. M. Smith. 1972. "Bayes Estimates for the Linear Model (with Discussion)," *Journal of the Royal Statistical Society, Series B*, 34: 1–41.

Little, R. J. A. 1985. "A Note about Models for Selectivity Bias," *Econometrica*, 53: 1469–1474.

McCullagh, P. and J. A. Nelder. 1989. *Generalised Linear Models*, 2nd ed. London: Chapman and Hall.

Robinson, W. D. 1950. "Ecological Correlations and the Behavior of Individuals," *American Sociological Reviews*, 15: 351–357.

Rosen, O., W. Jiang, G. King, and M. A. Tanner. 2001. "Bayesian and Frequentist Inference for Ecological Inference: The $R \times C$ Case," *Statistica Neerlandica*, 55: 134–156.

Selvin, H. C. 1958. "Durkheim's 'Suicide' and Problems of Empirical Research," *American Journal of Sociology*, 63: 607–619.

Simpson, E. H. 1951. "The Interpretation of Interaction in Contingency Tables," *Journal of the Royal Statistical Society, Series B*, 13: 238–241.

Skene, A. M. and J. C. Wakefield. 1990. "Hierarchical Models for Multi-centre Binary Response Studies," *Statistics in Medicine*, 9: 919–929.

Smith, A. F. M. and A. E. Gelfand. 1992. "Bayesian Statistics without Tears: A Sampling Resampling Perspective," *American Statistician*, 46: 84–88.

Spiegelhalter, D., A. Thomas, and N. Best. 1998. *WinBUGS: Bayesian Inference Using Gibbs Sampling, Manual v1.2.*, Imperial College, London and Medical Research Council Biostatistics Unit, Cambridge, available from www.mrc-bsu.cam.ac.uk\bugs.

Wakefield, J. C. 1996. "Bayesian Individualization via Sampling-Based Methods," *Journal of Pharmacokinetics and Biopharmaceutics*, 24: 103–131.

Wakefield, J. C. 2004. "Ecological Inference for 2×2 Tables (with discussion)," *Journal of the Royal Statistical Society, Series A*, 167: 385–445.

2 The Information in Aggregate Data*

David G. Steel, Eric J. Beh, and Ray L. Chambers

ABSTRACT

Ecological inference attempts to draw conclusions concerning individual-level relationships using data in the form of aggregates for groups in the population. The groups are often geographically defined. A fundamental statistical issue is how much information aggregate data contain concerning the relationships and parameters that we are trying to estimate. The information affects the standard errors of estimates as well as the power of any tests of hypothesis. It also affects the ability to tell, from the aggregate data, which different models under consideration are supported by the data.

In this chapter likelihood-based methods are considered. We show in general how aggregation affects the information matrix associated with the maximum likelihood estimates compared with the case when individual-level data are available. Hypothesis testing using aggregate data is also considered.

We apply this general approach to ecological inference in the case of several 2 by 2 tables and show how the information is affected by aggregation. Tests of the hypothesis that the parameters are constant across the groups are developed using aggregate data. We also consider how the addition of a small number of individual-level data obtained from a sample, ignoring the groups, increases the information concerning the parameters. The theory is illustrated through an example.

2.1 INTRODUCTION

The method of ecological analysis involves using aggregate data for a set of groups to make inferences concerning individual-level relationships. Typically the data available for analysis consist of the means or totals of variables of interest for geographical areas such as precincts, although the groups can be organizations such as schools or hospitals. Attention has focused on developing methods of estimating the parameters characterizing the individual-level relationships across the whole population, but also in some cases the relationships for each of the groups.

Applying standard methods used to analyze individual-level data, such as linear or logistic regression or contingency table analysis, to aggregate data will usually produce biased estimates of individual-level relationships. Thus much of the effort in ecological analysis has concentrated on developing methods of analyzing aggregate data that can produce unbiased, or less biased, parameter estimates. There has been less work done on inference procedures, such as constructing confidence intervals and hypothesis testing. Fundamental to these inferential issues is the question of how much information is contained in aggregate data and what evidence such data can provide concerning important assumptions and hypotheses.

* This research was supported by grants from the Australian Research Council. We would also like to thank John Rayner for some useful discussions.

In Section 2.2 we describe a general approach to determining the information in aggregate data and how it compares with the information in individual-level data for likelihood-based inference, including hypothesis testing. In Section 2.3 we illustrate how the approach applies in the case of data from several 2×2 tables. We also consider, in Section 2.4, the information contributed by aggregate and individual information when both are available. Section 2.5 gives empirical results based on some real data, illustrating the loss of information due to aggregation and how hypothesis testing and analysis of residuals can be done using aggregate data. Section 2.6 provides a brief discussion.

2.2 INFORMATION LOST BY AGGREGATION

Suppose that we have individual-level data $d^{(1)}$, which have associated probability function $f^{(1)}(d^{(1)}; \phi)$. The vector ϕ contains the parameters of the distribution of the individual-level data. Likelihood inference about the parameter vector ϕ would be based on the likelihood $L^{(1)}(\phi; d^{(1)}) = f^{(1)}(d^{(1)}; \phi)$ or the associated log likelihood

$$l^{(1)} \left(\phi; d^{(1)} \right) = \log L^{(1)} \left(\phi; d^{(1)} \right).$$

The score function for ϕ based on $d^{(1)}$ is

$$\mathrm{sc}^{(1)} \left(\phi; d^{(1)} \right) = \frac{\partial}{\partial \phi} l^{(1)} \left(\phi; d^{(1)} \right). \tag{2.1}$$

Maximum likelihood estimates (MLEs) would usually be obtained by solving

$$\mathrm{sc}^{(1)} \left(\phi; d^{(1)} \right) = 0, \tag{2.2}$$

resulting in the MLE $\hat{\phi}$.

For inference based on the MLEs we would also be interested in the (observed) information matrix

$$\mathrm{info}^{(1)} \left(\phi; d^{(1)} \right) = -\frac{\partial}{\partial \phi} \mathrm{sc}^{(1)} \left(\phi; d^{(1)} \right)$$

$$= -\frac{\partial^2}{\partial \phi \, \partial \phi^T} l^{(1)} \left(\phi; d^{(1)} \right). \tag{2.3}$$

The expected information is

$$\mathrm{Info}^{(1)} \left(\phi; d^{(1)} \right) = \mathrm{E} \left[\mathrm{info}^{(1)} \left(\phi; d^{(1)} \right) \right]. \tag{2.4}$$

The expectation is over the distribution of $d^{(1)}$. Under several regularity conditions the variance matrix of the asymptotic distribution of $\hat{\phi}$ is $[\mathrm{Info}^{(1)}]^{-1}$ (see for example Cox and Hinkley, 1974, Chapter 9).

Suppose we are interested in testing the hypothesis H_0. Let $\hat{\phi}_0$ be the MLE of ϕ under H_0. There are three common approaches to testing H_0:

1. The *likelihood ratio test* (LRT) is based on the likelihood ratio

$$R^{(1)} = \frac{L^{(1)} \left(\hat{\phi}_0; d^{(1)} \right)}{L^{(1)} \left(\hat{\phi}; d^{(1)} \right)},$$

and

$$-2 \log R^{(1)} = 2 \left[l^{(1)} \left(\hat{\phi}; \, d^{(1)} \right) - l^{(1)} \left(\hat{\phi}_0; \, d^{(1)} \right) \right]$$

is tested against the χ_q^2 distribution with $q = \dim\{\phi\} - \dim\{\phi_0\}$.

2. The *Wald test* is based on

$$W^{(1)} = \left(\hat{\phi} - \hat{\phi}_0 \right)^T \left[\text{Info}^{(1)} \left(\hat{\phi}; \, d^{(1)} \right) \right] \left(\hat{\phi} - \hat{\phi}_0 \right).$$

3. The *score test* is based on

$$\text{ST}^{(1)} = \text{sc}^{(1)} \left(\hat{\phi}_0; \, d^{(1)} \right)^T \left[\text{Info}^{(1)} \left(\hat{\phi}_0; \, d^{(1)} \right) \right]^{-1} \text{sc}^{(1)} \left(\hat{\phi}_0; \, d^{(1)} \right).$$

The score test does not require the calculation of $\hat{\phi}$, only $\hat{\phi}_0$, which in some situations will be an advantage over the Wald test. However, the Wald test does not require inversion of the information matrix. All these tests may be used to produce confidence regions for ϕ. Efron and Hinkley (1978) argue that it is preferable to use the observed rather than the expected information matrix for inference. We will follow this approach.

Instead of individual-level data, we have available the aggregate data $d^{(2)}$. Let $f^{(2)}(d^{(2)}; \phi)$ denote the associated probability function. Likelihood-based inference can then be undertaken using $f^{(2)}$. In general, deriving $f^{(2)}$ from $f^{(1)}$ may be difficult. Since $f^{(2)}$ is derived from $f^{(1)}$, it will depend on the same parameters as $f^{(1)}$. However, not all these parameters may be identifiable using aggregate data.

We assume that the individual-level data set comprises n individuals divided into p groups. In general, the n individuals are obtained from a sample of individuals, $S^{(1)}$, and the sample of p groups is $S^{(2)}$. The sample of individuals in group i is S_i. An important special case is when the samples are the entire finite population, i.e., $S^{(1)} = U^{(1)}$, $S^{(2)} = U^{(2)}$, and $S_i = U_i$. We will assume that any sampling involved is ignorable (for example, simple random sampling).

Breckling, Chambers, Dorfman, Tam, and Welsh (1994) described an approach for maximum likelihood inference using sample data. Sampling is a process by which data are unobserved or reduced, and aggregation is also a process that leads to the observed data being reduced. The basic results of Breckling et al. (1994) can then be applied to examine the effect of using aggregate data.

Let $\text{sc}^{(2)}(\phi; \, d^{(2)})$ and $\text{info}^{(2)}(\phi; \, d^{(2)})$ be the score function and observed information matrix based on $d^{(2)}$. The key results of Breckling et al. (1994) are

$$\text{sc}^{(2)} \left(\phi; \, d^{(2)} \right) = \text{E} \left[\text{sc}^{(1)} \left(\phi; \, d^{(1)} \right) \mid d^{(2)} \right], \tag{2.5}$$

$$\text{info}^{(2)} \left(\phi; \, d^{(2)} \right) = \text{E} \left[\text{info}^{(1)} \left(\phi; \, d^{(1)} \right) \mid d^{(2)} \right] - \text{Var} \left[\text{sc}^{(1)} \left(\phi; \, d^{(1)} \right) \mid d^{(2)} \right]. \tag{2.6}$$

The expectations in Equations 2.5 and 2.6 are over the distribution of $d^{(1)}$ conditional on $d^{(2)}$, that is, the individual-level data given the aggregate data. Hypothesis testing can also be done using this score function and information matrix as well as the likelihood based on $d^{(2)}$.

In some cases using Equation 2.5 to obtain the score function may be more convenient than direct differentiation of $l^{(2)} = \log f^{(2)}$. The result 2.6 is the key to determining the information loss due to the use of aggregate data. The variance–covariance matrix of the individual-level score function conditional on $d^{(2)}$ can be interpreted as the loss of information due to aggregation. In Section 2.3 we will illustrate this approach for the case of $p \, 2 \times 2$ tables, but the result can be applied in general.

Table 2.1 Individual-level data for group i			
	$Y=1$	$Y=0$	Total
$X=1$	n_{11i}	n_{12i}	$n_{1\bullet i}$
$X=0$	n_{21i}	n_{22i}	$n_{2\bullet i}$
Total	$n_{\bullet 1i}$	$n_{\bullet 2i}$	n_i

2.3 SEVERAL 2×2 TABLES

2.3.1 Data Available

Suppose that the individual-level data consist of p 2×2 tables giving the frequencies associated with two dichotomous variables, Y and X. Table 2.1 illustrates the data for group i.

It is assumed that the marginal frequencies for X are fixed, or conditioned upon, and that the values of Y are independent given X. Hence, for group i,

$$n_{11i} \sim \text{Bin}\,(n_{1\bullet i},\, \pi_{1i}), \qquad n_{21i} \sim \text{Bin}\,(n_{2\bullet i},\, \pi_{2i}),$$

where $\pi_{1i} = \text{Prob}(Y=1|X=1)$ and $\pi_{2i} = \text{Prob}(Y=1|X=0)$ for group i. The associated odds ratio is

$$\theta_i = \frac{\pi_{1i}}{1-\pi_{1i}} \frac{1-\pi_{2i}}{\pi_{2i}}.$$

Let $d_i^{(1)} = \{n_{11i},\, n_{1\bullet i},\, n_{\bullet 1i},\, n_i\}$ be the individual-level data for group i, and $d^{(1)} = \{d_i^{(1)},\, i \in S^{(2)}\}$ be the entire individual-level data set. In ecological inference the individual-level data are not available, so the values of n_{11i} are not available either. However, the marginal frequencies and n_i are available, giving the aggregate data $d_i^{(2)} = \{n_{1\bullet i},\, n_{\bullet 1i},\, n_i\}$ for group i and $d^{(2)} = \{d_i^{(2)},\, i \in S^{(2)}\}$ for the p groups.

2.3.2 Analysis Using Individual-Level Data

Let $\psi_i = (\pi_{1i},\, \pi_{2i})^T$ and $\phi = [\psi_1^T, \ldots, \psi_p^T]^T$. If no assumptions are made concerning the parameters ψ_i, each table could be analyzed separately with individual-level data. The likelihood for ψ_i based on $d_i^{(1)}$ is denoted $L_i^{(1)}(\psi_i;\, d_i^{(1)})$, and the log likelihood is

$$l_i^{(1)}\left(\psi_i;\, d_i^{(1)}\right) = n_{11i} \log \pi_{1i} + n_{12i} \log\,(1-\pi_{1i}) + n_{21i} \log \pi_{2i} + n_{22i} \log\,(1-\pi_{2i}).$$

The individual-level score function for ψ_i is

$$\text{sc}^{(1)}\left(\psi_i;\, d_i^{(1)}\right) = \begin{bmatrix} \dfrac{n_{11i} - n_{1\bullet i}\pi_{1i}}{\pi_{1i}\,(1-\pi_{1i})} \\ \dfrac{n_{\bullet 1i} - n_{11i} - n_{2\bullet i}\pi_{2i}}{\pi_{2i}\,(1-\pi_{2i})} \end{bmatrix}. \tag{2.7}$$

The resulting MLEs are

$$\hat{\psi}_i = (\hat{\pi}_{1i}, \ \hat{\pi}_{2i})^T = \left(\frac{n_{11i}}{n_{1\bullet i}}, \ \frac{n_{\bullet 1i} - n_{11i}}{n_{2\bullet i}} \right)^T.$$

The observed information matrix is

$$\text{info}^{(1)} \left(\psi_i; \ d_i^{(1)} \right) = \begin{bmatrix} \dfrac{n_{11i} \left(1 - 2\pi_{1i} \right) + n_{1\bullet i} \pi_{1i}^2}{\pi_{1i}^2 \left(1 - \pi_{1i} \right)^2} & 0 \\ 0 & \dfrac{\left(n_{\bullet 1i} - n_{11i} \right) \left(1 - 2\pi_{2i} \right) + n_{2\bullet i} \pi_{2i}^2}{\pi_{2i}^2 \left(1 - \pi_{2i} \right)^2} \end{bmatrix}, \tag{2.8}$$

and the expected information matrix is

$$\text{Info}^{(1)} \left(\psi_i; \ d_i^{(1)} \right) = \begin{bmatrix} \dfrac{n_{1\bullet i}}{\pi_{1i} \left(1 - \pi_{1i} \right)} & 0 \\ 0 & \dfrac{n_{2\bullet i}}{\pi_{2i} \left(1 - \pi_{2i} \right)} \end{bmatrix}. \tag{2.9}$$

It may be of interest to test whether there is evidence that the tables are homogeneous with respect to the conditional probabilities, i.e., $\pi_{1i} = \pi_1, \pi_{2i} = \pi_2$ for $i \in S^{(2)}$, which can be written as $\psi_i = \psi = (\pi_1, \ \pi_2)^T$ for all $i \in S^{(2)}$. This hypothesis may be of substantive interest, or it may be convenient for further analysis and interpretation. For example, if we have a sample of groups, then assuming group-specific parameters means that no inferences can be made concerning groups that are not in the sample. Even if all groups in the population of interest are included in $S^{(2)}$, the large number of groups may make interpretation of the analysis difficult if each group is assumed to have different parameter values. One approach to this issue is to allow for variation in ψ_i by including random effects, but for nonlinear models, this introduces considerable complexities in the analysis.

If $\psi_i = \psi$, then the log likelihood for ψ based on $d^{(1)}$ is

$$l^{(1)} \left(\psi; \ d^{(1)} \right) = \sum_{i \in S^{(2)}} l_i^{(1)} \left(\psi; \ d_i^{(1)} \right)$$

$$= n_{11\bullet} \log \pi_1 + n_{12\bullet} \log \left(1 - \pi_1 \right) + n_{21\bullet} \log \pi_2 + n_{22\bullet} \log \left(1 - \pi_2 \right).$$

Hence the tables can be collapsed, and the analysis can be based on the 2×2 table for the entire sample, $S^{(1)}$. The MLEs, score and information functions are as in Equations 2.7, 2.8, and 2.9 with the i for the elements of $d^{(1)}$ replaced with the summation subscript $\bullet$. That is,

$$\text{sc}^{(1)} \left(\psi; \ d^{(1)} \right) = \begin{bmatrix} \dfrac{n_{11\bullet} - n_{1\bullet\bullet} \pi_1}{\pi_1 \left(1 - \pi_1 \right)} \\ \dfrac{n_{\bullet 1 \bullet} - n_{11\bullet} - n_{2\bullet\bullet} \pi_2}{\pi_2 \left(1 - \pi_2 \right)} \end{bmatrix} \tag{2.10}$$

and

$$\text{info}_{11}^{(1)}\left(\psi;\,d^{(1)}\right) = \frac{n_{11\bullet}\left(1 - 2\pi_1\right) + n_{1\bullet\bullet}\pi_1^2}{\pi_1^2\left(1 - \pi_1\right)^2},$$

$$\text{info}_{21}^{(1)}\left(\psi;\,d^{(1)}\right) = 0, \qquad\qquad (2.11)$$

$$\text{info}_{22}^{(1)}\left(\psi;\,d^{(1)}\right) = \frac{\left(n_{\bullet1\bullet} - n_{11\bullet}\right)\left(1 - 2\pi_2\right) + n_{2\bullet\bullet}\pi_2^2}{\pi_2^2\left(1 - \pi_2\right)^2}.$$

The resulting MLEs are $\hat{\psi} = \left(\frac{n_{11\bullet}}{n_{1\bullet\bullet}},\,\frac{n_{\bullet1\bullet} - n_{11\bullet}}{n_{2\bullet\bullet}}\right)^T$.

The hypothesis $\psi_i = \psi$ can be tested using the likelihood ratio, Wald, or score test. The last two can be based on the observed or expected information matrix. Also the likelihood can be directly examined to see what evidence it provides (see Royall, 1997). For example, when the tables are homogeneous, $\phi_0 = [\psi^T, \ldots, \psi^T]^T$ and the score test using the observed information matrix is

$$ST^{(1)} = \sum_{i \in S^{(2)}} \text{sc}^{(1)}\left(\hat{\psi};\,d_i^{(1)}\right)^T \left[\text{info}^{(1)}\left(\hat{\psi};\,d_i^{(1)}\right)\right]^{-1} \text{sc}^{(1)}\left(\hat{\psi};\,d_i^{(1)}\right)$$

$$= \sum_{i \in S^{(2)}} ST_i^{(1)}.$$

The likelihood ratio is

$$R^{(1)} = \prod_{i \in S^{(2)}} \frac{L_i^{(1)}\left(\hat{\psi};\,d_i^{(1)}\right)}{L_i^{(1)}\left(\hat{\psi}_i;\,d_i^{(1)}\right)} = \prod_{i \in S^{(2)}} R_i^{(1)}.$$

2.3.3 Analysis Using Aggregate Data

In ecological inference the data available from each table are $d_i^{(2)}$, so that n_{11i} is not available. We could attempt an analysis without making any assumptions concerning ψ_i. This amounts to analyzing each group separately. Applying Equation 2.5 to Equation 2.7 immediately gives

$$\text{sc}^{(2)}\left(\psi_i;\,d_i^{(2)}\right) = \begin{bmatrix} \dfrac{\text{E}\left(n_{11i}\mid d_i^{(2)}\right) - n_{1\bullet i}\pi_{1i}}{\pi_{1i}\left(1 - \pi_{1i}\right)} \\[2em] \dfrac{n_{\bullet1i} - \text{E}\left(n_{11i}\mid d_i^{(2)}\right) - n_{2\bullet i}\pi_{2i}}{\pi_{2i}\left(1 - \pi_{2i}\right)} \end{bmatrix}.$$

Conditional on $d_i^{(2)}$, n_{11i} has a noncentral hypergeometric distribution (see for example McCullagh and Nelder, 1989: 257–259), and

$$\text{E}\left(n_{11i}\mid d_i^{(2)}\right) = \frac{P_1\left(\theta_i;\,d_i^{(2)}\right)}{P_0\left(\theta_i;\,d_i^{(2)}\right)},$$

where

$$P_r\left(\theta_i;\, d_i^{(2)}\right) = \sum_{j=a_i}^{b_i} \binom{n_{1\bullet i}}{j}\binom{n_{2\bullet i}}{n_{\bullet 1i}-j}\, j^r \theta_i^j.$$

The limits of the sum are the lower and upper bounds on n_{11i} given $d_i^{(2)}$, and are $a_i = \max(0,\, n_{\bullet 1i} - n_{2\bullet i})$ and $b_i = \min(n_{1\bullet i},\, n_{\bullet 1i})$. Denote $\mathrm{E}(n_{11i}|d_i^{(2)})$ by $\kappa_1(\theta_i;\, d_i^{(2)})$. Also

$$\mathrm{Var}\left(n_{11i}|d_i^{(2)}\right) = \frac{P_2\left(\theta_i;\, d_i^{(2)}\right)}{P_0\left(\theta_i;\, d_i^{(2)}\right)} - \kappa_1\left(\theta_i;\, d_i^{(2)}\right)^2$$

which will be denoted by $\kappa_2(\theta_i;\, d_i^{(2)})$.

From Equation 2.7,

$$\mathrm{Var}\left(\mathrm{sc}^{(1)}\left(\psi_i;\, d_i^{(1)}\right) | d_i^{(2)}\right)$$

$$= \kappa_2\left(\theta_i;\, d_i^{(2)}\right)\left[\begin{array}{cc} \dfrac{1}{\pi_{1i}^2\,(1-\pi_{1i})^2} & \dfrac{-1}{\pi_{1i}\pi_{2i}\,(1-\pi_{1i})\,(1-\pi_{2i})} \\[2ex] \dfrac{-1}{\pi_{1i}\pi_{2i}\,(1-\pi_{1i})\,(1-\pi_{2i})} & \dfrac{1}{\pi_{2i}^2\,(1-\pi_{2i})^2} \end{array}\right].$$

Applying Equation 2.6 with 2.7 and 2.8 gives

$$\mathrm{info}_{11}^{(2)}\left(\psi_i;\, d_i^{(2)}\right) = \frac{\kappa_1\left(\theta_i;\, d_i^{(2)}\right)(1-2\pi_{1i}) + n_{1\bullet i}\pi_{1i}^2 - \kappa_2\left(\theta_i;\, d_i^{(2)}\right)}{\pi_{1i}^2\,(1-\pi_{1i})^2},$$

$$\mathrm{info}_{21}^{(2)}\left(\psi_i;\, d_i^{(2)}\right) = \frac{\kappa_2\left(\theta_i;\, d_i^{(2)}\right)}{\pi_{1i}\pi_{2i}\,(1-\pi_{1i})\,(1-\pi_{2i})},$$

$$\mathrm{info}_{22}^{(2)}\left(\psi_i;\, d_i^{(2)}\right) = \frac{\left(n_{\bullet 1i} - \kappa_1\left(\theta_i;\, d_i^{(2)}\right)\right)(1-2\pi_{2i}) + n_{2\bullet i}\pi_{2i}^2 - \kappa_2\left(\theta_i;\, d_i^{(2)}\right)}{\pi_{2i}^2\,(1-\pi_{2i})^2}.$$

Setting $\mathrm{sc}^{(2)}(\psi_i;\, d_i^{(2)}) = 0$ yields the relationship

$$\pi_{1i}n_{1\bullet i} + \pi_{2i}n_{2\bullet i} = n_{\bullet 1i}$$

or

$$\pi_{2i} = \frac{n_{\bullet 1i}}{n_{2\bullet i}} - \frac{n_{1\bullet i}}{n_{2\bullet i}}\pi_{1i}, \tag{2.12}$$

which corresponds to the tomography line for group i discussed in King (1997: 80).

The aggregation of the data has resulted in each element of the information matrix being modified by a term proportional to $\kappa_2(\theta_i;\, d_i^{(2)})$ arising from the conditional variance of the individual-level score function. Also, n_{11i} is replaced by its expectation conditional on $d_i^{(2)}$.

For each group there is only one observed random variable $n_{\bullet 1i}$, and two parameters, unless some further assumptions are made. For p groups there are p observations $n_{\bullet 1i}$, $i \in S^{(2)}$, but $2p$ parameters. Hence standard asymptotic properties of likelihood-based methods cannot be relied upon. Beh, Steel, and Booth (2002) consider the likelihood associated with aggregate data for a single group. This is given by McCullagh and Nelder (1989: 353)

$$L_i^{(2)}\left(\psi_i;\, d_i^{(2)}\right) = (1 - \pi_{1i})^{n_{1\bullet i}}\, \pi_{2i}^{n_{\bullet 1i}}\, (1 - \pi_{2i})^{n_{2\bullet i} - n_{\bullet 1i}}\, P_0\left(\theta_i;\, d_i^{(2)}\right). \tag{2.13}$$

Wakefield (2001) uses the same likelihood, but presents it in the form of a convolution likelihood of two binomials.

Beh, Steel, and Booth (2002) show that the likelihood surface has a ridge along the tomography line 2.12. Along the tomography line the likelihood is minimized when $\pi_{1i} = \pi_{2i}$, i.e. at independence, and the maximum occurs at one of the ends of the tomography line. They also show that, except for cases when $n_{\bullet 1i}$ is very close to $n_{1\bullet i}$ or $n_{2\bullet i}$, the likelihood surface is not able to provide useful evidence concerning the values of π_{1i} and π_{2i} other than that they should be on the tomography line. Notice that the score and information function in this case can also be obtained directly from the likelihood $L_i^{(2)}$ given by Equation 2.13.

Beh, Steel, and Booth (2002) obtain the exact values of $\hat{\psi}_i = (\hat{\pi}_{1i},\, \hat{\pi}_{2i})^T$ that maximize the likelihood. Wakefield (2001) also obtains these values using an approximation. The resulting maximum of the likelihood $L_i^{(2)}(\hat{\psi}_i;\, d_i^{(2)})$ can also be obtained. Notice $\hat{\psi}_i$ is unique, except when $n_{1\bullet i} = n_{2\bullet i}$, in which case the likelihood is maximized at $(0, 1)^T$ and $(1, 0)^T$.

The inferential problem that arises from wishing to estimate $2p$ parameters from p observations can be tackled if we assume $\psi_i = \psi$ for all $i \in S^{(2)}$. Of course, this is a very strong assumption, and it is more realistic to assume that ψ_i varies in some way across the p groups. The variation may be related to group-level covariates z_i and random effects. However, analysis is relatively straightforward if the homogeneity assumption holds. More importantly, the question arises whether, in practice, it is possible from aggregate data alone to assess whether the homogeneity assumption is reasonable before attempting to use methods that allow for variation in ψ_i.

When $\psi_i = \psi$, we can obtain the score and information functions based on the aggregate data for the p groups in the sample by applying Equations 2.5 and 2.6 to 2.10 and 2.11 or by summing the score and information functions arising from each group with $\psi_i = \psi$. This gives

$$\mathrm{sc}^{(2)}\left(\psi;\, d^{(2)}\right) = \begin{bmatrix} \dfrac{\sum_i \kappa_1\left(\theta;\, d_i^{(2)}\right) - n_{1\bullet\bullet}\pi_1}{\pi_1\left(1 - \pi_1\right)} \\[4ex] \dfrac{n_{\bullet 1\bullet} - \sum_i \kappa_1\left(\theta;\, d_i^{(2)}\right) - n_{2\bullet\bullet}\pi_2}{\pi_2\left(1 - \pi_2\right)} \end{bmatrix},$$

$$\text{info}_{11}^{(2)}\left(\psi; d^{(2)}\right) = \frac{\sum_i \kappa_1\left(\theta; d_i^{(2)}\right)(1 - 2\pi_1) + n_{1\bullet\bullet}\pi_1^2 - \sum_i \kappa_2\left(\theta; d_i^{(2)}\right)}{\pi_1^2 (1 - \pi_1)^2},$$

$$\text{info}_{12}^{(2)}\left(\psi; d^{(2)}\right) = \frac{\sum_i \kappa_2\left(\theta; d_i^{(2)}\right)}{\pi_1\pi_2 (1 - \pi_1)(1 - \pi_2)},$$

$$\text{info}_{22}^{(2)}\left(\psi; d^{(2)}\right) = \frac{\left(n_{\bullet 1\bullet} - \sum_i \kappa_1\left(\theta; d_i^{(2)}\right)\right)(1 - 2\pi_2) + n_{2\bullet\bullet}\pi_2^2 - \sum_i \kappa_2\left(\theta; d_i^{(2)}\right)}{\pi_2^2 (1 - \pi_2)^2}.$$

Setting $\text{sc}^{(2)}(\psi; d^{(2)}) = 0$ gives the overall sample-level tomography line

$$\pi_1 n_{1\bullet\bullet} + \pi_2 n_{2\bullet\bullet} = n_{\bullet 1\bullet}.$$

The correlation between the two elements of the individual-level score function conditional on $d^{(2)}$, obtained from $\text{Var}[\text{sc}^{(1)}(\psi; d^{(1)})|d^{(2)}]$, is -1 and corresponds to the constraint arising from the tomography line.

Comparing $\text{info}^{(2)}$ with $\text{info}^{(1)}$, we see that in addition to the reduction in the diagonal elements, a positive term appears in the off-diagonal elements. This suggests that inferences concerning $\pi_1 - \pi_2$ will be particularly badly affected.

The same score function can be obtained directly from the likelihood of the aggregate data,

$$L^{(2)}\left(\psi; d^{(2)}\right) = \prod_{i \in S^{(2)}} L_i^{(2)}\left(\psi; d_i^{(2)}\right).$$

McCullagh and Nelder (1989: 353) obtain an equivalent score function for a different parameterization.

The equations $\text{sc}^{(2)}(\psi; d^{(2)}) = 0$ can be solved to obtain the estimates $\hat{\psi} = (\hat{\pi}_1, \hat{\pi}_2)^T$ under the hypothesis of homogeneity. This can be done in several ways, as reviewed by Beh and Steel (2002). Here we obtain the estimate of ψ using the Newton–Raphson iterative procedure

$$\psi^{(j+1)} = \psi^{(j)} - \alpha\, A^{-1}\left(\frac{\partial l}{\partial \psi}\right)\Bigg|_{\psi = \psi^{(j)}}$$

with the secant approximation of the hessian matrix A to accelerate convergence. Reddien (1986) comments that the use of this approximation is often preferred to the standard Newton–Raphson procedure and that its rate of convergence is both satisfactory and stable. The value of α is chosen such that $0 \le \alpha \le 1$ and dictates the step length taken on iteration of the procedure (see McCulloch and Searle, 2001: 269).

Once an estimate of the common probabilities, $\hat{\psi}$, is obtained, we can produce estimates of the group-specific proportions $\beta_i^b = n_{11i}/n_{1\bullet i}$ and $\beta_i^w = n_{21i}/n_{2\bullet i}$ by evaluating the expectation $\text{E}[n_{11i}|d^{(2)}] = \kappa_1(\hat{\theta}; d_i^{(2)})$ where $\hat{\theta}$ is the odds ratio calculated from $\hat{\psi}$. This gives the estimates $\hat{\beta}_i^b = \kappa_1(\hat{\theta}; d_i^{(2)})/n_{1\bullet i}$ and $\hat{\beta}_i^w = (n_{\bullet 1i} - \kappa_1(\hat{\theta}; d_i^{(2)}))/n_{2\bullet i}$. For each group these estimates of the proportions are obtained by projecting the estimates of the common probabilities, $\hat{\psi}$, onto the tomography line (Equation 2.12) for that group, using the expectation of the noncentral hypergeometric distribution $\kappa_1(\hat{\theta}; d_i^{(2)})$.

The likelihood ratio for testing the hypothesis $\psi_i = \psi$ is

$$R^{(2)} = \prod_{i \in S^{(2)}} \frac{L_i^{(2)}\left(\hat{\psi}; d_i^{(2)}\right)}{L_i^{(2)}\left(\hat{\psi}_i; d_i^{(2)}\right)} = \prod_{i \in S^{(2)}} R_i^{(2)}.$$

We will not use the Wald test, as $\text{info}^{(2)}$ is not defined at the $\hat{\psi}_i$ values. The score test based on the observed information matrix is

$$\text{ST}^{(2)} = \sum_{i \in S^{(2)}} \text{sc}^{(2)}\left(\hat{\psi}; d_i^{(2)}\right)^T \left[\text{info}^{(2)}\left(\hat{\psi}; d_i^{(2)}\right)\right]^{-1} \text{sc}^{(2)}\left(\hat{\psi}; d_i^{(2)}\right) = \sum_{i \in S^{(2)}} \text{ST}_i^{(2)}.$$

2.4 USING AGGREGATE AND UNIT-LEVEL DATA

In some situations it may be feasible to obtain both individual-level and aggregate data. For example, we may have a reasonably large number of groups and could consider choosing a small sample of individuals to supplement the aggregate data. Alternatively, we could have a reasonable size sample of individuals and consider supplementing it by some aggregate data. The latter case could be useful in producing estimates of group-specific quantities. This leads to the general issue of what is the relative value of the two types of data. This can help us decide at what sample size the information in the aggregate data has little additional value.

Suppose that we have a simple random sample, $S^{(0)}$ of n_0 individuals selected from the population of interest. We assume that the sampling fraction is small so that we can treat the data in $S^{(0)}$ as independent of that in $S^{(2)}$. The sample $S^{(0)}$ produces the data $d^{(0)}$. The aggregate and individual-level data can be combined, giving $d^{(c)} = \{d^{(2)}, d^{(0)}\}$. Because of the independence of the data sets, the score function and information matrices can be added, giving

$$\text{sc}^{(c)}\left(\phi; d^{(c)}\right) = \text{sc}^{(2)}\left(\phi; d^{(2)}\right) + \text{sc}^{(0)}\left(\phi; d^{(0)}\right),$$

$$\text{info}^{(c)}\left(\phi; d^{(c)}\right) = \text{info}^{(2)}\left(\phi; d^{(2)}\right) + \text{info}^{(0)}\left(\phi; d^{(0)}\right).$$

Consider the case of p 2×2 tables. Suppose that the group that each individual comes from is not known. This could be for reasons of confidentiality or because the sample was selected in a way that did not make recording the groups convenient. Then $d^{(0)} = \{n_{11}^{(0)}, n_{1\bullet}^{(0)}, n_{\bullet 1}^{(0)}, n^{(0)}\}$.

Assuming $\psi_i = \psi$, the information associated with $d^{(0)}$ is

$$\text{info}_{11}^{(0)}\left(\psi; d^{(0)}\right) = \frac{n_{11}^{(0)}\left(1 - 2\pi_1\right) + n_{1\bullet}^{(0)}\pi_1^2}{\pi_1^2\left(1 - \pi_1\right)^2},$$

$$\text{info}_{21}^{(0)}\left(\psi; d^{(0)}\right) = 0,$$

$$\text{info}_{22}^{(0)}\left(\psi; d^{(0)}\right) = \frac{\left(n_{\bullet 1}^{(0)} - n_{11}^{(0)}\right)\left(1 - 2\pi_2\right) + n_{2\bullet}^{(0)}\pi_2^2}{\pi_2^2\left(1 - \pi_2\right)^2}.$$

The addition of the unit-level data increases the diagonal elements of the information matrix and leaves the off-diagonal elements unchanged. Besides reducing the asymptotic variance of the estimates of π_1 and π_2, this will also dampen the correlation of the estimates, resulting in additional benefits for the estimation of $\pi_1 - \pi_2$.

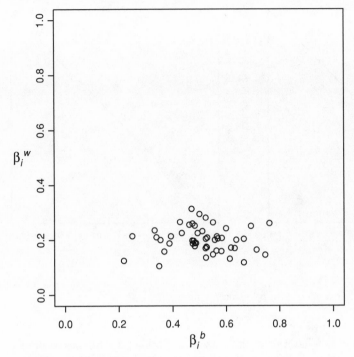

Figure 2.1. Plot of β_i^w versus β_i^b.

2.5 EXAMPLE

To illustrate the application of these results we will consider a simple example using data from the 1996 Australian census. The data corresponds to the census district (CD) level data for the city of Brisbane in Australia, where the individual level classifications are known. There are a total of 1541 CDs, but for simplicity we will focus our discussion on a random sample of 50 CDs.

For comparison, King's method is also applied to these data using the E_zI package (Benoit and King, 1998) with its default global parameters.

Consider the data with variables income and age, so that for CD i the classification of individuals is

$X = 1$ if a person is aged between 15 and 24 years,

$X = 0$ if a person is aged at least 25 years,

$Y = 1$ if a person's weekly income is between \$AU0 and \$AU159,

$Y = 0$ if a person's weekly income is at least \$AU160.

For the 50 CDs considered there are 22,323 individuals classified, with 4238 individuals aged between 15 and 24 years, and 5674 with a weekly income between \$AU0 and \$AU159. These values correspond to the marginal frequencies $n_\bullet$, $n_{1\bullet\bullet}$, and $n_{\bullet1\bullet}$, respectively. The proportion of people aged between 15 and 24 was 0.1898 and varied from 0.1053 to 0.2861 with a coefficient of variation 0.1970. A plot of the values of the group specific proportions β_i^b and β_i^w is given in Figure 2.1 and shows a considerable amount of variation.

Based on the individual-level data, we obtain $\hat{\pi}_1^{(1)} = 0.5054$ and $\hat{\pi}_2^{(1)} = 0.1953$, which have estimated standard errors of 0.0077 and 0.0029, respectively.

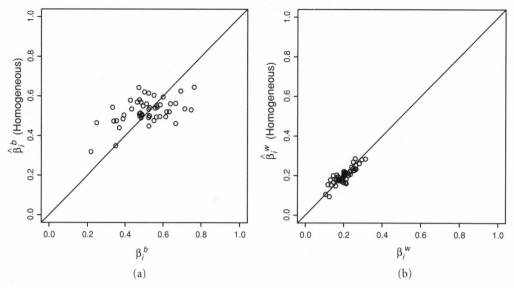

Figure 2.2. Plots of (a) $\hat{\beta}_i^b$ versus β_i^b and (b) $\hat{\beta}_i^w$ versus β_i^w, using $\kappa_1(\hat{\theta}^{(2)}; d_i^{(2)})$.

Based only on the aggregate-level data, the maximum likelihood estimates assuming homogeneous parameters and using the accelerated Newton–Raphson iterative procedure give $\hat{\pi}_1^{(2)} = 0.5184$ and $\hat{\pi}_2^{(2)} = 0.1922$ and estimated standard errors of 0.0353 and 0.0085, respectively. The initial values of π_1 and π_2 were set at 0.6 and 0.1966 so that the overall tomography line is satisfied. Instability of the convergence was experienced with $\alpha = 1$, so smaller steps were carried out throughout the iterative procedure with $\alpha = 0.4$. Using King's (1997) method via E_zI produced estimates $\hat{\pi}_1^{(2)} = 0.4769$ and $\hat{\pi}_2^{(2)} = 0.2020$ with estimated standard errors of 0.1606 and 0.0376 respectively. The point estimates obtained from the two methods are quite similar, although there is a large difference between the estimated standard errors. This may be due to the random effects incorporated into the King method, whereas our approach does not include any random variation in the group-specific parameters.

The estimates of the group-specific proportions β_i^b and β_i^w using King's approach and assuming homogeneity of the associated probabilities are very similar. In the latter approach, even though the probabilities π_{1i} and π_{2i} are assumed to be constant across the groups, the associated proportions, β_i^b and β_i^w, are not assumed to be constant across the groups. Figure 2.2 compares the individual-level proportions β_i^w and β_i^b with the estimates $\hat{\beta}_i^b$ and $\hat{\beta}_i^w$ obtained by considering the expectation $E[n_{11i} | d_i^{(2)}]$ using the parameter values $\hat{\pi}_1^{(2)}$ and $\hat{\pi}_2^{(2)}$, that is, $\kappa_1(\hat{\theta}^{(2)}; d_i^{(2)})$. These values are very similar to those produced when estimating β_i^b and β_i^w using King's approach, and these are produced in Figure 2.3. Chambers and Steel (2001) considered using the relative root-mean-square errors

$$V_1 = \frac{1}{\hat{\pi}_1^{(1)}}\sqrt{p^{-1}\sum_i \left(\hat{\beta}_i^b - \beta_i^b\right)^2}, \qquad V_2 = \frac{1}{\hat{\pi}_2^{(1)}}\sqrt{p^{-1}\sum_i \left(\hat{\beta}_i^w - \beta_i^w\right)^2}$$

to assess how well these estimates reproduce the true values. For the method assuming homogeneity between the groups, we have $V_1 = 0.1993$ and $V_2 = 0.1204$, while King's method produces the similar values $V_1 = 0.2066$ and $V_2 = 0.1317$. This indicates that for

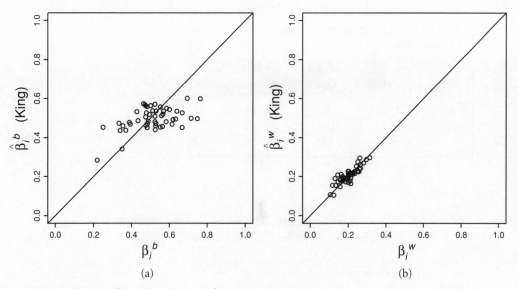

Figure 2.3. Plot of (a) $\hat{\beta}_i^b$ versus β_i^b and (b) $\hat{\beta}_i^w$ versus β_i^w, using King's methodology.

these CDs there is no advantage in allowing for group heterogeneity in the conditional probabilities.

Based on the individual-level parameter estimates $\hat{\pi}_1^{(1)}$ and $\hat{\pi}_2^{(1)}$, the information matrix and its inverse are

$$\text{info}^{(1)} = \begin{pmatrix} 16953.96 & 0 \\ 0 & 115075.3 \end{pmatrix},$$

$$\left[\text{info}^{(1)}\right]^{-1} = \begin{pmatrix} 0.00005898323 & 0 \\ 0 & 0.00000868996 \end{pmatrix}.$$

This gives the estimated standard errors $\widehat{\text{SE}}^{(1)}(\hat{\pi}_1^{(1)}|d^{(1)}) = 0.0077$ and $\widehat{\text{SE}}^{(1)}(\hat{\pi}_2^{(1)}|d^{(1)}) = 0.0029$.

The conditional expectation of this information matrix can be evaluated by replacing n_{11i} by its conditional expectation evaluated at $\hat{\theta}^{(2)}$. Doing so yields

$$\text{E}\left[\text{info}^{(1)}|d^{(2)}\right] = \begin{pmatrix} 16991.07 & 0 \\ 0 & 117205.8 \end{pmatrix},$$

which is very close to $\text{info}^{(1)}$.

Using $\hat{\pi}_1^{(2)}$, $\hat{\pi}_2^{(2)}$, and $\hat{\theta}^{(2)}$ from the Newton-Raphson procedure, we obtain

$$\text{Var}\left[\text{sc}^{(1)}|d^{(2)}\right] = \begin{pmatrix} 11927.53 & -19179.83 \\ -19179.83 & 30841.74 \end{pmatrix},$$

which has an associated correlation of -1. Applying Equation 2.6, the resulting information matrix based only on the aggregate level data is

$$\text{info}^{(2)} = \begin{pmatrix} 5063.538 & 19179.83 \\ 19179.83 & 86364.03 \end{pmatrix},$$

Table 2.2 Effect of aggregation on variance estimates: income by age

Parameter	$\widehat{\text{Var}}^{(2)}/\widehat{\text{Var}}^{(1)}$	Ind. sample equiv. to 50 CDs	Ind. sample equiv. per CD
π_1	21.2	1053	21
π_2	8.6	2596	52
$\pi_1 - \pi_2$	27.8	803	16

so that

$$\left[\text{info}^{(2)}\right]^{-1} = \begin{pmatrix} 0.0012436897 & -0.00027620009 \\ -0.00027620009 & 0.00007291774 \end{pmatrix};$$

therefore the estimated standard errors are $\widehat{\text{SE}}^{(2)}(\hat{\pi}_1^{(2)}|d^{(2)}) = 0.0353$ and $\widehat{\text{SE}}^{(2)}(\hat{\pi}_2^{(2)}|d^{(2)}) = 0.0085$.

The difference in the probabilities, $\pi_1 - \pi_2$, will often be of particular interest. From $\text{info}^{(1)}$ we obtain

$$\widehat{\text{Var}}^{(1)}\left[\hat{\pi}_1^{(1)} - \hat{\pi}_2^{(1)}|d^{(1)}\right] = \widehat{\text{Var}}^{(1)}\left(\hat{\pi}_1^{(1)}|d^{(1)}\right) + \widehat{\text{Var}}^{(1)}\left(\hat{\pi}_2^{(1)}|d^{(1)}\right)$$

$$-2\widehat{\text{Cov}}^{(1)}\left(\hat{\pi}_1^{(1)}, \hat{\pi}_2^{(1)}|d^{(1)}\right)$$

$$= 0.00005879863 + 0.000008480757 - 2 \times 0$$

$$= 0.00006727939.$$

Hence

$$\widehat{\text{SE}}^{(1)}\left[\hat{\pi}_1^{(1)} - \hat{\pi}_2^{(1)}|d^{(1)}\right] = 0.008202401.$$

From $\text{info}^{(2)}$,

$$\widehat{\text{Var}}^{(2)}\left[\hat{\pi}_1^{(2)} - \hat{\pi}_2^{(2)}|d^{(2)}\right] = \widehat{\text{Var}}^{(2)}\left(\hat{\pi}_1^{(2)}|d^{(2)}\right) + \widehat{\text{Var}}^{(2)}\left(\hat{\pi}_2^{(2)}|d^{(2)}\right)$$

$$-2\widehat{\text{Cov}}^{(2)}\left(\hat{\pi}_1^{(2)}, \hat{\pi}_2^{(2)}|d^{(2)}\right)$$

$$= 0.0012436897 + 0.00007291774 + 2 \times 0.00027620009$$

$$= 0.001869008,$$

giving

$$\widehat{\text{SE}}^{(2)}\left[\hat{\pi}_1^{(2)} - \hat{\pi}_2^{(2)}|d^{(2)}\right] = 0.04323203.$$

The estimated correlation between $\hat{\pi}_1^{(2)}$ and $\hat{\pi}_2^{(2)}$ obtained from $\text{info}^{(2)}$ is -0.917.

The effect of aggregation can be examined by looking at the ratio of the estimated variances obtained from $\text{info}^{(1)}$ and $\text{info}^{(2)}$. These are given in Table 2.2. Here the estimation of π_1 is

Table 2.3 Comparison of $\mathrm{Var}(\pi_1 - \pi_2)$ for the analysis of aggregate data and samples of individual-level data of various sizes

n_0	$\mathrm{Var}^{(c)}(\pi_1 - \pi_2)$	$\mathrm{Var}^{(0)}(\pi_1 - \pi_2)$
0	0.001869	–
1	0.001866	1.501876
10	0.001845	0.150188
50	0.001756	0.030037
100	0.001656	0.015019
500	0.001138	0.003004
1000	0.000818	0.001502
5000	0.000253	0.000300

more affected by aggregation than that of π_2, possibly because π_1 is larger and β_i^b varies more across the CDs. The increase in the asymptotic variance of the parameters π_1 and π_2 is more than the increase in the diagonal elements of the information matrix, i.e. more than 3.3 and 1.3 respectively. This is due to the large covariance term introduced by the aggregation. The estimation of $\pi_1 - \pi_2$ is affected even more than that of π_1, due to the effect of aggregation on the correlation of the estimates. In looking at these ratios, it must be remembered that the individual-level data consist of 22,323 people, whereas the aggregate data relate to 50 CDs, a ratio of 446. There are 4238 people who are 15–24 years old and who contribute to the estimation of π_1, an average of 84.8 people per CD. While there is clearly a loss of information through the use of aggregate data, it does not correspond to each CD being equivalent to an individual. In Table 2.2 we show the individual-level sample size required to obtain the same variance, and therefore standard error, as using these aggregate data for 50 CDs. For example, the sample of 50 CDs gives the same variance for the estimation of $\pi_1 - \pi_2$ as 803 individuals. Dividing by 50 gives an indication of the information per CD compared with the information per individual. For this example, on average, each CD is as useful as 16 individuals with regard to estimating $\pi_1 - \pi_2$. These results depend on the variation in the proportion of 15–24-year-olds across the CDs.

Using the results in Section 2.4 we can also examine the likely impact of supplementing aggregate data with individual-level survey data. This is shown in Table 2.3, which gives the variance $\mathrm{Var}^{(c)}$ of the estimate of $\pi_1 - \pi_2$ based on aggregate data for 50 CDs plus an independent sample of n_0 individuals for $n_0 = 0, 1, 10, 50, 100, 500, 1000$. For comparison, we also give the variance for these sample sizes when there is no aggregate data, $\mathrm{Var}^{(0)}$.

The results in Table 2.3 are consistent with the aggregate data being equivalent to 803 individuals.

We can also compare the use of individual and aggregate data in testing for homogeneity, using the likelihood ratio and score test as described at the end of Section 2.3. Both tests should be compared with χ_{98}^2, for which the critical value for a 5% test is 122.

For the likelihood ratio test the results are

$$-2\log R^{(1)} = 502.7287, \qquad -2\log R^{(2)} = 339.2903.$$

Both these values suggest that the null hypothesis of $\psi_i = \psi$ be rejected. The test statistic calculated from the individual-level data is larger, which is consistent with it having more

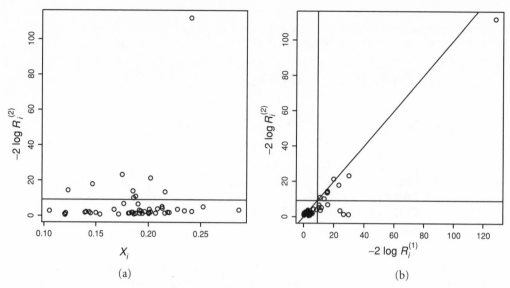

Figure 2.4. Plot of $-2\log R_i^{(2)}$ versus X_i and versus $-2\log R_i^{(1)}$.

power. Each of these test statistics can be decomposed into a term for each group, i.e.,

$$-2\log R^{(1)} = \sum_i \left(-2\log R_i^{(1)}\right), \qquad -2\log R^{(2)} = \sum_i \left(-2\log R_i^{(2)}\right).$$

Figure 2.4a gives a plot of $-2\log R_i^{(2)}$ versus $X_i = n_{1\bullet i}/n_i$, the proportion of people aged 15–24 years, for each CD. This plot may be useful as a diagnostic in identifying groups with large values which indicate that they are particularly affecting the statistical significance of the test. It will suggest those groups having parameters π_{1i} and π_{2i} which are statistically significantly different from the overall parameters values. It may also be useful in suggesting any trends in departures from homogeneity that may be related to X_i.

In examining these values we suggest comparing them with the 1% critical value of χ_2^2, i.e. 9.210. The horizontal and vertical lines on the figures correspond to this value.

Figure 2.4b gives a plot of $-2\log R_i^{(2)}$ versus $-2\log R_i^{(1)}$. Of the 17 cases that would be identified as statistically significant using individual-level data, 9 are also identified using the group-level data. Also, no cases that are identified as statistically nonsignificant using $-2\log R_i^{(1)}$ are identified as statistically significant using $-2\log R_i^{(2)}$. Hence, while there is, as expected, a loss of power in using the aggregate data, it is still possible to undertake a useful analysis of residuals.

Both the analyses of $-2\log R_i^{(1)}$ and $-2\log R_i^{(2)}$ identify one particular CD as having a large influence on the hypothesis test. This CD was investigated and found to have more than twice the usual population size, low values of β_i^b and β_i^w, and a reasonably high value of X_i. This is probably a CD in a newly developed area of the city.

A similar approach can be used with the score test, giving

$$\text{ST}^{(1)} = 496.8291, \qquad \text{ST}^{(2)} = 359.9741.$$

Figure 2.5 gives a plot of $\text{ST}_i^{(2)}$ versus X_i and $\text{ST}_i^{(1)}$.

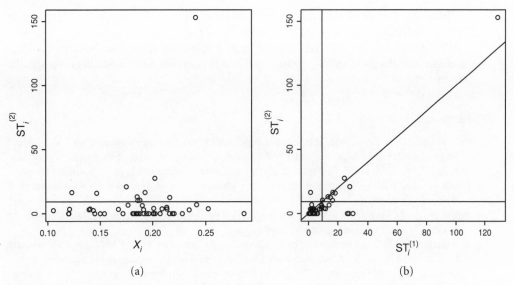

Figure 2.5. Plot of $\mathrm{ST}_i^{(2)}$ versus X_i and $\mathrm{ST}_i^{(1)}$.

Again these results both lead to the rejection of the null hypothesis. However, we encountered a problem with the score test. For 24 of the 50 CDs, $\mathrm{info}^{(2)}(\hat{\psi}; d_i^{(2)})$ was not positive definite, leading to a negative $\mathrm{ST}_i^{(2)}$ value. In our analysis we set such cases to zero. Numerically this situation arises because the subtraction of the estimate of the conditional variance of the score function for the CD reduces the diagonal elements and increases the off-diagonal elements too much. We are investigating modifications to the score test to overcome this difficulty. Even so, using $\mathrm{ST}_i^{(2)}$ identifies 10 of the 15 cases that $\mathrm{ST}_i^{(1)}$ would identify as having parameters statistically significantly different from the overall values. However, it also identified one case as statistically significant that was not so identified using $\mathrm{ST}_i^{(1)}$.

Signed residuals can also be determined and examined.

2.6 DISCUSSION

We have described a general approach to clearly identify the loss of information in using aggregate rather than individual-level data. Let Y_k denote the value of the response variable for individual k. In many situations determining the score function and information loss through aggregation will involve determining $\mathrm{E}(Y_k|d_i^{(2)})$, $\mathrm{Var}(Y_k|d_i^{(2)})$, and $\mathrm{Cov}(Y_k, Y_{k'}|d_i^{(2)})$ for $k, k' \in i$.

In the example of homogeneous 2×2 tables, this approach is not much simpler than direct use of the likelihood based on the aggregate data $d^{(2)}$. However, Equation 2.6 clearly shows the information loss. Much of the effect of aggregation in this case arises from the change to the off-diagonal elements of the information matrix.

The example considered in this chapter shows how we can test the hypothesis of the parameters of interest being constant across groups from aggregate data alone. Decomposing the resulting test statistics into contributions from each group enables an analysis of the impact that each group has on the hypothesis test. This can be useful in identifying groups with parameter values very different from the overall parameters.

The example suggests that residuals obtained from the likelihood ratio test using aggregate data are preferable to those obtained from the score test.

We are currently considering how the general approach applies in the more complex models, especially those including random effects to allow for the variation in group-specific parameters.

REFERENCES

Beh, E. J. and D. G. Steel. 2002. "Maximum Likelihood Estimation and Homogeneous 2 × 2 Tables." Preprint 3/02. School of Mathematics and Applied Statistics, University of Wollongong, Australia.

Beh, E. J., D. G. Steel, and J. G. Booth. 2002. "What Useful Information Is in the Marginal Frequencies of a 2 × 2 Table?" Preprint 4/02. School of Mathematics and Applied Statistics, University of Wollongong, Australia.

Benoit, K. and G. King. 1998. EZI: An Easy Program for Ecological Inference, version 2.02. Department of Government, Harvard University, Boston.

Breckling, J. U., R. L. Chambers, A. H. Dorfman, S. M. Tam, and A. H. Welsh. 1994. "Maximum Likelihood Inference from Sample Survey Data," *International Statistical Review*, 62, 349–363.

Chambers, R. L. and D. G. Steel. 2001. "Simple Methods for Ecological Inference in 2 × 2 Tables," *Journal of the Royal Statistical Society A*, 164, 175–192.

Cox, D. R. and D. V. Hinkley. 1974. *Theoretical Statistics*. London: Chapman and Hall.

Efron, B. and D. V. Hinkley. 1978. "Assessing the Accuracy of the Maximum Likelihood Estimator: Observed versus Expected Fisher Information (with Discussion)," *Biometrika*, 65, 457–487.

King, G. 1997. *A Solution to the Ecological Inference Problem*. Princeton, NJ: Princeton University Press.

McCullagh, P. and J. A. Nelder. 1989. *Generalized Linear Models*. London: Chapman and Hall.

McCulloch, C. E. and S. R. Searle. 2001. *Generalized, Linear, and Mixed Models*. New York: Wiley.

Reddien, G. W. 1986. "Newton–Raphson Methods," *Encyclopedia of Statistical Sciences*, 6, 210–212.

Royall, R. M. 1997. *Statistical Evidence: A Likelihood Paradigm*. London: Chapman and Hall.

Wakefield, J. 2001. "Ecological Inference for 2 × 2 Tables." Technical Report. Department of Statistics and Biostatistics, University of Washington.

3 Using Ecological Inference for Contextual Research

When Aggregation Bias Is the Solution as Well as the Problem

D. Stephen Voss

ABSTRACT

Gary King's ecological inference method represents a major breakthrough for analysts working with aggregate data because it is sensitive to contextual behavior patterns that previous methods had to assume away. King's critics underestimate the value of his method because they apply it to patently uninformative data, do not look for the contextual patterns that would improve estimation, and do not take advantage of the contextual knowledge that substantive experts would bring to an analysis. This chapter offers new diagnostic trials for the estimates from King's EI software, applied to data that have emerged from a genuine research agenda but for which the true values are known. Not only does the method do a superb job with typical precinct-level voting data, it even manages to produce solid estimates with inedequate county-level data once the analyst takes into account insights provided by the relevant scholarly literature. King's approach can and should be improved, but the imperfections provide no justification for using older methods of aggregate-data analysis or for relying solely on survey data such as exit polls.

INTRODUCTION

Debate over Gary King's proposed solution to the ecological inference problem (King, 1997) has begun to emerge in journals oriented toward statistics and political methodology. For the most part, this debate has operated at a theoretical level – evaluating properties of the estimators generated by King's method (as well as his supplementary software, EI and EzI). The tone of the debate has often been critical (Herron and Shotts, 2003; McCue, 2001; Rivers, 1998; Anselin and Cho, 2002; Cho, 1998; Freedman et al., 1998). At the same time, substantive applications using King's method have begun to appear in social-science journals (e.g., Burden and Kimball, 1998; Gay, 2001; Gimpel and Schuknecht, 2002; Liu, 2001; Lublin and Voss, 2002; Voss and Miller, 2001). Not only have these manuscripts successfully cleared the peer-review process for numerous respectable outlets, the authors also report concrete diagnostic checks that indicate the relative success of EI at solving difficult estimation problems.

Disagreement between theoretical critiques and substantive applications is not unique to aggregate-data analysis. Critics generally compare a method against ideal statistical properties, so the incentive is to identify data that illustrate methodological problems. Analysts, by contrast, generally compare a method against convenient alternatives; the incentive is to defend whichever statistical tools they select. Unfortunately, the pressures that drive apart theory and practice worsen in the instance of ecological inference. Success depends heavily upon the amount of information lost in the aggregation process and the contextual knowledge that an analyst exploits when trying to recapture lost information. Critics face little difficulty identifying data that will lead methods of ecological inference astray, whereas knowledgeable analysts can tweak performance out of a statistical tool that it would not exhibit if applied naively. The result is a dissonance that can only confuse practitioners waiting for the methodological literature's final verdict on a statistical innovation.

My purpose in this chapter is to lay out, in relatively accessible terms, why King's solution to the ecological inference problem represents a path-breaking development that should fundamentally change scholarly standards for what is acceptable in aggregate-data analysis. However, I do not simply summarize, in less-technical vocabulary, the various statistical virtues that King already has documented on behalf of his approach (1997, 1999, 2000, 2002). Rather, I focus on EI as a substantive resource for conducting what social scientists customarily call "contextual research." King's approach helps the analyst probe theoretically important contextual effects that undermined previous methods of ecological inference because these methods had to assume them away. Unlike the conventional forms of aggregate-data analysis that preceded it, King's approach holds out some possibility for pulling apart compositional and contextual patterns – that is, for determining the extent to which aggregate behavior varies from place to place because of changes in the balance of social groups composing each locale, and the extent to which aggregate behavior varies because of how each social group reacts to the context in which it operates.[1]

Pursuing this argument requires four distinct steps. The body of the chapter begins by embedding ecological inference within the needs of contextual research to show why they are inextricably linked. The aggregation bias that spoils conventional ecological inference derives in large part from the very same contextual effects central to social theories of human behavior. The second section reviews why King's method is sensitive to aggregation bias, which in turn means that it provides leverage for capturing otherwise elusive contextual effects. The third section explains why previous diagnostic tests do not give a good picture of EI's value for contextual research. The existing critiques analyze patently uninformative data and neglect to incorporate the sort of substantive insights that normally would be available to an analyst applying the method.[2]

The final section therefore exhibits King's approach in action to show how it is especially valuable for contextual research by analysts armed with informative data or with a significant background in the substance of their topics. In particular, it applies King's innovations to real data collected to address actual research questions in racial voting behavior, and it illustrates the unprecedented success of his statistical tools. Techniques of ecological inference still have far to go, and numerous enhancements still await practical implementation (as illustrated by the many essays in this volume). But all of the sound and fury generated by this scholarly ferment – which will give numerous reminders why EI is imperfect – should not distract practitioners from the simple fact that King's method is far superior to the tools upon which both scholars and policy makers previously relied. The criticism of King should not serve as an excuse to continue using those older methods.

HOW ECOLOGICAL ANALYSIS KILLED ECOLOGICAL INFERENCE

Contextual theories of political behavior generally characterize how individuals respond to their social environment. They recognize that individuals view political life through different

---

[1] Note that there is a third possibility, which is that behavior varies because of selection effects among the group members who gravitate to different locales. For purposes of this discussion, I conflate the two sorts of contextual patterns – the push vs. the pull of the environment – under the umbrella label of "contextual research." Distinguishing them is difficult to impossible with cross-sectional data, although greater insight might be gained from a dynamic approach to inference that incorporated variation across time (see Chapter 9 of this book).

[2] In other words, they do not even use *informally* the sort of prior knowledge that Bayesian innovations in ecological inference allow researchers to incorporate *formally* (see, for example, Chapters 1 and 6).

lenses depending upon the communities they inhabit. People experience different pressures and face different incentives because of where they happen to reside. Different memories and different symbols shape their political lives, and the schema that structure this emotion-laden raw material may be shared narratives that have emerged from a geographically bounded stream of communication (Couto, 1993). This complex, socially embedded perspective motivated many early empiricists in political science, including the "quintessential political scientist," V. O. Key, Jr. (Lucker, 2001; Natchez, 1985: 74, 94–99). It eventually faded in favor of highly individualistic approaches to political behavior grounded in social psychology, as epitomized by the Michigan model of voting behavior.[3]

Surveys encourage individualistic approaches to politics. They sample random people in isolation and ask for their subjective perceptions. Secondary analysis often explains opinion with opinion and preference with preference; the burden seldom falls on researchers to trace raw opinions back to any tangible source (Natchez, 1985: 64–67). In particular, analysts rarely consider the strongest community attachments that individuals might have – family, friends, church, school, neighborhood, county, newspaper – because they are localized.[4] Secondary analysts may not even possess the contextual information needed to allow such nuance. In work developed from such a data source, political actors inherently appear as disembodied souls. By contrast, aggregate statistics summarize the social environment shaping political behavior. They portray many of the external incentives and pressures that operate on political actors, especially those bounded by geography. With reliable methods of aggregate-data analysis, deeper insights about the social nature of politics would be possible – so the line between contextual analysis and aggregate-data analysis is hazy, and to some extent their fates have always been intertwined.

Sociologists recognized long ago the intimate connection between aggregation and attempts to contextualize human behavior. Indeed, the language we still use to discuss aggregate-data analysis reflects their awareness. They used biological metaphors to discuss how humans related to the pressures of a social environment, implicitly or explicitly comparing the process to a species interacting with its ecology. Ecological analysis, when applied to human behavior, meant studying contextual effects on how people acted and what they believed. Therefore, when aggregate-data analysis suffered a series of high-profile attacks that undermined confidence in available methods (e.g., Goodman, 1953; Robinson, 1950), the natural result was a decline in contextual studies.

Few early critics discussed the ironic tension between ecological inference and ecological analysis – the focus tended to be on fallacious conclusions rather than their substantive origin – yet it was precisely the importance of human ecology that made aggregate-data techniques for ecological inference so unreliable (Hauser, 1970). Contextual behavior undermined the very data conventionally available to study political context. For this reason, the two most common approaches to aggregate-data analysis assume that contextual effects do not exist. They require analysts to believe that members of demographic groups act the same way everywhere; demographic variation in their communities bears no relation to how people behave. "Homogeneous unit analysis," for example, requires the researcher to assume that places where a group is numerically dominant will be representative of how the group acts in more diverse places (MacManus, 1995: 45n). Linear "ecological regression,"

---

[3] Key wrote, in a letter recommending Gabriel Almond's promotion to full professor, "I'm enough of a reactionary myself to become annoyed when a political scientist picks up a smattering of social psychology . . . and proceeds to construct a system out of thin air" (Lucker, 2001: 204).

[4] The most obvious exception is the extensive, and valuable, body of work produced by R. Robert Huckfeldt (1986), including his work with coauthors such as Carol Kohfeld (1989) and John Sprague (1995).

meanwhile, explicitly assumes that all systematic behavioral variation is compositional, none is contextual (see the Introduction to this book).[5]

A quick formal exploration illustrates why linear ecological regression is almost useless in the presence of contextual effects.[6] Analysts regress an aggregate political outcome on the population density of each demographic group, and interpret the resulting coefficients as rates of behavior. Take the case of black (X_i) and white ($1 - X_i$) voting for the left-wing candidate in an election (V_i^L). The assumed linear relationship, across multiple areal units i, would take on the following form: [7]

$$V_i^L = \beta^b X_i + \beta^w (1 - X_i) + u_i,$$

where u_i is a complex residual to capture how voting differs from that predicted by the two coefficients.[8] This form of the regression lacks an intercept, but transforming the model to a bivariate version with a constant term is simple:

$$V_i^L = \beta^b X_i + \beta^w - \beta^w X_i + u_i$$
$$= \beta^w + (\beta^b - \beta^w) X_i + u_i.$$

Both political outcomes (V_i^L) and racial densities (X_i) usually appear in aggregate data. One generally lacks the frequencies that would appear in a cross-tabulation, though: the proportion of blacks (β^b) and whites (β^w) who supported the left-wing candidate.

The lack of an index for either parameter illustrates the common assumption that ethnic rates of behavior are constant across areal units, which is what makes a least-squares method of estimation so convenient. When this assumption is false – when members of an ethnic group do not, on average, behave the same way everywhere – the data may contain significant aggregation bias. Estimates from this simple model can fall quite far from the truth because they attribute contextual variation in one group's behavior to the other group.

Consider a simple contextual effect, in which whites support the left-wing candidate at a higher rate when they live in heavily minority areas (Voss and Lublin, 2001). The formula for left-wing support now contains a shifting parameter, β_i^w, which might be a linear function of racial density:

$$V_i^L = \beta^b X_i + \beta_i^w (1 - X_i) + u_i$$
$$= \beta_i^w + (\beta^b - \beta_i^w) X_i + u_i, \qquad \text{where } \beta_i^w = \gamma^0 + \gamma^1 X_i.$$

Naive ecological regression, performed on data of this sort, will not estimate the desired quantities (i.e., β^b and the weighted average of β_i^w, presuming all other assumptions of the

---

[5] A rival method, seldom used by analysts, rejects these assumptions. Called the "neighborhood model" (Freedman et al., 1991), it does not escape from the conundrum posed by data containing both compositional and contextual patterns. It simple reverses the error, assuming that all systematic variation in behavior is contextual, none compositional. Different demographic groups all would have to behave the same way in a given community.

[6] Some scholars call ecological regression "Goodman's method" after the man who popularized the idea (Goodman, 1953, 1959). However, most applications of the method violate the conditions for which he prescribed it, so I avoid the label. Note, incidentally, that my comments apply to ecological correlations as well.

[7] Areal units may be any geographically defined spaces important to analysts or policy makers. Examples include regions, provinces, states, counties, precincts, and legislative districts.

[8] This notation resembles Equation 0.4 in the Introduction, but it includes a catchall error term because that is what practitioners using the method customarily assume. Note, however, that this is not the well-behaved ordinary least squares error term, because it has to capture the effect of varying parameters (Zax, 2002).

model were correct). Instead, it would turn up the following:

$$V_i^L = \beta^b X_i + \beta_i^w (1 - X_i) + u_i$$
$$= \beta^b X_i + (\gamma^0 + \gamma^1 X_i)(1 - X_i) + u_i$$
$$= \beta^b X_i + \gamma^0 (1 - X_i) + \gamma^1 X_i (1 - X_i) + u_i$$
$$= [\beta^b + \gamma^1 (1 - X_i)] X_i + \gamma^0 (1 - X_i) + u_i.$$

The estimated white support for the left-wing candidate, therefore, will be γ^0 only – too low if γ^1 is positive. The estimated black support, meanwhile, will be too high. This is why analysts often estimate that Democratic support among blacks exceeds 100% (see King, 1997: 16).

Of course, one can adjust the model for this simple case of parameter variation. Applying the distributive property and then regrouping provides

$$= \beta^b X_i + \gamma^1 X_i - \gamma^1 X_i^2 + \gamma^0 - \gamma^0 X_i + u_i$$
$$= \gamma^0 + (\beta^b + \gamma^1 - \gamma^0) X_i - \gamma^1 X_i^2 + u_i.$$

One can compute the three parameters of interest after running that regression. However, if white and black vote choices *both* vary with the racial density of the locale, either directly or indirectly, then linear ecological regression is impossible because the parameters are underidentified. We would need not β^b but the weighted average of β_i^b:

$$= \beta_i^b X_i + \gamma^1 X_i - \gamma^1 X_i^2 + \gamma^0 - \gamma^0 X_i + u_i \quad (\text{where } \beta_i^b = \rho^0 + \rho^1 X_i)$$
$$= (\rho^0 + \rho^1 X_i) X_i + \gamma^1 X_i - \gamma^1 X_i^2 + \gamma^0 - \gamma^0 X_i + u_i$$
$$= \gamma^0 + (\rho^0 + \gamma^1 - \gamma^0) X_i + (\rho^1 - \gamma^1) X_i^2 + u_i.$$

It is impossible to compute the four parameters of interest that are now necessary.

The failure of conventional forms of ecological inference therefore amounts to more than just the danger of getting wrong answers, of committing an "ecological fallacy." For contextual analysis, they never provide any answers at all.

ENTER THE METHOD OF BOUNDS

King's (1997) approach offers some hope of capturing systematic geographical variation through a method of statistical inference. This is not the place to summarize King's proposed solution to the ecological-inference problem; a review appears in the Introduction to this book. However, the critical wrinkle for contextual analysis is King's use of the deterministic *method of bounds* (Duncan and Davis, 1953). The basic insight is fairly simple. Consider a locale in which the Democratic candidate wins 50% of the vote and 25% of the voters are black. Even if every black voted Democratic, whites would have to account for the remaining 25 percentage points of the Democratic candidate's votes. At least a third of whites mathematically must have voted that way (although more may have, if some blacks voted Republican). So the possible white vote in this hypothetical example does not extend from 0% to 100%; the minimum is 33%. Add up all the constraints on what is possible, maxima and minima, from areal unit to areal unit, and you may have quite a lot of information about larger electoral districts.

As the Introduction explains, EI identifies from the outset the complete set of possible rates of racial voting behavior – not for an electoral district as a whole, but for each areal unit it contains. Furthermore, EI goes beyond the simple method of bounds by considering

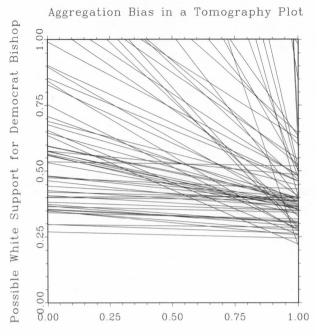

Possible Black Support for Democrat Bishop

Figure 3.1. Tomography plot illustrates all known information about the vote for U.S. Rep. Sanford Bishop in Georgia's 1996 2nd congressional district. Horizontal line segments represent all-white precincts; segments have greater black density as they become more vertical. The downward-cascading pattern shows that Bishop's white vote contained contextual effects: whites gave more support to the black Democrat when their locality contained greater black populations.

the two rates of group behavior simultaneously. It takes into account the linear relationship between how one group could have behaved and how the other could have in order to produce the final vote totals (see Equation 0.5 in the Introduction). EI therefore constrains estimates of *joint* behavior, reducing the range of estimates for each areal unit to a series of exclusive pairs.

By exploiting the deterministic information in the data so thoroughly, EI has the potential to detect and adjust for contextual patterns. This is best understood using the *tomography plot*, a graphical representation of the line segments for each areal unit in an analysis (see Figure 0.1 in the Introduction and its accompanying explanation). Figure 3.1 presents a plot containing line segments for a random selection of 25% of 1996 precincts in Georgia's second congressional district (see Voss and Lublin, 2001).[9] Horizontal lines correspond to precincts that are almost entirely white. They contain so few blacks that we know quite precisely how whites behaved but almost nothing about the blacks, which is why the slant of such a line only allows a small range of possible values on the Y-axis but any value on the X-axis. A segment becomes more vertical, however, as black voters increase proportionally. We are less sure how many whites supported the Democrat in these mixed counties, because the aggregate data also include a large black population.

[9] I should note that, strictly speaking, this plot does not simply contain deterministic information. I conducted a previous stage of EI to estimate the proportion of voters who were black. No assumptions about party preference by race were required to produce the figure.

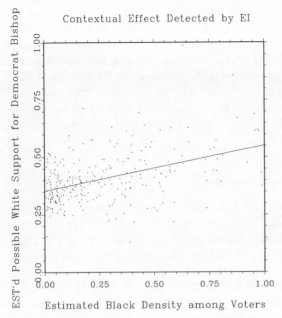

Figure 3.2. Basic EI results strongly indicate the presence of contextual effects (or aggregation bias) in the 1996 white vote for the Democratic incumbent Rep. Sanford Bishop. Whites sharing a mixed-race environment found the black moderate much more appealing than did those in heavily white precincts.

The narrow bounds that can appear for areal units often will push estimates from a basic EI analysis into a contextual pattern. This pattern alerts the analyst that the data contain aggregation bias. Figure 3.1 illustrates how the bounds inform ecological inference. The slanted lines often run up against the right edge of the unit square at a very high level of white support for the black Democrat, Sanford Bishop. The line segments cascade downward as they straighten out, though. All-white precincts are less likely to strike a high value on the right edge of the unit square. Their bounds indicate lower levels of white support for Bishop. White voters clearly supported the black Democrat at higher rates when they lived in a racially mixed context, and even the simplest versions of EI will capture this pattern by requiring each precinct estimate to be possible. Figure 3.2 shows how simple EI estimates run on these data follow a contextual pattern.

Not all examples of aggregation bias will be as obvious as the one I have selected here – but EI can pick up patterns in a large sample that are too subtle for the naked eye to detect. This is especially true when researchers approach an analysis with theoretical reasons to anticipate the contextual effect. In instances when researchers can hypothesize why voting rates might correlate with racial density, an extended version of King's model allows the introduction of covariates to explain systematic variation in group behavior (see Equation 0.10 in the Introduction). The model picks up contextual variation in the bounds and projects that pattern onto the remaining areal units whose bounds were not as informative. Bounding the estimates for each areal unit, and building up estimates for a larger electoral district based on those bounds, therefore allows EI to function even if both racial groups exhibit some degree of contextual behavior. It is not underidentified the way linear regression would be.

Of course, being able to produce estimates does not guarantee they will be good ones. Their quality depends upon how much information the bounds provide. Critics point out that King's method may underestimate the strength of contextual patterns, which are suppressed by the aggregation process (Anselin and Cho, 2002; Cho, 1998; Rivers, 1998). They worry about variation in estimates powered by residuals from a statistical analysis (Herron and Shotts, 2003; McCue, 2001). These are valid concerns. Researchers should understand the severity of the limits; methodologists should search for ways to alleviate the dangers. Nevertheless, the ability to detect even a healthy portion of that contextual variation takes King's method far beyond what practitioners were using for the five decades between first awareness of this problem (Robinson, 1950) and King's attempted solution (1997).

"IF IT IS SO USEFUL, THEN WHY ALL THE CRITICISM?"[10]

King's critics have complained that he was not explicit enough about when EI will be reliable and when it will be unreliable (Freedman et al., 1998: 1520). For the most part, these insights long precede King's book. An extensive literature has explored when data aggregation will throw away more or less information. King (1997: 88–89) also presented "scattercross graphs," as described by Leo Goodman (1959: 617–618), that provide a visual means of determining when the method of bounds will help make up for the limitations of ecological regression. Briefly, here are the rules of thumb that practitioners apparently need. Ecological inference will work better when:

1. The group of interest either constitutes a large majority of the overall population or is relatively segregated across areal units (which is more likely when areal units are very small).
2. Outcomes of interest approach unanimity in particular areal units, especially the ones with highly mixed populations.
3. Data contain numerous observations to insulate the estimation from errors due to chance.
4. The grouping of interest identifies a politically distinct population with internally similar behavior that differs from the behavior of other groups – that is, across-group variation outweighs within-group variation.
5. Within-group variation across areal units is effectively random, resulting from innumerable small sources rather than a few large but unmeasured influences.
6. Any systematic variation in a group's behavior across areal units does not respond to the balance among groups in each place, nor does it respond to other variables that are correlated with group density.
7. The researcher possesses sufficient knowledge of the subject matter to inform the estimation about possible sources of systematic within-group variation and to detect fallacious conclusions.

King's solution does not alter any of these generalizations. It still performs better with detailed data. It is still hindered by contextual patterns when bounds are uninformative. It still does not provide a panacea for analysts lacking substantive familiarity with their data.

---

[10] The heading quotes a question I was asked while presenting King's method at a conference workshop. I think it encapsulates how practitioners initially evaluate the startup costs necessary to learn a method. They may not weigh the methodological critiques themselves, assuming that "where there's smoke, there's fire."

Why King's Method Performs Better with Poor Data

The similarities between King's approach and ecological regression leads Douglas Rivers (1998: 442) to warn readers against thinking "that King has somehow relaxed the assumptions of ecological regression." He dismisses EI's "fanfare" and "notoriety" as undeserved because King's approach relies on assumptions that "include all those required for Goodman's estimator and then some." This critique is misleading at best. It implies that ecological regression is somehow a generalized form of King's approach, requiring fewer assumptions – which would make King's method more susceptible to faulty application. In fact, the reverse is the case. King's method is less vulnerable to faulty assumptions – not because the assumptions have become completely irrelevant, but because the method of bounds helps avoid analytical dependence on them.

Furthermore, some assumptions of ecological regression do not appear in King's method and therefore have been "relaxed" even in the sense that methodologists usually use the word (i.e., dropped). For example, EI does not assume that parameters are fixed. It does not assume that errors in prediction always have the same variance (i.e., homoskedasticity). By aggregating across areal units, EI computes direct estimates for the quantities of interest; it does not assume that the average aggregate behavioral pattern represents the average individual-level behavior pattern (Palmquist, 2002). Nor, thanks to King's use of the truncated bivariate normal distribution and the method of bounds, does EI assume linearity across the full range of data.[11]

Finally, it is worth noting that practitioners using EI are less vulnerable to faulty assumptions in another way – which is that the software includes both graphical and statistical diagnostics that often will indicate when assumptions are wrong. Indeed, not only do these diagnostics help experts check some of their basic ideas about the data-generation process, but the graphical and statistical tools sometimes have an independent substantive value; presenting them can help clarify the results of an analysis.[12] By contrast, aside from prior knowledge, about the only defense against faulty inference in ecological regression is observed nonlinearity in the relationship between racial density and outcome.[13] Also, linear methods of ecological inference, from correlations to multiple regressions, all lack meaningful standard errors that researchers regularly consult and that indicate the uncertainty contained within estimates (Zax, 2002).

A disadvantageous distribution of voters will inflate any specification error contained in the aggregate analysis many times over (Palmquist and Voss, 1996). Take one terrible case for ecological inference: when an analyst wishes to probe gender differences in behavior. Gender differences are especially resistant to aggregate-data analysis, unless one can incorporate outside information (see Chapter 6). Men and women usually live together – aside from places containing prisons, military bases, or other institutions that might skew the normal gender balance – so their populations are almost evenly divided. Furthermore, the fluctuations in gender that do occur across electoral units are almost completely irrelevant to politics; they are small, mostly random noise. Yet practitioners may not notice the

[11] Of course, GLS estimators for ecological regression could address some of these concerns, too (McCue, 2001: 109).
[12] For example, my analysis of 1996 congressional campaigns containing black candidates in white districts illustrated contextual effects in turnout and vote choice using the statistical and graphical diagnostics that King intended as tests for aggregation bias. (Voss and Lublin, 2001).
[13] Work by Brad Palmquist, summarized in Palmquist and Voss (1996), provides a method of gauging how much aggregation bias will foil linear ecological inferences, but his developments have not been sufficiently integrated by practitioners.

uselessness of naive ecological inferences based on data such as gender aggregates. Ecological correlations give a false sense of security, whereas King's software provides no such cover; standard errors advertise when an analyst tries to get milk from a stone.[14]

Why King's Method Performed Poorly with Horrible Data

Gary King's book (1997) already tests his method on real data. These examples illustrate the method's effectiveness, or at least its ability to warn analysts when something has gone wrong, although they are limited in quantity (Freedman et al., 1998: 1520). By contrast, critics have subjected King's approach to other diagnostic tests that point toward severe limitations (Anselin and Cho, 2002; Cho, 1998; Freedman et al., 1998, 1999). It may seem superfluous, at this point, to continue providing examples of the method in action – since success in a few data sets "does not prove anything" (Rivers, 1998: 443) and his model "works on some datasets but not others" (Freedman et al., 1998: 1520).

Nevertheless, the available slate of trials contain certain drawbacks that seem to call for a reconsideration. The initial trials were not representative of how King's method would work in most situations – let alone how it would perform in particularly useful situations. Leaving aside simulated data, King's method has been tested against:

- Aggregate data produced from a survey conducted during the 1984 California general election, in which the analyst attempted to estimate racial differences in education across 30 precincts (Cho, 1998: 153–160).
- Aggregate data produced from a survey conducted during a San Francisco city council race, in which the analyst attempted to estimate differences between Chinese and non-Chinese voters in their support for candidate Thomas Hsieh across 37 precincts (Cho, 1998: 160–161).
- Aggregate data produced from an exit poll conducted in Stockton during the 1988 presidential primary, in which the analyst attempted to estimate Jesse Jackson's support among Hispanics and non-Hispanics across 39 sample precincts (Freedman et al., 1998).
- Census-tract data from Los Angeles that contained 1980 demographics, in which the analyst attempted to estimate education, income, and home ownership for Hispanics and non-Hispanics across 1,409 tracts (Freedman et al., 1998).
- Census-tract data from Los Angeles that contained 1988 election statistics, in which the analyst attempted to estimate party registration for Hispanic and non-Hispanic registered voters (Freedman et al., 1998).
- County data from Texas that contained incidents of strokes, in which the analysts attempted to estimate stroke rates by gender (Anselin and Cho, 2002: 287–288).

How do these trials stack up against the conditions under which an analyst should expect optimal performance from an aggregate-data analysis technique? The data are notable, as a group, for the extent to which they deviate from conditions under which one ought to try ecological inference – and generally the few diagnostics they report from EI indicate as much.

Consider the following comparison of these data against the enumeration of optimal circumstances listed earlier. As far as a reader can judge, these trials apply King's method to data with very few homogeneous units. Blacks never exceed a third of the precinct population

---

[14] One pair of researchers at a recent conference concluded erroneously that EI was less successful than ecological correlations because EI had returned huge standard errors for gender-vote estimates (Peterson and Koloen, 2002). Essentially, they criticized EI because it was the bearer of bad news that they needed to hear.

in Cho's first example (see the giant standard errors in her initial analysis). The Chinese only exceed majority status in a handful of her precincts in the second example (see the slope of lines in the tomography plot as well as the large standard errors). The stroke analysis uses gender as its demographic category, probably the toughest case in ecological inference because of sharply limited compositional variation. Most of Freedman's examples use census tracts, long known for how seldom they approach homogeneity (Myers, 1954). With his exit-poll data, the standard error for Hispanics is more than four times as large as the one for non-Hispanics, suggesting that the data provided limited information about the minority group.[15]

Three of the examples include only a few dozen observations each. In some of these cases, it is unlikely that a researcher would have had to stop with so little data. For example, even if one were interested only in Jesse Jackson's Hispanic support in Stockton, the analysis would be stronger if it could borrow strength from related cases of Hispanic voting behavior nearby. Cho's education example not only includes few cases, it obviously requires covariates, which will tax the data more than usual.

Most of the trials attempt to predict socioeconomic data, which are known to vary widely within groups. Black education rates in Cho's first example jump from 1% to 90% across precincts! More importantly, socioeconomic status strongly shapes people's localized residential choices (see, e.g., Biggar and Martin, 1976), so minorities who reside in mixed-race or mixed-ethnicity settings are likely to have much higher status than those in all-minority ghettoes. The stroke data, meanwhile, were selected precisely because they exhibited significant spatial autocorrelation.[16] These examples were certain to be characterized by systematic variation within groups and by community-based similarities across them.

All of the political trials look at urban areas and yet make no reference to blacks – who stand apart for their heavy Democratic party support. Blacks simply fall into the non-Hispanic or non-Chinese categories, along with white Anglos. Anyone knowledgeable about racial politics should realize that combining whites and blacks into one group violates King's distributional assumptions, and probably introduces severe within-group variance while suppressing across-group variance.

None of the examples uses King's extended model to capture the contextual effect of group density directly. Only one uses the extended model at all: Cho introduces two covariates, income and age, while predicting racial education rates. Income helps, age hurts – which leads her to conclude that an analyst has no idea when a covariate might improve the situation. Yet EI's diagnostics clearly show that the income covariate was the right thing to use. In both the basic EI model and the version with an age covariate, standard errors from EI were so large that they swamped the estimates themselves. After Cho added the income covariate, though, the model suddenly behaved: it revised the estimate of black education rates upward by 50% and returned much smaller standard errors. One suspects that likelihood scores from the maximum-likelihood estimates also indicated the desirability of an income covariate.

---

[15] Freedman et al. (1999: 355) do not seem to understand the meaning of EI's standard errors. After King (1999) suggested that their data contain more information about non-Hispanics, they wrote: "It is not clear what sort of additional information would be available to King for non-Hispanics. ... Any error on the Hispanic side must be balanced by an error of the same size but the opposite sign on the non-Hispanic side." Yet their own table reveals that EI has reported much smaller standard errors for non-Hispanics than the program did for Hispanics (Freedman et al., 1998: 1519). The software reported errors proportional to the information available, and therefore to the true error, something the critics missed.

[16] They also might contain aggregation bias because of unaddressed simultaneity problems. *Ceteris paribus*, places where men die from strokes at high rates might tend to contain fewer men over the long term.

People who study subjects empirically should not reinvent the wheel. A scholarly liter-ature usually provides enough descriptive information that one can assess in advance the likely success of any particular inference, as I have done retrospectively with the existing trials. I severely doubt that scholars familiar both with ecological inference and with race and ethnicity would have been surprised by EI's poor performance in these hostile tests. Furthermore, a knowledgeable scholar would have balked at most of the biggest estimation errors even without the truth to guide choices: 91% of Hispanics as Democratic registrants, which will happen rarely across the country; standard errors so huge that the estimates are not substantively interesting; an estimate that whites with a college degree outnumbered blacks 4 to 1 when in fact blacks were more likely to have graduated from college. Even if it were true that theory and previous research provide "no clear way of distinguishing good models from bad models," they provide a lot more guidance than these particular trials brought to bear.

APPLYING EI WITH INFORMATIVE DATA OR CONTEXTUAL KNOWLEDGE

To illustrate how King's approach outperforms conventional methods of ecological inference by incorporating and then summarizing contextual information, I will apply his parametric model to the study of racial voting behavior in the U.S. south. In each case the goal is to fill in cross-tabulations between aggregate race data and aggregate political outcomes, thereby producing accurate estimates of voting behavior by race – exactly the sort of estimates ecological inference commonly would be called upon to produce in real voting or policy research. Before presenting the application, though, I should explain why racial voting behavior is a critical case for ecological inference, as well as why southern data are particularly helpful for assessing a method's contribution.

Why is race a good choice? First, racial categories are advantageous because they are highly segregated at low levels of aggregation but not terribly segregated at higher ones. They allow a test of King's method in a variety of situations. Second, racial behavior tends to be contextual, and in theoretically important ways. The nature of these contextual effects links specific substantive concerns of political scientists, sociologists, social psychologists, quantitative historians, constitutional-law scholars, and anthropologists, among others (e.g., Kousser, 1974; Pettigrew, 1985; Taylor, 1998; Voss, 2001). Third, voting-rights specialists depend upon ecological estimation. The U.S. Supreme Court declared racial bloc voting to be one component of a justiciable "vote dilution" claim in *Thornburgh v. Gingles* (478 U.S. 30-108), and litigants simply do not have state or local survey data available to establish or ward off constitutional claims. Analysts require some workable method of ecological inference to recapture data lost due to the secret ballot.

Of course, one could argue that selecting race stacks the deck in King's favor. Racial groups are more polarized in their partisan behavior than just about any other demographic category. Nevertheless, racial polarization is a fourth reason why race is a critical case for ecological inference. The survey-research revolution has not liberated those who study racial politics in the same way it has freed up work in other subfields. Politically sensitive topics resist objective measurement (Kuklinski, Cobb, and Gilens, 1997; Traugott and Price, 1992), so aggregate data naturally play a significant role in the study of race. Anyway, party choice is not the only form of racial voting behavior; registration and turnout do not polarize the races nearly as much. Race is a good choice for assessing the success of King's method.

Why southern data? First, the south makes sense because, among places with a substantial black population, that region has less residential segregation than the rest of the country (Massey and Denton, 1993). Estimation will be harder than usual. Second, my own research tends to focus on southern politics (e.g., Lublin and Voss, 2000a, 2000b, 2003; Voss, 1996), so I need not apply King's method blindly. Third, not only did southern states fuel the contextual study of racial voting (Heard, 1952; Key, 1949; Matthews and Prothro, 1966), they are the site of most redistricting litigation and thus typify the conditions under which King's method would shape public policy. Finally, and most importantly, a string of voting-rights cases have convinced the south's public officials that they need to invest in precise data collection. Sometimes the data reach such high quality that they include answers to questions that, in other locales, would require some form of statistical inference to probe.

County-Level Racial Voting Behavior

George Wallace's 1968 presidential campaign may have dealt the death blow to aggregate-data studies of voting behavior. White support for Wallace was so contextual, with support high in exactly the places where blacks were most numerous, that it completely skewed the techniques of ecological inference available at the time. Furthermore, the Wallace vote was only available to researchers at relatively high levels of aggregation, so aggregate data were (and are) quite poor.

An analysis by Schoenberger and Segal (1971: 585), for example, implied that Wallace received heavy black support in his 1968 presidential bid. The authors did not embrace this absurd conclusion, correctly attributing the findings to Wallace's heavy white support in the Black Belt, but lacked any statistical basis for their interpretation or any real estimates of white behavior. Not even additional methodological refinements, intended to counteract the "ecological fallacy," could remove their reliance on prior knowledge, or provide reliable estimates of how each race actually voted (Wasserman and Segal, 1973: 179). The complete inadequacy of aggregate-data analysis for contributing to this important topic of interest helped illustrate why the discipline needed to move toward surveys in the short term. The Wallace vote has even stumped researchers using more modern methods, including King's solution (Palmquist, 2002). It is therefore about as tough a real-life test as King's method could face.

Louisiana reports parish-level (i.e., county-level) voter registration broken down by race. If we consider the vote as a three-stage process – the decision to register, the decision to vote, the vote choice – the first stage of that process does not require estimation in this rare instance. Louisiana data are particularly useful for two other reasons. First, the state's registration data contained lots of idiosyncratic variation in 1968, all of which violates EI's assumptions. Some parishes purged their voter rolls of dead weight more frequently than others.[17] Some hosted federal election examiners eager to expand the voting rolls.[18] Second, all evidence indicates that very few blacks voted for Wallace. This strong prior on what the black estimate ought to be means that I can check King's method using multiple forms of racial behavior. It is precisely the combination of difficult data with known answers that makes the Louisiana case worthwhile as a test of King's method.

For my initial run, I did not take advantage of EI's more advanced features, such as modeling parameters of the truncated bivariate normal to vary with other relevant quantities. I want to compare the estimates from this simple EI analysis both with the real numbers

---

[17] In fact, eight parishes report more registered whites than they contained voting-age white adults (using 1970 census figures), and two similarly reported black registration exceeding possible levels. In those instances, I adjusted registration downward to 100% to keep it within possible bounds, but otherwise tolerated the measurement error contained in the numbers.

[18] Nine Louisiana parishes contained a federal examiner in 1966, according to the Matthews-Prothro data set maintained by Jim Alt (1994: 372–373).

Table 3.1 1968 registration estimates for Louisiana

Source	Registration White	Registration Black	Total
Truth	77.3	53.6	71.1
State data:			
Lower bound	60.9	0.0	
Upper bound	96.3	100.0	
Midpoint	*78.6*	*50.0*	71.2
Parish data:			
Lower bound	61.1	15.6	
Upper bound	90.7	99.3	
Midpoint	*75.9*	*57.5*	71.1
Naive ER	86.0 (4.0)	57.0 (9.6)	78.5
Weighted ER	77.9 (4.0)	60.0 (10.6)	73.2
Neighborhood	71.5	70.2	71.2
Homogeneous	85.4		
EI (simple)	76.7 (6.1)	55.2 (17.2)	71.1
EI (final)	77.1 (5.7)	54.0 (16.0)	71.1

Note: Methodological details of each estimation appear in the text. Parenthetical numbers are standard errors. No estimate of black behavior appears for homogeneous unit analysis because Louisiana contains no homogeneous black parishes.

and with estimates produced by other methods of aggregate-data analysis. The first row of Table 3.1 therefore reports the real racial registration rates: 53.6% of blacks and 77.3% of whites. I then report what an analyst lacking the truth would know to be true: the bounds for the state computed from state-level marginals, and the bounds for the state computed from parish-level marginals. The state bounds alone do not constrain black registration estimates at all, and only pinch possible white registration rates to a span of roughly 35 percentage points. The bounds based upon parish-level limitations squeeze the range of valid estimates for whites even more, and rule out the more extreme levels of black registration as well. The truth in this case clearly falls near to the midpoints between the bounds: 75.9% for whites and 57.5% for blacks.

Naive linear ecological regression produces quite impossible estimates: 86% registration for whites (more than two large standard deviations from the truth), and 57% registration for blacks. For the entire state, this implies a faulty 78.5% statewide registration rate. Faced by obviously incorrect implications, an analyst would know that ecological regression had failed. One solution would be to use a weighted analysis (Palmquist and Voss, 1997: 13). Therefore I repeated the ecological regression using weighted least squares. The white registration estimate then comes quite close – within a percentage point of the truth – but the black registration rate rises to more than six percentage points away. The overall estimates are still impossible, since they represent a 73.2% statewide registration rate.

Ecological regression does not produce parish-level estimates – 77.9% of whites and 60% of blacks presumably registered in each parish – but we can evaluate these figures as surrogate parish estimates by comparing them with the parish bounds that an analyst would know even without Louisiana's racial data. Together the estimates are impossible in all but, at best, two or three parishes (as indicated by how few of the tomography lines would cross that point). Even looking one race at a time, the white registration rate is impossible for 33 parishes: too low for 27 and too high for 6. The black registration rate is impossible for 14 parishes. That the bounds are so active signifies more than just the failure of linear regression; it also suggests that contextual effects may be biasing the estimates.

Another common method of analysis is to look at all-black units to determine black behavior and all-white units to determine white behavior. Unfortunately, only four of the 59 parishes used in my EI estimation contain more than a 90% white voting-age population, and none are more than 90% black.[19] The limits of this homogeneous unit approach are therefore obvious. The registration rate in the four white parishes, computed as a weighted average, comes to 85.4% percent – far higher than the true statewide rate. All-white parishes were not representative. The neighborhood model, which assumes that all races behave the same way in particular electoral units but differ across them, is similarly unimpressive. It estimates almost equal registration rates for blacks and whites when the true results are much more polarized.

Even a simple EI estimation clearly outperforms every method except weighted ecological regression. It estimates that 76.7% of whites registered, within a percentage point of the truth, and that 55.2% of blacks registered, within 2 percentage points of the truth. Given the wide variation from one parish to the next, these estimates are remarkable. The one drawback is that standard errors are very large. This is a reassuring drawback, though, since it means EI's standard errors reflect the high degree of uncertainty much better than those from naive ecological regression.

This simple EI run also predicts the true white registration rates in each parish amazingly well. Figure 3.3 presents a scatterplot of the EI estimates against the true white registration rates (a circle's radius indicates the size of the parish's white population). The solid slanted line, flanked by an 80% confidence interval, represents where cases would fall when estimates were exactly correct. Circles to the left of the line mean estimates were too low, those to the right that estimates were too high. As the graph shows, the bulk of parishes fall right on or around the solid line, indicating an excellent fit with the real answers. The exception is a handful of very small parishes with white voting estimates that are too low. In these rural parishes, black registration was below 25%, a known legacy of Jim Crow that no simple EI analysis captures because it violates the model's assumptions so severely.

EI partially adapts to the presence of aggregation bias, even when the researcher makes no overt attempt to model that bias, because requiring estimates to be possible will force them to follow contextual behavior in informative data. These data are far from informative. Nevertheless, consistent with previous research (Matthews and Prothro, 1966), the black registration estimates on average decrease 2.4 percentage points with a 10-percentage-point shift in black density. The basic version of EI therefore picked up some, but not all, of the true contextual pattern of aggregation bias. As the black density increased 10 percentage points, the real black registration rates decreased 4.1 percentage points, and the white rate climbed 1.4 percentage points.

I tried several refinements to the estimation – drawn from my knowledge of the southern politics literature, not from my knowledge of the true numbers. Two corrections to the basic model did appear useful – judging, for example, from how much they improved the log-likelihood score. I allowed parameters to react to the black density of the population, in keeping with previous literature. I also included a dummy variable for two areas historically known for their racial sensitivity: the Mississippi Delta parishes in the state's northeast

---

[19] There's no consensus on what constitutes a "homogeneous" place. I've used a 90% threshold. Lower levels might bring in more white places, but no Louisiana parish exceeded even a 70% black voting-age population, so estimating black behavior this way was impossible.

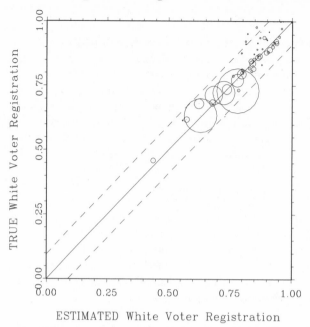

Predicting Parish Registration with Poor Data

ESTIMATED White Voter Registration

Figure 3.3. Parish-level estimates for Louisiana's 1968 white rate of voter registration are surprisingly accurate given the terrible quality of the data. The 45-degree angle represents perfect estimates. Those slightly above the line guessed too low for white registration; those below the line guessed too high. A few small delta counties violated the assumptions of King's EI, but while they probably inflated the standard error, they did not throw off the statewide estimate very much.

corner, and segregationist Judge Leander Perez's Plaquemines Parish. These refinements improved estimates, although the uncertainty remained high. Estimates for both races were within half a percentage point of the truth in this final model, and better reflected the aggregation bias in the true data. The black registration estimates decrease 3 percentage points, on average, with a 10-percentage-point increase in black density, and the white estimates inch upward (whereas in the simple analysis they remained static).

In sum, my EI estimation of Louisiana's 1968 parish registration rates is imperfect. Standard errors are quite conservative, given the amazing precision of the estimates, and a few intransigent parishes that violate the model assumptions do stump the program. Yet the main lesson of this exploration is that EI is resilient even in the most troublesome cases one is likely to face in real racial voting data – especially when one is armed with substantive knowledge. Nor, when faced by a tough case, does EI necessarily underestimate the uncertainty contained in its best estimates.

Normally the next stage would be to estimate turnout, using the racial registration estimates as a base (King, 1997: Chapter 15). However, since I possess the right answers for the initial estimation stage, I will use those instead. Estimating turnout, therefore, follows an identical procedure to that used in estimating registration in the previous test case. I know how many registered whites and blacks appear in each parish, and how many people voted, but I don't know how many of each voted. For this analysis, I allowed white turnout to increase as black density increased, since Wallace's antisegregation message played very well among Black Belt whites. I estimate that 79.5% of registered whites voted in the presidential election, whereas 59.2% of registered blacks did so. The findings resemble the 50–60% turnout rates estimated for Louisiana's registered blacks in 1966 (Campbell and Feagin, 1975: 136).

Of course, at this point most researchers might be willing to assume, say, a 1.5% rate of support for Wallace among black voters; turnout was the real source of uncertainty. But I'll carry it through for purposes of testing King's method, since it is exactly this stage of analysis that foiled old inference techniques soon after Wallace's campaign; they all returned estimates of black support for Wallace much too high to be realistic. The procedure is almost identical to the previous stage. We know the distribution of votes, and we possess estimates of turnout for each race (from the last stage), but we don't know the voting preferences.[20]

A simple EI analysis, with no embellishments, produces rather disheartening results: approximately one-quarter of black voters allegedly supported George Wallace (analysis not shown). Even this analysis is better than other ecological studies of the Wallace vote, which often implied greater support from blacks than from whites. Furthermore, this is a case in which prior knowledge can inform estimation without assuming the answers outright. EI can estimate aggregation bias informed by the contextual hypothesis that whites in parishes threatened by desegregation would be more supportive of Wallace.[21] This simple refinement removes the absurd numbers, as no previous statistical analysis of the aggregate Wallace vote has ever been able to do. Now 1.8% of blacks apparently backed Wallace, either by intent or not (which is surprisingly realistic given the large standard error of 6.2). And we have by far the best available estimate of Wallace's white support from each Louisiana parish, which comes to 57.1% at the state level.[22]

Precinct-Level Racial Voting Behavior

Precinct-level race and election data are widely available, especially from southern states that collect such information to document their compliance with the Voting Rights Act. For most states, the racial data come from aggregating Census voting-age population figures to the level of electoral units, as Lublin and Voss (2001) did in the Federal Election Project for 2000. Other states, such as North Carolina and Alabama, actually collect racial registration data, asking registrants to declare their racial category and aggregating those figures. A few states even keep track of turnout by race.

The availability of precinct-level data is the key to why King's method will work so consistently with modern racial voting studies. Residential segregation is still the norm in American society. A third of blacks live around few whites (Massey and Denton, 1993: 75–77), and many whites live in neighborhoods with only token black presence. The aggregation process discards relatively little information about these segregated voters, as far as producing racial estimates is concerned, limiting the scope of ecological inference necessary to produce accurate estimates. This sort of segregation is less severe in the south, where interracial contact has always been more common than in hypersegregated northern cities, yet still appears when data are measured at low levels.

Take Louisiana's racial registration figures for 1992. Out of 3,998 usable precincts, 11.6% are entirely uniform: 440 without a single black registered to vote, 25 with nothing but blacks. So we know the exact racial characteristics of 150,000 voters; no estimation is necessary and

---

[20] EI uses "multiple imputation" to account for the additional uncertainty that comes from using estimated turnout rates.

[21] EI options: `_Eeta=2` and `_EalphaW=0.5~0.1`.

[22] The standard error for this estimate is 1.4. It is, of course, possible that an analysis of Wallace's vote that drew strength from voting in other states would improve these estimates.

no uncertainty present.[23] A third of the state's precincts contained almost no blacks (i.e., fewer than 5% of registered voters), so that more than half of the white population resides in "homogeneous precincts." Another 260 precincts were almost exclusively black, containing more than a quarter of the black population. Using a lower standard, in which only 90% of the population must be uniform, means that 58% of Louisiana voters appeared in segregated locales where we have little doubt about what one racial category is doing.

The result of all this segregation is that, in many precincts, we know roughly how the dominant race behaved – a certainty that greatly informs statewide estimates as well. Leaving aside the uniform precincts, where we have no doubt at all, the range of possible white turnout is less than 10 percentage points in 1,829 precincts. The range of possible black turnout is equally narrow in 343 more. Thanks to the bounds imposed by racial registration rates in these informative precincts, white turnout for the state *must* have been between 75% and 88.9%, and black turnout between 51.5% and 87.9%. But results near these extremes would entail rather implausible behavior, the sort of thing a researcher with substantive expertise would know about, so it would be a safe bet estimates were somewhere within an even narrower range (Flanigan and Zingale, 1985).[24] The bounds work similarly for voting choices. Thanks to bounds imposed by racial turnout rates in each precinct, the white vote for Clinton must have been between 29.5% and 44%, the black vote between 54.3% and 97.7%, with the plausible results falling within even narrower ranges. The neighborhood model cannot be correct.

Segregation is one condition common to racial data that assists King's method. Another condition that adds to the certainty is extreme behavior.[25] When the phenomenon being studied approaches consensual levels, such as 0% or 100% of residents engaging in a partic- ular activity, then we know with fair certainty how people of all races behaved there. Racial voting behavior frequently runs up against this sort of boundary, since variance in voter choice can be quite high, with 9 in 10 black voters backing the Democratic party and rural whites heavily backing Republicans. In the Louisiana case, we see such extreme behavior with turnout as well, because most registered voters go to the polls.

The implications should be clear. Embedding the ecological inferences within known bounds on voting behavior does much of the work required to produce decent racial voting estimates. King's method therefore milks both the quality of contemporary data and the segregated nature of American society for the information they make available. His approach to ecological inference does add to the precision, especially when coupled with whatever substantive knowledge the researcher brings to bear, and the method's assumptions do not drive the results as much as King's critics suggest.

Nevertheless, it is worth observing how well King's method performs with such highly informative data. In particular, I will show how successful EI is at predicting racial turnout in Louisiana, the sort of thing a researcher normally must estimate (e.g., it is the first stage of double regression). Naturally Louisiana is a unique place, so one may be hesitant to extrapolate from there to other states. However, for purposes of gauging the success of King's method, there's no reason to think it poses a particularly easy trial. Segregation is not exceptionally high in Louisiana's cities, and turnout rates are not extraordinary. It also may seem unreliable to assume that, if EI works well predicting turnout, it will perform equally

---

[23] I am talking about estimation error here, not measurement error, which may be present to some degree.

[24] The real answers, which we know because Louisiana reports racial turnout, in fact were near the center of each range: 81.4% for whites and 71% for blacks.

[25] Note, however, that extreme behavior can have substantive costs as well (King, 2002). The low incidence of strokes in Texas means that Anselin and Cho (2002) are able to provide precise estimates of mortality rates – off by roughly 0.025 – but the low-event nature of their data may have complicated cross-gender comparisons.

Table 3.2 1991 turnout estimates for Louisiana

	Turnout		
Source	White	Black	Total
Truth	74.7	65.2	72.1
State data:			
Lower bound	61.6	0.0	
Upper bound	100.0	100.0	
Midpoint	*80.8*	*50.0*	72.4
Parish data:			
Lower bound	67.6	44.7	
Upper bound	82.4	83.9	
Midpoint	*75.0*	*64.3*	72.2
Naive ER	75.9 (0.2)	63.7 (0.3)	72.7
Weighted ER	75.3 (0.1)	63.5 (0.3)	72.2
Neighborhood	73.8	67.4	72.1
Homogeneous:			
Average	76.3	63.4	72.9
Weighted average	75.6	62.4	72.2
EI (simple)	75.4 (0.1)	63.3 (0.2)	72.2
EI (final)	74.9 (0.1)	64.5 (0.1)	72.2

Note: Methodological details of each estimation appear in the text. Numbers in parentheses are standard errors.

well predicting vote choices for which the truth cannot be known. Here too, however, my trial is more representative than one might assume. The main reason EI thrives is racial segregation, and that operates equivalently on both turnout and vote data.[26] Furthermore, voting behavior is more extreme than turnout in the contemporary period, so EI should get more purchase with votes.

I will use turnout from the 1991 Louisiana gubernatorial open primary; results are quite similar with other elections from the period.[27] The actual statewide turnout rates were 65.2% for blacks and 74.7% for everyone else, underscoring the faultiness of using a one-stage analysis (i.e., from population straight to vote choice without estimating turnout as an intermediate step). The state-level bounds are not particularly informative; we have no idea what the black turnout rate would be, and the white rate could be anything greater than 61.6% (all figures appear in Table 3.2). If we impose the absolute bounds individually on each precinct and add them up to statewide totals, however, we find that white turnout must be between 67.6% and 82.4%, while black turnout must be between 44.7% and 83.9%. The midpoints of these bounds would indicate white turnout of roughly 75%, and black turnout of 64.3%. The former is off the truth by only 0.3%, and the latter by just under a percentage point, so once again the bounds are pointing us in the right direction. There's

[26] Brad Palmquist breaks aggregation bias into two components, a specification shift representing the information lost by collecting areal data, and an inflation factor that can magnify the initial error severely. The inflation factor essentially represents traits of the areal units used in an analysis, and therefore would be similar for estimating turnout and for estimating vote choice. For race, the inflation factor tends to be quite low. See Palmquist and Voss (1996) for a summary.

[27] King's book (1997: 23) briefly used my 1990 Louisiana data, so I decided to explore the 1991 figures. They come after the rapid mobilization of voters during former Klansman David Duke's 1991 gubernatorial candidacy.

no guarantee of success in shooting from the hip this way, but it does reinforce Flanigan and Zingale's point (1985: 82–83) that the plausible bounds are usually narrower than the absolute bounds.[28]

The attractive precinct-level data permit most methods to approximate the truth. The neighborhood model, for example, estimates that white turnout was 73.8%, black turnout 67.4%. Naive ecological regression places those figures at 75.9% and 63.7% respectively. The white turnout estimate is 1.2 percentage points (or almost 19,000 voters) from the truth, one of the worst provided by any method, despite the highly informative data on whites. The estimates also imply a statewide turnout rate that was impossibly high. The worst of the simple methods is homogeneous precinct analysis. I tried it two ways this time: once with a simple precinct average, the other weighting that average by the number of registered voters in each precinct. Both are faulty, because white turnout is notably high in all-white precincts, and black turnout notably low in all-black precincts.

Weighted ecological regression does a nice job. It estimates that 75.3% of whites turned out, off by less than a percentage point. The black estimate is more disappointing, since it falls almost 2 percentage points from the truth, but given the less informative data for blacks, such an estimate still seems fairly strong. Furthermore, this time the joint estimates do not imply impossible statewide turnout rates. A simple EI run produces roughly the same estimates as weighted ecological regression: 75.4% of whites and 63.3% of blacks. The basic results do not indicate any aggregation bias: estimates of white and black turnout do not correlate with racial density. This is a case in which the EI diagnostics by themselves might leave an uninformed researcher satisfied.

However, I have a theoretical reason to expect that white turnout should decline in heavily black areas. Whites in integrated settings tend to have lower socioeconomic status than their segregated counterparts, and socioeconomic resources are an important determinant of political activity (Verba, Schlozman, and Brady, 1995: 513, 527). I therefore ended with a more complex EI analysis, allowing white turnout to vary as black density varied, without specifying the likely direction of the relationship.[29] Once again, EI did not detect all of the aggregation bias. As black population density increases 10 percentage points, white turnout declines 1.5 percentage points, on average. The estimated contextual effect is only a third as large, and therefore too low. Nevertheless, what bias EI did detect helped improve the estimates relative to the alternatives. The resulting estimates were 74.9% turnout for whites, 64.5% for blacks. In both cases, these estimates are closer to the truth than those from any other method used. The white estimate was only off by a fifth of a percentage point, and the black estimate by less than a percentage point as well.[30]

The hypothesis that white mobilization rates change with racial density emerges from a real-life research agenda. One theory suggests that whites mobilize when faced with a large black population in their locale (see Voss, 2000, for a literature review). By contrast, some scholars have noted a decline in white Anglo turnout in minority-dominated electoral districts (Gay, 2001; Barreto, Segura, and Woods, 2002). They interpret this decline as some sort of white demoralization caused by their minority status in elections. This is a clear

---

[28] For true behavior to approach one of the bounds would require consistently extreme behavior of a sort that should be familiar to a researcher with substantive expertise – such as with the well-known black vote for Democrats.

[29] The exact EI prior was `_EalphaW=(0~0.3)`. Other priors returned similar results, though.

[30] About the only sign of trouble was the small measures of uncertainty. I cannot rule out the criticism from King's critics that they are too low. King (2002) seems to acknowledge this problem himself. The measures of uncertainty are still helpful, though, because they appear to vary with the estimation error. Other diagnostics, such as checking that the true values did not fall consistently at the extremes of their posterior distributions (King, 1997: 213), looked adequate.

case of competing contextual theories. The evidence from Louisiana suggests that ecological inferences, such as those reported by Gay (2001), should be compatible with testing relatively strong contextual hypotheses. EI picked up enough of the true pattern that a test for ecological effects would have been strong and statistically significant in the correct direction. On the other hand, the results from Louisiana – along with my analysis of Georgia and Florida (Voss and Lublin, 2001) – reveal that those studying the effect of minority-dominated electoral districts need to rethink their interpretations. White turnout declines in heavily minority precincts regardless of whether the larger electoral environment is dominated by whites or blacks. EI's sensitivity to contextual effects therefore has contributed to an important substantive debate, debunking the white backlash idea yet calling into question the conventional wisdom on why white turnout declines in majority-minority districts.

The preceding analysis shows that precinct-level data are extremely useful for determining statewide behavior. Even fairly simple estimation methods come within a percentage point of true white behavior, and within two percentage points of true black behavior. The Louisiana data allow another test of EI's performance, however, which is to check the quality of precinct-level estimates it produces. EI might use the precinct data to generate excellent statewide estimates, but still be way off for individual areal units.[31] As it turns out, however, EI's estimates are amazingly accurate even at the precinct level. The estimates correlate heavily with the true white turnout rates: a coefficient of .93 when weighted by the number of registered whites, and .98 when weighted by the reciprocal of EI's reported precinct standard error (see Burden and Kimball, 1998: 539). The figures for blacks are naturally slightly lower, given the more limited information on black behavior, but still impressive: .87 when weighted by the number of registered blacks, and .94 when weighted by EI's reported level of confidence. It is worth noting that the cost of any survey with this level of local precision across an entire state would be astronomical, even if respondents could be trusted to report their turnout properly.

The EI estimation I ran took no notice of which precincts fell in which parishes. Although EI certainly would allow the researcher to adjust estimates according to county traits, none of my estimations took advantage of this option. Indeed, the estimation routine did not in any way attempt to optimize fit with parish behavior. It is worth investigating, therefore, how well the EI precinct estimates aggregate up to parish values. I created parish-level white (black) turnout estimates by averaging the figures for all precincts in a parish, weighted by the number of whites (blacks) contained in each.[32] The parish-level estimates end up almost as accurate as the statewide estimate, correlating with the truth at .99 for whites, .97 for blacks. The largest error for any parish's white turnout estimate is 2.3 percentage points, the largest error among blacks 3.6 percentage points. The average parish error is, of course, much smaller – under half a percentage point for both races (see Figure 3.4). Again, this level of success is astounding when considered in light of what surveys of similar precision would require.

One major concern with King's EI is that, like other methods of ecological inference, it may not pick up enough of the information missing in aggregate data to represent contextual effects accurately. Cho's critique (1998), for example, creates a hypothetical aggregate data set from survey data, and shows that King's method does not pick up the aggregation bias contained in her particular sample. Is his method equally limited for racial voting studies? This application indicates that, because of the virtues of precinct-level voting data, King's

---

[31] Accurate estimates still may not be useful for second-stage regressions if they introduce some kind of bias into the assessment of contextual effects (Herron and Shotts, 2003).

[32] The weighting is necessary to indicate the turnout level EI has estimated for the average person, rather than the average precinct (which is not particularly meaningful). See Voss (1996).

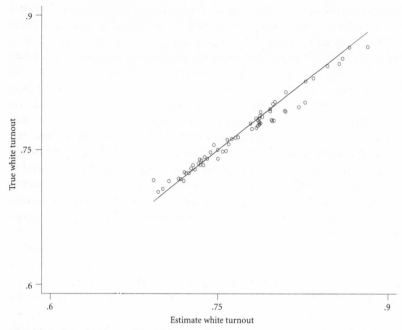

Figure 3.4. Parish-level predictive accuracy using precinct data. Each dot represents a Louisiana parish. The true turnout rates were provided by the state of Louisiana. The estimated numbers come from Gary King's EI, computed as a weighted average from precinct-level figures. The 45-degree line indicates where a parish would fall if the estimation were exactly correct. Dots above the line represent estimates that are too low; dots below it, too high.

method performs quite well. For example, I regressed EI's parish-level estimates on the parish black density, controlling for the true turnout. If EI falls prey to aggregation bias, errors in predicting the white voting rate should change with the black density and vice versa. However, the results do not indicate a statistically significant connection between the parish error and the racial demographics (analysis not shown); there is no evidence aggregation bias has made much difference to the parish-level figures.

Moving Beyond Aggregate Data

Some of King's critics reject ecological inference altogether, preferring the use of surveys. Of course, surveys have serious problems, going beyond sampling error to include refusals, deception, and questionnaire confusion. They are plagued with numerous sorts of bias (see, e.g., Burden, 2000: 390; Palmer and Duch, 2001), including an inability to measure racial attitudes reliably without taking special precautions (Kuklinski, Cobb, and Gilens, 1997; Traugott and Price, 1992). Almost all of the variables measured by a survey are contemporaneous, and separating out the causal order between two variables is difficult at best (see Hetherington and Globetti, 2002, for one recent attempt). However, it is worth considering how EI might stand up against survey analysis for the contextual study of voting behavior.

Most surveys either ask how people will vote in advance or ask how they voted afterward. Respondents asked this question after the fact misreport their voting at notably high levels, and those asked before the fact misreport whether they will really vote at all. Presumably the best survey of how people voted is an exit poll, since it only captures those who have voted and it catches them at a time when they have made the final decision but have not been contaminated by knowledge of the election results. Certainly it is common for journal reviewers, when faced with an aggregate-data analysis, to resist the conclusions unless they come accompanied by exit-poll analysis. Political scientists frequently use exit polls as a data source in studies of voting behavior, sometimes even using the data to assess contextual patterns (Carsey, 1995; Highton, 2002). Are exit polls a serious rival to ecological inference?

Below the presidential level, this is doubtful. Exit polls are rare except in particularly high-profile campaigns. More importantly, exit polls resemble other surveys in that they provide little leverage for testing behavior below the state level because they collect few observations in any one subdivision. They typically sample precincts to optimize overall estimates; nothing in their method should produce representative data at a lower level of aggregation. Even areal units as large as congressional districts may contain few respondents. For example, only 34 people from one precinct appeared in the 1996 Voter News Service data for Georgia's 2nd congressional district. The 11th district received slightly more coverage: four precincts with a total of 151 people. These numbers are not sufficient to test contextual theories. Nor is the sampling frame used in an exit poll likely to produce reliable estimates of behavior for demographic groups. Indeed, data weighted to maximize state-level accuracy may produce group-level estimates worse than what unweighted data would offer.

Compare the two methods as applied to 1996 congressional voting in Georgia. Because precinct-level data are available, aggregate-data analysis using King's method has a great deal of information with which to work. Out of 2,641 usable precincts, not a single black adult registered to vote in 109. Roughly 43% of Georgia's white adults and its 15.5% of its black adults are registered in precincts where their race predominates (i.e., more than 95% of population). Lower the threshold to 90%, and 61.4% of whites and 23.3% of blacks inhabit homogeneous precincts. The bounds are therefore helpful. Statewide racial turnout for the 1992 presidential contest must have fallen between 53.8% and 71.5% among whites, and between 24.1% and 79.3% among black. With 1992 congressional voting, similarly, the bounds on white turnout were tiny in four of Georgia's 11 districts (i.e., the range of possible white turnout was less than 10 percentage points). And the range only exceeded 20 percentage points in the three heavily black districts.

The Georgia VNS exit poll, by contrast, is completely unreliable below the state level. It does a wonderful job predicting the statewide presidential vote once data are weighted: 45.7% Clinton, 46.9% Dole, 6.3% Perot. When estimates are broken up by congressional district and by race, though, they are quite poor. It becomes clear that some combination of the sampling frame used by VNS and response bias among those polled results in invalid estimates of racial voting behavior by congressional district. Table 3.3 allows a district-by-district comparison between the VNS exit-poll results and the lower bound on white support for Clinton.[33] Of the eleven district-level estimates of white behavior, six are impossibly low. All but one of those errors exceeds five percentage points.

These errors are consistent, not random, and therefore extremely unlikely to result from sampling error. Clinton simply could not have won as many votes as he did in these districts if so few nonblacks had supported him, and the errors tend to be worst in the districts where we have the most aggregate information – that is, in the whiter districts. In Representative Newt Gingrich's 6th, for example, the exit-poll sample of 143 whites (when weighted) reported giving 23.3% of the vote to Clinton. However, looking at the precinct distribution of whites and votes, at least 29.1% of white voters must have done so. In the lily-white 9th,

---

[33] Producing the lower bounds required estimating white and black turnout first. But the need for turnout estimates cannot be the primary reason why I get disappointing results for exit-poll data. The polls perform especially badly in districts for which ecological inference must get very good estimates of white behavior.

Table 3.3 Presidential voting among Georgia whites, 1996

Congressional district	% black among voters	EI Lower bound	Exit-poll estimates 3-party% for Clinton	Impossible?	Minimum error
1	23.5	31.26	34.3	No	
2	26.8	30.95	39.2	No	
3	13.2	31.12	22.4	Yes	8.7
4	39.6	42.46	41.4	Yes	1.1
5	N/A	45.11	45.3	No	
6	3.2	29.11	23.3	Yes	5.8
7	8.9	33.16	37.6	No	
8	24.3	28.91	21.1	Yes	7.8
9	2.3	33.51	23.2	Yes	10.3
10	26.4	28.37	21.6	Yes	6.8
11	5.2	32.84	34.0	No	

Note: Exit-poll estimates were taken from the 1996 Voter News Service data provided to the ICPSR (archive 6989). The ecological inference estimates were produced using EI (Gary King's ecological inference software), with precinct-level racial registration data and election returns provided by the state of Georgia. "% black" represents the racial demographics estimated for those who turned out. The "EI lower bound" represents the minimum possible white three-party percentage for Clinton given estimated racial turnout rates.

the exit-poll estimate drawn from 99 whites is 23.2% for Clinton, whereas the actual white vote clearly was within half a percentage point of 34%. Exit polls are far off from what was possible, let alone from the truth. Polls containing this kind of error below the state level cannot assist with contextual analysis. Ecological estimates, while imperfect, surely seem better than any alternative for analyzing turnout or party choice at the ballot box. EI offers a critical corrective to political science's dependence on surveys.

CONCLUSION

Gary King's proposed solution to the ecological inference problem possesses all the virtues of methods previously used to analyze aggregate data. It takes advantage of the tangible information found in segregated locales, as homogeneous unit analysis does, since it precludes impossible results and borrows strength from the homogeneous places to estimate behavior in the mixed ones (King, 1997: 106–112). Similarly, it allows two-stage analysis much as ecological regression will, with the additional virtue of producing measures of uncertainty proportional to the real errors in estimation. Like the neighborhood model, the extended version does not require an analyst to ignore contextual patterns found in aggregate data. But it combines all of these traits into a unified model that constrains estimates according to the method of bounds and therefore is sensitive to both compositional and contextual patterns in the data. It produces low-level estimates with far more precision than surveys typically make available. EI is thus an important advance in the ability of researchers to conduct contextual analysis.

King's critics have ignored the vast improvement EI offers to scholars interested in contextualizing social behavior. Their applications did not give a fair representation of how EI usually performs. In particular, the applications presented in this chapter indicate that EI has taken us far enough to study voting behavior on exactly the sorts of questions – turnout and racial behavior – for which survey questions are unreliable and survey data limited in their contextual information. I tested King's EI using two Louisiana data sets in which the racial behavior was known. One was a 1968 parish-level data set where I knew racial rates of voter registration among black and white adults and also held a strong prior about racial voting preferences. The other was a 1991 precinct-level data set where I knew the racial turnout rates among those registered. These cases indicated that King's EI performs admirably, whether the comparison is (1) with other methods of aggregate-data analysis, (2) with the truth in data sets for which estimates can be evaluated, or (3) with the likely assistance that surveys might provide. King's EI run on precinct-level data produced estimates that were extremely close to the truth at the statewide, parish, and precinct levels. It also picked up some, but not all, of the contextual pattern contained in these data. The parish-level analysis, while clearly based on poor data, not only resulted in fairly precise estimates of voter registration, it also avoided the error committed by just about every aggregate-data analysis of the Wallace vote: the tendency to estimate high black support for the segregationist. Therefore, despite the criticism King's approach has faced and the limits it shows when applied to concocted data sets, it is unparalleled when applied to the actual sort of data needed for analyzing important social issues such as racial voting patterns.

As I have illustrated, the quality of EI estimates responds to an analyst's ability to anticipate contextual patterns and inform the software of these expectations – for example, by including covariates that capture the contextual effect directly (see Herron and Shotts, 2003, and the exchange that has followed). Of course, estimates shaped by a practitioner's instincts, field research, or theoretical arguments may face a greater burden of proof than estimates generated by a plug-and-chug equation that externalizes judgment. But developments within Bayesian statistics have created, even among quantitative researchers, a growing sense that analysts should not approach empirical inference under the pretense that they know nothing about the subjects they study. King's solution to the ecological inference problem fits comfortably within this trend of developing methods that succeed when analysts can incorporate what they have learned, a Bayesian approach that has received even greater development since the publication of his book (see Chapter 1 of this volume). My applications, guided by the relevant substantive literature, suggest that King's approach outperforms every commonly used alternative for ecological inference, incorporating the advantages of all of them while escaping the pitfalls of each. There is no reason, aside from ease of use, that would justify rejecting King's ecological-inference method in favor of the conventional competition.

REFERENCES

Alt, James E. 1994. "The Impact of the Voting Rights Act on Black and White Voter Registration in the South." In Chandler Davidson and Bernard Grofman (eds.), *Quiet Revolution in the South: The Impact of the Voting Rights Act, 1965–1990*. Princeton, NJ: Princeton University Press.

Anselin, Luc and Wendy K. Tam Cho. 2002. "Spatial Effects and Ecological Inference," *Political Analysis*, 10, Summer: 276–297.

Barreto, Matt A., Gary M. Segura, and Nathan D. Woods. 2002. "Rest Assured? Estimating the Potential Mobilizing or Demobilizing Effects of Overlapping Majority-Minority Districts." Paper presented at the annual meeting of the Midwest Political Science Association, Chicago, IL, April 25–28.

Biggar, Jeanne C. and Julia H. Martin. 1976. "Ecological Determinants of White and Black Immigration to Small Areas in Central Cities, 1965 to 1970," *Social Forces*, 55, September: 72–84.

Burden, Barry C. 2000. "Voter Turnout and the National Election Studies," *Political Analysis*, 8, Autumn: 333–345.

Burden, Barry C. and David C. Kimball. 1998. "A New Approach to the Study of Ticket Splitting," *American Political Science Review*, 92, September: 533–544.

Campbell, David and Joe R. Feagin. 1975. "Black Politics in the South: A Descriptive Analysis," *Journal of Politics*, 37, February: 129–162.

Carsey, Thomas M. 1995. "The Contextual Effect of Race on White Voter Behavior: The 1989 New York City Mayoral Election," *Journal of Politics*, 57, 221–228.

Cho, Wendy K. Tam. 1998. "Iff the Assumption Fits . . . : A Comment on the King Ecological Inference Solution," *Political Analysis*, 7: 143–163.

Couto, Richard A. 1993. "Narrative, Free Space, and Political Leadership in Social Movements," *Journal of Politics*, 55, February: 57–79.

Duncan, Otis Dudley and Beverly Davis. 1953. "An Alternative to Ecological Correlation," *American Sociological Review*, 18, December: 665–666.

Flanigan, William H. and Nancy H. Zingale. 1985. "Alchemist's Gold: Inferring Individual Relationships from Aggregate Data," *Social Science History*, 9, Winter: 71–91.

Freedman, David A., Stephen P. Klein, Jerome Sacks, Charles A. Smyth, and Charles G. Everett. 1991. "Ecological Regression and Voting Rights," *Evaluation Review*, 15, December: 673–711.

Freedman, David A., S. P. Klein, M. Ostland, and M. R. Roberts. 1998. "Review of 'A Solution to the Ecological Inference Problem,'" *Journal of the American Statistical Association*, 93, December: 1518–1522.

Freedman, David A., M. Ostland, M. R. Roberts, and S. P. Klein. 1999. "Response to King's Comment," *Journal of the American Statistical Association*, 94, March: 355–357.

Gay, Claudine. 2001. "The Effect of Black Congressional Representation on Political Participation," *American Political Science Review*, 95: 589.

Gimpel, James G., and Jason E. Schuknecht. 2002. "Political and Demographic Foundations for Sectionalism in State Politics: The Connecticut Case," *American Politics Research*, 30, March: 193–213.

Goodman, Leo A. 1953. "Ecological Regression and Behavior of Individuals," *American Sociological Review*, 18, December: 663–664.

Goodman, Leo A. 1959. "Some Alternatives to Ecological Correlation." *American Journal of Sociology*, 64, May: 610–625.

Hauser, Robert M. 1970. "Context and Consex: A Cautionary Tale," *American Journal of Sociology*, 75, January: 645–664.

Heard, Alexander. 1952. *A Two Party South?* Chapel Hill, NC: University of North Carolina Press.

Herron, Michael C. and Kenneth W. Shotts. 2003. "Using Ecological Inference Point Estimates as Dependent Variables in Second-Stage Linear Regressions," *Political Analysis*, 11 (Winter): 44–64.

Hetherington, Marc J. and Suzanne Globetti. 2002. "Political Trust and Racial Policy Preferences," *American Journal of Political Science*, 46, April: 253–275.

Highton, Benjamin. 2002. "White Voters and African-American Candidates for Congress." Paper presented at the annual meeting of the Midwest Political Science Association, Chicago, IL, April 25–28.

Huckfeldt, R. Robert. 1986. *Politics in Context: Assimilation and Conflict in Urban Neighborhoods*. New York: Agathon Press.

Huckfeldt, R. Robert and Carol W. Kohfeld. 1989. *Race and the Decline of Class in American Politics*. Urbana: University of Illinois Press.

Huckfeldt, R. Robert and John Sprague. 1995. *Citizens, Politics, and Social Communication: Information and Influence in an Election Campaign*. New York: Cambridge University Press.

Key, V.O. Jr. [1949] 1984. *Southern Politics in State and Nation*, new ed. Knoxville, TN: University of Tennessee Press.

King, Gary. 1997. *A Solution to the Ecological Inference Problem: Reconstructing Individual Behavior from Aggregate Data*. Princeton, NJ: Princeton University Press.

King, Gary. 1999. "The Future of Ecological Inference Research: A Comment on Freedman et al.," *Journal of the American Statistical Association*, 94, March: 352–355.

King, Gary. 2000. "Geography, Statistics, and Ecological Inference," *Annals of the Association of American Geographers*, 90: 601–606.

King, Gary. 2002. "Isolating Spatial Autocorrelation, Aggregation Bias, and Distributional Violations in Ecological Inference," *Political Analysis*, 10, summer: 298–300.

Kousser, J. Morgan. 1974. *The Shaping of Southern Politics: Suffrage Restriction and the Establishment of the One-Party South, 1880–1910.* New Haven, CT: Yale University Press.

Kuklinski, James H., Michael D. Cobb, and Martin Gilens. 1997. "Racial Attitudes and the 'New South,'" *Journal of Politics*, 59, 323–349.

Liu, Baodong "Paul." 2001. "The Positive Effect of Black Density on White Crossover Voting: Reconsidering Social Interaction Theory," *Social Science Quarterly*, 82, September: 600–613.

Lublin, David and D. Stephen Voss. 2000a. "Boll-Weevil Blues: Polarized Congressional Delegations into the 21st Century," *American Review of Politics*, 21, Fall & Winter: 427–450.

Lublin, David and D. Stephen Voss. 2000b. "Racial Redistricting and Realignment in Southern State Legislatures," *American Journal of Political Science*, 44, October:792–810.

Lublin, David and D. Stephen Voss. 2001. "Federal Elections Project." American University, Washington, DC, and the University of Kentucky, Lexington, KY.

Lublin, David and D. Stephen Voss. 2002. "Context and Francophone Support for Sovereignty: An Ecological Analysis." *Canadian Journal of Political Science*, 35, March: 75–101.

Lublin, David and D. Stephen Voss. 2003. "The Missing Middle: Why Median-Voter Theory Can't Save Democrats from Singing the Boll-Weevil Blues," *Journal of Politics*, 65, February: 227–237.

Lucker, Andrew M. 2001. *V. O. Key, Jr.: The Quintessential Political Scientist.* New York: Peter Lang.

Massey, Douglas S. and Nancy A. Denton. 1993. *American Apartheid: Segregation and the Making of the Underclass.* Cambridge, MA: Harvard University Press.

MacManus, Susan A. 1995. "The Appropriateness of Biracial Approaches to Measuring Fairness of Representation in a Multicultural World," *PS: Political Science and Politics*, 28, March: 42–47.

Matthews, Donald R. and James W. Prothro. 1966. *Negroes and the New Southern Politics.* New York: Harcourt Brace.

McCue, Kenneth F. 2001. "The Statistical Foundations of the EI Method," *The American Statistician*, 55, May: 106–110.

Myers, Jerome K. 1954. "Note on the Homogeneity of Census Tracts: A Methodological Problem in Urban Ecological Research," *Social Forces*, 32, May: 364–366.

Natchez, Peter B. 1985. *Images of Voting/Visions of Democracy: Voting Behavior and Democratic Theory.* New York: Basic Books.

Palmer, Harvey D. and Raymond M. Duch. 2001. "Do Surveys Provide Representative or Whimsical Assessments of the Economy?" *Political Analysis*, 9, Winter: 58–77.

Palmquist, Bradley L. 2002. "Unlocking the Aggregate Data Past – Which Keys Fit?" *Historical Methods*, 34 (Fall): 159–169.

Palmquist, Bradley L. and D. Stephen Voss. 1996. "Racial Polarization and Turnout in Louisiana: New Insights from Aggregate Data Analysis." Paper presented at the 54th Annual Meeting of the Midwest Political Science Association, Chicago, IL, April 18–20.

Palmquist, Bradley L. and D. Stephen Voss. 1997. "Racial Polarization in the Southern Electorate: Republican Votes for Duke in Louisiana." Paper presented at the 55th Annual Meeting of the Midwest Political Science Association, Chicago, IL, April 10–12.

Peterson, Geoff and Glory Koloen. 2002. "Examining the Ventura Vote: A Test of Ecological Regression." Paper presented before the Southwestern Political Science Association, New Orleans, LA, March 30.

Pettigrew, Thomas F. 1985. "New Black–White Patterns: How Best to Conceptualize Them?" *Annual Review of Sociology*, 11: 329–346.

Rivers, Douglas. 1998. "Review of 'A Solution to the Ecological Inference Problem,'" *American Political Science Review*, 92, June: 442–443.

Robinson, W.S. 1950. "Ecological Correlations and the Behavior of Individuals," *American Sociological Review*, 15: 351–357.

Schoenberger, Robert A. and David R. Segal. 1971. "The Ecology of Dissent: The Southern Wallace Vote in 1968," *Midwest Journal of Political Science*, 15: 583–586.

Taylor, Marylee C. 1998. "How White Attitudes Vary with the Racial Composition of Local Populations: Numbers Count," *American Sociological Review*, 63, August: 512–535.

Traugott, Michael W. and Vincent Price. 1992. "Exit Polls in the 1989 Virginia Gubernatorial Race: Where Did They Go Wrong?" *Public Opinion Quarterly*, 56, Summer: 245–253.

Verba, Sidney, Kay Lehman Schlozman, and Henry E. Brady. 1995. *Voice and Equality: Civic Voluntarism in American Politics*. Cambridge, MA: Harvard University Press.

Voss, D. Stephen. 1996. "Beyond Racial Threat: Failure of an Old Hypothesis in the New South," *Journal of Politics*, 58, November: 1156–1170.

Voss, D. Stephen. 2000. "Familiarity Doesn't Breed Contempt: The Political Geography of Racial Polarization." Doctoral dissertation, Harvard University Dept. of Government.

Voss, D. Stephen. 2001. "Huddled Masses or Immigrant Menace? The Black Belt Hypothesis Did Not Emigrate," *American Review of Politics*, 22, Summer: 217–232.

Voss, D. Stephen and David Lublin. 2001. "Black Incumbents, White Districts: An Appraisal of the 1996 Congressional Elections," *American Politics Research*, 29, March: 141–182.

Voss, D. Stephen and Penny Miller. 2001. "Following a False Trail: The Hunt for White Backlash in Kentucky's 1996 Desegregation Vote," *State Politics and Policy Quarterly*, 1, March: 63–82.

Wasserman, Ira M. and David R. Segal. 1973. "Aggregation Effects in the Ecological Study of Presidential Voting," *American Journal of Political Science*, 17: 177–181.

## PART TWO

4 Extending King's Ecological Inference Model to Multiple Elections Using Markov Chain Monte Carlo

Jeffrey B. Lewis

ABSTRACT

King's EI estimator has become a widely used procedure for tackling so-called ecological inference problems. The canonical ecological inference problem involves inferring the rate of voter turnout among two racial groups in a set of electoral precincts from observations on the racial composition and total voter turnout in each precinct. As a Bayesian hierarchical model, EI links information about the turnout by race in each precinct to information on turnout by race in other precincts through the assumption that turnout rates are independently drawn from a common distribution. In this way, strength is borrowed from other precincts in estimating the turnout rates by race within each precinct. Commonly, marginal turnout rates and racial compositions are observed for multiple elections within the same set of aggregate units. This chapter extends King's estimator to this case, allowing strength to be borrowed not only across precincts within the same election, but also across elections within precincts. The model is estimated via an MCMC algorithm, validated using simulated data, and applied to estimating voter turnout by race in Virginia during the 1980s.

4.1 INTRODUCTION

King's (1997) EI estimator has become a widely used procedure for tackling so-called ecological inference problems. The canonical ecological inference problem involves inferring the rate of voter turnout among two racial groups in a set of electoral precincts from observations on the racial composition and total voter turnout in each precinct.[1] As a Bayesian hierarchical model, EI links information about the turnout by race in each precinct to information on turnout by race in other precincts through the assumption that turnout rates are independently drawn from a common distribution. In this way, strength is borrowed from all precincts in estimating the turnout rates by race within each precinct. Commonly, marginal turnout rates and racial compositions are observed for multiple elections within the same set of precincts. This chapter extends King's estimator to this case, allowing strength to be borrowed not only across precincts within the same election, but also across elections within precincts.

One common use of EI is estimating turnout by race or estimating support for particular candidates by race. For example, EI has been used to assess claims about "racial block" voting that are often central to court cases involving legislative redistricting. The central question is whether voters of a particular racial or ethnic group in a state or locality habitually vote the same candidates. In these cases, election returns from various contests and across a number

---

[1] Here "precincts" may be electoral precincts or any other aggregate groupings of votes for which the racial composition is known.

of election cycles are typically available. While it is reasonable to assume that turnout rates or voting patterns in a given set of precincts are correlated across elections or contests, this additional source of information has not been exploited by previous estimators (one exception is Quinn, in this book, Chapter 9).

Given the difficulty of ecological inference and particularly the difficulty of estimating precinct quantities of interest, building a model that capitalizes on the commonalities that might exist across contests or elections at the precinct level is potentially fruitful. As demonstrated below, by borrowing strength across elections as well as across precincts, the mean square error of the precinct level predictions can be substantially improved. The model builds directly on King's EI. Turnout rates among whites and nonwhites across precincts are assumed to be drawn from a truncated bivariate normal distribution (TBVN). Whereas King's EI models the parameters of the truncated bivariate normal as election-specific, in the multielection model the parameters of the truncated bivariate normal distribution are determined by both precinct-specific and election-specific effects. In this way, the estimation of turnout rates by racial group are tied not only across precincts within elections as in King's model, but also across elections within precincts. The resulting seemingly unrelated ecological inference (SUEI) model is presented in detail below.[2]

The increased complexity introduced by the precinct-specific determinants of the underlying truncated bivariate normal that describes the distribution of the precinct-level turnout by race makes estimation by the standard maximization approach employed by King infeasible. Instead, the model is estimated by Markov chain Monte Carlo (MCMC). King's EI and the SUEI are members of a general class of hierarchical and mixture models that are known to be amenable to estimation by MCMC methods.

The estimator is applied to sets of simulated data and to electoral data from Virginia. Because the "true" values of the precinct quantities are known for the simulated data, the advantage of SUEI over King's EI can be directly assessed. For the Virginia data, the true values are not known. However, the estimates generated by each method can still be compared and the strength of the cross-election precinct effects assessed. Overall, SUEI and EI yield quite similar estimates of the aggregate quantities of interest, but in some cases the two models find quite different estimates of the precinct quantities. By borrowing strength across elections, SUEI is able to reduce the mean square error (MSE) of the precinct-level estimates in the simulated data by as much 40 to 50 percent. In the Virginia data sizeable cross-election dependencies are found and precinct-level estimates differ substantially from EI to SUEI.

4.2 KING'S EI MODEL

As presented in King (1997) and extensively discussed elsewhere, the basic EI model has as its foundation an identity, an independence assumption, and a distributional assumption that together form a simple mixture model. The identity says that in each precinct the total turnout rate must be the sum of the fraction of nonwhites that vote, and the fraction of whites that vote weighted by the fraction that each group comprises in the voting-age population of the precinct (see Introduction, Equation 4). Formally, let $\mathbf{T} = (T_1, T_2, \ldots, T_p)$ be the voter turnout rates in a set of p precincts, and $\mathbf{X} = (X_1, X_2, \ldots, X_p)$ be the fractions of the

---

[2] The notion of "seemingly unrelated" EI follows by analogy from the seemingly unrelated regression (Zellner, 1962) model in which linear regression models are connected only through correlations among their stochastic components. Here EI models that would otherwise be estimated separately are linked through a common precinct-specific stochastic component.

populations in each of the same set of precincts that is nonwhite. Then

$$T_i = \beta_i^b X_i + \beta_i^w (1 - X_i) \qquad \text{for } i = 1, \ldots, p, \tag{4.1}$$

where $\beta^b = (\beta_1^b, \beta_2^b, \ldots, \beta_p^b)$ and $\beta^w = (\beta_1^w, \beta_2^w, \ldots, \beta_p^w)$ are unobserved turnout rates among blacks and whites in the precincts. $\mathbf{T}$ and $\mathbf{X}$ are known from election returns and census data, while β^b and β^w are unknown quantities to be estimated. Because there are twice as many unknown quantities to be estimated as observations, additional assumptions must be made to identify the model. The (β^b, β^w) pairs for each precinct are assumed to be drawn independently from a common joint density. In particular, the (β^b, β^w) pairs are assumed to be drawn from a truncated bivariate normal distribution with parameters $\check{\psi} = (\breve{\mathfrak{B}}^b, \breve{\mathfrak{B}}^w, \breve{\sigma}_b, \breve{\sigma}_w, \breve{\rho})$.[3] The truncation is on the unit square, reflecting the logical bounds of β^b and β^w, which, as fractions of populations, must fall between zero and one.

Suppressing the precinct subscripts and noting that T is a linear function of the random quantities β^b and β^w, standard change-of-variables techniques yield the joint distribution of β^b and T.[4] As shown in Lewis (2002), the joint distribution of β^b and T is bivariate truncated normal with region of support $\{(\beta^b, T) \text{ s.t. } 0 \leq \beta^b \leq 1 \ \& \ \beta^b X \leq T \leq \beta^b X + (1 - X)\}$. Given that β^b and T are truncated bivariate normal, it is easy to show that $\beta^b | T$ is truncated normal (see King, 1997, or Lewis, 2002). Let f be the joint density of β^b and β^w, and g be the joint density of β^b and T. For simplicity, I will parameterize g by $\check{\psi}$ and X.[5]

In order to estimate the posterior distribution of $\check{\psi}$, King marginalizes the joint distribution of β^b and T with respect to β^b to find

$$g(T|X, \check{\psi}) = \int_0^1 g(\beta^b, T|X, \check{\psi}) d\beta^b.$$

Given the assumption of independent sampling, the likelihood of the observed data can be written as

$$L(\mathbf{T}|\mathbf{X}, \check{\psi}) = \prod_i g(T_i|X_i, \check{\psi}).$$

---

[3] This notation matches King (1997). King considers both the expectations and covariances of the distribution of β^b and β^w and the parameters of the truncated bivariate normal which describes the means and variances of the "corresponding untruncated variables" (p. 102). The later quantities are what constitute $\check{\psi}$. Also, see King's introduction (Equation 6 and surrounding text).

[4] X is taken to be a fixed quantity.

[5] The joint distribution of T and β^b is

$$g(\beta^b, T; \check{\psi}) = \frac{\phi_2(\beta^b, T; M(\check{\psi}))}{\int_0^1 \int_0^1 \phi_2(\beta^b, \beta^w; \check{\psi}) d\beta^b d\beta^w},$$

where ϕ_2 is the bivariate normal density function and M transforms the parameters of the joint distribution of β^b and β^w into the parameters of the joint distribution of β^b and T.

$$M : \left(\breve{\mathfrak{B}}^b, \breve{\mathfrak{B}}^w, \breve{\sigma}_b, \breve{\sigma}_w, \breve{\rho}\right) \longrightarrow \left(\breve{\mathfrak{B}}^b, \breve{\mathfrak{B}}^b X + \breve{\mathfrak{B}}^w (1 - X), \breve{\sigma}_b, \right.$$
$$\left. \sqrt{\breve{\sigma}_b^2 X^2 + \breve{\sigma}_w^2 (1 - X)^2 + 2\breve{\rho}\breve{\sigma}_b\breve{\sigma}_w X(1 - X)}, \frac{\breve{\sigma}_b X + \breve{\sigma}_w \rho (1 - X)}{\sqrt{\breve{\sigma}_b^2 X^2 + \breve{\sigma}_w^2 (1 - X)^2 + 2\breve{\rho}\breve{\sigma}_b\breve{\sigma}_w X(1 - X)}}\right).$$

These expressions hold for $0 \leq X < 1$. If $X = 1$, then $T = \beta^b$ and the joint distribution of T and β^b is simply the marginal distribution of β^b. In what follows, I avoid this technical nuisance by replacing X with $X - \epsilon$ in the data if $X = 1$.

Formulas for L are given in King (1997, Appendix D) and are not repeated here. The posterior distribution of $\breve{\psi}$ given the data is

$$P(\breve{\psi}|\mathbf{T}, \mathbf{X}) \propto L(\mathbf{T}|\mathbf{X}, \breve{\psi})p(\breve{\psi}), \tag{4.2}$$

where p is the joint prior distribution over $\breve{\psi}$.

Default options for King's computer implementation of EI place flat (improper) priors over $\breve{\mathfrak{B}}^b$ and $\breve{\mathfrak{B}}^w$, diffuse half-normal priors over $\breve{\sigma}^b$ and $\breve{\sigma}^w$, and an informative normal prior over the Fischer's Z transformation of $\breve{\rho}$. The informative prior on $\breve{\rho}$ effectively bounds estimates of its posterior mode away from 1 and -1. As noted by King, there is little information in the data about $\breve{\rho}$, and at extreme values of $\breve{\rho}$ the calculation of L becomes unreliable.[6] The prior distributions of each element of $\breve{\psi}$ are taken to be independent.

King's estimates the posterior distribution of $\breve{\psi}$ using numerical maximization of P to find the posterior modes and then uses normal asymptotic theory augmented with importance resampling to simulate draws from P.[7]

Given the posterior distribution of $\breve{\psi}$, the posterior distribution of each β_i^b (or β_i^w) given $\mathbf{T}$ and $\mathbf{X}$ can be formed as

$$P(\beta_i^b|\mathbf{T}, \mathbf{X}) = \int g(\beta_i^b|T_i, X_i, \breve{\psi})P(\breve{\psi}|\mathbf{T}, \mathbf{X})\, d\breve{\psi}. \tag{4.3}$$

While the integral in Equation 4.3 is difficult to evaluate directly, it is easy to draw samples from this density using Gibbs sampling. Suppressing the $\mathbf{X}$ and $\mathbf{T}$ from the notation, $\breve{\psi}^*$ is drawn from $P(\breve{\psi})$ using asymptotic normality and importance resampling, and then a draw is made from $g(\beta_i^b|T_i, X_i, \breve{\psi}^*)$ conditional on $\breve{\psi}^*$. Because $\beta^b|T$ is distributed truncated normal, $g(\beta_i^b|T_i, X_i, \breve{\psi}^*)$ can be sampled from using inverse CDF sampling. Samples from the posterior distribution of $\beta_i^b|T_i$ made in this way can be used to draw histograms or to calculate a posteriori expectations of these precinct-level quantities of interest.

Equation 4.3 reveals that through the assumption that all β^b and β^w pairs are drawn from a common distribution, EI "borrows strength" from data for other precincts in estimating the value of β^b in each precinct even though the draws for each precinct are a priori independent. By the accounting identity, given T_i, β^b and β^w are linearly dependent:[8]

$$\beta_i^w = \frac{T_i}{1 - X_i} - \frac{X_i}{1 - X_i}\beta_i^b.$$

Thus, the posterior distribution of β_i^w can be estimated using samples drawn from the distribution of β_i^b. King uses samples from the posterior distribution of the precinct β's to calculate other quantities of interest, such as the election-wide rates of turnout among blacks and whites.

4.2.1 MCMC Estimation of EI

As an alternative to King's procedure, I have implemented an MCMC estimator for the probability model described above. The estimator has the typical advantages of MCMC

---

[6] L requires the calculation of the bivariate normal integral over the unit square. This calculation can become noisy at extreme values of $\breve{\rho}$ or, more generally, whenever the area over the unit square is very small.

[7] In order to improve the normal approximation to the posterior distribution and to decrease the posterior correlations among the parameters, King first reparameterizes the posterior distribution, maximizing over the logs of $\breve{\sigma}_b$ and $\breve{\sigma}_w$, the Fischer's z transformation of $\breve{\rho}$, and $(\mathfrak{B}^b - 0.5)/(0.25 + \breve{\sigma}_b)$ and $(\mathfrak{B}^w - 0.5)/(0.25 + \breve{\sigma}_w)$ rather than $\mathfrak{B}^b$ and $\mathfrak{B}^w$.

[8] See (*This volume*) Introduction, p. 4, Equation 5 and surrounding text.

over King's procedure: it yields draws from the exact posterior distributions and is (in principle) more robust to numerical inaccuracies. It also has the typical disadvantages: lack of speed, difficulty in determining convergence, and so forth.

Rather than marginalizing β^b in forming the posterior distribution of $\check{\psi}$ as described above, in the MCMC approach the complete joint posterior distribution of $(\check{\psi}, \beta^b)$ is recovered. In this way, the joint distribution of the precinct quantities of interest are obtained directly from the estimation. Implementing MCMC using Gibbs sampling is straightforward. First, provisional values for $\check{\psi}$ are set. Next, values for β_i^b conditional on the provisional $\check{\psi}$, T_i, and X_i are drawn for $i = 1, 2, \ldots, p$. Then values of each element of $\check{\psi}$ are drawn conditional on the sampled values of the β^b, the values of the other elements of $\check{\psi}$, and the data. This process is then repeated. In the limit, the distribution of the sampled values will follow the joint posterior distribution of β^b and $\check{\psi}$ (see Gamerman, 1997).

As noted above, $g(\beta^b | T, X, \check{\psi})$ is truncated normal and can be sampled from using inverse CDF sampling. The more difficult distribution from which to sample is

$$P(\check{\psi} | \beta^b, \mathbf{T}, \mathbf{X}) \propto \left(\prod_i g(T_i, \beta_i^b | \check{\psi}) \right) p(\check{\psi}).$$

I use adaptive rejection Metropolis sampling (ARMS; Gilks, Best, and Tan, 1995) to draw from the conditional distribution of each element of $\check{\psi}$ conditional on the prior values of the other elements.[9] As shown by Gilks et al., ARMS allows sampling from arbitrary distributions that are known only up to a constant of proportionality. Suppressing the data and other parameters from the notation, we have, by the definition of conditional probability,

$$P(\check{\psi}_k | \check{\psi}^{-k}) \propto P(\check{\psi}).$$

Thus, the joint posterior (or a function proportional to it) can be used as the unnormalized density of the conditional posterior distributions of each element of $\check{\psi}$ conditional on the others.

The complete MCMC routine is:

1. Choose initial values $\check{\psi}$ for the parameters of the underlying TBVN distribution of β^b and β^w.
2. Draw values from the posterior distributions of β^b conditional on the current values of $\check{\psi}$, and the data, using inverse CDF sampling from these TN distributions.
3. Draw new values for each element of $\check{\psi}$ conditional on the previous values of the others, β^b, and the data, using ARMS.
4. Repeat from step 3.

4.2.2 Ecological Inference in Several Elections at Once

I now extend King's EI and the MCMC procedure to the case in which multiple elections are observed for the same set of geographic units (precincts).[10] In this extended model, precinct-level estimates of β^b and β^w for each of a series of elections are improved through the borrowing of strength, not only across precincts within elections, but also across elections within the same precinct.

---

[9] Computer routines implementing ARMS from user-written density functions are provided by Gilks et al. at http://www.mrc-bsu.cam.ac.uk/pub/methodology/adaptive_rejection/.

[10] Computer programs for estimating King's basic EI model using MCMC are available from the author.

Consider as set of elections $j = 1, 2, \ldots, J$ held in set of precincts $i = 1, 2, \ldots, p$. All of the general features of the EI model described above are maintained. In particular, the joint distribution of β_{ij}^b and β_{ij}^w is assumed to be bivariate truncated normal and independent of the X_{ij}. The identity

$$T_{ij} = X_{ij}\beta_{ij}^b + (1 - X_{ij})\beta_{ij}^w$$

holds. The parameters describing the joint distribution of β_{ij}^b and β_{ij}^w ($\check{\psi}_{ij}$) are the following:

$$\check{\mathfrak{B}}_{ij}^b = \check{\mathfrak{B}}_j^b + \mu_i^b,$$
$$\check{\mathfrak{B}}_{ij}^b = \check{\mathfrak{B}}_j^w + \mu_i^w,$$
$$\check{\sigma}_{ij}^b = \check{\sigma}_j^b,$$
$$\check{\sigma}_{ij}^w = \check{\sigma}_j^w,$$
$$\check{\rho}_{ij} = \check{\rho}_j.$$

The location of the TBVN distribution is a function of fixed precinct-specific and election-specific components. The dispersion parameters and correlation parameter have only election-specific components.[11] In order to separately identify the precinct and election location parameters, the expectations of the precinct location effects are assumed to be 0. In particular, I assume

$$\left(\mu_i^b, \mu_i^w\right) \sim \text{BVN}(\mathbf{0}, \mathbf{\Sigma})$$

for $i = 2, 3, \ldots, p$, where[12]

$$\mathbf{\Sigma} = \begin{bmatrix} \omega_b^2 & 0 \\ 0 & \omega_w^2 \end{bmatrix}.$$

The hyperparameters describing the variances of the precinct effects, ω_b^2 and ω_w^2, are given inverse chi-square priors.

The basic MCMC procedure described above is maintained, except that additional steps to allow Gibbs sampling from the conditional distributions of the additional parameters are added. The expanded procedure is:

1. Choose initial values $\check{\psi}_j$ for $j = 1, 2, \ldots, J$ for the parameters of the underlying TBVN distribution of β^b and β^w.
2. Choose initial values for μ_i^b and μ_i^w for $i = 1, 2, \ldots, p$.
3. Draw values from the posterior distribution of β_j^b conditional on $\check{\psi}_j$ for $j = 1, 2, \ldots, J$, μ_i^b and μ_i^w for $i = 1, 2, \ldots, p$, and the data, using inverse CDF sampling from these TN distributions.
4. Draw new values for each element of $\check{\psi}_j$, for $j = 1, 2, \ldots, J$ conditional on the previous values of the others, the current values of β^b, μ_i^b and μ_i^w for $i = 1, 2, \ldots, p$, and the data, using ARMS.

----

[11] Precinct-specific dispersion and correlation parameters are feasible, though using them adds substantial computational burden. Because the number of elections is typically small, the posterior distributions of the precinct variances and correlation components are unlikely to be very informative. If, on the other hand, one observed many elections in a small number of precincts the i and j, subscripts might reasonably be interchanged.

[12] The precinct effects are assumed to be independently drawn across precincts.

5. Draw new values for each element of μ^b and μ^w conditional on the other parameters and the current values of β_j^b for $j = 1, 2, \ldots, J$ and the data, using ARMS.
6. Draw new values for ω_b and ω_w conditional on μ_i^b and μ_i^w for $i = 1, 2, \ldots, p$ from the appropriate inverse chi-square distribution.
7. Repeat from step 3.

As noted by King (1997), there is relatively little information in the data about the parameters ρ_j for $j = 1, 2, \ldots, J$ that describe the correlation between β_{ij}^b and β_{ij}^w. In what follows, I restrict $\rho = 0$. The assumption that β_{ij}^b and β_{ij}^w are a priori independent is widely assumed in the literature (see, for example, King, Tanner, and Rosen, 1999, Introduction, p. 8; or Wakefield, 2001). This restriction greatly reduces the computational burden and numerical problems associated with the estimation.

Because the posterior distribution of the elements of $\tilde{\psi}$ are highly correlated (particularly if the degree of truncation is large), the MCMC routine converges slowly. Additionally, numerical failure of the bivariate normal density call can occur if the degree of truncation becomes too large.[13] To avoid these problems the values of $\mathfrak{B}_j^b$ and $\mathfrak{B}_j^w$ are assumed to lie in the interval $[-0.5, 1.5]$. This restriction is applied through a uniform prior on the $[-0.5, 1.5]$ interval for these parameters. Such a large restriction on the possible values of these theoretically unbounded parameters needs to be justified. In the next section, I demonstrate that truncated normal distributions with location parameters outside $[-0.5, 1.5]$ can be very closely approximated by truncated normal distributions with location parameters in that interval.

4.3 ESTIMATING THE TRUNCATED BIVARIATE NORMAL PARAMETERS WHEN THE DEGREE OF TRUNCATION IS LARGE

One of the main technical difficulties in implementing King's EI revolves around the estimation of the parameters of the truncated bivariate normal distribution when one or both of the location parameters are not in the interval $(0, 1)$. Figure 4.1 illustrates this problem in the simple case where the $\rho = 0$ and thus β^b and β^w follow univariate truncated normal distributions. The solid lines in the figure show the density over the unit interval when the location (μ) of the TN distribution is 2 and the dispersion (σ) is 0.25, 0.5, and 1.0. The dashed lines show the most similar TN distributions with location parameters equal to 5. The dotted lines show the most similar TN distributions with location parameters equal to 1.25. Note that in each case, the solid line is closely approximated by the dashed and dotted lines despite the disparity in the location parameters of the underlying distributions. Even if a large number of direct observations on β^b were available, it would be very difficult to infer the exact location and spread parameters of the underlying distribution. In the EI model, β^b is not directly observed. Uncovering the differences in the densities shown in Figure 4.1 through EI involves detecting small differences in *latent* distributions.

In and of itself, the fact that the likelihood will be locally very flat and skewed away from the unit interval when the true location parameter is not in the unit interval does not present a problem. However, in this case calculations of the likelihood becomes increasingly inaccurate as the estimated location parameter is moved off the unit interval. Thus, both the maximization procedures used by King and the MCMC techniques presented here can become unstable if the location parameters are allowed to stray too far from the unit interval.

---

[13] When $\rho = 0$ is imposed, the bivariate normal call becomes the product of univariate cumulative normal calls, greatly reducing the numerical inaccuracies.

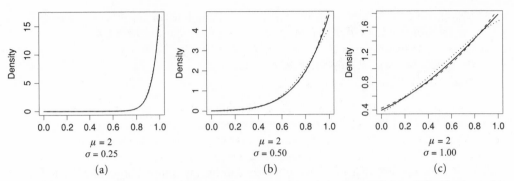

Figure 4.1. Discerning between truncated normal distributions. Truncated normal distributions with location parameters that lie beyond the support of the distribution can be closely approximated by other *TN* distributions. The solid line in each figure shows a *TN* density with location parameter equal to 2. The dashed line shows the closest *TN* density with location parameter equal to 5, and the dotted line shows the closest *TN* density with location parameter equal to 1.25.

On the other hand, the fact that TN distributions with very different parameterizations yield very similar densities implies not only that these parameters are difficult to estimate, but also that their exact values are not required to calculate the ultimate quantities of interest. These quantities of interest, such as the fraction of blacks that vote in each precinct or district-wide, are determined by densities that can be accurately estimated even if the parameters of the TN distribution cannot.

In what follows the values of the location parameters are restricted to fall between -0.5 and 1.5. This effectively avoids the numerical inaccuracies that arise when more extreme regions of the posterior density of the TBVN distribution are investigated, without appreciably affecting the posterior distributions of the precinct-level parameters of interest. Figure 4.2 shows how closely TN distributions with location parameters at 1.5 can approximate TN normal distributions with various location and dispersion parameters. The distance between distributions is measured by the Kullback–Liebler distances (Kullback and Liebler, 1951). The Kullback–Liebler distance between the true density f and the approximate density g is

$$I(f, g) = \int \ln \left(\frac{f(x)}{g(x)} \right) f(x) \, dx.$$

The distance I is commonly interpreted as the expected value of a likelihood-ratio test which attempts to discriminate between f and g using a single observation. The distances shown in Figure 4.2 are typically about 10^{-3}, often smaller, and in no case greater than 10^{-2}. By way of comparison, Figure 4.2 also shows the distances between the same set of TN distributions and truncated Student's t distributions with 80 degrees of freedom.[14] The truncated Student's t distribution with 80 degrees of freedom is chosen as a basis of comparison because its very close similarity to the normal is well known.[15] While the quality of the truncated Student's t approximation to the TN distributions is more variable, the overall quality of the

---

[14] Truncated Student's t distributions with the same location and dispersion parameters as the corresponding TN distributions are used for these comparisons.

[15] This comparison may be somewhat misleading because the region of truncation is often in the extreme tails where the Student's t and normal distribution differ most greatly. However, other similar heuristic comparisons yields similar results. For example, untruncated normal distributions with unit variance and means that differ by 0.045 have $I = 1 \times 10^{-4}$.

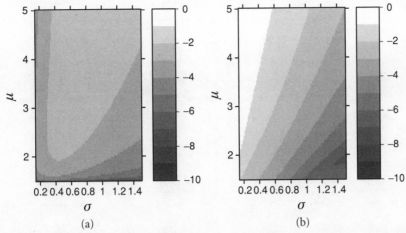

Figure 4.2. Level plots of Kullback–Liebler distances between truncated normal distributions on the interval $(0, 1)$ with the given parameters and (a) the closest truncated normal distribution with $\mu = 1.5$, (b) the corresponding Student's t distributions with 80 degrees of freedom. The scales of Kullback–Liebler distances are the order of magnitude $(\log_{10})$.

approximation is similar to that found when the TN with location parameter at 1.5 is used to approximate TN distributions with larger location parameters. Similar values for I are given by Aitchison and Shen (1980) for logistic normal approximations to Dirichlet distributions and are taken as evidence that logistic normal models can very closely approximate Dirichlet data.

4.4 APPLYING SUEI TO SIMULATED DATA

In this section, I report the results of the application of the SUEI estimator to simulated data that follow the probability models described above. These simulations reveal how the gains from SUEI vary as a function of: (1) the number of observed elections, (2) the correlation in X with precincts over time, and (3) when the conditions for aggregation bias are present in the data.

4.4.1 Validating the SUEI Model

I first consider simulated data that include five elections and 250 precincts. The main parameters of the TVBN distributions are $\mathfrak{B}^b = (1.00, 0.30, 0.60, 0.70, -0.10)$, $\mathfrak{B}^w = (0.40, 0.70, 0.40, 0.00, 0.30)$, $\sigma^b = (0.15, 0.07, 0.10, 0.05, 0.10)$, and $\sigma^w = (0.05, 0.07, 0.04, 0.12, 0.04)$.[16] The values of X are drawn from a uniform distribution on the interval $[0, 1/2]$ and are fixed across the elections within precincts, as would typically be the case with data on racial composition by precinct. The precinct effects are distributed normally across the precincts with a mean of 0 and standard deviations equal to 0.15 for μ^b and 0.10 for μ^w.

The posterior distributions of the estimated main truncated biviariate normal distributions are shown in Figure 4.3.[17] The "true" values of these parameters are shown as dots on

---

[16] The ρ parameters are all set equal to zero.

[17] These plots and other results presented are based on 500,000 MCMC iterations, of which the first 100,000 are discarded.

Election	$\bar{\mathfrak{B}}^b$	$\bar{\mathfrak{B}}^w$	σ^b	σ^w

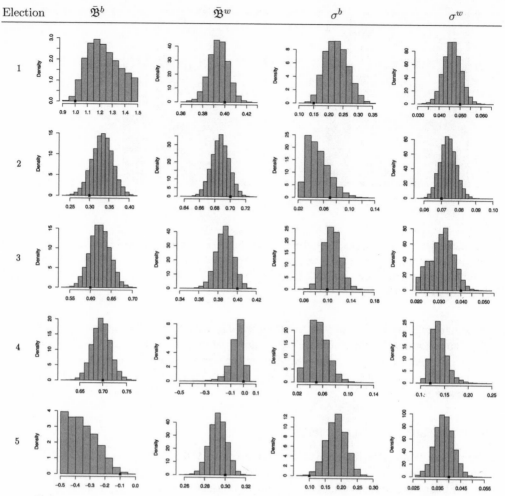

Figure 4.3. Estimates of model parameters from simulated data. The plots show histograms of the estimated posterior probabilities of of the model parameters. The dots on the axis of each graph indicate the "true" values of each parameter in the simulated data.

the axis of each histogram. In most cases, they fall near the bulk of the posterior mass. In few cases, they fall fairly far from the mass – in particular, in the case of $\mathfrak{B}^b$ for elections 1 and 5, where the true $\mathfrak{B}^b$'s are 1 and 0 respectively. In both cases, the posterior distributions lie mainly to the extreme side of the true value. Given the strong negative collinearity between $\mathfrak{B}^b$ and the corresponding σ^b when $\mathfrak{B}^b$ lies off (or, in this case, on the boundary) of the unit interval, the fact that the true σ^b's fall on the left edge of the posterior distributions associated with elections 1 and 5 comes as little surprise. However, it should be noted that for $\mathfrak{B}_4^w$, whose true value is 0, the posterior mass is much closer to true value. Here again the distribution is severely skewed away from the unit interval. As expected, the data are able to place low posterior probability on the values of $\mathfrak{B}_4^w$ that lie in the unit interval, but place relatively more weight on extreme values out of the unit interval.[18] While not shown in

---

[18] A key question is whether these posteriors are evidence that the MCMC estimator has not converged. However, there is little evidence that this is the case. Using a variety of starting values and rerunning the estimator

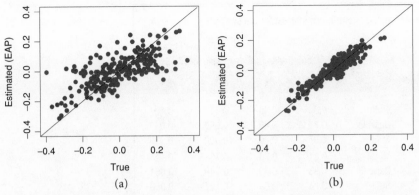

Figure 4.4. Estimated versus actual precinct effects: plots of the posterior mean estimates of the precinct effects against their "true" values in the simulated data: (a) nonwhite, (b) white.

Figure 4.3, the MCMC estimator is very effective at recovering the variation in the precinct effects, estimating ω_b to be 0.153 with a 95 percent credible interval of $(0.134, 0.172)$, and ω_w to be 0.095 with a credible interval of $(0.088, 0.112)$.

The expected a posteriori (EAP) precinct effects for each precinct in the simulated data are plotted against the true values in Figure 4.4. Both the true and estimated precinct effects for the nonwhite precinct populations exceed those from the white groups, as follows from the data, in which $\omega_b = 0.15$ and $\omega_w = 0.10$. The estimates of the μ^w generally correspond more closely to the true value. This is because the white group is considerably larger than the nonwhite group in most precincts, and thus the logical bounds on the precinct fractions of white turnout are typically tighter than those for nonwhite turnout.

The more important – and indeed central – question addressed by the simulation is how much improvement in the estimation of the ultimate quantities of interest result from the incorporation of precinct effects. Table 4.1 addresses this question. Here results of the SUEI model are compared with results of using King's EI estimator on each of the five sets of election data separately. This is not a perfect comparison, because the assumptions of SUEI and King's basic EI are not nested unless there are no precinct effects ($\omega_b = \omega_w = 0$). If truncation on the unit square is negligible, the two models are nearly nested. That is, the distribution β^b and β^w in each precinct will be a normal mixture (determined by the unobserved and in King's EI unidentified precinct effects) of nearly normal variables (the β's themselves). Because normal mixtures of normal variables are also normally distributed, without truncation King's EI and SUEI will be nested and the distributional assumptions of both models will simultaneously be satisfied. With truncation, however, this is no longer the case. The normal mixture of truncated normals that is the assumed distribution of β^b and β^w in SUEI is not the truncated normal distribution required for King's EI.[19] However, if the degree of truncation is relatively small or if the variance in the mixture that arises from the precinct effects is small relative to the election specific variation, the degree to which data generated under the SUEI assumptions differ from data generated under the standard EI assumptions will be relatively small. In these data, deviations of the simulated

consistently yielded similar posteriors. Applying King's estimator to the simulated data for a single election sometimes yields point estimates closer to the true modes; however, using the MCMC estimator on one election produces results similar to King's EI, suggesting that the difference results from the introduction of the precinct effects and not the MCMC procedure itself.

[19] This is because normal mixtures of truncated normals are not truncated normals.

Table 4.1 Estimated quantities of interest for the simulated data

Election		District-wide		Precinct-level std. dev./MSE	
		B^b	B^w	β^b	β^w
1	Truth	0.86	0.40	0.11	0.10
	Basic EI	0.86	0.40	0.099	0.043
	SUEI	0.87	0.40	0.088	0.033
2	Truth	0.31	0.70	0.16	0.12
	Basic EI	0.33	0.69	0.148	0.061
	SUEI	0.34	0.69	0.127	0.050
3	Truth	0.60	0.40	0.18	0.10
	Basic EI	0.62	0.39	0.150	0.059
	SUEI	0.62	0.39	0.122	0.043
4	Truth	0.70	0.10	0.15	0.09
	Basic EI	0.70	0.10	0.120	0.043
	SUEI	0.69	0.10	0.111	0.037
5	Truth	0.07	0.30	0.07	0.10
	Basic EI	0.06	0.30	0.071	0.030
	SUEI	0.08	0.29	0.070	0.030

Note: "Truth" rows give actual district-wide quantities and the actual standard deviation of the precinct-level quantities. The other rows give expected a posteriori estimates or mean square errors of those estimates across precincts.

data from the TBVN are sufficiently small that any observed differences between the EI and SUEI estimates do not follow from the fact that the simulated data were generated in a way that is not strictly consistent with the assumptions of King's EI.

Table 4.1 reveals that MSEs of the EAP estimates of the precinct quantities of interest are consistently smaller for SUEI than for King's EI. That is, as one would expect, borrowing strength improves the predictions of the precinct quantities. The gains are, however, modest. MSEs for β^w point estimates from the SUEI model are on average 11 percent smaller than the basic EI estimates; they are never larger, and at best are 19 percent smaller. For β^w the percentage improvements in the MSE of SUEI over basic EI are somewhat larger than for β^w, averaging 16 percent smaller, never larger, and at best 27 percent smaller. While these improvements are not huge, they are nonnegligible.

4.4.2 Investigating SUEI Efficiency Gains

I investigated how SUEI performed versus EI in three simulated data experiments. In the first experiment, I varied the number of observed elections. In the second experiment, I varied the correlation in X within precincts across elections. In the third experiment, I investigated the robustness of SUEI to aggregation bias. In all of these experiments, the same set of TBVN parameters was used for every election; $\check{\psi} = (0.8, 0.4, 0.1, 0.1, 0.0)$. The percent white (X) is assumed to be uniformly distributed over the interval $(0, 1)$ across precincts in each election. The number of precincts p, is set to 150. The standard deviation

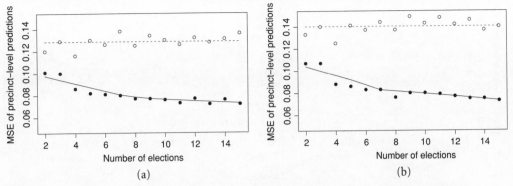

Figure 4.5. The average precinct-level mean squared error of (a) the β^b estimate and (b) the β^w estimate, as a function of the number of observed elections across 14 simulated data sets as described in the text.

of the precinct effects was set to 0.2 for both the white and nonwhite groups in each case. Large gains from SUEI would in some cases be possible if the TBVN parameters varied from election to election, but if we use the same probability model to generate each election in a given experimental trial, the results are easy to compare across methods and experiments.[20] In particular, because the marginal distribution of X and the parameters of the TBVN are the same in every election considered in all of these three experiments, the EI estimates should only vary as a function of sampling. On the other hand, as the number of elections is increased or as the correlation in X across elections decreases, the efficiency of SUEI should increase.

I begin by constructing a series of simulated data sets with the given parameter values. The first data set contains two elections, the second three elections, and so forth, up to the largest data set, which contains 15 elections. In contrast to the simulated data set presented in the previous subsection, here the values of X are independently drawn across elections, which (as shown below) increases the efficiency of SUEI estimates relative to the case in which X is fixed across elections.

Figure 4.5 shows the average MSE of the precinct-level quantities of interest across all precincts and elections for each of the data sets. The open circles show the MSE for standard EI estimates; the solid circles, for the SUEI estimates. The dashed line plots the trend in average MSE of the EI precinct-level estimates as the number of elections in the data is varied. The solid line plots the trend in the MSE of the SUEI estimates as the number elections is varied. Notice the dashed line is flat, reflecting the fact that EI does not borrow strength across elections. However, the quality of the SUEI estimates increases as more elections are observed and more information is pooled. Even when only two elections are observed, SUEI yields MSEs that are about 15 to 20 percent smaller than those produced by EI. With 15 observed elections the reduction in MSE approaches 50 percent. The graphs reveal diminishing returns to each additional observed election. Given the variances of the election-specific and precinct-specific components and leaving aside the truncations, the upper bound of the reduction in the precinct level MSE is approximately 55 percent.[21]

---

[20] The SUEI estimates are based on 100,000 iterations of the MCMC routine (the first 5,000 iterations are discarded).

[21] Leaving aside truncation, the MSE of the precinct quantities in EI would be $\sqrt{0.2^2 + 0.1^2} = 0.23$, as opposed to 0.10 if the precinct effects were known. Due to truncation, the MSEs are lower (about 0.13 for EI and 0.07 for SUEI with 15 elections).

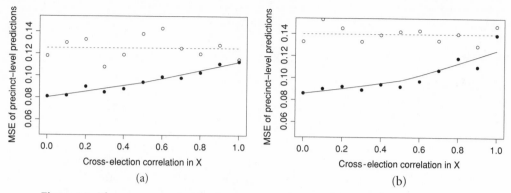

Figure 4.6. The average precinct-level mean squared error of (a) the β^b estimate and (b) the β^w estimate as functions of the correlation in X across elections as described in the text.

In the previous experiment, X was drawn independently across elections. Allowing X to vary within precincts across elections increases our ability to infer the values of the precinct-level effects and in part explains why I find larger gains in efficiency using SUEI in the this experiment than I did in the first simulated data set presented in the previous section. To see how the advantage of SUEI over EI varies as a function of the variation in X across elections, I created 11 simulated data sets. Each of the data sets includes eight elections generated by the same parameter values as the previous experiment, with one exception. In each of the data sets, the 150×8 matrix $\mathbf{X}$ is constructed by drawing from the distribution

$$\mathbf{X}_i^* \sim \mathrm{MVN}(\mathbf{0}, \mathbf{S}) \qquad \text{for } i = 1, \dots, p$$

for each precinct independently, where the 8×8 variance matrix $\mathbf{S}$ has ones along the main diagonal and $r \in [0, 1]$ in each of the off-diagonal entries. Thus, the pairwise correlation between any two columns of $\mathbf{X}^*$ is r. I then create $\mathbf{X}$ by taking the standard normal CDF of each element of $\mathbf{X}^*$. Across the 11 data sets, r is varied from zero (X is drawn independently across elections) to one (X is constant across elections). By construction, the marginal distribution of X in every election across the 11 data sets is uniform on the interval $[0, 1]$. Thus, as in the previous experiment, the (marginal) probability model generating each election is identical, and EI, which does not pool information across elections, should generate similar estimates for each election, regardless of the correlation in X across elections.

Figure 4.6 plots the MSEs of the estimates of precinct quantities of interest across the 11 simulated data sets. The dotted line representing the trend in the EI MSEs remains flat as the correlation in X across elections is increased. The advantage of SUEI over EI is greatest when X is drawn independently across elections, and least when X is identical across elections. This result follows from the fact that precinct effects can be more precisely estimated when there is variation in X across elections. Without variation in X (and without variation in the main parameters of TBVN across elections), SUEI can still recover some information about the precinct effects, in cases in which T is consistently higher or lower than average across elections; without variation in X, however, there is little information in the data to separate the overall pattern in turnout into nonwhite (μ^b) and white (μ^w) components. Nevertheless, the experiment reveals efficiency gains of 5 percent even when X and the parameters of the TBVN are constant across elections (the least favorable conditions for borrowing strength across elections).

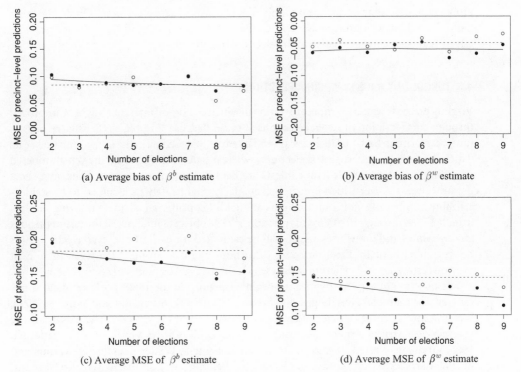

(a) Average bias of β^b estimate

(b) Average bias of β^w estimate

(c) Average MSE of β^b estimate

(d) Average MSE of β^w estimate

Figure 4.7. Average bias and MSE of precinct-level estimates as a function of the number of observed elections.

In a last set of experiments, I consider whether SUEI is more robust to data that violate the independence assumption, which is critical to avoiding bias in EI or ecological regression. In these experiments, I created data sets containing between two and nine elections which followed the same probability model as the previous experiments except that the cross-election correlation in X was fixed at 0.7, and $\breve{\mathfrak{B}}^b_{ij} = 0.8 + 0.4(X_{ij} - 0.5)$. Figure 4.7 shows the average bias and MSE of the EI and SUEI as a function of the number of elections. The top two panels reveal that SUEI was no more robust to aggregation bias than EI. When $\breve{\mathfrak{B}}^b$ (and, thus, β^b) is a function of X, estimates of β^b and β^w are biased. Increasing the number of elections does not reduce the bias in the SUEI estimates. However, the lower two panels reveal that even in the presence of bias, SUEI still reduces the MSE of the precinct-level prediction versus EI, and that advantage increases with the number of observed elections.

In other experiments, I ran SUEI and EI on data sets which included some elections in which the conditions for aggregation were present as well as some in which those conditions were not present. In those experiments, SUEI did somewhat decrease in the bias of the precinct-level estimates relative to EI, though the differences were not dramatic. The larger advantage of SUEI over EI when the independence assumption is violated may be found if the SUEI model is extended to allow the $\breve{\mathfrak{B}}^b$ and $\breve{\mathfrak{B}}^w$ to depend on X as in the extended EI model. I leave this extension to be investigated in future work.

While the results of these simulations are not definitive, they do yield some important observations. As the number of elections considered increases, the advantage (in terms of MSE) of SUEI over EI grows (to as much as 45 to 50 percent). Similarly as the racial compositions of the districts becomes more variable across elections, the advantage of SUEI grows, although some advantage is found even if X is fixed across elections. On the the other hand, I would have found smaller reductions in MSE from SUEI if the estimated precinct effects had been smaller relative to the election-specific effects.[22]

4.5 TURNOUT BY RACE IN VIRGINIA ELECTIONS

Virginia presents a good example of a setting in which ecological inference might be improved through consideration of several elections at once. Because Virginia elects its governors to four-year terms in odd-numbered years and its entire State senate in the odd-numbered years which do not have gubernatorial elections, whereas federal elections are in even-numbered years, important state or federal contests are held in Virginia every year. Thus, in a short period of years – over which precinct-level effects might safely be assumed to be stable – a sizable number of significant elections are held. I consider an example drawing on data from the 1984 through 1990 Virginia elections.[23] The object of inference is the rate of turnout among whites and nonwhites, which will be estimated for each of the seven elections. It is not possible to obtain direct measures of turnout by racial group.[24] However, there exist previous estimates and expert opinions which can be used as points of comparison.

The question of turnout by race in Virginia elections in the 1980s is of particular interest (see, for example, Hertzhog, 1994; Sabato, 1987, 1991; Strickland and Whicker, 1992; Traugott and Price 1992; Schexnider 1990; Morris and Bradley, 1994). The 1980s saw the emergence of African-American candidates for statewide office in Virginia and the nation. In 1985, Virginians elected an African-American, L. Douglas Wilder, lieutenant governor, and in 1989 they elected him governor. In 1988, the Republicans nominated Maurice Dawkins, an African-American, for the U.S. Senate. In 1984, Jesse Jackson won the Democratic caucus vote in Virginia (though he ran second to Mondale in national conventional delegates), and in 1988, Jackson captured a plurality (45 percent) of the Democratic primary vote. Thus, Virginia in the 1980s offers an interesting testing ground for theories about the electoral significance of race and, in particular, the effect of minority candidates on minority-voter mobilization.

An established literature presents theoretical foundations and empirical tests of the assertion that the race of candidates or office holders affects the political mobilization of racial minority and majority groups. For example, Tate claims that black participation is generally higher when black candidates are on the ballot, though her survey evidence suggests that most blacks disagree with the assertion that "blacks should always vote for black candidates when they run" (1994, p. 105). Nevertheless, Tate argues that high black turnout rates are often associated with precedent-setting candidacies (such as Wilder's). Bobo and Gilliam (1990) show that black political engagement is greater in cities with black mayors. Gay (2001) shows that white voter turnout is depressed and black voter turnout (sometimes) increased in districts held by black members of Congress. Kleppner (1985) reports that historically high black voter turnout was critical to Harold Washington's mayoral victory in Chicago in 1983. Similarly, high black voter turnout in states like Virginia is seen by some as critical to the success of black candidates (Strickland and Whicker, 1992).

The existing estimates of turnout by race in these elections come from Sabato (1991) and are based on turnout in 44 selected predominantly black precincts. The rate of turnout in

---

[22] Similarly, larger advantages would have been found if the precinct effects had accounted for a larger share of the variability in β^b and β^w.

[23] The data are from the ROAD data project (King et al., 1997).

[24] Indeed, Virginia does not collect information about the race of voters when they register.

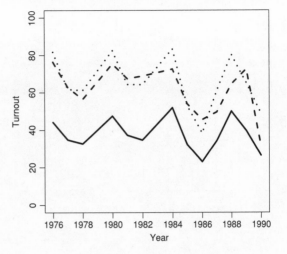

Figure 4.8. Estimates of black and white voter turnout from Sabato (1991). The dotted line shows white turnout, and the dashed line shows black turnout, in each case as a fraction of voter registration. The solid line shows total turnout as a fraction of the voting age population.

these precincts is taken as an estimate of black turnout statewide. Unfortunately, these estimates are for the percentage of registered voters that turn out to vote and not percentages of the total voting age populations. Because population data for the precincts are not available, the turnout rates as a fraction of voting age population cannot be estimated in a comparable way.[25] Turnout rates for blacks reported by Sabato are shown in Figure 4.8.[26] Interestingly, Sabato's results suggest that black turnout was higher than white turnout in the 1985 and 1989 races, in which Wilder was a candidate for lieutenant governor and governor. Black turnout was estimated to be lower than white turnout in 1986, when the black Republican Dawkins was a candidate for U.S. Senate, and in all of the other years in the eighties except 1981. By these estimates black turnout never exceeds white turnout by more than about 7.5 percentage points, though in some elections white turnout exceeds black turnout by as much as 17 percentage points.

In order to analyze turnout rates among whites and nonwhites using the ecological inference estimators developed above, I require election returns and racial composition data for a set of geographic units. Practically, this requires aggregating electoral returns to a level that corresponds to geographical units recognized by the Census Bureau. In the ROAD project, King et al. (1997) published electoral data for Virginia elections from 1984 to 1990 that are aggregated to the minor civil division (MCD) group level. In the main these are simply the Census Bureau's MCDs (for example, Alexandria, Berryville, or Quantico) except in cases where one or more electoral precincts (the lowest level of electoral aggregation) were shared across two or more MCDs. In these cases, the MCDs sharing precincts are grouped so that no electoral precinct is split across groupings. In total there are 257 MCD groups in the Virginia data, ranging widely in size from 506 to 183,000 voting age residents. The median Virginia MCD group has 7,363 voting age residents. Nonwhites make up 22 percent of the voting age residents statewide. The distribution of the nonwhite population across the MCD groups is shown in Figure 4.9. While many of the MCD groups have very small nonwhite populations, a small number of them are majority-minority.

[25] Similarly, because registration-by-race data are not available, ecological analysis of the sort developed here cannot be undertaken on the precinct-level data.

[26] Sabato does not give turnout rates for whites. In the figure, the white turnout rate is imputed from the total turnout rate and Sabato's black turnout rate under the assumption that 18 percent of the registered voters in Virginia were black during this period.

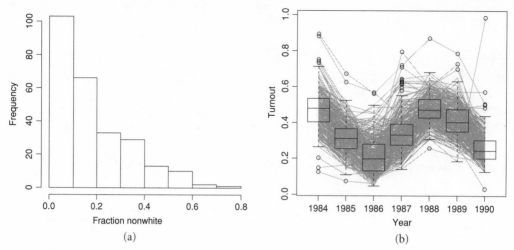

Figure 4.9. Virginia Ecological Election Data, 1984–1990: (a) racial composition, (b) turnout rates. Here (a) shows the distribution of nonwhite voters across Virginia minor civil division groups (MCD groups; see text for definition), and (b) shows boxplots for the turnout rates in each of the seven elections considered (as a percentage of voting age populations). Each gray line in (b) represents an MCD group.

The distribution of voter turnout across the elections is also shown in Figure 4.9.[27] The figure reveals cross-election and cross-precinct variation in overall voter turnout at the MCD-group level. As one would expect, voter turnout was highest in the presidential election years 1984 and 1988. Interestingly, the midterm elections of 1986 and 1990 had the lowest rate of turnout, even lower than the 1987 election in which no federal or statewide offices were contested. Closer inspection reveals that the 1987 election included a hotly contested statewide proposition that established the Virginia lottery, whereas the 1986 election did not involve a U.S. Senate contest, and Senator John Warner faced no Democratic opposition in his 1990 reelection campaign (Sabato, 1991). The gray lines in Figure 4.9 trace the turnout rates within each precinct over time. Notice that there appear to be many high- and low-turnout precincts. For example, the high and low outliers tend to be the same MCD groups over time. While not sufficient to demonstrate MCD-group effects in turnout by race, persistent differences in total turnout are consistent with the existence of those effects.

Table 4.2 presents estimates of the main truncated bivariate normal parameters as estimated by King's EI and SUEI. In all but one election, the 1986 midterm, the estimated parameters are very similar. The 1984 presidential election presents a good case of what we expect to find if the data are well conditioned and the degree of truncation in the assumed TBVN distributions is small.[28] The election-specific estimated location parameters, $\mathfrak{B}^b$ and $\mathfrak{B}^w$, are identical, and the estimated election-specific standard deviations are larger for King's EI than for SUEI. This is because some of the precinct-level variation in turnout that is captured by these parameters in King's EI is attributed to the precinct effect in SUEI. Table 4.3 shows the estimated standard deviations of the precinct effects. The standard deviation of the precinct effects for both whites and nonwhites is estimated to be about 0.09. Thus, in the 1984 presidential election, the estimates are consistent with the notion that the estimated σ^b from King's EI is decomposed to into election- and precinct-specific components

---

[27] Presentation of the turnout data in this way was suggested to me by James DeNardo.

[28] This should not be taken as implying that the data are in fact well conditioned. In particular, the these results are not informative about the existence of aggregation bias in the results.

Table 4.2 Estimates of truncated bivariate normal parameters for Virginia elections data: turnout by race, 1984–1990

Parameter	King EI			Precinct-effects EI		
	Mean	Std. Dev.	95% CI	Mean	Std. Dev.	95% CI
1984 Presidential						
$\mathfrak{B}^b$	0.55	0.02	(0.52, 0.59)	0.55	0.03	(0.49, 0.60)
$\mathfrak{B}^w$	0.46	0.01	(0.44, 0.47)	0.46	0.01	(0.47, 0.48)
$\breve{\sigma}^b$	0.12	0.02	(0.08, 0.16)	0.07	0.02	(0.04, 0.10)
$\breve{\sigma}^w$	0.12	0.005	(0.11, 0.13)	0.06	0.004	(0.06, 0.07)
1985 Gubernatorial						
$\mathfrak{B}^b$	0.47	0.01	(0.45, 0.50)	0.46	0.04	(0.42, 0.51)
$\mathfrak{B}^w$	0.27	0.01	(0.27, 0.29)	0.29	0.01	(0.27, 0.30)
$\breve{\sigma}^b$	0.03	0.02	(0.01, 0.07)	0.05	0.01	(0.03, 0.07)
$\breve{\sigma}^w$	0.10	0.003	(0.10, 0.11)	0.05	0.003	(0.04, 0.05)
1986 Midterm						
$\mathfrak{B}^b$	0.25	0.02	(0.21, 0.27)	−0.04	0.22	(−0.44, 0.27)
$\mathfrak{B}^w$	0.18	0.01	(0.16, 0.19)	0.19	0.01	(0.18, 0.22)
$\breve{\sigma}^b$	0.09	0.02	(0.05, 0.13)	0.35	0.11	(0.19, 0.53)
$\breve{\sigma}^w$	0.14	0.01	(0.13, 0.16)	0.10	0.01	(0.08, 0.11)
1987 State legislative						
$\mathfrak{B}^b$	0.25	0.03	(0.21, 0.30)	0.20	0.07	(0.09, 0.29)
$\mathfrak{B}^w$	0.36	0.01	(0.35, 0.37)	0.37	0.01	(0.35, 0.39)
$\breve{\sigma}^b$	0.10	0.02	(0.04, 0.14)	0.13	0.04	(0.08, 0.20)
$\breve{\sigma}^w$	0.12	0.005	(0.12, 0.13)	0.08	0.01	(0.07, 0.09)
1988 Presidential						
$\mathfrak{B}^b$	0.48	0.02	(0.45, 0.51)	0.48	0.03	(0.43, 0.53)
$\mathfrak{B}^w$	0.48	0.01	(0.47, 0.48)	0.48	0.01	(0.47, 0.50)
$\breve{\sigma}^b$	0.10	0.02	(0.07, 0.13)	0.03	0.01	(0.02, 0.06)
$\breve{\sigma}^w$	0.09	0.003	(0.09, 0.10)	0.03	0.003	(0.03, 0.04)
1989 Gubernatorial						
$\mathfrak{B}^b$	0.55	0.02	(0.52, 0.57)	0.55	0.03	(0.50, 0.60)
$\mathfrak{B}^w$	0.39	0.01	(0.38, 0.40)	0.39	0.01	(0.37, 0.40)
$\breve{\sigma}^b$	0.08	0.02	(0.05, 0.12)	0.06	0.02	(0.04, 0.09)
$\breve{\sigma}^w$	0.10	0.003	(0.10, 0.11)	0.04	0.003	(0.03, 0.04)
1990 Midterm						
$\mathfrak{B}^b$	−0.13	0.24	(−0.56, 0.16)	−0.10	0.23	(−0.46, 0.25)
$\mathfrak{B}^w$	0.27	0.01	(0.26, 0.28)	0.27	0.02	(0.27, 0.29)
$\breve{\sigma}^b$	0.29	0.07	(0.19, 0.42)	0.29	0.09	(0.15, 0.43)
$\breve{\sigma}^w$	0.10	0.003	(0.09, 0.11)	0.11	0.01	(0.10, 0.12)

Note: Posterior means, standard deviations, and credible intervals were calculated using King's computer procedures and the MCMC estimator described in the text.

Table 4.3 Estimated standard deviations of the precinct-specific effects on turnout by race across the seven elections, Virginia, 1984–1990

Parameter	Mean	Std. Dev.	95% CI
ω_b	0.09	0.04	(0.01, 0.14)
ω_w	0.09	0.01	(0.08, 0.10)

in SUEI. For example, the total nonwhite precinct-level variance is estimated in King's EI to be 0.12, and by SUEI to be $\sqrt{0.07^2 + 0.09^2} \approx 0.11$. As mentioned above, when the degree of truncation is negligible, both King's EI and SUEI imply that the precinct parameters follow bivariate normal distributions (both conditional and unconditional on the precinct effect). In such cases, precinct-level variance in King's EI will be decomposed into election- and precinct specific components as it is in the 1984 presidential election. Similar, results are obtained for the 1988 presidential election and the 1989 gubernatorial election.

In the remaining elections, differences in the estimated election-specific variance components between the two models cannot be directly attributed to the sort of decomposition described above. In these elections, the estimated election-specific variance components are larger in SUEI than in King's EI for at least one of the two racial groups. In the 1985 gubernatorial election, the EI estimated election-specific variance of β^b is not even larger than the precinct-specific variation found using SUEI. In most cases, the differences can be attributed to greater degrees of truncation combined with differences in the ways the two models respond to violations in the their distributional assumptions.

Despite differences in the estimated parameters of the underlying TBVN distributions, estimates of the aggregate quantities of interest are quite similar, as seen in Table 4.4. The maximum difference between the EI estimates and SUEI estimates are 5 percentage points for nonwhites and 1 percentage point for whites.[29] Interestingly, despite the additional efficiency that should be obtained from SUEI, the estimated posterior uncertainties in the EI estimates is generally smaller than those found for SUEI. This finding results in part from an understatement of posterior uncertainty from King's use of importance resampling and normal theory to construct estimates of the posterior uncertainty. The larger posterior uncertainties in SUEI also result from differing reactions of the two models to violations of their distributional assumptions.

The results presented in Table 4.4 support the notion that black turnout was elevated relative to white turnout in the two elections involving Douglas Wilder. In the 1985 and 1989 elections black turnout is estimated to have exceeded white turnout by about 15 to 25 percentage points. By comparison, in the 1987 state election, white turnout was estimated to exceeded nonwhite turnout by about 5 to 15 percentage points. In the two midterm elections, black and white turnout is estimated to have been quite similar. Although black turnout is estimated to have exceeded white turnout in 1986 and white turnout to have exceeded black turnout in 1990, in neither case is the difference within the 95 percent credible interval. The most anomalous case is the 1984 presidential election, in which black turnout is estimated to have exceeded white turnout by about 15 to 25 percent. While Jesse Jackson ran a strong campaign in the 1984 presidential primary, winning the Virginia caucus vote, it is not obvious that the effect of his campaign would extend to the general election six months later.

---

[29] That the maximum difference between EI and SUEI for whites is about 5 times smaller than for nonwhites follows directly from the fact that nonwhites comprise about 1/5 of the population.

Table 4.4 Estimates of the statewide quantities of interest: fractions of whites and nonwhites voting statewide

Parameter	King EI			Precinct-effects EI		
	Mean	Std. Dev.	95% CI	Mean	Std. Dev.	95% CI
1984 Presidential						
B^b	0.54	0.03	(0.50, 0.58)	0.53	0.04	(0.46, 0.59)
B^w	0.41	0.01	(0.40, 0.42)	0.42	0.01	(0.39, 0.44)
1985 Gubernatorial						
B^b	0.47	0.02	(0.44, 0.50)	0.44	0.04	(0.38, 0.50)
B^w	0.23	0.004	(0.22, 0.24)	0.24	0.01	(0.22, 0.26)
1986 Midterm						
B^b	0.25	0.02	(0.21, 0.27)	0.30	0.05	(0.22, 0.39)
B^w	0.21	0.01	(0.20, 0.22)	0.20	0.01	(0.17, 0.22)
1987 State legislative						
B^b	0.25	0.03	(0.20, 0.30)	0.22	0.04	(0.16, 0.28)
B^w	0.31	0.01	(0.29, 0.32)	0.32	0.01	(0.29, 0.33)
1988 Presidential						
B^b	0.46	0.02	(0.42, 0.43)	0.46	0.04	(0.40, 0.52)
B^w	0.45	0.01	(0.44, 0.46)	0.45	0.01	(0.43, 0.47)
1989 Gubernatorial						
B^b	0.53	0.02	(0.49, 0.56)	0.52	0.04	(0.46, 0.58)
B^w	0.34	0.01	(0.32, 0.36)	0.35	0.01	(0.33, 0.36)
1990 Midterm						
B^b	0.17	0.03	(0.14, 0.22)	0.22	0.04	(0.15, 0.30)
B^w	0.27	0.01	(0.25, 0.28)	0.26	0.01	(0.23, 0.28)

Overall, these estimates suggest that black voter turnout is systematically higher relative to white voter turnout than Sabato's estimates suggest. Several factors might account for these differences. The 44 predominantly black precincts use by Sabato could be atypical of turnout patterns statewide. Also, Sabato assumes that nonwhite and white behavior in these precincts is the same.[30] On the other hand, it is also quite possible that there is a relationship between voter turnout and racial composition. Key's (1949) racial threat hypothesis asserts that whites will be most motivated to vote against blacks in areas where blacks are most prevalent. Consistent with Key's hypothesis, Hertzog (1994) argues that "the single most significant factor in determining how white Virginians would vote in the 1980s was the percentage of black people living the voter's locality" (p. 163). If this is true, it is quite possible that for elections in which blacks are particularly mobilized, whites in predominantly black areas will be mobilized to vote as well (for the opposing candidate). In that case, the ecological inference models considered here, which assume that racial composition and turnout by each racial group are independent, will fail in such a way that the additional white turnout in areas with large black populations will be attributed to black voters. This effect is opposite to the usual aggregation bias result, in which voting rates in predominantly black areas are lower for both blacks and whites than in predominantly

---

[30] Without knowing the racial composition of these precincts, the influence of white turnout on Sabato's estimates cannot be assessed.

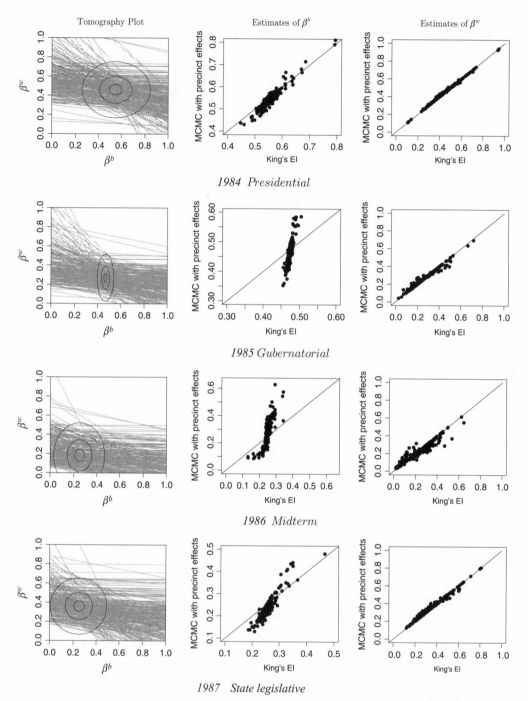

Figure 4.10. *MCD* group level tomography plots and estimates from King's *EI* and the precinct-effects *EI* model estimated by *MCMC*. The left panels show tomography plots of feasible values of β^b and β^w for each *MCD* group. The ellipses show probability contours of the *TBVN* parameters estimated by King's *EI*. The center and right panels show the *EAP* estimates of β^b and β^w respectively for each *MCD* group.

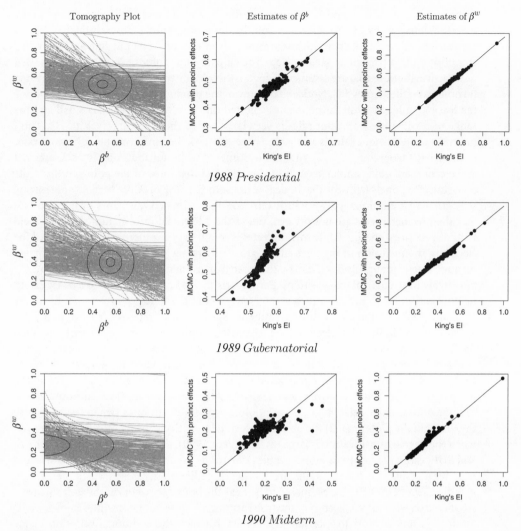

Figure 4.10. (*continued*)

white areas, leading the estimated black turnout to be lower relative to white turnout than is the true black turnout. Interestingly, Sabato's estimates indicates that black turnout is lower than the SUEI or EI estimates, not only in elections that involve black candidates, but in other elections as well, which undermines the idea that the differences between the two sets of estimates are due to aggregation bias resulting from racial threat. Further, the fact that Sabato's estimates which result in lower estimates of black turnout are based on the behavior of blacks (and whites) in the *most* heavily black precincts, makes less plausible the notion that there is a positive correlation between black or white turnout rates in an area and the fraction of blacks in that area. Overall, the EI and SUEI results regarding the aggregate quantities of interest are quite similar. Further, consistent with Sabato, the EI and SUEI results show higher black turnout relative to white turnout when Wilder was on the ballot.

As seen in the simulation, the real advantage in the SUEI estimator is in the improvement to the precinct-level (MCD-group-level) predictions. Figure 4.10 shows the MCD group turnout rates for whites and nonwhites as estimated by EI and SUEI along with King's so-called *tomography plot* for each election. In the tomography plot, each line represents the feasible values of black and white turnout given the total turnout rate and the racial composition in a particular MCD group. The ellipses show contour lines of the truncated normal distributions that are assumed to govern the joint distribution of white and nonwhite turnout (as estimated by EI). Notice that many of the precinct lines are very flat, indicating the feasible range of white turnout rates (plotted on the y-axis) is typically small and the range of feasible black turnout rates is very large (often the entire interval $[0, 1]$). Thus, inferring white turnout rates is a considerably easier task than inferring black turnout rates in these data. Consequently, EI- and SUEI-estimated white turnout rates in each precinct and election are quite similar, as indicated by the fact that most of the points in the white turnout (β^w) panels fall near the 45 degree lines. In the case of white turnout, borrowing strength across elections had very little effect on the estimated quantities of interest. Not that the precinct effects are not present; rather the additional information that they yield with respect to estimating white turnout rates is small. On the other hand, in several of the elections, the inclusion of precinct effects greatly increases the variation in the estimated turnout rates among blacks. That is, the posterior estimates are greatly effected by the borrowing of strength across elections. Particularly in 1985 and 1986, and to a lesser extent in 1987 and 1989, SUEI finds much greater variation in black turnout than does EI. In the 1984 and 1988 elections, variation in estimated black turnout rates made by EI and SUEI are similar, and in the 1990 election the EI estimates exhibit somewhat more variation than the SUEI estimates.

Overall, when the variation in black turnout rates is estimated to be large relative to the variation in white turnout rates (when the ellipses in the tomography plots are wide), the precinct effects add relatively less, and when the variation in black turnout rates is estimated to be small relative to the variation in white turnout rates (when the ellipses in the tomography plots are tall) the precinct effects add relatively more. Also, as noted above, when the degree of truncation is large (as in 1986 or 1990), the relationship between the EI and SUEI estimates becomes more complex due to the asymmetric effect that positive and negative precinct effects have on the precinct-level prediction in cases in which the election specific effect ($\mathcal{B}^b$ or $\mathcal{B}^w$) is estimated to lie near the boundary of or off the unit square.

Of course, without knowledge of the true turnout by whites and nonwhites in each MCD group it is not possible to ascertain the degree to which the additional variation in the SUEI estimates versus the EI estimates comports with "true" cross-MCD group variation in turnout rates. However, the estimates do suggest the existence of persistent cross-election variation in turnout rates, and those difference are reflected in the SUEI MCD group-level data predictions. Thus, the results presented here demonstrate how the analysis of several elections at once can be used to gain leverage on the behavior of voters within each precinct (MCD group).

4.6 DISCUSSION

The SUEI model maintains the central assumption found in Goodman (1959) and King (1997) of independence between the turnout rates within each racial group and the racial composition of the precincts. The violation of this assumption leads to aggregation bias (Robinson, 1950) when regression-like techniques (such as Goodman's ecological regression or King's EI) are applied. While the degree to which EI is more "robust" to violations of this assumption has been debated, it is important to note the centrality of the assumption and that its violation *will* lead to bias. King presents extensions to his model in which violations of this assumption are addressed, and those same extensions could be incorporated in the model presented here. Indeed, the MCMC estimator developed above can more easily and flexibly allow for dependences between the racial composition of the precincts and the turnout rates within each group. However, there is often little information in the data to estimate such dependences (Rivers, 2000). In this regard an extended SUEI which allows for nonindependence between the precinct quantities of interest and the racial composition of the district (as King's "extended" EI) holds some promise. If the structure of nonindependence is constant across elections, then borrowing strength across elections may help to estimate that structure. This extension remains for future work.

In both the simulated data and the empirical example, the district and state-wide estimates produced by King's basic EI model and the SUEI model are very similar. The advantage of the SUEI model is in the estimates of the precinct-level quantities of interest. In the simulated data, SUEI provides improvements in mean square error of 5 to 40 percent. Because the true precinct-level quantities are not known for the Virginia election data set, the degree of improvement cannot be directly assessed. However, the estimates suggest that a considerable amount of information about precinct-level turnout by race in any given election can be gleaned from other elections.

Substantively, the estimates support the widely held, but relatively unsubstantiated, claim that nonwhite turnout exceeded white turnout in several Virginia elections in the 1980s and particularly outpaced white turnout in the 1985 and 1989 elections, in which a African-American candidate, Douglas Wilder, was on the statewide ballot. While the results may be exaggerated by an ecological fallacy if whites in areas with large nonwhite populations turned out in disproportionately large numbers to vote against Wilder (as suggested by Key's (1949) racial threat hypothesis), the general finding appears clear.

This chapter demonstrates how King's EI model can be estimated using MCMC techniques and how cross-election precinct-level dependences can be estimated and used to improve precinct-level predictions. More generally, the MCMC approach laid out in this chapter can be applied of other extensions of King's model, including perhaps ways in which the assumption of independence between the racial composition of the district and turnout rates for each group might be relaxed. Using MCMC, the posterior distributions of these tenuously identified quantities might be more accurately assessed and reliably recovered than is possible using the asymptotic normal theory and importance resampling approach described by King (1997).

REFERENCES

Aitchison, J. and S. M. Shen. 1980. "Logistic-Normal Distributions: Some Properties and Uses," *Biometrica*, 67: 261–272.

Bobo, Lawrence and Franklin Gilliam. 1990. "Race, Sociopolitical Participation, and Black Empowerment." *American Political Science Review*, 84, June: 277–293.

Gamerman, Dani. 1997. *Markov Chain Monte Carlo: Stochastic Simulation for Bayesian Inference*. New York: Chapman & Hall.

Gay, Claudine. 2001. "The Effect of Black Congressional Representation on Political Participation." *The American Political Science Review*, 94, 3: 589–602.

Gilks, W. R., N. G. Best, and K. K. C. Tan. 1995. "Adaptive Rejection Metropolis Sampling," *Applied Statistics*, 44: 455–472.

Goodman, Leo. 1959. "Some Alternatives to Ecological Correlation." *American Journal of Sociology*, 64: 610–25.

Hertzog, Mark Wm. 1994. "White Flight in the Voting Booth: The Racial Composition of Localities and Partisan Voting in Virginia in 1980s." In Matthew Holden, Jr. (ed.), *The Challenge to Racial*

Stratification. National Political Science Review, Volume 4. New Brunswick, NJ: Transaction Publishers.

Key, V. O. 1949. *Southern Politics*. New York: Knopf.

King, Gary. 1997. *A Solution to the Problem of Ecological Inference: Reconstructing Individual Behavior from Aggregate Data*. Princeton, NJ: Princeton University Press.

King, Gary, Bradley Grofman, Greg Adams, Micah Altman, Kenneth Benoit, Claudine Gay, Jeffrey B. Lewis, Russ Mayer, and Eric Reinhardt. 1997. "The Record of American Democracy, 1984–1990." Harvard University, Cambridge, MA [producer], Ann Arbor, MI: ICPSR [distributor].

King, Gary, Martin Tanner, and Ori Rosen. 1999. "Binomial-beta hierarchical models for ecological inference," *Sociological Methods and Research*, 28, 61–90.

Kleppner, Paul. 1985. *Chicago Divided: The Making of a Black Mayor*. DeKalb, IL: Northern Illinois University Press.

Kullback, S. and R. A. Liebler. 1951. "On Information and Sufficiency." *Annals of Mathematical Statistics*, 22: 525–40.

Lewis, Jeffrey B. 2002. "Comment on McCue, K. F. 2001."The Statistical Foundations of the EI Method'" *The American Statistician*, 55: 106–110.

Morris, Thomas R. and Neil Bradley. 1994. "Virginia." In Chandler Davidson and Bernard Palmquist (eds.), *Quiet Revolution in the South: The Impact of the Voting Rights Act, 1965–1990*. Princeton: Princeton University Press.

Rivers, Douglas. 1998. "Review of 'A Solution to the Problem of Ecological Inference.'" *The American Political Science Review*, 92: 442–443.

Robinson, W. S. 1950. "Ecological Correlation and the Behavior of Individuals." *American Sociological Review*, 15: 351–357.

Sabato, Larry. 1981. *Virginia Votes, 1983–1986*. Charlottesville, VA: University of Virginia, Institute of Government.

Sabato, Larry. 1991. *Virginia Votes, 1987–1990*. Charlottesville, VA: University of Virginia, Institute of Government.

Schexnider, Alvin J. 1990. "The Politics of Pragmatism: An Analysis of the 1989 Gubernatorial Election in Virginia," *PS: Political Science and Politics*, 23, 3: 154–156.

Strickland, Ruth Ann and Marcia Lynn Whicker. 1992. "Comparing the Wilder and Gantt Campaigns: A Model for Black Candidate Success in Statewide Elections," *PS: Political Science and Politics* 25, 2: 204–212.

Tate, Katherine. 1994. *From Protest to Politics: The New Black Voters in American Elections*. Cambridge, MA: Harvard University Press.

Traugott, Michael W. and Vincent Price. 1992. "A Review: Exit Polls in the 1989 Virginia Gubernatorial Race: Where Did They Go Wrong," *Public Opinion Quarterly*, 36, 2: 245–253.

Wakefield, Jon C. 2001. "Ecological Inference for 2 × 2 Tables." Typescript Washington University.

Zellner, Arnold. 1962. "An Efficient Method of Estimating Seemingly Unrelated Regressions and Tests for Aggregation Bias," *Journal of the American Statistical Association*, 57: 348–368.

5 Ecological Regression and Ecological Inference*

Bernard Grofman and Samuel Merrill

ABSTRACT

We propose three methods of ecological inference that guarantee feasible solutions but are simpler to implement than the method of King (1997). Each procedure provides estimates at the level of the ecological unit as well as a more aggregated level. The first method uses a simple squared distance minimization algorithm on the tomographic line segments. The second also generates a distance minimization, but in a space keyed to the slopes and intercepts of possible regression lines. The third determines the regression line that minimizes the sum of the areas between it and pairs of constraint line segments that are generated by a variant of the Duncan–Davis method of bounds. The procedures are implemented on an Excel spreadsheet and are available over the Internet. We present empirical applications, for which the first and third methods yield results that are quite similar to those produced by King's algorithm.

5.1 INTRODUCTION

In ecological inference we seek to make use of data that is aggregated at the level of ecological units to make inferences about the behavior of individuals. The ecological fallacy (Robinson, 1950) occurs when relationships between variables that obtain at the aggregate level are not found at the individual level. In this chapter three methods of ecological inference are proposed that are simpler than the sophisticated statistical models offered by King and his colleagues.

King estimates the unknown parameters of interest using maximum likelihood estimation (MLE) methods on a truncated bivariate normal or Beta distribution overlaid on the tomographic lines in (β^b, β^w) space. The first of our three methods uses a simple squared distance minimization algorithm on the tomographic lines. The district level solution is that point on the district tomographic segment that minimizes the (weighted) sum of the squared distances to the feasible tomographic line *segments* for the ecological units. For each unit the estimates for the parameters of interest are the coordinates of the nearest point on the unit tomographic line segment to the district solution. The analytic solution we obtain from this method is very similar to that of the Goodman regression model, but – unlike regression – our approach guarantees feasible solutions at both the precinct and the district level.

The second and third methods we propose can each be thought of as forms of *constrained* Goodman ecological regression. The first of these latter methods generates a

* A previous version of this work was presented at the Ecological Inference Conference, June 17–18, 2002, at Harvard University, Cambridge, MA. The listing of authors is alphabetical. The first-named author is indebted for helpful conversations with John DiNardo and Anthony Salvanto, and for comments on a much earlier draft of this paper by Gary King. Errors remaining are solely the responsibility of the authors.

distance minimization in (m, b) space (where m and b are the slope and intercept of possible regression lines) rather than in (β^b, β^w) space. The last method operates in the original (X, T) space and finds the regression line that minimizes the sum of the areas between it and pairs of constraint line segments that are generated by a variant of the Duncan–Davis method of bounds.

These methods demonstrate that the contrast between ecological regression in the form proposed by Goodman (1953, 1959) and ecological inference of the sort described in King (1997) is too easily exaggerated. Each uses either King's extension of the Duncan–Davis (1953) method of bounds or a simple variant thereof. Each operates without any assumptions about the distribution of parameters, but bootstrap standard errors can be obtained to assess the results.

We compare the results of our methods with that of King for several artificial and real data sets. Our methods are implemented in Excel spreadsheets, which are available on the websites `http://www.cbrss.harvard.edu/events/eic/book.htm` and `http://course.wilkes.edu/Merrill/`. Two of the three methods produce results that are, in general, very close to those produced by King's algorithms.

5.1.1 Background

Since the critiques of scholars such as Robinson (1950), the use of ecological methods to attempt to specify individual level behavior from data that is available only at the level of ecological units has been both uncommon in the social sciences and highly suspect. It is now well known that ecological methods can sometimes yield quite misleading estimates, even of apparently simple statistics such as correlations. There have been a variety of attempts to resuscitate the use of ecological methods, such as the efforts of Goodman (1953, 1959) and Duncan and Davis (1953) to provide ecological estimates a solid statistical footing. In particular, these methods have been adopted for use in the analysis of racial bloc voting data in legal challenges to districting plans brought under the Voting Rights Act or the Fourteenth Amendment (Grofman, 2000).[1] But it is only following publication of Gary King's (1997) seminal work on ecological inference that the use of aggregate data on ecological units for purposes of directly inferring (mean levels of) *individual* behavior among individuals (entities) sorted into dichotomous or polychotomous categories has been undergoing a renaissance in political science research.

King (1997) argues that his approach to ecological inference is superior to Goodman's classic form of ecological regression for a number of reasons. Most notably, it makes use of all the information available about the data and the bounds on feasible parameter values, and guarantees that all estimates of unobservable individual parameters will be consistent with the feasible values for those parameters at the level of the ecological units used for analysis. While it is widely accepted that King (1997) represents a major advance on earlier methods such as Goodman's bivariate approach to ecological regression, King's approach to ecological inference has also been subject to strong attacks by scholars in both political science

---

[1] In voting rights challenges to districting plans (brought under Section 2 or Section 5 of the Voting Rights Act of 1965 as amended in 1982, or brought directly under the Fourteenth Amendment), analysis of voting by race was a legally mandated component of any litigation. Because survey data on local (or even state) elections is rarely available, analyses of the relationship between aggregate level voting patterns in the elections (usually measured at the precinct level) and the racial characteristics of these aggregate units has been used to make inferences about how members of each race are voting (Grofman and Migalski, 1988; Grofman, 1992). Despite the general disrepute of ecological methods over the past three decades, one area where ecological methods have been used by necessity is in the analysis of patterns of racial voting.

(Cho, 1998, 2001; Cho and Yoon, 2001; Anselin and Cho, 2002) and statistics (Freedman, Klein, Sachs, Smyth, and Everett, 1991; Freedman, Ostland, Roberts, and Klein, 1999). These authors argue that there are circumstances where his methods will be either inconclusive or wrong and that errors in inference may go undetected by his diagnostics. Others have argued that King overstates the distinctness of his approach from that of more traditional estimation techniques (McCue, 2001).

5.1.2 Proposed Methods

Our primary focus in this paper is not on critiques of ecological inference methods, but on offering three new methods of ecological inference that are easy to explain and very easy to calculate, e.g., using just an Excel spreadsheet. We suggest that each of these methods, which uses either King's extension of the Duncan–Davis method of bounds or a simple variant thereof, has many of the same nice properties as the methods proposed by King (1997) and King, Rosen, and Tanner (1999).[2] We will demonstrate that the contrast between Goodman-style ecological regression and ecological inference in the style of King is not so great as may appear.[3]

For simplicity of exposition, we will only look at bivariate analyses of the sort that can be done using the basic version of King's EZI computer program. We illustrate ecological methods as they might be applied to ascertain patterns of voting behavior in biracial contests involving at least one white candidate and one black candidate, using aggregate data (gathered, let us say, at the precinct level).[4] Here, we wish to understand what proportion of each group's votes go to a candidate identified with their own group.[5] Of course, our results have a much broader applicability than to the specific context of racial bloc voting.

We establish notation similar to that specified in Chapter 1:
For the ith *precinct*, let

X_i = proportion of the voters that are black,
T_i = proportion of the vote that goes to the black candidate,
β_i^b = proportion of black voters who vote for the black candidate,
β_i^w = proportion of white voters who vote for the black candidate.

For the entire *district*, let

X = proportion of the voters that are black,
T = proportion of the vote that goes to the black candidate,

---

[2] For more on this point see Grofman and Merrill (2002) and Silva de Mattos and Veiga (this volume, Chapter 15).

[3] Although this stark contrast is not King's own view (personal communication, 2001), we believe that, in large part because of the way the contrasts are emphasized in King (1997), most who have read this book have viewed King's method of ecological inference and Goodman's approach to ecological regression as almost completely opposite in nature.

[4] We will assume for convenience that we are only dealing with two groups of voters and that these two groups are mutually exclusive and exhaustive. As noted earlier, we refer to them as "black" and "nonblack," with "white" as a synonym for "nonblack." We also present our analyses for situations in which there is only one minority candidate, but extensions to situations with more than one minority candidate are straightforward.

[5] Analysis of racial bloc voting patterns is a context where it has been argued that the likely problems of ecological inference are minimized (Grofman, 1991, 1993, 2000). In that context, empirically, most methods yield very similar estimates, and methods such as standard ecological regression, when correctly applied and interpreted, have withstood legal challenges as well as challenges by expert witnesses skeptical of their accuracy.

B^b = proportion of black voters who vote for the black candidate,
B^w = proportion of white voters who vote for the black candidate.

The organization of this chapter is as follows.

We illustrate the direct link between the Goodman approach to ecological regression and the Duncan–Davis method of bounds, and we provide a theorem that allows us to derive a condition under which the results of the King (1997) approach and the answer obtained by ecological regression will be identical.

Next, we specify three "new" methods of ecological inference that use straightforward minimization algorithms that can be solved simply, e.g., using the Solver function in an Excel spreadsheet. For certain special cases, we can provide closed-form analytic solutions for these methods. Each of these methods draws, either directly or in transformed form, on King's (1997) seminal idea of using the Duncan–Davis (1953) method of bounds to construct line segments on which all feasible values of the unknown parameters must lie.

The first of these new methods operates in the same (β^b, β^w) space as that of King (1997). Rather than using MLE methods involving a truncated normal distribution or the Beta (see King, Rosen, and Tanner, 1999) or some other distribution, we solve a simple distance minimization problem to obtain the best-fitting joint prediction of the mean values of B^b and B^w. We then look at the projections from that point to the precinct-specific constraint boundaries (line segments) in (β^b, β^w) space to determine the best estimates of the individual β_i^b and β_i^w values.

The last two of our new methods can be viewed as variants of the Goodman ecological regression approach. They first produce a best estimate of the overall best-fitting bivariate regression, which yields feasible district values of B^b and B^w, and then use proximity to that line to generate precinct-specific estimates of the slopes m_i and intercepts b_i for the best-fitting overall regression lines for each precinct, from which the β_i^b and β_i^w values can be inferred. Empirically, we compare the results of our methods with the results of King's methods for artificial and real data sets.

5.2 ANALYZING THE LINK BETWEEN INDIVIDUAL BEHAVIOR AND BEHAVIOR RECORDED AT THE AGGREGATE LEVEL

We first illustrate the Duncan–Davis method and the simplest form of King's (1997) ecological inference model with an eleven-precinct set of hypothetical data (see Table 5.1) for which all methods will give essentially the same answer.

In each precinct, by the accounting identity,

$$T_i = \beta_i^b X_i + \beta_i^w (1 - X_i), \qquad (5.1)$$

and similarly, for the district as a whole,

$$T = \beta^b X + \beta^w (1 - X). \qquad (5.2)$$

While X and T are observable, the parameters of real interest, namely, the proportion of blacks who support the black candidate and the proportion of whites who support the black candidate, which we denote using β's, are unobservable. The problem is to get from the values we do know to those that we want to know about. By using the identity given

Table 5.1 Hypothetical illustrative eleven-precinct data set

Precinct	X_i Prop. black among voters	T_i Black cand. vote share	min β_i^b Min. black vote for black cand.	max β_i^b Max. black vote for black cand.	min β_i^w Min. white vote for black cand.	max β_i^w Max. white vote for black cand.
1	0.05	0.225	0.00	1.00	0.18	0.24
2	0.1	0.25	0.00	1.00	0.17	0.28
3	0.2	0.30	0.00	1.00	0.13	0.38
4	0.3	0.35	0.00	1.00	0.07	0.50
5	0.4	0.40	0.00	1.00	0.00	0.67
6	0.5	0.45	0.00	0.90	0.00	0.90
7	0.6	0.50	0.17	0.83	0.00	1.00
8	0.7	0.55	0.36	0.79	0.00	1.00
9	0.8	0.60	0.50	0.75	0.00	1.00
10	0.9	0.65	0.61	0.72	0.00	1.00
11	0.95	0.675	0.66	0.72	0.00	1.00
OVERALL MEAN	0.5	0.45	0.00	0.90	0.00	0.90
PRECINCT MEAN	0.5	0.45	0.18	0.89	0.04	0.75
GROUP POP	0.5	0.45	0.35	0.82	0.09	0.55

in Equation 5.1 above, which links T_i and X_i, with β_i^b and β_i^w, and combining it with our knowledge that vote proportions *must* lie between 0 and 1 (no ifs, ands, buts, or maybes), it is easy to show that any given pair of precinct values (X_i, T_i) gives rise to linear constraints on the feasible values of the β_i^b and β_i^w values for that precinct.

To see how this works, consider a simple example. Let us look at the data from Precinct 7 in Table 5.1. In that precinct, we have $X_i = 0.6$ and $T_i = 0.5$. Now, since 60% of the voters in the precinct are black and the black candidate got only 50% of the vote, *at most* five-sixths of the black voters (= 50%/60%) voted for the black candidate. On the other hand, even if all the white voters voted for the black candidate, since only 40% of the voters are white, *at least* one-sixth [= (50% − 40%)/60%] of the black voters must have supported the black candidate. Similarly, it is mathematically possible that every single white voter voted for the black candidate, and it is also possible that none of the white voters did so. By using data only from this precinct, the bounds we get on feasible patterns of black voting in the precinct do tell us that (given the actual X_i and T_i values) we must have between one-sixth and five-sixths of the black voters in that precinct supporting the black candidate, but the proportion of white voters who supported the black candidate could be anywhere between 0% and 100%.

The Duncan–Davis (1953) method can be used to get tight bounds either in precincts that are racially homogeneous or in precincts that vote lopsidedly for a candidate of one race. We have shown in Table 5.1 the maximum and minimum values of β_i^b and β_i^w for each of the eleven precincts. It is apparent that, for Precinct 1, the most heavily white precinct, although the bounds on the black vote are not at all informative, we can pin down the proportion of white voters supporting the black candidate as falling between 18% and 24%. Similarly, for Precinct 11, the most heavily black precinct, although the bounds on the white vote are not at all informative, we can pin down the proportion of black voters supporting the black candidate as falling between 66% and 72%.

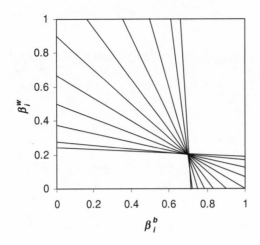

Figure 5.1. Tomographic plot for data in Table 5.1.

5.2.1 Tomographic Plots

When $X_i = 0.6$ and $T_i = 0.5$, not only is it true that $(\frac{1}{6}, 1)$ and $(\frac{5}{6}, 0)$ are feasible outcomes, but it is easy to see that all points on the line segment between the points $(\frac{1}{6}, 1)$ and $(\frac{5}{6}, 0)$ are also feasible, and are given by the equation

$$\beta_i^w = -\frac{3}{2}\beta_i^b + \frac{5}{4}$$

The only portion of this line that is of interest is the line segment containing the feasible values, i.e., the values on this line that lie at or between the points $(\frac{1}{6}, 1)$ and $(\frac{5}{6}, 0)$. We show in Figure 5.1 the precinct-based constraints on the joint (β_i^b, β_i^w) pairs for the data in Table 5.1. This type of joint constraint diagram, known as a *tomographic plot*, with values plotted in (β^b, β^w)*space*, was first introduced into the social sciences by King (1997) on p. 81 of his book, and used repeatedly thereafter.

Understanding what such a diagram shows is absolutely critical to understanding King's approach to the problem of reliable ecological inference and our own similar approaches. It is also critical to understanding alternative approaches such as the neighborhood model of Freedman et al. (1991).

Note that all the feasibility constraint lines in Figure 5.1 intersect at a single point (.70, .20). The parameter values at this intersection point correspond to the estimate for the mean value of the unobserved parameters we get from Goodman's ecological regression for the same data set. King's EZI algorithm also yields these same mean values for this data set, as it usually does when the tomographic segments meet at a point.

We now offer a simple result linking the values in the tomographic plots generated as the basis for King's method of ecological inference and the results of the classic Goodman ecological regression for the special case of the feasibility constraint lines intersecting at a single point.

Theorem 1. If the tomographic line segments used as the basis for King's ecological inference have a unique intersection, this intersection will be at a point, $(\hat{B}^b, \hat{B}^w)$, which corresponds to the (B^b, B^w) values derived from Goodman's method of bivariate ecological regression.

Proof. See Appendix 1.

Unfortunately, even when there is a unique intersection point of the tomographic plot lines, that intersection need not be within the unit square, i.e., need not be a feasible value.[6] Indeed, we might anticipate that, even in the absence of a unique intersection of the line segment bounds in the tomographic plot, when Goodman's ecological regression method yields a feasible estimate of mean (B^b, B^w) values, it is likely that the results of Goodman's approach and that of King's approach to ecological inference will not be far apart. The differences between the two approaches appear likely to arise when Goodman's ecological regression yields out-of-bounds estimates for one or more of the mean (or precinct specific) parameters. We will return to this issue, i.e., the circumstances under which different methods are likely to give rise to different answers, later in the chapter.

5.3 A SIMPLE DISTANCE MINIMIZATION ALGORITHM FOR ECOLOGICAL INFERENCE: METHOD I

It follows from equations (1) and (2) that

$$\beta_i^w = \frac{-X_i}{1 - X_i} \beta_i^b + \frac{T_i}{1 - X_i} \tag{5.3}$$

and

$$B^w = \frac{-X}{1 - X} B^b + \frac{T}{1 - X}. \tag{5.4}$$

In the example specified in Table 5.1, $B^w = -B^b + 0.9$, and similar equations hold for each precinct. Any pair of (B^b, B^w) values that lie on the district line segment specified in Equation 5.4 is compatible with the overall pattern of racial bloc voting in this data. But which point on this line segment is the most plausible estimate of this pair of values?

A simple approach is to look to see how far the various points on this line are from the other line segments in the tomographic plot. If, for example, there is a unique intersection of all the other line segments with each other, then the aggregate line-segment bound must also pass through that intersection. In this special case, it would seem that a very compelling case can be made for choosing the intersection point as our "best" estimate of the (B^b, B^w) values, at least if that point consists of jointly feasible values. In general, we can find the squared distance from each point on the aggregate line segment to each of the precinct line segments, and find the point that minimizes the (weighted) sum of those distances. Such distances will be interpreted later.

Our plan is to compute numerically – for each point on the overall tomographic constraint line defined by Equation (4) – the sum of the squared distances from that point to each of the precinct-level tomographic line *segments*. If the perpendiculars to the precinct-level tomographic lines intersect these lines at points in the feasible region, then a closed form solution for (B^b, B^w) can be derived (see Equations 5.13a and 5.13b below). If, instead, a perpendicular to a precinct-level tomographic line falls outside the feasible region, the shortest distance from a given point on the district line to the precinct-level segment must

---

[6] If, for example, the (X, T) values are (.3, .2), (.5, .5), and (.7, .8), the tomographic lines intersect at $\beta^b = 1.25$ and $\beta^w = -0.25$, which represent a point outside the unit square.

be computed to the nearer endpoint of the segment. The specifications of these endpoints P_1 and P_2 follow simple rules:[7]

$$\text{If } T_i \leq 1 - X_i \text{ then } P_1 = \left(0, \ \frac{T_i}{1 - X_i} \right);$$

$$\text{otherwise } P_1 = \left(\frac{T_i - (1 - X_i)}{X_i}, 1 \right). \tag{5.6a}$$

$$\text{If } T_i \geq X_i \text{ then } P_2 = \left(1, \ \frac{T_i - X_i}{1 - X_i} \right);$$

$$\text{otherwise } P_2 = \left(\frac{T_i}{X_i}, 0 \right). \tag{5.6b}$$

To implement this plan, it remains only to determine formulas for the points of intersection (to be used when they lie in the feasible region). As noted above, we have

$$\beta_i^w = \frac{-X_i}{1 - X_i} \beta_i^b + \frac{T_i}{1 - X_i} \tag{5.7}$$

as the equation for each precinct constraint line. If (B^b, B^w) lies on the aggregate constraint line, the line through this point and perpendicular to a precinct constraint line given by Equation 5.7 is given by

$$\beta_i^w = \frac{1 - X_i}{X_i} \beta_i^b + B^w - \frac{1 - X_i}{X_i} B^b. \tag{5.8}$$

The point of intersection of the precinct constraint line and this perpendicular is given by

$$\beta_i^b = \frac{X_i T_i - B^w X_i (1 - X_i) + B^b (1 - X_i)^2}{X_i^2 + (1 - X_i)^2} \tag{5.9}$$

and β_i^w can then be obtained from Equation 5.8.

In general, what we want to do is find the point on the district-level tomographic line that minimizes the sum of the squared distances from that point to all the line segments that define the precinct-specific joint bounds on the β_i^b and β_i^w values. First note that, from Equation 5.8,

$$\beta_i^w - B^w = \frac{1 - X_i}{X_i} \left(\beta_i^b - B^b \right),$$

---

[7] Note that the conditions on T_i in Equations 5.6a and 5.6b need not be complementary; it is the two conditions within 5.6a and within 5.6b that are complementary. In the degenerate case for which $X_i = 1$, if $T_i \leq 1 - X_i$ then $P_1 = (0, 1)$; if $T_i \geq X_i$ then $P_2 = (1, 0)$.

so that the square of the distance from (B^b, B^w) to the precinct constraint line, i.e., to the point of intersection given by Equation 5.9, is

$$d_i^2 = (\beta_i^b - B^b)^2 + (\beta_i^w - B^w)^2$$

$$= (\beta_i^b - B^b)^2 \frac{X_i^2 + (1 - X_i)^2}{X_i^2}. \qquad (5.10)$$

However, using Equation 5.9, we obtain

$$\beta_i^b - B^b = \frac{X_i T_i - B^w X_i (1 - X_i) - X_i^2 B^b}{X_i^2 + (1 - X_i)^2}.$$

Together with Equation 5.10, this implies that

$$d_i^2 = \frac{\left[T_i - X_i B^b - (1 - X_i) B^w \right]^2}{X_i^2 + (1 - X_i)^2}$$

$$= w_i^2 \left[T_i - X_i B^b - (1 - X_i) B^w \right]^2, \qquad (5.11)$$

where the weights w_i are given by

$$w_i = \frac{1}{\sqrt{X_i^2 + (1 - X_i)^2}}.$$

Note that the distance d_i can be interpreted as the weighted difference between the proportion of voters for the black candidate in the ith precinct and what that proportion would be if the proportions voting for the black candidate broken down by race were given by B^b and B^w, that is, the same as in the district as a whole. Hence, it makes sense to seek values of B^b and B^w that would minimize the squares of these differences. In fact, the numerator in Equation 5.11 is $(T_i - \hat{T}_i)^2$, where $\hat{T}_i$ is the ith fitted value under Goodman regression.

If all points of intersection are in the feasible region, we simply minimize $\sum_i d_i^2$ subject to the constraint that B^b and B^w are feasible (lie on the district constraint line), i.e., that

$$X B^b + (1 - X) B^w = T. \qquad (5.12)$$

Solving this constrained optimization problem by Lagrange multipliers, we obtain two linear equations in B^b and B^w:

$$B^b \sum_i w_i^2 X_i (X_i - X) + B^w \sum_i w_i^2 (1 - X_i)(X_i - X) = \sum_i w_i^2 T_i (X_i - X),$$

$$B^b X + B^w (1 - X) = T,$$

which yield the solutions

$$B^b = \frac{\sum_i w_i^2 (X_i - X)\left[(1-X)T_i - (1-X_i)T\right]}{\sum_i w_i^2 (X_i - X)^2},$$ (5.13a)

$$B^w = \frac{\sum_i w_i^2 (X_i - X)\left[X_i T - X T_i\right]}{\sum_i w_i^2 (X_i - X)^2}.$$ (5.13b)

Thus, in the special case in which all intersection points are in the feasible region, we have obtained closed-form solutions for B^b and B^w. These solutions are simple to compute on a spreadsheet and closely resemble the form of solutions to an ordinary least squares regression problem.[8] However, in solving our optimization problem, we are only interested in points of intersection (β_i^b, β_i^w) that specify *feasible* values for the respective precincts. Accordingly, if the point of intersection is outside the feasible region, we modify d_i^2 to be the squared distance to the nearer endpoint of the precinct line segment where it intersects the boundary of the feasible region. We then choose those values of B^b and B^w that lie on the district tomographic line and that minimize $\sum_i d_i^2$.

Standard errors and confidence intervals can be computed by a bootstrap method. This is done by repeated sampling with replacement from the data set, recomputing the parameter estimates, and determining the standard deviation of these estimates (see Efron and Tibshirani, 1993).

Each precinct-level estimate is the pair (β_i^b, β_i^w) that minimizes the expression $(\beta_i^b - B^b)^2 + (\beta_i^w - B^w)^2$. It is the intersection point of the perpendicular to the precinct tomographic line if this value is feasible, and otherwise is the nearest endpoint of the precinct tomographic line segment to the district solution point (B^b, B^w). These computations can be implemented in an Excel spreadsheet and are available on the websites http://www. cbrss.harvard.edu/events/eic/book.htm and http://course.wilkes. edu/Merrill/ through Internet Explorer.

District parameter estimates for Method I are presented later for several artificial and real data sets in Tables 2–4; precinct-level estimates are given for one real data set in Table 3. These results are discussed in Section 5.5.

If not all precincts are of equal size, we weight the d_i^2 by the number N_i of voters in precinct i, i.e., we minimize $\sum N_i d_i^2$. Equations 5.13a and 5.13b are replaced by

$$B^b = \frac{\sum_i w_i^2 N_i (X_i - X)\left[(1-X)T_i - (1-X_i)T\right]}{\sum_i w_i^2 N_i (X_i - X)^2},$$ (5.14a)

$$B^w = \frac{\sum_i w_i^2 N_i (X_i - X)\left[X_i T - X T_i\right]}{\sum_i w_i^2 N_i (X_i - X)^2}.$$ (5.14b)

---

[8] In this special case, the solution would be identical to the ordinary least squares solution if the weights w_i in Equation 5.13 were all identical.

5.4 EXTENDING THE DUNCAN–DAVIS METHOD OF BOUNDS TO DEVELOP TWO NEW FORMS OF GOODMAN'S ECOLOGICAL REGRESSION APPROACH: METHODS II AND III

King's ecological inference approach makes use of tomographic plots that constrain the values of unobservable individual-level parameters (β_i^b and β_i^w) to lie within feasible bounds for each of the ecological units. Ecological inference uses maximum likelihood methods to derive overall estimates of these unobservable parameters. We show that Goodman's approach to ecological regression can be adapted to make use of distance minimization methods that constrain the values of slope and intercept parameters so that the estimates of the unobservable individual-level parameters (β_i^b and β_i^w), and the mean values for those parameters, remain within feasible bounds. Indeed, we provide two different methods for doing so.

5.4.1 Adapting our Previous Distance Minimization Algorithm for Use in (m, b) Space Rather than (β^b, β^w) Space: Method II

Our first proposed integration of ecological inference and ecological regression uses a mathematical device to shift from the usual (X, T) space to a new space defined in terms of m and b, the slope and intercept parameters of the bivariate ecological regression. We derive the defining values for the line segments in that space from the Duncan–Davis (1953) method of bounds. Because

$$m = \beta^b - \beta^w$$

and

$$b = \beta^w,$$

we have

$$m = \left(b - \frac{T}{1-X} \right) \left(\frac{1-X}{-X} \right) - b = \frac{-b}{X} + \frac{T}{X}.$$

This expression may be rewritten as

$$T = mX + b.$$

For our example for which (X, T) = (.5, .45), the expression for the feasible overall line in (m, b) space is

$$m = -2b + 0.9.$$

Similar equations hold for each precinct.

Once we have constructed this set of equations, we apply the same methods as in the Section 5.3 to find the point on the line in the equation above that minimizes the (constrained) sum of squares to the various precinct-specific line segments. Only, now we are operating in (m, b) space rather than in (β^b, β^w) space.

The feasible region in (m, b) space is a diamond with corners at (0, 0), (0, 1), (−1, 1), and (0, 1). The squared distance from a point (m_0, b_0) on the district feasible line segment

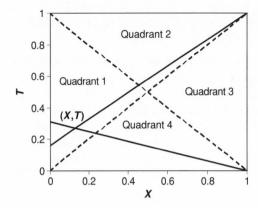

Figure 5.2. Quadrants for defining bounding lines for cones (dashed lines), with example of a pair of bounding lines through the point (X, T) (solid lines).

to a precinct feasible line segment is given by

$$d_i^2 = \frac{X_i^4}{(1 + X_i^2)^3}(b_0 + T_i - m_0 X_i)^2$$

if the foot of the perpendicular to the precinct line lies in the diamond, and otherwise by the distance to the nearest endpoint on that line segment. Because the transformation from the feasible square of (β^b, β^w) space to the diamond of (m, b) space alters distances, the minimization problems in Methods I and II are not identical. Simple examples show that precincts with symmetric patterns are treated symmetrically in (β^b, β^w) space, but not in (m, b) space.[9] As expected, Method II yields estimates for (B^b, B^w) that may be quite different from those obtained by King (1997) or by our Method I (or by our Method III below).

5.4.2 Operating Directly in (*X, T*) Space on the Set of Feasible Regression lines: Method III

Here we seek to build into the Goodman ecological regression approach the constraints on feasible values generated by the Duncan–Davis (1953) method of bounds. We now specify a pair of regression lines in the original (X, T) space that give bounds, for each ecological unit, for the jointly feasible values of m_i and b_i derived from the set of constraints on jointly feasible β_i^b and β_i^w values.

5.4.3 Defining the Cone of Feasible Values

Consider a point (X_i, T_i) that is an observed value for a given ecological unit (such as a precinct). If an ecological regression line passing through that point is to yield values of m and b that are feasible, it must be the case that the regression line intersects the line $X = 0$ somewhere between $T = 0$ and $T = 1$ and that it also intersects the line $X = 1$ somewhere

---

[9] For example, consider a district with three precincts with $(X_i, T_i) = (.3, .1)$, $(.5, .5)$, and $(.7, .9)$. The first and third precincts are symmetric in all respects and are equidistant from (and symmetric to) the district tomographic line segment in (β^b, β^w) space. In (m, b) space, however, the optimizing point on the district line is closest to an interior point on the feasible segment for precinct 1 but to an endpoint for the feasible segment for precinct 3. The distances involved are not the same.

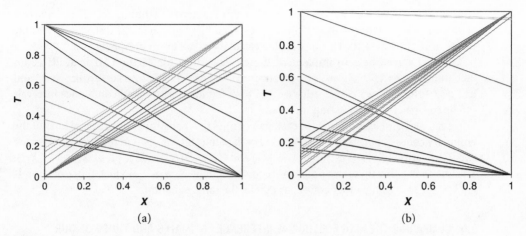

Figure 5.3. Bounding lines for cones of feasible values for 11 precincts for data from (a) Table 1, (b) Carter.

between $T = 0$ and $T = 1$. To see how these constraints apply, divide the unit square in standard (X, T) space into quadrants, as shown in Figure 5.2.

In quadrant 1, define a cone of feasible values passing through a point (X_i, T_i) by requiring that one defining (extremal) line of the cone pass through the point $(1, 0)$ and the other defining line pass through $(1, 1)$. Similarly, for points in quadrant 2, the defining lines of the cone must pass through $(0, 1)$ and $(1, 1)$; for points in quadrant 3 they must pass through $(0, 0)$ and $(0, 1)$; for points in quadrant 4 they must pass through $(0, 0)$ and $(1, 0)$. For points in quadrant 1, one of the two defining lines of the cone [that which passes through the point $(1, 0)$] must be a line whose m value is equal to $-T_i/(1 - X_i)$ and whose b value is equal to $T_i/(1 - X_i)$, while the other defining line [that which passes through the point $(1, 1)$] must be a line whose m value is equal to $(1 - T_i)/(1 - X_i)$ and whose b value is equal to $(T_i - X_i)/(1 - X_i)$.

In like manner, the cone of feasible regression lines for points in quadrant 2 is characterized by a bounding line with m value equal to $(1 - T_i)/(-X_i)$ and b value equal to 1, and a second bounding line with m value equal to $(1 - T_i)/(1 - X_i)$ and b value equal to $(T_i - X_i)/(1 - X_i)$. The cone for quadrant 3 is characterized by a bounding line with m value equal to T_i/X_i and b value equal to 0, and a second bounding line with m value equal to $(1 - T_i)/(-X_i)$ and b value equal to 1. Finally, the cone for quadrant 4 is characterized by a bounding line with m value equal to T_i/X_i and b value equal to 0, and a second bounding line with m value equal to $-T_i/(1 - X_i)$ and b value equal to $(T_i)/(1 - X_i)$. We can illustrate these boundary lines for the set of data in Table 5.1 (Figure 5.3a), and for an 11-precinct data set drawn from a real-world biracial legislative contest in the Deep South in the 1990s (Figure 5.3b; see also Section 5.5).

Our plan is to choose values of m and b that satisfy the district-wide constraint

$$T = mX + b,$$

i.e.,

$$m = (T - b)/X,$$

and minimize the sum of the areas between this line segment and the bounding line segments of the cones associated with the precinct values X_i and T_i. These areas are restricted to feasible values of X_i, i.e., $X_i \in [0, 1]$. The detailed calculations are given in Appendix 2.

An Excel spreadsheet to implement these calculations for Method III is available on the websites `http://www.cbrss.harvard.edu/events/eic/book.htm` and `http://course.wilkes.edu/merrill/`. Standard errors and confidence intervals can be constructed by bootstrap methods.

We can plot the (m, b) values for each pair of lines that constitute the extremal lines of the boundary cones as points in (m, b) space. For example, if (X_i, T_i) is in quadrant 1, then the two points are $(-T_i/(1 - X_i), T_i/(1 - X_i))$ and $((1 - T_i)/(1 - X_i), (T_i - X_i)/(1 - X_i))$. The line connecting these two points has equation $b = -X_i m + T_i$. In fact, the corresponding line for each of the other cones has exactly the same equation.

5.5 COMPARING THE KING ECOLOGICAL INFERENCE ESTIMATES AND THOSE OF OUR SIMPLIFIED APPROACHES

Aggregate parameter estimates produced by the basic version of King's (1997) MLE program and the estimates generated by our distance- or area-minimizing algorithms are typically similar to one another, but need not be identical. We show this in Table 5.2 for three hypothetical data sets (data sets A, B, and C).

The circumstances in which King's basic method and our least squares and area-minimizing approaches can be expected to give more divergent results occur when heavily truncated tomographic line segments pull the solution away from a more plausible

Table 5.2 Parameter estimates for B^b and B^w by alternative methods for artificial data sets

Data set	Parameter	King's method	Method I	Method II	Method III	Regression
				Value		
A	B^b	.838 (.005)	.830 (.023)	.839	.828 (.022)	.833 (.020)
	B^w	.282 (.005)	.290 (.017)	.281	.292 (.015)	.287 (.020)
B	B^b	.713 (.053)	.748 (.066)	.580	.656 (.069)	1.500 (.000)
	B^w	.287 (.053)	.252 (.077)	.420	.344 (.086)	−.500 (.000)
C	B^b	.917 (.024)	.829 (.083)	.672	.937 (.135)	1.007 (.035)
	B^w	.083 (.024)	.171 (.098)	.328	.063 (.166)	−.007 (.035)

Data set A:

X	0.10	0.18	0.26	0.34	0.42	0.50	0.58	0.66	0.74	0.82	0.90
T	0.34	0.37	0.44	0.50	0.53	0.52	0.64	0.59	0.69	0.75	0.79

Data set B:

X	0.30	0.34	0.38	0.42	0.46	0.50	0.54	0.58	0.62	0.66	0.70
T	0.10	0.18	0.26	0.34	0.42	0.50	0.58	0.66	0.74	0.82	0.90

Data set C:

X	0.10	0.15	0.20	0.80	0.85	0.90
T	0.05	0.15	0.25	0.75	0.85	0.95

Note: Bootstrap standard errors are given in parentheses.

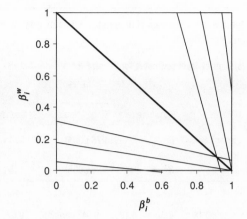

Figure 5.4. Tomographic plot for data set C. (Bold line is the district tomographic line.)

convergence of other, less-truncated tomographic line segments. A case in point is data set C (see Table 5.2 and Figure 5.4). Here the endpoints (.5, 0) and (1, .5) on tomographic line segments 1 and 6 have what appear to be inordinate effects on the parameter estimates for Method I. For this data set, Method III and King's method provide a more polarized but more plausible solution than Method I. The facts that not more than 50% of the blacks vote for the black candidates in Precinct 1 (in our example scenario) and not less than 50% of the whites vote for the black candidate in Precinct 6 may seem inconsistent with the rest of the district. Yet, given the small number of blacks in Precinct 1 and small number of whites in Precinct 6, such statistics may commonly occur due to random variation.

5.5.1 Weighting by Informativeness

Precincts that are mostly black are most informative in estimating B^b, whereas those that are mostly white are most informative in estimating B^w. Accordingly, we define a version of Method I *weighted by informativeness* by replacing the raw distance between (B^b, B^w) and a precinct tomographic line segment with a metric in which the coordinates are weighted by the proportions of blacks and whites. Thus, we define weighted squared distance

$$N_i \left[X_i \left(\beta_i^b - B^b \right)^2 + (1 - X_i) \left(\beta_i^w - B^w \right)^2 \right],$$

where N_i is the number of voters in precinct i, and where we recall that X_i and $1 - X_i$ are the proportions of blacks and whites, respectively, in the electorate. Given this weighting, if all minimizing points (β_i^b, β_i^w) do lie in the feasible region, the solution for (B^b, B^w) is identical with that of ecological regression.

For data set C, weighting the coordinates by the proportions of blacks and whites makes a substantial difference. The weighted estimates (see Table 5.4) for (B^b, B^w) are (.957, .043), in contrast to unweighted estimates of (.829, .171). King's estimates (.917, .083) are intermediate, and closer to our weighted estimates.

In practice, when we are looking at data from U.S. elections involving candidates of more than one race (especially data from the South), most methods are apt to yield values of at least the aggregate parameters B^b and B^w that are reasonably close to one another.[10] To

---

[10] In the specific context of racial bloc voting analyses, they are also likely to be not very different from the estimates generated by ecological regression, at least when those estimates are within (0,1) bounds (Grofman, 2000).

Table 5.3 Comparison of parameter estimates from methods I–III and King's method for the Carter 11-precinct data set

(a) District-level estimates for B^b and B^w

Data set	Parameter	King's method	Method I	Method II	Method III	Regression
				Value		
Carter 11-precinct sample	B^b	.978 (.005)	.974 (.043)	.940	.964 (.059)	.974 (.026)
	B^b	.136 (.005)	.138 (.016)	.155	.144 (.016)	.138 (.017)

Carter data:

X	0.13	0.67	0.16	0.04	0.33	0.02	0.04	0.02	0.31	0.99	0.95
T	0.27	0.69	0.20	0.14	0.39	0.23	0.16	0.16	0.43	0.96	0.95

Note: Bootstrap standard errors are given in parentheses.

(b) Precinct-specific estimates of β_i^b and β_i^w for the Carter data set

Precinct	β_i^b				β_i^w			
	King	Method I	Method II	Method III	King	Method I	Method II	Method III
1	0.9580	0.9783	0.9540	0.9556	**0.1672**	**0.1642**	**0.1678**	**0.1675**
2	**0.9683**	**0.9643**	**0.9503**	**0.9588**	0.1250	0.1331	0.1616	0.1443
3	0.9383	0.9587	0.8484	0.9927	**0.0591**	**0.0555**	**0.0765**	**0.0490**
4	0.9500	0.9730	0.8914	0.9786	**0.1063**	**0.1053**	**0.1087**	**0.1051**
5	0.9546	0.9602	0.9108	0.9701	**0.1119**	**0.1092**	**0.1335**	**0.1043**
6	0.9592	0.9760	1.0000	0.9346	**0.2151**	**0.2148**	**0.2143**	**0.2156**
7	0.9474	0.9739	0.9121	0.9703	**0.1272**	**0.1261**	**0.1287**	**0.1262**
8	0.9562	0.9745	0.9286	0.9635	**0.1438**	**0.1434**	**0.1443**	**0.1436**
9	0.9700	0.9921	0.9775	0.9542	**0.1874**	**0.1775**	**0.1840**	**0.1945**
10	**0.9683**	**0.9683**	**0.9680**	**0.9683**	0.1428	0.1380	0.1695	0.1416
11	**0.9924**	**0.9927**	**0.9905**	**0.9930**	0.1448	0.1391	0.1813	0.1322

Note: Estimates of β_i^b for majority black precincts and of β_i^w for majority white districts are indicated in bold.

see this consistency, we turn to working through two real-world examples: an 11-precinct sample of data (Carter data set) from a biracial legislative contest in a Deep South state in the 1980s, and a 284-precinct sample from the 1995 gubernatorial race in Louisiana, which included a prominent black candidate, Cleo Fields.[11] Our first data set was chosen to have a small number of precincts so as to demonstrate that even for small data sets, if patterns are clear enough, it is relatively easy to see what is happening.

For the Carter data set, King's EZI gets a mean value of (B^b, B^w) of (.978, .136) (see Table 5.3a). Our three estimates for the district parameters are (.974, .138), (.940, .155), and (.964, .144) for Methods I, II, and III, respectively. Note that, even though Method II has the potential to give results quite different from Methods I and III or from King's basic EZI program, in this real-world data set the three methods give results that are not very different. Furthermore,

---

[11] Cleo Fields was a state senator and former U.S. representative from majority black districts (see Voss, 1999, for further background).

Table 5.4 Comparison of Method I estimates, unweighted and weighted for informativeness

Data set	Parameter	Value		
		Method I unweighted	Method I weighted	King's method
Data set C	B^b	.829	.957	.917
	B^w	.171	.043	.083
Carter 11-	B^b	.974	.972	.978
Precinct set	B^w	.138	.139	.136
Cleo Fields	B^b	.874	.900	.901
284-precinct set	B^w	.025	.015	.014

for the Carter data set (see Table 5.4) the Method I estimates weighted for informativeness are (.972, .139), almost identical with the unweighted Method I estimates (.974, .138).

We can also compare precinct-specific values of β_i^b and β_i^w. We show those estimates for our three methods, along with the corresponding values from King's truncated normal MLE method, in Table 5.3b. Again there is very high consistency in the estimates, particularly – as expected – for estimates of β_i^b for majority black precincts and of β_i^w for majority white districts. These precincts are identified in bold in Table 5.3b. Indeed, the maximum difference between our Method I and King's method in estimating the β_i^b and β_i^w values for the majority race is 0.004, while the maximum difference for the corresponding estimates for the minority race is 0.027. These results are summarized in Figure 5.5, which plots the precinct-level estimates β_i^b (Figure 5.5a) and β_i^w (Figure 5.5b) for each of our three methods and King's method versus the black proportion of the population. It is apparent that – except for Method II – the estimates of β_i^b are almost identical to each other for heavily black precincts and that the estimates of β_i^w are almost identical to each other for heavily white precincts.

The Cleo Fields data set involves 284 precincts, many of which were heavily white or heavily black. We would expect these to be most informative about the voting behavior of the respective majority races. Table 5.4 compares the parameter estimates for Method I – weighted and unweighted – with those of King, for both the Carter and Cleo Fields data sets as well as for data set C. Unlike the Carter data set, the Cleo Fields data set shows significant differences when weighting is used; the weighted estimates of Method I are almost identical with those of King.

5.6 DISCUSSION

Since the least-squares and area minimization approaches we have offered are less general than King's method,[12] why might anyone care about results derived from them? There are several reasons. First, each generates closed-form solutions that are trivial to calculate, albeit the distribution of precinct specific values each generates cannot be characterized as a particular standard type (e.g., a truncated bivariate normal). In particular, because of the simplicity of the numerical calculations needed for our methods, it is practical to extend

---

[12] For example, to be comparable to the more advanced versions of King's program we would need to develop some explicit way of building in covariates.

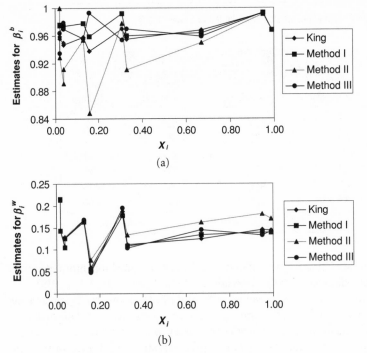

Figure 5.5. Precinct-level Estimates of (a) β_i^b and (b) β_i^w by King's method and our three methods for Carter data.

them from 2×2 to $m \times n$ tables, as has been shown by De Sio (2003). Second, each has a very simple mathematical exposition,[13] and can be described in reasonably intuitive terms.[14] Third, each offers either an indirect or a direct analogue to the OLS approach to ecological regression, but with the advantage that parameter results are constrained to feasible values. Fourth, although the following question needs considerable more investigation, based on our explorations so far, it appears likely that two of these simple methods (Methods I and III) will closely approximate the results generated by the basic MLE approach in King's (bivariate) EZI program. Finally, a comparison of the simple optimization aspects of our methods with the MLE approach of King, and comparisons among the three methods we introduce, shed some light on how ecological inference works and when it might be expected to fail.

APPENDIX 1. PROOF OF THEOREM 1

Theorem 1. If the tomographic line segment bounds used as the basis for King's ecological inference have a unique intersection, this intersection will be at a point, $(\hat{B}^b, \hat{B}^w)$, which corresponds to the (B^b, B^w) values derived from Goodman's method of bivariate ecological regression.

---

[13] The Monte Carlo nature of the MLE estimation procedure, combined with the complexities of estimating a truncated normal distribution, renders King's procedures much more complex than those we propose.

[14] Grofman and Merrill (2002) discuss criteria for a good solution to the problem of ecological inference, and Silva de Mattos and Veiga (this volume, Chapter 15) assess the predictive ability of several methods, including those of Goodman and King.

Proof. If $(\hat{B}^b, \hat{B}^w)$ lies on all the constraint lines of a tomographic plot, the coordinates $\hat{B}^b$ and $\hat{B}^w$ must satisfy

$$T_i = \hat{B}^b X_i + (1 - X_i)\hat{B}^w$$

for all i. Thus, after averaging, we have

$$T = \hat{B}^b X + (1 - X)\hat{B}^w$$

as well, where X and T are the (weighted) averages for the entire district. But the slope coefficient of ecological regression is given by

$$\hat{m} = \frac{\sum (X_i - X) T_i}{\sum (X_i - X)^2},$$

where

$$\begin{aligned}
\sum (X_i - X) T_i &= \sum (X_i - X)\left[\hat{B}^b X_i + (1 - X_i)\hat{B}^w\right] \\
&= \sum X_i - X)\left[X_i(\hat{B}^b - \hat{B}^w) + \hat{B}^w\right] \\
&= \sum (X_i - X)\left[(X_i - X)(\hat{B}^b - \hat{B}^w)\right] + \sum (X_i - X)\hat{B}^w \\
&= \sum (X_i - X)^2\left[\hat{B}^b - \hat{B}^w\right],
\end{aligned}$$

and where we have twice used the fact that $\sum (X_i - X) = 0$.

It follows that

$$\hat{m} = \hat{B}^b - \hat{B}^w.$$

But then the intercept of ecological regression is given by

$$\begin{aligned}
\hat{b} = T - \hat{m}X &= (\hat{B}^b X + (1 - X)\hat{B}^w) - (\hat{B}^b X - \hat{B}^w X) \\
&= \hat{B}^w,
\end{aligned}$$

so that $\hat{B}^b$ and $\hat{B}^w$ are equal to the parameter estimates of ecological regression. *q.e.d.*

APPENDIX 2. AREA CALCULATIONS FOR METHOD III

Before we tackle the general problem of minimizing the areas between the line $m = (T - b)/X$ and the bounding line segments of the cones associated with the precinct values X_i and T_i, we begin by specifying the area between any two lines contained in the range $X \in [0, 1]$. Let one line be $T_{(1)} = m_1 X + b_1$, and the other be $T_{(2)} = m_2 X + b_2$. These lines intersect at $X_c = -(b_2 - b_1)/(m_2 - m_1) = -\Delta b/\Delta m$, where $\Delta b = b_2 - b_1$ and $\Delta m = m_2 - m_1$.

There are two cases, depending on whether $X_c \in [0, 1]$, i.e., whether $0 \le -\Delta b/\Delta m \le 1$. We summarize cases and results in the table below:

Case	Intersection	Area between two lines
I	Outside $X_c \in [0, 1]$	$\left| \dfrac{\Delta m}{2} + \Delta b \right|$
II	Within $X_c \in [0, 1]$	$\left| \dfrac{(\Delta b)^2}{\Delta m} + \dfrac{\Delta m}{2} + \Delta b \right|$

To verify the results given in the table, we look at the relevant integrals. For case I, the area between the two lines is given by the absolute value of

$$\int_0^1 \left[T_{(2)} - T_{(1)} \right] dX = \int_0^1 \left[m_2 X + b_2 - m_1 X - b_1 \right] dX = \frac{1}{2} \Delta m + \Delta b.$$

Similarly, for case II, if $b_1 < b_2$, the areas between the two lines are given by

$$\int_0^{-\Delta b/\Delta m} \left[T_{(2)} - T_{(1)} \right] dX + \int_{-\Delta b/\Delta m}^1 \left[T_{(1)} - T_{(2)} \right] dX$$

$$= \int_0^{-\Delta b/\Delta m} \left[m_2 X + b_2 - m_1 X - b_1 \right] dX + \int_{-\Delta b/\Delta m}^1 \left[m_1 X + b_1 - m_2 X - b_2 \right] dX$$

$$= \int_0^{-\Delta b/\Delta m} \left[(\Delta m) X + \Delta b \right] dX - \int_{-\Delta b/\Delta m}^1 \left[(\Delta m) X + \Delta b \right] dX$$

$$= \frac{1}{2} \frac{(\Delta b)^2}{\Delta m} - \frac{(\Delta b)^2}{\Delta m} + \frac{1}{2} \frac{(\Delta b)^2}{\Delta m} - \frac{(\Delta b)^2}{\Delta m} - \frac{1}{2} \Delta m - \Delta b$$

$$= -\frac{(\Delta b)^2}{\Delta m} - \frac{1}{2} \Delta m - \Delta b.$$

If, instead, $b_1 \geq b_2$, the same result is obtained without the negative signs. In each case, the area is positive and hence is the absolute value of the expression. q.e.d.

Now, we can solve the general problem by finding the line whose b value minimizes the sum of the appropriate areas for each pairing between that line and the other lines in the set, subject to the constraint that the m and b values of that line must satisfy the equation $T = mX + b$.

REFERENCES

Anselin, Luc and Wendy Tam Cho. 2002. "Spatial Effects and Ecological Inference." *Political Analysis*, 10: 276–297.

Cho, Wendy Tam. 1998. "Iff the Assumption Fits . . . : A Comment on the King Ecological Inference Solution." *Political Analysis*, 7: 143–163.

Cho, Wendy Tam. 2001. "Latent Groups and Cross-Level Inferences." *Electoral Studies*, 20, 2: 243–263.

Cho, Wendy Tam and Albert H. Yoon. 2001. "Strange Bedfellows: Politics, Courts, and Statistics: Statistical Expert Testimony in Voting Rights Cases." *Cornell Journal of Law and Public Policy* 10, 2: 237–264.

De Sio, Lorenzo. 2003. "A Proposal for Extending King's EI Method to $m \times n$ Tables." Transcript: University of Florence.

Duncan, Dudley and Beverley Davis. 1953. "An Alternative to Ecological Correlation." *American Sociological Review*, 18: 665–666.

Efron, Bradley and Robert Tibshirani. 1993. *An Introduction to the Bootstrap*. London: Chapman and Hall.

Freedman, David, S.P. Klein, J. Sacks, C.A. Smyth and C.G. Everett. 1991. "Ecological Regression and Voting Rights." *Evaluation Review*, 15, 6: 673–711.

Freedman, David, M. Ostland, M.R. Roberts, and S.P. Klein. 1999. "The Future of Ecological Inference Research: A Comment on Freedman et al. – Response to King's Comment. *Journal of the American Statistical Association*, 94, 445: 355–357.

Goodman, Leo. 1953. "Ecological Regression and the Behavior of Individuals." *American Sociological Review*, 18, 6: 663–664.

Goodman, Leo. 1959. "Some Alternatives to Ecological Correlation." *American Journal of Sociology*, 64: 610–625.

Grofman, Bernard. l991. "Statistics without Substance: A Critique of Freedman et al. and of Clark and Morrison." *Evaluation Review*, 125, 6: 746–769.

Grofman, Bernard. 1992. "Expert Witness Testimony and the Evolution of Voting Rights Case Law." In Bernard Grofman and Chandler Davidson (eds.), *Controversies in Minority Voting: The Voting Rights Act in Perspective*. Washington, DC Brookings Institution.

Grofman, Bernard. 1993. "Voting Rights in a Multi-ethnic World." *Chicano-Latino Law Review*, 13, 15: 15–37.

Grofman, Bernard. 2000. "A Primer of Racial Bloc Voting." In Nathaniel Persily (ed.), *The Real Y2K Problem: Census 2000 Data and Redistricting Technology*. Brennan Center for Law and Justice, New York University, pp. 44–67.

Grofman, Bernard and Samuel Merrill, III. 2002. "What Does It Mean to Offer a 'Solution' to the Problem of Ecological Inference?" Typescript: University of California–Irvine.

Grofman, Bernard and Michael Migalski. l988. "Estimating the Extent of Racially Polarized Voting in Multicandidate Elections." *Sociological Methods and Research*, 16, 4: 427–454.

King, Gary. 1997. *A Solution to the Ecological Inference Problem*. Princeton, NJ: Princeton University Press.

King, Gary, Ori Rosen, and Martin Tanner. 1999. "Binomial-Beta Hierarchical Models for Ecological Inference." *Sociological Methods and Research*, 28, 1: 61–90.

McCue, Kenneth. 2001. "The Statistical Foundations of the EI Method." *American Statistician*, 55, 2: 106–110.

Voss, D. Stephen. 1999. "Racial Redistricting and the Quest for Legislative Diversity." Extensions of Remarks. *APSA Legislative Studies Section Newsletter* 22, July:11–14.

6 Using Prior Information to Aid Ecological Inference: A Bayesian Approach

J. Kevin Corder and Christina Wolbrecht*

ABSTRACT

This research concerns a long-standing historical question: How did previously disenfranchised women employ the ballot after suffrage extension in the United States? The absence of reliable survey data from the 1920s and the ecological fallacy have frustrated efforts to learn about the voting behavior of women in this period. The ecological inference problem is particularly difficult in the case of sex differences. In contrast to many other politically interesting groups (e.g., racial and ethnic minorities), women are generally not characterized by particular residential patterns; as a result, there is minimal variation in the percent female across units. We address this challenge, and the ecological inference problem generally, by (1) introducing new, highly disaggregated election returns and census data; (2) adding nonsample information from the historical context to inform our estimates (specifically, the previous electoral behavior of men and the easily defensible assumption that male turnout exceeds female turnout); and (3) taking advantage of the existence of one state, Illinois, where male and female ballots were tabulated separately in 1916 and 1920. We adopt and investigate the performance of a hierarchical binomial–normal model developed by Wakefield (2001). The results suggest that, while estimates can be highly contingent on investigator assumptions, a hierarchical strategy coupled with a limited number of uncontroversial assumptions can generate plausible estimates of turnout by gender.

6.1 INTRODUCTION

This research concerns a set of puzzles: (1) how did previously disenfranchised women employ the ballot after suffrage extension, and (2) how can individual-level relationships be inferred from aggregate data? These two questions have long been intertwined. The earliest political science article to identify what would become known as the ecological inference problem was a study of how newly enfranchised women cast their votes in a 1914 election (see King, 1997). Ogburn and Goltra (1919) were addressing a question of considerable scholarly and political interest: Did women employ the ballot – in this case, for substantive ballot initiatives – in some way distinct from that of long-enfranchised men? With the final struggle for ratification of the Nineteenth Amendment underway when the article was published, this was not merely a question for social scientists, but one of great concern to candidates, parties, and political observers.

The question of how American women employed their new right remains largely unanswered some eighty years later. The reason is a familiar one to students of ecological inference: As put simply by Ogburn and Goltra, "women's ballots are not distinguished from those of

* We gratefully acknowledge the support of the Faculty Research Program at the University of Notre Dame, the Research Development Award Program at Western Michigan University, and the National Science Foundation (SES-9905843 and 9905307).

men but are deposited in the same ballot box" (1919, p. 413). That is, we lack individual-level observations of electoral behavior and associated demographics, such as sex. Although Ogburn and Goltra report the results of a multivariate analysis of aggregate (precinct-level) female turnout and vote choice data, they were correct to be concerned about the reliability of their findings. An inability to overcome the ecological fallacy, combined with a lack of survey data from the 1920s, has meant that scholars have been unable to adequately examine the way in which a full half of the population was incorporated into the electorate.

Estimates of women's turnout after suffrage can allow us to investigate a number of important substantive puzzles concerning the political capabilities and preferences of women, the way in which any new voters adapt to their new right, and the stability of the electoral system. The first challenge, however, is to produce reliable estimates of female turnout. That task is the focus of this paper. The ecological inference problem is particularly difficult in the case of sex differences. In contrast to many other politically interesting groups (e.g., racial and ethnic minorities, immigrants, social classes), women are generally not characterized by particular residential patterns; as a result, there is minimal variation in the percent female across units.

We address this challenge, and the ecological inference problem generally, in three ways. First, we increase the variation in percent female and increase the number of observations by employing data at the lowest available level of aggregation. In a number of states, we are able to supplement available county-level data with previously untapped election and census records at the level of the Minor Civil Division (MCD), the primary geopolitical subdivisions of counties, and the urban ward. Second, we add nonsample information from the historical context to inform our estimation. Specifically, previous research and available records allow us to confidently assume that female turnout did not exceed male turnout in 1920. We also exploit the existence of an immediately prior election in which men's turnout is known: True male turnout in 1916 is used to inform our estimation of male and female turnout in 1920. Finally, we take advantage of the existence of one state, Illinois, where male and female ballots were tabulated separately in 1916 (Illinois granted women presidential suffrage in 1913) and 1920. True values from Illinois are used to verify assumptions and evaluate the estimates.

Building on the work of King (1997) and Wakefield (2001; this book, Chapter 1), we use a Bayesian approach to ecological inference to estimate the turnout of women in the 1920 presidential election. Specifically, we investigate the performance of a hierarchical binomial normal model developed in Wakefield (2001) and based on similar Bayesian approaches described in King, Rosen, and Tanner (1999). We identify the effects of various state-level priors on MCD-level estimates of male and female turnout. We summarize the effects of adding information via priors with a simple visual technique – comparing plots of estimated female turnout as a function of estimated male turnout across different settings of the priors.

The results suggest that, while estimates can be highly contingent on investigator assumptions, a hierarchical strategy coupled with a limited number of uncontroversial assumptions can generate plausible estimates of turnout by gender. The estimation strategy recovers the observed turnout of men and women in 1920 Illinois and demonstrates the utility of adding a limited amount of information, via assumption and hierarchy, to a complex estimation problem with limited information in the sample data.

6.2 DATA

In this Chapter, we estimate female turnout in three states: Illinois, Connecticut, and Massachusetts. We make no claim that this small selection of states is representative of the broader

Table 6.1 Sample States for Analysis

State	ICPSR[a] region	Party competition[b]	Electoral College vote share
Connecticut	New England	One-party Republican	1.3
Illinois	East North Central	One-party Republican	5.5
Massachusetts	New England	One-party Republican	3.4

[a] Inter-University Consortium for Political and Social Research.

[b] For each state, Burnham (1981) calculates the difference between the two parties' median shares of seats in the lower house of the state legislature over a particular period of electoral history. He terms this difference the "partisan lead." As Burnham (1981: p. 176) writes, "a median lead of 40 percent or more for either party . . . is indicative of one-party hegemony at the grass roots level." We consider states in that category to be one-party states. During the 1914–1930 period, 33 of the 48 states (69 percent) are one-party states.

American electorate in 1920. Instead, we select these three states to highlight the problems and prospects of Bayesian approaches to ecological inference. Illinois is particularly useful in that true values for the parameters of interest are observed. Connecticut is added to the sample because it is possible to fully merge census and election returns at the level of the MCD (and, for Hartford, the urban ward). The total number of observations is roughly equal to that in the Illinois data, suggesting that the influence of priors and data on posterior estimates should be comparable for these states. We also investigate Massachusetts, also fully merged at the MCD and ward level, but summing to a much larger number of observations (nearly 450). In the broader project that motivated this paper, we examine a larger sample of states that provides variation in substantive conditions, such as region, party competition, and date of female enfranchisement. Table 6.1 displays the states examined in this analysis and their relevant characteristics.

Our goal is to employ election returns and census information at the lowest available level of aggregation in each state. This data collection strategy provides several important advantages. Smaller areal units provide greater variation in the various electoral behaviors and demographic characteristics of interest. A major advantage of aggregate-level analysis is the ability to locate behavior within its social and political context. By using the lowest available level of aggregation, we are able to be quite specific about the environments in which men and women participated in elections in the 1920s. We also increase the number of observations; in Connecticut alone, we move from 8 counties to 177 MCDs and urban wards. (The most important improvement over county-level data, which we do not exploit in this paper, is the ability to discriminate between rural and urban areas.)

Aggregate-level election returns, particularly at the level below the county, have not been systematically located and preserved (for a recent exception, see King and Palmquist, 1997). Fortunately, in both Connecticut and Massachusetts, MCD-level election returns are available from state publications.[1] In Illinois, however, MCD-level returns are not centrally published or archived. A county-by-county search located original MCD-level records for

---

[1] Specifically: *Connecticut Statement of Vote* (various years) and Massachusetts Public Document No. 43 (various years). In Connecticut, these data are supplemented by newspaper reports of the ward-level returns. For further information on the data, consult the overview and state-specific documentation on the project website (http://catt.friedmann.wmich.edu).

Table 6.2 Geographic units of sample states

State	Aggregation type	Number of observations	Average voting age population
Connecticut	Minor Civil Division	167	4,526
	Urban ward	10	8,279
Illinois	County	95	20,141
	City	1	21,550
	County less urban wards	1	29,440
	Ward	35	8,660
	Minor Civil Division	102	2,712
Massachusetts	Minor Civil Division	372	5,980
	MCD grouping	6	16,700
	Ward	109	10,850

8 of 102 counties covering 51 percent of the 1920 population (including Cook county and Chicago wards).[2] Election returns are merged with available demographic data published by the U.S. Census. Before 1930, the Census only reported MCD population totals. Beginning in 1930, other demographic characteristics, including sex, race, nativity, and age, are reported at the MCD level. We use a combination of census data from the county and MCD levels in 1920 and 1930 to estimate the number of voting age males and females in each MCD. Where redistricting and annexing led to changes in MCD boundaries, we aggregate several MCDs together into MCD groupings.[3] The geographic units used in the analysis are described in Table 6.2.

6.3 USING ECOLOGICAL INFERENCE TO ESTIMATE MALE AND FEMALE TURNOUT

Ecological inference relying on the marginal distribution of gender is particularly challenging. At high levels of aggregation the proportion female varies only slightly – from .49 to .54 across fourteen Massachusetts counties, for instance. At lower levels of aggregation, such as the urban ward, the proportion of women varies from .40 to .60. But extreme concentrations of men and women are observed only very rarely and represent distinct social anomalies. Women only make up 20 percent of the population in 1920 Dannemora, NY, for example, but most of the males are incarcerated in the town's state prison. Since the proportion of women varies only nominally, the information in the data, represented by the logical boundaries for male and female turnout, is more limited than for ecological inference problems involving demographic characteristics such as race or nativity. Tomography plots, a visual summary of the logically possible combinations of male and female turnout in each MCD, are reproduced for the states of Illinois and Connecticut as Figure 6.1. There are a few MCDs where the logical boundaries are highly informative – areas where turnout is very high or very low – but the logical boundaries for most MCDs are quite wide.

A second complication of the gender and vote data is aggregation bias. The Illinois data reveal severe aggregation bias in 1920. Since the State of Illinois recorded ballots of men and

---

[2] Source: *Blue Book of the State of Illinois* (various years), *Chicago Daily News Almanac and Year-Book* (various years), and original Statements of Vote held by county offices.

[3] For more information on the process of merging census and election data or for information on the estimation of MCD level census data, consult the project website (http://catt.friedmann.wmich.edu)

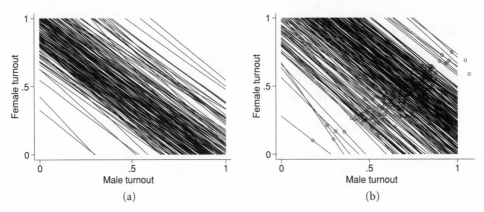

Figure 6.1. Tomography plots, 1920: (a) Connecticut; (b) Illinois (true values displayed).

women separately, we can observe true female turnout at the MCD, ward, or county level. Figure 6.2 summarizes the true relationship between female turnout and male turnout in Illinois. Each point identifies an MCD (or county) pair of observed male and female turnout. Since every point is below the main diagonal, there were no observed MCDs or urban wards or counties where female turnout exceeded male turnout in Illinois. In fact, male turnout exceeded female turnout by an average of over 25 percent. The ecological relationship between MCD proportion women and MCD aggregate turnout in Illinois and Massachusetts appears in Figure 6.3. As the proportion of women increases, aggregate turnout increases. The (mistaken) ecological inference is that women vote at higher levels than men. To overcome these problems of aggregation bias and wide logical bounds, we introduce nonsample information, in the form of historical data and uncontroversial substantive assumptions, to the problem.

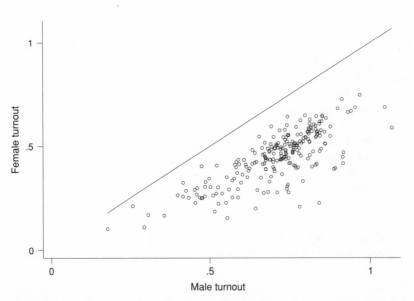

Figure 6.2. Female turnout by male turnout, Illinois, 1920.

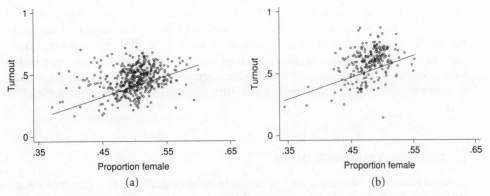

Figure 6.3. Aggregate turnout as a function of proportion female, 1920: (a) Massachusetts; (b) Illinois.

6.4 NONSAMPLE INFORMATION AND ECOLOGICAL INFERENCE

Approaches to ecological inference that rely exclusively on the logical boundaries implied by the MCD marginals or rely on strong assumptions about the absence of aggregation bias will fail in applications that are grounded in exploring gender differences. There is substantial aggregation bias, and the logical boundaries are quite wide. An alternative strategy is to locate and exploit nonsample information to improve estimates of female turnout. If there is a single claim that is common to proponents of the variety of approaches to ecological inference, it is that information outside of the sample data should inform estimates of parameters of interest. King (1997) and Achen and Shively (1995) directly describe the problem of ecological inference as an effort to narrow logical bounds by adding information. King, Rosen, and Tanner (1999) introduce a Bayesian modeling approach that relies on a hierarchical structure to introduce information from the aggregate to the estimates of quantities at lower levels of aggregation. Wakefield (2001) describes a more general hierarchical modeling strategy with the goal of understanding how elementary hierarchical structure and assumptions influence estimates. We adopt the Bayesian approach introduced by Wakefield to investigate the voting behavior of women. We extend the model by introducing two types of nonsample information.

Historical data on electoral behavior present a number of different types of information that a Bayesian modeling strategy could exploit. First, since only men were allowed to vote for some time, estimation of male and female turnout in 1920 offers a unique opportunity to incorporate out-of-sample information. Male turnout in the most recent previous presidential election (1916) is observed in Illinois (where male and female ballots are counted separately) and in other sample states (where the franchise was limited to males in 1916). These data can be collected and observed at the same level of aggregation that we use to estimate parameters in 1920. For this paper, we rely on priors for the state-level turnout of males to improve model performance at lower levels of aggregation.

Historical experience can also be applied to the problem in the form an uncontroversial assumption or constraint. Based on a variety of newspaper reports, election returns (from Illinois), and an extensive scholarly literature, male turnout is expected to be higher than female turnout. Newer, inexperienced voters are expected to be at least somewhat less active in exercising the right to vote and overcoming hurdles of procedure and information that affect levels of participation. New female voters were particularly hampered by strong social norms against female political activity. The assumption of lower female turnout holds at both high levels of aggregation (the state level) and lower levels of aggregation (such as the MCD). This assumption, coupled with the logical boundaries implied by the table marginals, suggests much narrower bounds for MCD-level outcomes than the unconstrained logical bounds would imply. In Section 6.7, we introduce a rejection sampling approach to constrain estimates to satisfy the assumption that male turnout exceeds female turnout at the MCD level.

6.5 INTRODUCING PRIOR INFORMATION

We use a hierarchical binomial normal model to estimate male and female turnout at the MCD level. Each observation (ward or MCD) is treated as a separate 2×2 table with known marginals (numbers of men and women and numbers of voters and nonvoters) and unknown interior cells (number of women voters). The model, elaborated by Wakefield (2001; this book, Chapter 1), describes the observed total number of votes cast in the MCD as a draw from a binomial distribution with parameters z_i and n_i. The probability that an individual votes (z_i) is the weighted sum of two independent probabilities: the probability of a vote by a female (p_{i1}) and the probability of a vote by a male (p_{i2}). (This step also introduces an accounting identity, the logical boundaries that are implied by the data.) Only three pieces of information from the MCD enter the likelihood: the number of votes cast (V), the number of males (M), and the number of females (F). The gender-specific probability of turnout in each MCD (p_{i1}, p_{i2}) is approximated normally via transformation to the logistic (θ_{i1}, θ_{i2}). The formal representation is uncomplicated:

$$V_i \sim \text{bin}(z_i, n_i),$$

$$z_i = x_i p_{i1} + (1 - x_i) p_{i2},$$

$$x_i = \frac{F_i}{M_i + F_i}$$

$$n_i = F_i + M_i,$$

$$p_{i1} = \frac{\exp(\theta_{i1})}{1 + \exp(\theta_{i1})},$$

$$p_{i2} = \frac{\exp(\theta_{i2})}{1 + \exp(\theta_{i2})}.$$

The primary assumptions of the modeling process are that the transformed probability of male turnout for each MCD observation (θ_{i2}) is drawn from a single underlying normal distribution and that the transformed probability of female turnout in each MCD is drawn from a separate underlying normal distribution. There are a number of alternative distributional assumptions to this binomial–normal model, depending on the approximation used for the total votes observed (binomial count or normal proportion) and the assumptions about how the unobserved and separate male and female probabilities are distributed (normal, Student's t, beta).

The hierarchy is introduced by specifying the normal distribution that describes the MCD logits. A highly aggregated (in this case, state-level) prior describes the location and precision of the normal distribution. Four pairs of hyperparameters (A_k, B_k) (C_k, D_k) introduce

Table 6.3 Summary statistics for male turnout: mean and precision in the scale of estimation, simple proportion, and population-weighted (actual) state turnout

Year	State	n	Mean (logit)	Precision (logit)	Turnout (unweighted)	Turnout (actual)
1916	Connecticut	177	0.42	3.55	0.601	0.515
1916	Illinois	234	1.29	1.21	0.760	0.681
1920	Illinois	234	0.95	2.11	0.707	0.643
1916	Massachusetts	477	0.18	3.44	0.540	0.505

information into the model:

$$\theta_{i1} \sim \text{norm}(\mu_1, \tau_1),$$

$$\theta_{i2} \sim \text{norm}(\mu_2, \tau_2),$$

$$\mu_1 \sim \text{norm}(A_1, B_1),$$

$$\mu_2 \sim \text{norm}(A_2, B_2),$$

$$\tau_1 \sim \text{gamma}(C_1, D_1),$$

$$\tau_2 \sim \text{gamma}(C_2, D_2).$$

At the second stage, each MCD-level probability is treated as a draw from a normal distribution with mean μ and precision τ.[4] The state-level mean is drawn from a normal distribution, and the precision from a gamma distribution. In most applications, this state-level mean and precision would be specified in a way that added little information to the model. A uniform distribution or nearly flat normal distribution centered around zero would be appropriate for the mean (implying values of 0.00 for A_k and 0.0001 for B_k). A similarly uninformative prior would be introduced for the gamma distribution. Our strategy is to instead introduce and exploit prior information about the mean and the precision of this state-level distribution – introducing information about both the normal distribution of the state-level mean and the gamma distribution for the state-level precision – to improve model estimates.

Data on male turnout in the 1916 election suggest a number of characteristics that should also describe the 1920 elections and that can be introduced as priors. Using data from the 1910 and 1920 census and 1916 election returns, we estimate turnout at the MCD level for the 1916 election. The logit for estimated male turnout in each state in 1916 and, as observed, in 1920 Illinois are reported in Table 6.3. The observed summary statistics for male behavior in 1916 are the state-level priors that we exploit to estimate 1920 turnout at the MCD level.[5] These data can also verify the adequacy of the distributional assumptions of the model. The distribution of the logit of male turnout in 1916 Illinois is displayed in Figure 6.4. The normal distribution would appear to provide a reasonable approximation for the observed distribution of male turnout.

---

[4] In Bayesian modeling contexts, the dispersion parameter of the normal distribution is typically designated not as the standard deviation or variance (σ^2), (but as the precision $(\tau = 1/\sigma^2)$.

[5] The expected value for gamma(C_k, D_k) is C_k/D_k. Here C_k and D_k should be selected to return an expected value equal to the observed precision in 1916.

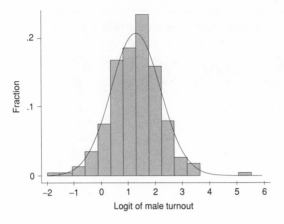

Figure 6.4. Distribution of male turn-out, 1916 Illinois (with normal overlay).

The implications of adding prior information in this context are not well understood. As noted in Chapters 1 and 2 in this volume, hierarchical modeling strategies for ecological inference are special in that the addition of more first-stage (MCD) observations does not result in more influence of the data on the posterior estimates. Even in very large samples, there is a limited amount of information about the parameters of interest. As a consequence, second- and third-stage assumptions, about both the form and the parameters of the distribution that generates the data, will always exert a substantial influence on posterior estimates. Further, the use of informed priors of any sort is not common practice in published political science work using Bayesian approaches (particularly Markov Chain Monte Carlo (MCMC) methods).

6.6 FINDINGS

Our strategy is to estimate a series of models, first varying the priors for the state mean (A_k), then the precision of the prior for the state mean (B_k), and finally the parameters of the gamma distribution (C_k, D_k) that are used to estimate the state-level variance of male and female turnout. The parameters of each model are estimated via MCMC as implemented in WINBUGS. The complete code for the binomial normal model (exclusive of the data) is included as an appendix to this chapter. To reduce the influence of starting points on the estimated parameters, we run five chains (each representing an independent simulation) with widely dispersed starting points for each model. A total of 350,000 simulations are performed for each model, with the first 100,000 observations discarded. The monitored chains are thinned to 2,500 observations for each node, and the mean of these observations serves as the point estimate. We do not report convergence diagnostics for each chain in each model, but convergence was monitored for both state-level and MCD-level parameters for each of the 30 models estimated. An elementary convergence diagnostic, Gelman and Rubin's R, indicates that the chains converge (see Gelman and Rubin, 1992). Within-chain autocorrelation, however, does remain large for a small number of MCD nodes. Experimentation with longer chain lengths, of 1,000,000 iterations or more, did not indicate a higher degree of convergence or result in substantively different posterior estimates.

Each model is summarized with a plot of female turnout as a function of male turnout. This graphical strategy reveals how the mean and variance of male and female turnout changes as priors are updated and permits direct comparison with the observed relationship in Illinois (reproduced as Figure 6.2 above). Each estimated pair of male and female turnout will fall along the tomography lines represented in Figure 6.1. In Section 6.7, we investigate the effects of an auxiliary MCD-level assumption, that the male turnout (p_{i2}) exceeds female turnout (p_{i1}).

6.6.1 Implications of Changes in the Expected Mean of Male Turnout

We assume that the true state-level male turnout is located between the level slightly above male turnout observed in 1916 and total observed turnout of men and women in 1920. This assumption implies two substantive claims: Male state-level turnout was higher than female turnout in 1920, and male turnout declined or only modestly increased after 1916. The justification for the former assumption (male turnout exceeds female turnout) is described above. There are several reasons to expect that male turnout declined after 1916. The 1920 election occurred during a period of generally declining turnout following the 1896 realignment. With the return to normalcy, the 1920 election itself was widely regarded as uninteresting and noncompetitive; Harding was elected president with over 61 percent of the vote, the largest landslide thus far in American history (Degler, 1964). Between 1916 and 1920, male turnout in presidential elections in Illinois, for instance, fell from 67.5% to 64.3%. The expectation that turnout generally was on the decline during this period has been noted often by scholars as a factor confounding attempts to disentangle the effects of female enfranchisement (Kleppner, 1982). On the other hand, the attention given to and the novelty of women's voting may have spurred men to vote at higher rates than they had in 1916; a number of newspaper reports, for example, suggested heightened participation by men due to women's entrance in to the electorate. In Illinois, men's turnout increased by nearly 5 percentage points, from 62.8 to 67.5 percent, between 1912 and the first Presidential election that included women voters in 1916. We therefore test the effect of alternative priors that imply that men's turnout either increased marginally after 1920 due to the introduction of women as voters or decreased substantially due to the lack of competition.

To measure the effect of choosing the prior (A_2), we select (1) a value that implies male turnout was just above female turnout (within 1 percentage point), (2) a value that implies male turnout was somewhat higher than in 1916, and (3) the midpoint between (1) and (2). The influence of priors is summarized in Figures 6.5, 6.6, and 6.7. Each figure represents estimates for one state. Each panel represents one set of priors. Precisions and other prior information (the parameters of the gamma distribution) are held constant for each state.

The effects of decision about priors are not the same across the sample states. In Illinois, the posterior point estimates for the hierarchical model with diffuse priors (a naive model) are very similar to the posterior point estimates for the models with more precise priors. Introduction of a hierarchy alone, without informed priors, generated estimates consistent with expectations and close to true values. In Connecticut, a diffuse prior resulted in wildly implausible estimates, with female turnout exceeding male turnout by large margins in some MCDs. Figure 6.6 suggests that modest differences in priors result in nontrivial changes in the estimates (estimated mean male turnout increases from to 52 to 60 percent as the location parameter is increased from 0.18 to 0.42). The introduction of an informative prior that implies male turnout remained at or near 1916 levels results in posterior point estimates that also conform to the MCD-level expectation that male turnout should exceed female turnout. There are no MCD observations above the main diagonal in the lower panels of Figure 6.6. But, in Massachusetts, a number of observations remain above the main diagonal, even with precise priors that result in mean male turnout remaining at 1916 levels. These observations, which are mostly urban wards in Boston, are areas where published registration figures indicate female turnout is quite low. These observations both violate the

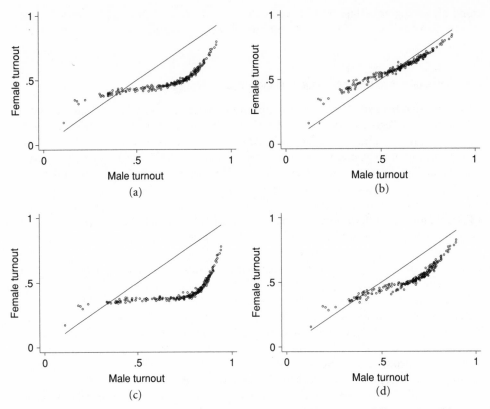

Figure 6.5. Influence of the location of state-level priors (Illinois): (a) diffuse prior; (b) $\mu_1 \sim$ norm(0.40, 20.00); (c) $\mu_1 \sim$ norm(0.76, 20.00); (d) $\mu_1 \sim$ norm(1.17, 20.00).

MCD-level assumption and are directly inconsistent with the historical record. We address this problem in Section 6.7, below.

6.6.2 Implications of Changes in the Precision of the Expected Mean Male Turnout

The locations of priors for the mean of male and female turnout are accompanied by precisions (B_k). High levels of precision imply estimates will lie close to the prior location. Lower levels of precision do not introduce as much information into the estimation procedure. The observed influence of the prior is a function of both the precision and the number of observations in the data set, so the appropriate level for the precision will be dependent on the number of observations. Applications that rely on noninformed priors typically use very low precisions (0.001) to permit a wide variance for the simulation of state-level parameters. We experiment with higher levels of precision (from 0.01 to 50.00) to learn how precisions of this magnitude affect estimates from data sets of varying size (from 177 observations in Connecticut to 447 observations in Massachusetts).[6]

---

[6] Precisions lower than 0.50 often result in numerical problems with the MCMC simulations. Low precisions permit draws of extremely high and low values for θ_k to be introduced, which imply turnout probabilities approaching zero and one. The logistic distribution is relatively compact, with most observed values between -3 and $+3$), so precisions on the order of 0.50, which loosely bound the logit, are reasonable starting points to test the effects of adding information.

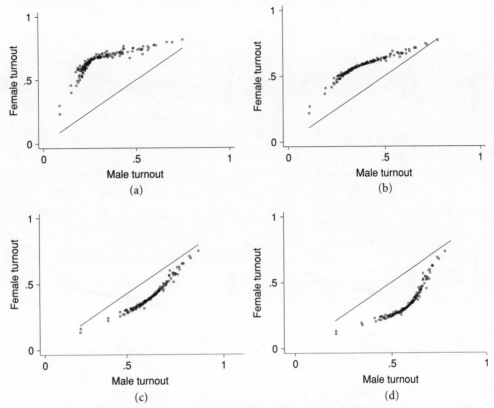

Figure 6.6. Influence of the location of state-level priors (Connecticut): (a) diffuse prior; (b) $\mu_1 \sim$ norm$(-0.03, 5.00)$; (c) $\mu_1 \sim$ norm$(0.18, 5.00)$; (d) $\mu_1 \sim$ norm$(0.42, 5.00)$.

As with the location parameter, the effects of increasing precision vary across the sample states. At low levels of precision ($B_k=1.00$), the posterior estimates are also quite imprecise. But the precision also affects the estimated mean turnout, and the magnitude of the effect is, as expected, related to the number of observations. Using the Connecticut data, a precision of 1.00 introduced sufficient information to generate a posterior estimate quite different from the posterior generated with a diffuse prior. A precision of 20.00 or more was required to produce similar effects with the Massachusetts data. Figure 6.8 displays the effects of high precisions on the Connecticut estimates; Figure 6.9 displays the effects of identical precisions on the Massachusetts estimates.

6.6.3 Implications of Changes in the Parameters of the Gamma Distribution

Historical data on turnout also provide information about the expected value of the variance of MCD observations about the state mean. The state-level precision is drawn from a gamma distribution that can be centered around observed 1916 values for males. Unlike the parameters for the mean, changes in the parameters of the gamma distribution have fairly modest effects on the turnout estimates. For each simulation, the parameters of the gamma distribution are set at the same values for men and women, implying similar variances at the MCD level. The Illinois data indicate that this assumption is reasonable. Connecticut MCD estimates for three very different settings of the gamma distribution are summarized

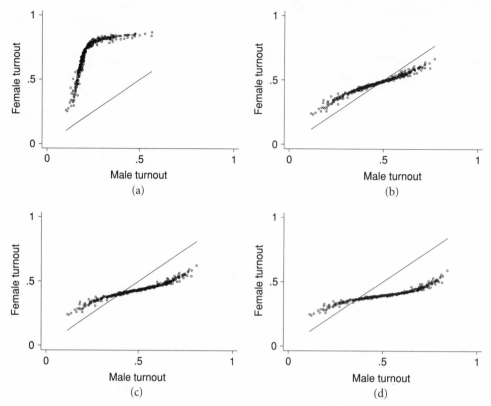

Figure 6.7. Influence of the location of state-level priors (Massachusetts): (a) diffuse prior; (b) $\mu_1 \sim$ norm(-0.09, 50.00); (c) $\mu_1 \sim$ norm(0.04, 50.00); (d) $\mu_1 \sim$ norm(0.14, 50.00).

in Figure 6.10. The mean for each pair of hyperparameters is the same, but the standard deviation varies across the panels. The top left panel introduces the least information; the lower right panel introduces the most information. The estimated mean male turnout increases from 0.50 to 0.53 as the level of information in the gamma prior is increased.

6.7 USING MCD-LEVEL ASSUMPTIONS TO IMPROVE ESTIMATES

The Bayesian approach recovers observed values in the state of Illinois and generates plausible estimates for a number of MCDs in Connecticut and Massachusetts. There are important exceptions – estimates for a limited number of MCDs and wards in Illinois suggest female turnout exceeds male turnout, and we know that this is not the case. The same result is observed in Massachusetts and persists even when high levels of precision are introduced. One way to address the problem observations is to sample from the distribution that describes the MCD-level parameters of interest and truncate the sample to satisfy the assumption that male turnout exceeds female turnout at the level of the MCD ($p_{i2} > p_{i1}$ or, in the notation of the introduction to this book, $\beta_i^b > \beta_i^w$).

The point estimates for female turnout at the MCD level summarize a chain of observed output from the MCMC simulations. Given the mean and the standard deviation of each chain, we use a simple rejection algorithm to draw 2500 values from the target distribution that satisfy two additional constraints: female turnout is less than average turnout, and

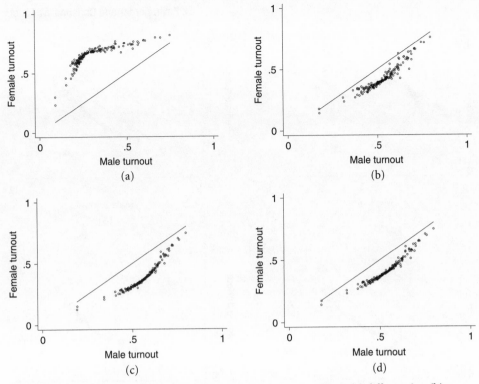

Figure 6.8. Influence of the precision of state-level priors (Connecticut): (a) diffuse prior; (b) $\mu_1 \sim$ norm(0.18, 1.00); (c) $\mu_1 \sim$ norm(0.18, 10.00); (d) $\mu_1 \sim$ norm(0.18, 50.00).

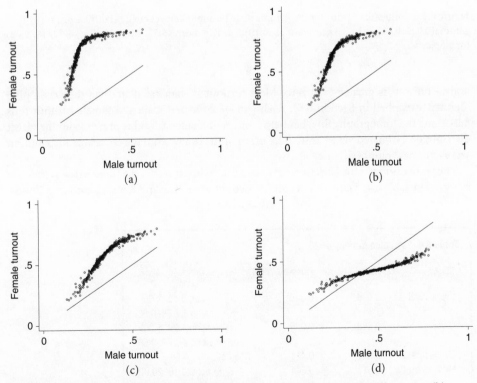

Figure 6.9. Influence of the precision of state-level priors (Massachusetts): (a) diffuse prior; (b) $\mu_1 \sim$ norm(0.04, 1.00); (c) $\mu_1 \sim$ norm(0.04, 10.00); (d) $\mu_1 \sim$ norm(0.04, 50.00).

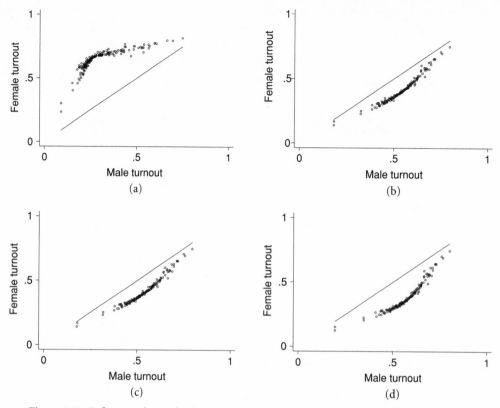

Figure 6.10. Influence of prior for the gamma distribution (Connecticut): (a) diffuse prior; (b) $\tau_i \sim$ gamma(0.035, 0.01); (c) $\tau_i \sim$ gamma(0.35, 0.10); (d) $\tau_i \sim$ norm(3.55, 1.00). Here $\mu_1 \sim$ (0.18, 5.00) for all panels.

female turnout is greater than zero. Male turnout is then calculated via the accounting identity (described in Section 6.5). Each pair of estimated male and female turnout thus falls along the tomography line, lies below the main diagonal, and is drawn from the target distribution estimated via MCMC. The mean of the draws from the truncated distribution serves as a new point estimate.

The point estimates for 1920 turnout in three sample states, and the Illinois true values, are reported in Table 6.4. The estimated difference between male and female turnout in Illinois

Table 6.4 Estimated turnout, 1920

State	Male turnout	Female turnout	Priors
Connecticut	0.614	0.248	$\mu_2 \sim$ norm(0.42, 2.00) $\tau_i \sim$ gamma(1.75, 0.50)
Illinois	0.698	0.355	$\mu_2 \sim$ norm(1.29, 5.00) $\tau_i \sim$ gamma(0.60, 0.50)
Illinois (actual)	0.643	0.411	[n/a]
Massachusetts	0.519	0.341	$\mu_2 \sim$ norm(0.18, 20.00) $\tau_i \sim$ gamma(1.70, 0.50)

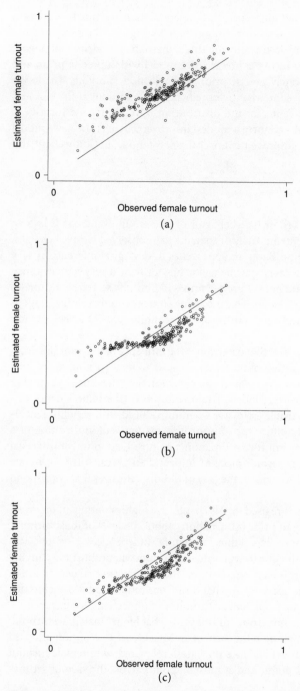

Figure 6.11. Estimated and observed female turnout, 1920 Illinois: (a) diffuse prior; (b) $\mu_1 \sim$ norm(1.18, 20.00); (c) $\mu_1 \sim$ norm(1.18, 5.00); with truncation ($p_{i1} < p_{i2}$).

is somewhat higher than the observed difference, but the population-weighted correlation between observed and actual male turnout in Illinois is 0.95. Figure 6.11 compares the estimated and actual values for female turnout for three alternative modeling strategies: the hierarchical model with diffuse priors, a hierarchical model with a precise prior, and a hierarchical model with a moderately precise prior after rejection sampling. The lower panel indicates that the final model somewhat overpredicts female turnout at the tails and somewhat underpredicts it at the center of the distribution. Overall, female turnout is slightly underpredicted. These results confirm a modest improvement over the naive model in Illinois and suggest a substantial improvement over the naive model in Connecticut and Massachusetts.

6.8 CONCLUSION

In research situations where observed or true behavior of one group of interest is known and this observation is related either temporally or spatially to unobserved sample behavior, information can be incorporated into Bayesian approaches to ecological inference at very high levels of aggregation. In some cases, past behavior may provide a very narrow range of plausible values for one group and permit precise priors to limit the search for estimates along the tomography line at the MCD level. This modeling strategy could exploit highly aggregated survey data, when available, to generate priors that condition MCD-level estimates on known quantities.

We identify a crucial model parameter that determines the influence of the prior information on posterior estimates – the location of the assumed mean of male turnout at the state level. If survey data are available to describe this mean behavior, then the crucial parameter can be specified with some confidence. Under certain conditions (the Illinois data), this prior information can produce plausible estimates when introduced with very little precision. In other cases (Massachusetts), this type of prior information is of limited use for a number of observations. To further improve estimation, we introduce an uncontroversial assumption at the MCD level. This second piece of information permits us to generate plausible estimates for all observations and, in the case of Illinois, estimates that correspond with observed behavior.

Estimates produced by the procedure used in this chapter are highly contingent on investigator assumptions (or the quality of prior information) about the level of male turnout. In the case of Illinois, the elementary hierarchical structure, independent of priors, was sufficient to generate estimates both close to true values and somewhat robust to changing priors. A precise prior at the highest level of aggregation (the state) permitted generation of estimates at very low levels of aggregation (the MCD) in Connecticut and Massachusetts. But, depending on the location of the prior, female turnout in Connecticut, for instance, either lagged a full 28 points behind male turnout or was somewhat higher than male turnout. Incorporation of additional information in the form of an MCD-level assumption imposed via rejection sampling reduced this dependence on state-level priors, with female turnout lagging male turnout by at least 17 points and at most 37 points across the various settings of the priors.

Full disclosure of assumptions and explicit consideration of the implications of changing these assumptions helps to communicate the level of uncertainty associated with each set of estimates in this application. Incorporation of more specific MCD-level priors for a limited number of observations (e.g., use of registration data from Boston wards) or consideration of spatial structure may permit estimation of parameters of interest without placing such a premium on assumptions about state-level outcomes.

APPENDIX. WINBUGS CODE

```
model for (i in 1:ntab)
# MCD Likelihood
V1920[i] ~ dbin(z[i], n[i])
z[i] <- (x[i] * p1[i]) + ((1 - x[i]) * p2[i])
x[i] <- F1920[i] / (M1920[i]+F1920[i])
n[i] <- F1920[i] + M1920[i]
p1[i] <- exp(theta[i, 1]) / (1 + exp(theta[i, 1]))
p2[i] <- exp(theta[i, 2]) / (1 + exp(theta[i, 2]))
# Second stage
theta[i,1] ~ dnorm(mu[1], tau[1])
theta[i,2] ~ dnorm(mu[2], tau[2])
# Third stage priors
mu[1] ~ dnorm(-0.44, 20.00)
mu[2] ~ dnorm(1.17, 20.00)
tau[1] ~ dgamma(0.50, 0.50)
tau[2] ~ dgamma(0.50, 0.50)
# Stste-level parameters of interest
mean[1]<- mean(p1[])
mean[2]<- mean(p2[])
# initial conditions
list(mu = c(-0.44, 1.17), tau = c(0.50, 2.0))
```

REFERENCES

Achen, Christopher H. and W. Phillips Shively. 1995. *Cross-Level Inference.* Chicago: University of Chicago Press.

Burnham, Walter Dean. 1981. "The System of 1896: An Analysis." In Paul Kleppner, Walter Dean Burnham, Ronald P. Formisano, Samuel P. Hays, Richard Jensen, and William G. Shade (eds.), *The Evolution of American Electoral Systems.* Westport, CT: Greenwood Press.

Degler, Carl N. 1964. "American Political Parties and the Rise of the City: An Interpretation." *Journal of American History*, 51, June: 41–59.

Gelman, A. and D. B. Rubin. 1992. "Inference from Iterative Simulation Using Multiple Sequences." *Statistical Science*, 7: 457–511.

King, Gary. 1997. *A Solution to the Ecological Inference Problem: Deconstructing Individual Behavior from Aggregate Data.* Princeton, NJ: Princeton University Press.

King, Gary and Bradley Palmquist. 1997. "The Record of American Democracy, 1984–1990." *PS: Political Science and Politics*, 30, December: 746–747.

King, Gary, Ori Rosen, and Martin Tanner. 1999. "Binomial–Beta Hierarchical Models for Ecological Inference." *Sociological Methods and Practice*, 28: 61–90.

Kleppner, Paul. 1982. "Were Women to Blame? Female Suffrage and Voter Turnout." *The Journal of Interdisciplinary History*, 12, Spring: 621–643.

Ogburn, William F. and Inez Goltra. 1919. "How Women Vote: A Study of an Election in Portland, Oregon." *Political Science Quarterly*, 34: 413–433.

Wakefield, Jonathan. 2001. "Ecological Inference for 2 × 2 Tables." Working Paper no. 12. Center for Statistics and the Social Sciences, University of Washington.

7 An Information Theoretic Approach to Ecological Estimation and Inference*

George G. Judge, Douglas J. Miller, and Wendy K. Tam Cho

ABSTRACT

The purpose of this chapter is to formulate and demonstrate information theoretic, moment-based approaches to processing and recovering information from aggregate voter data. In the context of the ecological inference problem, we focus on the recovery of unknown conditional vote counts for a precinct or district, given the observed number of votes for each candidate and the number of voters in demographic categories. The unknown and unobservable vote counts are interpreted as conditional probabilities of micro voting decisions. The problem of recovering the unknown probabilities from the macro data is initially formulated as an ill-posed or underdetermined inverse problem. The solution procedures are based on the Cressie–Read power-divergence criterion, and examples from the recent ecological inference literature are used to illustrate the characteristics of the estimators. In the second part of the chapter, we cast the information recovery problem in terms of a moment-based estimation problem and suggest solutions for recovering the unknown response parameters and corresponding marginal probabilities.

7.1 INTRODUCTION

In the social sciences, many of the data used for estimation and inference are available only in the form of averages or aggregate outcomes. Given this type of data restriction, researchers often use probabilities to represent information concerning the unknown and unobservable parameters of the underlying decision process. As a case in point, political scientists often face the question of how to process and recover information concerning voter behavior from precinct- or district-level data. These data are in many cases limited to aggregate vote counts, and individual-specific information about voters in a precinct is seldom available.

Efforts to recover micro information from aggregate data generally result in ill-posed inverse problems which yield a multitude of feasible "solutions" due to the lack of sufficient information. In other words, ill-posed problems are fundamentally indeterminate because there are more unknowns than data points. Consequently, there is not enough information available from the data to uniquely solve the problem using traditional rules of logic. Seminal developments for coping with this long-standing methodological challenge include Robinson (1950), Goodman (1953, 1959), Duncan and Davis (1953), Freedman, Klein, Sacks, Smyth, and Everett (1991), Achen and Shively (1995), and King (1997). Ill-posed inverse problems are not unique to political science, and the literature is littered with possible

---

* The authors gratefully acknowledge the many generous comments and suggestions provided by Bruce Cain, David Freedman, Marian Grendar, Gary King, T. C. Lee, Jeffrey Lewis, Ken McCue, Art Owen, and Rogério Silva de Mattos, without implying their agreement with the full content of the paper.

solutions to related estimation and inference problems in economics and other fields (see for example Golan, Judge, and Miller, 1996).

Given the importance of ecological estimation and inference problems in political science, we propose information theoretic procedures to recover estimates of the unknown conditional probabilities used as a basis for understanding voter behavior. In these problems, it is often possible to select feasible solutions or estimates that conform to the observed data, but the question lurking in the background is "what do these estimates mean, or what question are they answering?"

Because the information theoretic and other formulations are based entirely on aggregate data that are limited, partial, and incomplete, the recovered conditional probabilities may not be appropriate for answering a range of important voter behavior questions. Hence, to make efficient use of aggregate election data, we must find some way to introduce additional structure into the modeling and information recovery process. One way to proceed is to specify a conceptual framework that provides a plausible basis for the underlying data generation process. Toward this end, in the second part of this chapter, we suggest moment-based formulations that exploit the theoretical underpinnings of voter behavior and introduce important behavior parameters that facilitate the presentation and interpretation of the results. One purpose for adding this information or model structure is to provide a basis for converting a fundamentally ill-posed inverse problem into a well-posed problem. By reformulating the problem, we recover information at the appropriate level of aggregation on important voter response parameters along with the unknown conditional probabilities. The resulting formulations are semiparametric in the sense that the joint distribution of the underlying data is unspecified, apart from a finite set of moment conditions. These components form the basis for recovering the unknown response parameters and corresponding conditional probabilities and are used as standard operational tools in econometric information processing and recovery problems (Mittelhammer, Judge, and Miller, 2000). There certainly are many possible ways to approach ill-posed problems, so we emphasize that one must proceed cautiously when considering the significance of the estimates.

This chapter proceeds as follows: In Section 7.2, we develop notation consistent with the basic problem and develop a corresponding basis for modeling the aggregate data that focuses on the unknown conditional probabilities. In Section 7.3, we model the data as both a pure and a noisy inverse problem, suggest a solution, and interpret the recovered conditional probabilities. In Section 7.4, we suggest moment-based formulations that exploit the theoretical underpinnings of voter behavior and introduce important behavior parameters that facilitate the presentation and interpretation of the results. In Section 7.5, we discuss the implications of the models and the proposed solutions as a basis for learning about voter behavior. Some examples based on real and synthetic data are presented in the Appendix.

7.2 NOTATION AND BASIC INVERSE MODEL

To develop a model that will reflect the characteristics of voter response, consider the observed outcomes for a particular election across $i = 1, \ldots, m$ electoral units (e.g., precincts or districts). Each unit has $j = 1, \ldots, g$ types of individual voters and $k = 1, \ldots, c$ vote choices (e.g., candidates for office or propositions, including perhaps an abstention or no-vote category). For convenience and without loss of generality, we will adopt a framework where the election units are precincts and the vote choice is a set of candidates. For each precinct, the observed data are the number of votes for each candidate, $N_{i \cdot k} = \sum_{j=1}^{g} N_{ijk}$, and the number of voters in each group, $N_{ij \cdot} = \sum_{k=1}^{c} N_{ijk}$. The total number of ballots cast

Table 7.1 Known and unknown components of the voter problem

Group	Candidate				Count
	1	2	3	4	
1	$\beta_{11} N_{1\cdot}$	$\beta_{12} N_{1\cdot}$	$\beta_{13} N_{1\cdot}$	$\beta_{14} N_{1\cdot}$	$N_{1\cdot}$
2	$\beta_{21} N_{2\cdot}$	$\beta_{22} N_{2\cdot}$	$\beta_{23} N_{2\cdot}$	$\beta_{24} N_{2\cdot}$	$N_{2\cdot}$
3	$\beta_{31} N_{3\cdot}$	$\beta_{32} N_{3\cdot}$	$\beta_{33} N_{3\cdot}$	$\beta_{34} N_{3\cdot}$	$N_{3\cdot}$
	$N_{\cdot 1}$	$N_{\cdot 2}$	$N_{\cdot 3}$	$N_{\cdot 4}$	N

in the precinct is $N_i = \sum_{j=1}^{g} \sum_{k=1}^{c} N_{ijk}$. For any secret ballot, the total number of votes cast by each group for particular candidates in the election is unknown and *unobserved*. Given the observed data, our initial objective is to formulate an inverse model that will permit us to estimate N_{ijk}, the unobserved number of votes cast in precinct i by voters of type j for candidate k, from the sample of voters who voted in the election.

For the purposes of formulating the basic inverse model, the data may be stated in terms of the observed row or column proportions, i.e., for precinct i, $n_{i\cdot k} = N_{i\cdot k}/N_i$ or $n_{ij\cdot} = N_{ij\cdot}/N_i$. The inverse problem may be equivalently stated in terms of the proportion of voters in each category, $\beta_{ijk} = N_{ijk}/N_{ij\cdot} = n_{ijk}/n_{ij\cdot}$, where $\sum_{k=1}^{c} \beta_{ijk} = 1$ for each i and j. In this context, β_{ijk} may be interpreted as the conditional probability that voters in precinct i and group j voted for candidate k, where the conditioning indices are i and j. For example, in a study of split-ticket voting, the index j may represent votes for each of g national candidates from different parties, and the index k may represent the local candidates. The objective in this case would be to estimate the conditional probability that voters selected candidate k in the local election given that they voted for candidate j in the national election. In another application such as a study of polarized voting, the conditioning index j may represent characteristics of the electorate such as race or gender.

7.2.1 Modeling Voting Behavior as an Inverse Problem

The components of this information recovery problem for a particular precinct (i suppressed) are summarized in Table 7.1. The observed numbers of ballots cast by registered voters in the groups ($N_{j\cdot}$) are the row sums, and the observed numbers of votes received by the candidates ($N_{\cdot k}$) are the column sums. What we do not know and cannot observe is the number of votes cast by each group, N_{jk}, or the proportion of votes cast by each group for each candidate, n_{jk}. If the conditional probabilities β_{jk} were known, we could derive the unknown number of voters as $N_{jk} = \beta_{jk} N_{j\cdot}$. However, the conditional probabilities are unobserved and not accessible by direct measurement. Thus, we are faced with the cross-level inference problem, an inverse problem where we must use indirect, partial, and incomplete macro measurements as a basis for recovering the unknown conditional probabilities. The probability space interpretation gives the problem some minimal structure and provides a basis for learning from the data in a highly ambiguous situation.

The symbols in Table 7.1 and the corresponding data provide a limited basis for understanding voter behavior. If we are to improve our basis for recovering voter response information from partial incomplete data, we must introduce some structure into the modeling process. One bit of structure comes from the realization that the conditional probabilities β_{jk} must satisfy the row sum and column sum conditions, $\sum_{k=1}^{c} \beta_{jk} = 1$ and $\sum_{j=1}^{g} \beta_{jk} N_{j.} = N_{.k}$. Some additional structure may be imposed, based on a substantive theory about the particular behavior being examined and the elicitation of prior nonsample information, and we can exploit this model structure to facilitate presentation and interpretation.

If we make use of the column sum conditions, we have the relationship

$$n_{i.k} = \sum_{j=1}^{g} n_{ij.} \beta_{ijk} \tag{7.1}$$

for $i = 1, \ldots, m$ and $k = 1, \ldots, c$. To formalize our notation, we let $\mathbf{x}(i) = (n_{i1.} \; n_{i2.} \cdots n_{ig.})'$ represent the $g \times 1$ vector of proportions for each of the groups $j = 1, \ldots, g$ in precinct i, and let $\mathbf{y}(i) = (n_{i.1} \; n_{i.2} \cdots n_{i.c})'$ represent the $c \times 1$ sample outcome vector of vote proportions for each candidate $k = 1, \ldots, c$ in precinct i. Then, the relationship among the observed marginal proportions and unknown conditional probabilities may be written as

$$\mathbf{y}'(i) = \mathbf{x}'(i) \mathbf{B}(i) . \tag{7.2}$$

The component $\mathbf{B}(i) = (\boldsymbol{\beta}_{i1} \; \boldsymbol{\beta}_{i2} \cdots \boldsymbol{\beta}_{ic})$ is an unknown and unobservable $g \times c$ matrix of conditional probabilities, and $\boldsymbol{\beta}_{ik} = (\beta_{i1k} \; \beta_{i2k} \cdots \beta_{igk})'$ is the $g \times 1$ vector of conditional probabilities associated with precinct i and candidate k. If we rewrite $\mathbf{B}(i)$ in $gc \times 1$ vectorized form as $\boldsymbol{\beta}(i) = \text{vec}(\mathbf{B}(i)) = (\boldsymbol{\beta}'_{i1} \; \boldsymbol{\beta}'_{i2} \cdots \boldsymbol{\beta}'_{ic})'$, then we may rewrite Equation 7.2 as

$$\begin{bmatrix} y_1(i) \\ y_2(i) \\ \vdots \\ y_c(i) \end{bmatrix} = \begin{bmatrix} \mathbf{x}'(i) & \mathbf{0} & \cdots & \mathbf{0} \\ \mathbf{0} & \mathbf{x}'(i) & \cdots & \mathbf{0} \\ \vdots & \vdots & \ddots & \vdots \\ \mathbf{0} & \mathbf{0} & \cdots & \mathbf{x}'(i) \end{bmatrix} \begin{bmatrix} \boldsymbol{\beta}_{i1} \\ \boldsymbol{\beta}_{i2} \\ \vdots \\ \boldsymbol{\beta}_{ic} \end{bmatrix}, \tag{7.3}$$

or more compactly as $\mathbf{y}(i) = (\mathbf{I}_c \otimes \mathbf{x}'(i)) \boldsymbol{\beta}(i) = \mathbf{X}(i)\boldsymbol{\beta}(i)$, where $\mathbf{X}(i) = (\mathbf{I}_c \otimes \mathbf{x}'(i))$ and $\otimes$ denotes the Kronecker product. We may extend the formulation to include observations for $m \geq 2$ precincts by stacking the vectors $\mathbf{y}(i)$ and $\boldsymbol{\beta}(i)$ to form

$$\begin{bmatrix} \mathbf{y}(1) \\ \mathbf{y}(2) \\ \vdots \\ \mathbf{y}(m) \end{bmatrix} = \begin{bmatrix} \mathbf{X}(1) & \mathbf{0} & \cdots & \mathbf{0} \\ \mathbf{0} & \mathbf{X}(2) & \cdots & \mathbf{0} \\ \vdots & \vdots & \ddots & \vdots \\ \mathbf{0} & \mathbf{0} & \cdots & \mathbf{X}(m) \end{bmatrix} \begin{bmatrix} \boldsymbol{\beta}(1) \\ \boldsymbol{\beta}(2) \\ \vdots \\ \boldsymbol{\beta}(m) \end{bmatrix}, \tag{7.4}$$

or $\mathbf{y} = \mathbf{X}\boldsymbol{\beta}$.

Given the relationships 7.2 to 7.4 as a way of modeling the underlying data process, we view each election as an experiment. The sample data underlying Table 7.1 are viewed as the outcome of an election experiment. Consequently, we represent these sample data as having a systematic component (Equation 7.2) and a random component ε_{ik}, and write the statistical model expressing the data sampling process as

$$n_{i.k} = \sum_{j=1}^{g} n_{ij.} \beta_{ijk} + \varepsilon_{ik}, \tag{7.5}$$

or

$$y = X\beta + \epsilon, \tag{7.6}$$

where the noise vector ϵ is supported on a nonempty and bounded set and is assumed to have mean $E[\epsilon] = 0$ and finite covariance matrix Σ. The errors represent sampling variation in the observed column $(n_{i \cdot k})$ relative to the true but unobserved marginal probability that voters in precinct i vote for candidate k.

Using this weak model specification, we initially solve the problem by using the observed data outcomes $y = X\beta$ to represent the population moments, $E[y] = E[X\beta + \epsilon]$. Under this form, the absence of sampling errors and other stochastic noise components in Equations 7.2–7.4 implies that the problem of recovering β from observed y and X is a pure inverse problem. For each precinct-specific problem 7.3, note that the matrix $X(i)$ has dimension $c \times gc$ and is underdetermined and generally not invertible. Thus, under traditional mathematical inversion procedures, the voter pure inverse (VPI) problem is said to be ill posed, and the solution space for the problem contains arbitrary parameters. The question we now face is whether or not there is a plausible basis for reasoning in situations like this where the information we possess specifies only a feasible set of functions. Moving in the direction of a plausible solution basis, we note that the unknown conditional probabilities must satisfy some additional conditions such as additivity and nonnegativity, and the solution to the pure inverse problem 7.2 must satisfy the estimating functions $y = X\beta$.

7.3 SOME INFORMATION THEORETIC SOLUTIONS

7.3.1 Choosing the Criterion Function

Given the inverse model specified in Section 7.2.1, the long journey in defining a solution begins with the selection of a goodness-of-fit criterion. If we recognize and maintain the distinction that the unknown elements β_{ijk} are conditional probabilities rather than joint probabilities, then our pure voting inverse model is similar to allocating values to each of the cells in a contingency table. Consequently, the Cressie–Read power-divergence (CRPD) statistic (Cressie and Read, 1984; Read and Cressie, 1988; Baggerly, 1998) is a pseudodistance measure that may be used to compare elements in the set of feasible conditional probabilities implied by the available data. For a discrete probability distribution w defined with respect to $i = 1, \ldots, n$ possible outcomes, the CRPD statistic

$$I(\mathbf{w}, \mathbf{q}, \lambda) = \frac{2}{\lambda(1+\lambda)} \sum_i w_i \left[\left(\frac{w_i}{q_i} \right)^\lambda - 1 \right], \tag{7.7}$$

measures the pseudodistance between $\mathbf{w}$ (i.e., conditional probabilities in the VPI problem) and a set of reference weights $\mathbf{q}$. The reference weights may be based on additional or prior information that the researcher may want to bring to bear upon the estimation. The discrete weights must satisfy $(w_i, q_i) \in (0, 1) \times (0, 1) \ \forall i$ and $\sum_i w_i = \sum_i q_i = 1$. Read and Cressie note that Equation 7.7 encompasses a family of empirical likelihood estimation objective functions that includes:

1. The Kullback–Leibler directed divergence or discrimination information statistic (Kullback, 1959; Gokhale and Kullback, 1978)

$$I(\mathbf{w}, \boldsymbol{q}, \lambda \to 0) \propto \sum_{i=1}^{n} w_i \ln\left(\frac{w_i}{q_i}\right) \tag{7.8}$$

and

$$I(\mathbf{w}, \boldsymbol{q}, \lambda \to -1) \propto \sum_{i=1}^{n} q_i \ln\left(\frac{q_i}{w_i}\right). \tag{7.9}$$

Note that $I(\mathbf{w}, \boldsymbol{q}, \lambda \to 0) + I(\mathbf{w}, \boldsymbol{q}, \lambda \to -1)$ is a symmetric distance function.

2. Pearson's chi-square statistic (Pearson, 1900)

$$I(\mathbf{w}, \boldsymbol{q}, \lambda = 1) = \sum_{i=1}^{n} \frac{(w_i - q_i)^2}{q_i}. \tag{7.10}$$

3. The modified chi-square statistic (Neyman, 1949)

$$I(\mathbf{w}, \boldsymbol{q}, \lambda = -2) = \sum_{i=1}^{n} \frac{(q_i - w_i)^2}{w_i}. \tag{7.11}$$

4. The squared Matusita or Hellinger distance

$$I(\mathbf{w}, \boldsymbol{q}, \lambda = -1/2) \propto \sum_{i=1}^{n} \left(\sqrt{w_i} - \sqrt{q_i}\right)^2. \tag{7.12}$$

Read and Cressie note that the CRPD statistic is strictly convex in its arguments and may be used as a criterion function for minimum-distance estimation. Given uniform reference weights $q_i = n^{-1} \; \forall i$, the negative of Equation 7.7 also encompasses other prominent statistics:

1. The empirical likelihood statistic (Owen, 1988, 1990)

$$-I(\mathbf{w}, \boldsymbol{q}, \lambda \to -1) \propto \sum_{i=1}^{n} \ln w_i. \tag{7.13}$$

2. Shannon's entropy (Shannon, 1948) or the exponential empirical likelihood (DiCicco and Romano, 1990; Corcoran, 2000) statistic

$$-I(\mathbf{w}, \boldsymbol{q}, \lambda \to 0) \propto -\sum_{i=1}^{n} w_i \ln w_i. \tag{7.14}$$

3. The Simpson or Gini statistic

$$-I(\mathbf{w}, \boldsymbol{q}, \lambda = 1) = 1 - \sum_{i=1}^{n} w_i^2. \tag{7.15}$$

In these cases, the minimum-distance estimation problem is solved by maximizing the criterion function with respect to $\mathbf{w}$.

7.3.2 Solution to a Pure Inverse Problem

Under the minimum CRPD estimation criterion, an estimator for the VPI problem may be derived by minimizing the estimation criterion (Equation 7.7) for this problem,

$$\frac{2}{\lambda(1+\lambda)} \sum_{i=1}^{m} \sum_{j=1}^{g} \sum_{k=1}^{c} \beta_{ijk} \left[\left(\frac{\beta_{ijk}}{q_{ijk}} \right)^{\lambda} - 1 \right] \tag{7.16}$$

(given some λ), subject to the column-sum condition 7.1 and the row-sum (additivity) condition

$$\sum_{k=1}^{c} \beta_{ijk} = 1 \qquad \forall \, i, j \,. \tag{7.17}$$

The Lagrange expression for this constrained minimization problem is

$$L(\beta, \alpha, \gamma) = \frac{2}{\lambda(1+\lambda)} \sum_{i=1}^{m} \sum_{j=1}^{g} \sum_{k=1}^{c} \beta_{ijk} \left[\left(\frac{\beta_{ijk}}{q_{ijk}} \right)^{\lambda} - 1 \right]$$

$$+ \sum_{i=1}^{m} \sum_{k=1}^{c} \alpha_{ik} \left(n_{i \cdot k} - \sum_{j=1}^{g} n_{ij \cdot} \beta_{ijk} \right) + \sum_{i=1}^{m} \sum_{j=1}^{g} \gamma_{ij} \left(1 - \sum_{k=1}^{c} \beta_{ijk} \right), \tag{7.18}$$

where α_{ik} and γ_{ij} are Lagrange multipliers for the constraints 7.1 and 7.17, respectively. The necessary condition for $\widehat{\beta}_{ijk}$ is

$$\frac{\partial L}{\partial \beta_{ijk}} = \frac{2}{\lambda} \left(\frac{\widehat{\beta}_{ijk}}{q_{ijk}} \right)^{\lambda} - \frac{2}{\lambda(1+\lambda)} - \widehat{\alpha}_{ik} n_{ij \cdot} - \widehat{\gamma}_{ij} = 0, \tag{7.19}$$

and the solution for the conditional probabilities is

$$\widehat{\beta}_{ijk} = q_{ijk} \left[\frac{1}{1+\lambda} + \frac{\lambda}{2} \left(\widehat{\alpha}_{ik} n_{ij \cdot} + \widehat{\gamma}_{ij} \right) \right]^{1/\lambda}. \tag{7.20}$$

In general, the solution does not have a closed-form expression and must be stated in intermediate form as a function of the optimal Lagrange multipliers, $\widehat{\alpha}_{ik}$ and $\widehat{\gamma}_{ij}$. Consequently, the optimal values of the Lagrange multipliers must be determined numerically. We note that as $\lambda \to 0$ in Equation 7.16, the estimating criterion is

$$\sum_{i=1}^{m} \sum_{j=1}^{g} \sum_{k=1}^{c} \beta_{ijk} \ln \left(\frac{\beta_{ijk}}{q_{ijk}} \right), \tag{7.21}$$

and the intermediate solution for the constrained optimal β_{ijk} is

$$\widehat{\beta}_{ijk} = \frac{q_{ijk} \exp \left(\widehat{\alpha}_{ik} n_{ij \cdot} \right)}{\sum_{k=1}^{c} q_{ijk} \exp \left(\widehat{\alpha}_{ik} n_{ij \cdot} \right)}. \tag{7.22}$$

The elements $\widehat{\alpha}_{ik}$ are the optimal values of the Lagrange multipliers on the constraint 7.1. Under uniform reference weights ($q_{ijk} = c^{-1} \, \forall i, j$), the negative criterion is proportional to

$$-\sum_{i=1}^{m}\sum_{j=1}^{g}\sum_{k=1}^{c} \beta_{ijk} \ln \beta_{ijk}, \qquad (7.23)$$

and the minimum CRPD problem is known in the information theory literature as the method of maximum entropy (Jaynes, 1957a, 1957b) for pure inverse problems. Illustrative examples using real and synthetic data are given in the Appendix.

7.3.3 Incorporating Bounds on the Conditional Probabilities

Given the high degree of ambiguity resulting from the aggregate data, we can follow Duncan and Davis (1953) and use Equation 7.1 to refine the constraint set on the conditional probabilities by placing upper and lower bounds on each β_{ijk}. As indicated by King (1997), the constraint 7.1 implies that the lower bound on β_{ijk} is $Z_{ijk1} = \max(0, (n_{i \cdot k} - (1 - n_{ij \cdot}))/n_{ij \cdot})$, and the upper bound is $Z_{ijk2} = \min(1, n_{i \cdot k}/n_{ij \cdot})$. Given the bounds, β_{ijk} may be expressed as a convex combination $\beta_{ijk} = \sum_{h=1}^{2} \varphi_{ijkh} Z_{ijkh}$ for $\varphi_{ijkh} \geq 0$ such that $\varphi_{ijk1} + \varphi_{ijk2} = 1$. In this case, we may specify reference weights q_{ijkh} on each of the upper and lower bounds such that $\beta_{ijk}^{0} = \sum_{h=1}^{2} q_{ijkh} Z_{ijkh}$ is a presample estimate of the unknown β_{ijk}.

After incorporating the bounding information, the reformulated VPI problem may now be solved by minimizing

$$\frac{2}{\lambda(1+\lambda)} \sum_{i=1}^{m}\sum_{j=1}^{g}\sum_{k=1}^{c}\sum_{h=1}^{2} \varphi_{ijkh}\left[\left(\frac{\varphi_{ijkh}}{q_{ijkh}}\right)^{\lambda} - 1\right], \qquad (7.24)$$

subject to reparameterized versions of Equations 7.1 and 7.17:

$$n_{i \cdot k} = \sum_{j=1}^{g} n_{ij \cdot} \sum_{h=1}^{2} \varphi_{ijkh} Z_{ijkh}, \qquad (7.25)$$

$$1 = \sum_{k=1}^{c}\sum_{h=1}^{2} \varphi_{ijkh} Z_{ijkh}, \qquad (7.26)$$

plus the additivity constraint on the new weights,

$$\varphi_{ijk1} + \varphi_{ijk2} = 1. \qquad (7.27)$$

Setting up and solving the first-order conditions leads to the solution

$$\widehat{\varphi}_{ijkh} = q_{ijkh}\left[\frac{1}{1+\lambda} + \frac{\lambda}{2}\left(\widehat{\alpha}_{ik} n_{ij \cdot} Z_{ijkh} + \widehat{\gamma}_{ij} Z_{ijkh} + \widehat{\rho}_{ijk}\right)\right]^{1/\lambda}, \qquad (7.28)$$

where the point estimator of the bounded conditional probability is

$$\widehat{\beta}_{ijk} = \sum_{h=1}^{2} \widehat{\varphi}_{ijkh} Z_{ijkh}. \qquad (7.29)$$

If we let $\lambda \to 0$ in the criterion function 7.16, we are led to the constrained minimization problem

$$\sum_{i=1}^{m} \sum_{j=1}^{g} \sum_{k=1}^{c} \sum_{h=1}^{2} \varphi_{ijkh} \ln \left(\frac{\varphi_{ijkh}}{q_{ijkh}} \right) , \tag{7.30}$$

subject to the constraints 7.25 to 7.27. The intermediate solution for the constrained optimal φ_{ijkh} may be expressed as

$$\widehat{\varphi}_{ijkh} = \frac{q_{ijkh} \exp \left(\widehat{\alpha}_{ik} n_{ij\cdot} Z_{ijkh} + \widehat{\gamma}_{ij} Z_{ijkh} \right)}{\sum_{h=1}^{2} q_{ijkh} \exp \left(\widehat{\alpha}_{ik} n_{ij\cdot} Z_{ijkh} + \widehat{\gamma}_{ij} Z_{ijkh} \right)} , \tag{7.31}$$

and the estimator of the conditional probabilities is Equation 7.29. Illustrative examples for these formulations using real and synthetic data are given in the Appendix.

7.3.4 The Noisy Voter Inverse Problem

The pure voter inverse problem of Sections 7.3.2 and 7.3.3 is one plausible way to model information recovery from aggregate election data. However, if we view each election as an experiment, then Table 7.1 represents the outcome of an election experiment. Because it may be unrealistic to assume that the vote counts and the shares (proportions) are perfectly observed, in the spirit of much of the research in the ecological inference area, we turn to the following sampling model that has both systematic and stochastic components that represent the sampling process as in Equation 7.5:

$$n_{i\cdot k} = \sum_{j=1}^{g} n_{ij\cdot} \beta_{ijk} + \varepsilon_{ik} , \tag{7.32}$$

or in the form of a linear statistical model

$$y = X\beta + \epsilon . \tag{7.33}$$

The random $mgc \times 1$ noise vector ϵ is assumed to have mean $E[\epsilon] = 0$ and finite covariance matrix Σ. At this point, we assume that the X's are measured without error. We refer to the resulting estimation problem as the voter noisy inverse (VNI) problem.

7.3.4.1 Incorporating Bounds on the Characteristics of the Noise

The properties of $\varepsilon_{ik} \in [0, 1]$ may be derived from the known properties of $n_{i\cdot k}$ in Equation 7.5 or 7.32. First, we may be able to refine the plausible subset of the error space for a given sample by using the method of bounds to determine the plausible upper and lower bounds on ε_{ik}. The largest possible positive difference between $n_{i\cdot k}$ and the systematic component occurs if the conditional probabilities assigned to each group j in column k are zero (i.e., $\beta_{ijk} = 0$), and the upper bound is simply $n_{i\cdot k}$. Accordingly, the largest possible negative difference occurs if $\beta_{ijk} = 1$ for each j in column k, and the lower bound is $n_{i\cdot k} - 1$.

Second, we may refine the bounds to reflect the statistical properties of ϵ. Under the standard sampling conditions commonly assumed for the problem, ϵ is a mean-zero process with finite covariance Σ. Further, $n_{i\cdot k}$ is a $\sqrt{N_i}$-consistent estimator of the marginal probability $\beta_{i\cdot k}$ such that $n_{i\cdot k} \overset{p}{\to} \beta_{i\cdot k}$ and is asymptotically normal as $\sqrt{N_i} (n_{i\cdot k} - \beta_{i\cdot k}) \overset{d}{\to}$

$N(0, \beta_{i\cdot k}(1 - \beta_{i\cdot k}))$. Consequently, we know the bounds should be centered about zero. Let $V_{ik1} = \delta_{ik}(n_{i\cdot k} - 1)/\sqrt{N_i}$ be the lower bound and $V_{ik2} = \delta_{ik}n_{i\cdot k}/\sqrt{N_i}$ be the upper bound for each error term (where $\delta_{ik} > 0$ may be distinct for each i and k). To directly impose the mean-zero property of ϵ, we may specify symmetric (about zero) bounds, $V_{ik1} = -\delta_{ik}\max(n_{i\cdot k}, 1 - n_{i\cdot k})/\sqrt{N_i}$ and $V_{ik2} = -V_{ik1}$.

Given the error bounds, each ε_{ik} may be expressed as a convex combination

$$\varepsilon_{ik} = w_{ik1}V_{ik1} + w_{ik2}V_{ik2}, \tag{7.34}$$

where $w_{ikr} > 0$ for $r = 1, 2$ and $w_{ik1} + w_{ik2} = 1$. Then Equation 7.32 may be reformulated as

$$n_{i\cdot k} = \sum_{j=1}^{g} n_{ij\cdot} \sum_{h=1}^{2} Z_{ijkh}\varphi_{ijkh} + \sum_{r=1}^{2} V_{ikr}w_{ikr}. \tag{7.35}$$

By construction, there exist simplex-valued weights $\{\varphi_{ijkh}\}$ and $\{w_{ikr}\}$ such that Equation 7.35 holds for the observed sample. Through Equation 7.35, the VNI problem may now be based on the linear statistical model 7.33 plus the bounding information on β_{ijk} and ε_{ik}. Thus, the VNI problem may be solved by formulating it as a minimum-distance estimation problem and determining an appropriate set of weights for the unknown conditional probabilities and error components. As before, the problem specification allows for reference weights on the unknown parameters, q_{ijkh} for φ_{ijkh} and q_{ikr}^{w} for w_{ikr}.

7.3.4.2 The Solution

As in Sections 7.3.2 and 7.3.3, we solve the extended VNI problem by minimizing the CRPD criterion subject to the complete set of constraints. In particular, we minimize

$$\sum_{i=1}^{m}\sum_{j=1}^{g}\sum_{k=1}^{c}\sum_{h=1}^{2} \varphi_{ijkh} \ln\left(\frac{\varphi_{ijkh}}{q_{ijkh}}\right) + \sum_{i=1}^{m}\sum_{k=1}^{c}\sum_{r=1}^{2} w_{ikr} \ln\left(\frac{w_{ikr}}{q_{ikr}^{w}}\right), \tag{7.36}$$

subject to Equation 7.35 plus

$$\sum_{k=1}^{c}\sum_{h=1}^{2} \varphi_{ijkh}Z_{ijkh} = 1, \tag{7.37}$$

$$\varphi_{ijk1} + \varphi_{ijk2} = 1, \tag{7.38}$$

$$w_{ik1} + w_{ik2} = 1. \tag{7.39}$$

The necessary conditions yield the intermediate solutions for the weights

$$\widehat{\varphi}_{ijkh} = \frac{q_{ijkh}\exp\left(\widehat{\alpha}_{ik}n_{ij\cdot}Z_{ijkh} + \widehat{\gamma}_{ij}Z_{ijkh}\right)}{\sum_{h=1}^{2} q_{ijkh}\exp\left(\widehat{\alpha}_{ik}n_{ij\cdot}Z_{ijkh} + \widehat{\gamma}_{ij}Z_{ijkh}\right)}, \tag{7.40}$$

$$\widehat{w}_{ikr} = \frac{q_{ikr}^{w}\exp\left(\widehat{\alpha}_{ik}V_{ikr}\right)}{q_{ik1}^{w}\exp\left(\widehat{\alpha}_{ik}V_{ik1}\right) + q_{ik2}^{w}\exp\left(\widehat{\alpha}_{ik}V_{ik2}\right)}. \tag{7.41}$$

After the optimal Lagrange multipliers $\widehat{\alpha}_{ik}$ and $\widehat{\gamma}_{ij}$ are numerically determined, the estimates $\widehat{\beta}_{ijk}$ are computed as in Equation 7.29. In the Appendix, a data set is used to illustrate the noisy inverse formulation and compare it with the pure inverse formulation. In general, the introduction of the noise components weakens the constraints and moves the estimate in the direction of the initial unbounded pure outcome.

The ill-posed and underdetermined character of the pure and noisy inverse problems implies that a unique solution does not exist. Each "solution" is merely an algorithm for inferring a function (conditional probabilities) that is consistent with the available information (constraints) and the estimation criterion. Accordingly, we have developed a feasible solution method based on information theoretic and empirical likelihood concepts and tools. Under the noisy inverse formulation, it is possible to demonstrate that under standard regularity conditions on $n_{i \cdot k}$ (stated in Section 7.3.4.1) $\hat{\beta}_{ijk}$ is a $\sqrt{N_i}$-consistent and asymptotically normal estimator. The large-sample properties of the estimator present a basis for inference about the minimum CRPD model of voting behavior.

7.3.5 Remarks

One of the great questions of political science revolves around the ideal of representation. Do our political institutions promote or inhibit fair representation of the masses? This is a difficult question to answer, and there are few mechanisms through which we can gain insight into it. One mechanism, however, is the election process. Elections can be seen as natural experiments where we are able to observe repeatedly the behavior of the citizenry and its response to political institutions over time. Although it is difficult to make large-scale changes in our political structures, policies and platforms certainly change in response to each election, and this process is ongoing. To gain maximal insight, we would ideally like to know how preferences map to choices in a variety of contextual settings. Surveys usually cannot capture these varieties of settings, whereas aggregate returns can. Moreover, an analysis of aggregate data allows us to study those rarer instances in which institutions do shift and we want to see how that change in structure alters the mapping of preferences to choice.

The formulations in this section allow us to tap into these types of questions on a macro level. We can observe how a macro unit such as a precinct behaves across elections and through time. We can moreover, through the information theoretic formulations, observe how this behavior changes as a function of precinct characteristics such as urban–rural or minority composition or the strengths of major party affiliations.

These formulations are based on aggregate data, and so the results necessarily apply directly to the aggregate units only. The connection to individual-level behavior is clearly indirect. Nonetheless, if one needs to provide an interpretation of individual behavior based on aggregate data, the estimated conditional probabilities from the information theoretic approach are a plausible basis. These conditional probability estimates are admittedly only one way to summarize the aggregate data, but using this trajectory to arrive at a "solution" is attractive in several ways. First, the information theoretic procedure provides a solution to the ill-posed inverse problem that is consistent with the possible underlying data-generating process. Second, this procedure provides an especially appealing solution in that the outcomes represent voter counts that could have occurred in the greatest number of ways given the data constraints (see Section 2.2 in Golan, Judge, and Miller, 1996, for details). Third, political science theories rarely provide an adequate basis for specifying the random mechanism by which the observed data are generated. As previously noted, the proposed approach is semiparametric and does not require a fully specified likelihood function. Fourth, the information theoretic procedures allow one to stay within the general framework while using additional nonsample information to condition the solution.

7.4 RECOVERING INFORMATION ON INDIVIDUAL BEHAVIOR

In the approach to information recovery for the inverse problems in Section 7.3, we only use the observed macro data relating to voter groups and candidates. Since one uses aggregate data as an input, one gets information relevant at the aggregate level as output. For many voter behavior questions, these aggregated estimates may not provide an adequate basis for inference in either a positive or a normative sense. Ultimately, we are interested in micro (individual voter) behavior, and this is the topic to which we now turn.

Viewing each election as an experiment, we use Equations 7.32 and 7.33 as a basis for modeling the sampling process. We noted that it may be unrealistic to assume that the vote counts and voter group shares (i.e., the $n_{ij.}$'s or the $\mathbf{x}$'s) are measured without error. If we let $\mathbf{x}^*$ be the observed voter group shares from Equation 7.33 and $\mathbf{x}$ be the true unobservable voter shares, then we may model $\mathbf{x}^*$ as

$$\mathbf{x}^* = \mathbf{x} + \mathbf{u}, \tag{7.42}$$

where $\mathbf{u}$ is an unobserved noise vector. Therefore, the underlying statistical model is

$$y = \mathbf{x}\beta + \epsilon, \tag{7.43}$$

but the observable version of Equation 7.33 is

$$y = \mathbf{x}^*\beta + \epsilon^*, \tag{7.44}$$

where

$$\epsilon^* = \epsilon - \mathbf{u}\beta. \tag{7.45}$$

If the measurement errors in $\mathbf{x}$ are independent of ϵ and mutually uncorrelated, then ϵ^* is a mean-zero noise vector with covariance $\mathbf{\Sigma} + \beta\beta'\sigma_u^2\mathbf{I} = \mathbf{\Omega}$. In the statistical model based on the observable data, $\mathbf{x}^*$ is correlated with the random matrix ϵ^*. Thus, the usual linear model condition that the right-hand-side explanatory variables are orthogonal in expectation to the error process is violated. Further, traditional estimation rules based on $\mathrm{E}\left[\mathbf{x}^{*\prime}\epsilon^*\right] = \mathbf{0}$ will have questionable statistical properties when this condition does not hold.

To mitigate the effect of the measurement errors, we use additional information that we identify in the form of instrumental variables. This source of information makes use of the fact that precincts may vary in their individual demographic characteristics and that this variation may be related to the corresponding unknown and unobservable voter group shares and conditional probabilities. Given the economic, political, and social differences between precincts, it seems likely that the group shares and conditional probabilities β_{ijk} may vary over individuals, precincts, and/or time. To reflect this potential heterogeneity in the micro behavior, we assume that the β_{ijk}'s are conditional on a set of explanatory instrumental variables, and that these covariates reflect the individual, spatial, or temporal differences in voter decisions. Thus, the instrumental variable (IV) approach provides a method for estimating causal effects in a measurement error or simultaneous equation model framework. The covariates may include measures of economic performance such as the local level of unemployment, political characteristics such as incumbency, or demographic variables such as the average age of the electorate. Using this information, along with the observed macro data discussed in Section 7.3, it is possible to form a set of estimating equations as a basis for recovering the unknown conditional probabilities and identifying the effect of the explanatory variables on the corresponding conditional probabilities. The ultimate success of the moment-based specification depends on a plausible theory of micro voter behavior that helps to identify the important behavior-conditioning factors.

Returning to the statistical model 7.42 where the observed $\mathbf{x}^*$'s are now stochastic explanatory variables that are correlated with the noise vector ϵ^*, one useful way to model the data sampling process is to consider y and $\mathbf{x}^*$ as endogenous, jointly determined random variables. In this context, the statistical model becomes a system of relations

$$y = \mathbf{x}^*\beta + \epsilon^* \tag{7.46}$$

and

$$\mathbf{x}^* = \mathbf{A}\pi + \mathbf{u}, \tag{7.47}$$

where $\mathbf{A}$ is a set of instrumental variables that are correlated with $\mathbf{x}^*$ but uncorrelated with ϵ^* and $\mathbf{u}$. Under this formulation, the simultaneous or structural equation statistical model results, and traditional estimation and inference procedures apply directly to the model (see Chapter 17 in Mittelhammer, Judge, and Miller, 2000, for more details).

In practice, the source of measurement error is varied and specific to the application being considered. In general, we expect that some measurement error will be evident in the $\mathbf{X}$ variable. For example, in the voting rights context, errors in the $\mathbf{X}$ variable are commonplace, since the variable of interest, racial turnout proportions, is rarely accessible. Instead, one must rely on a proxy variable such as racial registration proportions or racial population proportions. Using a proxy variable leads to the type of measurement error mentioned above.

7.4.1 Moment-Based Model Formulation

To link the β_{ijk} to the explanatory instrumental variables, we rewrite the noisy inverse statistical model 7.33 as

$$\mathbf{A}'y = \mathbf{A}'\mathbf{X}\beta + \mathbf{A}'\epsilon. \tag{7.48}$$

The explanatory variables $\mathbf{A}$ are assumed to be uncorrelated with the noise components. Consequently, we can form the following set of estimating equations:

$$\mathrm{E}\left[\mathbf{A}'\left(\mathbf{Y} - \mathbf{X}\beta\right)\right] = \mathbf{0} \tag{7.49}$$

and the sample analog

$$T^{-1}\mathbf{A}'\left(\mathbf{Y} - \mathbf{X}\beta\right) \xrightarrow{p} \mathbf{0} \qquad \text{as } T \to \infty. \tag{7.50}$$

The individual components of the moment conditions may be stated in scalar form as

$$T^{-1}\sum_{t=1}^{T}\mathbf{A}'_{ti}\left[n_{ti\cdot k} - \sum_{j=1}^{g}n_{tij\cdot}\beta_{tijk}\right] = 0 \tag{7.51}$$

for each i and k. To allow for heteroskedasticity across precincts and possible temporal correlation, we assume regularity conditions on ϵ such that Equation 7.51 holds under an appropriate weak law.

The moment condition (7.51) may be extended to include the reparameterized conditional probabilities β_{tijk} and noise components ε_{tik} as in Section 7.3. The voter inverse problem with noise and time-varying conditional probabilities may be solved by minimizing the CRPD objective function

$$I(\varphi, \mathbf{w}, \lambda) = \frac{2}{\lambda(1+\lambda)} \sum_{t=1}^{T} \sum_{i=1}^{m} \sum_{j=1}^{g} \sum_{k=1}^{c} \sum_{h=1}^{2} \varphi_{tijkh} \left[\left(\frac{\varphi_{tijkh}}{q_{tijkh}} \right)^{\lambda} - 1 \right]$$

$$+ \frac{2}{\lambda(1+\lambda)} \sum_{t=1}^{T} \sum_{i=1}^{m} \sum_{k=1}^{c} \sum_{r=1}^{2} w_{tikr} \left[\left(\frac{w_{tikr}}{u_{tikr}} \right)^{\lambda} - 1 \right] \qquad (7.52)$$

subject to the estimating equations

$$\sum_{t=1}^{T} \mathbf{A}'_{ti} \left[n_{ti \cdot k} - \sum_{j=1}^{g} n_{tij \cdot} \sum_{h=1}^{2} Z_{tijkh} \varphi_{tijkh} - \sum_{r=1}^{2} V_{tikr} w_{tikr} \right] = \mathbf{0} \qquad (7.53)$$

plus the additivity conditions

$$\sum_{k=1}^{c} \sum_{h=1}^{2} \varphi_{tijkh} Z_{tijkh} = 1 , \qquad (7.54)$$

$$\varphi_{tijk1} + \varphi_{tijk2} = 1 , \qquad (7.55)$$

$$w_{tik1} + w_{tik2} = 1 . \qquad (7.56)$$

The intermediate solution may be stated in terms of the Lagrange multipliers

$$\widehat{\varphi}_{tijkh} = \frac{q_{tijkh} \exp \left(\widehat{\alpha}'_{ik} \mathbf{A}_{ti} Z_{tijkh} n_{tij} + \widehat{\gamma}_{tij} Z_{tijkh} \right)}{\sum_{h=1}^{2} q_{tijkh} \exp \left(\widehat{\alpha}'_{ik} \mathbf{A}_{ti} Z_{tijkh} n_{tij} + \widehat{\gamma}_{tij} Z_{tijkh} \right)} . \qquad (7.57)$$

The minimum-CRPD estimator of the time-varying conditional probability is

$$\widehat{\beta}_{tijk} = \sum_{h=1}^{2} \widehat{\varphi}_{tijkh} Z_{tijkh} . \qquad (7.58)$$

The Lagrange multiplier $\widehat{\alpha}_{ik}$ provides a basis for evaluating the effect of the instrumental variables on the solution.

In general, the estimators for the moment-based model formulation will also be consistent and asymptotically normal under standard regularity conditions. For example, the consistency result stated in Equation 7.50 and a related assumption regarding the asymptotic normality of $T^{-1/2} \mathbf{A}'(\mathbf{Y} - \mathbf{X}\beta)$ may be used to establish the asymptotic properties. To illustrate the basic statistical properties of the moment-based formulation, we conduct a series of Monte Carlo simulation exercises for a cross-sectional version of the model with $m = 20$ and $m = 50$ precincts or districts. Overall, the replicated estimates of the model parameters exhibit smaller sample bias and variance as the number of precincts, m, increases. We discuss further details regarding the composition of the replicated sampling process and the simulation results in the Appendix.

7.4.1.1 Remarks

Applications of the ecological inference problem are often in areas where the estimates are highly consequential. For instance, in the voting rights arena, the decision of a judge to grant or deny relief under the Voting Rights Act turns entirely on an ecological inference. How the system of representation plays out in our democracy is closely tied to how this type of legislation is enforced. Hence, not allowing for measurement error in this context especially could have great ramifications. Moreover, this is a circumstance where measurement error is known to pose a problem. In particular, the voter group shares are often based on registration rates (which can be obtained for a small set of localities) or population figures (which are easily obtainable), but the variable of interest is racial turnout rates (which are very difficult to obtain). Using one as a proxy for the other may be necessary, but also clearly problematic.

Some scholars have suggested a "double regression" approach to alleviate this problem (Kousser, 1973; Grofman, Handley, and Niemi, 1992). This method embodies the same idea as the minimum-CRPD method, but does not take any additional information into account. The proposed instrumental variables approach allows one to incorporate the large literature on voter turnout to help mitigate the effect of the undisputed measurement error. Although the success of this formulation is dependent on a plausible theory of micro-level behavior, the uncertainty can be assuaged by reliance on solid empirical studies in an extensive substantive literature. While the formulations proposed here are at the macro level, they incorporate information that has been empirically verified at the micro level.

7.4.2 The Discrete Choice Voter Response Model

In this section, we focus on obtaining and using micro data about individual voters in a precinct. Our objective is to use these micro data to estimate the effects of political, social, economic, and demographic variables on voter behavior and to recover the corresponding marginal (conditional) probabilities. We envision a situation where detailed survey data are collected on variables that characterize the voters in the precinct and indicate how each person voted in a particular contest. Given micro data that reflect the individual characteristics of a sample of voters, we model voter response as a discrete binary choice problem.

To develop this model, we use the unordered multinomial statistical response model. In this context, consider an unordered multinomial discrete choice problem with an experiment (survey) consisting of N trials (voters in a precinct), in which binary random variables $y_{1j}, y_{2j}, \ldots, y_{Nj}$ are observed. The binary outcomes $\{y_{ij}\}$ are observed for voters $i = 1, \ldots, N$ and candidates $j = 1, 2, \ldots, J$ in a given precinct. The candidate indices may be reordered without loss of generality so that the candidates represent J unordered categories. The observed outcome is $y_{ij} = 1$ if and only if voter i casts a vote for candidate j, and $y_{ij} = 0$ otherwise.

Let the probability that voter i casts a vote for candidate j be p_{ij}, and assume that the voting decision is related to a set of explanatory variables $\mathbf{a}_i$ through the model

$$p_{ij}(\boldsymbol{\beta}) \equiv P\left(y_{ij} = 1 \mid \mathbf{a}_i, \boldsymbol{\beta}_j\right) = G\left(\mathbf{a}_i'\boldsymbol{\beta}_j\right) > 0 \tag{7.59}$$

for each i and j. In particular, $\mathbf{a}_i' = (a_{i1}, a_{i2}, \ldots, a_{iK})$, $\boldsymbol{\beta}_j$ is a $K \times 1$ vector of unknown response parameters, and $G(\cdot)$ is a function that links the probabilities p_{ij} with the linear combination $\mathbf{a}_i'\boldsymbol{\beta}_j$ such that $G(\mathbf{a}_i'\boldsymbol{\beta}_j) \in [0, 1]$ and $\sum_{j=1}^{J} G(\mathbf{a}_i'\boldsymbol{\beta}_j) = 1$.

Suppose the observed outcomes of y_{ij} are noisy, so that the underlying binary random variables may be modeled as

$$Y_{ij} = G\left(\mathbf{a}_i'\beta_j\right) + \varepsilon_{ij} = p_{ij} + \varepsilon_{ij}, \tag{7.60}$$

where the ε_{ij} are noise components. The binary response model may be written in matrix form as

$$Y = p + \epsilon, \tag{7.61}$$

where each component is an $NJ \times 1$ vector. We assume $\mathrm{E}\left[\epsilon\right] = \mathbf{0}$ and that $\mathbf{cov}\left(\epsilon\right)$ is a finite positive semidefinite matrix. Note that this matrix is rank-deficient due to the additivity property of the choice probabilities, $\sum_{j=1}^{J} p_{ij} = 1$.

If we follow McFadden (1974), Manski and McFadden (1982), or Maddala (1983), we may solve the problem with the traditional maximum likelihood approach. Under the log-likelihood function

$$\ln \mathrm{L}\left(\beta; \mathbf{a}\right) = \sum_{i=1}^{N} \sum_{j=1}^{J} y_{ij} \ln G\left(\mathbf{a}_i'\beta_j\right), \tag{7.62}$$

the solution is the multinomial logit estimator if G is the logistic CDF, and the multinomial probit estimator if G is the multivariate normal (Gaussian) CDF.

Rather than adopt a fully parametric specification, we extend the ideas outlined in Section 7.4.1 and use a moment-based approach for estimation and inference. In this context, we use the observed outcomes of y and the $N \times K$ matrix of explanatory variables $\mathbf{a}$ to recover information about the *unknown* and *unobservable* model components p and β. For the multinomial choice problem, this information may be written as an inverse problem with noise that is linear in p:

$$\left(\mathbf{I}_J \otimes \mathbf{a}'\right) y = \left(\mathbf{I}_J \otimes \mathbf{a}'\right) p + \left(\mathbf{I}_J \otimes \mathbf{a}'\right) \epsilon. \tag{7.63}$$

The inverse problem has KJ moment relations and NJ unknown conditional probabilities. Assuming the orthogonality condition $\mathrm{E}[(\mathbf{I}_J \otimes \mathbf{a}')\,\epsilon] = \mathbf{0}$ holds, we can form an unbiased estimating function

$$\mathrm{E}\left[\left(\mathbf{I}_J \otimes \mathbf{a}'\right)\left(Y - p\right)\right] = \mathbf{0}, \tag{7.64}$$

with sample analog

$$N^{-1}\left(\mathbf{I}_J \otimes \mathbf{a}'\right)\left(Y - p\right) = \mathbf{0}. \tag{7.65}$$

If $N > K$ (as is often the case), the inverse problem based on this set of estimating equations is ill posed.

One way to solve the ill-posed inverse problem and recover information about the unknown model components is to use the CRPD criterion introduced in Section 7.3. For expository simplicity, we focus on the special case of CRPD that results in Shannon's entropy functional. Under this information criterion, we can solve the following extremum problem:

$$\max_{p} -p' \ln p, \tag{7.66}$$

subject to the moment constraints

$$\left(\mathbf{I}_J \otimes \mathbf{a}'\right) \mathbf{y} = \left(\mathbf{I}_J \otimes \mathbf{a}'\right) \mathbf{p} \tag{7.67}$$

and the additivity constraints

$$[\mathbf{I}_N \quad \mathbf{I}_N \quad \cdots \quad \mathbf{I}_N] \, \mathbf{p} = \mathbf{1}, \tag{7.68}$$

where the matrix on the left-hand side is $N \times NJ$, and $\mathbf{1}$ is an $N \times 1$ vector of 1's.

The information theoretic solution to the inverse problem may be derived from the necessary conditions for this inverse problem. The intermediate form of the solution is

$$\widehat{p}_{ij} = \frac{\exp\left(-\mathbf{a}_i' \widehat{\boldsymbol{\lambda}}_j\right)}{\Omega_i\left(\widehat{\boldsymbol{\lambda}}\right)} = \frac{\exp\left(\mathbf{a}_i' \widehat{\boldsymbol{\beta}}_j\right)}{\Omega_i\left(\widehat{\boldsymbol{\beta}}\right)}, \tag{7.69}$$

where $\widehat{\boldsymbol{\lambda}}_j$ is the $K \times 1$ vector of optimal Lagrange multipliers for the jth moment constraint. The expression represents only an intermediate solution to the inverse problem, because $\widehat{p}_{ij}$ is a function of $\widehat{\boldsymbol{\lambda}}_j$, which must be numerically determined. As indicated, the inverse problem may also be stated in terms of the response parameters $\widehat{\boldsymbol{\beta}}_j = -\widehat{\boldsymbol{\lambda}}_j$. Finally, the denominator component or partition function takes the form

$$\Omega_i\left(\widehat{\boldsymbol{\beta}}\right) = \sum_{j=1}^{J} \exp\left(\mathbf{a}_i' \widehat{\boldsymbol{\beta}}_j\right). \tag{7.70}$$

Thus, by making use of the micro data in this multinomial context, we can recover estimates of the response parameters $\boldsymbol{\beta}_j$ and the corresponding marginal probabilities. Further, the solution to the inverse problem has the same mathematical form as the logistic multinomial probability model (Mittelhammer, Judge, and Miller, 2000, Chapter 20).

The intermediate solution may be substituted back into the Lagrange expression to form a concentrated objective function

$$M(\boldsymbol{\lambda}) = \mathbf{y}'\left(\mathbf{I}_J \otimes \mathbf{a}\right) \boldsymbol{\lambda} + \sum_{i=1}^{N} \ln \Omega_i\left(\boldsymbol{\lambda}\right), \tag{7.71}$$

which is identical to the log-likelihood function for the multinomial logit problem (Maddala, 1983: 36). Consequently, the asymptotic properties of the multinomial logit estimator also apply to the information theoretic solution in this inverse problem, and the sampling results may be used to form inferences regarding voter response to changes in the explanatory variables. The solution to the inverse problem will not coincide with the multinomial logit case if we use other members of the CRPD criterion family as the objective function. However, related large-sample properties may be derived under comparable regularity conditions.

7.4.2.1 Remarks

Precincts represent an aggregate unit, which moreover is aggregated at an arbitrary level. Precinct behavior is interesting in some contexts, but another challenge is reconstructing individual-level behavior. Knowing how people vote is instrumental to understanding the dynamics and consequences of our political structures. Surveys provide one means of accomplishing this task. However, surveys have clear weaknesses that could be overcome with aggregate data. The discrete choice formulations developed here provide a method for utilizing survey information in conjunction with the aggregate data, and thus allow one to draw from the strengths of both levels of data. For a discussion of this type of model in an epidemiology context, see Wakefield and Salway (2001).

The discrete choice formulations provide but one way to bridge the chasm between the macro and micro estimates. They enable us to condition on a set of covariates to make this link from the macro to the micro. There have been many studies seeking to link covariates to voter choice at the micro level. We look to these studies to guide the choice of explanatory variables for the discrete choice formulations in Section 7.4. In particular, many of these studies have established a clear empirical link between voter preferences and socioeconomic variables such as age, income, and education. In addition, the socioeconomic variables can be used to design a survey that would elicit information on individual attitudes and how these characteristics map to attitudes. Indeed, we are more generally interested in mapping attitudes to characteristics rather than the more narrow question of how attitudes map to vote preferences. The former mapping is much more general and would allow us to engage in a wider range of prediction. Campaign strategists, after all, are most interested in forming effective targeting strategies based on individual characteristics, not individual vote preferences per se.

Although there are many ways to transform this problem into a well-posed inverse problem, our formulation here is attractive because it has many of the same nice features as the one discussed in Section 7.3. In particular, the procedure has a base in information theory and empirical likelihood theory that permits semiparametric inference and allows the incorporation of nonsample information when available.

7.5 IMPLICATIONS

Ecological inference problems provide an interesting challenge for polimetricians. The secret ballot is designed to maintain a wall of secrecy around individual vote preferences, and it has done so very successfully. As a result, the data generated from any election are partial and incomplete. Consequently, the corresponding estimation and inference models present themselves as underdetermined and ill-posed inverse problems. While our goal is to obtain information in terms of conditional probabilities as a basis for expressing the micro processes underlying the macro outcome data, these conditional probabilities are unobserved and unobservable. This means few, if any, bets on the values of the unknowns will ever be collected.

Although many theories about voting behavior exist, there does not appear to be one overarching micro theory that encompasses all of the empirical and theoretical research on the topic. Few have even discussed, or even seem willing to discuss, the prospects of constructing a micro foundation for aggregate outcomes. This lack of model structure creates presentational and interpretational problem and results in insufficient information on which to specify a data sampling process that might be consistent with the observed data outcomes. Hence, traditional estimation and inference procedures appear to be ill suited to deal with ecological data. The use of creative assumptions to achieve tractability and well-posed mathematical and statistical models leads in many cases to erroneous interpretations and conclusions. No one ever said ecological inference was easy.

Building on the productive efforts of many polimetricians, in an effort to make some progress on these interesting problems and challenges, we have considered nontraditional methods of thinking about this problem. This approach recognizes that the problem of sorting out voter behavior that is modeled in terms of unknown probabilities while making use of only aggregate data constraints results in an ill-posed inverse problem. In seeking a basis for reasoning in this logically indeterminate situation, we have modeled the ecological inference problem as a pure and a noisy inverse problem. In this context, to choose a "solution" from the set of feasible solutions, the Cressie–Read statistic was used to identify a family of goodness-of-fit or pseudodistance measures. This solution provides a useful way to summarize a micro system that is consistent with the observed macro counterpart.

This formulation is also attractive in that it provides a straightforward way to include prior nonsample information, is amenable to a multiplicity of precincts, can easily include spatial and intertemporal aspects, and is easy to implement. Furthermore, it allows one to alleviate problems such as measurement error by incorporating an instrumental variables framework that may be employed along with the moment conditions to provide a basis for recovering estimates of response parameters and the corresponding marginal probabilities related to voter preferences. Finally, in order to bridge these estimates to the micro level, we view the ecological inference problem as a discrete choice problem. This permits the recovery of response parameters related to voter characteristics, and again recovery of corresponding marginal (conditional) probabilities.

It is worth noting that the application of maximum entropy methods has been explored in the ecological inference context (Johnston and Pattie, 2002). However, extensions of the method which we explore (e.g., cross-entropy) and the introduction of information theoretic techniques are novel in the study of ecological inference.

Under the instrumental variables and discrete choice formations, estimation and inference proceed in the context of sampling theory and provide a sampling basis for evaluating performance. To a large extent, the information-processing and recovery rules described are nontraditional and do not assume information about the underlying sampling distributions, which is unknown. These nonparametric or semiparametric formations permit one to stay within the realm of sampling theory but allow one to avoid the rigidity of likelihood functions and proceed on the basis of a finite set of moment conditions.

In looking ahead toward ways to think about ecological inference problems, semiparametric and nonparametric formulations of the random coefficient models seem to be promising avenues. In this framework, one may replace unknown functions with reasonable nonparametric estimators rather than the maximum likelihood estimator that constrains the parametric setting. One possibility in this connection is sieve empirical likelihood estimation and testing procedures. Alternatively, the Bayesian method of moments offers a basis for recovering conditional probabilities without the usual Bayesian likelihood and prior distributions.

The writing of this chapter, which led to a trek into the world of ecological inference, has been a very rewarding experience. It has reminded us that aggregate analyses that lead to invalid micro inferences also have implications and consequences other than statistical ones. It is also refreshing for economists to be reminded that the problem of recovering micro-level effects from an aggregate counterpart is not unique to economic data.

APPENDIX. ILLUSTRATIVE EXAMPLES

Information-Theoretic Formulation

To illustrate the properties of the information theoretic approach, we consider a special case of the VPI problem based on an election with $k = 4$ candidates in some precinct. Suppose that N votes were cast for the candidates, and that we record the individual votes as

$x_i = k$ for $i = 1, \ldots, N$ and $k = 1, \ldots, 4$. Because of the secret ballot, individual records are unknown, and thus we only have the average vote outcome from the election, $\overline{x}$. Further, suppose we believe that the candidates are equally likely to win the election *ex ante*. The objective of our VPI problem is to estimate the proportion β_k of votes that each candidate received, based on this very limited information. Within the context of Section 7.3, we solve the problem by maximizing the CRPD objective function with uniform reference weights and $\lambda \to 0$,

$$-\sum_{k=1}^{4} \beta_k \ln \beta_k , \tag{7.72}$$

subject to

$$\sum_{k=1}^{4} \beta_k k = \overline{x} , \tag{7.73}$$

$$\sum_{k=1}^{4} \beta_k = 1 , \tag{7.74}$$

by choice of $\beta_k \geq 0$. The intermediate solution to the VPI problem is

$$\widehat{\beta}_k = \frac{\exp\left(-\widehat{\alpha}k\right)}{\sum_{k=1}^{4} \exp\left(-\widehat{\alpha}k\right)} , \tag{7.75}$$

where $\widehat{\alpha}$ is the optimal Lagrange multiplier for the constraint 7.73.

Although the problem is stated as a constrained maximization, the computational burden may be reduced by concentrating the estimation problem. Following the discussion of Equation 7.71 for the discrete choice problem in Section 7.4.2, we can substitute the intermediate solution 7.75 back into the Lagrange equation for the problem defined by Equations 7.72 to 7.74. The resulting concentrated objective function

$$M(\alpha) = \alpha\overline{x} + \ln\left[\sum_{k=1}^{4} \exp\left(-\alpha k\right)\right] \tag{7.76}$$

is strictly convex in α, and the optimal value of the Lagrange multiplier may be computed by minimizing $M(\alpha)$. We can then evaluate Equation 7.75 at $\widehat{\alpha}$ to determine the estimated vote shares. Thus, the estimates for the VPI problem may be computed with any software package that solves unconstrained optimization problems (e.g., maximum likelihood or nonlinear least squares estimation). In general, we can form concentrated objective functions for any of the minimum-CRPD problems stated in this chapter, and we provide additional examples in the following subsection.

The simple VPI problem is very similar to Jaynes's famous dice problem in which we must assign probabilities to the six faces of a die based on the observed average outcome of N rolls. In our case, we have four unknown probabilities β_k and only two pieces of available information. To demonstrate the solution to our simple VPI problem, we report the conditional probabilities for five different values of $\overline{x}$ in Table 7.2. Note that all of the minimum CRPD solutions to this problem based on uniform reference weights are discrete uniform when $\overline{x} = 2.5$. Otherwise, the estimated conditional probabilities are monotonically increasing if $\overline{x} > 2.5$ and monotonically decreasing if $\overline{x} < 2.5$.

Table 7.2 Solutions to the simple VPI problem

	Candidate			
$\bar{x}$	1	2	3	4
1.5	0.648	0.235	0.086	0.031
2.0	0.421	0.277	0.182	0.120
2.5	0.250	0.250	0.250	0.250
3.0	0.120	0.182	0.277	0.421
3.5	0.031	0.086	0.235	0.648

Variants of King's Ohio Voter Problem

To further demonstrate the minimum CRPD procedure, we consider the simple problem presented by King (1997) in his Table 1.2. For a particular Ohio precinct, King reports the number of votes for the two major parties plus the number of nonvoters ($c = 3$) in the 1990 Ohio for the state House of Representatives election. King also reports the number of registered black and white voters in the Ohio precinct ($g = 2$). The data provided by King are the row and column sums in Table 7.3. For example, there are 221 black registered voters in the precinct, and 92 votes were cast for the Republican candidate. The associated VPI problem is to estimate the number of votes cast for each party (including no-vote tallies) conditional on the race of the voter. In effect, we have $g(c - 1) = 4$ unknown probabilities and $g - 1 = 2$ pieces of information (after normalization), and King's problem is clearly underdetermined.

The problem is solved using the minimum-CRPD estimator with uniform reference weights and $\lambda \to 0$. The objective function is Equation 7.23, and the intermediate solution for the constrained optimal β_{ijk} is a special case of Equation 7.22:

$$\widehat{\beta}_{jk} = \frac{\exp\left(-\widehat{\alpha}_k n_{j\cdot}\right)}{\sum_{k=1}^{3} \exp\left(-\widehat{\alpha}_k n_{j\cdot}\right)} \, . \tag{7.77}$$

To compute the optimal Lagrange multipliers $\widehat{\alpha}_k$, we minimize the concentrated objective function

$$M(\alpha) = \sum_{k=1}^{3} n_{\cdot k} \alpha_k + \sum_{j=1}^{2} \ln\left[\sum_{k=1}^{3} \exp\left(-\alpha_k n_{j\cdot}\right)\right] . \tag{7.78}$$

The predicted vote counts appear in the individual cells in the table, and the estimated conditional probabilities are reported in parentheses. Without access to the individual ballots, we cannot know the true values of the elements β_{ijk} in this example. However, we do know that the solution is consistent with a reasonable set of regularity conditions and with what is known about the set of feasible conditional probabilities β_{ijk}. Further, the estimated voter counts have maximum multiplicity under the Shannon entropy criterion. That is, the conditional distribution that maximizes Equation 7.23 is coincident with the set of cell-specific vote outcomes that may be realized in the largest number of ways given the row and column sum constraints (see Section 2.2 in Golan, Judge, and Miller, 1996, for more details).

Table 7.3 Estimates for the Ohio voter problem

	Candidate			
Group	Democrat	Republican	No Vote	Count
VPI problem				
Black	56.8	46.0	118.2	221
	(0.2570)	(0.2080)	(0.5350)	
White	73.2	46.0	364.8	484
	(0.1512)	(0.0951)	(0.7536)	
	130	92	483	705
VPI problem with bounded probabilities				
Black	67.0	47.0	107.0	221
	(0.3030)	(0.2130)	(0.4840)	
	[0, 0.588]	[0, 0.416]	[0, 1]	
White	63.0	45.0	376.0	484
	(0.1300)	(0.0930)	(0.7770)	
	[0, 0.269]	[0, 0.190]	[0.541, 0.998]	
	130	92	483	705
VNI problem with bounded probabilities and errors				
Black	64.9	45.9	110.2	221
	(0.2940)	(0.2080)	(0.4990)	
	[0, 0.588]	[0, 0.416]	[0, 1]	
White	65.1	46.1	372.8	484
	(0.1350)	(0.0950)	(0.7700)	
	[0, 0.269]	[0, 0.190]	[0.541, 0.998]	
	130	92	483	705
	[−0.031, 0.031]	[−0.033, 0.033]	[−0.026, 0.026]	

To demonstrate the effect of the bounds on β_{ijk}, we solve the bounded VPI problem and present the results in Table 7.3. For this version of the VPI problem stated in Section 7.3.3, the weights on the bounds are special cases of Equation 7.31:

$$\widehat{\varphi}_{jkh} = \frac{\exp\left(-\widehat{\alpha}_k n_{j\cdot} Z_{jkh} - \widehat{\gamma}_j Z_{jkh}\right)}{\sum_{h=1}^{2} \exp\left(-\widehat{\alpha}_k n_{j\cdot} Z_{jkh} - \widehat{\gamma}_j Z_{jkh}\right)} . \qquad (7.79)$$

The concentrated objective function for this problem,

$$M(\boldsymbol{\alpha}, \boldsymbol{\gamma}) = \sum_{k=1}^{3} \alpha_k n_{\cdot k} + \sum_{j=1}^{g} \gamma_j + \sum_{j=1}^{2} \sum_{k=1}^{3} \ln\left[\sum_{h=1}^{2} \exp\left(-\alpha_k n_{j\cdot} Z_{jkh} - \gamma_j Z_{jkh}\right)\right], \qquad (7.80)$$

is derived by substituting the intermediate solution back into the Lagrange equation, and the optimal Lagrange multipliers $\widehat{\alpha}_k$ and $\widehat{\gamma}_j$ are computed by unconstrained minimization of $M(\boldsymbol{\alpha}, \boldsymbol{\gamma})$. The solution values of β_{ijk} are computed from the optimal weights $\widehat{\varphi}_{jkh}$ as in Equation 7.29, and the estimates appear in parentheses below the estimated vote counts. The associated Duncan–Davis bounds appear below in brackets. In five of six cells, the upper or lower bounds narrow the feasible set to a proper subset of $[0, 1]$. Also, the estimated conditional probabilities are near (but not exactly at) the center of the bounded intervals. Relative to the unbounded results, note that the bounding information has effectively shifted votes from the no-vote category to the Democrat columns for black voters. For whites, the shift is from the Democrat category to the no-vote column. Of course, we do not know that this solution is better than the unbounded pure solution, because the cell values are unobservable.

To illustrate the case with bounds and $\lambda \to 0$ from Section 7.3.4.2, we solve the Ohio voting example in terms of the extended VNI problem with bounds on β_{ijk} and ε_{ik}. We use the bounds on β_{ijk} stated in Table 7.3, and the upper and lower bounds appear below the estimates in the table. The error bounds are selected to be symmetric about zero with $\delta_{ik} = 1$. The upper and lower error bounds are stated below the column counts at the bottom of Table 7.3. The intermediate solution for φ_{jkh} takes the same form as in the bounded VPI problem, but the optimal values of α and γ for this problem will be different due to the presence of the noise term. The concentrated objective function is

$$M^*(\alpha, \gamma) = M(\alpha, \gamma) + \sum_{k=1}^{3} \ln \left[\exp\left(-\alpha_k V_{k1}\right) + \exp\left(-\alpha_k V_{k2}\right) \right], \qquad (7.81)$$

and the term added to $M(\alpha, \gamma)$ represents the presence of the noise terms.

Relative to the two preceding demonstrations, note that the estimates for the bounded VNI problem represents an intermediate case—some of the mass shifted to form the bounded VPI estimates has reverted to the unbounded VPI case. In effect, the noise components weaken the constraints for the VNI problem, and the solution can move closer to the unbounded outcome. Although the column sums are not strictly required to match the observed values, note that they do in this solution. Further, the use of wider error bounds reduces the tendency for the column sums to be satisfied by the estimated conditional probabilities.

This is a fairly simplistic example that could be extended easily in several ways. For instance, under the usual scenarios, candidates are far from equally likely to win the election *ex ante*. The equally likely assumption can be weakened so that we can incorporate our fairly accurate ability to predict election outcomes long before they occur. In an actual application of this approach, we will be able to capitalize on the information provided by a larger number of precincts. This example supplies estimates for just one precinct. Presumably, the numerous precincts that would constitute a data set would supply additional information. We could perhaps take advantage of information underlying some manifested spatial autocorrelation among the precincts (for work in this area, see Anselin and Cho, 2002; Calvo and Escolar, 2002; Gotway and Young, 2002; and Haneuse and Wakefield, 2002).

Given the large uncertainty that surrounds these estimates, it is difficult to choose among these three demonstrations. One might be inclined to the VNI formulation with bounds simply because the bounds are deterministic information that one would like to incorporate and the errors certainly seem to be important and plausible features as well. Interestingly, however, none of these demonstrations produces substantively different results. And even without explicitly incorporating the bounds, the estimates for the VPI problem are within the bounds. This lack of variation in the estimates is especially true for the Republican candidate, for whom the range of vote counts is minuscule (45–47), as is the range of vote proportions. The range for the Democratic candidate is larger, but still not large enough to be interesting. The bounds in this case are relatively narrow, so it is surprising that they would not have a greater effect.

Lastly, we note that the estimates in these cases, especially when the bounds are incorporated, appear to tend toward the center of the possible range of values, and that the estimates

Table 7.4 Simulation results for the moment-based formulation

Parameter	True value	m = 20 Average	m = 20 Std. dev.	m = 50 Average	m = 50 Std. dev.
α_{11}	0.1	0.1288	0.94	0.1378	1.13
α_{12}	0.2	0.1559	1.49	0.1890	1.64
α_{13}	0.3	0.2795	1.87	0.3002	0.25
α_{21}	0.4	0.4296	0.95	0.4385	1.12
α_{22}	0.5	0.4580	1.49	0.4886	1.63
α_{23}	0.6	0.5998	1.87	0.5997	0.24
α_{31}	0.7	0.7276	0.94	0.7381	1.13
α_{32}	0.8	0.7570	1.49	0.7890	1.64
α_{33}	0.9	0.8826	1.87	0.9001	0.26
α_{41}	1.0	1.0303	0.95	1.0394	1.13
α_{42}	1.1	1.0578	1.50	1.0856	1.62
α_{43}	1.2	1.1795	1.86	1.1988	0.23

for the white group and the black group tend to be similar. This is not particularly surprising, as one might initially guess that the estimated voter counts would have maximum multiplicity toward the center rather than toward either end of the range of possibilities. In this sense, one might believe that this estimator would produce estimates consistent with the conclusion that different groups of voters tend to act similarly. The implications for using this estimator in a voting rights case, then, can be quite consequential, since the charge in those cases is to determine whether there is polarized voting among the groups in the electorate and the inclination of the estimator is to provide group estimates that are similar.

Moment-Based Formulation

We now demonstrate the sampling properties of the estimator for the moment-based model formulation in Section 7.4.1. In particular, we consider a cross-sectional version of the model based on $m = 20$ and $m = 50$ precincts with $g = 3$ voter types and $c = 4$ candidates. Three instrumental variables $\mathbf{A}_i$ are used for each precinct, and these include a constant (i.e., vector of ones) and two nonconstant instruments generated as pseudorandom standard normal variables (fixed in repeated samples). We also simplify the formulation stated in Section 7.4.1 by using uniform reference weights for the conditional probabilities and by ignoring the bounds on the conditional probabilities. Following the notation in Equation 7.57, we denote the associated Lagrange multipliers for this version of the model as α_{kh}, where $k = 1, \ldots, 4$ and $h = 1, \ldots, 3$. The row-sum values are the same for each precinct: $n_{i1.} = 0.3$, $n_{i2.} = 0.25$, and $n_{i3.} = 0.45$. The mean values of the column-sum values $n_{i \cdot k}$ are derived from Equation 7.1 based on a set of "true" conditional probabilities that are functions of the observed instrumental variables $\mathbf{A}_i$ and the true values of the Lagrange multipliers α_{kh} (see Table 7.4 for the true values). To represent sampling variability in the candidate shares as in Equation 7.5, we add Gaussian noise components with mean zero and variance 0.0001 to the mean values of $n_{i \cdot k}$ for $k = 1, 2, 3$. The noisy value of $n_{i \cdot 4}$ is recovered by normalization: $n_{i \cdot 4} = 1 - n_{i \cdot 1} - n_{i \cdot 2} - n_{i \cdot 3}$.

The sampling process is replicated for $m = 20$ and $m = 50$ precincts over 500 Monte Carlo trials. The estimated Lagrange multipliers are saved from each trial, and the sample mean and standard deviation of the estimates for each α_{kh} are reported with the true parameter values in Table 7.4. Given that this is a cross-sectional sample ($T = 1$), the regularity conditions stated in Section 7.4.1 do not directly apply to this case. However, we find that the sample means of the $\widehat{\alpha}_{kh}$'s are close to the true parameter values and that the simulated standard deviations are stable. The sampling results are especially encouraging in that we are not relying on time series observations ($T = 1$) and the largest value of m is small relative to typical numbers of precincts. Further, the efficiency of the moment-based estimator may be improved by allowing for spatial correlation among the precincts.

REFERENCES

Achen, C. H. and W. P. Shively. 1995. *Cross-Level Inference.* Chicago: University of Chicago Press.

Anselin, L. and W. K. T. Cho. 2002. "Spatial Effects and Ecological Inference," *Political Analysis*, 10, 3: 276–297.

Baggerly, K. 1998. "Empirical Likelihood as a Goodness of Fit Measure," *Biometrika*, 85, 3: 535–547.

Calvo, E. and M. Escolar. 2002. "The Local Voter: Exploring a Geographically Weighted Approach to Cross-level Inference."

Corcoran, S. 2000. "Empirical Exponential Family Likelihood using Several Moment Conditions," *Statistica Sinica*, 10: 545–557.

Cressie, N. and T. Read. 1984. "Multinomial Goodness of Fit Tests," *Journal of the Royal Statistical Society, Series B*, 46: 440–464.

DiCicco, T. and J. Romano. 1990. "Nonparametric Confidence Limits by Resampling Methods and Least Favorable Families," *International Statistics Review*, 58: 59–76.

Duncan, O. and B. Davis. 1953. "An Alternative to Ecological Correlation," *American Sociological Review*, 18: 665–666.

Freedman, D., S. Klein, J. Sacks, C. Smyth, and C. Everett. 1991. "Ecological Regression and Voting Rights (with Discussion)," *Evaluation Review*, 15: 659–817.

Gokhale, D. and S. Kullback. 1978. *The Information in Contingency Tables.* Marcel Dekker.

Golan, A., G. Judge, and D. Miller. 1996. *Maximum Entropy Econometrics: Robust Estimation with Limited Information.* Wiley.

Goodman, L. 1953. "Ecological Regression and the Behavior of Individuals," *American Sociological Review*, 18: 663–664.

Goodman, L. 1959. "Some Alternatives to Ecological Correlation," *American Journal of Sociology*, 64: 610–625.

Gotway, C. A. and L. J. Young. 2002. "A Spatial View of the Ecological Inference Problem." In G. King, M. A. Tanner, and O. Rosen (eds.), *Ecological Inference: New Methodological Strategies.* Cambridge University Press.

Grofman, B., L. Handley, and R. Niemi. 1992. *Minority Representation and the Quest for Voting Equality.* Cambridge University Press.

Haneuse S. and J. Wakefield. 2002. "Ecological Inference Incorporating Spatial Dependence." In G. King, M. A. Tanner, and O. Rosen (eds.), *Ecological Inference: New Methodological Strategies.* Cambridge University Press.

Jaynes, E. T. 1957a. "Information Theory and Statistical Mechanics I," *Physical Review*, 106: 620–630.

Jaynes, E. T. 1957b. "Information Theory and Statistical Mechanics II," *Physical Review*, 108: 171–190.

Johnston, R. and C. Pattie. 2000. "Ecological Inference and Entropy-Maximizing: An Alternative Estimation Procedure for Split-Ticket Voting," *Political Analysis*, 8: 333–345.

King, G. 1997. *A Solution to the Ecological Inference Problem.* Princeton University Press.

King, G. 1999. "The Future of Ecological Inference Research: A Reply to Freedman, et al.," *Journal of the American Statistical Association*, 94: 352–355.

Kousser, J. 1973. "Ecological Regression and the Analysis of Past Politics," *The Journal of Interdisciplinary History*, 4, Autumn, 2: 237–262.

Kullback, S. 1959. *Information Theory and Statistics.* Wiley.

Kullback, S. 1971. "Marginal Homogeneity of Multidimensional Contingency Tables," *Annals of Mathematical Statistics*, 42: 594–606.

Maddala, G. S. 1983. *Limited-Dependent and Qualitative Variables in Economics*. Cambridge University Press.

Manski, C. and D. McFadden. 1982. "Alternative Estimates and Sample Designs for Discrete Choice Analysis." In C. Manski and D. McFadden (eds.), *Structural Analysis of Discrete Data with Econometric Applications*. The MIT Press.

McFadden, D. 1974. "The Measurement of Urban Travel Demand," *Journal of Public Economics*, 3: 303–328.

Mittelhammer, R., G. Judge, and D. Miller. 2000. *Econometric Foundations*. Cambridge University Press.

Neyman, J. 1949. "Contributions to the Theory of the χ^2 Test." In *Proceedings of the First Berkeley Symposium on Mathematical Statistics and Probability*, pp. 239–273.

Owen, A. 1988. "Empirical Likelihood Ratio Confidence Intervals for a Single Functional," *Biometrika*, 75: 237–249.

Owen, A. 1990. "Empirical Likelihood Ratio Confidence Regions," *Annals of Statistics*, 18: 90–120.

Pearson, K. 1900. "On a Criterion That a Given System of Deviations from the Probable in the Case of a Correlated System of Variables is Such That it Can Be Reasonably Supposed to Have Arisen from Random Sampling," *Philosophical Magazine, 5th Series*, 50: 157–175.

Read, T. and N. Cressie. 1988. *Goodness-of-Fit Statistics for Discrete Multivariate Data*. Springer-Verlag.

Robinson, W. S. 1950. "Ecological Correlations and the Behavior of Individuals." *American Sociological Review*, 15: 351–357.

Shannon, C. 1948. "A Mathematical Theory of Communication," *Bell System Technical Journal*, 27: 379–423.

Wakefield, J. and R. Salway. 2001. "A Statistical Framework for Ecological and Aggregate Studies." *Journal of the Royal Statistical Society, Series A*, 164: 119–137.

8 Ecological Panel Inference from Repeated Cross Sections[*]

Ben Pelzer, Rob Eisinga, and Philip Hans Franses

ABSTRACT

This chapter presents a Markov chain model for the estimation of individual-level binary transitions from a time series of independent repeated cross-sectional (RCS) samples. Although RCS samples lack direct information on individual turnover, it is demonstrated here that it is possible with these data to draw meaningful conclusions on individual state-to-state transitions. We discuss estimation and inference using maximum likelihood, parametric bootstrap, and Markov chain Monte Carlo approaches. The model is illustrated by an application to the rise in ownership of computers in Dutch households since 1986, using a 13-wave annual panel data set. These data encompass more information than we need to estimate the model, and this additional information allows us to assess the validity of the parameter estimates. We examine the determinants of the transitions from have-not to have (and back again) using well-known socioeconomic and demographic covariates of the digital divide. Parametric bootstrap and Bayesian simulation are used to evaluate the accuracy and the precision of the ML estimates, and the results are also compared with those of a first-order dynamic panel model. To mimic genuine repeated cross-sectional data, we additionally analyze samples of independent observations randomly drawn from the panel. Software implementing the model is available.

8.1 INTRODUCTION

It has sometimes been argued that King's ecological inference model can be adapted and fruitfully applied to independent repeated cross-sectional (RCS) samples (see, e.g., Penubarti and Schuessler, 1998; King, Rosen, and Tanner, 1999). To date, however, surprisingly little research has been devoted to the development of cross-level inference models that draw panel conclusions from nonpanel data.[1] Moreover, the existing approaches to ecological panel inference are implicitly or explicitly grouping methods, which suffer from small-sample-size restrictions. The individual observations are typically grouped into a limited number of observed covariate patterns, based on time-invariant characteristics (e.g., sex, race). For each covariate pattern, the margins of a transition table are obtained by aggregating

---

[*] The data for the Socio-Economic Panel used in this paper were collected by Statistics Netherlands and were made available by the Scientific Statistical Agency of the Netherlands Organization for Scientific Research. Our program *CrossMark* implements all the simulations and estimations reported here. It is programmed in Delphi but distributed as a standalone program running under Windows. The program (including documentation) is free software and available from the first author (`b.pelzer@maw.kun.nl`).

[1] Studies that are related to this topic include Franklin (1989), Moffitt (1990, 1993), Sigelman (1991), Mebane and Wand (1997), Penubarti and Schuessler (1998). The model presented by Quinn in Chapter 9 of this volume is also of relevance. The framework discussed here has, in its basic form, been proposed by Moffitt (1990, 1993). Pelzer, Eisinga, and Franses (2002) discuss the (dis)similarities between this model and the ecological panel inference (EPI) method of Penubarti and Schuessler (1998) and the two-stage auxiliary instrumental variables (2SAIV) approach of Franklin (1989).

within the groupings, and this aggregate information is subsequently used to track changes in the dependent variable of interest. Obviously, such grouping methods are likely to face difficulties (such as sparse-data problems) if the number of covariates and/or the number of repeated cross sections become large.

In this chapter we consider a transition inference model for RCS data with a more dynamic and more flexible structure. In the model proposed here, the micro observations need not be divided into (fixed) groups to obtain sample aggregates. In fact, the variation in the individual covariates is utilized as part of the estimation procedure. The model therefore takes full advantage of the individual survey data and provides full information on the effects of covariates entering the model.

There are several reasons for investigating dynamic models for RCS data. One is the lack of genuine panel data. Panel designs are, rightfully, highly regarded for the opportunity they offer to measure transitions of state or value from repeated observations on the same sample units. For many research issues, however, adequate panel data are rather hard to come by or simply unavailable. Another major difficulty is that panel data are potentially subject to nonsampling biases. An important such bias is sample attrition that results from the progressive loss of (often selective groups of) respondents willing to participate in the data collection. While nonresponse is also a limitation for cross-sectional surveys, it is a more serious problem for panel data because nonresponse often accumulates over time. A related limitation is that it is often difficult to ensure that changes in the target population are reflected in the panel. While panels are typically designed to be representative of the population at the beginning of the study, the panel ages over time, and few panels are, in addition to providing longitudinal data, also designed to permanently provide fully representative information of the population by continuous renewal of the sample.

A large number of cross-sectional surveys conducted by public and private organizations are repeated at regular time intervals. These repeated cross-sectional surveys do not suffer from panel mortality and reflect changes in the universe that cannot be taken into account by a panel study. Estimating individual transitions from such data has an air of performing an impossible task, of obtaining information from nowhere. Indeed, it is often argued that panel data are absolutely needed to study individual-level change (e.g., Kish, 1987: 167). While individual change is obviously only *visible* in panel data, we will show that this argument is not correct and that data from successive, separately drawn samples can be used to validly estimate transitions using a model that is no more magical than the use of "plug-in" estimates and bridging assumptions in other areas of statistical modeling.

The outline of this chapter is as follows. Section 8.2 presents a Markov transition model for repeated cross sections designed to deal specifically with binary responses. The model has its origins in the work of Moffitt (1990, 1993). We briefly review its main features and discuss maximum likelihood (ML), parametric bootstrap, and Markov chain Monte Carlo (MCMC) approaches to estimation and inference. Section 8.3 considers an application of the model to the rise in computer penetration rates in Dutch households from 1986 to 1998, using annual panel data from the Socio-Economic Panel (SEP) survey of Statistics Netherlands. We examine the determinants of the transitions from "have-not" to "have" (and back again) using well-known socioeconomic and demographic covariates of the digital divide. Parametric bootstrap and Bayesian simulation are used to evaluate the accuracy and the precision of the RCS Markov ML estimates, and the results are also compared with those of a first-order dynamic panel model. To mimic genuine RCS data, we additionally analyze samples of independent observations randomly drawn from the panel. The summary in Section 8.4 concludes the chapter.

8.2 ESTIMATING TRANSITIONS FROM RCS DATA

8.2.1 Binary Transition Model

Obviously, the estimation of dynamic models with repeated cross-sectional data is hampered by the lack of information about lagged variables. Let y_{it} denote the observed response for the binary random variable y of unit i at time period t. The crucial characteristic of RCS data is that y_{it} is observed, but $y_{i\,t-1}$ is not. Consequently, no estimate of the serial covariance of successive y_{it} is available in RCS data. This does not imply that dynamic models cannot be estimated with repeated cross sections. However, it does imply that estimation of the unobserved transitions is possible only by putting certain constraints on the transitions for unit i and/or time period t.

Consider a 2×2 transition table in which the internal cell values sum to unity across rows. If we define $p_{it} = P(y_{it} = 1)$, $\mu_{it} = P(y_{it} = 1 \mid y_{i\,t-1} = 0)$, and $\lambda_{it} = P(y_{it} = 0 \mid y_{i\,t-1} = 1)$, then we have the well-known accounting equation

$$E(y_{it}) = p_{it} = \mu_{it}(1 - p_{i\,t-1}) + (1 - \lambda_{it})p_{i\,t-1}, \tag{8.1}$$

which is recognized as the equivalent of Equation 0.4 presented in the Introduction to this book. This identity is the critical equation that needs to be solved in estimating dynamic models with repeated cross sections, as it relates the marginal probabilities (p_{it} and $p_{i\,t-1}$) to the entry (μ_{it}) and exit (λ_{it}) transition probabilities. A more concise form for the same equation is $p_{it} = \mu_{it} + \eta_{it} p_{i\,t-1}$, so that $\eta_{it} = 1 - \lambda_{it} - \mu_{it}$. It is also sometimes convenient to define $\kappa_{it} = 1 - \lambda_{it} = P(y_{it} = 1 \mid y_{i\,t-1} = 1)$. If we recursively substitute for p_{it} in Equation 8.1 and derive its reduced form in terms of past μ_{it} and λ_{it}, then we get

$$p_{it} = \mu_{it} + \sum_{\tau=1}^{t-1}\left[\mu_{i\tau} \prod_{s=\tau+1}^{t} \eta_{is}\right] + p_{i0} \prod_{\tau=1}^{t} \eta_{i\tau}. \tag{8.2}$$

This is the model equation that will be used in this chapter. It is obviously not uniquely solvable with RCS data without identifying constraints. Several types of restrictions may be used in this context.

One is to impose some direct restraint on the patterns of the unobserved μ_{it} and λ_{it}. For example, the parameters in Equation 8.2 are clearly identifiable with RCS data if we take the transition probabilities to be homogeneous with respect to both units i and time periods t. With the assumption that $\mu_{it} = \mu$ and $\lambda_{it} = \lambda$ for all i and t, the long-run value of p_{it} in Equation 8.2 reduces to $p_{it} = \mu/(\mu + \lambda)$ (see, e.g., Ross, 1993: 152–153). Models with this type of homogeneity have been studied extensively in the statistical literature, and they have been applied in various economic, social, and political science studies (see Pelzer, Eisinga, and Franses, 2002, for additional references).

The model proposed here uses a different type of restriction. This restriction may be imposed if the cross-sectional data include covariates $\mathbf{x}_{it}$ that are measurable in the past (by "backcasting"), and if the current and the lagged $\mathbf{x}_{it}$ affect μ_{it} and λ_{it}. In that case, the covariates $\mathbf{x}_{it}, \mathbf{x}_{i\,t-1}, \ldots, \mathbf{x}_{i1}$ can be employed to obtain current and backward predictions of the entry ($\mu_{it}, \mu_{i\,t-1}, \ldots, \mu_{i1}$) and exit ($\lambda_{it}, \lambda_{i\,t-1}, \ldots, \lambda_{i2}$) transition probabilities, by specifying

$$\mu_{it} = F(\mathbf{x}_{it}\beta) \quad \text{and} \quad \lambda_{it} = 1 - F(\mathbf{x}_{it}\beta^*). \tag{8.3}$$

In these equations β and β^* are two different sets of k-dimensional parameters associated with two potentially different sets of (time-invariant or time-varying) k-dimensional covariates $\mathbf{x}_{it}$, and F is the – in this paper logistic – link function. Estimates of the model parameters are obtained by substituting Equation 8.3 into 8.2.

The critical identifying restriction used here is that the regression parameters are taken to be constant over time, but this constancy assumption may easily be relaxed if we have a sufficient number of repeated cross sections. We may use a semiparametric approach that assumes the parameters to be constant within but different across discrete time periods, or we can model the parameters as a function of time using polynomials or splines. For example, in our empirical illustration below, we introduce time variation into the model by allowing the baseline entry rates (i.e., the constant parameter) to become a first-degree polynomial in time. This is accomplished simply by including the variable time in the model. It is important to note that the underlying Markov chain is not assumed to be homogeneous in the model proposed here, implying that the entry and exit transition probabilities may vary across both units i and time periods t. Also note that to obtain p_{it}, we actually integrate (sum) over all possible unobserved state-to-state transition paths for each individual unit i, starting at $t = 1$ and ending at the cross-sectional observation period t. This implies that the probabilities are estimated as a function of all the available cross-sectional samples, rather than simply the observations from the current time period.

Other, perhaps more implicit assumptions underlying the application of the model are that $p_{i0} = 0$, that all the covariates $\mathbf{x}_{it}$ included in the model should have known values in the past, and that the estimation of the entry and exit transitions depend exclusively on variations in the covariates observed. With respect to the first assumption, it should be noted that p_{i1} is the first observed outcome and p_{i0} the value of the state prior to the first outcome. It is generally difficult to incorporate the prior state into the model, and we could invoke the restriction that $p_{i1} = 0$, the consequence of which would be that $p_{i1} = \mu_{i1}$. However, because in many applications the latter assumption is untenable, we prefer to use a separate logistic function for the cross section at $t = 1$, i.e., $P(y_{i1} = 1) = F(\mathbf{x}_{it}\delta)$. The δ-parameters are estimated simultaneously with the entry and exit parameters of interest at $t = 2, \ldots, T$, and they are estimated as a function of all cross-sectional data, rather than simply the observations at $t = 1$.

If some of the covariates are "nonbackcastable" (i.e., if their past history is unknown), the model may be modified by estimating two different sets of parameters for both μ_{it} and λ_{it}: one for the current transition probability estimates and a separate one for the preceding estimates. If we denote the time-dependent covariate with unknown past history by $\mathbf{v}_{it}$ and the associated parameter vector representing the effect on μ_{it} by ζ, then we have $\text{logit}(\mu_{it}) = \mathbf{x}_{it}\beta^{**} + \mathbf{v}_{it}\zeta$ for cross section t, and $\text{logit}(\mu_{it}) = \mathbf{x}_{it}\beta$ for the cross sections $1, \ldots, t - 1$. This specification allows one to express the current transition probability estimates as a logistic function of both backcastable and nonbackcastable variables. A similar model may be specified for λ_{it}. It should be noted here that in our application below we assume that $\beta^{**} = \beta$.

If the assumption that all relevant variables are included in the model is not a realistic one, it may be useful to include an individual-specific random error term ε_i in the linear predictor of the transition probabilities to allow for omitted variables, at least insofar as these variables are time-invariant for each individual. In this logistic–normal mixture model we have $\text{logit}(\mu_{it}) = \mathbf{x}_{it}\beta + \gamma_0\varepsilon_i$ and $\text{logit}(1 - \lambda_{it}) = \mathbf{x}_{it}\beta^* + \gamma_1\varepsilon_i$, where γ_0 and γ_1 are coefficients of the random variable ε_i having zero mean and unit variance. To estimate the parameters, the (marginal) likelihood of this model may be integrated with respect to the distribution of ε_i using the Gauss–Hermite quadrature approximation. While likelihood inference about the parameters is possible, it is worth noting that accurate estimation of γ_0 and γ_1 from the data themselves is difficult, unless the number of observations is large. As unobserved heterogeneity is not examined in the empirical application below, we will not elaborate on this topic here. Pelzer, Eisinga, and Franses (2002) provide further details.

Finally, it may be useful to outline the commonalities and differences between the ecological analysis of aggregate data and the Markov model for repeated cross-sectional data proposed here. As noted by Sigelman (1991) and Penubarti and Schuessler (1998), drawing panel inferences at the micro level from repeated cross sections constitutes an ecological inference problem. To demonstrate this point, consider the following partially observed transition table for a population in which there is an absence of both recruitment (immigration or birth) and losses (emigration or death):

	$Y_t = 0$	$Y_t = 1$	
$Y_{t-1} = 0$			N^0_{t-1}
$Y_{t-1} = 1$			N^1_{t-1}
	N^0_t	N^1_t	N

In this closed population the marginal distributions are known and fixed, and the ecological inference problem arises because the aggregate measures of change are observed, but the interior cells are not. The two margins provide (at least some) information on the cells, and the accounting identity ensures that the Duncan and Davis (1953) bounds (also termed Fréchet bounds in the statistical literature) will obtain. If we have available a sufficiently large number of transition tables for consecutive time points, an ecological inference model such as that presented by Quinn in Chapter 9 of this volume may be applied to the data.

The situation is somewhat different if the data are drawn from a time series of independent samples of the population of interest. In that case, the marginal values are estimates of the true population parameters and thus themselves subject to error (Tam Cho, 1998). And this implies that the bounds too will be known only up to sampling error. If the sample sizes are large, one may be willing to take the margins as fixed and error-free and use the samples to obtain the marginal proportions of the transition table, as presented in the left panel below:

	$Y_t = 0$	$Y_t = 1$				$Y_t = 0$	$Y_t = 1$	
$Y_{t-1} = 0$			p^0_{t-1}		$Y_{t-1} = 0$			
$Y_{t-1} = 1$			p^1_{t-1}		$Y_{t-1} = 1$			
	p^0_t	p^1_t	1			p^0_{it}	p^1_{it}	1

If the data are limited to y_{it}, we could apply the inference model proposed here, using a Markov model with constant terms only. If we additionally observe covariates, we could also aggregate the micro data into covariate patterns, as in Penubarti and Schuessler (1998), to obtain the marginal distributions of the transition table for each pattern and thus ranges of feasible entries that are consistent with the margins. King's EI could then be used to exploit the information provided by the bounds (using covariate patterns as equivalents to precincts in the analysis of voting). The number of patterns obviously should not be too large relative to the sample size, to obtain reasonably reliable aggregates. Hence the method is likely to suffer from small-sample-size restrictions.

Also note that in using this grouping method, inferences are at the level of individuals sharing the same values of the observed covariates, that is, at the level of the covariate patterns, rather than at the level of individuals. This allows one to trace fixed groups over time rather than individuals, whose covariate values might change. Thus, the method is applicable only if we have a sufficient number of observations for every covariate value and if, in addition, the covariates are time-invariant (so that the sample population can be divided into groups with fixed membership). It faces difficulties in cases of time-varying or nonbackcastable covariates, and these difficulties increase if the number of repeated cross sections becomes large.

The empirical application discussed in Section 8.3 may be used to illustrate the issue. The covariates used in that example include education, age, number of household members, income, and time. The number of covariate patterns observed is 10,510, and the average number of observations per pattern is 2.5. Even if we were to categorize the variable age into three different age categories, as is done in the estimation procedure, the number of covariate patterns would still be large (1,053) and, accordingly, the number of observations per group low (about 25 on average). That is, the group sizes in this example are simply too small for us to ignore the presence of sampling error. And this implies that the data at hand cannot be used to fruitfully compare the performance of our model with the EI grouping method. That is a very interesting and important topic, but one left for future research with other data.

As indicated, what is special for the current model is that the information available in the repeated cross sections is fully exploited. In the model proposed here, there is no grouping of the data, and in the extreme case each individual unit may have its own covariate pattern. This means, as illustrated in the right panel above, that in our procedure only one of the margins (y_{it}) is available for inference, and the other one ($y_{i\,t-1}$) is not. And this in turn implies that in our model the repeated cross sections themselves cannot provide any deterministic, informative restrictions on the entries. Consequently, the inference problem in the model proposed here is greater (in the sense of having a larger number of unknowns) than in the applications where the margins are (assumed to be) known. The approach proposed here is to completely express the marginal probabilities p_{it} in terms of μ_{it} and κ_{it}, recursively, so that estimating the latter automatically renders the former. Also, Equation 8.1 may be rearranged into $\mu_{it} = p_{it}/(1 - p_{i\,t-1}) - p_{i\,t-1}/(1 - p_{i\,t-1})\kappa_{it}$, where $\kappa_{it} = 1 - \lambda_{it}$. This expression resembles the equation that King (1997) termed the "tomography line" (i.e., Equation 0.5 in the Introduction to this book). Since the estimated marginal probabilities p_{it} and $p_{i\,t-1}$ are guaranteed to lie in the (0, 1) range, bounds are enforced on the maximum likelihood estimators of μ_{it} and κ_{it}. These upper and lower limits are not informative as in the Duncan and Davis (1953) methods of bounds, however, but rather logical limits implied by the model.

8.2.2 Estimation and Simulation

8.2.2.1 Maximum Likelihood Estimation

The method of maximum likelihood may be used to estimate the parameters in Equation 8.3 – plugged into 8.2 – along with their (co)variances. For a sample of n statistically independent observations – where each observation is treated as a single draw from a Bernoulli distribution – with success probability p_{it}, the model 8.2 has the log likelihood function

$$\ell\ell = \sum_{t=1}^{T} \sum_{i=1}^{n_t} \ell\ell_{it} = \sum_{t=1}^{T} \sum_{i=1}^{n_t} [y_{it} \log(p_{it}) + (1 - y_{it}) \log(1 - p_{it})],$$

where T is the number of cross sections and n_t the number of units of the cross-sectional sample at time period t. Maximization of this function has to be performed iteratively and requires the derivatives of the log likelihood with respect to the (vector of) parameters, θ, say. If we suppress subscript i to ease notation, the first derivatives with respect to θ are

$$\frac{\partial \ell\ell_t}{\partial \theta} = \frac{y_t - p_t}{p_t(1 - p_t)} \cdot \frac{\partial p_t}{\partial \theta},$$

where

$$\frac{\partial p_t}{\partial \theta} = \frac{\partial \mu_t}{\partial \theta} + \frac{\partial p_{t-1}}{\partial \theta}\eta_t + p_{t-1}\frac{\partial \eta_t}{\partial \theta}.$$

If θ is used to estimate μ_t, then $\partial \mu_t/\partial \theta = \mathbf{x}_t \mu_t(1 - \mu_t)$ and $\partial \eta_t/\partial \theta = -\partial \mu_t/\partial \theta$. If it is used for λ_t, then $\partial \mu_t/\partial \theta = \mathbf{0}$ and $\partial \eta_t/\partial \theta = \mathbf{x}_t \lambda_t(1 - \lambda_t)$. The values for $\partial p_t/\partial \theta$ can be obtained by recursive substitution, setting $p_0 = 0$ and $\partial p_0/\partial \theta = \mathbf{0}$, and starting from $\partial p_1/\partial \theta = \partial \mu_1/\partial \theta = \mathbf{x}_1 \mu_1(1 - \mu_1)$. The second derivatives are

$$\frac{\partial^2 \ell\ell_t}{\partial \theta\, \partial \theta'} = -\frac{(y_t - p_t)^2}{p_t^2(1 - p_t)^2} \cdot \frac{\partial p_t}{\partial \theta} \cdot \frac{\partial p_t}{\partial \theta'} + \frac{y_t - p_t}{p_t(1 - p_t)} \cdot \frac{\partial^2 p_t}{\partial \theta\, \partial \theta'},$$

where

$$\frac{\partial^2 p_t}{\partial \theta\, \partial \theta'} = \frac{\partial^2 p_{t-1}}{\partial \theta\, \partial \theta'} \cdot \eta_t + \frac{\partial p_{t-1}}{\partial \theta'} \cdot \frac{\partial \eta_t}{\partial \theta} + \frac{\partial^2 \mu_t}{\partial \theta\, \partial \theta'} \cdot (1 - p_{t-1}) - \frac{\partial \mu_t}{\partial \theta'} \cdot \frac{\partial p_{t-1}}{\partial \theta},$$

with $\partial^2 \mu_t/\partial \theta\, \partial \theta' = \mathbf{x}_t' \mathbf{x}_t \mu_t(1 - \mu_t)(1 - 2\mu_t)$. Again, if we set $\partial^2 p_0/\partial \theta\, \partial \theta' = \partial p_0/\partial \theta = \partial p_0/\partial \theta' = \mathbf{0}$, the values for $\partial^2 p_t/\partial \theta\, \partial \theta'$ can be obtained recursively, starting from $\partial^2 p_1/\partial \theta\, \partial \theta' = \partial^2 \mu_1/\partial \theta\, \partial \theta'$.

The parameter estimates may be obtained by Newton's method, which uses the Hessian matrix of the actual second derivatives. To speed up computation, we may avoid calculating the exact Hessian by approximating it instead by the expected second derivatives, and use Fisher's method of scoring. Here we will follow the latter approach. In addition to providing parameter estimates, the Fisher optimization algorithm produces as a by-product an estimate of the asymptotic variance–covariance matrix of the model parameters, given by the inverse of the estimated information matrix evaluated at the converged values of the estimates. Each element of the inverse of the information matrix is a minimum variance bound for the corresponding parameter, and the positive square roots of the diagonal elements of this matrix (i.e., the standard errors of the estimated coefficients) may be used for significance tests and to construct confidence intervals.

According to asymptotic theory, ML estimators become progressively more unbiased and more normally distributed, and achieve the minimum possible variance more closely, as the sample size increases (see, e.g., King, 1989). However, these asymptotic assumptions may be violated in our complex Markov chain model. Moreover, the estimators in our model have essentially unknown properties for small to moderate sample sizes, and we cannot present any guidelines as to when a sample is sufficiently large for the asymptotic properties to be closely approximated. It is therefore important to investigate the behavior of the estimators of the parameters in Equation 8.2 by examining their finite-sampling distribution. The bootstrap and MCMC simulations provide useful tools in this situation.

8.2.2.2 Parametric Bootstrap Simulation

The bootstrap uses Monte Carlo simulation to empirically approximate the probability distribution of the parameter estimates and other statistics, rather than relying on assumptions about its shape that may only be asymptotically correct. The technique used here is the model-based parametric bootstrap (Davison and Hinkley, 1997). For the parametric bootstrap, resamples are taken from the original data via a fitted parametric model to create replicate data sets, from which the variability of the quantities of interest can be assessed. In the repeated simulations, it is assumed that both the form of the deterministic component of the model and the nature of the stochastic component are known. Bootstrap samples are generated using the same fixed covariates as in the original sample and a set of predetermined values for the parameters, allowing only the stochastic component to change randomly from sample to sample. By this means, many bootstrap samples are generated, each of which provides a set of estimates of the parameters that may then be examined for their bias, variance, and other distributional properties and used for bootstrap confidence intervals and hypothesis testing. The parametric bootstrap resampling procedure is implemented here according to the following algorithm:

1. Estimate the unknown parameter θ according to the model 8.2, using the original sample $\{x_{it}, y_{it}\}$, $i = 1, \ldots, n_t$, $t = 1, \ldots, T$, with the estimate denoted as $\hat{\theta}$, and obtain the fitted values $\hat{p}_{it}$ of the probability that the binary dependent variable $y_{it} = 1$.
2. For each x_{it} in the original sample $\{x_{it}, y_{it}\}$, generate a value of the bootstrap dependent variable y_{it}^* by random sampling from a Bernoulli distribution with success probability given by $\hat{p}_{it}$.
3. Use the bootstrap sample $\{x_{it}, y_{it}^*\}$ to fit the parameter estimate θ^*.
4. Repeat Steps 2 and 3 R times, yielding the bootstrap replications denoted as $\hat{\theta}_1^*, \ldots, \hat{\theta}_R^*$. The empirical distribution of these replications is used to approximate the finite-sample distribution of $\hat{\theta}$.

In this study we look at the density of the values of $\hat{\theta}^*$ under resampling of the fitted model to examine the bias and variance and to see if it is multimodal, skewed, or otherwise nonnormal. To obtain an accurate empirical approximation, we use $R = 5,000$ replications of the original data set. While the bootstrap estimates of bias and variance under the fitted model are important in their own right, parametric resampling may also be useful in testing problems when standard approximations do not apply or when the accuracy of the approximation is suspect. The key to applying the bootstrap for hypothesis testing is to transform the data so that the null hypothesis is true in the bootstrap population. That is, we simulate data under the null hypothesis, so that bootstrap resampling resembles sampling from a population for which the null hypothesis holds (Hall and Wilson, 1991). The bootstrap hypothesis test compares the observed value in the original sample with the R values $\hat{\theta}_1^*, \ldots, \hat{\theta}_R^*$, which are obtained from samples independently generated under the null model that satisfies H_0. The bootstrap P-value may then be obtained by $p^*(\hat{\theta}) = P(\hat{\theta}^* \geq \hat{\theta} \mid H_0) = R^{-1} \sum_{i=1}^{R} I(\theta^* \geq \hat{\theta})$, where the indicator $I(\cdot)$ equals one if the inequality is satisfied and zero if not (Davison and Hinkley, 1997). We reject the null hypothesis if the selected significance level exceeds $p^*(\hat{\theta})$.

8.2.2.3 Markov Chain Monte Carlo Simulation

Another powerful tool next to MLE and parametric bootstrap is Bayesian simulation, which is easily implemented using Markov chain Monte Carlo (MCMC) methods. Bayesian data analysis is not concerned with finding the parameter values for which the likelihood reaches the global maximum. It is primarily concerned with generating samples from the posterior distribution of the parameters given the data and a prior density, and this distribution may be asymmetric and/or multimodal. Other advantages of the Bayesian approach include the possible incorporation of any available prior information and the ability to make inferences on arbitrary functions of the parameters or predictions concerning specific individual units in the sample (see Pelzer and Eisinga, 2002). A popular method for MCMC simulation is Metropolis sampling (Tanner, 1996). The Metropolis sampler obtains a chain of draws from the posterior multivariate distribution $\pi(\theta \mid y)$ of the parameter θ. In sampling from the unknown target distribution, the algorithm uses a known auxiliary density A – e.g., a (multivariate) uniform or normal distribution – to select candidate parameters θ^c. The Metropolis algorithm proceeds as follows:

1. Choose a starting value for the parameter (e.g., the ML estimates).
2. Randomly draw the parameter θ^c from A, a symmetric proposal distribution with mean equal to the previous draw θ and an arbitrary variance.
3. If $\pi(\theta^c \mid y) \geq \pi(\theta \mid y)$, add the candidate θ^c to the chain of draws. If $\pi(\theta^c \mid y) < \pi(\theta \mid y)$, calculate the ratio $r = \pi(\theta^c \mid y)/\pi(\theta \mid y)$, and add θ^c with probability r to the chain of draws.
4. If the candidate θ^c is not added to the accepted draws in Step 3, add θ, so that two successive elements of the chain have the same parameter value θ. Else proceed with the next step.
5. Repeat Steps 2–4 K times, yielding a sample from the posterior distribution of θ.

In the Markov chain sampling used here, we assumed a priori that we are ignorant of the values of the parameters (i.e., have a vague prior belief). This implies that $\pi(\theta \mid y)$ equals the likelihood of θ. Once stationarity has been achieved, a value from a chain of draws from the Metropolis algorithm is supposed to have the same distribution as the target density. We ran the Metropolis algorithm $K = 100{,}000$ times, excluding an initial burn-in of 10,000 samples, and subsequently obtained the mean, standard deviation, and limits of the 95% credibility interval of θ.

8.3 APPLICATION

8.3.1 PC Penetration in Dutch Households

The major concern of this section is how the RCS Markov model performs in practice. The empirical application is concerned with modeling the rise in computer penetration rates in Dutch households in the 1986–1998 period using data from the Socio-Economic Panel (SEP) collected by Statistics Netherlands. The reason for using this 13-wave annual household panel study is that it offers the opportunity to check the estimation results against the panel findings. However, it is important to note that in the RCS Markov analysis below the panel data are treated as if they were observations of a temporal sequence of 13 independent cross-sectional samples. That is, no use is made of information about lagged values of y_{it}.

The binary dependent variable y_{it} is defined to equal one if the household owns a personal computer and zero if not. Table 8.1 reports the proportions of Dutch households with a PC in 1986–1998 along with the observed entry and exit transition rates. As can be seen, there is a marked upward time trend in PC ownership, from 12% in 1986 to 57% in 1998. While the entry rates (i.e., $\bar{y}_t \mid y_{t-1} = 0$) also show an increase over time, the exit rates (i.e., $(1 - \bar{y}_t) \mid y_{t-1} = 1$) show erratic change.

Table 8.1 Proportions of PC ownership in Dutch households over time, 2208 cases

Year	$\bar{y}_t$	$\bar{y}_t \mid y_{t-1} = 0$	$(1 - \bar{y}_t) \mid y_{t-1} = 1$
1986	.12		
1987	.15	.05	.10
1988	.20	.08	.12
1989	.24	.08	.13
1990	.28	.08	.08
1991	.31	.09	.09
1992	.36	.11	.09
1993	.38	.10	.13
1994	.41	.10	.09
1995	.44	.13	.11
1996	.48	.13	.07
1997	.51	.14	.09
1998	.57	.19	.07

It is clear from previous studies which structural determinants explain systematic variation in the presence of a PC in homes. The most important covariates – in the Netherlands as elsewhere – are educational attainment, age, the size of the household, and household income (see, e.g., OECD, 2001). These variables are included in the SEP household study, but they would generally also be available in a repeated cross-sectional survey. The time-varying variable age of head of household (hereafter *age*) is categorized into three different age categories (18–34, 35–54, and 55+ years). The time-varying variable number of household members is constructed from cross-sectional information about the number and the ages of the children in the household and the presence of a spouse. It is assumed that a family with children has two adults. The variable highest completed education of head of household (hereafter *education*) is taken to be fixed over time. In addition to these backcastable variables, the analysis also includes the temporary, nonbackcastable covariate household income. The variable used here is the standardized (i.e., corrected for size and type of household) disposable household income, categorized into quintiles.

8.3.2 RCS Markov Model

8.3.2.1 Maximum Likelihood

The first model fitted was a time-stationary Markov chain with constant terms only. This model produces the parameters $\beta(\mu_t) = -2.543$ and $\beta^*(\lambda_t) = -3.310$ and a log-likelihood value LL $= -15,895.214$. These estimates imply constant transition probabilities $\mu = .073$ and $\lambda = .035$, and hence predicted rates that underestimate the observed sample frequencies reported in Table 8.1. The model was subsequently modified to a nonstationary, heterogeneous Markov model by adding the covariates reported above. In analyzing the data with this model, it became apparent that the covariates have a substantial effect on the transition from have-not to have, but that they contribute little to the explanation of the reverse transition. We therefore decided to model the exit transitions using a constant term only. Further, it turned out that the inclusion of a linear time trend in the prediction of obtaining a computer appreciably improves the fit. We therefore included the variable time in the

Table 8.2 *ML*, parametric bootstrap, and *MCMC* estimates of *RCS* Markov model and *ML* estimates of first-order panel model, observations 26,364

	ML^a	RCS Markov Bootstrap[b]		MCMC[b]		Panel ML^a
$\delta(p_{t=1})$						
Constant	−3.713 (.202)	−3.718	(.205)	−3.754	(.232)	−3.606 (.276)
		[4.137	−3.318]	[−4.225	−3.327]	
Education	0.382 (.054)	0.381	(.055)	0.393	(.056)	0.364 (.072)
		[0.271	.489]	[0.288	.504]	
Age 35–54	−0.058 (.119)	−0.057	(.121)	−0.037	(.120)	0.092 (.170)
		[−0.294	.181]	[−0.284	.197]	
Age 55 and over	−0.852 (.162)	−0.859	(.165)	−0.842	(.178)	−0.782 (.252)
		[−1.201	−.551]	[−1.207	−.513]	
No. of household members	0.331 (.042)	0.332	(.043)	0.327	(.038)	0.310 (.061)
		[0.248	.417]	[0.249	.397]	
$\beta\,(\mu_{t=2,\dots,13})$						
Constant	−6.336 (.121)	−6.344	(.124)	−6.339	(.130)	−5.116 (.138)
		[−6.586	−6.110]	[−6.605	−6.105]	
Education	0.368 (.023)	0.369	(.023)	0.365	(.026)	0.245 (.029)
		[0.323	.413]	[0.310	.414]	
Age 35–54	0.137 (.049)	0.137	(.050)	0.129	(.049)	−0.098 (.067)
		[0.042	.238]	[0.037	.224]	
Age 55 and over	−1.364 (.066)	−1.365	(.065)	−1.362	(.067)	−1.270 (.089)
		[−1.494	−1.240]	[−1.499	−1.226]	
No. of household members	0.421 (.018)	0.422	(.018)	0.425	(.020)	0.375 (.023)
		[0.387	.457]	[0.389	.470]	
Income	0.438 (.015)	0.438	(.015)	0.438	(.016)	0.230 (.022)
		[0.408	.468]	[0.403	.467]	
Time	0.218 (.009)	0.218	(.009)	0.219	(.010)	0.171 (.008)
		[0.201	.236]	[0.198	.240]	
$\beta^*(\lambda_{t=2,\dots,13})$						
Constant	−2.292 (.132)	−2.300	(.133)	−2.307	(.198)	−2.284 (.039)
		[−2.576	−2.058]	[−2.779	−1.938]	
$\ell\ell$	−12,895.106					−7,766.304

[a] Standard errors in parentheses.
[b] The mean is reported as the point estimate, the standard deviation in parentheses, and the 95th percentile interval in brackets. The parametric bootstrap results are based on $R = 5,000$ bootstrap samples from the original data, and the MCMC findings on $K = 100,000$ Metropolis sampler posterior estimates.

model. This inclusion implies, as indicated in Section 8.2.1, that we drop the assumption of a time-constant intercept and allow the baseline entry rates to increase linearly over time. The results are reported in the second column of Table 8.2.

The top part of the table gives the estimated effects on the marginal probabilities p_{i1}. The table indicates that both education and the number of household members positively affect the presence of a PC in homes. While there is no significant difference in PC ownership between the 18–34-year age group and those aged 35–54, ownership is significantly more widespread among the younger age group than among those aged 55 and over. The middle part of Table 8.2 presents the effects on the transition from have-not to have with respect to PC ownership. The results show that educational attainment of head of household, household size, household income, and time have a positive effect on obtaining a computer. This finding confirms the conclusion of cross-sectional studies that computer ownership has spread most rapidly among affluent, well-educated families with children (OECD, 2001). The coefficients of the age terms again imply similar entry rates among the younger and middle age groups. The older age group has considerably lower access rates. The parameter estimate of the constant term for λ_{it} is shown in the bottom part of the table. An intercept of -2.292 implies a time-constant exit transition probability of $\lambda = .092$ (i.e., $\kappa = .908$), which perfectly matches the observed mean frequency of .092.

8.3.2.2 Parametric Bootstrap

As indicated, the benefit of parametric simulation is that the bootstrap estimates give empirical evidence that likelihood theory can be trusted, while providing alternative methods for calculating measures of uncertainty if that theory is unreliable. To examine the sampling distribution of the parameter estimates, we generated $R = 5{,}000$ bootstrap samples according to the algorithm given in Section 8.2.2.2. Table 8.2 provides for each parameter the mean and the sample standard deviation of the bootstrap estimates. In some applications of likelihood methods the variability of likelihood quantities may be grossly over- or underestimated. As the table shows, however, the misestimation is small enough to be unimportant here. The bootstrap mean values are close to the ML estimates, and the sample standard deviations are similar to the likelihood-based standard errors. The bootstrap estimates of bias and other distributional properties are given in Table 8.3.

The ML estimates of the model parameters appear to be only slightly biased, the largest absolute bias being 0.0086. When the estimated bias is expressed as a percentage of the parameter estimate (not reported in Table 8.3), the largest differences between standard theory and the bootstrap results are found for the parameter $\delta(p_{i1})$ of the age 35–54 dummy, for which the percentage bias is 1.85%. All other parameters have percentage biases less than 1%. The parameters also tend to have a small bias compared to the magnitude of their standard deviation. A frequently applied rule of thumb is that a good estimator should be biased by less than 25% of its standard deviation (Efron and Tibshirani, 1993). As can be seen in Table 8.3, the ratios of estimated bias to standard deviation are all much smaller than 0.25. Small values are also found for the root mean square error, which takes into account both standard deviation and bias. The bootstrap sample variance may be compared with the estimated ML variance using a chi-square test to examine whether the sample variance from the bootstrap is significantly larger than the variance from ML (Ratkowsky, 1983). For none of the parameters is the bootstrap variance significantly in excess of the ML variance. The largest value was again found for the $\delta(p_{i1})$ parameter of the age 35–54 dummy. The statistic $\chi^2 = (N-1)(\hat{\sigma}^2_{\text{bootstrap}}/\hat{\sigma}^2_{\text{ML}})$ is distributed as chi-square with 4,999 degrees of freedom (df), a transform of which may be closely approximated by the standard normal distribution, yielding, for this dummy variable, $z = \sqrt{2\chi^2} - \sqrt{2\,\text{df}-1} = 1.857$.

Table 8.3 also reports the skewness, the excess kurtosis, and the Jarque–Bera (1980) statistic, which may be used to test whether the estimators are normally distributed. The null hypothesis of normality is only rejected for the constant and the age 55+ parameter of $\delta(p_{i1})$, and for the constant term parameter of $\beta^*(\lambda)$. The distribution of the latter is somewhat peaked, and all three estimates have an extended tail to the left. The normal approximation is least accurate for the $\beta^*(\lambda)$ constant. However, even for this estimate the deviation from normality is negligible. The same goes for the distribution of κ $[= (1 + \exp(\beta^*(\lambda)))^{-1}]$,

Table 8.3 Parametric bootstrap estimates, based on R = 5000 bootstrap samples

	Bias $\times 10^2$	Bias÷sd	rmse	Skewness	Excess kurtosis	Jarque–Bera
$\delta(p_{t=1})$						
Constant	−.493	−.024	.205	−.098*	.094	9.812*
Education	−.089	−.016	.055	−.008	.061	0.796
Age 35–54	.107	.009	.121	.032	−.026	1.008
Age 55 and over	−.729	−.044	.165	−.179*	.104	28.954*
No. of household members	.128	.030	.043	.028	−.078	1.985
$\beta\,(\mu_{t=2,\ldots,13})$						
Constant	−.862	−.070	.124	−.033	−.012	0.931
Education	.066	.029	.023	−.050	−.037	2.405
Age 35–54	.040	.008	.050	.070	−.067	5.225
Age 55 and over	−.059	−.009	.065	−.052	.000	2.285
No. of household members	.084	.047	.018	.010	−.025	0.224
Income	.065	.043	.015	−.032	.044	1.260
Time	.022	.025	.009	.008	−.104	2.338
$\beta^*(\lambda_{t=2,\ldots,13})$						
Constant	−.789	−.059	.133	−.293*	.296*	89.691*

Note: The bootstrap estimate of bias ($= \bar{\theta}_{\text{bootstrap}} - \theta_{\text{ML}}$) is multiplied by 100, and rmse $= \sqrt{\text{sd}^2 + \text{bias}^2}$. The standard errors of skewness and excess kurtosis are 0.035 and 0.069, respectively. The Jarque–Bera (1980) test statistic for normality has an asymptotic χ_2^2 distribution; the 5% critical value is 5.991.
* Significant at the .05 level.

shown in Figure 8.1a. The histogram shows no visible departure of the κ estimates from those expected for a normally distributed random variable.

8.3.2.3 Markov Chain Monte Carlo

The Metropolis sampler posterior estimates for each parameter are reported in Table 8.2. The findings are based on $K = 100{,}000$ samples, excluding 10,000 samples for initial settling. Inspection of the posterior means reveals that there are no gross discrepancies in magnitude with the ML estimates. The MCMC standard deviations and the ML standard errors are also similar to one another. The same goes for the 95th percentile intervals of the parametric bootstrap estimates and the Bayesian credibility intervals. Thus Bayesian and frequentist methods for obtaining estimates produce roughly similar results.

In sum, according to both parametric bootstrap and MCMC simulations, the maximum likelihood estimators in this application are almost unbiased, with a variance close to the minimum variance bound, and a distribution close to normal. This implies that the ML point estimates of the parameters are accurate and that the inverse of the Fisher information matrix may be used as a good estimate of the covariance matrix of the parameter estimates.

8.3.3 Dynamic Panel Model

It is compelling to compare the RCS Markov ML estimates with the corresponding parameter estimates of a dynamic panel model that allows for first-order dependence. Most directly

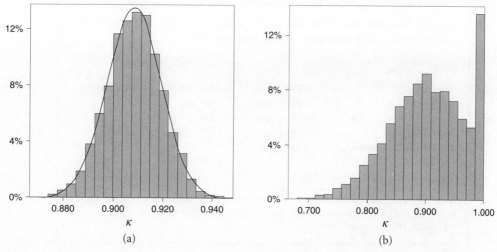

Figure 8.1. Histogram of ML estimates of κ (a) for 5000 bootstrap samples from the original full data, with normal curve superimposed, and (b) for 5000 cross-sectional samples of 2208 observations, one observation per household.

related to the RCS Markov model is a panel model that specifies a separate logistic regression for $P(y_{it} = 1 \mid y_{i\,t-1} = 0, 1)$, and includes $y_{i\,t-1}$ as an additional predictor. This model can conveniently be written in a single equation as logit $P(y_{it} = 1 \mid y_{i\,t-1} = 0, 1) = \mathbf{x}_{it}\beta + y_{i\,t-1}\mathbf{x}_{it}\alpha$, where $\alpha = \beta^* - \beta$ (see Amemiya, 1985; Diggle, Liang, and Zeger, 1994; Beck, Epstein, Jackman, and O'Halloran, 2001).

The results of applying this logistic model to the binary panel data are shown in the rightmost columns of Table 8.2. A comparison of the RCS Markov and panel estimates indicates that most of the findings are insensitive to the choice of model. The point estimates of all parameters, except perhaps the coefficients for age 35–54 and those for income, are rather similar, and the standard errors also correspond.

Note that the standard errors of the entry parameters are somewhat smaller for the RCS Markov model than for the panel data analysis. This may seem to be counterintuitive, as it would appear to show that more efficient estimates are produced when lagged y_{it}-values are unknown than when they are known. It should be noted, however, that the two models differ in the number of observations per parameter. The RCS Markov model uses 24,336 observations (excluding the observations at $t = 1$) to estimate seven β (μ_t) and one $\beta^*(\lambda)$ parameter, hence 3,042 observations per parameter. In the panel model we have 16,431 observations to estimate seven β (μ_t) parameters – i.e., 2,347 observations per parameter – and 7,905 observations to estimate $\beta^*(\lambda)$. This explains, at least intuitively, the somewhat smaller (larger) standard errors of the entry (exit) parameters in the RCS Markov model. The differences are modest, however, and inferences about the parameters do not change appreciably with the choice of model. Moreover, the two models predict equal transition probabilities μ_{it} and λ_{it} for all individual cases (not reported), and the accuracy of the two models as judged by a ROC curve analysis is almost identical (the area under the ROC curve for the $(y_t \mid y_{t-1} = 0)$ observations is 0.763 for the RCS Markov model and 0.768 for the panel model).

Only with respect to the likelihood is the RCS Markov model clearly inferior to the panel model. However, the two models differ in the computation of p_{it} and thus

Table 8.4 Mean and standard deviation ($\div \sqrt{13}$) of the *RCS* Markov *ML* estimates for 5,000 samples of 2,208 observations, one for each household

	$\delta(p_{t=1})$	$\beta\,(\mu_{t=2,\dots,13})$	$\beta^*(\lambda_{t=2,\dots,13})$ [a]
Constant	−3.845 (.199)	−6.426 (.120)	−2.389 (0.260)
Education	0.403 (.046)	0.366 (.027)	
Age 35–54	−0.045 (.118)	0.147 (.045)	
Age 55 and over	−0.785 (.160)	−1.423 (.063)	
No. of household members	0.343 (.032)	0.431 (.018)	
Income		0.447 (.015)	
Time		0.223 (.010)	

Note: Each sample is drawn without replacement and consists of 13 sets – one for each time period – of size 156. The standard deviation, divided by $\sqrt{13}$, is reported in parentheses.
[a] Excluding 440 samples with $\beta^*(\lambda_t) \leq -8$ (i.e., $\kappa > .9996$).

also of the likelihood. In binary panel data, the marginal probability p_{it} is either μ_{it} or $1 - \lambda_{it}$, conditional on $y_{i\,t-1}$, and the likelihood contribution can be written as $\ell_{it} = \mu_{it}^{y_{it}(1-y_{i\,t-1})}(1 - \lambda_{it})^{y_{it}y_{i\,t-1}}(1 - \mu_{it})^{(1-y_{it})(1-y_{i\,t-1})}\lambda_{it}^{(1-y_{it})y_{i\,t-1}}$. In the RCS Markov model, however, the marginal probability p_{it} is always a weighted sum of two probabilities – μ_{it} and λ_{it} – weighted by p_{it}, and the likelihood is given by $\ell_{it} = [\mu_{it}(1 - p_{i\,t-1}) + (1 - \lambda_{it})p_{i\,t-1}]^{y_{it}}[(1 - \mu_{it})(1 - p_{i\,t-1}) + \lambda_{it}p_{i\,t-1}]^{1-y_{it}}$. This implies that even if panel and RCS data produce identical transition probabilities μ_{it} and λ_{it}, the two likelihood functions may differ because of $p_{i\,t-1}$. The likelihood values are identical only if $p_{i\,t-1}$ is equal to $y_{i\,t-1}$; that is, if the lagged covariates perfectly predict the previous response.

8.3.4 Samples of Independent Observations

As indicated, in the RCS Markov model the panel data are treated as independent cross sections, implying that there is no information on autocov($y_{it}, y_{i\,t-1}$) available in the data file used for analysis. Nevertheless, the best way to make sure that the results are not artifacts is to analyze independent observations. To do so, we randomly draw (without replacement) samples of 2,028 different households from the (2,028×13 =) 26,364 panel observations, where each sample consists of 13 separate sets – one for each time period – of 156 households. Hence each household is selected only once in the "cross-sectional" sample. The total number of possible "cross-sectional" samples in our application is approximately $10^{2,242}$ [$\approx \prod_{s=0}^{12}(2,028 - s \times 156)!/156!(2,028 - 156 - s \times 156)!$]. We randomly drew 5,000 samples and analyzed each data set separately, using maximum likelihood estimation.

Table 8.4 reports the average values of the parameters across the samples along with the standard deviation divided by $\sqrt{13}$. A comparison of Tables 8.2 and 8.4 suggests that for almost all parameters the mean values are close to the MLE obtained for the original full sample size. The only noticeable difference is in the constant term parameter of $\beta^*(\lambda)$. This mismatch can be explained by referring to the distribution for κ, shown in Figure 8.1b. For several "extreme," small samples the true maximum of the likelihood function is attained when κ takes the boundary value $\kappa = 1$. This implies that the true MLE of $\beta^*(\lambda)$ is minus infinity and the Fisher optimization algorithm thus fails to converge.

Since the resample size is much smaller than the original sample size, it is not surprising that there is a large drop in efficiency relative to the estimates from the original full sample. However, dividing the standard deviations by $\sqrt{26,364/2,208} = \sqrt{13}$ scales them back to the standard errors of the parameters in the original sample. As can be seen, the standard deviations in Table 8.4 agree well with the ML standard errors reported in Table 8.2, the exception again being the constant parameter of $\beta^*(\lambda)$.

8.3.5 Parametric Bootstrap Test

Under parametric bootstrap, hypothesis testing is remarkably easy. We simply need to fit the hypothesized null model, generate bootstrap replications under the assumptions of this model, and calculate the measure we wish to test, both for the real data and for the R sets of bootstrap data. If the value from the real data is among the 5% most extreme values in the combined set of $R + 1$ values, the hypothesis is rejected at the .05 level of significance. For illustrative purposes, we selected a single sample from the "cross sections" of size 2,028, with ML estimates close to those reported in Table 8.2. The estimated value for κ in this sample was .916. Now consider testing the hypothesis $H_0 : \kappa \geq .999$ against the one-sided alternative $H_1 : \kappa < .999$ ($H_0 : \kappa = 1$ would be a theoretically implausible hypothesis to test for all cases). In $R = 4,999$ bootstrap resamples from H_0, we found 51 values less then or equal to .916, so the p^*-value is $51/5,000 = .0102$. This finding leads us to reject the null hypothesis for this particular sample.

8.4 SUMMARY

Repeated cross-sectional surveys have become an important data source for research over the past decades. The accumulation of these surveys offers researchers from various disciplines a growing opportunity to analyze longitudinal change. Dynamic models for the analysis of repeated cross sections are, however, relatively rare, and one may even argue that there is an increasing lag between the availability of data and models to analyze them.

The results presented here illustrate the usefulness of exploiting repeated cross-sectional surveys to identify and to estimate 0–1 transition probabilities, which are generally thought to be nonestimable from RCS data. The bootstrap and MCMC findings for the PC ownership example suggest that the maximum likelihood RCS Markov model produces reliable estimates in large samples. It also turns out that, in our empirical application at least, the RCS Markov model performs almost as well as a first-order dynamic panel model. To rule out artificial results, samples of independent observations from the panel data were also analyzed, with similar results to those for the full sample.

This paper has made some necessary first steps in exploring a largely unknown area, and many relevant topics could not be covered here. For example, in some contexts (e.g., the empirical illustration discussed here) it is pretty clear from previous studies or theory which covariates are likely to be important and how they are related, at least qualitatively, to the dependent variable of interest. In other cases, especially in complex data from an unfamiliar field, covariate selection may be far from obvious. An important part of the analysis is then a preliminary analysis to search for a suitable model. This involves not just inspecting the adequacy of the initial model, but doing so in a way that will suggest an improvement of the model and bring to light possibly unsuspected features of the data.

A difficult problem in model specification is that it is not always possible from the data themselves to obtain a clear indication of how to improve the model (and how important it is to do so). It may also happen that different models fit the data roughly equally well and that any choice between them has to be made on grounds external to the data.

Further, it is obvious that estimating the "nonestimable" is possible only by making assumptions. The validity of the assumptions, however, cannot be assessed from the data under study. Consequently, findings are always conditional on the appropriateness of the assumed model, which in a fundamental sense is not testable. An appropriate statistical framework then is to consider how sensitive the results are to model assumptions. An important subject for future work is therefore to develop sensitivity analysis tools (such as influence diagnostics) and to study the stability of the results under different model specifications and small modifications or perturbations of the data.

Topics to be studied by further Monte Carlo work are the distributional properties of the estimators in different model specifications and the sensitivity of inference procedures to varying sample sizes. In addition to the parametric bootstrap, nonparametric resampling could be used to examine the robustness of specification. Nonparametric simulation requires generating artificial data without assuming that the original data have some particular parametric distribution. Finally, although the impetus behind developing the methodology presented here came from the intent to dynamically model RCS data, it would be of interest to apply the model to panel data with missing observations for y_{t-1}. The Markov chain model could then be used, in conjunction with a first-order panel model for observations with nonmissing y_{t-1}, to obtain model-based imputations for the missing data.

REFERENCES

Amemiya, Takeshi. 1985. *Advanced Econometrics*. Oxford: Basil Blackwell.

Beck, Nathaniel, David Epstein, Simon Jackman, and Sharyn O'Halloran. 2001. "Alternative Models of Dynamics in Binary Time-Series–Cross-Section Models: The Example of State Failure." Paper presented at the 2001 Annual Meeting of the Society for Political Methodology, Atlanta GA.

Davison, A. C. and D. V. Hinkley. 1997. *Bootstrap Methods and their Application*. Cambridge: Cambridge University Press.

Diggle, Peter J., Kung-Yee Liang, and Scott L. Zeger. 1994. *Analysis of Longitudinal Data*. Oxford: Clarendon Press.

Duncan, Otis Dudley and Beverly Davis. 1953. "An Alternative to Ecological Correlation," *American Sociological Review*, 18: 665–666.

Efron, Bradley and Robert J. Tibshirani. 1993. *An Introduction to the Bootstrap*. New York: Chapman and Hall.

Franklin, Charles H. 1989. "Estimation across Data Sets: Two-Stage Auxiliary Instrumental Variables Estimation (2SAIV)," *Political Analysis*, 1: 1–23.

Hall, Peter and Susan R. Wilson. 1991. "Two Guidelines for Bootstrap Hypothesis Testing," *Biometrics*, 47: 757–762.

Jarque, Carlos M. and Anil K. Bera. 1980. "Efficient Tests for Normality, Homoscedasticity and Serial Independence of Regression Residuals," *Economics Letters*, 6: 255–259.

King, Gary. 1989. *Unifying Political Methodology. The Likelihood Theory of Statistical Inference*. Cambridge: Cambridge University Press.

King, Gary. 1997. *A Solution to the Ecological Inference Problem: Reconstructing Individual Behavior from Aggregate Data*. Cambridge: Cambridge University Press.

King, Gary, Ori Rosen, and Martin Tanner. 1999. "Binomial–beta Hierarchical Models for Ecological Inference," *Sociological Methods and Research*, 28: 61–90.

Kish, Leslie. 1987. *Statistical Design for Research*. New York: Wiley.

Mebane, Walter R. and Jonathan Wand. 1997. "Markov Chain Models for Rolling Cross-Section Data: How Campaign Events and Political Awareness Affect Vote Intentions and Partisanship in the United

States and Canada." Paper presented at the 1997 Annual Meeting of the Midwest Political Science Association, Chicago.

Moffitt, Robert. 1990. "The Effect of the U.S. Welfare System on Marital Status," *Journal of Public Economics*, 41: 101–124.

Moffitt, Robert. 1993. "Identification and Estimation of Dynamic Models with a Time Series of Repeated Cross-sections," *Journal of Econometrics*, 59: 99–123.

OECD. 2001. "Understanding the Digital Divide." Pdf file available at http://www.oecd.org/pdf/ M00002000/M00002444.pdf (June 2003).

Pelzer, Ben and Rob Eisinga. 2002. "Bayesian Estimation of Transition Probabilities from Repeated Cross Sections," *Statistica Neerlandica*, 56: 23–33.

Pelzer, Ben, Rob Eisinga, and Philip Hans Franses. 2002. "Inferring Transition Probabilities from Repeated Cross Sections," *Political Analysis*, 10: 113–133.

Penubarti, Mohan and Alexander A. Schuessler. 1998. *Inferring Micro from Macrolevel Change: Ecological Panel Inference in Surveys*. Los Angeles: University of California.

Ratkowsky, David A. 1983. *Nonlinear Regression Modeling: A Unified Practical Approach*. New York: Marcel Dekker.

Ross, Sheldon M. 1993. *Introduction to Probability Models*, 5th ed. San Diego, CA: Academic Press.

Sigelman, Lee. 1991. "Turning Cross Sections into a Panel: A Simple Procedure for Ecological Inference," *Social Science Research*, 20: 150–170.

Tam Cho, Wendy K. 1998. "If the Assumption Fits . . . : A Comment on the King Ecological Inference Solution," *Political Analysis*, 7: 143–163.

Tanner, Martin. 1996. *Tools for Statistical Inference*. New York: Springer.

## PART THREE

9 Ecological Inference in the Presence of Temporal Dependence*

Kevin M. Quinn

ABSTRACT

Researchers have realized for some time that the quality of ecological inferences depends critically on the quality of the prior assumptions one makes. In many applications, the most uncontroversial piece of background knowledge is that the interior cell probabilities of interest exhibit substantial stability over time. Seen this way, temporal dependence is not a nuisance to be statistically accounted for, but rather an important piece of background knowledge that can be used by researchers to form more accurate prior distributions for the interior cell probabilities of interest. In this manuscript we develop a class of Bayesian hierarchical models that can be used for ecological inference where there is *a priori* reason to believe temporal dependence is present. A version of the model is applied to simulated data as well as data on voting registration by race in Louisiana counties over a 14-year period. Within the context of these data, the proposed dynamic model performs reasonably well.

9.1 INTRODUCTION

Researchers have realized for some time that the quality of ecological inferences depends critically on the quality of the prior assumptions one makes. This is true regardless of whether the prior assumptions are explicitly stated, as in a Bayesian analysis, or are left implicit. The key to making reasonable ecological inferences then is seen to be, to a large extent, dependent upon one's ability to formulate reasonable prior beliefs about the process under study.

In many applications, the most uncontroversial piece of background knowledge is that the interior cell probabilities of interest exhibit substantial stability over time. Seen this way, temporal dependence is not a nuisance to be statistically accounted for, but rather an important piece of background knowledge that can be used by researchers to form more accurate prior distributions for the interior cell probabilities of interest.

In this chapter we develop a class of Bayesian hierarchical models that can be used for ecological inference where there is *a priori* reason to believe temporal dependence is present. These models are based on the ecological inference model of Wakefield (2001) along with the work of Besag et al. (1991, 1995) and West and Harrison (1997) on Markov random field priors. While these models are somewhat more complicated than other approaches for directly incorporating prior information into models for ecological inference, they have the advantage that the prior distribution they employ is oftentimes easier to specify confidently, given what we know about many social processes.

A model of this kind is applied to data on voting registration by race in Louisiana counties over a 14-year period. The advantage of using these data is that the interior cell counts are

* This research was supported under NSF grant SES 01-36679 as well as by the Center for Statistics and the Social Sciences with funds from the University Initiatives Fund at the University of Washington.

actually observed, which allows one to examine the performance of the model under study. Within the context of these data, the proposed dynamic model performs reasonably well. Nonetheless, it should be emphasized that it is possible to construct examples where the model will perform poorly.

This chapter is organized as follows. Section 9.2 details the proposed dynamic model and places it within the context of previous work on ecological inference and temporal dependence. Section 9.3 discusses the Markov chain Monte Carlo (MCMC) algorithm used to fit the model, and briefly comments on other possible approaches. Section 9.4 looks at the performance of the model in some simulated data examples. In Section 9.5 we turn attention to the application of voting registration by race in Louisiana from 1975 to 1988. Section 9.6 concludes.

9.2 A MODEL FOR ECOLOGICAL INFERENCE IN THE PRESENCE OF TEMPORAL DEPENDENCE

Consider the following partially observed contingency table for time period t:

	$Y_t = 0$	$Y_t = 1$	
$X_t = 0$	Y_{0t}		r_{0t}
$X_t = 1$	Y_{1t}		r_{1t}
	c_{0t}	c_{1t}	N_t

In many social science applications, X may represent a background characteristic such as race, sex, or educational background, while Y may represent a social action such as voting, registering to vote, or committing a crime. Throughout the chapter we assume that our data consists of a sequence of such partially observed tables indexed by time $t = 1, \ldots, T$.

Although the table margins (c_{0t}, c_{1t}, r_{0t}, and r_{1t}) are observed, the need for ecological inference arises because the interior cell counts (y_{0t} and y_{1t}) are unobserved. The goal of ecological inference is to estimate the interior cell counts, or equivalently, to estimate $P(Y_t = 0 | X_t = 0)$ and $P(Y_t = 0 | X_t = 1)$. In what follows we will use the notation $\beta_{jt} = P(Y_t = 0 | X_t = j)$ for $j = 0, 1$.

9.2.1 Likelihood

Following Wakefield (2001), we can write the likelihood function for T tables as the product of a convolution of binomial mass functions

$$L(\boldsymbol{\beta}_0, \boldsymbol{\beta}_1) = \prod_{t=1}^{T} \sum_{y_{0t}=u_{0t}}^{u_{1t}} \binom{r_{0t}}{y_{0t}} \binom{r_{1t}}{c_{0t} - y_{0t}} \beta_{0t}^{y_{0t}} (1 - \beta_{0t})^{r_{0t} - y_{0t}} \beta_{1t}^{c_{0t} - y_{0t}} (1 - \beta_{1t})^{r_{1t} - c_{0t} + y_{0t}},$$

(9.1)

where $\boldsymbol{\beta}_j$ denotes the vector of T conditional probabilities $\beta_{j1}, \ldots, \beta_{jT}$ for $j = 0, 1$, $u_{0t} = \max(0, c_{0t} - r_{1t})$, and $u_{1t} = \min(r_{0t}, c_{0t})$. This model results from the assumption that $Y_{jt} | r_{jt} \sim Binomial(r_{jt}, \beta_{jt})$ for $j = 0, 1$ and that, conditional on $\boldsymbol{\beta}_0$ and $\boldsymbol{\beta}_1$, the cell counts are independent across tables. In what follows, we maintain this conditional independence assumption and model temporal dependence through the prior distributions for $\boldsymbol{\beta}_0$ and $\boldsymbol{\beta}_1$.

Working with this likelihood directly will generally prove to be infeasible. When N_t is large (as it will typically be in social science applications) it will be reasonable to employ

Wakefield's (2001) asymptotic approximation to Equation 9.1 given by the following:

$$\tilde{L}(\beta_0, \beta_1) = \prod_{t=1}^{T} \frac{1}{\sqrt{r_{0t}\beta_{0t}(1 - \beta_{0t}) + r_{1t}\beta_{1t}(1 - \beta_{1t})}}$$

$$\times \exp\left[-\frac{(c_{0t} - r_{0t}\beta_{0t} - r_{1t}\beta_{1t})^2}{2(r_{0t}\beta_{0t}(1 - \beta_{0t}) + r_{1t}\beta_{1t}(1 - \beta_{1t}))}\right]. \tag{9.2}$$

9.2.2 Prior Specification

A defining aspect of ecological inference is that the posterior distribution depends crucially on the prior distribution even as the sample size goes to infinity. This suggests at least two approaches to inference. The first, embodied by Wakefield's (2001) baseline model and less formally by Duncan and Davis's (1953) method of bounds, focuses solely on the information in the likelihood through the use of uniform priors on $(\beta_0 \ \beta_1)$. A second approach, exemplified by the work of King (1997) and King, Rosen, and Tanner (1999) and by the hierarchical models proposed by Wakefield (2001), seeks to construct reasonable prior distributions by pooling information across tables via various hierarchical prior specifications.

The first approach is useful in that it provides a solid baseline against which to compare the results from other model specifications. Nonetheless, in most cases, the bounds on the model parameters may be so wide that the results from the baseline model are of limited practical use.

The second approach remedies this problem, but it does so at a price. The specification of an informative prior distribution results in a more sharply peaked posterior distribution, which leads to more certain inference. However, because of the lack of information in the likelihood function, one's inferences are determined, to a large extent, by the choice of prior specification.

The current chapter is closely allied with the second approach above in that it presents ways to formulate reasonable, informative prior distributions for tables observed over time. The major difference is that it is often easier to specify the prior distributions described below because researchers often have reasonably good information about how much temporal stability the interior cell probabilities exhibit even if they don't have good information about the overall level of the cell probabilities. For other approaches to ecological inference with temporally dependent data see Pelzer, Eisinga, and Franses (Chapter 8 of this volume) and Lewis (Chapter 4).

We begin by reparameterizing so that the transformed parameters are unbounded. Let

$$\theta_{jt} \equiv \log\left(\frac{\beta_{jt}}{1 - \beta_{jt}}\right), \qquad j = 0, 1, \quad t = 1, \dots, T.$$

The starting point for our prior specification is the assumption that *a priori* θ_{jt} follows a simple random walk in time. Formally,

$$\theta_{jt} = \theta_{j(t-1)} + \epsilon_{jt}, \qquad j = 0, 1, \quad t = 2, \dots, T,$$

where

$$\epsilon_{jt} \sim \mathcal{N}\left(0, \sigma_j^2\right).$$

It can be shown[1] that this random walk prior corresponds to the following (improper) joint density for $\boldsymbol{\theta}_j$, $j = 0, 1$:

$$p(\boldsymbol{\theta}_j|\sigma_j^2) \propto \sigma_j^{-T} \exp\left(-\frac{1}{2\sigma_j^2}\boldsymbol{\theta}_j'\mathbf{W}\boldsymbol{\theta}_j\right),   \tag{9.3}$$

where $\mathbf{W}$ is the $T \times T$ matrix with typical off-diagonal element

$$w_{ts} = \begin{cases} -1 & \text{if } t \text{ and } s \text{ are neighboring time periods,} \\ 0 & \text{otherwise} \end{cases}$$

and typical diagonal element $w_{tt} = \sum_{s \neq t} |w_{ts}|$. In other words, $\mathbf{W}$ has the form

$$\mathbf{W} = \begin{bmatrix} 1 & -1 & & & & & \\ -1 & 2 & -1 & & & 0 & \\ & -1 & 2 & -1 & & & \\ & & \cdot & \cdot & \cdot & & \\ & & & \cdot & \cdot & \cdot & \\ & 0 & & & -1 & 2 & -1 \\ & & & & & -1 & 1 \end{bmatrix}.$$

Note that $\mathbf{W}$ does not have full rank, and consequently $p(\boldsymbol{\theta}_j|\sigma_j^2)$ is not a proper density. As result, this prior does not specify the overall level of $\boldsymbol{\theta}_j$ – an arbitrary constant can be added to $\boldsymbol{\theta}_j$ without changing the value of the right hand side of Equation 9.3.

It is informative to look at the implied prior distribution for θ_{jt} given the elements of $\boldsymbol{\theta}_j$ other than θ_{jt}. Let ∂_t denote the set of time periods directly adjacent to time period t, and $\boldsymbol{\theta}_{j(-t)}$ the vector composed of the elements of $\boldsymbol{\theta}_j$ other than θ_{jt}. Besag et al. (1991, 1995) show that

$$\theta_{jt}|\boldsymbol{\theta}_{j(-t)}, \sigma_j^2 \sim \mathcal{N}\left(\sum_{s \in \partial_t} \frac{-w_{ts}\theta_{js}}{w_{tt}}, \frac{\sigma_j^2}{w_{tt}}\right).   \tag{9.4}$$

In words, the conditional prior mean of θ_{jt} is a weighted average of the neighboring values of θ_j, and the conditional prior variance is inversely proportional to the sum of the weights from neighboring time periods.

Attempts at estimating a covariance between $\boldsymbol{\theta}_0$ and $\boldsymbol{\theta}_1$ resulted in models that were extremely weakly identified. Rather than trying to estimate such a covariance parameter, we simply assume that $\boldsymbol{\theta}_0$ is *a priori* independent of $\boldsymbol{\theta}_1$. Of course, as we will see later, this does not preclude the possibility that $\boldsymbol{\theta}_0$ is *a posteriori* dependent on $\boldsymbol{\theta}_1$.

We complete the prior specification by adopting a conjugate prior distribution for σ_0^2 and σ_1^2. More specifically, we assume that σ_j^2 follows an inverse gamma distribution with shape $\nu_j/2$ and scale $\delta_j/2$ for $j = 0, 1$. The posterior density for (β_0, β_1) is then proportional to the likelihood in Equation 9.1 times the densities $p(\boldsymbol{\theta}_0|\sigma_0^2)$ and $p(\boldsymbol{\theta}_1|\sigma_1^2)$ given in Equation 9.3 times the inverse gamma priors for σ_0^2 and σ_1^2.

---

[1] For instance, see Clayton (1996). See also Besag et al. (1991, 1995) and West and Harrison (1997).

One of the major benefits of this class of prior distributions is that the level of θ_{jt} is left unspecified. Since θ_{jt} is defined to be the log odds of $Y_t = 0$ given $X_t = j$, the researcher is simply required to specify beliefs for the odds ratio $\exp(\theta_{jt} - \theta_{j(t-1)})$, which corresponds to e raised to the power of the increment of the random walk. For instance, suppose we believe that the expected values of the endpoints for the 95% prior credible interval for the odds ratio above will be 1.25 and 0.8. This implies that the endpoints for the log odds ratio $(\theta_{jt} - \theta_{j(t-1)})$ will be $\log(1.25) = 0.223$ and $\log(0.8) = -0.223$. Given that the increments of the random walk are assumed to be Gaussian, these endpoints correspond to approximately $2\sigma_j$. This means that we should set ν_j and δ_j so that $E[\sigma_j] = 0.5\log(1.25)$.

It should be noted that more complicated dynamics can be modeled using the same framework. For instance, suppose one is willing to assume that the logit of the cell probabilities evolves according to

$$\theta_{jt} = 2\theta_{j(t-1)} - \theta_{j(t-2)} + \epsilon_{jt}, \qquad j = 0, 1, \quad t = 3, \ldots, T,$$

where

$$\epsilon_{jt} \sim \mathcal{N}\left(0, \sigma_j^2\right).$$

Such a model corresponds to the assumption that the expected value of the current value of θ_j is the linear extrapolation of the two preceding values of θ_j (Clayton, 1996). However, as a word of warning, such a prior specification produced wildly misleading results when applied to the Louisiana voter registration data analyzed later in this chapter.

It is also worth mentioning that this same setup can be used to model spatial and spatiotemporal dependence. The only difference is that the neighborhood structure would now be based on both spatial and temporal proximity. See Haneuse and Wakefield (Chapter 12 of this volume) for details.

It is straightforward to extend this model to include the effects of measured covariates on the cell probabilities. For instance, it is possible to assume that θ_{jt} is given by the following:

$$\theta_{jt} = \mathbf{z}_{jt}\boldsymbol{\alpha}_j + \eta_{jt} + \epsilon_{jt}, \qquad j = 0, 1, \quad t = 1, \ldots, T,$$

where $\mathbf{z}_{jt}$ is the vector of covariates specific to row j and time t, and η_{jt} is now assumed to follow a random walk in time. Model fitting via Markov chain Monte Carlo is straightforward (see Besag et al., 1991, 1995 for a similar setup in a nonecological inference framework).

9.3 MODEL FITTING

Bayesian inference for the model discussed above centers on the posterior distribution for $(\beta_0, \beta_1, \sigma_0^2, \sigma_1^2)$. We use MCMC methods to construct an approximate sample from this posterior distribution. The MCMC strategy employed is the following.

To begin one scan of the MCMC algorithm we sample $[\beta_{0t}, \beta_{1t}|\beta_{0(-t)}, \beta_{1(-t)}, \sigma_0^2, \sigma_1^2]$ using a Metropolis–Hastings step for $t = 1, \ldots, T$. The posterior full conditional distribution here is simply proportional to the contribution of the tth table to the likelihood in Equation 9.1 times the prior for θ_{0t} in Equation 9.4 times the prior for θ_{1t} in Equation 9.4. As a practical matter we use the approximate likelihood in Equation 9.2 in place of the exact likelihood. Candidate values of (β_{0t}, β_{1t}) are generated from a uniform distribution defined on the extended tomography line for table t times a univariate normal distribution that is perpendicular to the tomography line. The length of the tomography line on which the uniform distribution is defined is extended so that at the endpoints of the extended tomography line ± 2 standard deviations of the perpendicular normal density are outside the square $[0, 1]^2$. Through simulation experiments it was found that setting the standard deviation of the perpendicular normal density equal to $2.6528\sqrt{N_t}$ resulted in a somewhat overdispersed candidate generating distribution. The advantage to this candidate generating distribution is that it closely approximates the underlying likelihood surface (although not necessarily the posterior surface, which will be more concentrated on one section of the tomography line) and it is proportional to a univariate normal density, making it easy to evaluate and sample from. Both of these facts make the Metropolis–Hastings sampling of the cell probabilities fairly quick.

The next step after sampling the cell probabilities for the T tables is to sample $[\sigma_0^2, \sigma_1^2 | \beta_0, \beta_1]$. Because of the model's conditional independence assumptions, we have $p(\sigma_0^2, \sigma_1^2 | \beta_0, \beta_1) = p(\sigma_0^2 | \beta_0) p(\sigma_1^2 | \beta_1)$, which allows us to sample these parameters in two separate steps. Once again because of the model's conditional independence assumptions, $p(\sigma_j^2 | \beta_j)$ is proportional to the density $p(\theta_j | \sigma_j^2)$ given in Equation 9.3 times the inverse gamma prior density for σ_j^2. Multiplication of these densities reveals that $p(\sigma_j^2 | \beta_j)$ is an inverse gamma density with shape $(v_j + T)/2$ and scale $(\delta_j + \theta_j' \mathbf{W} \theta_j)/2$. A simple Gibbs step can thus be used to sample $[\sigma_j^2 | \beta_j]$ for $j = 0, 1$.

Other MCMC approaches are certainly possible. In particular, some gains in simulation efficiency might be had by sampling from the joint full conditional for $[\beta_0, \beta1 | \sigma_0^2, \sigma_1^2]$ rather than from the univariate full conditionals. The problem here is finding a reasonably good candidate generating density so that the acceptance rate of the Metropolis–Hasting sampling isn't extremely low.

The raw C++ code to fit these models, along with an R interface to the C++ code, is available at http://scythe.wustl.edu/mcmcpack.html.

9.4 SIMULATED DATA EXAMPLES

In order to get some sense of how the dynamic model developed above performs, we present results from three simulated data sets. In each case we compare the performance of the dynamic model, using three different prior specifications, with the performance of Wakefield's basic hierarchical model, also using three different prior specifications. In each simulated data set there are 20 time periods. The row sums are fixed at $r_{0t} = 3500$ and $r_{1t} = 1500$ for all t. The interior cell probabilities are then varied, and the interior cell counts are generated from the appropriate binomial distributions.

The first simulated example assumes that $\theta_{0t} = 0.921 + 0.0789t$ and $\theta_{1t} = -0.1053 + 0.1053t$ for $t = 1, \ldots, 20$. Figure 9.1 presents a tomography plot of these data in which the tomography lines have been color-coded according to their temporal position. Here we see that the linear dependence on the logit scale is clearly visible on the color-coded tomography plot.

Figures 9.2 and 9.3 present the results from the dynamic model and Wakefield's hierarchical model respectively. In each case, three prior specifications were employed: one in which $\delta_0 = \delta_1 = 0.05$ and $v_0 = v_1 = 1$, another in which $\delta_0 = \delta_1 = 0.5$ and $v_0 = v_1 = 1$, and a third in which $\delta_0 = \delta_1 = 3$ and $v_0 = v_1 = 1$. Looking at these figures, we see that the dynamic model tends to perform somewhat better than the basic hierarchical model in that its point estimates are generally closer to the true values. As we would expect, Figure 9.3 shows that the hierarchical model tends to shrink all of the point estimates to the average level across the tables, while the dynamic model allows for more local variability. The true

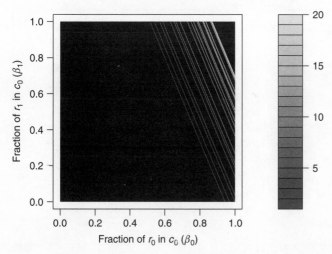

Figure 9.1. Dynamic tomography plot from first simulated data set. The tomography lines are color-coded according to their temporal location.

values of β_{0t} and β_{1t} are inside the 95% credible intervals regardless of which model is fitted. In short, both models do reasonably well on this data set, with the dynamic model doing slightly better.

The second simulated example assumes that $\theta_{0t} = ((t-10)/8)^2$ and $\theta_{1t} = ((t-9)/10)^2$ for $t = 1, \ldots, 20$. Figure 9.4 presents a tomography plot of these data in which the tomography lines have been color-coded according to their temporal position. Here we see the the U-shaped trajectories of the cell probabilities expressed by the fact that the tomography lines from first time periods tend to cluster with the tomography lines from the later periods. Note also that almost no information about the level of β_1 is conveyed in the bounds.

Figures 9.5 and 9.6 present the results from the dynamic model and Wakefield's hierarchical model respectively. In each case, three prior specifications were employed: one in which $\delta_0 = \delta_1 = 0.05$ and $\nu_0 = \nu_1 = 1$, another in which $\delta_0 = \delta_1 = 0.5$ and $\nu_0 = \nu_1 = 1$, and a third in which $\delta_0 = \delta_1 = 3$ and $\nu_0 = \nu_1 = 1$. Regardless of prior specification, each of the models does a reasonably good job of estimating β_0. This is due, to a very large extent, to the amount of information available in the bounds. On the other hand, neither model does a great job of estimating β_1. This is due to a lack of information in the bounds for these parameters. In summary, the two models (under all of the prior specifications) perform about equally well on this simulated data set.

The third simulated example assumes that $\theta_{0t} = ((t-10)/8)^2$ and $\theta_{1t} = 0.947 + 0.053t$ for $t = 1, \ldots, 20$. Figure 9.7 presents a tomography plot of these data in which the tomography lines have been color-coded according to their temporal position. Here the temporal pattern is more difficult to see in the tomography plot. We can see that in the later time periods there are semi-informative bounds on β_{1t} and there are always fairly informative bounds on β_{0t}.

Figures 9.8 and 9.9 present the results from the dynamic model and Wakefield's hierarchical model respectively. In each case, three prior specifications were employed: one in which $\delta_0 = \delta_1 = 0.05$ and $\nu_0 = \nu_1 = 1$, another in which $\delta_0 = \delta_1 = 0.5$ and $\nu_0 = \nu_1 = 1$, and a third in which $\delta_0 = \delta_1 = 3$ and $\nu_0 = \nu_1 = 1$. Once again, both models do a reasonable job of estimating β_0, with the slight caveat that the dynamic models' estimates seem to be

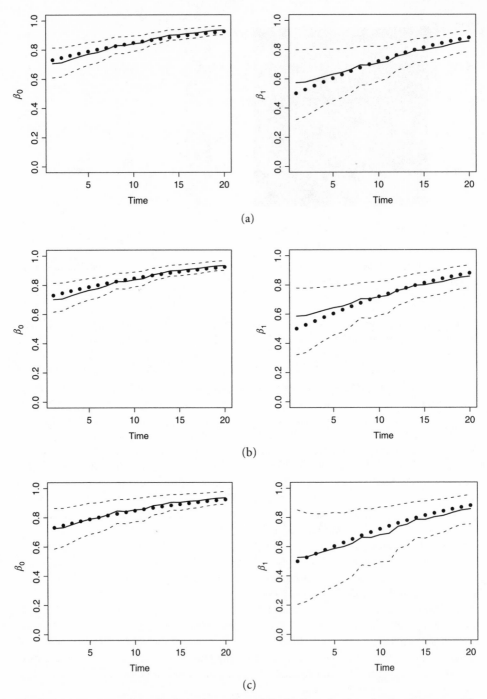

Figure 9.2. Summary of results from dynamic models fitted to the first simulated data set. The solid circles correspond to the true values of β_{0t} and β_{1t} that generated the data, the solid lines correspond to the estimated posterior means of these parameters, and the dashed lines correspond to the 2.5th and 97.5th posterior percentiles for these parameters. (a) $\delta_0 = \delta_1 = 0.05$ and $\nu_0 = \nu_1 = 1$; (b) $\delta_0 = \delta_1 = 0.5$ and $\nu_0 = \nu_1 = 1$; (c) $\delta_0 = \delta_1 = 3$ and $\nu_0 = \nu_1 = 1$.

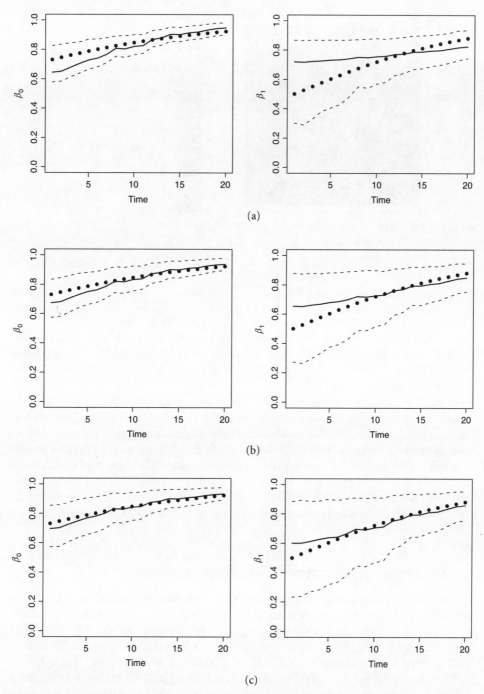

Figure 9.3. Summary of results from hierarchical models fitted to the first simulated data set. The solid circles correspond to the true values of β_{0t} and β_{1t} that generated the data, the solid lines correspond to the estimated posterior means of these parameters, and the dashed lines correspond to the 2.5th and 97.5th posterior percentiles for these parameters. (a) $\delta_0 = \delta_1 = 0.05$ and $v_0 = v_1 = 1$; (b) $\delta_0 = \delta_1 = 0.5$ and $v_0 = v_1 = 1$; (c) $\delta_0 = \delta_1 = 3$ and $v_0 = v_1 = 1$.

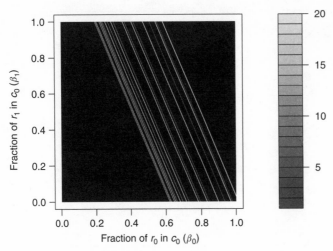

Figure 9.4. Dynamic tomography plot from second simulated data set. The tomography lines are color-coded according to their temporal location.

somewhat falsely precise. Neither model does a very good job of estimating β_1; this is partly due to the lack of information in the bounds and also partly because both models implictly use information in the bounds on β_0 to estimate β_1. Since β_{0t} and β_{1t} are following different paths through time, this biases the estimates of β_1 (the cell probabilities with the least informative bounds).

In summary, the dynamic model slightly outperformed the hierarchical model when the cell probabilities exhibited fairly strong linear trends. In the other simulated data examples the two models performed about equally well. Perhaps the most important point to take from these examples is the role of the exact priors used on the variance parameters in these models may not be important as long as they are not too informative. The three prior specifications used in these examples had prior modes for the variance parameters at 0.01667, 0.1667, and 1.000. On a logit scale these are fairly large differences in prior beliefs. Nonetheless, the posterior results changed only minimally across prior specifications. In large part this was because the priors used were all fairly diffuse with ν_j set equal to 1 for $j = 0, 1$.

9.5 APPLICATION: VOTER REGISTRATION IN LOUISIANA, 1975–1988

To see how the model discussed above performs on real data, we look to data relating race and voter registration in 52 Louisiana counties from 1975 to 1988.[2] These data are available at the Record of American Democracy (King et al., 1997) project website (http://hdc-www.harvard.edu/ROAD/) and have been previously analyzed by King (1997) and King et al. (1999). Also see Haneuse and Wakefield (Chapter 12 of this volume). These data are well suited to our present purposes in that they are fairly typical of the types of data political scientists wish to use to make ecological inferences, they have a moderate time dimension,

---

[2] The original data set contained data from 64 counties over 1975–1990. Of these, 12 were removed because of what appeared to be bad outliers and/or coding inconsistencies. Similarly, 1989 and 1990 were removed because of data problems in the 1989 data.

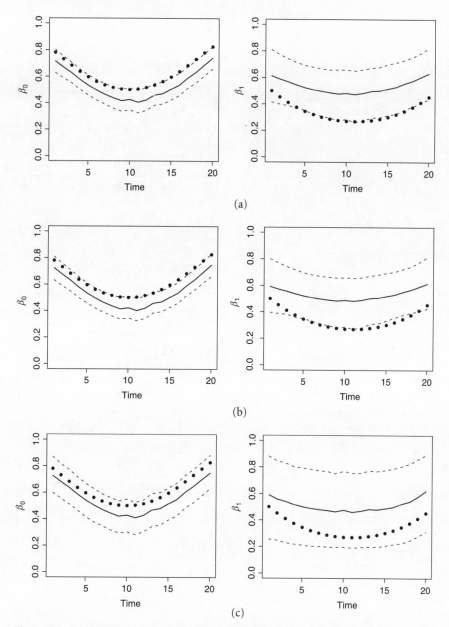

Figure 9.5. Summary of results from dynamic models fitted to the second simulated data set. The solid circles correspond to the true values of β_{0t} and β_{1t} that generated the data, the solid lines correspond to the estimated posterior means of these parameters, and the dashed lines correspond to the 2.5th and 97.5th posterior percentiles for these parameters. (a) $\delta_0 = \delta_1 = 0.05$ and $\nu_0 = \nu_1 = 1$; (b) $\delta_0 = \delta_1 = 0.5$ and $\nu_0 = \nu_1 = 1$; (c) $\delta_0 = \delta_1 = 3$ and $\nu_0 = \nu_1 = 1$.

and, most importantly, the actual interior cell counts are known, so that we can assess how well our model performs.

We are interested in how voter registration (coded as registered and not registered) varies by race (coded as black and white). The inference problem can be summarized in the table:

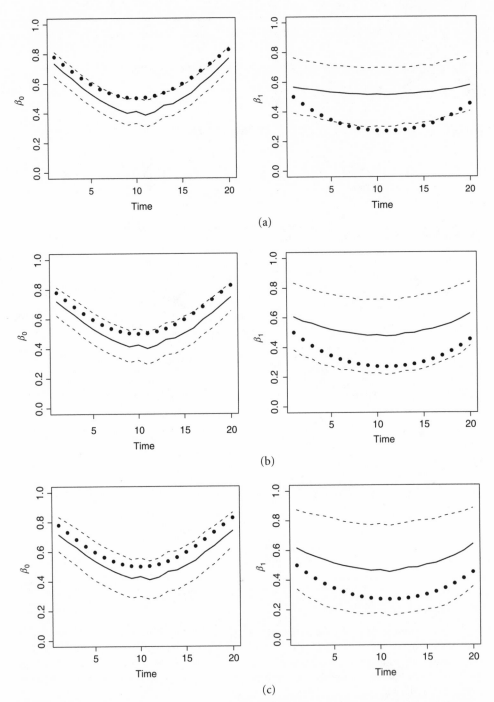

Figure 9.6. Summary of results from hierarchical models fitted to the second simulated data set. The solid circles correspond to the true values of β_{0t} and β_{1t} that generated the data, the solid lines correspond to the estimated posterior means of these parameters, and the dashed lines correspond to the 2.5th and 97.5th posterior percentiles for these parameters. (a) $\delta_0 = \delta_1 = 0.05$ and $v_0 = v_1 = 1$; (b) $\delta_0 = \delta_1 = 0.5$ and $v_0 = v_1 = 1$; (c) $\delta_0 = \delta_1 = 3$ and $v_0 = v_1 = 1$.

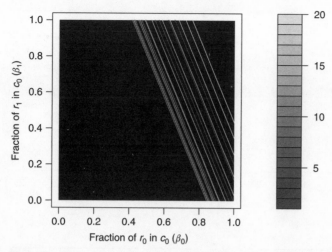

Figure 9.7. Dynamic tomography plot from third simulated data set. The tomography lines are color-coded according to their temporal location.

	Regist. $Y_t = 0$	Not regist. $Y_t = 1$	
White $X_t = 0$	Y_{0t}		r_{0t}
Black $X_t = 1$	Y_{1t}		r_{1t}
	c_{0t}	c_{1t}	N_t

for time period t in a particular county. In what follows we make the (unrealistic, but conservative) assumption that the logits of the cell probabilities are independent across counties and thus that each county-specific time series of tables can be analyzed separately. Within a particular county, inference focuses on β_{0t} (the conditional probability that a citizen is registered to vote at time t given that s/he is white) and β_{1t} (the conditional probability that a citizen is registered to vote at time t given that s/he is black).

The dynamic model with a simple random walk prior on (θ_0, θ_1) was fitted to these data. Here ν_j was set equal to 1 and δ_j was set equal to 0.03 for $j = 0, 1$. This corresponds to a vague prior belief that σ_j is 0.1, which implies $\exp(\theta_{jt} - \theta_{j(t-1)})$ should generally be roughly between 0.82 and 1.22. On a probability scale, this implies that if $\beta_{j(t-1)} = 0.75$, then our best guess is that β_{jt} will be between 0.71 and 0.79 about 95% of the time.

Wakefield's (2001) baseline model with Beta(1, 1) priors was also fitted to these data as a point of comparison.

Figure 9.10 displays the posterior mean values of β_{0t} and β_{1t} from the dynamic model and the baseline model together with the observed fractions of registered whites and registered blacks in each county–year. From the figure we see that the point estimates for probabilities that whites are registered are very similar for the dynamic model and for the baseline model. This is to be expected, as the bounds on these probabilities are generally quite informative for most county–years. On the other hand, we see that the dynamic model point estimates for β_1 are generally closer to the observed fraction of registered blacks than are the estimates from the baseline model. The bottom panels in Figure 9.10 show that the dynamic model's point estimates of β_0 tend to be slightly lower than the baseline model's estimates, and the dynamic model's estimates of β_1 tend to be noticeably higher than the baseline model's estimates.

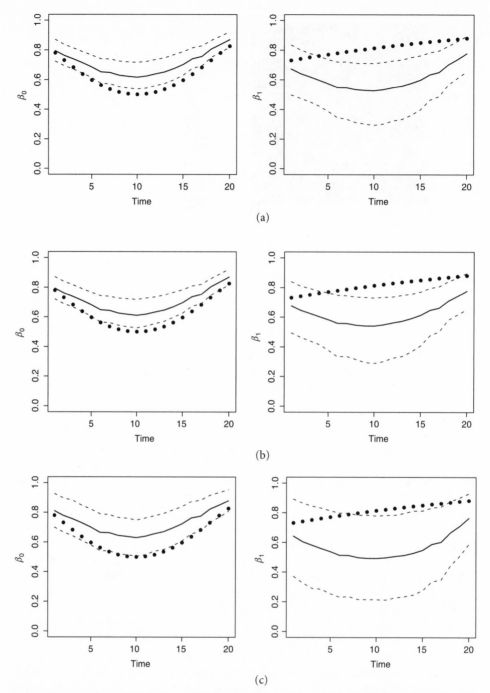

Figure 9.8. Summary of results from dynamic models fitted to the third simulated data set. The solid circles correspond to the true values of β_{0t} and β_{1t} that generated the data, the solid lines correspond to the estimated posterior means of these parameters, and the dashed lines correspond to the 2.5th and 97.5th posterior percentiles for these parameters. (a) $\delta_0 = \delta_1 = 0.05$ and $\nu_0 = \nu_1 = 1$; (b) $\delta_0 = \delta_1 = 0.5$ and $\nu_0 = \nu_1 = 1$; (c) $\delta_0 = \delta_1 = 3$ and $\nu_0 = \nu_1 = 1$.

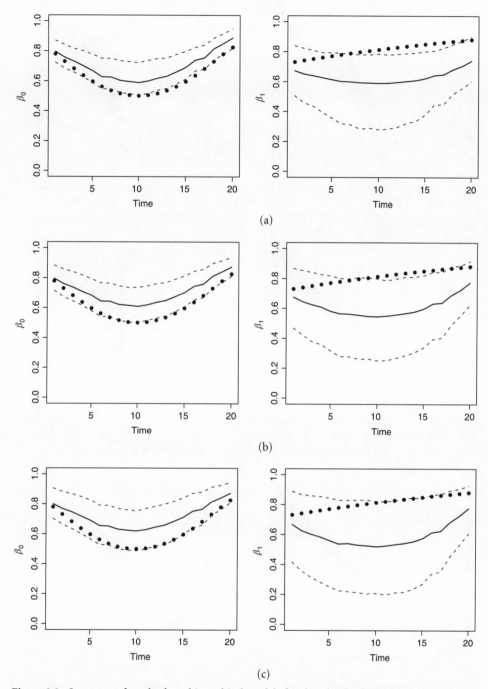

Figure 9.9. Summary of results from hierarchical models fitted to the third simulated data set. The solid circles correspond to the true values of β_{0t} and β_{1t} that generated the data, the solid lines correspond to the estimated posterior means of these parameters, and the dashed lines correspond to the 2.5th and 97.5th posterior percentiles for these parameters. (a) $\delta_0 = \delta_1 = 0.05$ and $\nu_0 = \nu_1 = 1$; (b) $\delta_0 = \delta_1 = 0.5$ and $\nu_0 = \nu_1 = 1$; (c) $\delta_0 = \delta_1 = 3$ and $\nu_0 = \nu_1 = 1$.

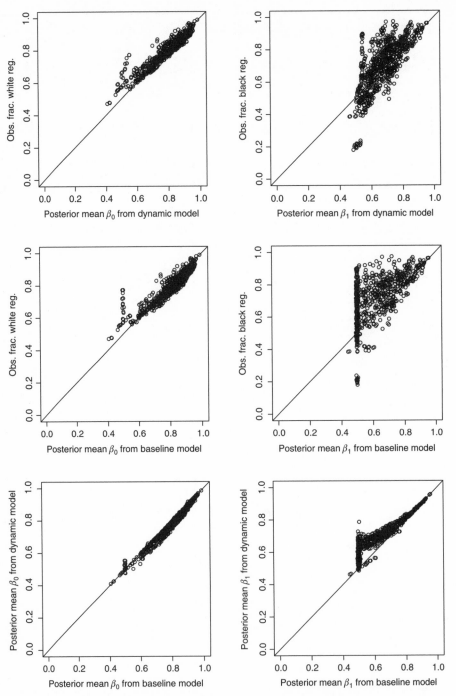

Figure 9.10. Summary of Bayesian point estimates of cell probabilities for all counties and time periods.

Table 9.1 Performance of the dynamic model relative to the baseline mode

Parameter	MSE	Avg. difference between point estimate and obs. fraction	Empirical 90% coverage	Empirical 50% coverage
β_0 (dynamic)	0.0059	0.0272	0.8365	0.4299
β_0 (baseline)	0.0139	0.0356	0.9973	0.8159
β_0 (hierarch.)	0.0060	0.0286	0.8777	0.4615
β_1 (dynamic)	0.0212	0.0802	0.8352	0.4286
β_1 (baseline)	0.0809	0.1170	0.9973	0.8173
β_0 (hierarch.)	0.0281	0.0876	0.8695	0.4629

Table 9.1 presents some measures of the performance of the dynamic model relative to the baseline model. The first column contains the posterior mean squared error between β_{jt} and the observed fraction of registered voters in race j in year t. As we would expect given the much smaller posterior variance of β_{jt} in the dynamic model, the posterior distribution of the cell probabilities is much closer to the true fractions under the dynamic model than under the baseline model. This is true for both β_0 and β_1. The posterior mean square difference between β_{0t} and the observed fraction of registered whites is about 2.4 times larger in the baseline model than in the dynamic model, while for β_{1t} the ratio is about 3.8.

To check whether these differences between the baseline model and the dynamic model were solely due to the lower posterior variability of β_{jt} under the dynamic model than under the baseline model, we computed the mean distance between the posterior mean of β_{jt} and the observed fraction of registered voters in race j in year t. This information is presented in the second column of Table 9.1. Here we see that this distance is about 1.3 times larger in the baseline model than in the dynamic model for the white registration probabilities, and about 1.5 times larger in the baseline model than in the dynamic model for the black registration probabilities.

Finally, to get a sense of overall model adequacy, we calculated the empirical fraction of the time that the observed fraction of registered voters in race j fell within the central 90% and 50% Bayesian credible interval. Here we would expect that a correct model would have empirical coverage probabilities close to the nominal values of 0.90 and 0.50. This information is presented in the third and fourth columns of Table 9.1. Here we see that (not unexpectedly) the baseline model is overly conservative while the dynamic model is somewhat falsely precise.

While all of these summary measures are interesting in this example, it should be emphasized that in actual applications where ecological inference is necessary these quantities can't be calculated, since the interior cell counts are not observed.

Finally, we turn our attention to the results from 6 counties that are roughly typical of the results from all 52 counties. Looking at the results from county 1 in Figure 9.11, we see that the estimates from the dynamic model are more in line with the observed fractions of registered blacks and whites than the baseline estimates are. Here we see that the dynamic model makes use of the information from the few years in which there are informative bounds on β_{1t} to shrink the estimates of β_{1t} in years where the bounds are uninformative.

Looking at the results from county 57 in Figure 9.12, we see a case in which the bounds on β_{1t} are never informative. As we would expect given the tight bounds on β_{0t}, both the baseline model and the dynamic model do an accurate job of estimating β_{0t}. However, neither model does a great job of estimating β_{1t}, although the dynamic model estimates are always closer to the observed fraction of registered blacks. Two things are particularly interesting to note in this case. First, the key for the dynamic model to work reasonably well is to have some information in the bounds for at least a few time points. Second, the dynamic model estimates are not simply a smoothed version of the baseline posterior means as one might expect. Instead, as we can see in Figure 9.12, the dynamic model estimates of β_{1t} are uniformly greater than the baseline estimates for all time periods. What appears to be happening here is that the ridgelike likelihood function together with the random walk prior is shrinking β_{1t} towards β_{0t}. Likewise, β_{0t} is shrinking toward β_{1t}. Quick inspection of the results from all of the counties shows that this seems to be always the case.

The results from county 59, which are presented in Figure 9.13, demonstrate that even a few informative bounds can greatly improve the estimates over the baseline model. Here, there are only two years (1975 and 1988) in which the bounds on β_{1t} are informative. Nonetheless, this small amount of information greatly improves the estimates of β_{1t}. Indeed, if we look at the posterior modes of β_{1t} instead of the posterior means, the results are even more accurate. Again, it is also worth noting that the posterior means of β_{1t} are being pulled closer to β_{0t} despite the assumption of *a priori* independence.

The results in Figure 9.14 for county 99 show a situation in which there are tight bounds on both β_{0t} and β_{1t}. Here the dynamic model performs extremely well. Note the slight bimodality in the posterior distribution of $\beta_{0(1980)}$ and $\beta_{1(1980)}$ from the dynamic model. The reason for this is that the tomography lines separate into two clusters, as can be seen in Figure 9.14a.

The results from county 105 in Figure 9.15 show a situation in which the dynamic model performs well even though the bounds on β_{1t} are only minimally informative. Again, note that β_{0t} and β_{1t} are being shrunk towards each other despite the assumption of prior independence.

Finally, the results from county 115 presented in Figure 9.16 show a situation where things go badly wrong. Here the bounds are not informative for β_{1t}, and the true fraction of registered blacks is far away from 0.5. The dynamic model shrinks the values of β_{1t}, and to a lesser extent β_{0t}, towards 0.5. Here the dynamic model produces misleading estimates for both β_{0t} and β_{1t}.

9.6 DISCUSSION

A key feature of ecological inference is that the results are noticeably dependent upon the researcher's choice of prior distributions even as the sample size goes to infinity. This forces researchers to carefully consider the prior specifications employed in any analysis of ecological data. A primary goal to help ease this task should be the development of classes of prior distributions that (a) can be easily elicited from substantive experts, (b) accord well with the substantive phenomena under study, and (c) lead to reasonable inferences with actual (nonsimulated) ecological data.

This chapter is an initial attempt to specify a class of prior distributions that meet these criteria. It makes use of an intrinsic autoregressive prior for the logits of the cell probabilities. Such a prior distribution has previously been used in spatial statistics and image processing (Besag et al., 1991, 1995) and in time series modeling (West and Harrison, 1997). In the present context we have looked only at temporal dependence, although it is in principle straightforward to model spatial or spatiotemporal dependence with such prior distributions as well (see Haneuse and Wakefield, Chapter 12 of this volume). Proper specification of this prior distribution requires the researcher to consider the size of the odds ratio given

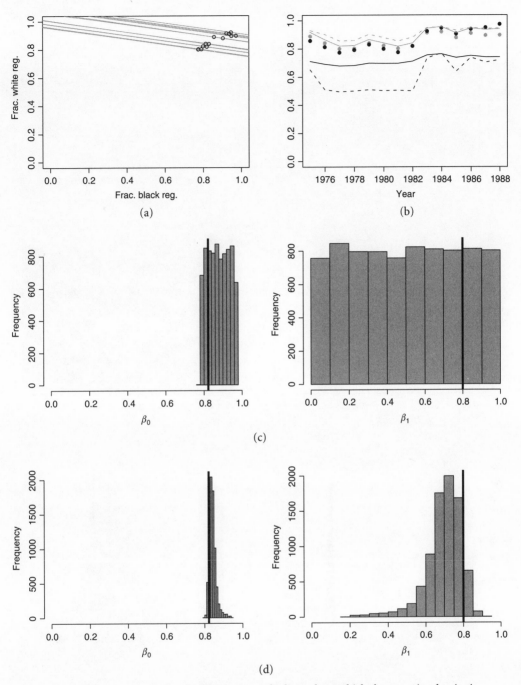

Figure 9.11. Results from county 1. (a) The tomography lines along which the posterior density is concentrated. (b) The observed fraction of registered voters (dots), and the posterior means of β_{jt} from the dynamic model (solid lines) and the baseline model (dashed lines), for blacks (black lines and dots) and whites (light blue lines and dots). The remaining graphs are histograms of β_0 and β_1 for 1980 from (c) the baseline model and (d) the dynamic model, along with the observed fraction registered (the vertical black lines).

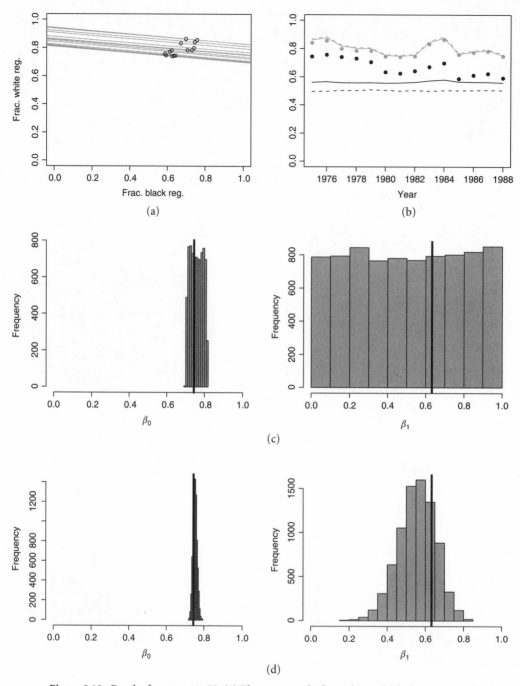

Figure 9.12. Results from county 57. (a) The tomography lines along which the posterior density is concentrated. (b) The observed fraction of registered voters (dots), and the posterior means of β_{jt} from the dynamic model (solid lines) and the baseline model (dashed lines), for blacks (black lines and dots) and whites (light blue lines and dots). The remaining graphs are histograms of β_0 and β_1 for 1980 from (c) the baseline model and (d) the dynamic model, along with the observed fraction registered (the vertical black lines).

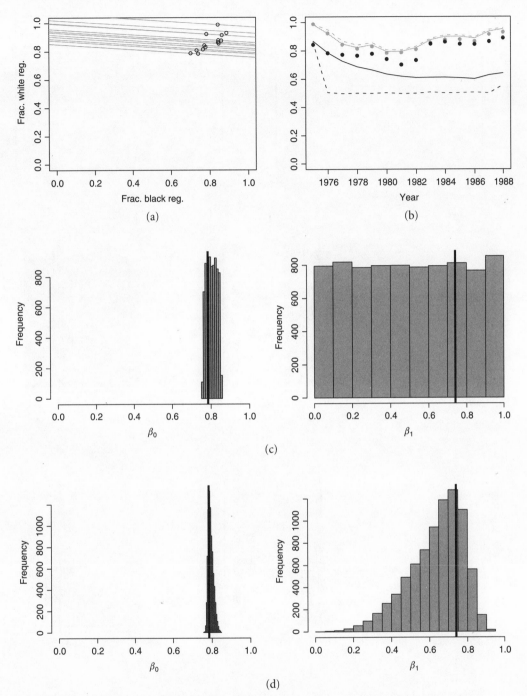

Figure 9.13. Results from county 59. (a) The tomography lines along which the posterior density is concentrated. (b) The observed fraction of registered voters (dots), and the posterior means of β_{jt} from the dynamic model (solid lines) and the baseline model (dashed lines), for blacks (black lines and dots) and whites (light blue lines and dots). The remaining graphs are histograms of β_0 and β_1 for 1980 from (c) the baseline model and (d) the dynamic model, along with the observed fraction registered (the vertical black lines).

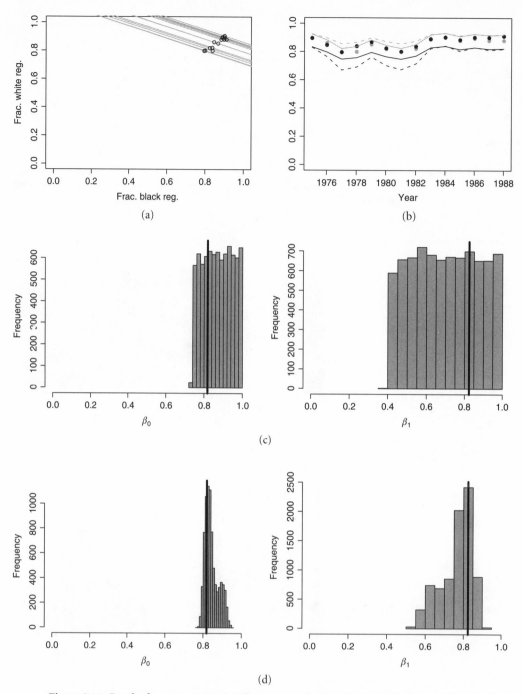

Figure 9.14. Results from county 99. (a) The tomography lines along which the posterior density is concentrated. (b) The observed fraction of registered voters (dots), and the posterior means of β_{jt} from the dynamic model (solid lines) and the baseline model (dashed lines), for blacks (black lines and dots) and whites (light blue lines and dots). The remaining graphs are histograms of β_0 and β_1 for 1980 from (c) the baseline model and (d) the dynamic model, along with the observed fraction registered (the vertical black lines).

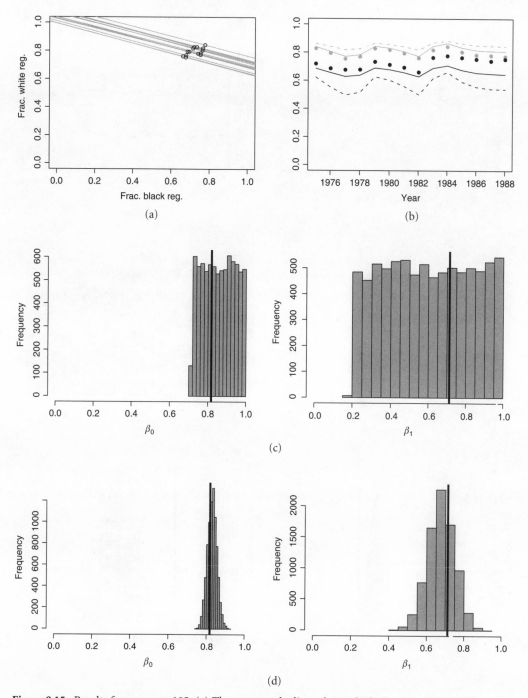

Figure 9.15. Results from county 105. (a) The tomography lines along which the posterior density is concentrated. (b) The observed fraction of registered voters (dots), and the posterior means of β_{jt} from the dynamic model (solid lines) and the baseline model (dashed lines), for blacks (black lines and dots) and whites (light blue lines and dots). The remaining graphs are histograms of β_0 and β_1 for 1980 from (c) the baseline model and (d) the dynamic model, along with the observed fraction registered (the vertical black lines).

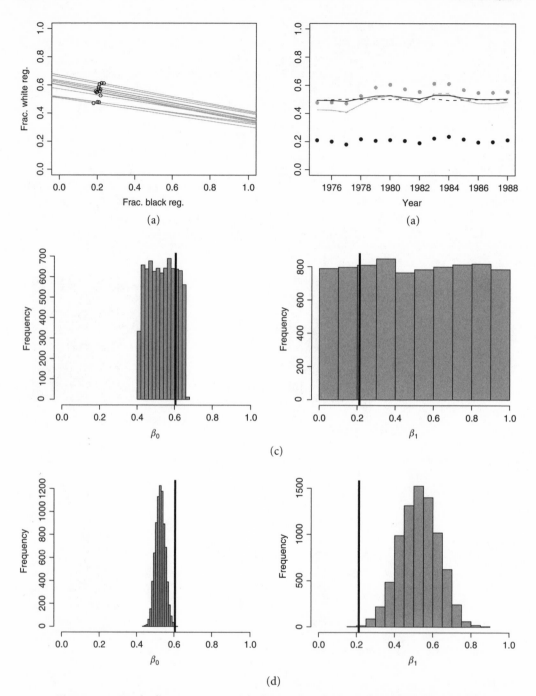

Figure 9.16. Results from county 115. (a) The tomography lines along which the posterior density is concentrated. (b) The observed fraction of registered voters (dots), and the posterior means of β_{jt} from the dynamic model (solid lines) and the baseline model (dashed lines), for blacks (black lines and dots) and whites (light blue lines and dots). The remaining graphs are histograms of β_0 and β_1 for 1980 from (c) the baseline model and (d) the dynamic model, along with the observed fraction registered (the vertical black lines).

by $\exp(\theta_{jt} - \theta_{j(t-1)})$ and is thus reasonably easy. The dynamics postulated by this prior distribution are also reasonable for many social science applications where the underlying temporal process is reasonably smooth. Finally, an analysis of the data on race and registration from Louisiana counties shows that a model that employs this prior distribution yields reasonable results.

In principle, the models discussed in this paper for 2×2 tables can be extended to deal with the general $r \times c$ table case (see Section 5 of Wakefield, 2001, as well as King et al. 1999). Nonetheless, the lack of information in generic $r \times c$ tables with r and c greater than 2 suggests that efficient model fitting may be quite complicated – perhaps requiring modified MCMC algorithms and/or additional identifying assumptions.

Nonetheless, there is still much work to be done – both within the context of ecological inference models for temporally dependent data and within the context of ecological inference models more generally. First, more thought needs to be given to methods for accurately eliciting prior beliefs from substantive experts. Prior distributions are necessary for ecological inference. Consequently, accurate prior distributions are required to obtain accurate measures of posterior uncertainty about model parameters.

Second, still more work needs to be done on model checking and sensitivity analysis. What happens to the posterior distribution if a uniform prior is used for the cell probability with the most informative bounds (the probability that a white citizen is registered, in the Louisiana example) while an intrinsic autoregressive prior is used for the other cell probability (the probability that a black citizen is registered, in the Louisiana example)? What happens if an informative prior is specified for the overall level of θ_j? What happens if the increments of the random walk process are assumed to be Student-t random variables rather than Gaussian random variables? Can we reject certain types of dynamic processes as reasonable data-generating processes based solely on the information in the margins of the table? All of these questions are unanswered.

Finally, developing models that explicitly model spatiotemporal dependence rather than just spatial or temporal dependence is clearly of interest. In many applications, we expect the interior cell probabilities to exhibit both temporal and spatial dependence. While this might seem to be a major nuisance from a classical econometric perspective, it is actually a tremendous source of background information that can be used to improve one's inferences through the specification of informative prior distributions. Of course, as is often the case in ecological inference, incorrect specification of the prior distribution can lead to incorrect posterior inference even in very large samples. For this reason, more complicated prior distributions require more thorough sensitivity analysis and accurate elicitation of real subjective prior beliefs.

REFERENCES

Besag, Julian, Jeremy York, and Annie Mollié. 1991. "Bayesian Image Restoration with Two Applications to Spatial Statistics," *Annals of the Institute of Statistics and Mathematics*, 43: 1–59.

Besag, Julian, Peter Green, David Higdon, and Kerrie Mengersen. 1995. "Bayesian Computation and Stochastic Systems," *Statistical Science*, 10: 3–66.

Clayton, David G. 1996. "Generalized Linear Mixed Models." In W. R. Gilks, S. Richardson, and D. J. Spiegelhalter (eds.), *Markov Chain Monte Carlo in Practice*. London: Chapman & Hall.

Duncan, Otis Dudley and Beverly Davis. 1953. "An Alternative to Ecological Correlation." *American Sociological Review*, 18: 665–666.

King, Gary. 1997. *A Solution to the Ecological Inference Problem*. Princeton, NJ: Princeton University Press.

King, Gary, Bradley Palmquist, Greg Adams, Micah Altman, Kenneth Benoit, Claudine Gay, Jeffrey B. Lewis, Russ Mayer, and Eric Reinhardt. 1997. "The Record of American Democracy, 1984–1990," Harvard University, Cambridge, MA [producer], Ann Arbor, MI: ICPSR [distributor].

King, Gary, Ori Rosen, and Martin A. Tanner. 1999. "Binomial–Beta Hierarchical Models for Ecological Inference," *Sociological Methods and Research*, 28: 61–90.

Wakefield, Jonathan. 2001. "Ecological Inference for 2 × 2 Tables." Working Paper no. 12. Center for Statistics and the Social Sciences, University of Washington.

West, Mike and Jeff Harrison. 1997. *Bayesian Forecasting and Dynamic Systems.* New York: Springer-Verlag.

10 A Spatial View of the Ecological Inference Problem*

Carol A. Gotway Crawford and Linda J. Young

ABSTRACT

The ecological fallacy that often results from ecological inference has long been a contentious issue in sociology, geography, epidemiology, and statistics. Several different solutions to the ecological inference problem have been proposed in these different disciplines. When grouped data are created by spatial aggregation, as is typically the case with Census data, the ecological inference problem can be considered as a special case of what is known in the field of geostatistics as the change-of-support problem (COSP). In this chapter, we give a brief overview of the causes of the ecological inference problem as it arises in geographical correlation studies. We relate the aggregation and specification biases resulting from the ecological fallacy to the scale and aggregation effects underlying the modifiable areal unit problem (MAUP) in geography. We introduce the COSP in spatial statistics, and show that the ecological inference problem and the MAUP, as well as the map overlay operations conducted within geographical information systems (GISs), are all special cases of the COSP. Geostatistical solutions to simple COSPs indicate a general solution strategy for these problems. We review some of these solutions and discuss some of the most recent statistical solutions to COSPs.

10.1 INTRODUCTION

Much of the literature on the ecological inference problem focuses on inferring internal cell counts of an $r \times c$ contingency table (often a 2×2 table) from the marginal totals. Individuals are divided into areal regions (e.g., census tracts, voting districts) and then cross-classified by other variables (e.g., sex, race). In this context, Klein and Freedman (1993), Cleave, Browne, and Payne (1995), and King (1997) provide comprehensive discussions of the ecological inference problem and various solutions to it. An overview of these is given in the Introduction by King, Rosen, and Tanner. In much of this discussion, the spatial aspects of the aggregation into areal regions are not explicitly considered. Often, however, the cause of specification bias in ecological inference is the failure to incorporate relevant spatial information about individuals (Klein and Freedman, 1993).

The chapters by Calvo and Escolar (Chapter 11) and Haneuse and Wakefield (Chapter 12) present new methods that use spatial information to improve traditional solutions to the ecological inference problem. In this chapter, we help to set the stage for their development by focusing on some of the issues that arise in obtaining spatial information about individuals from geographically aggregated data. In this context, we summarize the causes of the ecological inference problem from the viewpoint of spatial statistics. We relate the aggregation and specification biases resulting from the ecological fallacy to the scale and

---

* We appreciate the assistance of J. Felix Rogers, National Center for Environmental Health, who allowed us to impose our statistical curiosity on his study.

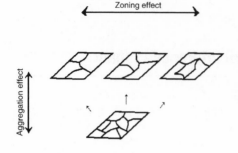

Figure 10.1. Aggregation and zoning issues in the MAUP. (Adapted from Wong, 1996.)

grouping effects underlying the modifiable areal unit problem (MAUP) in geography. We introduce the change-of-support problem (COSP) in spatial statistics and show that the ecological inference problem and the MAUP are both special cases of the COSP. Geostatistical solutions to simple COSPs indicate a general solution strategy for these problems. We review some of these solutions and discuss some of the most recent statistical solutions to COSPs.

10.2 THE MODIFIABLE AREAL UNIT PROBLEM

The *modifiable areal unit problem* (MAUP) is a geographic manifestation of the ecological fallacy where inference based on data aggregated to a particular set of geographical regions may change if the same data are aggregated to a different set of geographical regions. For example, Openshaw and Taylor (1979) considered 99 counties in Iowa and constructed all possible groupings of these counties into larger districts. When considering the correlation between the percentage of Republican voters and the percentage of elderly voters, 12 districts could be contrived to produce correlations ranging from −0.97 to +0.99. Moreover, there seemed to be no obvious relation between the spatial characteristics of the districts and the variation in the resulting correlation coefficients.

The MAUP is actually two interrelated problems. The first problem is that different results and inferences are obtained when data are grouped into increasingly larger areal units. This is often referred to as the *scale effect* or *aggregation effect*. It is analogous to the *aggregation bias* in ecological inference resulting from the grouping of individuals. Another problem occurs that is analogous to the *specification bias* in ecological inference that results from the differential distribution of confounding variables created by grouping (Morgenstern, 1982). This second problem, often termed the *grouping effect* or the *zoning effect* in spatial analysis, reflects the variability in results due to alternative formations of the areal units leading to differences in unit shape at the same or similar scales (Openshaw and Taylor, 1979; Openshaw, 1984; Wong, 1996). These problems are illustrated in Figure 10.1.

The decades of research on the MAUP and the ecological inference problem have clearly identified the source of these problems. The smoothing effect that results from averaging is the underlying cause of both the scale problem in MAUP and aggregation bias in ecological studies. As heterogeneity among units decreases through aggregation, the uniqueness of each unit and the dissimilarity among units are reduced. As Openshaw (1984) noted, "whether the ecological fallacy problem exists or not depends on the nature of the aggregation. A completely homogeneous grouping system would be free of this problem." There is, however, another mitigating factor: spatial autocorrelation. The decrease in variability is moderated by the positive autocorrelation among the original observations and exacerbated by negative autocorrelation (Arbia, 1986, and Cressie, 1993, both illustrate the effect of autocorrelation on the variance of the sample mean). When areal units are similar to begin

<table>
<tr><td colspan="3">Table 10.1 Examples of the univariate change-of-support problem</td></tr>
</table>

The nature of the process is	But we observe or analyze instead	Examples in spatial analysis
Points	Points	Point kriging; prediction of undersampled variables
Points	Areal	Ecological inference; geographical correlation studies
Areal	Points	Use of areal centroids; spatial smoothing; block kriging
Areal	Areal	The MAUP; areal interpolation; incompatible/misaligned zones
Surfaces	Points	Trend surface analysis; environmental monitoring; exposure assessment
Surfaces	Areal	Remote sensing; multiresolution images; image analysis

Source: Modified from Arbia (1989).

with, the aggregation process results in much less information loss than it does with highly dissimilar units. To further compound the problem, the aggregation process itself induces positive spatial autocorrelation, particularly if the aggregation process allows overlapping units (e.g., moving averages).

The smoothing effect and resulting alterations in the spatial autocorrelation of the units are not just the sources of the scale effect in the MAUP, but are sources of the zoning effect as well. The MAUP does not exist, or at least its effects are much less pronounced, when areal units are aggregated in a noncontiguous or spatially random fashion (Gehlke and Biehl, 1934; Blalock, 1964). Only when contiguous units are combined, altering the spatial autocorrelation among the units, is the zoning effect of MAUP most apparent. Because the variation among the original areal units is not uniform over the entire region, merging smaller units is analogous to smoothing different combinations of spatial neighbors. Depending on the similarity of the neighbors, different zoning rules can lead to different analytical results.

10.3 SPATIAL STATISTICS AND THE CHANGE-OF-SUPPORT PROBLEM

With the recent advances in geographical information systems (GISs), the scale and zoning problems in the MAUP and the ecological inference problem are now almost routinely encountered in analyses that use spatial data. They can occur naturally or be artificially induced by the measurement process or analytical considerations. Frequently, the spatial process of interest is inherently of one form, but the data we observe are of another form. For example, sometimes the data are just not available at the desired scale of interest. Meteorological processes occur over a continuum, but we can record only point observations on that surface. At times, individual-level inference is desired, but to ensure data confidentiality, only aggregate data are available. These situations are special cases of the *change-of-support problem* (COSP) in geostatistics. The term *support* refers to the geometrical size, shape, and spatial orientation of the regions associated with the measurements (see, e.g., Olea, 1991). Changing the support of a variable (typically by averaging or aggregation) creates a new variable. This new variable is related to the original one, but has different statistical and spatial properties. The problem of how the spatial variation in one variable relates to that of the other variable is the COSP. The COSP often results from the different forms of spatial data: points, lines, areas, and surfaces. Thus, both the ecological inference problem and the MAUP are COSPs. Table 10.1, modified from Arbia (1989), delineates some common COSPs.

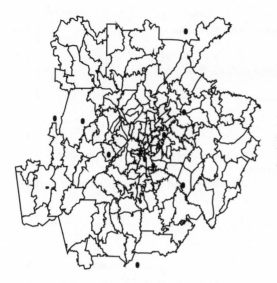

Figure 10.2. The bivariate COSP. ZIP codes and locations of air pollution monitors in the Atlanta metropolitan area (From Tolbert et al., 2000.)

In the spatial sense, these are all univariate problems in that there is just one spatial response variable of interest. The bivariate COSP, where there are two spatial variables of differing supports, has received limited attention in the literature (Cressie, 1996). The bivariate COSP brings with it additional issues best conveyed with an example. Consider the study, described in Tolbert et al. (2000), designed to measure the effect of air quality on asthma exacerbation in metropolitan Atlanta. Perhaps for data confidentiality reasons or for practical reasons of time and cost involved in geocoding address information, the numbers of asthma cases and controls were reported by ZIP code. Air quality, quantified by various indices such as ozone concentration, was measured at several monitoring stations throughout metro Atlanta (Figure 10.2). In terms of the health outcome of interest (asthma), this is an ecological inference problem, because inferences about people are to be made from aggregated data at the ZIP-code level. However, another COSP problem arises in linking the exposure and health outcome information together, because the two variables of interest have inherently different scales: disease pertains to individuals, but air quality varies over a continuous surface. This latter issue is slightly different from those discussed previously. The restriction of air quality to the individual results from a desire to draw inferences about the "cause" of the disease. The inability to measure the "air quality of an individual" (without extreme inconvenience to the individuals in the study), and not aggregation, causes the COSP problem. Inferential issues for these problems have been discussed in Cressie (1996).

The COSP has been studied in many different disciplines, although the term COSP has rarely been used except within the field of geostatistics. In addition to the MAUP and the ecological inference problem, numerous other terms have been introduced to describe one or more facets of the COSP as well as various "solutions" to it: spatial data transformations; the scaling problem; inference between incompatible zonal systems; pycnophylactic geographic interpolation; block kriging; the polygonal overlay problem; areal interpolation; inference with spatially misaligned data; contour reaggregation; and multiscale and hierarchically scaled modeling. We choose to use the term "change of support" to describe the problems inherent in all of these approaches because it provides a unifying framework and offers many insights into possible solutions.

10.4 SOLUTIONS TO THE CHANGE-OF-SUPPORT PROBLEM

Many solutions have been proposed to different COSPs. Of course there is no unique solution to any COSP, since any proposed solution must make untestable assumptions about the information lost in aggregation. Thus, the solutions inherently differ with respect to the assumptions made, the validity of these assumptions, and the nature of any extra information used to reconstruct the missing individual-level statistics. One source of extra information readily available in all spatial problems is the support of the geographical regions. Some solutions to COSPs take explicit account of the shapes and orientations of the spatial units and not just their size. Many solutions, however, are incomplete, taking account only of the relative sizes between the units. In a previous paper, we provided an overview of the many different solutions to COSPs, emphasizing current statistical approaches (Gotway and Young, 2002). From our critical review, we found that most solutions to COSPs had a common theme: they all build a model from point support data (even if no observations were taken at this level of support) and then develop methods to optimally estimate important parameters. In the following sections, we focus on one particular set of solutions, spatial smoothing methods, that provide one solution to the ecological inference problem in spatial statistics.

10.4.1 Spatial Smoothing of Aggregated Data

Much of the spatial data we work with today is geographically aggregated and standardized to produce rates for each geographic region. The rates are often displayed on a chloropleth map, and the map is then used to compare regions and make inference about individuals. However, the rates have different variances, and this variation also changes across the map. Spatial smoothing has often been suggested to reduce this problem, and many smoothers are available. Most of these delineate each region by its centroid and then use some sort of interpolation between centroids to compute smoothed estimates. In doing so, the supports of the data are ignored (in most applications, even the areas of the regions are ignored). In this section, we describe some approaches that take explicit account of the different supports in obtaining smoothed estimates.

Let $X(A_1), \ldots, X(A_n)$ denote the aggregated data (counts or totals) observed in regions A_i within a domain $D \subset \Re^2$, and let the area of region i be denoted by $|A_i|$. Tobler (1979) suggested one of the earliest smoothers of aggregated data. He assumed the existence of an underlying intensity function, $\lambda(x, y)$, which is nonnegative and has a value for every location $\mathbf{s} = (x, y) \in D$. Thus, the underlying population is assumed to be distributed according to a spatial density function proportional to $\lambda(\mathbf{s})$, and the number of people in any region A is $X(A) = \int_A \lambda(\mathbf{s}) \, d\mathbf{s}$. Tobler suggested that such an intensity function should be smooth and that adjacent regions should influence each other in the estimation process. Thus, he suggested choosing $\lambda(x, y)$ to minimize

$$\int \int \left[\left(\frac{\partial^2 \lambda}{\partial x^2} \right)^2 + \left(\frac{\partial^2 \lambda}{\partial y^2} \right)^2 \right] dx \, dy, \tag{10.1}$$

subject to the constraints $\lambda(\mathbf{s}) \geq 0$ and

$$\int_{A_i} \lambda(\mathbf{s}) \, d\mathbf{s} = X(A_i) \qquad \text{for } i = 1, \ldots, n. \tag{10.2}$$

When applied to point data, the intensity surface that minimizes Equation 10.1 is the surface of minimum curvature. The minimum curvature method produces smooth surfaces from irregularly spaced data that are visually pleasing and constrained to have maxima and minima only at data locations. In the case of areal data, with the additional constraint of Equation 10.2, the surface is constrained to preserve volume: the intensity process integrates to the observed data for each region. Tobler (1979) called this constraint the *pycnophylactic property* (or volume-preserving property). Both Tobler (1979) and Dyn, Wahba, and Wong (1979) have proven the existence and uniqueness of the solution to this constrained minimization problem.

The solution requires specification of boundary conditions, and Tobler suggested forcing either the intensity surface or its gradient to be zero at the boundary of the domain. The boundary conditions will affect the smoothness properties of the surface, particularly near the edges of the domain. Dyn, Wahba, and Wong (1979) suggested an alternative smoothness criterion,

$$\int \int \left(\frac{\partial^2 \lambda}{\partial x^2} + 2\frac{\partial^2 \lambda}{\partial x \, \partial y} + \frac{\partial^2 \lambda}{\partial y^2} \right) dx \, dy,$$

which allows the solution and its gradient to be free and determined by the data.

Brillinger (1990, 1994) considered a different optimization criterion based on a locally weighted analysis. In this approach, the problem is to estimate the value of $\lambda(x, y)$ based on a linear combination of aggregate data values, i.e., $\hat{\lambda}(\mathbf{s}) = \sum_{i=1}^{n} w_i X(A_i)$. Each weight, $w_i(x, y)$, determines the effect of region A_i on location (x, y). In geostatistics, this is an adaptation of what is called the *block kriging* predictor (see Cressie, 1993, 1996). The weights are chosen to minimize the prediction mean squared error and are given by

$$\Sigma w = \sigma.$$

The elements of Σ are the covariances among the aggregated data,

$$\mathrm{cov}(X(A_i), X(A_j)) = \int_{A_j} \int_{A_i} C(\mathbf{u}, \mathbf{v}) \, d\mathbf{u} \, d\mathbf{v}; \qquad (10.3)$$

the elements of σ are the covariances between the areal data and "data" at point $\mathbf{s}$,

$$\mathrm{cov}(X(\mathbf{s}), X(A_i)) = \int_{A_i} C(\mathbf{u}, \mathbf{v}) \, d\mathbf{u} \, d\mathbf{v};$$

and $C(\mathbf{u}, \mathbf{v})$ is the underlying, point-to-point covariance function $C(\mathbf{u}, \mathbf{v}) = \mathrm{cov}(X(\mathbf{u}), X(\mathbf{v}))$, for $\mathbf{u}, \mathbf{v} \in D$.

The covariance function $C(\mathbf{u}, \mathbf{v})$ cannot be estimated directly from aggregate data. Cressie (1993) suggested a practical approach to building a point-level model in which a parametric form for $C(\mathbf{u}, \mathbf{v})$ is assumed and the theoretical covariance on the right hand side of Equation 10.3 is equated to the empirical covariance function of $X(A)$, estimated and modeled from available data. Gelfand, Zhu, and Carlin (2001) eloquently implement this idea with Gaussian data using Bayesian hierarchical models and Gibbs sampling. Because $\lambda(x, y)$ is an intensity function of a spatial point pattern (and not an underlying random field as is assumed in geostatistics), Brillinger (1990, 1994) used $C(\mathbf{u}, \mathbf{v}) = K(\mathbf{u} - \mathbf{v})$, where $K(\cdot)$ is a kernel function integrating to 1. Thus, the weights are approximately (because the A_i are disjoint, so Σ is approximately diagonal) equal to

$$w_i(x, y) = \frac{1}{|A_i|} \int \int_{A_i} K(x - u, y - v) \, du \, dv.$$

Given the weight function, a locally weighted estimate of the underlying intensity can be obtained by maximizing the weighted log likelihood of the data. Thus, for smoothing rates, $X(A_i)/N_i$, with $X(A_i) \sim \text{Poisson}(N_i\lambda(\mathbf{s}))$, the locally weighted estimate of λ at (x, y) is

$$\hat{\lambda}(x, y) = \frac{\sum_i w_i(x, y) X(A_i)}{N_i \sum_i w_i(x, y)}.$$

Müller, Stadtmüller, and Tabnak (1997) adapted Brillinger's ideas to the estimation of the intensity function of disease incidence, where the total number of disease cases and the total population at risk are available for each region. They developed a modified version of locally weighted least squares where the squared differences between observations and local fits are integrated over the regions.

These approaches all force the intensity estimates to allow for the differing supports of the regions A_i. Thus, these smoothing methods are one solution to the area–point COSP (the ecological inference problem). Integrating the intensity estimates over different domains is a solution to the area–area COSP (the MAUP).

10.4.2 Case Study: Georgia Health Care District 9

Rogers et al. (2000) presented the results of a case–control study of the risk of having a very low birth weight (VLBW) baby, one weighing less than 1,500 grams at birth. The data were obtained from the National Center for Environmental Health, Centers for Disease Control and Prevention. The study area comprised contiguous counties in southeastern Georgia, constituting Georgia Health Care District 9 (GHCD9) (Figure 10.3). Cases were identified from all live-born, singleton infants born between April 1, 1986 and March 30, 1988. Controls, babies born in the same area during the same period weighing more than 2,499 grams at birth, were identified from birth registries. Further details of the case identification and control selection procedures, as well as other variables recorded during the study, are described in Rogers et al. (2000). The methods used in this paper are based on a total of 230 cases and 550 controls.

Of interest in this paper is the use of aggregated data (here, the number of cases and controls per county) to obtain a smoothed map of the relative risk of observing a case rather than a control at location $\mathbf{s}$ in GHCD9. We assume that the original, but unobserved, point case and control data result from spatial point processes with underlying intensity functions $\lambda_1(\mathbf{s})$ and $\lambda_2(\mathbf{s})$, respectively. Each intensity function is proportional to the corresponding spatial density function associated with the probability of observing a case or a control at any particular location in the study area. Comparison of the two estimated intensity functions provides a way to estimate the spatial variation in the risk for a VLBW baby in GHCD9. Thus, $r(\mathbf{s}) = \lambda_1(\mathbf{s})/\lambda_2(\mathbf{s})$ is the relative risk of VLBW at location $\mathbf{s}$.

If the individual-level case and control data were available, density estimation methods could be used to estimate the intensity functions (e.g., Bithell, 1990; Kelsall and Diggle, 1995, 1998). With aggregate data, these density estimation methods cannot be used to estimate the individual-level risks. The methods developed by Brillinger (1990, 1994) and Müller et al. (1997) described in Section 10.4.1 could be used with rates of VLBW, but the

0   15   30   60   Miles

Figure 10.3. Counties of Georgia Health Care District 9.

underlying intensity functions are not guaranteed to be nonnegative and are not constrained to preserve volume (cf. Equation 10.2). Thus, we adapt Tobler's (1979) method, described in Section 10.4.1, to the constrained estimation of relative risk. The intensity of each process is estimated separately from the case and control counts associated with each county. Each intensity surface is constrained to satisfy the volume-preserving property. The estimated relative risk surface is then $\hat{\lambda}_1(\mathbf{s})/\hat{\lambda}_2(\mathbf{s})$ and is shown in Figure 10.4.

To provide some evaluation of this approach, we also obtained the original case and control data. The address information was geocoded to provide point spatial data projected onto the Universal Transverse Mercator (UTM) grid system. Density estimation methods developed by Bithell (1990), Kelsall and Diggle (1995), and Kelsall and Diggle (1998) were then used to estimate the spatial variation in risk from the point-level case–control data (Figure 10.5).

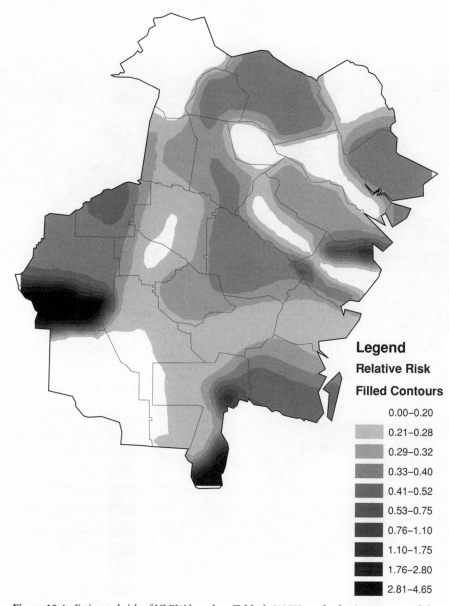

Figure 10.4. Estimated risk of VLBW based on Tobler's (1979) method using aggregated data.

Comparing the two maps, one obvious conclusion is that the risk map computed using Tobler's method is not as smooth as the risk map estimated from the point case–control data. This is expected, both because some information lost in aggregation can never be recovered and because of the volume-preserving constraints. The effects of these constraints will be most pronounced when two regions close together have very different risks. The risk map based on the point case–control data tends to smooth out these differences. This is evident in the northern part of the maps: The small, oval county in the north-central part of GHCD9, Evans County, had no VLBW babies. Tobler's method constrains the risk surface to zero here; the density estimation method applied to the case–control point data smooths over

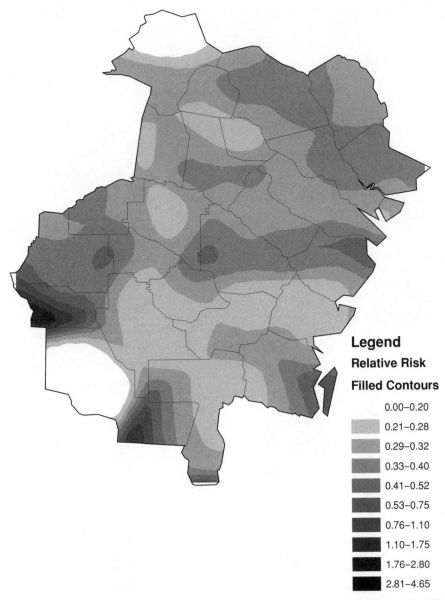

Figure 10.5. Estimated risk of VLBW based on density estimation methods (Bithell, 1990; Kelsall and Diggle, 1995, 1998) using point data.

this small area. Although in areas like these the maps clearly differ, consistent patterns also exist between the maps. Both maps indicate that the westernmost part of GHCD9, comprising Atkinson, Coffee, and Jeff Davis, seems to have a higher risk, overall, while the swath composed of parts of the southern counties (parts of central and eastern Ware, eastern Charlton, south Bradley, and Glynn) appears to have an overall lower risk for VLBW babies.

This case study has illustrated one method for inferring individual-level behavior (disease risk, population density, crime intensity) from geographically aggregated data that explicitly uses the support of the areal regions. Obtaining individual-level inference is easy; assessing the quality of such inferences, particularly in a spatial setting, is not. Comparison with the relative risk map produced from individual-level case–control data, both visually (as described here) and quantitatively by comparing population estimates over different Census units, indicates this type of approach gives reasonable results. In this example, the geocoded case–control point data (and Census population data) were available for comparison. In most studies, this type of data will not be available, and it will be difficult to ascertain how well this approach works in any given application. More thorough investigation, with different types of point data and through simulation, will allow evaluation of the general method and comparison with other approaches described earlier and reviewed in Gotway and Young (2002).

10.5 SUMMARY

In this chapter, we have given an overview of the COSP in spatial statistics, as it relates to the ecological inference problem that arises when aggregate data are used to make inferences. We have demonstrated how spatial smoothing methods that explicitly allow for the changes in support can be used to disaggregate spatial data and allow inferences about individuals.

A number of issues still need to be resolved with the use of these methods. Constraining the intensity functions so they satisfy volume-preserving properties seems like a reasonable requirement; intuitively we should not be able to have more cases or controls than we started with, nor less. These constraints do affect the intensity estimates and the resulting risk surface. Neither risk map is the true map (both are based on estimates and assumptions), and it is difficult to say which map is closer to reality. Thus, we have to wonder whether the features introduced by the constrained smoothing are realistic, and we have to entertain the possibility that unconstrained risk maps, even those constructed from point case–control data, are too smooth. As all of these methods are relatively new, little is known about the properties of spatial intensity estimation methods even with point-level data. Finding an objective way to evaluate these approaches (and others with the same goals) is important, although such a study seems difficult.

Both Brillinger (1990, 1994) and Müller et al. (1997) derived standard errors for the estimates produced from their approaches to spatial smoothing of aggregate data. Brillinger (1990, 1994) also adapted his method to include relevant covariate information. Locally weighted least squares regression is often used for multivariate regression, so adapting the method of Müller et al. (1997) to include covariates seems straightforward. For some reason, statisticians have not embraced Tobler's (1979) method, so these derivations have not been done (at least to the best of our knowledge). Volume-preserving constraints will certainly make such derivations more complex. All of these methods assume independent data and thus ignore any spatial correlations among the aggregate data.

Spatial support should be an important component of spatial data analysis; a circle is inherently different from a rectangle, even if they have the same area. However, explicitly allowing for support in statistical methods adds a great deal of complexity to already complex problems. The practical implications of ignoring support are difficult to measure. The first step is the development of viable approaches for solving COSPs. Interest in these problems is now considerable, and good progress is being made.

REFERENCES

Arbia, G. 1986. "The Modifiable Areal Unit Problem and the Spatial Autocorrelation Problem: Towards a Joint Approach," *Metron*, 44: 391–407.

Arbia, G. 1989. "Statistical Effect of Data Transformations: A Proposed General Framework." In M. Goodchild and S. Gopal (eds.), *The Accuracy of Spatial Data Bases*, London: Taylor and Francis, pp. 249–259.

Bithell, J. F. 1990. "An Application of Density Estimation to Geographical Epidemiology," *Statistics in Medicine*, 9: 691–701.

Blalock, H. M. 1964. *Causal Inferences in Nonexperimental Research*. Chapel Hill, NC: University of North Carolina Press.

Brillinger, D. R. 1990. "Spatial–temporal Modeling of Spatially Aggregate Birth Data," *Survey Methodology*, 16: 255–269.

Brillinger, D. R. 1994. "Examples of Scientific Problems and Data Analyses in Demography, Neurophysiology, and Seismology," *Journal of Computational and Graphical Statistics*, 3: 1–22.

Cleave, N., P. J. Brown, and C. D. Payne. 1995. "Evaluation of Methods for Ecological Inference," *Journal of the Royal Statistical Society, Series B*, 159: 55–72.

Cressie, N. 1993. *Statistics for Spatial Data*. New York: Wiley.

Cressie, N. 1996. "Change of Support and the Modifiable Areal Unit Problem," *Geographical Systems*, 3: 159–180.

Dyn, N., G. Wahba, and W. H. Wong. 1979. "Discussion of Tobler (1979), 'Smooth Pycnophylactic Interpolation for Geographical Regions,'*Journal of the American Statistical Association*, 74: 530–535.

Gehlke, C. E. and K. Biehl. 1934. "Certain Effects of Grouping upon the Size of the Correlation Coefficient in Census Tract Material," *Journal of the American Statistical Association*, supplement 29, pp. 169–170.

Gelfand, A. E., L. Zhu, and B. P. Carlin. 2001. "On the Change of Support Problem for Spatio-temporal Data," *Biostatistics*, 2: 31–45.

Gotway, C. A. and L. J. Young. 2002. "Combining Incompatible Spatial Data," *Journal of the American Statistical Association*, 97: 632–648.

Kelsall, J. E. and P. J. Diggle. 1995. "Non-parametric Estimation of Spatial Variation in Relative Risk," *Statistics in Medicine*, 14: 2335–2342.

Kelsall, J. E. and P. J. Diggle. 1998. "Spatial Variation in Risk: A Nonparametric Binary Regression Approach," *Applied Statistics*, 47: 559–573.

King, G. 1997. *A Solution to the Ecological Inference Problem*. Princeton, NJ: Princeton University Press.

Klein, S. P. and D. A. Freedman. 1993. "Ecological Regression in Voting Rights Cases," *Chance*, 6: 38–43.

Morgenstern, H. 1982. "Uses of Ecologic Analysis in Epidemiologic Research," *American Journal of Public Health*, 72: 1336–1344.

Müller, H. G., U. Stadtmüller, and F. Tabnak. 1997. "Spatial Smoothing of Geographically Aggregated Data, with Application to the Construction of Incidence Maps," *Journal of the American Statistical Association*, 92: 61–71.

Olea, R. A. 1991. *Geostatistical Glossary and Multilingual Dictionary*. New York: Oxford University Press.

Openshaw, S. 1984. *The Modifiable Areal Unit Problem*. Norwich, England: Geobooks.

Openshaw, S. and P. Taylor. 1979. "A Million or So Correlation Coefficients." In N. Wrigley (ed.), *Statistical Methods in the Spatial Sciences*. London: Pion, pp. 127–144.

Rogers, J. F., S. J. Thompson, C. L. Addy, R. E. McKeown, D. J. Cowen, and P. Decouflé. 2000. "Association of Very Low Birth Weight with Exposures to Environmental Sulfur Dioxide and Total Suspended Particulates," *American Journal of Epidemiology*, 151: 602–613.

Tobler, W. 1979. "Smooth Pycnophylactic Interpolation for Geographical Regions (with Discussion),"*Journal of the American Statistical Association*, 74: 519–536.

Tolbert, P. E., J. A. Mulholland, D. L. MacIntosh, D. L. F. Xu, D. Daniels, O. J. Devine, B. P. Carlin, M. Klein, J. Dorley, A. J. Butler, D. F. Nordenberg, H. Frumkin, P. B. Ryan, and M. C. White. 2000. "Air Pollution and Pediatric Emergency Room Visits for Asthma in Atlanta," *American Journal of Epidemiology*, 151: 798–810.

Wong, D. W. S. 1996. "Aggregation Effects in Geo-referenced Data." In D. A. Griffith (ed.), *Advanced Spatial Statistics*. Boca Raton, FL: CRC Press, pp. 83–106.

11 Places and Relationships in Ecological Inference

Uncovering Contextual Effects through a Geographically Weighted
Autoregressive Model*

Ernesto Calvo and Marcelo Escolar

ABSTRACT

One of the most salient but less studied features of ecological inference is the presence of spatial
structure inducing aggregation bias in the observed data. This lack of attention is due to the fact that in
most ecological inference models aggregation bias and spatial aggregation bias have been confounded.
In this article we take advantage of a geographically weighted auto-regressive approach (GW-AR) to
ecological inference that incorporates information about the underlying sources of spatial aggregation
bias in ecological inference. We then show how this spatial information can be incorporated into most
ecological inference methods as a covariate. Finally, we use Monte Carlo simulations to study the
performance of the adjusted EI and Goodman models in the presence of spatial effects.

11.1 INTRODUCTION

One of the most salient but less studied features of ecological inference is the presence of
spatial structure inducing aggregation bias in the observed data. This lack of attention is due
to the fact that in most ecological inference models aggregation bias[1] and spatial aggregation
bias[2] have been confounded into one and the same thing. However, provided that we know
the location of the observable ecological units, there exists considerable more information
about spatial aggregation bias than about most other nonspatial sources of bias.

In this chapter we take advantage of a geographically weighted auto regressive approach (GW-AR) to ecological inference that incorporates information about the underlying
sources of spatial aggregation bias in ecological data. This spatial information can be then
incorporated into most ecological inference methods, although we will focus on spatial auto
regressive controls for the Goodman regression and King's EI. In doing so, we will also shed
light on the different performance of the standard Goodman and EI models in the presence
of spatial effects (Anselin and Tam Cho, 2002; King, 2002; Calvo and Escolar, 2003) and
their different local estimates (Herron and ßhotts, 2003; Adolph and King, 2003).

There are a number of different procedures that can be used to explore spatial aggregation bias in ecological data. Geographically weighted regression (GWR) provides a theoretically sound and computationally simple alternative within the classical framework. We also

---

* We thank Charles Brunsdon, Noah Kaplan, Gary King, Sebastien Haneuse, Keith Poole, Jon Wakefield, and
  an anonymous reader for their comments and suggestions. In particular, we thank Sebastien Haneuse and Jon
  Wakefield for their advice in programming the distance-weighted WinBugs alternative provided in the Appendix.
[1] The "grouping-induced correlation between X_i and e_i-error term" (King, 1997: 55).
[2] The correlation between X_i and a spatially nonstationary error term, the result of the data being explained by
  different spatial regimes. See also "Extreme Spatial Heterogeneity" in Anselin (1988).

provide a distance weighted MCMC alternative in the Apendix, in the spirit of that presented by Haneuse and Wakefield in Chapter 12 of this volume.

The order of presentation of this article is as follows: first, in Sections 11.2 and 11.3, we introduce a common statistical perspective to discuss local contexts and global relationships. We then describe the GW-AR approach to control for spatial effects in ecological inference. In Section 11.6 we provide Monte Carlo evidence on the performance of the GW-Goodman and GW-EI models. The results converge with previous literature showing that in the presence of spatial effects EI may provide estimates that are both biased and closer to the true β_i^b than Goodman's β_i^b (Voss, Chapter 3 in this volume; Anselin and Tam Cho, 2002; Herron and Shotts, 2003). Finally, in Section 11.7, we exemplify the method with an analysis of the relationship between the Peronist vote and turnout in Argentina.

11.2 CONTEXTUAL EFFECTS AND GLOBAL RELATIONSHIPS

Maps can be read in many ways. They provide information about the shortest route to our destination, but they also provide information about social structures and processes. Poverty maps are meaningful because wealth is not randomly distributed in cities; southern and northern Democrats have geographically distinctive political agendas; and city areas like Chinatown, the Magnificent Mile, or Cabrini Green in Chicago all express different social structures and relationships that construct these locations as meaningful *places*. Yet, is it only recently that we have started to explore the statistical implications of this diversity in political science rather than just searching for a solution to its *problematic* effects (Ward and Gleditsh, 2002; Kohfeld and Sprague, 2002; Anselin and Tam Cho, 2002).

In a strictly statistical sense location matters, just as places matter in a much more substantive way. People with similar incomes choose different neighborhoods to live in for reasons that shape their school choices, and select schools for reasons that affect their vote, and decide their vote for reasons that are not unrelated to their housing and neighbor preferences. Similarly, party machines can register voters more successfully in some counties, close races for local candidates can drive voters to turn out in larger numbers in one state but not in others, and even differences in the average age of citizens across different Florida counties may have a significant impact on the state level of their political participation or their vote.

In most ecological inference methods these peculiarities are construed as noise, even though this "noise" often displays a fairly systematic spatial structure.[3] It usually expresses contextual relationships that shape our variables of interest, affecting the estimation of *global* parameters by the continuous intervention of a geographically located world. And, while these spatial effects are usually the result of local omitted variables (King, 1996; Agnew, 1996a, 1996b), it is generally impossible to take account of all the contextual variables that shape social phenomena over space. As is often observed in public opinion, preferences among different groups of voters tend to display trends over time in response to significant political events. For example, in panel data it is often observed that the support for a candidate shifts up or down for all voters in a sample in response to a political scandal even though different group preferences continue to be affected by other intervening variables like wealth or education. Similarly, a candidate's scandal in a local community can move the average vote for party i down, holding other meaningful variables constant. As a result, spatially structured data often displays large margin errors, heteroscedastacity, and highly uninformative scatterplot distributions (Anselin, 1988).

---

[3] See Haneuse and Wakefield (Chapter 12) and Voss (Chapter 3) for exceptions.

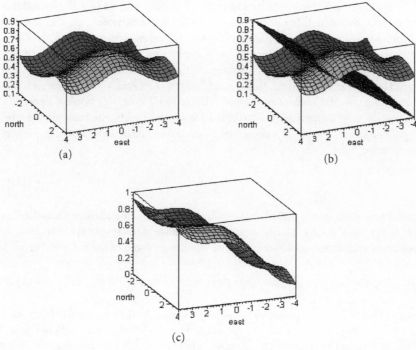

Figure 11.1. Spatial dependence in the vote for party i.

The geographic extent to which these *neighborhood effects* (Johnston, 1986a, 1986b) depress voting, however, is much more than a factor to be corrected. It provides information as to how communities are linked, what populations fall within the influence area of a particular territorial politics and how these contextual *topographies* are linked to other socially relevant phenomena (Fotheringham and O'Kelly, 1989; Anselin, 1988; Sui and Hugill, 2002). In other words, how much a *place* (contextual variables) explains social phenomena and how global the relationships really are.

11.3 LINEAR RELATIONSHIPS AND NON-LINEAR SPACES

Imagine a three-dimensional Euclidean representation of the party A vote in the unrealistically square city depicted in Figure 11.1.

The geography of this city is mapped by its east and north coordinates, and y_i describes the mean vote for party A in every coordinate i of its spatial surface. In the absence of spatial effects, the average local vote y_i in any particular east-north region of the city would be similar to the city's average (Guillorel and Levy, 1992). However, in the presence of spatial effects, different regions of the city would be characterized by different expected local means.[4] For example, in the area represented by the coordinates $[2, -2]$[5] of Figure 11.1a the mean expected vote for party A is around 35%. Meanwhile, in the area $[0, 1]$ the mean expected vote for party A is close to 65%.

---

[4] Spatial non-stationarity, spatial regimes (quantitative geography), and random fields (statistics, image technology) are growing research areas analyzing the properties of spatial structures.

[5] The first number indicates the east coordinate, and the second number indicates the north coordinate.

These differences could be explained by a number of global variables (e.g. the spatial distribution of wealthy voters in different regions of the city), local variables (e.g. the financial scandal of local alderman Smith), or diffusion effects (the degree of integration of the City's media, transportation, etc.). Mean differences in y_i could also be explained by the endogenous properties of the covariates if the distribution of the white and black vote has a spatial structure (see Haneuse and Wakefield, this book, Chapter 12) if racial polarization leads to higher turnout in particular regions of the data (King, 1997; Voss, this book, Chapter 3).

Without introducing further variables to allow for spatial effects, the basic model presented in Figure 11.1a presumes that y_i is to some degree explained by an underlying spatially heterogeneous structure s_i.

$$y_i = f(s_i) + u_i \tag{11.1}$$

Because spatial non-stationarity means that nearby observations are clustered together, an instrument for $f(s_i)$ in Equation 11.1 is provided by the more familiar spatial auto regressive model in which $\mathbf{W}y_j$, contiguous observations of y_i, explain some of the variation in y_i:

$$y_i = \rho \mathbf{W} y_j + u_i, \tag{11.2}$$

where $\mathbf{W}$ is a contiguity matrix whose elements are 1 if y_j is next to y_i and 0 otherwise, ρ is a parameter indicating the magnitude of variation in y_i as the mean value of contiguous observations change, and u_i is the stochastic error term.

Now assume that an exogenous variable X_i is both linearly related to y_j and linearly increasing from east to west, as shown in Figure 11.1b.[6] If we were unaware of the spatial structure in Figure 11.1b, we might run the basic Goodman regression and obtain OLS estimates of the global parameters of interest by the equation:[7]

$$y_i = \beta^w + (\beta^b - \beta^w)X_i + u_i. \tag{11.3}$$

This model, however, provides a linear approximation to Figure 11.1c rather than to the more appropriate data generation process described by Figure 11.1b. Therefore, the omitted spatial structure of Figure 11.1a will lead to inefficient and often biased ecological estimates of the parameters of interest.

There are currently a large number of tests that can be used to detect spatial effects[8] but in many cases a visual exploration of the relationship between the residuals and the east north coordinates (Figure 11.2) will clearly show the presence of contextual effects in the data.[9]

Provided that the social process that generated y_i corresponds to that depicted in Figure 11.1b, the basic Goodman identity should be corrected to allow for the presence of spatial effects in the data:

$$y_i = \beta^w + (\beta^b - \beta^w)X_i + \overset{*}{f}(s_i) + u_i, \tag{11.4}$$

---

[6] We impose the east–west restriction so that we can represent more intuitively the linear relation between X_i and y_i on the city's surface.

[7] We use $y_i = \beta^w + (\beta^b - \beta^w)X_i + u_i$ instead of the more familiar $y_i = \beta^b X_i + \beta^w(1 - X_i) + u_i$ to be consistent with Figure 11.1. See Grofman and Merrill, this book, Chapter 5.

[8] Some popular alternatives include Moran's I, which estimates the correlation between every observation y_i and its neighbors y_j; and Geti's G, which provides local correlation estimates for every point in the map.

[9] These two plots were obtained from the Monte Carlo simulations that will be presented in the next section.

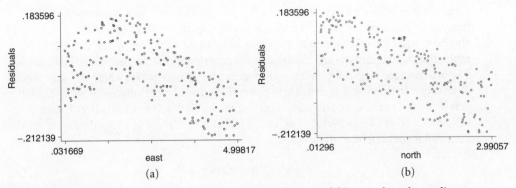

Figure 11.2. Spatial dependence in the residuals of the Goodman model (east and north coordinates of the precinct centroids).

or,

$$y_i = \beta^b X_i + \beta^w (1 - X_i) + f(s_i) + u_i. \tag{11.5}$$

To those familiar with the general additive model (GAM), Equations 11.4 and 11.5 should ring familiar (Hastie and Tibshirani, 1990). Turnout is here explained as a linear function of black and white turnout (standard Goodman model) while $f(s_i)$ estimates the non-linear spatial structure in the data. The basic problem, however, is that we lack an appropriate instrument to assess the non-linear structure of spatial (contextual) effects.

Luckily, quantitative geographers, regional scientists, and epidemiologists have developed a number of models to deal with issues of spatial heterogeneity and auto-correlation in their data. In the next section we will focus on a distance-weighted alternative and introduce a geographically weighted auto regressive control (GW-AR) for ecological inference in the presence of spatial effects. Using Brunsdon, Charlton, and Fotheringham's (1997) geographically weighted regression, we show that it is possible to recover a spatial vector parameter S that provides substantive information about the relative impact of context and its spatial structure.

11.4 GEOGRAPHICALLY WEIGHTED REGRESSION AND ITS ALTERNATIVES

Controlling for spatial effects means modeling the assumption that values in adjacent geographic locations are likely to be linked to each other by some underlying spatial structure. This spatial structure may be itself the result of other omitted local variables or some diffusion mechanism that force y_i to be spatially dependent on contiguous values.[10]

11.4.1 Contiguity

As we already showed in Equation 11.2, one way to take account of such spatial structure would be to use an extra explanatory variable describing the mean value of the dependent

---

[10] Note that spatial structure on the dependent variable y_i always implies auto-correlation. However, spatial structure may or may not result in aggregation bias (extreme spatial heterogeneity). Recovering the underlying spatial structure present in a particular data set should both improve the efficiency of the estimates in cases of auto-correlation and control for omitted spatial effects when spatial dependence leads to aggregation bias.

variable for neighboring observations. Such a procedure would be equivalent to including a time lag in time series analysis. In ecological data, a spatial matrix lag of mean y_i values can also be entered into the equation. However, in contrast with time series, the matrix lag is multi dimensional and the lags modeled in the equation cannot be considered exogenous.[11] The matrix of the lagged dependent variables can be written as $\mathbf{Wy}$, where w_{ij} describes an observation in location j as adjacent to point i if $w_{ij} = 1$ or not adjacent if $w_{ij} = 0$. Notice that if $w_{ij} = 1$, then y_i and y_j are geographically located next to each other. Therefore, y_j will be entered as a lagged value of y_i, and y_i will also be entered as a lagged value of y_j. The extended model can be written as:

$$\mathbf{y} = \mathbf{XB} + \rho\mathbf{Wy} + \varepsilon \qquad (11.6)$$

where ρ is the coefficient for the adjacent mean variable.[12]

As with standard time series auto regressive models, the number of auto regressive lags can vary; e.g. a first-order spatial lag would include observations that are contiguous to w_{ij}, second-order spatial lags would be contiguous to the first-order lag of w_{ij}, etc. In contrast with time series, however, observations that are distant may still be related to w_{ij}. Therefore, it is important to model the entire spatial structure of the data into $\mathbf{Wy}$. Such an alternative is possible through kriging, through the expansion method (Casseti), or through a geographically weighted regression of the residuals.

A common variation for the model just described is the auto-regressive error model, which assumes that the error term is spatially dependent as described in the following equation:

$$\mathbf{y} = \mathbf{XB} + (I - \rho\mathbf{W})^{-1}\varepsilon \qquad (11.7)$$

As in standard time series analyses, Equation 11.7 can be estimated by decomposing the spatially dependent error vector ε into a grid that describes the spatial trend ρ, and the usual stochastic error u_i-recovering the spatial structure in the error term.

11.4.2 Distance Weights: GWR

An alternative to contiguity matrices are distance-weighting schemes, modeling the assumption that nearby observations y_j have more influence in the estimation than observations that are further away. Seven years ago Brunsdon, Fotheringham and Charlton (1996) created GWR for exploring what they define as spatial nonstationarity: the condition by which "a simple 'global' model cannot explain the relationship between sets of variables" (p. 1).

Similar to King's EI (1996), GWR estimates local parameters for every observation i in a data set but, unlike EI, it uses distance weights to reestimate the changing relationship among variables within different spatial regimes. Such weights give declining salience to cases that are further away geographically, as measured by the distances from each observation to all others in the data set. The distances are usually computed from the geographical center

---

[11] We use the notation of Brunsdon, Fotheringham and Charlton (2000) to describe the spatial auto regressive model.

[12] Taking Equation 11.6, subtracting $\rho\mathbf{Wy}$ from both sides and factoring we have that: $(I - \rho\mathbf{Wy})\mathbf{y} = \mathbf{XB} + \varepsilon$. After transforming the X matrix (Brundsdon, Fotheringham, and Charlton, 2000), we obtain a spatial auto-regressive model $\mathbf{y} = (I - \rho\mathbf{W})^{-1}\mathbf{XB} + (I - \rho\mathbf{W})^{-1}\varepsilon$, where the variance-covariance matrix $\text{Cov}(y) = \sigma^2[(I - \rho\mathbf{W})^{-1}]'\,(I - \rho\mathbf{W})^{-1}$. The last two equations are equivalent to those of the standard OLS, but with an error term that is a linear transformation of the original spatially dependent vector ε. The main problem is, therefore, finding an acceptable value of ρ to substitute into the ecological inference model to control for the spatial structure present in the ecological data.

of each observation (the centroid) entered in the estimation process by their east north coordinates. Examples of different geographical centroids are the east north center of a precinct, a *circuito*, or a state.

GWR implements one local regression model for every observation of the data set according to the equation:

$$y_i = \sum_k \beta_k(e_i, n_i) X_{ik} + \varepsilon_i \qquad (11.8)$$

where y_i is the expected local mean; β_k are the estimated local parameters β_o through β_k; (e_i, n_i) is a distance weighting function for the i observation by its east–north coordinates; and X_{ik} describes the explanatory variables which may include a vector of ones, X_{io}, if there is a constant. The model assumes that data near to point i have more influence in the estimation of $\beta_k(e_i, n_i)$ than observations that are further away from i. In matrix notation, GWR can be written as

$$\mathbf{B}_{(ei,ni)} = \left(\mathbf{X}^T \mathbf{W}_{(ei,ni)} \mathbf{X}\right)^{-1} \mathbf{X}^T \mathbf{W}_{(ei,ni)} y \qquad (11.9)$$

where $\mathbf{W}$ is a matrix of weights whose off-diagonal elements are zero and whose diagonal elements $w_{i1}, \ldots, w_{in}$ provide a decay functions for points further away from i. Notice that a number of different weights can be used to estimate this local regression. For example, if all $w_{i1} = 1$ then no decay is represented by this matrix and the local regression model will be identical to the global OLS. On the other hand, if $w_{i1} = 1$ for 50% of the sample whose observations are closer to i, all local regressions in $w_{i1} = 1$ will be identical to the OLS estimated for the full subsample.

The problem of how to find an optimum weight to describe the spatial structure of the data requires assumptions about either the proper distance-decay function and/or the proper subsample of points. As usual, under- and over-smoothing are some problems that can arise from a poorly calibrated model. The most common choice for distance weights is Gaussian, which gives declining weights to observations as

$$\mathbf{W}_{i1} = \exp\left(-d_{i1}^2/h^2\right) \qquad (11.10)$$

where d describes the distance from observation i to observation 1, and h describes a smoothing bandwidth. As h increases, the level of smoothing increases; therefore, the local regression parameter β_{ki} converges to the global parameter β_k.[13] As h decreases, the local estimates become more spiked and the parameter becomes more distinctly local.

As can be shown, a geographically weighted Goodman regression can be implemented within this framework by specifying Equation 11.8 as

$$y_i = \beta_{(ei,ni)}^b X_i + \beta_{(ei,ni)}^w (1 - X_i) + \varepsilon_i. \qquad (11.11)$$

In general, however, we lack theoretical reasons to assume that the full model will vary over space. More importantly, there are good reasons to think that changing the spatial scale of support for the model (MAUP) will result in similar spatial aggregation problems over the newly restricted subsample when estimating β_i^b and β_i^w. Rather, the alternative we present below is to model the spatial structure of the error term directly to build a semiparametric auto-regressive error model.

---

[13] As noted by Beck and Jackman, "least square can be thought as an infinitely smooth scatterplot smoother" (1998: p. 606).

11.4.3 A Semiparametric Model Using the GWR

Now that the GWR has been presented, we can write again Equation 11.5 as

$$y_i = f(e_i, n_i) + \sum_k \beta_k X_{ik} + \varepsilon_i \qquad (11.12)$$

where the dependent variable y_i is explained by a set of linear predictors β_k and a non-parametric spatial structure $f(e_i, n_i)$ over the east–north coordinates. If we knew the error term, ε_i, a spatial smoothing could be applied to estimate the full equation. However, as ε_i is unknown, we have to both estimate $\hat{f}(e_i, n_i)$ and $\hat{\beta}$ as a two stage model. First we have to smooth the error term

$$\hat{f}(e_i, n_i) = \sum_i w_{(ei, ni)} u_i \qquad (11.13)$$

to find an instrument for the true spatial structure $f_{(e_i, n_i)}$. Then, we can use the estimated $\hat{f}(e_i, n_i)$ to estimate $\hat{\beta}$. As shown by Hastie and Tibshirani (1990) and by Brunsdon, Fotheringham, and Charlton (2000); a semiparametric model with only one smoother can be analytically derived.[14] Therefore, it is not necessary to iterate between $\hat{f}(e_i, n_i)$ and $\hat{\beta}$ for convergence.[15]

We can then use this semiparametric GWR procedure to estimate Equation 11.5.

11.5 THE PROCEDURE

The estimation procedure for a GWR Goodman or King model requires four relatively simple steps.

1. First, we compute the naïve Goodman regression model regressing X and $1 - X$ on y, saving the predicted values and the residuals. Population weights may also be entered in this stage if necessary, as shown in the Peronist example of Section 11.7.
2. Second, we map (using ArcView or an equivalent) the spatial structure of the residuals and conduct tests of spatial auto correlation between our *residuals* and the *predicted* turnout, i.e., we perform Moran's I, GWR Monte Carlo testing. A scatterplot of the residuals against the east and north coordinates of the data can also provide a simple visual test for spatial aggregation bias.
3. In the presence of spatial auto-correlation we compute a geographically weighted regression of the *predicted* $\hat{y}_i$ on the first stage *residuals* and save the local parameter B_i-technically equivalent to estimating an instrument for the spatial distribution of the error in Equation 11.13. We can obtain the parameter B_s because GWR fits a regression line for every observation of our data set. Because we are regressing the predicted dependent variable of the original Goodman model on the residuals, B_s will have mean 0 and a GW variance 1, describing the spatial structure of the error term in the first stage.
4. Finally, for a GWR Goodman: (a) we regress the new model

$$y_i = \beta^b X_i + \beta^w (1 - X_i) + \beta^3 B_s + u_i \qquad (11.14)$$

---

[14] Hastie and Tibshirani (1990): p. 118. Fotheringham, Brunsdom, and Charlton (2000): p. 180.
[15] However, iteration as it will be described below can prevent oversmoothing in some applications, particularly in the presence of local outliers.

where β^b describes blacks' turnout, β^w describes whites' turnout, β^3 describes the direct effect of the spatial parameters B_s on the ecological inference estimate, and u_i describes the stochastic error. It is important to note that by using the parameter B_s to predict the spatial structure of β^b and β^w, we can obtain both local estimates and aggregate quantities of interest, as in King's EI. GWR-Goodman will provide, therefore, local estimates that will be much closer to King's EI. If the non-linear spatial parameter B_s explains no variation in the dependent variable y_i, the results will be similar to the standard Goodman regression. For iterating the procedure, we predict a new dependent variable $\hat{y}_i$ from the previous model and repeat steps 1, 3 and 4. As in most semiparametric smoothing techniques, there are small efficiency gains by iterating the procedure. However, more important than iterating the procedure is properly choosing bandwidths and kernel functions.[16] (b) We run the GWR EI model by entering the B_s parameter estimated in (3) as a covariate Z^{bw} and Z^{bb}. No second stage is required.

11.6 A SIMPLE MONTE CARLO TEST OF THE GW-AR APPROACH TO ECOLOGICAL INFERENCE

How well does GW-AR recover the underlying spatial structure observed in the data? In this section we provide a preliminary answer to this question. In doing so, we also provide new evidence on the relative performance the Goodman regression and King's EI in the presence of spatial effects (Anselin and Tam Cho, 2002; King, 2002).

Because the underlying spatial structure that generated the data is unknown, and omitted local and global variables are at work, Monte Carlo experiments are particularly well suited to test the performance of spatially heterogeneous ecological inference models. We can (i) produce a dependent variable Y that is a function of X, $(1 - X)$ and a known spatially heterogeneous structure $f(s)$; (ii) evaluate the performance of ecological inference methods when this spatial structure is not entered into the model; and (iii) evaluate how close the recovered GW-AR spatial parameters B_s are to the designed spatial structure.

There has been considerable debate as to the proper data generation process to test for spatial heterogeneity and spatial auto correlation in ecological inference (Anselin and Tam Cho, 2002; King, 2002; Adolph and King, 2002). Therefore, it seems appropriate to briefly describe the Monte Carlo design used in this article.

Following King (2002), we generated the data using an untruncated random effects model design with $\beta^b \sim N(.4, .02)$, $\beta^w \sim N(0.6, 0.02)$ and $X \sim N(0.6, 0.04)$. The true spatial structure was created by imposing a wiggling functional form to the east-north coordinates of a virtual city, as in Figure 1a. This wiggling spatial structure was $S_i = ((sin(east) + (cos(north))/10 - 0.015$; with $east, north \sim U(-5, 5)$. Using a uniform distribution on the east and north coordinates provides an even squared grid, while the sin(east) and cos(north) over the specified range $[-5, 5]$ generates a wiggling spatial structure similar to Figure 11.1a.[17] The range of variation of the spatial structure was thus reduced from $[-2, 2]$ to $[-0.2, 0.2]$ and a remainder (0.015) was substracted to guarantee that the mean of the spatial structure was 0. Notice that the spatial structure has mean 0 but no variance, to reduce the

---

[16] It is worth noticing that this procedure describes a semiparametric auto-regressive error model. Therefore, the B_s parameter is not entered as a weighting function of the original equation $y_i = \beta_i^b + \beta_i^w (1 - X)$ but as an instrument for the underlying spatial structure in in the dependent variable y_i. For further details see "Semiparametric smoothing approaches" in Brunsdon, Charlton, and Fotheringham (2000) and Hastie and Tibshirani (1990).

[17] Many other distributions are possible by either shifting the scale of the east and north coordinates or using a different functional form.

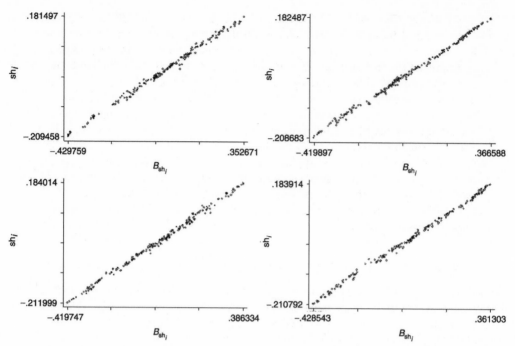

Figure 11.3. Scatterplot of the true spatial structure and the GWR parameter (Monte Carlo simulations a, b, c, and d).

error-in-variables attenuation bias (Adolph and King, 2002). Normal error terms, on the other hand, were introduced into the parameters β_i^b and β_i^w. The basic equation generated was therefore

$$y_i = \beta_i^b X + \beta_i^w (1 - X_i) + S_i. \tag{11.15}$$

This model has certain nice features for testing spatial effects, including the fact that it will generally stay within bounds but does not require explicit truncation or the presumption of a truncated bivariate normal distribution. However, avoiding more extreme truncation data sets will also result in a larger number of within bound Goodman estimates. This should be taken into consideration when comparing the relative performances of the Goodman and EI models (see Silva de Mattos and Veiga, this book, Chapter 15). The distance-weighted grid imposed on the data also has many advantages over contiguity matrices. First, complex spatial structures with different functional forms can be incorporated in this grid to analyze the estimation problems that occur as a result of the observable units being further apart, different in size, unevenly spread, etc. We gave similar population weights to every precinct ($N = 1$ for every i) and no aggregation bias different from the noted spatial aggregation bias was imposed on the data.

In Figure 11.3 we show that there is a good fit between true spatial structure S_i and the parameter B_s recovered from the residuals in the first Monte Carlo simulation. In fact, in all simulations the r^2 between the true and the recovered spatial structure was above 0.9. The quality of this fit, however, should in general vary as a function of the level of association between the spatial structure S_i and y_i and the noise in the data, as in any GAM model.

Table 11.1 Goodman, EI, GW-AR-Goodman and GW-AR-EI

Model	β^b	β^w
EI	.468 (.085)	.5061 (.123)
Goodman	.401 (.104)	.608 (.155)
GWEI	.405 (.042)	.6011 (.03)
GW-Goodman	.404 (.029)	.603 (.041)

In Table 11.1 we provide comparative information of the global parameters β^b and β^w estimated by EI, Goodman, GW-EI, and GW-Goodman regressions. The dispersion of the global parameters β^b and β^w around the true (designed) values in the uncorrected models is considerably higher than in corrected models.

More importantly, in only 36% of the naïve Goodman and 67% of EI were the β^b estimates in the 0.35–0.45 interval including the true value of 0.4. Comparative kernels of the naïve Goodman and EI models with their GW-AR show the corrected models to provide a more adequate fit to the data. In the corrected models, the percentage of global β^b within the 0.35–0.45 interval was 89% for the GW Goodman and 90% for the GW EI.

Together with Table 11.1, the kernel graphs in Figure 11.4 provide some interesting evidence of the impact of spatial effects on the standard Goodman and EI estimates. In

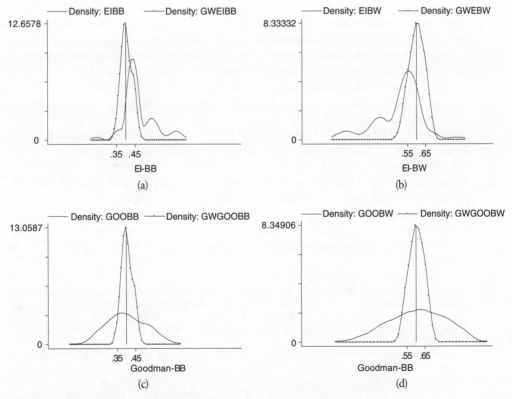

Figure 11.4. Kernel density estimates for EI and GW.

Figure 11.4a we see a kernel density graph of EI and GW-EI β^b estimates. As we can see, the uncorrected EI is biased to the right and shows two smaller modes away from the expected mean of 4.

By contrast, the corrected GW-EI is centered on the expected value of $\beta^b = 0.4$ and displays a narrower variance. Figure 11.4b displays kernel estimates for the EI and GW-EI β^w with results comparable to those of Figure 4.1. We again observe bias to the left which is corrected in the GW-EI model. In Figure 11.4c and 11.4d, the uncorrected Goodman models are on average centered on the proper values $\beta^b = 0.4$ and $\beta^w = 0.6$. However, the variance is extremely large, which would lead us to expect a rather large number of estimated models with unreliable global estimates.

As noted by Voss, this book, Chapter 3, there is extensive debate as to the performance of EI in recovering both local quantities of interest and more adequate global estimates than those of the Goodman model. Extensive applied research displaying sensible results contrast with Monte Carlo evidence showing EI to produce biased estimates in the presence of spatial effects (Anselin and Tam Cho, 2002; Calvo and Escolar, 2003).

The Monte Carlo evidence presented in Figure 11.4a to 11.4d may explain some of these conflicting accounts. The figure shows that the global EI estimates are closer to the true expected values $\beta^b = 0.4$ and $\beta^w = 0.6$ and display smaller variances than Goodman's estimates. However, the global β^b and β^w estimates are biased.[18] Moreover, the kernel density estimates for the uncorrected EI show that in the presence of spatial effects EI may often flip backwards, finding local maxima away from the true global β^b and β^w.[19]

The standard Goodman regression estimates, on the other hand, show wider variances and display a large number of estimates further away from the true values of 0.4 and 0.6. However, the average of these estimates remains unbiased. EI would then appear to produce more sensible results for researchers, although there is little guarantee that those results are in fact centered around the true mean. However, it is worth noticing that the use of a weakly truncated Monte Carlo design overstates the number of *reasonable* estimates produced by the Goodman regression. To conclude, in the GW corrected models, the GW-EI and GW-Goodman global estimates are practically identical.

Analyzing two of the simulated data sets in more detail provides further insights into the estimation of precinct-level quantities of interest in the presence of extreme spatial heterogeneity.[20] First, it is worth noticing that in the presence of spatial aggregation bias the local quantities of interest can diverge dramatically from the true local values even when the proper global estimates are computed.

For example, in Figure 11.5 we provide comparative estimates of local quantities of interest for the first two Monte Carlo simulations produced by our Stata script (test 1 and test 2). The plots in Figure 11.5 show that the global β^b and β^w estimates of test 1 in the uncorrected model (a) are centered near the true design values of 0.4 and 0.6 respectively. The local β_i^b and β_i^w, however, provide a poor fit to the true local parameters. In the case of test 2 we can

---

[18] King (2002) suggested that the Monte Carlo evidence provided by Anselin and Tam Cho (2002) may be faulty, the result of a poorly designed spatial experiment. He pointed out that truncation was imposed on the data, perhaps leading to some sort of selection bias. We obtained similar results to Anselin and Tam Cho, however, implementing King's suggested Monte Carlo design. There was no truncation and no replacement in our simulated data sets.

[19] Sign reversals were also found by Anselin and Tam Cho (2002), Calvo and Escolar (2003) and Herron and Shotts (2002).

[20] In all simulations the r^2 between the true and the recovered spatial structure was above .9. The quality of this fit, however, should in general vary as a function of the level of association between the spatial structure and Y.

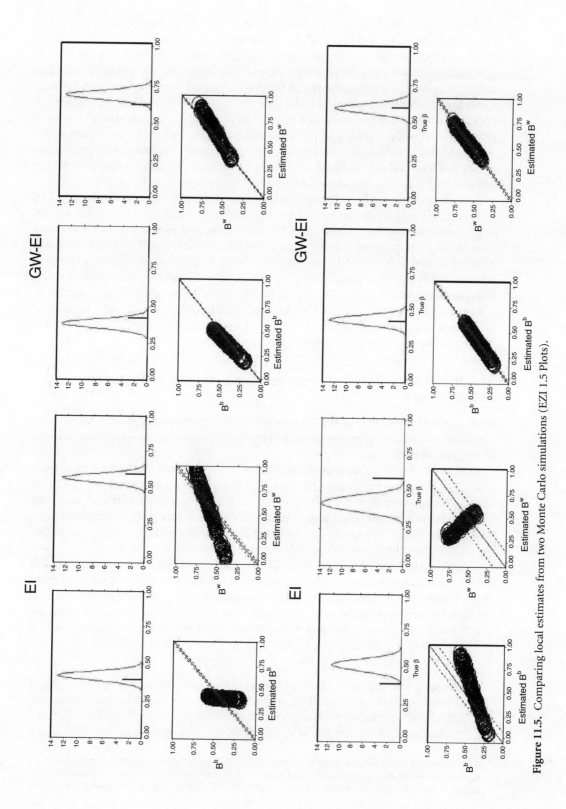

Figure 11.5. Comparing local estimates from two Monte Carlo simulations (EZI 1.5 Plots).

observe that both the true global β^b and β^w lie outside of EI estimates (kernel plots). The local estimates are also significantly different from their design values.

The fact that confidence intervals of test 1 are significantly narrower than those of test 2 does not conform to any substantive information about the performance of EI in finding proper local estimates, raising doubts on the exact relationship between the global β^b estimates and the local precinct bounds. The information added by the GW-AR parameter B_s does provides both EI and Goodman with information to fit different local mean values. In general, the GW-Goodman and GW-EI local parameters are similar. However, given that EI also fits β_i^b and β_i^w within the local bounds, some differences will surface particularly in the presence of local outliers. To obtain similar results, the local Goodman estimates should be adjusted by minimizing the distance from the point estimates to the bounds.[21]

In summary, compared with the standard Goodman regression, the uncorrected EI model was closer to the true but biased estimates of the global β^b and β^w parameters, as noted in previous research (Anselin and Tam Cho, 2002; Calvo and Escolar, 2003). These results were obtained using the random effects model and the Monte Carlo procedure proposed by King (2002) and adding a spatial structure sh_i. On the other hand, the GW-Goodman and GW-EI models provided adequate, and similar, global and local parameters in our Monte Carlo simulations.

In the next section we use the GW-AR procedure to control for spatial effects in the estimation of the Peronist turnout in the city of Buenos Aires and revisit the problem of obtaining proper local estimates of the quantities of interest.

11.7 AN ECOLOGICAL INFERENCE OF THE PERONIST TURNOUT IN 1999 IN THE CITY OF BUENOS AIRES

Analyzing the Peronist vote in Argentina is in itself an important research agenda. However, for reasons of space and presentation, we will restrict our analysis to the estimation problems as they appear in the data.

In Figure 11.6 we map the spatial distribution of turnout (top) and of the Peronist vote (middle) and precinct size (bottom) in the City of Buenos Aires. The figure shows significant spatial structure in all three cases. Turnout is considerably lower in the northeast part of the city. The Peronist vote is significantly higher in the south, where there are larger numbers of registered voters. This would lead us to expect a spatially induced positive correlation between the Peronist vote and the number of registered voters.

Estimating the Peronist turnout in the City of Buenos Aires provides an interesting and challenging case for ecological inference, because it combines a number of different problems: (i) there is evidence of aggregation bias across precincts with different population sizes, (ii) there is evidence of spatial aggregation bias across different locations, and (iii) there are significant differences in the spatial structure and distribution of the ecological units. A preliminary review of the first two problems may help to clarify some of the distinctions we have shown in this article.

1. The nonspatial aggregation bias can be readily observed in the increasing proportion of Peronist voters in more populated precincts. These precincts also have higher turnout levels for all voters across the board. A preliminary observation of the naive Goodman residuals against the number of voters shows that differently sized precincts have a

---

[21] However, we do not have a theory to explain why the minimum distance from the predicted β_i^b (or the posterior β_i^b) to the local bounds provides an acceptable local estimate for our model (Herron and Shotts, 2002: p. 2). We will revisit this problem in the next section using the example of the Peronist vote in the City of Buenos Aires.

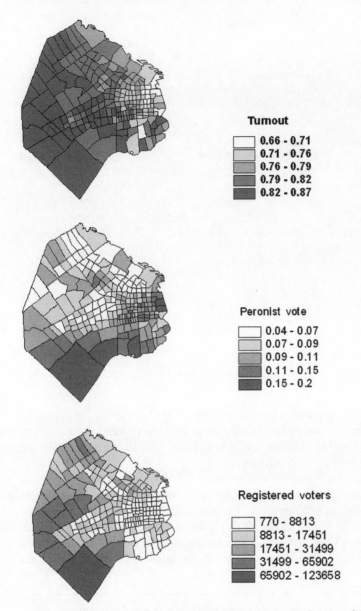

Turnout

	0.66 - 0.71
	0.71 - 0.76
	0.76 - 0.79
	0.79 - 0.82
	0.82 - 0.87

Peronist vote

	0.04 - 0.07
	0.07 - 0.09
	0.09 - 0.11
	0.11 - 0.15
	0.15 - 0.2

Registered voters

	770 - 8813
	8813 - 17451
	17451 - 31499
	31499 - 65902
	65902 - 123658

Figure 11.6. Turnout, registered voters, and Peronist vote in the City of Buenos Aires.

distinctive behavior that is also correlated with the Peronist vote (Figure 11.7c, bottom left). This aggregation problem results in severely biased Goodman coefficients if the model is run without population weights.

2. The spatial aggregation bias can be observed in the significant relation between the residuals of the Goodman equation and the east–west dimension (Figure 11.7a). The north–south dimension also displays significant heteroscedasticity, which should increase the variance around the estimated mean (Figure 11.7b).

Since we do not have precinct-level true values for Peronist turnout but we do have voting booth values, we decided to approach the estimation process as a modifiable areal unit

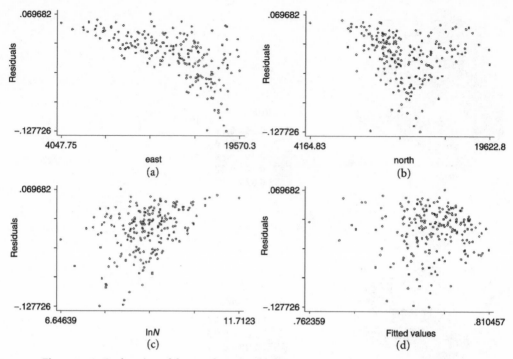

Figure 11.7. Exploration of the Goodman residuals against N and the east–west coordinates.

problem (MAUP). We used our precinct-level data to recover the booth-level parameters of Peronist and non-Peronist turnout rather than the individual voters' parameters. In total, 6509 voting booths were used to estimate baseline models of Peronist turnout, which we then compared with our precinct-level aggregates.

As shown in Table 11.2, both baseline models show the Peronist turnout to be above the other parties' turnout. However, we have little reason to believe that this is due to a particularly higher mobilization capacity and expect this difference to be the result of other variables at work (Calvo and Escolar, 2003). Substantive aggregation bias leads to poor estimates for the naïve Goodman model when population weights are not entered in the model. On the other hand, the global estimates of the weighted Goodman model are

Table 11.2 Estimates of Peronist and non-Peronist turnout in the city of Buenos Aires, all models

	Baseline Goodman	Baseline EI	Goodman w/o pop weights	Goodman w pop weights	EI	GW-Goodman	GW-EI
B^{PJ}	.889	.8961	.528***	.88***	.793***	.859***	.877***
	(.011)	(.04)	(.09)	(.066)	(.015)	(.02)	(.012)
B^{NP}	.801	.80	.822***	.80***	.811***	.805***	.802***
	(.001)	(.001)	(.009)	(.007)	(.0015)	(.002)	(.0012)
Rho	–	.0929	–	–	.720	–	−.1077
B_s	–	–	–	–	–	.889***	
N	6509	6509	209	209	209	209	209

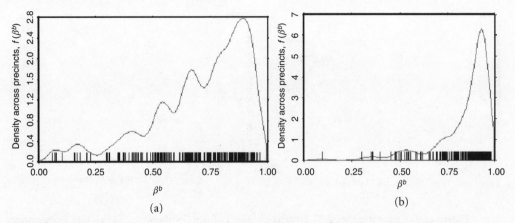

Figure 11.8. Comparative kernel plots of EI (a) and GW-EI (b) Local B_i^b Estimates; (EZI 1.5 "Results" plots).

particularly close to the baseline values, although there is a high variance around the mean estimated B^{PJ}.

The EI estimates are considerably better than those of the unweighted Goodman regression, but worse than the weighted Goodman. The B^{PJ} estimates of EI are 8% below the baseline estimates and below the reported non-Peronist turnout B^{NOPJ}. These results are particularly problematic at the local level, where a rather large number of feasible (within bounds) but unlikely local estimates were computed by EI (Figure 11.8).

Now we turn our attention to the geographically weighted models. The GW-EI estimates are similar to the baseline estimates. Also, the kernel of the local B^{PJ} estimates displays only one mode, compared with three in the uncorrected model (Figure 11.8). Therefore, as expected, the spatial parameter B_s provides EI with information to produce narrower precinct estimates. The GW-Goodman estimates, however, were 2% below the baseline estimates, which is farther from the true values estimated by the weighted Goodman regression. Still, the corrected model displays more adequate standard errors that include the baseline estimates at $p < 0.1$ and provides local B^{PJ} estimates like those of EI.

One of the most appealing advantages of EI for many researchers is the possibility of obtaining local estimates that can either provide rich descriptions of the geographic nature of social relationships or new data to conduct further research. There has been, however, little debate about what makes these local estimates good estimates. One of the most interesting problems that emerge from comparing the local B_i^{PJ} from EI and GW-Goodman (Figure 11.9) is that while the spatial structure is clearly the same, the scale for the B_i^{PJ} estimate varies substantively.[22] That is, while the local estimates for EI B_i^{PJ} go from a minimum turnout of 0.06 to a maximum of 0.96, the range of the GW-Goodman goes from 0.70–0.894. However, the high correlation between the two sets of estimates shows the same contextual effects generating these different local estimates.

When we compare the GW-EI and the GW-Goodman estimates, the relation between the two sets of local estimates fades because much of the local variation in EI's B_i^{PJ} is now explained by the covariate Z^{PJ}. However, the range of variation in B_i^{PJ} for the corrected GW-EI is still significantly larger than that of the GW-Goodman model. These differences

---

[22] It is worth noticing that the local B_i^{NOPJ} estimates of EI and GW-Goodman were almost identical, as a result of tighter bounds for EI estimates. Less informative bounds, far away from the TBN core, were more problematic.

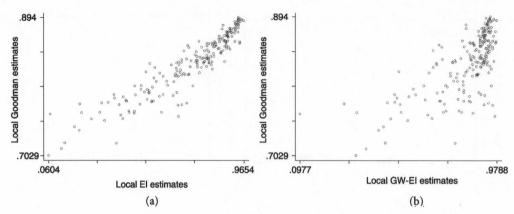

Figure 11.9. Comparing local PJ turnout estimates of the Goodman vs. EI (a), and Goodman vs. GW-EI (b) models.

are the result of different regions of the data not being explained by the original TBN in EI but still forced within the local bounds.

While EI does provides researchers with tools that described these extreme observations to be characterized by less informative bounds, researchers have usually reported these estimates, and used them for second stage analysis, without acknowleading the different information provided by these local estimates.

The problem is not less dramatic for the GW-Goodman model. Smoothing the spatial surface of the ecological relationship to allow for local variations in the mean estimates allows researchers to obtain local values that will not be forced within the observed bounds. However, they generally will fall outside the unit square of the precinct bounds. An alternative modification to the GW-Goodman model would be to minimize the distance between the model's local estimates and the precinct bounds, generating B_i^{PJ} similar to those of EI (see Merrill and Grofman, Chapter 5 in this volume). We do not, however, have a theory that provides a rational for such minimization strategy. After all, if the local B_i^{PJ} in region g is poorly explained by the overall model, why would the closest point from the model's estimate to the bound be a better predictor of the true local quantity of interest than any other point in the unit square?

11.8 CONCLUDING REMARKS

In this chapter we have described a simple distance-weighted auto-regressive model to control for spatial aggregation bias (extreme spatial heterogeneity) in ecological inference. Using Monte Carlo simulations with a random effects untruncated design (King, 2002) we find that EI produces biased estimates in the presence of spatial effects as previous literature has shown (Anselin and Tam Cho, 2002; Calvo and Escolar, 2003). The geographically weighted auto-regressive parameters B_s was able to restore the spatial independence properties of the ecological data and produce more adequate global estimates, as shown both by the Monte Carlo evidence and the analysis of the Peronist vote. The use of a geographically weighted control also allowed us to compute local estimates within the classical Goodman framework and compare them with EI's local estimates. The results show EI to produce feasible, but unlikely, local estimates with a wider range of variance than the estimates produced by GW-Goodman. Such results are problematic both when local estimates are used for descriptive purposes and when they are used in second-stage inference (Herron and Shotts, 2002). In our view, considerably more research is needed to define statistically acceptable local estimates that fall within the local bounds.

APPENDIX A. A DISTANCE-WEIGHTED WINBUGS MODEL FOR ECOLOGICAL INFERENCE IN THE PRESENCE OF SPATIAL DEPENDENCE

We provide here a distance-weighted alternative to the intuitive model of Haneuse and Wakefield (this book, Chapter 12). In our example, the distance-weighted model also estimates separate spatial structures for whites and blacks. Unlike Haneuse and Wakefield, who proposed estimating two separate binomial equations (one for blacks and one for whites), we estimate a logistic general linear model with only one binomial equation, which facilitated convergence for the two different spatial structures. The model derives directly from King's random error treatment of the Goodman identity. Following King (1997:96) we define the local parameters β_i^b and β_i^w as functions of the global means, B^b and B^w and two spatially dependent error terms, ϵ_i^b and ϵ_i^w:

$$\beta_i^b = B^b + \epsilon_i^b,$$
$$\beta_i^w = B^w + \epsilon_i^w.$$

Substituting these parameters into the Goodman identity equation, we have $y_i = (B^b + \epsilon_i^b)X_i + (B^w + \epsilon_i^w)(1 - X_i)$ and replacing the ϵ_i^b and ϵ_i^w by Diggle, Tawn, and Moyeed's (1997) spatially correlated matrix of error terms we obtain

$$y_i = B^b X_i + B^w(1 - X_i) + S_i$$

where

$$S_i = \sigma_b^2\{1 - \rho(u_b^2)\}X_i + \sigma_b^2\{1 - \rho(u_w^2)\}(1 - X_i).$$

Following Diggle, Tawn, and Moyeed (1998), similar to the GWR approach in our paper, we presume a distribution function for the spatial auto correlation ρ as a zero-mean stationary Gaussian process with variance σ_b^2 and a correlation function

$$\rho(u_i^b) = \exp[-(\alpha d)^k].$$

Where $\alpha > 0$ provides an estimate of the declining correlation with distance d, and $0 < k < 2$ describes the level of smoothing over observations.

The Winbugs Model

Using the "*spatial.exp*" function in WinBugs, it is possible to estimate the model described. The model is a close relative of universal kriging, with two zero-mean stationary Gaussian spatial smoothers. Hierarchically centering the spatial structures both follows from the formal model and facilitated convergence. We use x[i] and y[i] to describe the east and north spatial coordinates, z[i] to describe the percent of black voters usually written as X_i, and t[i] for T_i. Finally, we take advantage of WinBugs flexibility to compute and sample from the precinct level *quantities of interest* for blacks (qibbi[i]) and whites (qibwi[i]).

```
model
{ W[1:N] ~ spatial.exp(mu[], x[], y[], w.tau, w.phi, 1)
M[1:N] ~ spatial.exp(mu[], x[], y[], m.tau, m.phi, 1)
for (i in 1:N){
t[i] ~ dnorm(g[i], taup[i])
taup[i] <- p[i] / (g[i] * (1 - g[i]))
logit(g[i]) <- betab * z[i] + betaw * (1 - z[i]) + space[i]
space[i] <- (M[i] * z[i]) + (W[i] * (1 - z[i]))
mu[i] <- 0
## quantities of interest
qibbi[i] <- exp(M[i] + betab) / (1 + (exp(M[i] + betab)))
qibwi[i] <- exp(W[i] + betaw) / (1 + (exp(W[i] + betaw)))
## un-transformed quantities of interest
qib[i] <- M[i] + betab
qiw[i] <- W[i] + betaw
}
betaw ~ dnorm(.001,.001)
betab ~ dnorm(.001,.001)
w.phi ~ dunif(.001,5)
m.phi ~ dunif(.001,5)
w.tau ~ dgamma(.01,.01)
m.tau ~ dgamma(.01,.01)
}
```

REFERENCES

Adolph, Christopher, Michael C. Herron, Gary King, and Kenneth W. Shotts. 2003. "A Consensus on Second Stage Analyses in Ecological Inference Models," *Political Analysis*, 11, 1: 86–94.

Agnew, J. 1996a. "Mapping Politics: How Context Counts in Electoral Geography," *Political Geography*, 15, 2: 129–146.

Agnew, J. 1996b. Maps and Models in Political Studies: a Reply to Comments. *Political Geography*, 15, 2: 165–167.

Agnew, J. 1987. *Place and Politics: The Geographical Mediation of State and Society*. London: Allen and Unwin.

Anselin, Luc. 1988. *Spatial Econometrics: Methods and Models*. London: Kluwer Academic.

Anselin, Luc and Wendy K. Tam Cho. 2002. "Spatial Effects and Ecological Inference," *Political Analysis*, 10, 3: 276–297.

Beck, N. and S. Jackman. 1998. "Beyond Linearity By Default: Generalized Additive Models," *American Journal of Political Science*, 42, 1: 596–627.

Brunsdon, C., A. Stewart Fotheringham, and M. Charlton. 2000. *Quantitative Geography: Perspectives on Spatial Data Analysis*. London. Sage Publications.

Brundson, C., A. Stewart Fotheringham, and M. Charlton. 1996. "Geographically Weighted Regression: a Method for Exploring Spatial Nonstationarity," *Geographical Analysis*, 28, 4: 281–298.

Calvo, Ernesto and Marcelo Escolar. 2003. "A Geographically Weighted Approach to Ecological Inference," *American Journal of Political Science*, 47, 1: 188–209.

Flint, Collin. 1996. "Whither the Individual, Whither the Context," *Political Geography* 15, 2: 147–151.

Fotheringham, A. and M. O'Kelly. 1989. *Spatial Interaction Models: Formulations and Applications*. Amsterdam: Kluwer Academic.

Fotheringham, Stewart, M. E. Charlton, and C. Brunsdon. 1997. "Two Techniques for Exploring Non-stationarity in Geographical Data" *Geographical System*, 4:59–82.

Guillorel H. and J. Levy. 1992. "Space and Electoral System", *Political Geography*, 11, 2: 205–224.

Hastie, Trevor and R. J. Tibshirani. 1990. *Generalized Additive Models*. London: Chapman and Hall.

Herron, Michael and Kenneth W. Shotts. "Using Ecological Inference Point Estimates as Dependent Variables in Second-Stage Linear Regression," *Political Analysis*, 11, 1: 44–64.

Johnston, R. J. 1986a. "A Space for Place (or a Place to Space) in a British Psychology," *Environment and Planning A*, 19: 599–618.

Johnston, R. J. 1986b. "The Neighborhood Effect Revisited: Spatial Science or Political Regionalism," *Environment and Planning D*, Society and Space 4: 41–55.

Kohfeld, Carol and John Sprague. 2002. "Race, Space, and Turnout," *Political Geography*, 21, 2: 175–193.

King, G. 1996. "Why Context Should Not Count," *Political Geography*, 15, 2: 159–164.

King, G. 1997. *A Solution to the Ecological Inference Problem: Reconstructing Individual Behavior from Aggregate Data*. Princeton: Princeton University Press.

King, Gary. 2002. "Isolating Spatial Autocorrelation, Aggregation Bias, and Distributional Violations in Ecological Inference," *Political Analysis*, 10, 3: 298–300.

Sui, D. Z., and P. J. Hugill. 2002 "A GIS-Based Spatial Analysis on Neighborhood Effects and Voter Turn-Out: a Case of Study in College Station, Texas," *Political Geography*, 21: 159–173.

Ward, Michael D. and Kristian S. Gleditsh. 2002. "Location, location, location: an MCMC approach to modeling spatial context with categorical variables," *Political Analysis*, 10, 3: 244–260.

12 Ecological Inference Incorporating Spatial Dependence

Sebastien Haneuse and Jonathan Wakefield

ABSTRACT

Ecological inference for a series of 2×2 tables suffers from an inherent lack of identifiability. Any attempt at a solution to this inferential problem must either (a) incorporate additional information or (b) make assumptions. Without further information and given the data in the margins alone, critical assumptions, such as that of no contextual effects, remain untestable. This suggests a strategy of reporting a series of models based on a range of plausible assumptions, and thus performing a sensitivity analysis with respect to the untestable assumptions. The work of this paper is motivated by a voter-registration example from the U.S. state of Louisiana in 1990, where each 2×2 table represents one of 64 parishes. When aggregation is on the basis of geography, as in our example, it is intuitive that spatial effects may have a role in an ecological inference analysis. Thus far, such a role has received little attention in the literature. In this paper, we draw on the spatial epidemiological and biostatistical literature and consider the inclusion of a hierarchical spatial model into a sensitivity analysis for ecological inference. We outline issues regarding specification, interpretation, and computation for this particular model when applied to the Louisiana example. A small simulation study suggests that, in the presence of spatial effects, traditional approaches to ecological inference may suffer from incorrect estimation of variability, while models that explicitly allow for spatial effects have generally better performance.

12.1 INTRODUCTION

At the most fundamental level the difficulties in ecological inference for 2×2 tables are generated by a lack of identifiability of key quantities. We only observe the margins of a series of 2×2 tables, while the quantities of interest are derived from the internal cells. Any attempt at a "solution" to this problem must overcome this inherent nonidentifiability by either (a) collecting additional information or (b) making assumptions. Additional information can be in the form of a sample of individuals for which the cross-classification is available (Wakefield, 2004) or in the form of informative priors in a Bayesian analysis (see Chapters 1 (Wakefield) and 6 (Corder and Wolbrecht) of this book). Assumptions can be made directly about the quantities of interest or by imposing some structure on the underlying model that is assumed to generate the data. For the latter case, biases arise when these assumptions, which are generally untestable given the data in the margins alone, are inappropriate. Thus a reasonable strategy, in the absence of individual-level data, would be to report a series of models that are based on a range of plausible assumptions. One can then proceed by examining consistencies and inconsistencies across the results, performing a sensitivity analysis to untestable assumptions (see Chapter 13 (Salway and Wakefield)).

266

Although there is an extensive literature aimed at addressing biases that arise in approaches to the ecological inference problem, the role of spatial effects has not been extensively investigated. In particular, the consequences of having spatial effects present and whether taking account of them is beneficial for estimation have received little attention. In this paper, we draw on the spatial epidemiological and biostatistical literature to investigate how one might incorporate spatial effects into a model for ecological inference. This opens a new avenue for plausible models that may be incorporated into a sensitivity analysis. One common approach to incorporating spatial effects is to adopt a random effects specification. In spatial epidemiology such random effects models describe heterogeneity in disease rates across areas, some of which is assumed to be spatially structured and the remainder unstructured. In this paper, we adopt a random effects specification for an underlying model, which is assumed to generate the (unobserved) internal cells of the 2×2 tables, within an overall *hierarchical spatial model* for ecological inference.

The structure of the paper is as follows. Section 12.2. briefly outlines a motivating example of voter registration in Louisiana from 1990, the notation used throughout the paper, and the problem formulation. Spatial effects in ecological inference are discussed in Section 12.3, as are some of the connections between political science and spatial epidemiology. In Section 12.4 we provide an outline of a spatial model commonly used in epidemiology, including specification, interpretation, and computational issues. Section 12.5 describes and reports on a series of simulations aimed at identifying the effect of spatial dependence and assessing the success of the proposed spatial model. Section 12.6 returns to the voter registration data taken from Louisiana in 1990. Finally, Section 12.7 provides some discussion and concluding remarks.

12.2 NOTATION AND PROBLEM FORMULATION

The data that we use to motivate this paper is voter registration data from Louisiana in 1990 (also see Chapter 1 of this book). Specifically, the data consist of parish-level totals of registration in three categories (Democrat, Republican, and independent) as well as parish-level totals of race in three categories (black, white, and other). For the purposes of this paper we concentrate on the problem of examining Democrat–Republican registration versus black–white race in $n = 64$ parishes. Although there are currently 65 parishes in the state of Louisiana, data for two parishes, St. Martins Parish North and St. Martins Parish South, were collected as a combined total. Throughout this paper we use notation in which race is indexed by j ($j = 0$ denotes blacks and $j = 1$ denotes whites), and parishes by i, $i = 1, \ldots, n$. Thus, for parish i, we may write down a 2×2 table which provides a cross-classification of race and registration, as in Table 12.1.

Let $\hat{p}_{ji} = Y_{ji}/N_{ji}$, denote the race–parish-specific registration probabilities for the Republican party, had we observed the internal cells (Y_{0i} and Y_{1i}) of Table 12.1. Further, consider

Table 12.1 2×2 table for parish i

	Democrat	Republican	
Black		Y_{0i}	N_{0i}
White		Y_{1i}	N_{1i}
	$N_i - Y_i$	Y_i	N_i

the overall race-specific probabilities of registering Republican, $\bar{p}_j$, defined as a weighted average of the race–parish-specific probabilities, weighted by the size of the race-specific population total in each parish:

$$\bar{p}_0 = \frac{\sum_{i=1}^{n} N_{0i}\, \bar{p}_{0i}}{\sum_{i=1}^{n} N_{0i}}, \qquad \bar{p}_1 = \frac{\sum_{i=1}^{n} N_{1i}\, \bar{p}_{1i}}{\sum_{i=1}^{n} N_{1i}}. \tag{12.1}$$

It is these quantities that are often of interest in ecological inference. However, the internal cells of Table 12.1 are unobserved in an ecological study. Given the ecological data (N_{0i}, N_{1i}, Y_i) alone, the $\bar{p}_{ji}$ cannot be *directly* computed and therefore neither can ($\bar{p}_0$, $\bar{p}_1$). For our purposes of methods comparison, we consider the goal of ecological inference to compute ($\bar{p}_0$, $\bar{p}_1$) using the ecological data alone, which requires the imputation of the internal cells of Table 12.1. Using the observed marginal quantities, we may compute the observed marginal probability of being black in parish i, denoted $x_i = N_{0i}/N_i$, and the observed marginal probability of registering Republican, denoted $\tilde{q}_i = Y_i/N_i$. Given the fixed race margin, we can write down the basic accounting identity that relates the marginal Republican registration probability, $\tilde{q}_i$, to the two unknown race-specific probabilities, $\bar{p}_{0i}$ and $\bar{p}_{1i}$, via the known marginal probability of being black, x_i:

$$\tilde{q}_i = \bar{p}_{0i} x_i + \bar{p}_{1i}(1 - x_i). \tag{12.2}$$

The accounting identity 12.2 highlights the nonidentifiability issue, since there are an infinite set of ($\bar{p}_{0i}$, $\bar{p}_{1i}$) that are consistent with ($\tilde{q}_i$, x_i). Thus, simplifying assumptions in the model, from that of a saturated model involving $2n$ unknown quantities, are needed. One of the strongest assumptions is that of the ecological regression model (Goodman, 1953), where race-specific probabilities are assumed to be constant in expectation across all parishes. That is, $E[\bar{p}_{0i}|x_i] = p_0$ and $E[\bar{p}_{1i}|x_i] = p_1$. This assumes that the natural heterogeneity in the race-specific probabilities across parishes can be absorbed into a single linear regression-type error term. Several approaches have been put forward to better accommodate this heterogeneity. These include the *nonlinear neighborhood model* (Freedman et al., 1998), which assumes that there is heterogeneity across parishes but not across races within a parish (i.e. $\bar{p}_{0i} = \bar{p}_{1i} = \tilde{q}_i$); the *extended Goodman model* (Achen and Shively, 1995), which specifies the probabilities as linear functions of race (i.e. adding quadratic terms into Equation 12.2), and hierarchical modeling approaches. The latter include a model based on a truncated bivariate normal distribution (King, 1997), and a beta-binomial hierarchical model (King, Rosen, and Tanner, 1999). Each specification assumes that the heterogeneity across the race-specific probabilities takes on a specific form – in particular, a form that has no spatial structure (beyond that due to neighboring parishes having similar x_i values).

The approach that we take in this paper is to postulate the existence of an underlying model, which is assumed to generate the internal cells of Table 12.1. The underlying model is specified in terms of a set of population-based parameters $p_{ji} = P(\text{register Republican} \mid \text{race } j, \text{parish } i)$, which are interpreted as probabilities in a hypothetical infinite population. These should be distinguished from the $\bar{p}_{ji}$, which are single realizations from this data-generating mechanism, and therefore not necessarily equal to the p_{ji}. We can think of the p_{ji} as the underlying propensity to register Republican for race j in area i, whereas the $\bar{p}_{ji}$ reflects the actual registration for the Republican party on a specific date. The p_{ji} are assumed to be unknown constants, while we might have observed a different sets of $\bar{p}_{ji}$ if the registration process were repeated. To solve the nonidentifiability problem, we adopt a specific structure to this underlying model, parameterized in terms of the p_{ji}, and in particular a structure which allows explicitly for spatial effects. The models of King (1997) and King, Rosen, and Tanner (1999) are alternative specifications of the underlying model. Thus, under this paradigm the goal of the analysis shifts from one of *imputation* of the $\tilde{p}_{ji}$ to one of *estimation* of the p_{ji}. However, since the totals N_i in Table 12.1 are large (ranging from 4,421 to 218,000), we assume that $\tilde{p}_{ji}$ and p_{ji} are the same and therefore do not distinguish between the two goals. Notice, however, that the hypothetical p_{ji} need not satisfy the accounting identity 12.2 with respect to the observed ($\tilde{q}_i$, x_i). Wakefield (2004) provides the likelihood function for a single 2×2 table, which allocates mass to values of (p_{0i}, p_{1i}) which do not satisfy Equation 12.2.

The notation that we adopt differs slightly from that of the Introduction to this book. Our notation (see also Chapters 1 (Wakefield) and 13 (Salway and Wakefield)) is consistent with that found in the biostatistics–epidemiology literature and also aims to emphasize the difference between the proportions $\tilde{p}_{ji}$ and the parameters p_{ji}. In our notation, the observed data are ($\tilde{q}_i$, x_i, N_i) from n 2×2 tables, while in the notation of the Introduction the observed data are (T_i, X_i, N_i) from p 2×2 tables. There the unobserved race–parish-specific proportions are denoted (β_i^b, β_i^w), whereas we use ($\tilde{p}_{0i}$, $\tilde{p}_{1i}$). The race-specific weighted averages are denoted (B^b, B^w) in the Introduction, whereas we use ($\tilde{p}_0$, $\tilde{p}_1$).

12.3 SPATIALLY STRUCTURED REGISTRATION PROBABILITIES

Achen and Shively (1995) examine the issue of aggregation bias, which is defined as the failure of a model based solely on aggregated data to estimate parameters, extensively in an individual-level model. They allude to the role of spatial effects via their *intraconstituency spatial autocorrelation*, which is described as the " . . . tendency of individuals in the same geographic unit to resemble each other in unmeasured ways" (p. 96). In fact, Achen and Shively equate their intraconstituency spatial autocorrelation with aggregation bias in Goodman's ecological regression. They indicate that in order to avoid aggregation bias one would need to adjust for variables that represent how individuals group themselves into geographical units. Alternatively, if such variables are unmeasured, then unbiased estimation relies on the assumption that they are unassociated with the regressor, which in our case is race x_i. Their spatial autocorrelation is closely related to the issue that we consider in this paper. Here, we explicitly consider how the registration probabilities themselves exhibit spatial structure *across* the geographical area. This spatial structure is likely due to unmeasured factors, such as income, which have a spatial pattern and are predictive of the registration probabilities. In the model we outline below, these unmeasured factors are incorporated via random effects, which are assumed to be at the parish level and therefore common to all individuals within the parish. Thus, they could be viewed as similar in nature to the intraconstituency spatial autocorrelation. However, whereas Achen and Shively in their description of the spatial component assume that it is area-specific, we in addition allow the spatial effects (i.e. the strength of dependence of the p_{ji}'s on the spatially structured unmeasured factor) to differ between the two races.

Anselin and Cho (2002) provide an excellent discussion of the links between spatial effects and ecological inference as well as describing a range of plausible spatial models. They also present a Monte Carlo simulation study examining the impact of spatially structured heterogeneity on the results of the Goodman model and the EI model (King, 1997) above and beyond aggregation bias. They show that under their data-generating system both approaches produce unbiased estimates regardless of the strength of the spatial structure.

However, they also show that the estimates from these two models experience higher variability across simulations when spatial effects are present. They do not, however, examine the performance of the models by comparing the model-based variability (standard errors reported by the procedures) with the "true" simulation-based variability (variability in estimates across simulations). Furthermore, although they consider various forms of spatial structure, they do not propose how one might proceed in an applied setting, that is, how one would model spatial patterns in the residuals.

In this paper we turn to the extensive spatial epidemiology literature on the analysis of aggregated disease counts. The motivation for the research in this field comes from several sources: readily available geographically indexed health and population data, and advances in computing, geographical information systems, and statistical methodology. Applications of spatial models include disease mapping, assessment of risk in relation to a point or line source, cluster detection, and geographical correlation studies. The latter, which are also referred to as ecological studies (Richardson and Monfort, 2000), aim to assess disease risk associations between sets of variables measured on groups, and then relate these assessments to risk at the level of the individual. Differences in risk estimates at the different levels of inference are often referred to as *ecological* or *cross-level* bias. In ecological studies in spatial epidemiology, the presence of residual spatial dependence is viewed as a nuisance. In the context considered here, it is viewed as something that may be beneficial for the estimation of race-specific probabilities. Chapter 13 (Salway and Wakefield) provides a comparison of the approaches to ecological inference in epidemiology, political science, and sociology.

One of the main problems in many spatial epidemiology applications is the sparseness of events, due to the statistical rarity of diseases (such as most forms of cancer). This leads to highly variable estimates of risk. In addition, inference can be highly prone to enumeration errors in the data, so that small changes (especially in the number of disease cases) can have a great impact. To overcome these issues, and to provide a more robust method of estimation, it is common to adopt a hierarchical model linking all the risk estimates across areas. This results in a form of smoothing where the risk estimates are able to "borrow strength" from each other via the structure of the model. Lindley and Smith (1972) showed that, in terms of mean squared error, related hierarchical models tend to provide better estimates than methods that use the data from a single area only. In the context of ecological inference in political science, it would be of interest to examine whether the adoption of a hierarchical model may help overcome the nonidentifiability problem by linking probabilities across areas. This is generally not necessary in spatial epidemiology, since a constant exposure effect is assumed across areas. In the political science context, this would be equivalent to assuming that the difference between blacks and whites in the race-specific probabilities is constant across areas.

To numerically quantify the extent of spatial dependence, as an initial data exploratory step, we use three statistics: Moran's I statistic (Moran, 1948), Geary's c statistic (Geary, 1954), and a nonparametric rank-based statistic, which we denote by D (see the Appendix for details of each of these statistics). Each bears a close resemblance to the conventional correlation coefficient, with positive spatial dependence being indicated by large values of I and small values of both c and D. These *autocorrelation statistics*, as well as other statistics for detecting spatial dependence and clustering, are described in detail by Wakefield, Kelsall, and Morris (2000). To obtain measures of statistical significance we employ a permutation test (see for example Lehmann, 1986). In such a test, the sampling distribution of the test statistic is computed by repeatedly permuting the data across the parishes (in our case 10,000 times) and evaluating the test statistic each time. A histogram of the resulting test statistics provides an approximation to the sampling distribution. The significance level (for a one-sided test of no positive spatial dependence) can then be evaluated by counting the number of test statistics whose value is more extreme (having larger I and smaller c and D) than the test statistic observed for the original data.

These statistics have been used in spatial epidemiology, but, as pointed out by Besag and Newell (1991), their use is dangerous when the summary measures (for example, probabilities or rates) have nonconstant uncertainties that have spatial structure. For example, in spatial epidemiology rural areas tend to have low populations and therefore highly variable disease rates. Since these areas tend to be contiguous (since population size has spatial structure), it is likely that the high and low disease rates are contiguous, giving the impression of spatial dependence. In the political science context the events are not rare and the populations (parish sizes in our example) tend to be large, so that the problems of instability are not great. However, the proportion black, x_i, is likely to have strong spatial structure, and if race is an important predictor of behavior, then spatial structure may be induced in the overall probabilities $\bar{q}_j$. In modeling, we are interested in the residual spatial variability after allowing for the variability induced by the x_i. Hence careful interpretation of the three summary statistics is required. In general, we would not advocate their use beyond an initial exploratory step, particularly with small sample sizes.

12.4 HIERARCHICAL SPATIAL MODEL

12.4.1 Specification and Interpretation

The model that we adopt is a three-stage hierarchical model for the hypothetical probabilities $\{p_{ji}\}$, $j = 0, 1, i = 1, \ldots, n$, adapted from the spatial epidemiology literature. The basic idea is to build plausible models for each set of race-specific probabilities, which are linked to the observed data via the accounting identity 12.2 and through a likelihood function.

12.4.1.1 Stage 1

At the first stage, for the observed marginal probability of registering Republican we adopt a normal approximation to the convolution likelihood. Chapter 1 of this book outlines the convolution likelihood and examines the normal approximation in detail. Thus, for parish i, we assume

$$\frac{Y_i}{N_i} \sim \mathcal{N}\left(q_i, \sigma_i^2\right), \tag{12.3}$$

where $q_i = p_{0i}x_i + p_{1i}(1 - x_i)$ and $\sigma_i^2 = N_i^{-1}\{p_{0i}(1 - p_{0i})x_i + p_{1i}(1 - p_{1i})(1 - x_i)\}$.

12.4.1.2 Stage 2

The second stage adopts, for each race, a random effects specification for the logit transformed race–parish-specific probabilities. In particular, for race j and parish i, we assume

$$\text{logit}(p_{ji}) = \mu_j + U_{ji} + V_{ji}, \tag{12.4}$$

where μ_j is a race-specific mean (on the logit scale), $\vec{U}_j = (U_{j1}, U_{j2}, \ldots, U_{jn})^T$ is the race-specific vector of spatially structured random effects, and $\vec{V}_j = (V_{j1}, V_{j2}, \ldots, V_{jn})^T$ is the race-specific vector of nonspatial random effects, $j = 0,1$. The model assumes that heterogeneity in the logit(p_{ji})'s across the geography (64 parishes) around the race-specific mean μ_j can be decomposed into two components, one exhibiting spatial structure and the other exhibiting no structure. This specification of structured and unstructured random effects was first suggested by Besag, York, and Mollie (1991) in the context of disease mapping. The two sets of random effects may be interpreted in a variety of ways. Here we adopt an interpretation in terms of allowing for unmeasured covariates and for potential errors in the observed N_{1i} and Y_i (Wakefield, Best, and Waller, 2000). In particular, the vector $\vec{U}_j$ may represent unmeasured socioeconomic factors which vary smoothly across the state of Louisiana. The vector $\vec{V}_j$, in addition to unmeasured covariates that do not exhibit spatial structure, may also represent enumeration anomalies which we may not expect to have any structure. It is important to note that these random effects are introduced at the parish level, and are consequently assumed to be constant for all individuals of race j within parish i. Consequently, in terms of unmeasured covariates, the random effects are univariate summaries of the combined effects of the joint distributions of these unmeasured covariates within each parish.

Our approach is to adopt a fully Bayesian framework by not only making distributional assumptions on both sets of random effects but also specifying prior distributions for the resulting hyperparameters. Typically, normal distributions are used for the random effects, although robust alternatives are possible (see the discussion of Besag, York, and Mollie, 1991). For the nonspatial random effects we assume that, for race j, the V_{ji} are independently and identically distributed according to a $\mathcal{N}(0, \sigma_{vj}^2)$ distribution, where $\sigma_{vj}^2 > 0$ reflects the amount of unstructured race-specific between-parish heterogeneity. Specification of the vector of spatially structured random effects, $\vec{U}_j$, requires more care. Initially, suppose we adopt an n-dimensional normal distribution

$$\vec{U}_j \sim \mathcal{N}(\vec{0}, \ \sigma_{uj}^2 \Sigma_j),$$

where σ_{uj}^2 reflects the amount of overall variability in the U_{ji}, and Σ_j is a race-specific positive definite correlation matrix. There are many frameworks that we may adopt for the specification of the elements of Σ_j to represent spatial dependence between U_{ji} and U_{jk} for $i \neq k$. Modeling could proceed by specifying an explicit joint model for these correlations, for example specifying the (i, k) element of Σ_j as $\Sigma_{j,ik} = \exp[-\phi d_{ik}]$, where $\phi > 0$ and d_{ik} is the distance between the centroids of parishes i and k. For a fixed distance between two parishes, smaller values of ϕ correspond to stronger correlation, and larger values to weaker correlation. This specification has been implemented but is highly expensive computationally (for details see Wakefield, Best, and Waller, 2000).

As an alternative to the joint specification, we may exploit standard properties of the multivariate normal distribution to obtain a *conditional* specification. Let $Q_j = \Sigma_j^{-1}$ be the precision matrix, and $Q_{j,ik}$ denote the (i, k) element of the matrix Q_j. As reviewed by Besag and Kooperberg (1995), we may write down the set of n conditional distributions

$$U_{ji}|U_{jk} = u_{jk}, \ k \neq i, \ \sim \mathcal{N}\left(\sum_{k=1}^n W_{j,ik} u_{jk}, \ \sigma_{uj}^2 D_{j,ii}\right), \tag{12.5}$$

where $W_{j,ii} = 0$, $W_{j,ik} = -Q_{j,ik}/Q_{j,ii}$, and $D_{j,ii} = Q_{j,ii}^{-1}$. The specification given by 12.5 indicates that, for $i = 1, \ldots, n$, the distribution of the ith parish's random effect, U_{ji}, conditional on the set of random effects for all other parishes is normally distributed with mean equal to a weighted average of those random effects and variance proportional to the constant σ_{uj}^2. From this *conditional* specification we can retrieve the joint specification via the relationship $Q_j = D_j^{-1}(I - W_j)$, where D_j is an $n \times n$ diagonal matrix containing elements $D_{j,ii}$ for $i = 1, \ldots, n$, I is an $n \times n$ identity matrix, and W_j is an $n \times n$ matrix containing elements $W_{j,ik}$ for $i, k = 1, \ldots, n$. The specification 12.5 is often referred to as a *Gaussian autoregression*.

A common model is the *intrinsic Gaussian conditional autoregression* (ICAR) considered by Besag et al. (1991) and given by

$$ U_{ji}|U_{jk} = u_{jk}, \ k \neq i, \ \sim \ \mathcal{N}\left(\frac{1}{m_i} \sum_{k \in \delta_i} u_{jk}, \ \frac{\omega_{uj}^2}{m_i} \right), \qquad i = 1, \ldots, n, \qquad (12.6) $$

where δ_i is the set of indices for the neighbors of parish i, and m_i is the number of neighbors for parish i. This model is a special case of 12.5 with $W_{j,ik} = 1$ if parish i and parish k are adjacent and 0 otherwise, and $D_{j,ii} = 1/m_i$. The model has intuitive appeal in that it assumes that the spatially structured random effect for parish i, given all the other parishes, has mean equal to the average of the random effects for the neighboring parishes and precision proportional to the number of neighboring parishes. This specification is also the limiting form of a more general model where the conditional mean is multiplied by a scaling factor $\lambda \in (0, 1)$. The parameter λ, together with the weight matrix W_j, dictates the degree of spatial dependence in the U_{ji}. At one extreme $\lambda = 0$ corresponds to the case where the conditional mean in 12.6 does not depend on neighboring values, thereby limiting the amount of spatial dependence between the U_{ji}. Spatial dependence may still be induced via the m_i, for example, if there is clustering of small (or large) parishes. At the other extreme, $\lambda = 1$, which is the specification in 12.6, corresponds to the case where the conditional mean is exactly the average of the neighboring values. This increases the potential for spatial dependence in the model by inducing fairly strong local smoothing across the U_{ji}.

In this paper we adopt 12.6 for the spatial component of the heterogeneity in the logit(p_{ji})'s. By setting λ equal to 1 we explicitly assume that the spatial component of the overall heterogeneity exhibits a high degree of spatial correlation. The freely varying parameter ω_{uj}^2 dictates the magnitude of heterogeneity that is attributed to the spatial component, with the remaining heterogeneity being captured by the unstructured component and more specifically the parameter σ_{vj}^2. The extent to which the logit transformed probabilities exhibit spatial dependence relies on an interplay between the magnitudes of ω_{uj}^2 and σ_{vj}^2.

One feature of the conditional specification 12.6 is that, given our specific choices of W_j and λ, the model does not yield a positive definite precision matrix Q_j. Hence the corresponding joint specification does not exist. A benefit of this, however, is that the model is nonstationary and so may be able to reflect more spatially irregular behavior. On the technical side, we may remedy the lack of a full joint specification by including a separate intercept term (as we do with μ_j) and imposing the constraint that the u_{ji} sum to zero. This results in an identifiable model for the random effects. Instead of the sum-to-zero constraint, one could alternatively constrain one of the U_{ji} to equal zero or omit the overall mean μ_j. It is also important to note that the variance ω_{uj}^2 is interpreted as a conditional variance, which is emphasized by the change in notation from σ_{uj}^2 to ω_{uj}^2 in 12.6. A disadvantage, therefore, of the specification 12.6 is that it is difficult to compare σ_{vj}^2 and ω_{uj}^2 directly, since one is interpreted marginally and the other conditionally. Even though the marginal variance for the ICAR distribution does not exist, we compute the *empirical marginal variance*, denoted here by $\widehat{V}[U_{ji}]$, described in the next section, via simulation. We finally comment on the choice of the neighborhood, where we take as neighbors two areas that share a common boundary, as is usual. This choice has its origins in applications with regular arrays, and so the model is more reasonable for geographies that are not too irregular. Louisiana is reasonable in this respect. Wakefield, Best, and Waller (2000) discuss a variety of other issues pertaining to this model.

12.4.1.3 Stage 3

At the third stage we make a priori distributional assumptions regarding the hyperparameters introduced at the second stage: $(\mu_0, \mu_1, \sigma_{v0}^2, \sigma_{v1}^2, \omega_{u0}^2, \omega_{u1}^2)$. Since the range of values on the logit scale is $(-\infty, \infty)$, the mean parameters μ_j can take on any value, and therefore a fully uninformative prior would be a flat prior on the entire real line. While uninformative on the logit scale, this results in a prior distribution on the probability scale that puts nearly all of its mass on two values: 0 and 1. In nonecological applications with *regular* models, the choice of the third-stage distributions has less impact. As discussed by Wakefield (2004), this is not the case in ecological studies. For our application, we chose to adopt logistic priors, with location 0 and scale 1, for both μ_0 and μ_1, which results in a flat prior on the probability scale which lies on the unit interval $(0, 1)$.

For the variance components, a common choice for an uninformative prior has been a Gamma(ϵ, ϵ) distribution for the inverse variance (precision), with ϵ small (Spiegelhalter, Thomas, Best, and Lunn, 2000). Kelsall and Wakefield (1999) point out that this prior is not consistent with very small amounts of variability, and for their specific data analysis they suggest a Gamma(0.5, 0.0005) as an alternative. For our application, due to the multitude of problems faced by ecological inference, the choice of the prior distribution for the (inverse) variance components requires even more care. As discussed in Chapter 1 of this book, in the context of ecological inference the lack of information in the margins indicates that an uninformative prior is not a good choice. The approach that we take is geared specifically to the Louisiana data.

Initially, before we describe the derivation of the variance priors, we empirically examine the marginal variability for the ICAR model 12.6. Given a fixed value of ω_u^2, we may draw independent samples from an ICAR distribution, $\{U_1^{(d)}, \ldots, U_{64}^{(d)}\}$ for $d = 1, \ldots, D$, where D is the number of samples drawn. See the Appendix for details. For each draw we compute the following *empirical marginal variance*:

$$\widehat{V}\left[U_i^{(d)}\right] = \frac{1}{63} \sum_{i=1}^{64} \left(U_i^{(d)} - \bar{U}^{(d)}\right)^2,$$

where $\bar{U}^{(d)}$ is the mean of the draw. Via simulation, for any value of ω_u^2 and for the specific spatial structure of the Louisiana geography, we find that

$$\frac{\text{Mean}(\widehat{V}[U_i])}{\omega_u^2} \approx 0.49. \tag{12.7}$$

That is, the conditional variance is larger, on average across simulations from Equation 12.6, than the empirical marginal variance by a factor of approximately 2. Now, consider the total marginal variance (TMV) of the sum of the two random effects. When decomposing variability into spatial and unstructured components, this total will remain fixed. Therefore, the two variance components will be negatively related and, in particular, are unlikely to be both large simultaneously. At one extreme the spatial component $\widehat{V}[U_{ji}]$ would contribute all of the total marginal variability, while at the other extreme it would make zero contribution. In reality, $\widehat{V}[U_{ji}]$ will account for a portion of the total, with the remainder of the variability being accounted for by σ_{vj}^2. Our approach is to derive a prior distribution for the total marginal variability and then use it as a prior distribution for unstructured (marginal) variance component. For the spatial (conditional) variance component, an adjustment is made via the ratio in Equation 12.7. Although, as we point out above, there will likely be negative dependence between the two variance components (in particular in the posterior), we assume a priori independence.

Assume that the logit(p_{ji}) is normally distributed about some mean μ_j. Using properties of the normal distribution, we find that 95% of the centered logits will lie in the interval $(-\theta, \theta)$, where θ can be solved for via

$$\text{TMV} \approx \left(\frac{\theta}{1.96}\right)^2. \tag{12.8}$$

Alternatively, we may postulate a value for θ and then solve for the TMV using Equation 12.8. Suppose, a priori, we expect 95% of the race-specific registration probabilities, for either race, to lie in the interval (0.01, 0.50), so that the corresponding logits lie in the interval $(-4.60, 0.00)$. Solving, we find that $\theta = 2.3$, which results in a maximal point value for the total marginal variability of 1.38. The strategy that we adopt is to pick a Gamma distribution on the precision scale which assigns sufficient weight to a plausible range of values on the (marginal) variance scale based on this point value. A numerical search was performed such that the resulting Gamma distribution, after transformation back onto the variance scale, had (0.05, 1.38) as its 5th and 95th percentiles respectively. The choice of the 5th percentile was arbitrary but, it was felt, would allow for small enough amounts of variability. This resulted in Gamma(1.50, 0.23) priors for the inverses of $\{\sigma_{v0}^2, \sigma_{v1}^2\}$. For the inverses of the spatial (conditional) variance components we performed a similar search using (0.10, 2.82) as the 5th and 95th percentiles. These percentiles were chosen on the basis of Equation 12.7. This resulted in Gamma(1.52, 0.49) priors for the inverses of $\{\omega_{u0}^2, \omega_{u1}^2\}$.

As a final note, this procedure is sensitive to the smallest selected probability (i.e. 0.01 above). Small changes in this lower bound will likely result in large changes on the logit scale and consequently the value of θ.

12.4.2 Simulation from the Prior

Before we implement the analysis, we examine realizations from the joint prior specification for the model in order to examine graphically the effect of spatial dependence. In addition, this allows us to evaluate the autocorrelation statistics described earlier in a setting in which we know the extent of spatial dependence. This is done by simulating from the specified prior distributions and examining the resulting probabilities. Assuming the hyperparameters are independent a priori, we can simulate from each of the prior distributions using the Louisiana geography data, where, for each realization, we fix the values of the x_i to be equal to those in the original data. In particular, it is instructive to examine single realizations of the joint prior distribution for all 64 parish-specific probabilities, for various values of the underlying second-stage hyperparameters. It is useful to examine various strength combinations of the unstructured and spatially structured random effects and the resulting probabilities plotted on the Louisiana geography. We do this by initially fixing the total marginal variance on the logit scale for the parish-specific probabilities. The total marginal variability can be thought of as a mixture of the two sources of (marginal) variability, and we control the mixture via the parameter $\gamma \in (0, 1)$. For a fixed value of γ we specify the contributions from the two sources of variability as follows:

$$\sigma_v^2 = (1 - \gamma)\text{TMV}, \qquad V[U_i] = \gamma\,\text{TMV}.$$

Thus, for $\gamma = 0$ all of the TMV is unstructured, while at the other extreme for $\gamma = 1$ all of it is spatially structured. The empirical marginal variance for the spatially structured random effects is controlled by simulating a realization from an ICAR distribution with $\omega_u^2 = 1.0$ and appropriately rescaling the resulting U_i. The rescaling preserves the strength of spatial structure in the U_i, since, as described in Section 4.1.2, the strength of the spatial structure is governed by the weight matrix, W_j.

Figure 12.1 provides four realizations from the joint prior for the parish-specific probabilities. For each realization, there are three sets of probabilities of registering Republican:

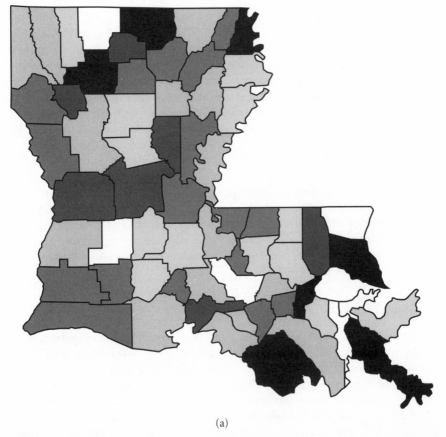

(a)

Figure 12.1. Simulated priors for Louisiana on the logit scale, where γ_0 and γ_1 denote the proportions of the variability that is spatially structured. Darker regions represent parishes with higher probabilities of registering Republican, and the cutoffs are common to all maps within a single row. Numbers represent p-values for the test of no positive spatial dependence based on Moran's I statistic. (a) Blacks ($\gamma_0 = 0.05$): 0.822. (b) Whites ($\gamma_1 = 0.05$): 0.961. (c) Combined: 0.770. (d) Blacks ($\gamma_0 = 0.05$): 0.892. (e) Whites ($\gamma_1 = 0.95$): <0.001. (f) Combined: <0.001. (g) Blacks ($\gamma_0 = 0.05$): 0.806. (h) Whites ($\gamma_1 = 0.95$): < 0.001. (i) Combined: 0.007. (j) Blacks ($\gamma_0 = 0.95$): 0.011. (k) Whites ($\gamma_1 = 0.05$): 0.591. (l) Combined: 0.190.

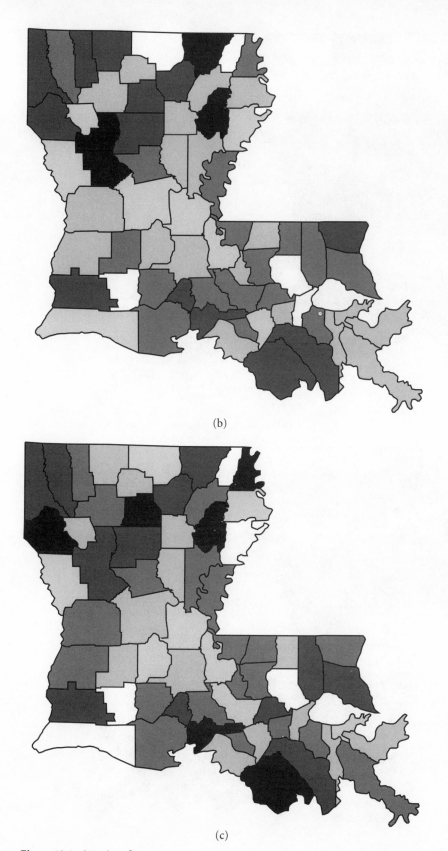

(b)

(c)

Figure 12.1. (*continued*)

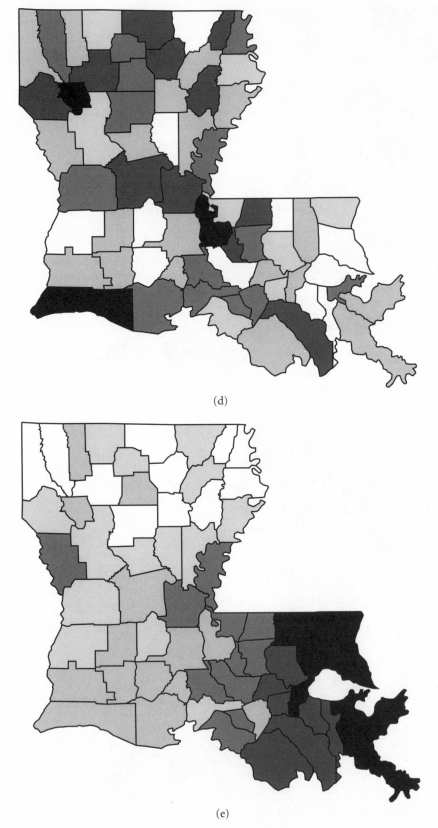

(d)

(e)

Figure 12.1. (*continued*)

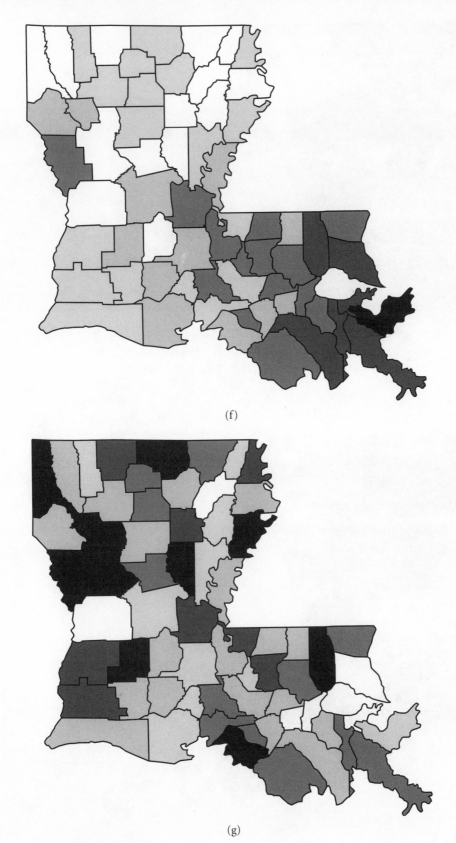

(f)

(g)

Figure 12.1. (*continued*)

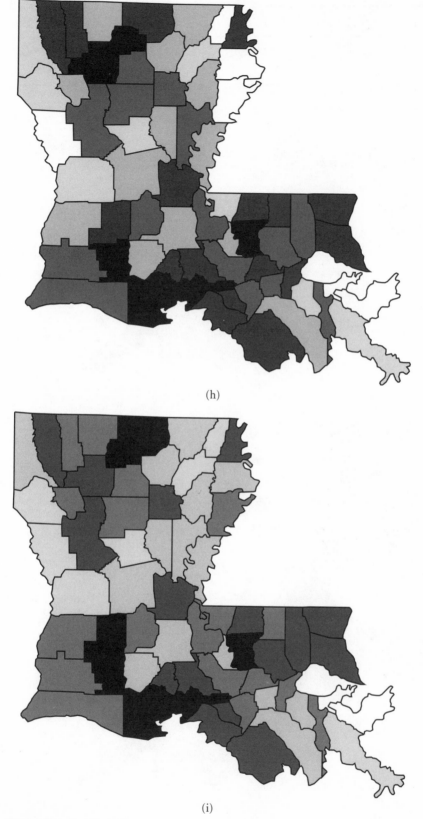

(h)

(i)

Figure 12.1. (*continued*)

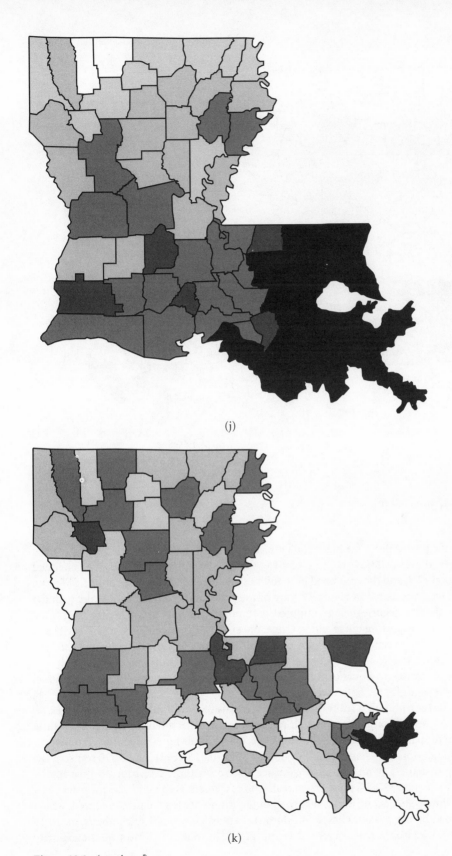

(j)

(k)

Figure 12.1. (*continued*)

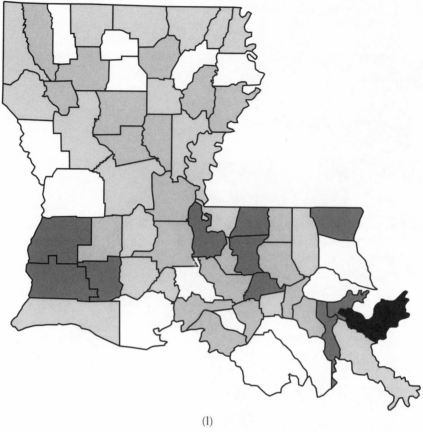

(1)

Figure 12.1. (*continued*)

race-specific probabilities for blacks (p_{0i}), race-specific probabilities for whites (p_{1i}), and the combined probabilities (q_i). In each case, the race-specific probabilities are generated via Equation 12.4, and the combined probabilities are computed via the accounting identity 12.2. The plots presented in Figure 12.1 are of the probabilities on the logit scale, with the cutoffs for the six categories being computed by combining all three sets of logit-transformed probabilities and splitting the resulting range into six equally spaced intervals. In each case, darker regions represent parishes with higher probabilities of registering Republican. For each realization the x_i are taken to be those from the 1990 Louisiana data. In addition, the mean parameter in Equation 12.4 is set to 0.5 for both races, and the total marginal variability is set to 1.0 for both races.

Figure 12.1a–c present a realization where γ equals 0.05 for both blacks and whites, so that only 5% of the variability for each race is spatially structured. The plots show little indication of spatial structure, as we would expect. The resulting p-values for permutation tests based on Moran's I statistic (see Section 12.3) are 0.822, 0.961, and 0.770 respectively, indicating that there is no statistical evidence (based on these tests) for positive spatial dependence. Figure 12.1d–i present two realizations where γ is equal to 0.05 for blacks and 0.95 for whites. That is, for whites nearly all of the variability is spatially structured, which is confirmed by the p-values based on Moran's I statistic (< 0.001 for both Figure 12.1e and 12.1h). We also see from Figure 12.1f and 12.1i that, since the whites are the majority race, spatial structure in the white probabilities induces spatial structure in the combined probabilities (p-values < 0.001 and 0.007 respectively).

Figure 12.1d–i also highlight a difficulty that is common when dealing with maps of this kind: although spatial structure may be present, it may not be obvious (which is why we include two realizations for this case). In particular, both Figure 12.1e and 12.1h represent probabilities where there is a high degree of spatial dependence across the Louisiana geography. The spatial dependence is clear in Figure 12.1e but much less so in Figure 12.1h. Consequently, it is important to not depend on assessing the degree of spatial dependence solely by eye. In addition to plots such as Figure 12.1, it may be worthwhile to compute autocorrelation statistics (and associated tests of significance) to quantify numerically the degree of spatial dependence, as well as to fit spatial models such as those described here.

Finally, Figure 12.1j–l provide a realization where γ equals 0.95 for blacks and γ equals 0.05 for whites. We find that although there are spatial effects for the black probabilities (p-values $= 0.011$), they do not induce spatial effects in the combined probabilities (p-value $= 0.190$).

12.4.3 Implementation

In the Bayesian paradigm, estimation and inference can proceed via direct evaluation of the required integrals or via approximations, analytic or numerical. Given the complex structure of the model and the large number of unknown parameters, we implement the model using Markov chain Monte Carlo (MCMC) (see, for example, Gilks, Richardson, and Spiegelhalter, 1996). In particular, we use the Metropolis–Hastings sampling algorithm, which is implemented in the freely available WinBUGS statistical software package (Spiegelhalter et al., 2003). The Appendix provides sample WinBUGS code used for one of the hierarchical models of Section 12.6. The specific functions used to fit the ICAR spatial model are provided in the GeoBugs add-on module (Thomas, Arnold, and Spiegelhalter, 2002).

One critical issue is the adequate monitoring of the resulting Markov chains to ensure proper convergence. This is especially important in applications such as ecological inference, where the nonidentifiability in the first-stage likelihood will result in a relatively flat posterior. For all subsequent analyses that are based on the margins of Table 12.1, we ran three Markov chains simultaneously from three different starting points. Furthermore, we ran each chain for 1 million iterations, discarding the first quarter as a burn-in period (to remove dependence on the initial points). To ensure the proper mixing of the chains and subsequent convergence, we examine time series plots of the resulting samples for each of the hyperparameters. Since the distribution of the variance components on their original scale is asymmetric, assessment of convergence was performed after log transformation.

For some of the models, problems with convergence were encountered. In particular, it was found that convergence was not achieved in any model that attempted to include a spatial component for both races. Initially, the chains were run for a further 1 million iterations, but this yielded no improvements. This problem persisted even in idealized situations, such as the simulations described in the next section. The problems are due to a lack of information in the likelihood, where the model is unable to distinguish all of the types of variability from the data provided in the margins alone. We were able to solve these convergence problems by incorporating a more informative prior at the third stage of the model. In particular, for the analysis of the Louisiana data we used much stronger priors on the variance components for the blacks, to impose low levels of variability. We also constrained the standard logistic prior of the mean parameter for both races to lie on the interval $(-\infty, 0)$, which corresponds to the interval $(0, 0.5)$ on the probability scale. While this helped considerably in improving convergence, it may be an unrealistic approach, since we may not have access to such strong prior information. Therefore we feel that attempting to fit these full models, where both races have a spatial component, will not be feasible in most applied settings.

The convergence problems also motivated the use of a modified version of the model which only allows one of the races to have a spatial component. That is, we consider models where either ω_0^2 or ω_1^2 equal zero. In the limited range of examples that we consider in the simulations of Section 12.5 and in the analysis of the Louisiana data of Section 12.6, running these models was more successful and we did not experience convergence problems.

12.5 SIMULATIONS

Here we report three sets of simulations carried out to investigate the effect of spatial dependence on ecological inference. Given the scope of the potential ways in which we may specify spatial dependence, we do not view these as being in any way comprehensive. The first two simulations examine traditional approaches to ecological inference; simple ecological regression (ER) and King's EI solution (implemented in the freely available EZI software, Benoit and King, 2001). The third simulation examines the performance of the hierarchical spatial model of Section 12.4. In each case, the simulations have been generated under an idealized scenario where other problems encountered in ecological inference, such as contextual effects and bias due to an asymmetric distribution for the x_i's (see Wakefield, 2004, for discussion regarding this issue), have been minimized. Although this is somewhat artificial, it enables the isolation of the effect of spatial dependence. Throughout, we adopt the same geography as the Louisiana data.

Simulation of spatially dependent data using the ICAR specification is not trivial and requires care. The approach that we adopt is to simulate race-specific registration probabilities from Equation 12.4, setting $(\mu_0, \mu_1) = (0, 0)$. This corresponds to medians on the probability scale of 0.5 for both blacks and whites. In addition, we fix the total marginal variability (on the logit scale) at 1.0 for both races. Throughout we assume that the variability for blacks is unstructured (i.e., $\sigma_{v0}^2 = 1.0$ and $\omega_{u0}^2 = 0$), while for whites we vary the contribution of the spatial component to the total marginal variability, via the mixing parameter γ introduced in Section 12.4.2. We consider five cases, $\gamma = 0.0, 0.2, 0.4, 0.6, 0.8$, to reflect increasing contributions of the spatial component for whites. In each case, simulated data sets had race–specific registration probabilities, with roughly symmetric distributions around 0.5 for both blacks and whites. Typically, the 75th and 95th percentiles were around 0.66 and 0.83. To ensure that our simulations reflect the direct impact of spatial dependence, we simulate the x_i's from a U(0,1) distribution. A single set of x_i's was generated, and the same set was used for all data sets. Using these x_i and the simulated race–parish-specific probabilities, we computed the marginal probabilities of registering Republican: $q_i = p_{0i}x_i + p_{1i}(1 - x_i)$. Contextual effects are not present, since p_{ji} is independent of x_i in Equation 12.4. For each case a total of 5000 data sets were generated via the scheme outlined above.

We evaluate the various ecological inference procedures via the comparison between model-based and simulation-based variability (see Section 12.3) and with the use of two summary measures. For the variability comparison, if the model-based standard error estimates are appropriate (i.e., they take proper account of the underlying variability in the data), then we would expect them to be equal to the simulation-based standard error estimates.

The first summary measure examines the performance of the procedure by comparing the resulting estimate of $\bar{p}_j$, the overall race-specific probability 12.1, with the actual value.

Table 12.2 Simulation results for ecological regression (ER) and King's EI model in the presence of increasing spatial effects

Mixing Parameter[a]	Blacks				Whites			
	PB[b]		Variability $V[\bar{p}_0]$		PB[b]		Variability; $V[\bar{p}_1]$	
γ	Mean	SD	Simulation[c]	Model[d]	Mean	SD	Simulation[c]	Model[d]
ER								
0.0	−0.21	5.31	2.13	1.66	0.01	6.05	2.42	2.06
0.2	−0.05	4.95	1.88	1.66	−0.13	5.74	2.18	2.06
0.4	0.02	4.92	1.77	1.66	−0.21	5.73	1.92	2.06
0.6	−0.26	5.13	2.01	1.67	0.11	5.94	1.82	2.07
0.8	−0.03	5.26	1.98	1.68	−0.17	6.06	1.77	2.08
EI								
0.0	0.01	5.06	1.78	0.36	−0.21	5.77	2.40	0.48
0.2	0.54	5.17	1.75	0.33	−0.79	5.98	2.18	0.44
0.4	0.57	4.64	1.48	0.34	−0.99	5.63	1.96	0.45
0.6	−0.21	4.85	1.91	0.36	0.01	5.51	1.46	0.48
0.8	−0.51	5.13	2.09	0.36	0.34	5.92	1.94	0.47

[a] Degree of contribution by spatial component to total marginal variability for whites.
[b] Mean and standard deviation of the percentage bias Equation (12.9) over all simulated data sets.
[c] Variance of the reported point estimates × 1000.
[d] Average of the reported squared standard errors × 1000.

If we denote the actual value of $\bar{p}_j$ for simulated data set s by $\bar{p}_{s,j}$ and the estimate by $\hat{\bar{p}}_{s,j}$, then the *percentage bias* (PB) for data set s is computed as follows:

$$\mathrm{PB}_{s,j} = \frac{\hat{\bar{p}}_{s,j} - \bar{p}_{s,j}}{\bar{p}_{s,j}} \times 100, \qquad j = 0, 1. \tag{12.9}$$

We can think of Equation 12.9 as examining the overall performance of the procedure towards the goal of estimating $\bar{p}_j$, $j = 0, 1$.

The second summary measure examines the performance at the parish level. If we denote the true race–parish-specific probabilities of registering Republican for simulated data set s by $p_{s,ji}$ and their corresponding estimates by $\hat{p}_{s,ji}$, then we compute the following *goodness of fit* (GoF) measure for data set s:

$$\mathrm{GoF}_{s,j} = \frac{1}{64} \sum_{i=1}^{64} \frac{|\hat{p}_{s,ji} - p_{s,ji}|}{\bar{p}_{s,j}}, \qquad j = 0, 1. \tag{12.10}$$

For each of the summary measures, values reported are averages and standard deviations taken across the simulated data sets.

Table 12.2 summarizes the results of the simulations for ecological regression and King's EI model. The results for ecological regression are based on all 5000 data sets, while the results for EI, due to its computational intensiveness, are based on the first 100 data sets for each value of γ. From Table 12.2 we find that ecological regression performs very well in terms

Table 12.3 Simulation results based on 25 repetitions examining ecological regression, EI, and four variants of the hierarchical model of Section 12.4, in the presence of strong spatial effects ($\gamma = 0.8$).

Model	Mean PB[a]		Mean GoF[b]		Rank of GoF$_1^c$				
	Blacks	Whites	Blacks	Whites	1st	2nd	3rd	4th	5th
ER	0.45	−0.74	3.41	3.57	0	0	0	0	25
EI	0.70	−1.01	2.12	2.47	1	9	11	4	0
Internal	0.02	0.01	0.02	0.02	–	–	–	–	–
Neither	0.51	−0.79	2.10	2.45	1	15	8	1	0
Whites only	0.32	−0.50	1.99	2.21	23	0	1	1	0
Blacks only	0.37	−0.59	2.20	2.53	0	1	5	19	0

[a] Mean percentage bias Equation 12.9 over the 25 simulated data sets.
[b] Mean goodness of fit measure Equation 12.10 over the 25 simulated data sets × 10.
[c] Ranking of GoF measure Equation 12.10 for whites across the 25 simulations.

of PB for both races, although there is quite a lot of variability in the PB across simulations. In particular, we find that the extent of bias does not seem to depend on the level of spatial dependence. We also find that for both races the measure of variability reported by ecological regression does not depend on the amount of spatial structure in the white probabilities. For the black probabilities the variability is consistently overestimated, although the extent of the overestimation does not seem to depend on the value of γ. For the whites we find that the true (simulation-based) variability decreases as the amount of spatial structure increases. When there is no spatial structure, ecological regression underestimates the variability, and when there is strong spatial structure it overestimates it. For the EI model we again find that there is little indication of bias, and what bias we find does not seem to be associated with the amount of spatial structure in the white probabilities. For both races, the estimates of variability reported by EI are much too small, which would result in confidence intervals (based on standard errors reported by EI) which would be too tight. Since these results are only based on 100 data sets for each value of γ, it is not clear to what extent we can interpret patterns in the simulation-based variability.

For the hierarchical spatial model of Section 12.4 the computational burden is very high, and we therefore consider only 25 data sets, taken from the case where $\gamma = 0.80$. Table 12.3 provides a comparison of six models applied to these 25 data sets. The six models include ecological regression, EI, and four variants of the hierarchical spatial model. The first variant, termed "Internal," uses the random effects specification of the hierarchical model but assumes that the internal cells are known. That is, it models the two sets of race-specific registration probabilities via (4) directly. The second variant, termed "Neither," assumes that all heterogeneity for both races is unstructured, while the third, "Whites only," incorporates a spatial component for whites but not blacks. The final model, "Blacks only," incorporates a spatial component for blacks but not whites.

From Table 12.3, we see that the "Whites only" model outperforms each of the other models that are solely based on the ecological data. Ecological regression performs well overall, but very poorly at the parish level. EI performs poorly overall, but quite well at the parish level. However, the "Whites only" spatial model performs better, on average, at both the state level and the parish level, and for both races, than each of the other ecological models.

Table 12.3 also provides the ranking of the GoF measure 12.10 for whites across the 25 simulations. We find that the "Whites only" model provides the best fit, in terms of this particular measure, for 23 out of the 25 data sets. We find similar results for the GoF for blacks. For the PB, although the "Whites Only" model performs better on average, the rankings for either race show no preference for any of the models.

12.6 ANALYSIS OF LOUISIANA DATA

12.6.1 Analysis Based on Internal Data

Although in typical applications of this methodology one would not observe the internal cells for the n 2 × 2 tables, in our example we do have access to them. We initially present a brief analysis of the internal data, the results of which will become the basis of comparison for subsequent analyses based solely on the margins.

Figure 12.2 presents three plots that examine the race–parish-specific registration probabilities for the Louisiana data. Figure 12.2a shows that there is quite a lot of variation in the probabilities for whites (ranging from 0.072 to 0.418), while there is very little variation in the probabilities for blacks (ranging from 0.005 to 0.079). This is also clear from Figure 12.2b and 12.2c, which plot the parish-specific probabilities versus the observed probability of being black, x_i, for blacks and whites respectively. From these plots we see that in nearly all of the 64 areas whites form the majority, with x_i ranging from 0.042 to 0.588. Of the 64 parishes, only 5 have the majority of individuals black. Using the internal data, we are

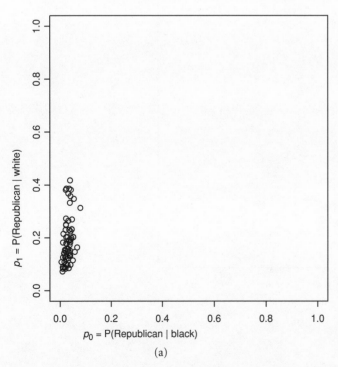

(a)

Figure 12.2. Race-specific registration probabilities, $\hat{p}_{ji}$, based on the internal cells: (a) parish-specific registration probabilities, black vs. white; (b) black parish-specific registration probabilities vs. proportion black; (c) white parish-specific registration probabilities vs. proportion black.

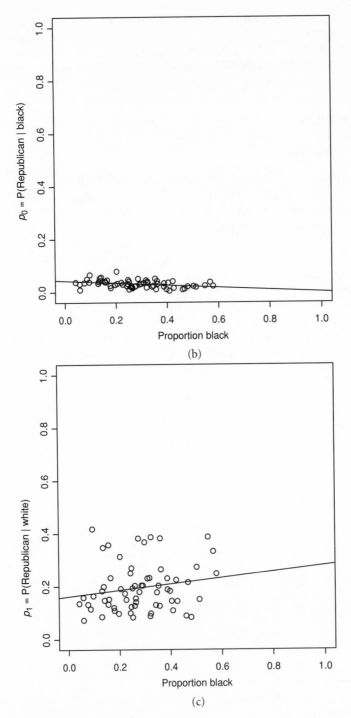

(b)

(c)

Figure 12.2. (*continued*)

able to directly compute the main quantities of interest, $\bar{p}_0$ and $\bar{p}_1$. We find that the overall weighted probability of registering Republican is 0.035 for blacks and 0.254 for whites (see Table 12.5 below).

We can also use the internal data to examine the extent to which issues such as aggregation bias due to contextual effects and spatial dependence will affect an analysis based solely on the data provided in the margins. Figure 12.2b and 12.2c indicate the extent of any contextual effects, where the behavior of individuals in a parish depend on the racial mixture. From Figure 12.2b, the negative slope indicates that the tendency for blacks to register Republican decreases as the proportion black in the area increases. Likewise, the positive slope in Figure 12.2c indicates that the tendency for whites to register Republican increases as the proportion black in the area increases. However, it is unlikely that contextual effects play a large role here. For blacks, the slope is -0.042, which is very close to zero. From this figure, we find that a 10% increase in the proportion black is associated with a decrease of 0.0042 in the expected probability of registering Republican. A 50% increase in the proportion black is associated with a decrease of 0.02 in the expected probability of registering Republican. For whites, the slope is 0.117, which is positive and somewhat larger in magnitude. Thus, a 50%

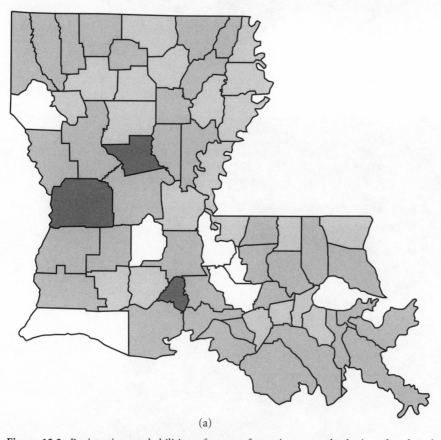

(a)

Figure 12.3. Registration probabilities, after transformation onto the logit scale, plotted on the Louisiana geography. For each plot the cutoffs on the logit scale between the six levels are $\{-4.48, -3.65, -2.82, -1.99, -1.16\}$ (or equivalently, $\{0.011, 0.025, 0.056, 0.120, 0.238\}$ on the probability scale). (a) Blacks (logit) probabilities $\bar{p}_{0i}$; (b) white (logit) probabilities $\bar{p}_{1i}$; (c) combined (logit) probabilities $\bar{q}_i$.

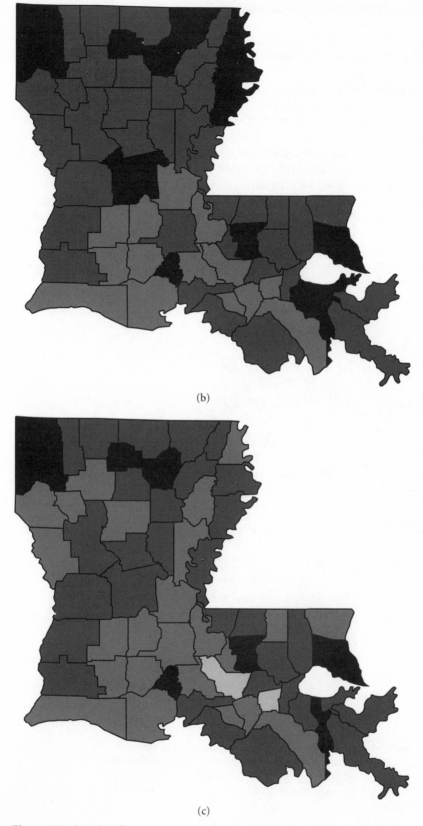

(b)

(c)

Figure 12.3. (*continued*)

Table 12.4 Autocorrelation statistics for the 1990 voter registration data for Louisiana

| Data | Statistic (p-value[a]) | | |
	Moran's I	Geary's c	Nonparametric D
N_i	0.14 (0.025)	0.83 (0.136)	17.17 (0.000)
x_i	0.15 (0.016)	0.73 (0.002)	17.70 (0.000)
$\tilde{p}_{0i}$	0.15 (0.020)	0.89 (0.127)	20.83 (0.214)
$\tilde{p}_{1i}$	0.20 (0.008)	0.79 (0.014)	18.68 (0.005)
$\tilde{q}_i$	0.15 (0.022)	0.85 (0.070)	19.17 (0.015)
logit($\tilde{p}_{0i}$)	0.15 (0.021)	0.89 (0.138)	20.83 (0.209)
logit($\tilde{p}_{1i}$)	0.23 (0.002)	0.77 (0.006)	18.68 (0.005)
logit($\tilde{q}_i$)	0.19 (0.006)	0.84 (0.043)	19.17 (0.015)

[a] p-values are based on a permutation test with 10,000 repetitions.

increase in the proportion black is associated with roughly a 0.06 increase in the expected probability of registering Republican.

Figure 12.3 examines the registration probabilities, after transformation onto the logistic scale, plotted on the Louisiana geography. The first two plots indicate the probabilities for blacks and whites; the third presents the combined probabilities that we would observe from the ecological data. For each of the plots the same six groupings are used, with darker shades representing areas with higher (Republican) registration probabilities. The cutoffs between the six groups are based on the combined (logit-transformed) probabilities and split the range into six equally spaced intervals. From Figure 12.3a and 12.3b, since the colors hardly overlap, it is clear that the white probabilities are higher than the black probabilities. In Figure 12.3a there does not seem to be any discernable pattern among the black probabilities; from Figure 12.3b there may be an indication of a cluster of parishes in the south and southwest where registration probabilities for whites are lower compared to the rest of Louisiana. This may be indicative of spatial structure among whites, although interpretation is difficult.

Table 12.4 provides the autocorrelation statistics of Section 12.3 for the race-specific probabilities as well as the combined probabilities. Overall, the results are consistent with the observations from Figure 12.3. We do note, however, that there is a disparity between the results for the black probabilities ($\tilde{p}_{0i}$), where inference based on Moran's I statistic would indicate significant spatial dependence (at the 0.05 level). Inference based on either of the other two statistics would not be significant. Although this disparity may be a result of the very little variation in the black probabilities (see Figure 12.2b), this illustrates the caution that is needed in interpretation of these autocorrelation statistics.

The first column of Table 12.6 below provides the results of applications of the spatial model outlined in Section 12.4 to the internal Louisiana data. This model is termed the "internal" model. However, two separate models are fitted, applying Equation 10.4 to each race. For each parameter, posterior medians and 90% credibility intervals (CIs) are reported. Since these results are based on the internal data, we consider them to be the gold standard (in terms of the second-stage hyperparameters) when examining the performance of the other models which are based on the margins alone. The variances in Table 12.6 correspond to variability on the logit scale, and we see again that there is less overall marginal variability in the blacks ($0.072 + 0.194 = 0.266$) than in the whites ($0.132 + 0.187 = 0.319$). A considerably larger proportion of the total marginal variability is attributable to the spatial component for whites (41%) than for blacks (27%).

12.6.2 Analysis Based Solely on Margins

Before we examine the use of the spatial model outlined in Section 12.4, we pause to analyze the Louisiana data using a few traditional methods for ecological inference. In particular, we examine the plot of tomography lines, the neighborhood model, two versions of ecological regression, and King's EI model. The two versions of ecological regression that we consider are the simple model (labeled ER-OLS), and a weighted version where the regression is weighted by the total population N_i (labeled ER-WLS).

Figure 12.4 presents graphical summaries, and Table 12.5 presents numerical results. In particular, Table 12.5 provides the resulting point estimates of the overall probabilities for each race, 90% confidence intervals, the PB Equation 12.9, and the GoF measure Equation 12.10. For EI, the analysis was carried out in the freely available EzI software (Benoit and King, 2003).

Having the benefit of the internal data, it is clear from Table 12.5 that none of these models are satisfactory. In a typical application, we would be unaware of this. One clue to potential problems, however, is that the results are not consistent across the non-neighborhood models, especially for $\bar{p}_0$. Table 12.5 also provides the results of the application of the hierarchical spatial model of Section 12.4 to the data provided in the margins alone. The first model, labeled "Neither," only includes unstructured random effects and makes no attempt to model the spatial structure fixing $\omega_{vj}^2 = 0$ for $j = 0$, 1. The second model, labeled "Whites only," only incorporates spatial effects for the whites, holding $\omega_{v0}^2 = 0$, and the third model, labeled "Blacks only," holds $\omega_{v1}^2 = 0$. The final model incorporates spatial effects for both races, but to ensure convergence stronger priors at the third stage are needed (see Section 12.4.2).

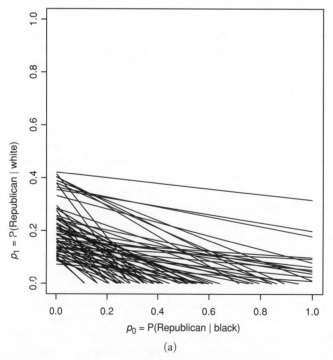

(a)

Figure 12.4. Results of traditional analyses of the Louisiana 1990 voter registration data: (a) tomography lines; (b) neighborhood model; (c) ecological regression (OLS and WLS).

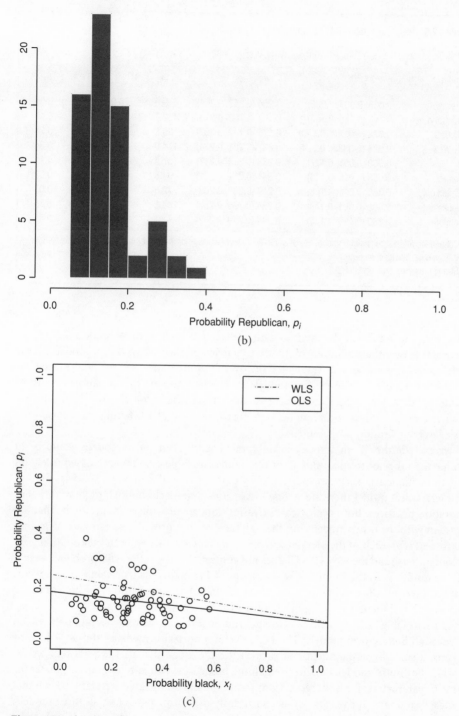

Figure 12.4. (*continued*)

Table 12.5 Results for the 1990 Louisiana voter registration data

Model	Overall probability (90% CI)[a] Black ($\bar{p}_0$)	White ($\bar{p}_1$)	PB Black	White	GoF Black	White
Internal	0.035 (0.034, 0.035)	0.254 (0.253, 0.254)	0.0	0.0	0.02	0.00
Neighborhood	0.181 (0.160, 0.203)	0.197 (0.180, 0.215)	422.6	−22.1	3.32	0.19
ER-OLS	0.073 (−0.004, 0.150)	0.175 (0.142, 0.207)	109.8	−31.2	1.21	0.28
ER-WLS	0.078 (−0.008, 0.164)	0.237 (0.201, 0.274)	124.0	−6.5	1.35	0.34
EI	0.089 (0.051, 0.127)	0.233 (0.218, 0.247)	157.5	−8.2	1.64	0.11
Neither	0.068 (0.016, 0.146)	0.241 (0.211, 0.261)	94.8	−5.0	0.69	0.05
Whites only	0.060 (0.011, 0.158)	0.244 (0.206, 0.263)	72.6	−3.8	0.48	0.03
Blacks only	0.085 (0.021, 0.178)	0.234 (0.199, 0.259)	144.5	−7.6	0.66	0.05
Both[b]	0.059 (0.013, 0.125)	0.244 (0.219, 0.262)	72.1	−3.8	0.65	0.05

[a] Confidence interval for neighborhood, ER-OLS, ER-WLS, and EI; posterior credibility interval for Internal, Neither, Whites only, Blacks only, Both.
[b] Strong prior (see Section 12.4.2).

Again, with the benefit of the internal data, we see that each of these models provide an improvement over the traditional methods. In particular, the "Whites only" model and the "Both" model provide similar results for the overall probabilities and the percentage bias. This is not surprising, since the first model reflects the structure that we know to exist in the internal data, while the second incorporates strong priors. We also see from the GoF measures that the "Whites only" model is doing the best job of estimating the race-specific parish-level registration probabilities.

If we exclude the "Both" model, in an applied setting our only recourse would be to examine the range of results from all of the models in Table 12.5 that are based solely on the data in the margins. From the results of both ecological regression models, EI, and each hierarchical model there are strong indications that blacks and whites have different registration practices. Both ecological regression models provide estimates of $\bar{p}_0$ that are consistent with the other models, but the weighted version provides an estimate of $\bar{p}_1$ that is consistent with each of the hierarchical models. For $\bar{p}_0$, however, both the resulting 90% CIs contain zero, and the 90% OLS CI does not contain the true value. This problem persists with the results from the EI model, where neither CI contains the true values. By contrast, all of the Bayesian CIs contain the true values. Overall, however, without the benefit of the true values it is difficult to distinguish between the hierarchical models.

We turn to Table 12.6 to provide a heuristic argument that allows us to distinguish between the Bayesian hierarchical models. The table outlines posterior medians and 90% CI's for the second-stage hyperparameters in each of the hierarchical spatial models that we fit. Ignoring the "Both" model, the three remaining models provide similar point estimates for the mean parameters, for both races. Comparing these with the gold standard, we see that the mean parameter for blacks, μ_0, is consistently overestimated across all three models, while the mean parameter for the whites, μ_1, is consistently underestimated (this is to be expected, given the constraints imposed by the accounting identity 12.2). For whites, the 90% CIs are comparable for the "Neither" and "Whites only" models, while the 90% CI for μ_0 in the "Blacks only" model is considerably wider. For μ_1, we see that the 90% CIs are similar across all models. Thus, it is difficult to distinguish between the models on the basis

Table 12.6 Posterior medians and 90% credibility intervals for second-stage hyperparameters

Parameter	Internal	Neither	Whites only	Blacks only	Both[a]
μ_0	−3.55	−2.82	−3.00	−3.02	−2.85
	(−3.64, −3.46)	(−4.22, −2.12)	(−4.76, −2.10)	(−6.62, −2.15)	(−4.42, −2.18)
σ^2_{v0}	0.19	0.23	0.32	0.39	0.11
	(0.10, 0.30)	(0.06, 1.03)	(0.08, 1.50)	(0.08, 7.92)	(0.07, 0.16)
ω^2_{u0}	0.22	−	−	0.55	0.10
	(0.09, 0.65)			(0.13, 8.81)	(0.07, 0.15)
$\widehat{V}[U_{0i}]$	0.07	−	−	0.30	0.05
	(0.03, 0.17)			(0.06, 3.88)	(0.02, 0.11)
μ_1	−1.52	−1.63	−1.61	−1.65	−1.62
	(−1.61, −1.43)	(−1.86, −1.43)	(−1.88, −1.44)	(−1.88, −1.43)	(−1.83, −1.45)
σ^2_{v1}	0.19	0.36	0.21	0.34	0.24
	(0.08, 0.30)	(0.26, 0.52)	(0.10, 0.37)	(0.24, 0.49)	(0.12, 0.40)
ω^2_{u1}	0.31	−	0.35	−	0.32
	(0.12, 0.84)		(0.13, 0.87)		(0.13, 0.81)
$\widehat{V}[U_{1i}]$	0.13	−	0.14	−	0.13
	(0.06, 0.26)		(0.06, 0.28)		(0.05, 0.26)

[a] Strong prior (see Section 12.4.3).

of the mean parameters. Looking at the results of the "Neither" model, we can interpret the variance components σ^2_{vj}, $j = 0, 1$, as the overall marginal variability (on the logit scale) for the blacks and whites respectively. We see for blacks that there is less overall marginal variability than for whites (0.23 compared to 0.36). We also find that there is much less posterior uncertainty in the estimate for σ^2_{v1} than σ^2_{v0} in this model.

We can examine the impact of incorporating spatial effects into the model by comparing the "Whites only" model and the "Blacks only" model with the "Neither" model. For the "Whites only" model we find that the point estimate of the variance component for the blacks, σ^2_{v0}, increases from 0.23 to 0.32, and the 90% CI widens. Looking at the hyperparameters for whites, we see that in the "Whites only" model the total marginal variability has been decomposed into marginal (spatially) structured variability and marginal unstructured variability. In fact, it seems that the model was able to decompose the variability quite successfully ($0.14 + 0.21 = 0.35 \approx 0.36$). In addition, the 90% CIs do not reflect excessive increased posterior uncertainty after the introduction of spatial effects for whites. This suggests that there does seem to be an important spatial component for whites across the parishes.

Comparing the "Blacks only" model with the "Neither" model, we see that the point estimate for the total marginal variability in whites decreases from 0.36 to 0.34. For blacks, we see that the decomposition of the total marginal variance has not been as successful. In particular, the total of the marginal spatially structured variance and the marginal unstructured variance far exceeds the total provided in the "Neither" model ($0.30 + 0.39 = 0.69 > 0.23$). In addition, we find that the 90% CIs for all of the hyperparameters for blacks are very wide, indicating a much larger degree of posterior uncertainty. Thus, given the trouble that this model is experiencing in estimating two separate variance components, and given that the "Neither" model indicates little overall variability, one is inclined to ignore the possibility of spatial effects for blacks.

Based on this heuristic argument, it seems that the "Whites only" model is doing a better job of explaining the variability in the data. Comparing this model with the model based on the internal data (first column of Table 12.6), we see that there is very close correspondence in the point estimates, as well as 90% CI's for whites, and reasonable correspondence for blacks.

12.7 DISCUSSION

It is clear that sources of bias in the ecological inference problem are numerous and complex. As a result it seems no single model will capture all of the subtleties involved. In political science, the biggest hurdle that one faces in ecological inference is the assumption of no contextual effects. In our example, this translates into assuming that the registration behavior of either race within a parish does not depend on the racial mixture within the parish. Without further information, either in the form of detailed prior information (see Chapter 6 of this book) or information directly regarding the internal cells, the validity of any model rests on this untestable assumption. Conditional on the assumption of no contextual effects, as Wakefield (2004) discusses, the most reasonable approach to the ecological inference problem is to present the results from a broad range of analyses, performing, in a sense, a sensitivity analysis. In epidemiology, sensitivity analyses are performed to examine the (potential) effects of unmeasured covariates, and in particular unmeasured confounders (see Chapter 13 of this book). In the context of this paper, a sensitivity analysis examines the impact of different modeling assumptions required to overcome the problem of nonidentifiability. With regard to choosing between the modeling assumptions, the issue becomes moot if the results are consistent across all models. However, if the results are not consistent across all models, then it becomes less clear how to proceed. Examination of these inconsistencies may itself provide clues as to which direction to move in, although this is not guaranteed. Sensitivity analysis in the context of modeling assumptions is an area of research which needs further attention.

One gap in the range of approaches that are commonly used is the lack of exploitation of spatial effects. In contexts where aggregation is determined by geography, as in the context of this chapter, it seems intuitive that incorporating spatial effects could enhance our ability to perform estimation and inference and perhaps even to control aggregation bias. In this chapter we provide a preliminary examination of the role that spatial effects take on in this problem as well as investigate the application of one particular hierarchical spatial model that is commonly used in spatial epidemiology.

The simulations of Section 12.5 indicate that techniques such as ecological regression and King's EI solution are likely to yield substantially incorrect estimates of the variability of their point estimates. This results in confidence intervals that have incorrect coverage. Our simulations also indicate that a model that incorporates spatial effects, when they exist, may also help in the estimation of quantities of interest, and therefore provide a closer correspondence to results based on the internal data (see Table 12.3). The analysis of Section 12.6.2 also indicates the potential for these models. Having access to the internal data, we see that the hierarchical model of Section 12.4 provides estimates of the overall probabilities that are closer to the truth (i.e., to those based on the internal data), and also provide considerably better overall fit to the internal data across the 64 parishes. In practice, however, one would not have the benefit of the internal data, and so, as pointed out above, the only reasonable course of action is to fit a broad range of models and report the results from each. For the Louisiana data, we were able to provide a heuristic argument for choosing between the models. It is uncertain that such a heuristic approach will work for a typical ecological inference analysis, where the internal cells are not available. The arguments do fit within those of an overall sensitivity analysis, however, and there may in fact be other explanations for the observed results. For example, the failure of the "Blacks only" model to recover estimates comparable to those of the "Internal" model may be a result of the sparsity of information regarding blacks and not necessarily a lack of spatial variability. Finally, we acknowledge the possibility of contextual effects in the Louisiana voter registration data of 1990. We again emphasize that, given the data in the margins alone, it is not possible to consider contextual effects explicitly, and consequently a cautionary note should always be added to any ecological inference analysis.

In this chapter, we have considered a single framework for a spatial model and for one special case of it. The framework that is outlined in Section 12.4.1 is very flexible, and many of the choices that we have made could be adjusted. For the spatial components our choice of the weight matrices, W_j, assumes that spatial dependence is a function of two parishes being adjacent. Other choices include assuming that spatial dependence is a function of physical distance (say between centroids of the parishes). The model that we adopted uses a conditional specification for the spatially structured random effects. This is due to our experience in spatial epidemiology, where conditionally specified models are both computationally tractable with MCMC and relatively simple. Finally, we have concentrated on a situation where there is no further information other than that provided in the margins of Table 12.1. In particular, we assume no information regarding other covariates, such as income. Both ecological regression and EI are able to incorporate other covariates. However, it is unclear how model selection might proceed, and, as Achen and Shively (1995) point out, aggregation bias can be worsened by adjusting for inappropriate covariates. One benefit of the model outlined in Section 12.4 is its ability to take account of unmeasured covariates (both unstructured and spatially structured) via the random effects, although one cannot, in general, adjust for unmeasured confounders via the inclusion of random effects. Since the random effects are race-specific, the model allows the unmeasured covariates to be race-specific. This would be important if, for example, income were different between the races (within a parish), or perhaps if the effect of income on registration behavior were different between the races. However, the model is flexible enough to allow race-independent random effects (i.e. effects shared by both races within a parish), V_i and/or U_i, which could replace terms in Equation 12.4 for both races. For example, we may consider a situation where we believe, a priori, that the spatial variation is due to some external event that is independent of race but varies across areas. In such a case we would replace Equation 12.4 with

$$\text{logit}(p_{ji}) = \mu_j + U_i + V_{ji}.$$

There are also several other frameworks that one could consider in an ecological inference analysis. One such framework could be adopted from the work of Knorr-Held and Best (2001). In the spatial epidemiology context, their shared-component model assumes that the underlying risk surface is composed of $K < n$ flat surfaces, within each of which the risk is constant (Knorr-Held and Raber, 2000). This would translate into some natural grouping of the parishes where the race-specific registration probabilities are constant across parishes within the group, but vary across groups. One could interpret this as a "local" ecological regression, where the assumptions of ecological regression are appropriate over each of the K surfaces. Another framework is that of Calvo and Escolar, outlined in Chapter 11. Their framework examines spatial variation in the residuals from an ecological regression. They then use a geographically weighted regression approach, effectively estimating an extra spatially varying covariate and adding it to the accounting identity 12.2. While their model makes far fewer assumptions, which is certainly a desirable property, it does not allow heterogeneity, and in particular spatially structured heterogeneity, to be race-specific. This would not be appropriate in the voter registration example of this chapter.

The results of this chapter are far from being conclusive, and there are a great many avenues for further research. These include examining the variety of approaches outlined above. In addition, to have a better understanding of when these models are appropriate or necessary, it is important to thoroughly examine the effects of spatial dependence via more extensive simulations. In Section 12.6.1, we used autocorrelation statistics to examine the extent of spatial dependence in the $\hat{p}_{ji}$. It would be extremely useful to develop a diagnostic measure to determine the amount of spatial dependence based on the data in the margins alone. This avenue will likely prove difficult, since spatial dependence in the race-specific probabilities will not necessarily translate into spatial dependence in the marginal probabilities, and vice versa. There may be scenarios, however, where this is the case. The question would then be how reasonably (since, as with nearly all assumptions, necessary for ecological inference, it would be untestable) these scenarios apply to any particular data set.

APPENDIX

12.A.1 Simulation from the Intrinsic Gaussian Conditional Autoregression

As pointed out in Section 12.4, the joint specification for the ICAR does not exist. Thus, to generate a single realization we adopt an algorithm outlined in Besag and Kooperberg (1995). Following their Corollary 3.2, we constrain the final random effect, $U_{j,64}$, to equal 0. Again, let Q_j be the corresponding precision matrix in the joint specification (which will not be of full rank, and hence not invertible) for the ICAR. Then for $i = 1, \ldots, 63$, let $W_{ji} = U_{ji} - U_{j,64} = U_{ji}$. Further, let I denote the 63×63 identity matrix and $\overrightarrow{-1}$ the 63×1 vector of -1's. Thus, we have $\vec{W}_j = A\vec{U}_j$, where $A = (I|\overrightarrow{-1})$ is the concatenation of I and $\overrightarrow{-1}$. Taking $\bar{A} = (I|\vec{0})^T$ to be the generalized inverse of A, and $Q_{Wj} = \bar{A}^T Q_j \bar{A}$ to be the precision matrix for $\vec{W}_j$, then we find that $\Sigma_j = \bar{A} Q_{Wj}^{-1} \bar{A}^T$ is a generalized inverse of Q_j. Hence one may generate random deviates from an ICAR(ω_j^2) distribution by simulating from a multivariate normal distribution with a vector of zeros as the mean vector and variance–covariance matrix Σ_j. Again, this is subject to the constraint that the final random effect is always equal to zero.

12.A.2 Autocorrelation Statistics

Here we briefly overview the autocorrelation statistics used in the paper. Let W_{ik} denote some measure of "closeness" between parish i and parish k. In our application we use $W_{ik} = 1$ if parishes i and k are adjacent, and $W_{ik} = 0$ otherwise. This is not the only choice, and another common choice is to base W_{ik} on some distance measure (say between the centroids) of parishes i and k. Let $\bar{p}_j$ denote the mean of $\hat{p}_{ji}, i = 1, \ldots, n$, and r_{ji} denote the ranks of $\hat{p}_{ji}, i = 1, \ldots, n$. Then the autocorrelation statistics of Section 12.3 are defined as follows:

Moran's I statistic:

$$I = \frac{n \sum_i \sum_k W_{ik}(\hat{p}_{ji} - \bar{p}_j)(\hat{p}_{jk} - \bar{p}_j)}{(\sum_i \sum_k W_{ik}) \sum_l (\hat{p}_{jl} - \bar{p}_j)^2}.$$

Geary's c statistic:

$$c = \frac{(n-1) \sum_i \sum_k W_{ik} (\hat{p}_{ji} - \hat{p}_{jk})^2}{(\sum_i \sum_k W_{ik}) \sum_l (\hat{p}_{jl} - \bar{\hat{p}}_j)^2}.$$

Nonparametric D statistic:

$$D = \frac{\sum_i \sum_k W_{ik} |r_{ji} - r_{jk}|}{\sum_i \sum_k W_{ik}}.$$

12.A.3 WinBUGS Code

The following is sample WinBUGS code for the "Whites only" model of Section 12.6.2. In this model, it is assumed that the black probabilities exhibit only unstructured variation, while the white probabilities may exhibit both unstructured and spatial structured variation. Note that in the WinBUGS formulation, variance components for both the normal and ICAR distributions are specified in terms of precision parameters (i.e. inverse variances). In the code below, q[i] represents the marginal probability of registering Republican (p_i) in parish i.

```
model
{
  for ( i in 1 : ntabs ) ## ntabs = 64
  {
## 1st Stage Likelihood (for the observed data)
  Z[i] ~ dnorm( q[i], tau.q[i] )
  Z[i] <- Y[i] / N[i]
  tau.q[i] <- N[i] / ((p[i, 1] * (1 - p[i, 1]) * x[i]) + (p[i, 2]
    * (1 - p[i, 2]) * (1 - x[i])))

  prep[i] <- (p[i, 1] * x[i]) + (p[i, 2] * (1 - x[i]))
  p[i, 1] <- exp( mu[1] + Vb[i] ) / (1 + exp( mu[1] + Vb[i]))
  p[i, 2] <- exp( mu[2] + Uw[i] + Vw[i] ) / (1 + exp( mu[2] + Uw[i] + Vw[i]))

## Unstructured random effects
  Vb[i] ~ dnorm( 0, tau.v[1] )
  Vw[i] ~ dnorm( 0, tau.v[2] )

## Compute marginal quantities
  x[i] <- N0[i] / N[i]
  N[i] <- N0[i] + N1[i]
  }

## ICAR distribution for spatially structured random effects
Uw[1:ntabs] ~ car.normal( adj[], weights[], num[], tau.u )
for(k in 1:sumNumNeigh)
{
  weights[k] <- 1
}

## Third stage priors
  mu[1] ~ dlogis(0, 1)
```

```
mu[2] ~ dlogis(0, 1)
tau.u ~ dgamma(1.519157, 0.4943456)
tau.v[1] ~ dgamma(1.4999566, 0.2269434)
tau.v[2] ~ dgamma(1.4999566, 0.2269434)

## Quantities of interest to monitor
params[1] <- mu[1]
params[2] <- log( 1 / tau.v[1] )
params[3] <- mu[2]
params[4] <- log( 1 / tau.u )
params[5] <- log( pow( sd( Uw[1:ntabs] ), 2 ) )
params[6] <- log( 1 / tau.v[2] )
params[7] <- inprod( p[,1], N0[] ) / sum( N0[] )
params[8] <- inprod( p[,2], N1[] ) / sum( N1[] )
}
```

REFERENCES

Achen, C. H. and W. P. Shively. 1995. *Cross-Level Inference*. Chicago: University of Chicago Press.

Anselin, L. and W. T. Cho. 2002. "Spatial Effects and Ecological Inference," *Political Analysis*, 10, 3: 276–297.

Benoit, K. and G. King. 2001. EzI for Windows 9x/NT/2000, v2.7. http://gking.harvard.edu/stats.shtml.

Benoit, K. and G. King. 2003. "EzI: A(n Easy) Program for Ecological Inference, Version 2.7." http://gking.harvard.edu/stats.

Besag, J. and C. Kooperberg. 1995. "On Conditional and Intrinsic Autoregressions," *Biometrika*, 82: 733–746.

Besag, J. and J. Newell. 1991. "The Detection of Clusters in Rare Diseases," *Journal of the Royal Statistical Society, Series A*, 154: 143–155.

Besag, J., J. York, and A. Mollie. 1991. "Bayesian Image Restoration with Applications in Spatial Statistics," *Annals of the Institute of Statistics and Mathematics*, 43: 1–59.

Freedman, D. A., S. P. Klein, M. Ostland, and M. R. Roberts. 1998. Review of: 'A Solution to the Ecological Inference Problem'. By G. King. *Journal of the American Statistical Association*. 93: 1518–22.

Geary, R. C. 1954. "The Contiguity Ratio and Statistical Mapping," *The Incorporated Statistician*, 5: 115–145.

Gilks, W. R., S. Richardson, and D. J. Spiegelhalter. 1996. *Markov Chain Monte Carlo in Practice*. New York: Chapman and Hall.

Goodman, L. 1953. "Ecological Regressions and the Behavior of Individuals," *American Sociological Review*, 18: 663–666.

Kelsall J. E. and J. C. Wakefield, 1999. Contribution to: "Bayesian models for spatially correlated disease and exposure data." By N. G. Best, L. A. Waller, A. Thomas, E. M. Conlon, and R. Arnold. In *Bayesian Statistics* 6. Proceedings of the Sixth Valencia International Meeting. J. M. Bernado, J. O. Berger, A. P. Dawid, and A. F. M. Smith (editors). Oxford University Press.

King, G. 1997. *A Solution to the Ecological Inference Problem*. Princeton, NJ: Princeton University Press.

King, G., O. Rosen, and M. A. Tanner. 1999. Binomial-beta hierarchical models for ecological inference. *Sociological Methods and Research*, 28: 61–90.

Knorr-Held, L. and G. Raber. 2000. "Bayesian Detection of Clusters and Discontinuities in Disease Maps," *Biometrics*, 56: 13–21.

Knorr-Held, L. and N. Best. 2001. "A Shared Component Model for Detecting Joint and Selective Clustering of Two Diseases," *Journal of the Royal Statistical Society, Series A*, 164: 73–85.

Lehmann, E. L. 1986. *Testing Statistical Hypotheses*, 2nd ed. Springer-Verlag.

Lindley, D. and A. Smith. 1972. "Bayes Estimates for the Linear Model," *Journal of the Royal Statistical Society, Series B*, 34: 1–41.

Moran, P. A. P. 1948. "The Interpretation of Statistical Maps." *Journal of the Royal Statistical Society, Series B*, 10: 243–251.

Richardson, S. and C. Monfort. 2000. "Ecological Correlation Studies." In P. Elliot, J. C. Wakefield, N. G. Best, and D. Briggs (eds.), *Spatial Epidemiology: Methods and Applications*. Oxford University Press, pp. 205–220.

Spiegelhalter, D. J., A. Thomas, N. G. Best, and D. Lunn. 2003. *WinBUGS User Manual, Version 1.4.* Cambridge, U.K.: Medical Research Council Biostatistical Unit.

Thomas, A., N. G. Best, R. Arnold, and D. J. Spielgelhalter. 2002. *GeoBUGS User Manual, Version 1.1.* London: Imperial College School of Medicine.

Wakefield, J. C. 2004. "Ecological Inference for 2 × 2 Tables," *Journal of the Royal Statistical Society, Series A.*

Wakefield, J. C., N.G. Best, and L. A. Waller. 2000. "Bayesian Approaches to Disease Mapping." P. Elliot, J. C. Wakefield, N. G. Best, and D. Briggs (eds.), In *Spatial Epidemiology: Methods and Applications.* Oxford University Press, pp. 104–127.

Wakefield, J. C., J. E. Kelsall, and S. E. Morris. 2000. "Clustering, Cluster Detections, and Spatial Variation in Risk." In P. Elliot, J. C. Wakefield, N. G. Best, and D. Briggs (eds.), *Spatial Epidemiology: Methods and Applications.* Oxford University Press, 128–152.

## PART FOUR

13 A Common Framework for Ecological Inference in Epidemiology, Political Science, and Sociology

Ruth Salway and Jonathan Wakefield

ABSTRACT

Ecological studies arise within many different disciplines. This chapter describes common approaches to ecological inference in an environmental epidemiology setting, and compares these with traditional approaches in political science and sociology. These approaches vary considerably, both in their use of terminology and notation, and in the relative importance of the various issues that make ecological analyses problematic. The aims of this chapter are twofold. Firstly, we describe ecological inference in an epidemiology setting, where the interest is in the relationship between disease status and exposure to some potential risk factor. We concentrate on those issues which are of particular concern in epidemiology, for example the presence of additional (possibly unmeasured) covariates, termed confounders. Secondly, we seek to unite the current work in epidemiology, political science, and sociology by clarifying differences in terminology, by describing commonly used approaches within a common statistical framework, and by highlighting similarities and differences between these approaches. Often different models can be attributed to different sets of underlying assumptions; we emphasize that such assumptions are crucial in the conclusions drawn from ecological data, and their appropriateness should be carefully considered in any specific situation. Combining approaches from all three disciplines gives a broad range of possible assumptions and available techniques from which to choose.

13.1 INTRODUCTION

Ecological studies arise within many different disciplines; in this chapter we consider ecological inference from an epidemiology perspective and compare it with approaches in political science and sociology. Although all three disciplines utilize ecological data, commonly used approaches vary considerably, and there is very little communication between epidemiology, on the one hand, and sociology and political science, on the other. Although methods in one discipline may not always be applicable in another, in general many of the concerns addressed are common to all.

When using ecological data to make inference about individuals, bias may occur due to aggregating data within areas; this bias is known as *aggregation bias* (Achen and Shively, 1995) in the social sciences, and as *ecological bias* (Richardson and Monfort, 2000) in epidemiology. A more general term used in sociology is *cross-level bias* (Firebaugh, 1978), which refers to bias that occurs when data are available at one level but inference is made at a different level (so it can also refer to bias that arises from using individual data to make inference about areas).

In Section 13.2 we describe how ecological studies arise in epidemiology. The common problem is to make individual-level inference in the presence of possible ecological bias; one of the ways in which epidemiological approaches differ is in explicitly concentrating

303

on the underlying causes of bias. We follow such an approach throughout this chapter; first, we identify the main sources of ecological bias, and then we consider the effect on inference of each source separately. We introduce a general statistical model in Section 13.3 that allows us to explicitly model three of the main sources of bias. These are bias due to unmeasured covariates, bias due to the presence of contextual effects, and bias due to the model parameters varying between areas, and are discussed in Section 13.4. This model will provide the framework for this chapter and will be used to link approaches to ecological inference in the three disciplines.

Section 13.5 discusses some of the primary issues in ecological analysis in epidemiology. We discuss the aims of ecological analyses, and describe the general approaches that are used to tackle the sources of bias. Section 13.5.2 introduces the use of hierarchical models to model overdispersion, and Sections 13.5.3 and 13.5.4 consider two ideas from general epidemiology that may be applied to ecological analyses when the availability of data is limited. The first is that of choosing between competing explanations, in the presence of little information from the data themselves, on the basis of *plausibility*. The second demonstrates the use of a sensitivity analysis to investigate the possible effects on inference of unobserved confounding.

We compare and contrast the epidemiology and social science approaches to ecological inference in Section 13.6. We focus on a scenario in which the data are discrete and consist of one 2 × 2 table for each area; the links between this model and the more general framework of Section 13.3 are highlighted in Section 13.6.1. One of the important differences between epidemiology and political science is that in the latter it may be the unobserved individual data that are of interest rather than underlying probabilities (which is essentially a difference between prediction and causality); the differences are discussed in Section 13.6.2. Section 13.6.3 focuses on the situation in which the underlying probabilities vary between areas. Section 13.7 considers some common models used in social science and relates them to those used in epidemiology, and Section 13.8 provides a concluding discussion.

Throughout this chapter we will use terminology from epidemiology, so that the outcome of interest is a disease indicator; an individual with the disease is known as a *case*, and a disease-free individual a *noncase*. The covariate of interest, a potential risk factor for the disease, is called the *exposure* variable, and we are specifically interested in the nature of the relationship between the disease indicator and exposure to the risk factor, after control for confounding variables. Roughly speaking, a confounder is a variable that is related to both the response and the exposure, does not lie on the causal pathway between exposure and response, and is not caused by the response (see Rothman and Greenland, 1998, for more discussion). So, for example, the disease indicator may be whether an individual has a respiratory disease, such as asthma. The exposure may be discrete, for example a genetic trait, or it may be continuous, for example the sulfur dioxide concentration in ambient air in the neighborhood of the individual. Similarly confounders may be discrete (for example gender) or continuous (for example, dietary measures such as fat consumption). For both confounders and exposures, continuous variables may be artificially discretized. Although this reduces information, a large number of categories allows for flexible risk–exposure–confounder relationships, and for interactions to be considered.

In a political science application, the response may correspond to voter turnout, with a "case" being a voter and a "noncase" being a nonvoter. The "exposure" is race, which is discrete for example, with two categories, black and white. A possible confounder in this example might be income, which we might expect to be related to both voter turnout and race. The problem of determining causality between exposure and disease in the presence of confounding variables is central to epidemiology. The equivalent problem in political science might be to assess the causal relationship between race and voting behavior, controlling for income.

13.2 ECOLOGICAL INFERENCE IN EPIDEMIOLOGY

Determining causality in any observational study is problematic, since exposures are not randomly assigned to individuals. A major cause of bias in observational studies is that due to confounding; consequently, many epidemiologic analytical techniques are concerned with controlling for confounding factors. This general philosophy extends to ecological studies; the aim is usually to make inference for individuals concerning the relationship between disease and exposure in the presence of confounding. By many epidemiologists ecological studies are viewed with skepticism. This view would seem too pessimistic, however. Ecological studies are not only useful hypothesis-generating mechanisms, but can also add to the totality of evidence when building a case for a disease risk–exposure relationship (Morgenstern, 1998). The appeal of ecological studies is that they can utilize routinely available data (and so are relatively inexpensive to carry out) and can cover a broad geographical area, thus taking advantage of large exposure contrasts and large populations; both of these factors increase power.

Historically, epidemiologists have concentrated on methods developed for contingency tables. A typical analysis with binary exposure and disease variables would initially examine the marginal observed association (that is, collapsing across confounder stratum), before examining the effects of stratification (confounder) variables such as age and sex, perhaps following a test for heterogeneity of the association across stratifying variables, that is, a test for effect modification. Chapter 3 of Breslow and Day (1987) and Chapter 4 of Breslow and Day (1980) provide an excellent introduction to such approaches. More recently, a more explicit model-based approach has grown in popularity (Clayton and Hills, 1993). The advantages of such an approach are that universal statistical principles can be followed in a more general modeling setting, and problems of small cell counts can be avoided to some extent by smoothing across cells. In addition the assumptions that lead to particular estimators can be made explicit, which is particularly important in ecological studies. Stratified analyses can often be viewed as a special case of the more general framework.

Hence the current focus in ecological models in epidemiology is on explicitly modeling the risk–exposure relationship and estimating effect parameters. The disease–exposure relationship is often nonlinear. Diseases are usually rare in a statistical sense. Ecological studies are particularly important in environmental epidemiology in examining the effects of air pollution (Pope and Dockery, 1996) and water quality (see, for example, Maheswaran et al., 1999). Often the scale is international; for example, Yasui et al. (2001) examine the ecological association between incidence of breast cancer and incidence of non-Hodgkins lymphoma, and Prentice and Sheppard (1990) describe an ecological approach to studying the relationship between total dietary fat intake and incidence of breast cancer. Numerous studies have also examined the ecological association between measures of socioeconomic status and different health outcomes; see Singh and Siahpush (2002) and the references contained therein. Richardson and Monfort (2000) and Wakefield (2003) provide further examples of ecological studies.

In a model-based approach we are interested in the underlying individual parameters (and derived probabilities) of disease. This is consistent with the search for causal relationships and may be contrasted with a predictive approach in which it is not estimates of parameters that are of concern, but rather imputation in which the missing cell entries are the target of inference. The objective of most epidemiological studies is to estimate the change in disease risk attributable to a specific factor for a rare disease. This can be expressed on various scales, for example, as a *risk difference*, or as a *relative risk* of disease for each area. Typically a risk difference is used with a linear model and represents the additive difference between the disease risk of, for example, an exposed individual and an unexposed individual. Relative risks are more natural in a log-linear framework and represent the multiplicative increase in disease risk in the exposed population relative to the unexposed population. No exposure effect (that is, when the risk of an exposed and unexposed individual is the same) corresponds to a risk difference of 0, or a relative risk of 1.

13.3 STATISTICAL MODEL

In this section we introduce notation that allows us to separate different sources of ecological bias. We begin by describing an explicit model at the level of the individual (following Richardson, Stucker, and Hémon, 1987; Prentice and Sheppard, 1995; and Wakefield and Salway, 2001). We are interested in examining individual relationships; it is advantageous to specify models in terms of individual parameters, as this links ecological inference to individual inference. By stating an underlying model we are also better equipped to make explicit the assumptions of any analysis and to identify the plausibility of such assumptions. This approach is of particular benefit when attempting to identify causal relationships.

The notation in this chapter differs from that used in the Introduction to this book, for the latter does not extend easily to an epidemiology context. However, it is consistent with that used in Chapters 1 and 12.

Suppose we have a study area partitioned into a disjoint set of m areas, with area i containing N_i individuals, $i = 1, \ldots, m$. The response is a Bernoulli random variable Y_{ij} representing the disease outcome of individual j in area i, $i = 1, \ldots, m$, $j = 1, \ldots, N_i$, over a specific time period, with $Y_{ij} = 1$ corresponding to a case and $Y_{ij} = 0$ a noncase. Similarly, we let X_{ij} represent the univariate exposure of individual j in area i. In our general formulation, X_{ij} may be a discrete variable with two or more categories, or it may be continuous. It is straightforward to extend this model to consider multiple exposures (for example, three different air pollutants), but for notational simplicity we will assume it is univariate. We begin with an individual risk–exposure model for a noninfectious disease (so that outcomes on different individuals within an area may assumed to be independent, after controlling for risk factors). The model takes the form

$$Y_{ij}|q_{ij} \sim_{\text{ind}} \text{Bernoulli}(q_{ij}),$$

where

$$q_{ij} = \text{P}(Y_{ij} = 1 | X_{ij}, Z_{ij}, X_i, \text{ area } i),$$

and

$$g(q_{ij}) = \beta_{0i} + \beta_{1i}(X_{ij} - X_i) + \beta_2 X_i + \gamma Z_{ij} + \delta_i, \qquad (13.1)$$

where "ind" is an abbreviation for *independently distributed*, and we have assumed linearity on a scale determined by a link function $g(\cdot)$. Here X_i is the mean exposure in area i, and Z_{ij} is a univariate individual-level confounder (again the extension to multiple confounders is straightforward).

The model 13.1 allows for the possibility of confounding, contextual effects, effect modification, and overdispersion, including spatial dependence:

- The effect of an individual's exposure relative to the area-level average exposure is given by β_{1i}; this is the effect parameter of interest, and is an area-specific exposure effect, so that we have effect modification (also known as interaction) by area.
- We also allow the baseline risk parameter β_{0i} to vary between areas.
- The parameter β_2 measures a contextual effect due to exposure, that is, an effect due to the overall average exposure in the area beyond the effect of an individual's personal exposure. Contextual effects in the exposure will be present if $\beta_{1i} \neq \beta_2$.
- The presence of confounding is represented through the covariate Z_{ij} and the associated nuisance parameter γ. This may be a within-area confounder (a variable measured at the level of the individual – for example, a behavioral variable), or a between-area confounder, in which case $Z_{ij} = Z_i$ (a characteristic of the area – for example, income disparity or access to health services). The model does not allow confounder effects to vary by region, or for a contextual effect in the confounder, but it is general enough to allow a number of possible sources of bias to be illustrated.
- Finally, the random effect error term δ_i may or may not have spatial structure.

The model 13.1 incorporates a link function $g(\cdot)$, which allows for a nonlinear risk–exposure relationship. Suitable link functions include a logit link, which constrains the probabilities q_{ij} to lie between 0 and 1, or a log link as an approximation when q_{ij} is small (that is, the disease is rare). The latter model is frequently used in epidemiology, where disease counts in an area are small relative to the population size. This corresponds to a multiplicative risk–exposure relationship, with

$$E[Y_{ij}|X_{ij}, X_i, Z_{ij}] = \exp\left\{\beta_{0i} + \beta_{1i}(X_{ij} - X_i) + \beta_2 X_i + \gamma Z_{ij} + \delta_i\right\}.$$

Great care is required to interpret the parameters of this model (since we cannot increase an individual's exposure and keep the average the same). If we increase the exposure for all individuals in area i by one unit, then for each individual in area i we have

$$\frac{P[Y_{ij} = 1|X_{ij} = x + 1, X_i = \bar{x}_i + 1, Z_{ij}]}{P[Y_{ij} = 1|X_{ij} = x, X_i = \bar{x}_i, Z_{ij}]} = \exp(\beta_{1i} + \beta_2),$$

which gives an interpretation to the sum of the two effect parameters when Z is kept constant for all individuals and the two individuals that are compared are in the same area (since we need the parameters β_{0i} to cancel).

We are concentrating upon a linear link function in this chapter, in which case, if we increase the exposure for all individuals in area i by one unit, the risk difference is given by

$$P[Y_{ij} = 1|X_{ij} = x + 1, X_i = \bar{x}_i + 1, Z_{ij}] - P[Y_{ij} = 1|X_{ij} = x, X_i = \bar{x}_i, Z_{ij}]$$
$$= \beta_{1i} + \beta_2.$$

Again, under a causal interpretation we may consider two individuals j and j' in the same area i whose exposures differ by one unit and who have the same value of Z, to obtain

$$P[Y_{ij} = 1|X_{ij} = x + 1, X_i = \bar{x}_i, Z_{ij} = z] - P[Y_{ij'} = 1|X_{ij'} = x, X_i = \bar{x}_i, Z_{ij'} = z]$$
$$= \beta_{1i}.$$

Suppose that neither the baseline risk parameter β_{0i} nor the effect parameter β_{1i} depend on i. Now, consider two areas i and i' whose mean exposures differ by one unit, and consider two individuals, j in area i, and j' in area i', who have the same value of Z but whose exposures differ by one unit. Then

$$P[Y_{ij} = 1 | X_{ij} = x + 1, X_i = \bar{x}_i + 1, Z_{ij} = z] - P[Y_{i'j'} = 1 | X_{i'j'} = x, X_i = \bar{x}_i, Z_{ij'} = z]$$

$$= \beta_2.$$

The above considerations illustrate the care that must be taken in parameter interpretation.

The linear model is somewhat unrealistic in that no constraints are placed on q_{ij}, which must be between 0 and 1, since it is a probability. In practice such a simplistic model will be suitable in only a few situations, for example as an approximation for low levels of exposure and small exposure effects. In general, fitting a linear model when the true relationship is nonlinear can introduce serious bias (Greenland, 1992). However, nonlinearity introduces additional problems of mathematical complexity which make the exposition less easy to follow. Many of the results follow for a log-linear model, and where differences occur, they are noted in the text.

In an ecological study only area-level data are available. Typically these data consist of the area means X_i, Y_i, and perhaps Z_i. In epidemiology the ecological data usually consist of counts of cases within each area, $Y_{i+} = \sum_j Y_{ij}$; since $Y_i = Y_{i+}/N_i$, these are interchangeable, for the population sizes are known (at least in principle, although data anomalies may be problematic; see Wakefield and Elliott, 1999). The disease counts Y_{i+} and mean Y_i correspond to T_i' and T_i respectively in the notation of the Introduction.

Here we will formulate the ecological model in terms of disease counts, Y_{i+}. We derive the model induced at the ecological level in Equation 13.1 by aggregating over individuals within each area. In general the form of this ecological model will depend on the joint within-area distribution of X_{ij}, Z_{ij}:

$$E[Y_{i+} | X_{ij}, Z_{ij}] = N_i \, E_{X_{ij}, Z_{ij}}[q_{ij} | X_i, Z_i],$$

where the expectation is with respect to the joint distribution of $(X_{ij}, Z_{ij}) | X_i, Z_i$. Here, we assume that both exposure and covariate are discrete binary variables, with

$$X_{ij} | \pi_{xi} \sim_{\text{ind}} \text{Bernoulli}(\pi_{xi}),$$

and

$$Z_{ij} | \pi_{zi} \sim_{\text{ind}} \text{Bernoulli}(\pi_{zi}),$$

so that, for example, the probability of an individual in area i being exposed is given by $P(X_{ij} = 1 | \pi_{xi}) = \pi_{xi}$. Under these circumstances,

$$Y_{i+} | \pi_{xi}, \pi_{zi} \sim_{\text{ind}} \text{Binomial}\{N_i, q_i\},$$

with

$$q_i = \beta_{0i} + \beta_2 \pi_{xi} + \gamma \pi_{zi}. \tag{13.2}$$

The term $\beta_{1i}(X_{ij} - X_i)$ has disappeared, since $E[X_{ij} - X_i] = 0$ when we average over an area. Equation 13.2 depends only on the area-specific probabilities (π_{xi}, π_{zi}) because we have a linear relationship; in general, a nonlinear relationship will result in an additional term involving the joint probability $\pi_{xzi} = P(X_{ij} = 1, Z_{ij} = 1 | \pi_{xzi})$ (Lasserre,

Guihenneuc-Jouyaux, and Richardson, 2000). Similarly, the joint distribution needs consideration when we have effect modification by Z.

In the more general situation where exposures may be continuous and the link function is nonlinear, the expression for the marginal risk q_i will depend on higher moments of the within-area exposure–confounder distribution, such as the variance–covariance matrix (Richardson et al., 1987; Wakefield and Salway, 2001).

Typically we do not know the underlying population parameters π_{xi} and π_{zi} and must use estimates, for example the means X_i and Z_i. In this case, $X_{ij}|X_i$ are not independent and the binomial distribution is an approximation to the true distribution of disease counts (although with large N_i this should not be a problem). We have

$$E[Y_i|X_i, Z_i] = q_i = \beta_{0i} + \beta_2 X_i + \gamma Z_i, \tag{13.3}$$

but the variance will be smaller than under a binomial model. The true distribution is a convolution of binomials (Chapter 1).

The main difference between this model and that of the Introduction is that here we have explicitly described the individual-level relationship. The focus is clearly on estimating the individual-level parameters β_{0i}, β_{1i} (and hence the underlying individual probabilities), rather than the unobserved cell proportions. The relationship between these two depends on the form of the individual model (via the choice of link function and whether confounding, contextual effects or effect modification is present). This is discussed further in Section 13.6.1.

The simplest case of the model 13.2 (which is unrealistic in practice) is when we have no confounding (so $\gamma = 0$), no contextual effects (so $\beta_{1i} = \beta_2$), and nonvarying baseline risk and effect estimates (so the parameters β_{0i}, β_{1i} do not vary between areas). Then Equation 13.3 becomes

$$E[Y_i|X_i] = \beta_0 + \beta_1 X_i, \tag{13.4}$$

or, written in terms of the relative risk $\theta = p_1/p_0$, where $p_x = P(Y_{ij} = 1|X_{ij} = x)$,

$$E[Y_i|X_i] = p_0 + p_0(\theta - 1)X_i \tag{13.5}$$

(also considered by Plummer and Clayton, 1996: 116). In this special case, the ecological model takes the same form as the individual-level model, with the same parameters. It is well documented (for example, Piantadosi, Byar, and Green, 1988) that in this case estimates derived from the ecological model will be unbiased estimates of the underlying individual-level parameters. This result requires a linear relationship between X_{ij} and Y_{ij}; with other link functions, the ecological model will not in general take the same form (Richardson et al., 1987), even in the absence of confounding, contextual effects, and effect modification, unless there is no within-area variability in areas (in a political science context, an example would be each area containing individuals of one race only). The distinction between linear and nonlinear forms is important in epidemiology, since risk–exposure relationships are often multiplicative. The bias that may arise in fitting an ecological model of the same form as the individual-level model is known as *pure specification bias* (Greenland, 1992).

13.4 SOURCES OF ECOLOGICAL BIAS

We will now see how the ecological parameter estimates behave when the simple case of no confounding, no contextual effects, and no effect modification, as in Equation 13.4, does

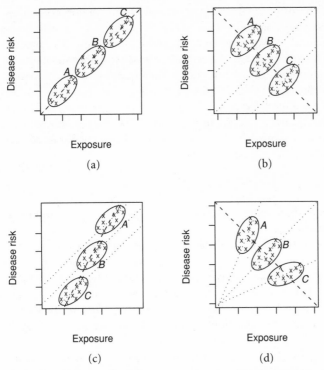

Figure 13.1. Types of ecological bias for a linear model. In each case, the dotted lines represent the relationship within areas, and the dashed line represents the ecological relationship. (a) No ecological bias. (b) Negative bias due to between-area confounding, within-area confounding, confounding by group, or contextual effects. (c) Positive bias due to between-area confounding, within-area confounding, confounding by group, or contextual effects. (d) Negative bias due to effect modification.

not hold. We will consider three situations: when unmeasured confounders are present, when contextual effects are present, and when the parameters β_{0i}, β_{1i} vary between areas. Throughout we assume a linear link.

Figure 13.1 illustrates the effect of different types of ecological bias for three areas, A, B, and C. In each case, the dotted lines represent the individual relationships between disease and exposure within each area, and the dashed line represents the ecological relationship. The figure is based on the individual model in Equation 13.1, with a linear link function; that is,

$$E[Y_{ij}|X_{ij}, X_i, Z_{ij}] = \beta_{0i} + \beta_{1i}(X_{ij} - X_i) + \beta_2 X_i + \gamma Z_{ij}.$$

Figure 13.1a illustrates the straightforward case where there is no confounding or contextual effect and the parameters do not vary between areas. In this case, the individual-level model is

$$E[Y_{ij}|X_{ij}] = \beta_0 + \beta_1 X_{ij},$$

and the ecological model is

$$E[Y_i|X_i] = \beta_0 + \beta_1 X_i.$$

In this case there is no bias, and the individual and ecological regression lines are equal.

Figure 13.1b and 13.1c illustrate two situations where there is bias. In both cases, the individual effect parameter is the same for each area (so the dotted lines are parallel), but the baseline risk (where each line crosses the Y axis) differs. As a result the ecological estimate of the exposure effect is biased. In case (b) the relationship between disease and exposure within areas is positive, but the ecological effect is negative (so that what is sometimes called a *protective effect* has been induced). In case (c) both relationships are positive, but the ecological effect is an overestimate of the individual effect.

These situations can arise for a linear model in one of four ways. Firstly, they can arise when the baseline risk parameter β_{0i} varies between areas, that is, the individual-level model is

$$E[Y_{ij}|X_{ij}] = \beta_{0i} + \beta_1 X_{ij}.$$

The ecological-level model becomes

$$E[Y_{ij}|X_i] = E[\beta_{0i}|X_i] + \beta_1 X_i,$$

so bias is caused when there is correlation between X_i and β_{0i}. For ease of explanation suppose

$$E[\beta_{0i}|X_i] = a + bX_i,$$

so that

$$E[Y_{ij}|X_i] = a + (b + \beta_1)X_i.$$

If the true individual effect is positive ($\beta_1 > 0$), a negative correlation ($b < 0$) will result in underestimating the effect parameter; in extreme cases ($b < -\beta_1$) this will cause a negative ecological effect as in case (b). A positive correlation ($b > 0$) will cause the ecological effect parameter to be greater than the individual effect, as in case (c). That the baseline risk appears to vary by area could be due to data anomalies in the population or disease counts.

Secondly, such bias can be caused by an unmeasured confounder, acting either between or within areas. For a between-area confounder the individual-level model is

$$E[Y_{ij}|X_{ij}, Z_i] = \beta_0 + \beta_1 X_{ij} + \gamma Z_i,$$

and so we have

$$E[Y_{ij}|X_i] = \beta_0 + \beta_1 + \gamma E[Z_i|X_i],$$

leading to bias as with the previous example. If we write $\beta_{0i} = \beta_0 + \gamma E[Z_i|X_i]$, then we have

$$E[Y_{ij}|X_i] = \beta_{0i} + \beta_1 X_i,$$

showing how the variation of baseline risk by area has been induced; thus β_{0i} and X_i will always be correlated (since Z_i is a between-area confounder), and bias will result as described above.

Similarly, for a within-area confounder the individual-level model is

$$E[Y_{ij}|X_{ij}, Z_{ij}] = \beta_0 + \beta_1 X_{ij} + \gamma Z_{ij}$$
$$= \beta_{0i} + \beta_1 X_{ij},$$

with $\beta_{0i} = \beta_0 + \gamma E[Z_{ij}|X_i]$. In this case, there will again be bias, since Z_{ij} and X_{ij} are correlated, leading to β_{0i} and X_i being correlated. It is possible for a within-area confounder Z_{ij} to be correlated with X_{ij} (since it is a within-area confounder) without the averages Z_i being correlated with X_i (that is, it need not also be a between-area confounder). Hence an unmeasured within-area confounder may not cause ecological bias, although often Z will be a confounder at both levels. If Z_{ij} is both a within-area confounder and a between-area confounder and if Z_i is measured and Z_{ij} unmeasured, then no bias will result with a linear model. This is not the case for a nonlinear model, where omission of a within-area confounder will lead to bias, even if the area-level confounder is measured.

Finally, this type of bias may be due to contextual effects, where the individual-level model is

$$E[Y_{ij}|X_{ij}, X_i] = \beta_0 + \beta_1(X_{ij} - X_i) + \beta_2 X_i \qquad (13.6)$$
$$= \beta_{0i} + \beta_1 X_{ij},$$

with $\beta_{0i} = \beta_0 + (\beta_2 - \beta_1)X_i$, so that

$$E[Y_{ij}|X_i] = \beta_{0i} + \beta_1 X_i,$$

with β_{0i} depending on X_i. So a contextual effect acts in the same way as a between-area confounder, since β_{0i} and X_i will always be correlated and thus cause ecological bias. For this model we end up with

$$E[Y_{ij}|X_i] = \beta_0 + \beta_2 X_i, \qquad (13.7)$$

so only the contextual effect can be estimated. If we rewrite Equation 13.6 in a form that is more familiar in the social sciences,

$$E[Y_{ij}|X_{ij}, X_i] = \beta_0 + \beta_1 X_{ij} + \beta_2^* X_i,$$

then we obtain

$$E[Y_{ij}|X_i] = \beta_0 + (\beta_1 + \beta_2^*)X_i,$$

illustrating that we are estimating the combined effects of individual and contextual effects in an ecological study.

Figure 13.1d illustrates a different source of bias, due to effect modification, that is, when the effect parameter β_{1i} is different in each area (dotted lines all have different slopes). Here the individual model is

$$E[Y_{ij}|X_{ij}] = \beta_0 + \beta_{1i} X_{ij}.$$

An individual study would calculate separate estimates for each effect parameter, corresponding to the slopes of the dotted lines; each of these effects is positive. However, an ecological study estimates the dashed line, and concludes that there is a protective effect.

This occurs because β_{1i} is negatively related to X_i; here we have decreasing slopes with increasing exposure. In this example each area has the same baseline parameter β_0, and so all three dotted lines cross at the same point on the Y axis (at $Y = \beta_0$).

If we have (say) $\beta_{1i} | X_i \sim N(\beta_1, \sigma^2)$ and a linear model, then an ecological analysis with a constant effect parameter across areas would provide an unbiased estimator of β_1.

We now describe in more detail each of unmeasured confounding, contextual effects, and parameters that vary across areas.

13.4.1 Unmeasured Confounding

As described earlier, a confounder is a covariate that is related to both the outcome and the exposure (and is not on the causal pathway, and is not affected by the response). Suppose we have two populations in the age range 20–45, one that is exposed to air pollution and has a high rate of asthma, and the second that is unexposed and has a low rate of asthma. Suppose we also know that the exposed population contains more smokers than the unexposed population, and that smoking is associated with asthma. In this situation we do not know if there is a true association between air pollution and asthma or whether it is just due to differences in smoking behavior; smoking is said to be a confounder. In ecological studies confounders can act within areas, between areas, or both. In any observational study it is always possible that an observed association is due to unmeasured confounding, and (as already mentioned) much of analytical epidemiology is concerned with designs and analysis strategies that attempt to minimize bias due to confounding.

Bias due to confounding arises from omitting either within-area or between-area confounders from the model. Greenland and Robins (1994) give examples that demonstrate such biases; it is possible for the individual disease–exposure relationship to act in one direction, while the ecological data indicate a relationship in the opposite direction (this is illustrated in Figure 13.1b). A within-area confounder would also act as a confounder in an individual study. In a linear model, the aggregated within-area confounder will appear in the ecological model as an area-level confounder, unless the average exposure and the average confounder are uncorrelated across areas. As discussed by Greenland and Robins (1994), within-area confounding becomes more problematic when dealing with a nonlinear risk–exposure relationship, since within-area variability in confounders means that including a simple average value for an area is not sufficient to control for confounding. Instead we need to control for the *within-area confounder distribution* (there is a further increase in complexity when we have multiple confounders).

Between-area confounding is analogous to the usual confounding in an individual-level study, since the area is the level of analysis. Between-area confounders include covariates that represent characteristics of the area such as whether the area is urban or rural, or the average income in the area. In both these cases the confounder is often acting as a surrogate for the area average of important unmeasured individual-level characteristics. However, identifying such confounders may not be straightforward. Often it is the case that a variable is a confounder at both levels. If the variables are known, they may be included as between-area confounders in the ecological model 13.3. The specific form of the model should always be assessed, since, as always, there is no *a priori* reason why the effects should be additive. Unfortunately, checking the form of the ecological risk model is impossible when only ecological-level data are available (though a plausible form may be known from individual-level studies, in animal or man).

It is of theoretical interest to examine the likely size and direction of bias due to omitted confounders, and in practice methods for addressing the sensitivity to unmeasured confounding are of interest (see Section 13.5.4). For the remainder of this section, we will assume that there are no contextual effects, and that parameters do not vary between areas.

In the model 13.1 confounding is introduced through the final term with $\gamma \neq 0$, and with Z_{ij} and X_{ij} correlated. From Equation 13.3 we can see that if the area averages for the confounder, Z_i, are known, they can be included in the model and the parameter estimates will be unbiased. This is not the case for other link functions, where typically the ecological model involves terms which are unobserved in practice (Wakefield, 2003). If the average area-level confounder is not included in the model, then the estimates of the parameters (β_0, β_1) will be biased. This bias will depend on the strength of the relationship between the confounder and the outcome (γ) and on the extent of dependence between the confounder and the exposure as measured through $E[Z_i|X_i]$.

The true individual model with no contextual effects or effect modification is

$$E[Y_{ij}|X_{ij}, Z_{ij}] = \beta_0 + \beta_1 X_{ij} + \gamma Z_{ij}. \tag{13.8}$$

Omitting the confounder gives the "true" ecological model:

$$E[Y_i|X_i] = \beta_{0i} + \beta_1 X_i + \gamma E[Z_i|X_i],$$

where β_1 is the effect parameter which is of interest. Suppose that the confounder, Z_{ij}, is binary. Then we can write this model in terms of the probabilities $q_x = P(Z_{ij} = 1|X_{ij} = x)$, that is, the distribution of the confounder given the exposure variable, assuming for simplicity that this relationship is constant across areas. So

$$E[Z_i|X_i] = q_0 + (q_1 - q_0)X_i,$$

and the ecological model becomes

$$E[Y_i|X_i] = (\beta_0 + \gamma q_0) + \{\beta_1 + \gamma(q_1 - q_0)\} X_i. \tag{13.9}$$

Suppose we fit the ecological model assuming that there is no confounding. So we obtain estimates of the parameters, β^*, from

$$E[Y_i|X_i] = \beta_0^* + \beta_1^* X_i. \tag{13.10}$$

Then from Equation 13.9,

$$\beta_0^* = \beta_0 + \gamma q_0, \tag{13.11}$$

$$\beta_1^* = \beta_1 + \gamma(q_1 - q_0). \tag{13.12}$$

Note that if $q_1 = q_0$ (so that X and Z are independent) or if $\gamma = 0$ (so Z_{ij} is not associated with Y_{ij}), there is no bias in the effect parameter β_1^*. Otherwise the effect parameter is biased by a component that depends on γ, the relationship between disease and confounder, and q_0, q_1, the relationship between exposure and confounder. If the confounder is positively associated with both the disease and the exposure, then the bias will be positive and the estimator $\hat{\beta}_1^*$ will overestimate β_1. If they are of opposite signs, then the bias in $\hat{\beta}_1^*$ will be negative; so if β_1 is positive, then it is possible for $E[\hat{\beta}_1^*]$ to be negative. The larger the true effect β_1, the less likely this change of sign is to occur. Wakefield (2003) discusses the above and more general situations with a log link risk model and continuous exposures and confounders.

13.4.2 Contextual Effects

Contextual effects are area-level summary variables, such as the average exposure in an area, that affect the individual's outcome in addition to the individual-level variable. For example, an individual's health might be affected both by their own level of poverty and also by the general level of poverty in the area in which they live (sometimes such effects are known as neighborhood effects). In epidemiology contextual effects are often surrogates for combinations of unmeasured risk factors. In other disciplines contextual effects arise unambiguously; for example, in education the class IQ as well as individual IQ may be predictive of performance. In this example it is clear that the class IQ is a potentially relevant variable. In epidemiology, the area or neighborhood over which the contextual variable should be calculated is less clear.

Studies at the level of the individual can include a group average term in the analysis. However, at an ecological level it is not possible to distinguish between the effect of the term representing the aggregated individual variable and the contextual effect. This is illustrated by the comparison of the ecological regression and linear neighborhood models; see for example Chapter 1 and Equation 13.6, leading to Equation 13.7. This demonstrates that even if the interest is in the contextual effect $\beta_2 - \beta_1$, this cannot be estimated from the ecological data alone (Greenland, 2002).

As discussed above and illustrated in Figure 13.1, contextual effects can be considered as a special case of a between-area confounder (writing $Z_{ij} = X_i$), and so much of the discussion of between-area confounding above is applicable to contextual effects. The main difference is that no matter how many ecological data are available, the individual and contextual effects cannot be estimated separately. This is a fundamental difficulty of ecological inference, on which the social sciences literature concentrates.

13.4.3 Parameters That Vary between Areas

If one or more of the parameters vary between areas, in an individual-level analysis we can fit a separate model for each area or include area as a covariate in the model. However, ecological data do not contain enough information to estimate separate effect parameters for each area without imposing additional assumptions (King, 1997), since there are more parameters to be estimated than there are data points. If the baseline risk β_{0i} varies between areas, then the underlying risk for an unexposed individual will depend on the area in which the individual belongs. For example, unexposed individuals in different areas are at different baseline risk of asthma, due both to differences in unmeasured individual-level risk factors, and to true area effects such as different levels of health care in different areas. When the effect parameter β_{1i} varies between areas, the effect of being exposed is different for different areas. So, for example, the effect of air pollution on an individual's risk of asthma will depend on where they live.

When the baseline risk β_{0i} varies randomly (so that the coefficient is uncorrelated with X_i) due to unmeasured factors between areas, then it can be modeled as a random effect as discussed in Section 13.5.2. Such variation can arise through unmeasured variables that have no association with the exposure, or through data anomalies, again without association with the exposure. When the parameter β_{0i} varies systematically between areas, it is sometimes referred to as *confounding by group* (Greenland and Morgenstern, 1989). This can then be considered as a special case of an unmeasured between-area confounder, by writing $\beta_{0i} = \beta_0 + \gamma Z_i$. The inclusion of random effects cannot in general control for confounding.

Effect modification occurs when β_{1i} varies between areas. It may arise from a multiplicative interaction term at the individual level. This could be due to the presence of an unmeasured variable that changes across areas and has an interaction at the individual level, or to data anomalies that are associated with exposure (Greenland, 1992). Hence effect modification is distinct from confounding: a confounder is a nuisance variable which causes bias in the effect estimate (and can theoretically be controlled for), while effect modification is a property of the effect of interest.

In an ecological study, it might be thought that the ecological model would estimate the average effect parameter across all areas, that is, $\bar{\beta}_1 = E[\beta_{1i}]$. However, if confounding by group or effect modification which is dependent on X_i is present, this is not the case. Greenland and Morgenstern (1989) partition the ecological estimate into components due to confounding by group and to effect modification. Assuming no confounders and no contextual effects in the model 13.1 for simplicity, we have

$$E[Y_{ij}|X_{ij}] = \beta_{0i} + \beta_{1i}X_{ij}.$$

If we then fit the ecological model $E[Y_i|X_i] = \beta_0^* + \beta_1^* X_i$, we have (Greenland and Morgenstern, 1989)

$$\hat{\beta}_1^* = \frac{\text{cov}(X_i, Y_i)}{\text{var}(X_i)} = \frac{\text{cov}(X_i, \beta_{0i} + \beta_{1i}X_i)}{\text{var}(X_i)}$$

$$= E[\beta_{1i}] + \frac{\text{cov}(X_i, \beta_{0i})}{\text{var}(X_i)} + \frac{\text{cov}(\{X_i - E[X_i]\}X_i, \beta_{1i})}{\text{var}(X_i)}, \qquad (13.13)$$

using the identity

$$\text{cov}(XZ, X) = E[Z]\text{var}(X) + \text{cov}(X\{X - E[X]\}, Z).$$

The first term in Equation 13.13 is the average parameter across areas; $\hat{\beta}_1^*$ will be an unbiased estimator for the average effect $\bar{\beta}_1$ if the remaining terms are zero. The second and third terms can be viewed as bias components. The second term is attributable to confounding by group; it will be zero if $\beta_{0i} = \beta_0$, that is, if the baseline risk does not vary between areas, or if β_{0i} is uncorrelated with X_i. The third term is due to effect modification, and it will be zero if $\beta_{1i} = \beta_1$, or if β_{1i} is uncorrelated with X_i. So in a linear model it is when the area-specific parameters depend on the mean area exposure that problems arise.

It can be seen from this partition that the smaller the between-area variance in exposure means, $\text{var}(X_i)$, the larger the bias in the estimate $\hat{\beta}_1^*$, and so the bias is theoretically unbounded. Similar results can be obtained for other link functions, although in these cases there is an additional term representing pure specification bias. This additional term arises because of within-area variability in the exposure and is present even if parameters do not vary between areas. In these cases, bias can also occur due to effect modification even when β_{1i} is uncorrelated with X_i.

13.5 ISSUES IN ECOLOGICAL INFERENCE IN EPIDEMIOLOGY

13.5.1 Ecological Bias in Epidemiology

It is worth reiterating that determining causality in any observational study is problematic, since the existence of unmeasured variables (confounders) that induce bias in the observed association can never be disproved. The interpretation of ecological results in the presence of unmeasured confounding is thus of central importance, and the approaches described in subsequent sections reflect this.

The environmental epidemiology literature in general is less concerned with contextual effects. Contextual effects in the exposure variable are less common in chronic disease epidemiology, in contrast to infectious disease epidemiology, in which an individual's risk of disease may depend both on personal immunity and on the immunity of those around. In noninfectious-disease epidemiology, contextual effects are more likely to occur in confounders (such as deprivation) than in environmental exposures. There is a large literature in social epidemiology, especially on the effect of living in an area of low socioeconomic status, beyond that of a person's own socioeconomic status (see Smith, 2000; Singh and Siahpush, 2002; and the references therein). Contextual effects are often a proxy for other unmeasured variables, but, as illustrated, contextual effects and individual-level effects cannot both be estimated if aggregate data only are available. In the example given above, the socioeconomic status of an area is considered a surrogate for other characteristics of the area or individuals within it. If all these characteristics were available, the contextual effect would disappear. Sheppard (2003) discusses various issues relating to the estimation of contextual effects in an environmental epidemiology context.

In epidemiology we would always expect effect modification to be present, but it is usual to assume that the variability in effects is small. Sufficient data to estimate area-specific effects are generally not available, since in a typical study diseases are rare.

A common assumption in environmental epidemiology is that the exposure effect is constant across both area and confounders. Stratifying the analysis by one or more confounders allows a separate effect for each confounder group. A major disadvantage is the unavailability of ecological data at the levels necessary; for example, stratification by age would require incidence rates and exposure variables for each age group in each area, and the latter are unlikely to be available. This is closely related to the consideration of mutual standardization, in which (for example) age-standardized disease rates must be regressed on age-standardized exposures; otherwise bias will result (Rosenbaum and Rubin, 1984). It is usually assumed that the exposure distributions are at least approximately constant across strata.

13.5.2 Overdispersion and Random Effects

Overdispersion occurs when the variance of the response exceeds that predicted from the model. Model-based standard errors will be inappropriate if the model does not allow for overdispersion. Overdispersion can arise for a variety of reasons, including the omission of important variables, errors in the data (including the response, the population counts, and exposures and confounders; see Wakefield and Elliott, 1999), and misspecifying the functional form of the mean. Often the first explanation will be the main source, and if overdispersion is found, it is an indication that variables associated with the outcome are unmeasured; if these variables are confounders, then estimators will be biased. The level of overdispersion can therefore be used as an informal indicator of the extent of unmeasured confounding, and a large value for the overdispersion parameter suggests that caution should be exercised when interpreting observed associations.

The introduction of random effects to represent the unexplained sources of variation between areas can help to address the problem of overdispersion by giving more appropriate standard errors, though it cannot control for unmeasured confounding. Wakefield (2004a) gives a more detailed discussion of the role that random effects play in an ecological study. Spatial as well as unstructured random effects may be included.

Data anomalies are an example of features that may be accommodated for using nonspatial random effects, and many unmeasured risk factors, such as environmental exposures, will have spatial structure. Besag, York, and Mollie (1991) originally introduced a model with both unstructured and spatial random effects, in the context of disease mapping, and Clayton, Bernardinelli, and Montomoli (1993) included such effects in an ecological regression setting. Following these authors, we write the residual relative risk (on the linear predictor scale) as $\delta_i = V_i + U_i$ in the model 13.1. The component V_i represents unstructured effects which are independent and identically distributed from some distribution, typically the normal. The component U_i represents spatially structured area-specific random effects which display dependence between U_i and $U_{i'}$, $i' \neq i$. The choice of this model is more difficult than for the independent random effects, and inference is much more likely to be influenced by the specific choice made. One possibility is a conditional autoregressive (CAR) model, with the limiting *intrinsic* form being a common choice. Richardson and Monfort (2000) offer a review of the use of Bayesian hierarchical models in an ecological setting, and include a description of this choice. Chapter 12 of this book describes their use to allow for spatial dependence between areas in a political science context. Clayton et al. (1993) state that the U_i terms are an attempt to control for "confounding by location." The estimated regression coefficient may change from those obtained from a model containing nonspatial random effects only, and one never knows whether a genuine part of the exposure effect has been erroneously removed. Both estimates may be reported, and it is a judgment call whether the effect should be estimated from local or global exposure contrasts (corresponding to the inclusion and exclusion of spatial random effects, respectively).

Suppose that in the linear model there is a single unmeasured variable, Z. To illustrate how random effects might take account of unmeasured variables, suppose the ecological model is

$$E[Y_i | X_i] = \beta_0 + \beta_1 X_i + \gamma E[Z_i | X_i].$$

If X and Z are independent (so Z is not a confounder), then there is no bias in estimation of the effect parameter, and we have

$$E[Y_i | X_i] = \beta_0 + \beta_1 X_i + \gamma E[Z_i] \tag{13.14}$$

and

$$Y_i = E[Y_i | X_i] + \delta_i,$$

with $\delta_i = \gamma\{Z_i - E[Z_i]\}$. If Z_i is a confounder, then there will be bias in the estimator of the effect of X. Particular distributional assumptions for the random effects distribution correspond to different assumptions about the distribution of Z_i across areas.

An advantage of hierarchical models is that they allow strength to be borrowed from other areas in a structured way, thus smoothing rates which in areas with low populations may be highly unstable (Clayton and Kaldor, 1987). The assumption of constant baseline probabilities across areas is also avoided. As for any Bayesian approach, the choice of priors is important, particularly for the variance components in the random effects distributions and for spatial dependence parameters. Ecological studies are particularly sensitive to prior choice (Chapters 1 and 12 of this book). Since nonhierarchical models for ecological data have shown themselves to be highly sensitive to the choice of model, it is no surprise that hierarchical models behave similarly.

13.5.3 Plausibility

Causality cannot be proved from observational studies, but conclusions can be reached on the basis of *plausibility*. In epidemiology, rather than relying on a single study, evidence about a potential relationship is collected from a variety of different studies, each with its own strengths and weaknesses. Biological mechanisms and animal studies are also important. Thus evidence is gradually built up, and is combined in the hope of providing a consistent story. An obvious example is the causal relationship now known to exist between smoking and lung cancer. No single observational study provides incontrovertible evidence of this association, but many different observational studies in humans, and experimental studies in animals, have shown associations. One of the important early arguments was given by Cornfield et al. (1959) who used a sensitivity study to show that the strength of unmeasured confounding required to explain away the observed association was highly implausible. For a review of the health effects of smoking, see Doll (1998).

Another term for plausibility is *coherence*. See Rosenbaum (2002, Chapter 9), in which the author states, "A coherent pattern of associations is one that is, at each of many points, in harmony with existing knowledge of how the treatment should behave if it has an effect."

One drawback of ecological studies is that if we do not obtain individual-level data, then we have no way of checking the form of the individual-level model. Conclusions will depend on this underlying model, but there is nothing in the ecological data to help us distinguish between competing explanations. Often, however, it can be argued that one explanation is more plausible than another. For example, ecological data cannot say whether a linear or a log-linear model is more suitable. However, information from other sources might suggest that the relationship is more likely to be multiplicative, and so a log link is the more appropriate choice. One of the advantages of taking the approach advocated in this chapter, of stating methods in terms of an explicit underlying individual-level model, is that it allows the explicit statement and critique of required assumptions.

13.5.4 Sensitivity to an Unmeasured Confounder

In this section we describe a sensitivity analysis approach to address the problem of unmeasured confounding, illustrating the idea of plausibility discussed in the previous section. Rothman and Greenland (1998) provide background on the use of sensitivity analyses in general in epidemiology, and Wakefield (2003) specifically in the area of ecological studies. The basic idea can also be applied to other situations, such as sensitivity to contextual effects, pure specification bias, spatial dependence, classification errors, and selection bias. Unfortunately, there is no information in the data about the extent of bias from these sources, though external sources can provide invaluable information. For example, local knowledge can inform us on the accuracy of population counts and of disease registries. If the observed association is large, then, as we shall see, it is more difficult to explain it away with unmeasured confounding.

Here we concentrate on sensitivity to an unmeasured confounder. The approach for an ecological analysis is as follows. We start from the proposed individual-level model, which includes the unmeasured confounder; for the purposes of the sensitivity analysis we assume that this model is correct, and so includes the "true" parameter. We derive the appropriate ecological level model and compare this with the fitted model to give an expression for the estimated parameter in terms of the "true" parameter. We can then use this expression with various assumptions about the unobserved confounder to give estimates of the "true" parameter. Finally, we consider how plausible such assumptions are. For example, we may conclude that unmeasured confounding cannot plausibly explain a result (as with the smoking–lung-cancer example).

Suppose we fit the simple model 13.10, assuming no confounding, contextual effects, or effect modification:

$$E[Y_i|X_i] = \beta_0^* + \beta_1^* X_i,$$

and obtain an observed effect estimate $\hat{\beta}_1^*$. Suppose, however, that there is evidence of overdispersion; this suggests that unmeasured confounding is present and the true individual model is Equation 13.8:

$$E[Y_{ij}|X_{ij}, Z_{ij}] = \beta_0 + \beta_1 X_{ij} + \gamma Z_{ij},$$

with corresponding ecological model

$$E[Y_i|X_i] = \beta_{0i} + \beta_1 X_i + \gamma E[Z_i|X_i].$$

From Section 13.4.1 (Equation 13.12) we have

$$\beta_1^* = \beta_1 + \gamma(q_1 - q_0).$$

We know that $\hat{\beta}_1^*$ is a potentially biased estimator of β_1; we are interested in the extent to which this is a real relationship rather than due to ecological bias. In particular:

• Is the association of sufficient size that it cannot be plausibly explained away by ecological bias?
• Can we obtain an approximate adjusted estimate (or a range) of relative risk?

We use the expression for the bias given above to examine these questions.

We will consider a simple artificial example, comparing the incidence of respiratory diseases in boys under five and the average air pollution (low or high) for a set of areas. We let $Y_{ij} = 0\,(1)$ denote respiratory-disease nonincidence (incidence), and $X_{ij} = 0\,(1)$ represent unexposed (exposed), for the jth individual in area i. Hence Y_i and X_i are the average disease incidence and exposed, respectively, in area i. Across areas, the incidence rates vary between 0% and 24%, and the proportion exposed to high air pollution varies between 6% and 99%. This example should be viewed as merely illustrative, for studies such as this are far more complicated (for example, involving more than two levels of the primary exposure of specific interest and multiple secondary exposures).

We fit the basic ecological model 13.10 and obtain

$$E[Y_i|X_i] = 0.06 + 0.04 X_i,$$

so $\hat{\beta}_1^* = 0.04$. If we accept this result at face value, we have a risk difference of 0.04, or a relative risk of 1.6; so this evidence suggests that a child exposed to high air pollution has a 60% greater risk of respiratory disease than an unexposed child. However, we do not believe here the assumption of no confounding; there are many potentially important missing variables, such as genetic components and child, parent, household, and lifestyle characteristics. An obvious confounder that has been overlooked is poverty (which is a surrogate for lifestyle and behavioral characteristics and is related to many diseases). We are interested in knowing if air pollution really causes the observed increased incidence of asthma, or whether it is due to the differing levels of poverty in the study.

Table 13.1 Sensitivity analysis results

		θ				
		1.1	1.2	1.5	2	4
	0.1	–	–	–	0.40	0.13
γ	0.2	–	–	0.40	0.20	0.07
	0.5	0.80	0.40	0.16	0.08	0.03

Note: The strength of the linear relationship between disease and confounder is represented by γ, and q_0 and q_1 are the probabilities of poverty for unexposed and exposed individuals, respectively, that is, $q_x = P(Z_{ij} = 1 | X_{ij} = x)$, $x = 0, 1$. For given γ and $\theta = q_1/q_0$, the table shows the necessary value of q_0 for a confounder to explain away the observed association. Inadmissible q_x, in which probabilities outside of (0, 1) are obtained, are shown as dashes.

If the observed effect were entirely due to poverty and not to air pollution, then the true effect would be $\beta_1 = 0$. Substituting $\beta_1 = 0$ and $\beta_1^* = 0.04$ in Equation 13.12 gives

$$0.04 = \gamma(q_1 - q_0).$$

We will look at a range of possible values for γ, q_0, and q_1 which satisfy this expression. In this example both γ and $q_1 - q_0$ must have the same sign (since we know their product is positive). We will assume that they are both positive, so the confounder, poverty, is more likely among those exposed to air pollution, and the confounder is positively associated with respiratory disease risk (which, as just stated, is typical of a variable such as poverty). We will also write $q_1 = \theta q_0$; so θ is the relative risk of poverty for exposed individuals relative to unexposed, so that θ represents how much more prevalent the confounder is among exposed than unexposed individuals. This reformulation aids interpretation of the sensitivity analysis; however, it should be noted that θ must be constrained so that both q_0 and q_1 lie between 0 and 1.

For a range of values of γ and θ, Table 13.1 illustrates some possible values that q_0 could take for us to observe a coefficient of 0.04, when the real coefficient is 0; inadmissible solutions (where the probabilities q_x are not between 0 and 1) are shown as dashes. Values for γ represent a range of beliefs about the strength of the relationship between disease and confounder on an additive scale.

This table gives some idea of the characteristics of a missing confounder that would be wholly responsible for the observed effect. In this example, the observed risk difference of 0.04 is less likely to be caused solely by a relatively weak confounder (with $\gamma = 0.1$), since, for example, this would require the probability of poverty for an unexposed individual to be 0.13, and the probability for an exposed individual to be four times as likely, that is 0.52. If a moderate unmeasured confounder ($\gamma = 0.2$) is responsible for the association between respiratory disease and air pollution, it would need to be around 1.5–4 times more prevalent among exposed children than among unexposed children. A stronger confounder (with $\gamma = 0.5$) would need very little difference in poverty between exposed and unexposed groups.

The final step is to interpret this in terms of the study and form a conclusion as to how likely it is that such a confounder exists. We know from other studies that poverty has a reasonably strong effect on most diseases, at least compared to most environmental sources of pollution (Carstairs, 2000). If we assume that respiratory diseases follow a similar pattern, then it is likely that poverty is at least a moderate confounder. We then have to consider how much more prevalent we would expect poverty to be among children exposed to high air pollution than among those not exposed; this is measured by θ. It depends very much on the study design. If, for example, the main sources of air pollution for the study area were major locations of heavy industry, then we would expect poorer areas to be close to the industry, and $\theta = 1.5$ or higher would be reasonable. In this case we would conclude that although our study suggests a link between pollution and asthma, it can easily be explained by unmeasured confounding. If the source of air pollution in the study was pollution from proximity to major roads, depending on the area in which the study is based, we may expect less difference in poverty between exposed and unexposed areas. In this hypothetical example we would conclude that the true effect is unlikely to be as great as was observed.

If, as is always the case in practice, there are multiple confounders, then it is far easier to create plausible scenarios which explain away observed associations. Of course, if such confounders are negatively associated with either disease or exposure, they could also be masking a true association. Such issues lead naturally into the planning of a study that is carefully designed to examine this relationship. If only small risk differences are envisaged in an ecological study, then the study should not be carried out, since biases due to within-area variability in exposures and confounders, and pure specification bias, are likely to dominate the observed association.

Approaches to sensitivity in the same spirit have been considered in the social sciences, but in a less formal manner. See for example, Flanigan and Zingale (1985) and Achen and Shively (1995, Chapter 8).

13.6 ISSUES IN ECOLOGICAL INFERENCE IN SOCIOLOGY AND POLITICAL SCIENCE

In the previous section we have described a number of issues relating to ecological inference in epidemiology, with an emphasis on spatial epidemiology and in particular on issues of confounding. We have kept this discussion as general as possible; a link function enables a range of choices for suitable models, and exposures and confounders may be either discrete or continuous.

In this section, we look at how the issues in epidemiology discussed above fit in the wider picture and compare the results with those in other disciplines. We consider some of the specific concerns of sociology and political science and see how they relate to the model that we have described, and we demonstrate the links between these approaches and those in epidemiology. We also identify differences between the disciplines.

13.6.1 Ecological Inference for 2×2 Tables

In the social sciences data often consist of discrete outcome and predictor variables, and so the ecological data consist of a series of cross-classified data that may be represented by a set of 2×2, or more generally, $r \times c$ tables, as described in the Introduction to this book. In this chapter we have used slightly different notation, concentrating on the underlying probabilities rather than the unobserved cell entries. Table 13.2 establishes notation for the data on the left, and for the underlying probability model on the right; the ecological data consist of the margins of the left table only. The left-hand table may be compared to Table 0.1 in the Introduction; here we have represented the actual numbers in each cell, rather than the proportions. The proportions β_i^b and β_i^w defined in the Introduction correspond to the fractions $n_{11i}/\{N_i X_i\}$ and $n_{01i}/\{N_i(1 - X_i)\}$, respectively, in our notation.

Table 13.2 Cell counts for the individual data (left) and the underlying probabilities (right) for a generic 2×2 table in area i

		Y					Y		
		0	1				0	1	
X	0	n_{00i}	n_{01i}	$N_i(1 - X_i)$	X	0	$1 - p_{0i}$	p_{0i}	$1 - \pi_{xi}$
	1	n_{10i}	n_{11i}	$N_i X_i$		1	$1 - p_{1i}$	p_{1i}	π_{xi}
		$N_i - Y_{i+}$	Y_{i+}	N_i			$1 - q_i$	q_i	1

We now focus on the underlying marginal probabilities in the case of a binary exposure $P(Y_{ij} = 1 | X_{ij} = x) = p_{xi}$, where i indexes areas, $i = 1, \ldots, m$; j indexes individuals within areas, $j = 1, \ldots, N_i$; and $x = 0, 1$ (these probabilities are marginal because we have averaged over contextual effects and confounders). The ecological model for the disease rate Y_i in terms of these probabilities is given by

$$E[Y_i | X_i] = P(Y_{ij} = 1 | X_{ij} = 0) P(X_{ij} = 0 | X_i) + P(Y_{ij} = 1 | X_{ij} = 0) P(X_{ij} = 0 | X_i)$$
$$= p_{0i} + (p_{1i} - p_{0i}) X_i; \tag{13.15}$$

that is, a linear ecological model with intercept p_{0i} and slope $p_{1i} - p_{0i}$. The ecological relationship between disease rates Y_i and proportion exposed X_i will be linear regardless of the form of the individual model, even if confounding or contextual effects are present. In the latter case, although the model is still of this form, the difference is in interpretation and imputed cell entries will depend greatly on whether contextual effects are assumed to be present or absent.

The ecological model 13.15 is in terms of the probabilities (p_{0i}, p_{1i}), rather than the regression parameters (β_{0i}, β_{1i}) which we have focused upon in previous sections. However, these parameters are related. In the case of a linear link function we have

$$p_{0i} = \beta_{0i} + (\beta_2 - \beta_{1i}) X_i + \gamma E[Z_{ij} | X_{ij} = 0],$$
$$p_{1i} = \beta_{0i} + \beta_{1i} + (\beta_2 - \beta_{1i}) X_i + \gamma E[Z_{ij} | X_{ij} = 1]. \tag{13.16}$$

In general the relationship between the probabilities and the regression parameters is not straightforward, depending on contextual effects and on the relationship between the confounder and the predictor X. The interpretation of the probabilities is complicated when confounding or contextual effects are present. For a linear link function, and in the absence of additional variables, Z (so that $\gamma = 0$), and contextual effects (so that $\beta_2 = \beta_{1i}$), the probabilities and parameters are simply related by

$$p_{0i} = \beta_{0i},$$
$$p_{1i} = \beta_{0i} + \beta_{1i}. \tag{13.17}$$

13.6.2 Fractions versus Probabilities

In this chapter we have so far concentrated on estimating the parameters of a hypothetical model in which there is an infinite population within each area, in which case these probabilities correspond to the proportion of category x whose response is $Y = 1$. Many methods in the political science literature – for example, the method of bounds (Duncan and Davis, 1953) and King's EI method (King, 1997) – are concerned with estimating (*predicting*) the unobserved cell entries (or equivalently, the fractions β_i^b and β_i^w as defined in the Introduction). Which of these is of interest will depend upon the particular application; it is important to distinguish between the two, however, since they are not interchangeable. We note, however, that building a causal model will generally aid in producing a good predictive model. In an individual-level study where the proportions are observed, they can be used as estimates of the underlying probabilities ($\hat{p}_{0i} = \beta_i^w$ and $\hat{p}_{1i} = \beta_i^b$), and if the number of individuals in each group-by-area margin is large, these estimates will be accurate, regardless of the existence of contextual effects and confounding. By contrast, ecological estimates of the fractions will only be accurate under very strict conditions.

Estimating the unobserved proportions is a missing data or imputation problem. The fractions are of interest when the actual numbers in the table are required – for example, in court cases concerning voting rights of minorities (see, for example, Freedman et al., 1991), or in a public health context where, for example, the actual numbers of elderly people with a disease in an area might be required in order to determine allocation of health resources. In these cases, the data in the table represent the entire population of interest; we are only concerned with the individuals eligible to vote in that specific election, or with the diseased individuals in that specific public health area. If the missing data were available, we would report the numbers in the table, and would not typically be interested in further statistical analysis.

The underlying probabilities are of interest when we are concerned with examining causal relationships between variables. In this case, the data in the table represent samples, and we wish to extrapolate to a wider population. For example, if a study of air pollution and asthma is conducted in a particular study area, we will generally be interested in applying the conclusions to a wider region. In this situation, if we had the individual data, we would model the observed data as a function of exposure and confounders in order to obtain estimates (with associated interval estimates) of the risk attributable to exposure.

Whether predictive or causal inference is required, the use of a causal model in which variation is modeled in terms of the primary predictor X, confounders, and contextual effects is likely to be advantageous. In many areas of political science the fractions have traditionally been taken as the primary target of interest. In historical voting studies, such as determining voting patterns for Hitler's National Socialist German Worker's Party in 1930 (Hamilton, 1982) we may want to know the probabilities in an underlying model for political theory, to examine how different demographic, religious, and occupational groups were voting. Usually, in epidemiology and sociology, underlying causal relationships are of interest, and these may be addressed by estimating regression coefficients in a probabilistic model. We reiterate that most applications would benefit from thinking in terms of an individual-level model, since this allows one to think about variables that may be distorting relationships that are of interest.

13.6.3 Probabilities That Vary between Areas

In social science applications the probabilities vary between areas, and this must be acknowledged to obtain accurate area-level estimates. (When estimating average causal relationships, however, we may not need to acknowledge such variability under certain assumptions, such as a linear model with randomly varying coefficients; see Equation 13.13.) However, without additional data or assumptions, it is not possible to estimate separate probabilities for each area, since we have $2m$ quantities of interest and just m observed data points. In this section we see how nonconstant probabilities arise as a result of the sources of bias that we have considered.

From Equation 13.16 we can see that there are three ways in which the probabilities p_{0i}, p_{1i} may vary between areas:

- if one or both of the parameters (β_{0i}, β_{1i}) vary between areas;
- if contextual effects are present;
- if there is unmeasured confounding.

The last two ways correspond to the conditions given by Firebaugh (1978) for *cross-level bias* to be present. If contextual effects or confounding is present, this will result in the probabilities being dependent on *context*; in general, we might expect probabilities to vary as a result of all three causes.

Probabilities that depend on context have been modeled in sociology and political science by

$$p_{0i} = a_0 + b_0 X_i,$$
$$p_{1i} = a_1 + b_1 X_i. \tag{13.18}$$

We will show how this assumption corresponds to different assumptions about contextual effects and confounding in the general individual model with a linear link function, that is,

$$E[Y_{ij}|X_{ij}, X_i, Z_{ij}] = \beta_{0i} + \beta_{1i}(X_{ij} - X_i) + \beta_2 X_i + \gamma Z_{ij}.$$

For this model, as derived previously, the marginal probabilities are given by

$$p_{0i} = \beta_{0i} + (\beta_2 - \beta_{1i})X_i + \gamma E[Z_{ij}|X_{ij} = 0],$$
$$p_{1i} = \beta_{0i} + \beta_{1i} + (\beta_2 - \beta_{1i})X_i + \gamma E[Z_{ij}|X_{ij} = 1]$$

(from Equation 13.16).

Suppose that we have constant regression probabilities, so that $\beta_{0i} = \beta_0$ and $\beta_{1i} = \beta_1$ (and that the contextual effects of interest are $\beta_2 - \beta_1$). Then the marginal probabilities in terms of the regression parameters are given by

$$p_{0i} = \beta_0 + (\beta_2 - \beta_1)X_i,$$
$$p_{1i} = \beta_0 + \beta_1 + (\beta_2 - \beta_1)X_i.$$

Here it is clear that if contextual effects are present, both probabilities will vary linearly with X_i. This corresponds to the model 13.18 with

$$a_0 = \beta_0,$$
$$a_1 = \beta_0 + \beta_1,$$
$$b_0 = \beta_2 - \beta_1, \tag{13.19}$$
$$b_1 = \beta_2 - \beta_1.$$

The *extended ecological regression* model given by Equation 13.18 is discussed extensively by Achen and Shively (1995). At the ecological level its use leads to

$$q_i = a_1 + (a_0 + b_1 - a_1)x_i + (b_0 - b_1)x_i^2,$$

and so an additional constraint must be imposed for identifiability. A common choice is to set either b_0 or b_1 to zero. Here, we see that the model we have derived in terms of the regression parameters (as summarized in Equation 13.19) corresponds to the alternative constraint that $b_0 = b_1$, and to an assumption that the contextual effect is the same for both exposure groups (and this parameter is not identifiable from the quadratic model).

The identifiability constraint should be chosen by consideration of what is appropriate for the data in hand, rather than on tractability of the model. For example, in an epidemiology context in which X represents poverty (with $X = 0$ and 1 representing poor and nonpoor), the constraint $b_0 = 0$ means that a poor individual's risk does not depend on the average poverty in the area, while $b_1 = 0$ means that a nonpoor individual's risk does not depend on the average poverty in the area. Carrying out analyses with several values of b_0 and b_1 has the same flavor as the sensitivity analyses described in Section 13.5.4.

The marginal probabilities may also vary as a result of an unmeasured confounder. Assuming that $\beta_{0i} = \beta_0$ and $\beta_{1i} = \beta_1$, we have

$$p_{0i} = \beta_0 + \gamma E[Z_{ij}|X_{ij} = 0],$$
$$p_{1i} = \beta_0 + \beta_1 + \gamma E[Z_{ij}|X_{ij} = 1].$$

These probabilities will be correlated with X_i if the values of $q_x = E[Z_{ij}|X_{ij} = x], x = 0, 1$, are correlated with X_i. For example, if q_0, q_1 are linearly related to the mean exposure X_i, then

$$E[Z_{ij}|X_{ij} = 0] = c_0 + d_0 X_i,$$
$$E[Z_{ij}|X_{ij} = 1] = c_1 + d_1 X_i.$$

This gives Equation 13.18 with

$$a_0 = \beta_0 + \gamma c_0,$$
$$b_0 = \gamma d_0,$$
$$a_1 = \beta_0 + \beta_1 + \gamma c_1,$$
$$b_1 = \gamma d_1.$$

Confounding is not often discussed explicitly in the sociology and political science literature. The general term *specification bias* is sometimes used in the sociology literature to refer to incorrect specification of the individual model; an aggregate model which ignores within-area confounding is a particular instance of this in which the model is incorrect because it omits important covariates. Between-area confounders may arise as a result of the way groups are formed. Thus between-area confounders can be seen in terms of *aggregation bias* in the sociology literature (for example, Langbein and Lichtman, 1978), in which the allocation of people into areas may depend on the response, the exposure, or both, possibly through the effect of other variables.

Although the sociology and political science literatures are much concerned with probabilities that vary between areas, an investigation into this variation is not the usual approach. Thus, although the underlying reasons for varying probabilities may differ, the method of analysis will be the same. This is in contrast to the approach in epidemiology (for example, Greenland and Morgenstern, 1989), where the source of variation is identified and influences the choice of approach. All three types of bias cause the probabilities to vary between areas, but the implications for analysis are different. For example, Section 13.4.3 showed that effect modification cannot be removed by controlling for confounders. Hence it is beneficial to identify the reasons for the variability in probabilities across areas.

13.7 RELATIONSHIP BETWEEN MODELS IN EPIDEMIOLOGY AND SOCIAL SCIENCE

A common approach to inference in the social sciences is *ecological regression* (Goodman, 1953, 1959). We let $\tilde{p}_{xi}$ denote the fractions responding for $X = x$. If the fractions are constant in expectation ($E[\tilde{p}_{0i}|X_i] = \tilde{p}_0$, $E[\tilde{p}_{1i}|X_i] = \tilde{p}_1$), which would arise if the underlying probabilities were common across areas ($p_{0i} = p_0$, $p_{1i} = p_1$), then

$$E[Y_i|X_i] = \tilde{p}_0 + (\tilde{p}_1 - \tilde{p}_0)X_i. \tag{13.20}$$

This model now has only two parameters, and can be fitted with ecological data. This is Equation 13.4 with $\beta_0 = \tilde{p}_0$ and $\beta_1 = \tilde{p}_1 - \tilde{p}_0$; in the epidemiology literature the parameters may also be written in terms of the relative risk (as we did in Equation 13.5). Goodman discussed fitting this model, conditional on many caveats, to obtain $\tilde{p}_0 = \hat{\beta}_0$ and $\tilde{p}_1 = \hat{\beta}_0 + \hat{\beta}_1$; Achen and Shively (1995) give expressions for the standard errors of these estimates.

A least squares approach to estimation in this model is often used, which implicitly assumes that the variance is constant; as noted earlier in Section 13.3, the true variance is nonconstant. While this has been considered, it is of secondary importance compared to other assumptions such as the existence of contextual effects. Achen and Shively (1995) argue that more sophisticated models allowing for nonconstant variance are not of practical importance, since over the typical ranges for a political science application the variances of $\bar{X}_i$ and Y_i are similar and vary so little as not to be a problem. In epidemiology diseases are typically rare and studies are based on small counts. In such cases, assuming a constant variance will give very poor estimates of the standard errors. To remedy this the log disease rate may be regressed on X_i, or (preferably) a Poisson log-linear model may be used (as described in Chapter 1); see Richardson and Monfort (2000) for further details.

The most serious drawbacks of ecological regression are the assumptions of constant probabilities across areas and of the absence of contextual effects. The former is unrealistic in practice because for most applications we expect demographic and area characteristics to modify the probabilities. In terms of the model 13.1, ecological regression means assuming that there are no contextual effects, no unmeasured confounders, and no effect modification, and these are again implausible assumptions in most situations. Goodman (1959) was aware that the constancy assumption would not be valid in general, but suggested that the method might be appropriate when the expected values of $\tilde{p}_{0i}$ and $\tilde{p}_{1i}$ are constant, and $\tilde{p}_{0i}$ and $\tilde{p}_{1i}$ do not systematically vary with X_i (this will occur if the parameters β_{0i}, β_{1i} vary randomly across areas), although predictions for particular areas may still be poor. This is consistent with Section 13.4.3, where we demonstrated that we have an unbiased estimate of the average $E[\beta_{1i}]$ if the parameters β_{0i} and β_{1i} (and hence the probabilities p_{0i} and p_{1i}) are uncorrelated with X_i. In such a case we would be estimating the average marginal probabilities p_{0i}, p_{1i} across areas. It is well known that least squares has robust estimation properties for regression parameters but is poor for prediction (since the distribution of the error terms is needed for this).

Freedman et al. (1991) proposed an alternative model, the (nonlinear) neighborhood model with the assumption that there is no difference in the two probabilities of disease in each area; that is, $p_{0i} = p_{1i} = q_i$. This corresponds to an assumption of no exposure effect, that is, $\beta_1 = 0$. The marginal probability q_i may vary due to unmeasured characteristics, summarized at the area level. A special case, the linear neighborhood model, allows this common probability to vary between areas depending on the average exposure, that is, $q_i = a + bX_i$. The probability q_i may vary due to contextual effects or between-area confounding (with confounding by group being one potential explanation). The resulting ecological model is

$$E[Y_i|X_i] = a + bX_i,$$

which is indistinguishable from ecological regression (Equation 13.20), but the interpretation of the coefficients is very different. Freedman's assumption corresponds to assuming that there is no individual exposure effect, but that apparent differences in probabilities between areas are due to X_i.

The linear neighborhood model is not generally used in practice, since its assumptions are even more restrictive than Goodman's regression; indeed, this model was initially proposed to discredit Goodman regression by demonstrating that a different assumption (which is uncheckable from the data alone) gives rise to a different conclusion, but an identical ecological mean model. This further illustrates the fundamental difficulty in ecological analyses: assumptions are crucial and can drastically affect the conclusions of a study, and are often uncheckable from the ecological data alone. In Sections 13.5.3 and 13.5.4 we stressed the importance of choosing assumptions based on context and checking their importance via a sensitivity analysis.

In epidemiology, hierarchical models may be used to deal with spatial and residual variation, as described in Section 13.5.2. In the political science literature, King (1997) proposed the *ecological inference* (EI) method, a particular form of hierarchical model that addresses the problem of probabilities that vary between areas. Wakefield (2004b) and Chapter 1 of this book describe the general use of hierarchical models. In the basic model it is assumed that the disease probabilities p_{0i}, p_{1i} are independent of X_i, so there are no contextual effects or unmeasured confounding, and probabilities vary only due to random effect modification (that is, they do not depend on exposure). Expressed in terms of the three types of ecological bias, it can be seen that this is a strong assumption, and substantial bias may arise if it is violated (e.g. Cho, 1998).

King's EI method is popular among political scientists because it provides estimation in the presence of random effect modification, and user-friendly software is available. However, it may produce poor estimates if confounding, contextual effects, or structured effect modification are present (Cho, 1998). The method can be extended to incorporate confounders (King, 1997: Chapter 9; this book, Introduction); the fractions $\hat{p}_{0i}$, $\hat{p}_{1i}$ are regressed on an area-level variable Z_i. One specific case often considered is when $Z_i = X_i$; that is, the probabilities depend on the average exposure. However, strong prior information is required for stable information whenever such regressions are carried out (Wakefield, 2004b). The problem is also avoided if additional individual-level data are available.

An approach that has been taken (see for example, the references in Herron and Shotts, 2004), but is incorrect, is to obtain estimates of p_{0i}, p_{1i} and then to regress these on area-level variables, in a two-stage approach. An analogous approach in epidemiology would be to control for confounding variables, and then to regress area-level relative risks upon area-level variables of interest. The problem is that the effect of the latter variables may be distorted unless the stratification variables are independent of the variables of interest (that is, are not confounders). For example, suppose we wish to investigate the effect of an environmental exposure, and wish to control for the confounder, poverty (and for the sake of exposition we assume that individuals in areas of high poverty are more likely to receive high exposure). If we control *a priori* for poverty using data from the study region (via internal standardization), then we will have removed some of the effect of exposure, and we then will overestimate the effect of poverty. In epidemiology external rates for the stratification variables are often used to avoid this problem, or simultaneous estimation of the exposures and confounders is carried out. This issue is closely related to that of mutual standardization.

13.8 CONCLUSIONS

In this chapter we have summarized some of the issues that are relevant to ecological inference in epidemiology, and shown how these relate to work in sociology and political science. Although the motivations for ecological studies differ, the approaches have much in common when one translates the different notations and languages used. The social sciences literature does not generally state a model at the level of the individual. By specifying a common framework, we have seen how different models actually correspond to different sets of underlying assumptions, and have identified similarities between approaches.

We have identified three main sources of bias: parameters that vary between areas, the presence of contextual effects, and the presence of confounding. Each discipline deals with these considerations in different ways and with different emphasis and terminology; however, we have seen that there is substantial overlap. In particular, although confounding is not explicitly considered in sociology and political science, we have seen how one of the main concerns, probabilities varying between areas, can be naturally interpreted as due to unmeasured confounding. We can thus borrow ideas from epidemiology to help deal with nonconstant probabilities from this source, by attempting to control for confounders.

There are differences in the context and the form of the data in different disciplines. In epidemiology the rarity of diseases allows a log-linear model to be used, which is more tractable than a logistic form. The sparsity of cases means that effect modification is rarely considered, and hierarchical models are often used for stable estimation. Nonrare outcomes obviously provide more information, but following the individual modeling approach described here is more difficult when using the logistic model. Another important difference is the emphasis on causality in epidemiology. Prediction does not require an explicit causal model, and in political science, when the interest is in the actual numbers of people voting, the problem becomes one of imputation of missing values, rather than estimation of underlying parameters. However, a modeling approach will often be beneficial for prediction. The extensions to continuous variables, which are more common in epidemiology, are not necessarily of use for political science problems, although they may be of some interest in sociology.

In sociology and political science, the focus on the unobserved fractions may obscure consideration of an underlying model, and does not explicitly allow identification of the reasons for variation between areas. Nonconstant probabilities can be due to contextual effects or to confounding or varying parameters. The main difference in the underlying approach to ecological inference is that political science is concerned with capturing the variation between areas, but is less interested in the actual source of the variation. On the other hand, epidemiology attempts to model the actual source of variation; this is better for making predictions for individuals in unobserved areas with particular exposure distributions, which is of more interest when the emphasis is on causality. There are other advantages to examining these different sources separately; for example, a method that reduces bias from confounding may not reduce bias from effect modification (Greenland and Morgenstern, 1989).

Additionally, since a major concern in epidemiology is controlling for potential confounders, it is important to be able to isolate bias from this source.

Assumptions in ecological inference are crucial. Often restrictive assumptions are necessary to be able to carry out an analysis, and ecological inference is highly sensitive to such assumptions. Since these assumptions cannot typically be checked from ecological data alone, we emphasize the idea of drawing conclusions on the basis of consistency of results across different modeling assumptions. In epidemiology, ecological inference is considered more plausible if consistent across different studies (which may correspond to different areas or different time periods) and if supported by biological mechanisms. In the social sciences, having different study areas with different distributions across the grouping variable is desirable, in particular where the proportions in each group, x_i, are nearly uniformly distributed across the interval $(0, 1)$. When cell counts are of interest, studies in different areas are still useful for consistency arguments. A related idea is that of a sensitivity analysis, such as that described in Section 13.5.4, which enables us to see how sensitive results are to different assumptions and provide some insight into the importance of possible biases and the uncertainty of results.

In this chapter we have concentrated on highlighting areas in epidemiology that offer benefits to sociology and political science, in particular the specification of explicit models. However, there is much to be gained in the other direction. The study of contextual effects is becoming of increasing interest in epidemiology, although as yet very little consideration has been given to contextual effects in an ecological model in environmental epidemiology. This is one area where epidemiology can benefit from the existing work in sociology. Another such area is that of effect modification. Although rare diseases and small areas frequently mean that effect modification cannot be studied, it may be possible in some studies with nonrare diseases, such as asthma, to take advantage of the current work in this area. The simplifications when dealing with a single binary exposure (for example, the ecological regression model) are not widely exploited in epidemiology.

Hierarchical models have proved useful in all disciplines. They provide a flexible way of incorporating assumptions and prior knowledge into the analysis, allow probabilities to vary between areas (including the possibility of spatial variation), and can easily incorporate the explicit modeling of observed confounders. In particular the choice of model can be tailored to the particular study; the routine use of any single model in all situations is not a good strategy.

Not all approaches in one discipline are suitable for use in another. However, the problems are sufficiently similar that there is much to be gained by being aware of work in different areas. Identifying links between one discipline and another is not straightforward; this chapter has concentrated on making some of these links explicit through the use of a common individual model.

REFERENCES

Achen, C. H. and W. P. Shively. 1995. *Cross-level Inference*. University of Chicago Press.
Besag, J., J. York, and A. Mollie. 1991. "Bayesian Image Restoration with Two Applications in Spatial Statistics," *Annals of the Institute of Statistics and Mathematics*, 43: 1–59.
Breslow, N. and N. Day. 1987. *Statistical Methods in Cancer Research, Volume 2 – The Analysis of Cohort Studies*. Oxford: Oxford University Press.
Breslow, N. and N. E. Day. 1980. *Statistical Methods in Cancer Research, Volume 1 – The Analysis of Case–Control Studies*. Scientific Publications No. 32. Lyon: International Agency for Research on Cancer.

Carstairs, V. 2000. "Socio-economic Factors at Areal Level and Their Relationship with Health." In P. Elliott, J. C. Wakefield, N. G. Best, and D. J. Briggs (eds.), *Spatial Epidemiology: Methods and Application*, Chapter 4. Oxford: Oxford University Press.

Cho, W. K. T. 1998. "Iff the Assumption Fits. . . : A Comment on the King Ecological Inference," *Political Analysis*, 7: 143–163.

Clayton, D. and M. Hills. 1993. *Statistical Models in Epidemiology*. Oxford Science Publications.

Clayton, D. and J. Kaldor. 1987. "Empirical Bayes Estimates of Age-Standardized Relative Risks for Use in Disease Mapping," *Biometrics*, 43: 671–681.

Clayton, D. G., L. Bernardinelli, and C. Montomoli. 1993. "Spatial Correlation in Ecological Analysis," *International Journal of Epidemiology*, 22: 1193–1202.

Cornfield, J., W. H. Haenszel, E. C. Hammond, A. M. Lilienfeld, M. B. Shimkin, and E. L. Wynder. 1959. Smoking and Lung Cancer: Recent Evidence and a Discussion of Some Questions," *Journal of the National Cancer Institute*, 22: 173–203.

Doll, R. 1998. "Uncovering the Effects of Smoking: Historical Perspective," *Statistical Methods in Medical Research*, 7: 87–117.

Duncan, O. D. and B. Davis. 1953. "An Alternative to Ecological Correlation," *American Sociological Review*, 18: 665–666.

Firebaugh, G. 1978. "A Rule for Inferring Individual-Level Relationships from Aggregate Data," *American Sociological Review*, 43: 557–572.

Flanigan, W. and N. Zingale. 1985. "Alchemist's Gold: Inferring Individual Relationships from Aggregate Data," *Social Science History*, 9: 71–92.

Freedman, D. A., S. P. Klein, J. Sacks, C. A. Smyth, and C. G. Everett. 1991. "Ecological Regression and Voting Rights," *Evaluation Review*, 15: 673–711.

Goodman, L. A. 1953. "Ecological Regressions and the Behavior of Individuals," *American Sociological Review*, 18: 663–664.

Goodman, L. A. 1959. "Some Alternatives to Ecological Correlation," *Americal Journal of Sociology*, 64: 610–625.

Greenland, S. 1992. "Divergent Biases in Ecologic and Individual-Level Studies," *Statistics in Medicine*, 11: 1209–1223.

Greenland, S. 2002. "A Review of Multilevel Theory for Ecologic Analyses," *Statistics in Medicine*, 21: 389–395.

Greenland, S. and H. Morgenstern. 1989. "Ecological Bias, Confounding and Effect Modification," *International Journal of Epidemiology*, 18, 1: 269–274.

Greenland, S. and J. Robins. 1994. "Invited Commentary: Ecologic Studies – Biases, Misconceptions and Counterexamples," *American Journal of Epidemiology*, 139, 8: 747–764.

Hamilton, R. 1982. *Who Voted for Hitler?* Princeton, NJ: Princeton University Press.

Herron, M. and K. W. Shotts. 2004. "Logical Inconsistency in King-Based Ecological Regressions," to appear in American Journal of Political Science.

King, G. 1997. *A Solution to the Ecological Inference Problem*. Princeton University Press.

Langbein, L. I. and A. J. Lichtman. 1978. *Ecological Inference*. Beverley Hills, CA: Sage Publications.

Lasserre, V., C. Guihenneuc-Jouyaux, and S. Richardson. 2000. "Biases in Ecological Studies: Utility of Including Within-Area Distribution of Confounders," *Statistics in Medicine*, 19: 45–59.

Maheswaran, R., S. Morris, S. Falconer, A. Grossinho, I. Perry, J. Wakefield, and P. Elliott. 1999. "Magnesium in Drinking Water Supplies and Mortality from Acute Myocardial Infarction in North West England," *Heart*, 82: 455–460.

Morgenstern, H. 1998. "Ecologic Study." In P. Armitage and T. Colton (eds.), *Encyclopedia of Biostatistics*, Vol. 2. Wiley, pp. 1255–1276.

Piantadosi, S., D. P. Byar, and S. B. Green 1988. "The Ecological Fallacy," *American Journal of Epidemiology*, 127, 5: 893–904.

Plummer, M. and D. Clayton. 1996. "Estimation of Population Exposure," *Journal of the Royal Statistical Society, Series B*, 58: 113–126.

Pope, C. A. and D. Dockery. 1996. "Epidemiology of Chronic Health Effects: Cross-Sectional Studies." In R. Wilson and J. Spengler (eds.), *Particles in Our Air: Concentrations and Health Effects*. Boston: Harvard University Press, pp. 149–167.

Prentice, R. L. and L. Sheppard. 1990. "Dietary Fat and Cancer: Consistency of the Epidemiologic Data and Disease Prevention That May Follow from a Practical Reduction in Fat Consumption," *Cancer Causes Control*, 1: 87–97.

Prentice, R. L. and L. Sheppard. 1995. "Aggregate Data Studies of Disease Risk Factors," *Biometrika*, 82, 1: 113–125.

Richardson, S. and C. Monfort. 2000. "Ecological Correlation Studies." In P. Elliott, J. C. Wakefield, N. G. Best, and D. J. Briggs (eds.), *Spatial Epidemiology: Methods and Application*, Chapter 11. Oxford: Oxford University Press.

Richardson, S., I. Stucker, and D. Hémon. 1987. "Comparison of Relative Risks Obtained in Ecological and Individual Studies: Some Methodological Considerations," *International Journal of Epidemiology*, 16, 1: 111–120.

Rosenbaum, P. and D. Rubin. 1984. "Difficulties with Regression Analyses of Age-Adjusted Rates," *Biometrics*, 40: 437–443.

Rosenbaum, P. R. 2002. *Observational Studies*, 2nd ed. New York: Springer-Verlag.

Rothman, K. J. and S. Greenland. 1998. *Modern Epidemiology*. Lippincott-Raven.

Sheppard, L. 2003. "Insights on Bias and Information in Group-Level Studies," *Biostatistics*, 4: 265–278.

Singh, G. K. and M. Siahpush. 2002. "Increasing Inequalities in All-Cause and Cardiovascular Mortality among US Adults Aged 25–64 Years by Area Socio-economic Status, 1969–1998," *International Journal of Epidemiology*, 31: 600–613.

Smith, G. D. 2000. "Learning to Live with Complexity: Ethnicity, Socioeconomic Position and Health in Britain and the United States," *American Journal of Public Health*, 90: 1694–1698.

Wakefield, J. and P. Elliott. 1999. "Issues in the Statistical Analysis of Small Area Health Data," *Statistics in Medicine*, 18: 2377–2399.

Wakefield, J. C. 2003. "Sensitivity Analyses for Ecological Regression," *Biometrics*, 59: 9–17.

Wakefield, J. C. 2004a. "A Critique of Statistical Aspects of Ecological Studies in Spatial Epidemiology," *Ecological and Environmental Statistics*, to appear.

Wakefield, J. C. 2004b. "Ecological Inference for 2 × 2 Tables, *Journal of the Royal Statistical Society, Series A*, to appear.

Wakefield, J. C. and R. E. Salway. 2001. "A Statistical Framework for Ecological and Aggregate Studies," *Journal of the Royal Statistical Society, Series A*, 164: 119–137.

Yasui, Y., J. Potter, J. Stanford, M. Rossing, M. Winget, M. Bronner, and J. Daling. 2001. "Breast Cancer Risk and "Delayed" Primary Epstein–Barr Virus Infection," *Cancer Epidemiology, Biomarkers and Prevention*, 10: 9–16.

14 Multiparty Split-Ticket Voting Estimation as an Ecological Inference Problem*

Kenneth Benoit, Michael Laver, and Daniela Giannetti

ABSTRACT

The estimation of vote splitting in mixed-member electoral systems is a common problem in electoral studies, where the goal of researchers is to estimate individual voter transitions between parties on two different ballots cast simultaneously. Because the ballots are cast separately and secretly, however, voter choice on the two ballots must be recreated from separately tabulated aggregate data. The problem is therefore of one of making ecological inferences. Because of the multiparty contexts normally found where mixed-member electoral rules are used, furthermore, the problem involves large-table ($R \times C$) ecological inference. In this chapter we show how vote-splitting problems in multiparty systems can be formulated as ecological inference problems and adapted for use with King's (1997) ecological inference procedure. We demonstrate this process by estimating vote splitting in the 1996 Italian legislative elections between voters casting party-based list ballots in proportional representation districts and candidate-based plurality ballots in single-member districts. Our example illustrates the pitfalls and payoffs of estimating vote splitting in multiparty contexts, and points to directions for future research in multiparty voting contexts using $R \times C$ ecological inference.

INTRODUCTION

Split-ticket voting is a common focus of interest in the field of electoral studies. It is concerned with identifying and analyzing patterns in the way that voters behave when faced with two distinct voting choices that give them the option of dividing their vote between different parties. Vote-splitting opportunities may be presented by institutional frameworks, such as having two types of votes to cast simultaneously in a mixed-member system; having a runoff election in systems where failure to reach a minimum vote percentage in a first round of elections allows voters a second opportunity to vote in a runoff; or even having the possibility of casting multiple votes for the same office (possibly preferential or transferable votes). Other possibilities for observing vote splitting are presented by votes for separate offices, whether simultaneously elected (as when congressional and presidential elections coincide) or temporally separate (as in estimating voter transitions between two sequential elections).

Faced with the possibility of dividing their vote between parties, voters may choose to maintain a consistent *ticket* by casting two ballots for the same party, or to split their ticket by voting for different parties on different ballots. The manner in which they split their vote offers observable implications on a wide variety of theoretical explanations of voting behavior, such as the investigation of strategic voting (Laver, 1987), instrumental or expressive

* Thanks to Raj Chari, John Haslett and David Jackson for comments, and to Gary King and Jeff Gill for help with the estimation issues.

voting (Benoit, Giannetti, and Laver, 2002), a voter's desire to produce divided government (Fiorina 1996), byproducts of ballot mechanisms (Beck, 1997), the efficacy of campaigning (Burden and Kimball, 1998), or the approval or rejection of potential governments (Strøm, Budge, and Laver, 1994) – making the estimation of split-ticket voting an issue of keen interest to researchers in electoral studies.

The potential wealth of theoretically informative behavior yielded by ticket splitting has been limited, however, by the difficulty of estimating the phenomenon. Because anonymously and separately cast ballots are not linked by any identifying information, the only way to estimate split-ticket voting from actual election results is by using aggregate data. Surveys offer an indirect alternative for measuring individual-level ticket splitting, but these suffer from a variety of additional problems, such as overstating voter turnout and overstating support for winners (see Burden and Kimball, 1998: 534), as well as providing too few cases at the district level to allow for reliable estimation of behavior in the context where the behavior actually takes place. The only directly observable phenomena typically available to researchers, therefore, are voting results aggregated at some unit of electoral geography, such as precinct, district, state, or region. Each electoral unit can then be thought of as providing a table whose rows and columns are defined by voters exercising categories of choice on two separate ballots. The problem created by the anonymity of the voter and the absence of any linking information between the two ballots is that the cell values are unknown. The problem, therefore, is the well-known one of having to make ecological inferences about individual behavior based on aggregate data, requiring statistical techniques appropriate to this problem.

Our attention in this chapter focuses on using techniques of ecological inference to estimate split-ticket voting under *mixed-member* electoral systems. Used in various forms in New Zealand, Italy, Germany, Russia, and Hungary – to name but a few examples – the mixed-member electoral system provides two distinct political contexts for voting.[1] One of these is a proportional representation (PR) context in which choices are made in relation to party lists in multimember constituencies. The other is a single-member district (SMD) context in which choices are made in relation to individual candidates, typically using a plurality rule. A popular compromise for countries seeking a balance between majoritarian and proportional principles, mixed-member systems are now used in a substantial number of post-Communist states as well (Moser, 1999; Shugart and Wattenberg, 2001b). Elections held under mixed-member systems provide political scientists with fascinating natural laboratories within which to analyze the behavior of the same set of voters in different strategic settings under otherwise controlled conditions, confronting the same party system and the same issue space at the same moment in time. Analyses of vote splitting in such systems not only are descriptively interesting to scholars concerned with a particular political system, but have also been used more generally to explore alternative theoretical accounts of voting behavior. Vote splitting has been studied closely in New Zealand, for instance, since its switch from first-past-the-post to that system in 1996 (e.g., Johnston and Pattie, 1999, 2000; Banducci, Karp, and Vowles, 1998). Italy also adopted the mixed-member system for first use in its 1994 election, prompting numerous studies of its effects on voter choice (see Benoit, Giannetti, and Laver, 2002); so did Japan (Reed and Thies, 2001).

The difficulty of estimating split-ticket voting under mixed-member rules, however, is substantially greater than the same problem studied in the traditional U.S. or British contexts. This is because the mixed-member electoral system is almost always associated with a multiparty system. The number of unknowns to be estimated is multiplied by having

---

[1] For an excellent general discussion of mixed-member electoral systems, see Shugart and Wattenberg (2001a).

more than two or three categories of vote choice on each dimension of the voter transition table. In the language used elsewhere in this book (e.g., Judge, Miller, and Cho, Chapter 7), the ill-posed inverse problem in multiparty split-voting studies is even more ill-posed than in typical two-party applications. Our ability to estimate and analyze split-ticket voting in multiparty contexts, therefore, is directly linked to advances in ecological inference that make reliable and accurate estimates possible.

In what follows we demonstrate how split-ticket voting under mixed-member electoral rules can be expressed as an ecological inference problem and estimated using an extension of King's (1997) ecological inference technique (referred to hereafter as EI) suited for $2 \times C$ tables. Our data comes from the 1996 elections to the Italian Chamber of Deputies, where we have observed both PR and plurality voting by party in a total of 475 single-member districts. First, we frame the problem of vote splitting by partitioning voters according their political preferences and voting behavior. Next, we partition the observable aggregate data into a framework corresponding to the partition of voter types. We then adapt the EI procedure to estimate at the district level the relative proportions of each type of individual voter from the partitioned aggregate data, using the extended EI model incorporating additional contextual information in the form of district-level covariates. In addition to reviewing important diagnostic information from the EI estimations to provide a methodological evaluation of our results, we also analyze and characterize these results in a substantive empirical context. Finally, we offer suggestions for taking the Italian estimates further and for extending our approach to other contexts.

VOTING IN THE ITALIAN MIXED-MEMBER ELECTORAL SYSTEM

Electoral Politics and Background

The Italian mixed-member electoral system involves 475 single-member districts, in which candidates compete in plurality elections, as well as 26 multimember constituencies (*circoscrizioni*), in which a total of 155 seats are allocated by PR, giving a total legislature of 630 seats.[2] (For a brief but clear description, see D'Alimonte, 1998.) Though the new electoral system was intended to bring about a reduction in the number of parties, what in fact happened was that Italian political parties retained their separate identities, organizing themselves into opposing "cartels" with preelection agreements that shared out the candidacies in the single-member districts. Electoral politics in the 1996 elections had thus been structured around two major electoral coalitions, the *Polo della Libertà*, on the right, and the *Ulivo*, on the left.[3]

Since nearly every Italian party also establishes a list to contest the multimember constituencies, almost every Italian voter may vote for his or her most preferred party in the PR element of the election. When it comes to the plurality ballot, however, a voter's first-choice party may well not be contesting the single-member constituency in which the voter lives. It may be replaced instead by another party from the same cartel to which the first-choice

---

[2] The number of PR seats a party will eventually obtain is determined by subtracting the plurality vote share of second-placed candidates in the districts where a party has won a seat from the PR vote share of that party at the constituency level. This is a *partial deduction*, known as the *scorporo*.

[3] In 1996, the *Ulivo* consisted of the Greens (Fed. Dei Verdi), the Prodi alliance (Pop–SVP–PRI–UD–Prodi), the Democratic Party of the Left (PDS), the Dini List (PPI), and PS d'Az. Although not formally part of the *Ulivo* cartel, the Refounded Communists (RC) is also included because of the nature of its exclusivity pacts in 1996, which functioned like the formal cartel agreements. *Polo* consisted of CCD–CDU, Forza Italia (FI), and the *Alleanza Nazionale* (AN).

party belongs. The different choices facing voters in single- and multimember constituencies confront Italian voters with important strategic decisions.

A Model of Voting Behavior in Italy's Mixed-Member System

Our focus in this paper is on substantive and procedural issues pertaining to the estimation of vote-splitting between cartels, rather than the empirical confirmation of a theoretical model of voting behavior. Nonetheless, it is useful to distinguish between two broad categories of voters. This is the distinction, introduced by Brennan and Lomaski (1993) and developed by Schuessler (2000) and by Brennan and Hamlin (2000), between *instrumental* and *expressive* voters. Essentially, the instrumental value of a vote "derives from the contribution the vote makes to bringing about the desired electoral outcome" (Brennan and Lomaski, 1993: 23). The expressive, or "intrinsic," value of a vote, on the other hand, "is the value that the voter places on expressing a preference for *a*, rather than *b*, in and of itself (i.e., independent of any effect of the voting act on the electoral *outcome*" (Brennan and Lomaski, 1993: 23; emphasis in original).

The PR element in a mixed-member election provides strong incentives for voters to vote "sincerely" for their most-preferred parties. For most voters, their first-choice party is available on the ballot, giving their vote maximum value as an expression of political preference. For instrumental voters, voting for the first-choice party increases the probability of this party getting into government and changing policy outputs; it increases the party's claim on cabinet seats should it succeed in getting into government, thereby increasing its impact on policy outputs; and it increases the allocation of SMD candidacies within the electoral cartel in future elections, thereby increasing its chances of success in the future. For these reasons, therefore, we assume that voters who have genuine (instrumental or expressive) preferences for a specific political party will always vote for this party on their PR ballot.

The plurality element in the election, on the other hand, may or may not result in one of the two big cartels offering a given voter his or her most-preferred party. If it does offer a voter the most-preferred party, then we assume the voter will also cast his or her plurality vote for this party's candidate. For the same reasons outlined in the previous paragraph, both instrumental and expressive voters are likely to cast their plurality ballot in a *party-loyal* fashion. This will be true in all constituencies except those in which some third party is predicted to have a serious chance of success. In such constituencies, some voters may face a strategic decision. For some instrumental voters, it may possibly be the case that a voter will do better by voting *strategically*, not for his or her most-preferred party, but for the party best placed to defeat a less-preferred rival. Otherwise the instrumental voter should still vote for his or her most-preferred party.

A much more common situation in the plurality election is that one of the two big cartels does not offer a voter his or her most-preferred party, but a candidate from another party in the same electoral cartel. We can think of such voters as being *disappointed*, or *frustrated*, since their first-choice party is not on offer. The problem examined in this paper consists of estimating the proportions of disappointed voters who behave in one of two possible ways.

One way that disappointed voters can behave is to vote for the candidate sponsored by the cartel of their most-preferred party. For a variety of reasons, voters may choose to cast their plurality vote in this *cartel-loyal* manner. For disappointed instrumental voters, voting for another party in the same cartel increases the probability that their most-preferred party will be a member of the winning cartel, will go into government, will receive cabinet seats, and will thereby have some impact on public policy. Disappointed instrumental voters thus use their vote to have an effect on which cartel wins the election, and hence place their most-preferred party in the strongest position. Disappointed expressive voters, in contrast, are likely to switch their vote to the party on offer that is next highest in their expressive ranking. Since, as we have seen, many matters other than policy may determine expressive returns, this party may or may not be in the same cartel as their first-choice party, but it is quite possible that it is indeed in the same cartel.

The other way that disappointed voters can behave is to switch their votes to a candidate who is outside the cartel of their most-preferred party – in other words, in a cartel-disloyal fashion. Cartel switching is something that might be quite logical for disappointed expressive voters, since expressive returns can be derived from a wide range of matters that are quite unrelated to cartel membership. We note that voting for a noncartel party (one that is not *Polo* or *Ulivo*) offers an additional option for cartel disloyalists. For example, a disappointed voter whose most preferred party is in the *Polo* cartel, upon finding that the *Polo* cartel sponsored a candidate in her single-member district from a party different from her most preferred, could be cartel-disloyal by voting either for the *Ulivo* candidate, or for a noncartel candidate (from a party not sponsored by either *Polo* or *Ulivo*).

The bottom line is that the nature of Italian elections under the mixed-member electoral system allows us to partition Italian voters into three exclusive and exhaustive sets. The first set consists of people who vote for some party in the PR election and, finding the same party available in the SMD election, vote for it again. We call these voters *party loyalists*. The second set consists of voters who vote in the PR election for their most preferred party and, finding this party unavailable in the SMD election, vote for a different party in the same electoral cartel as their most preferred party. We term these voters *cartel loyalists*. The third set comprises those who vote in the PR election for some party and, finding this party unavailable in the SMD election, vote for a party that is not in the same electoral cartel as their PR choice. We term this final category of voters *cartel disloyalists*. Having defined the basic types of voter we consider, we now need to define some quantities that will allow us to partition the observed aggregate data.

Formal Statement of the Model

For each SMD in Italy we define, and can observe, the following quantities:

N The total number of votes in the district.[4]

P_u The plurality vote for the candidate running under the *Ulivo* cartel label.

P_p The plurality vote for the candidate running under the *Polo* cartel label.

P_o The sum of the plurality vote(s) for the candidate(s) running under other cartel or noncartel party labels, defined as $N - P_u - P_p$.

L_u The list votes (at the district level) for the party endorsing the candidate running as *Ulivo*.

L_p The list vote (at the district level) for the party endorsing the candidate running as *Polo*.

L_o The sum of the list votes (at the district level) for the parties endorsing the candidates that are running as neither *Ulivo* nor *Polo*.

---

[4] Because the number of valid votes differs for each ballot type in a single district, the total number of valid candidate SMD votes seldom equals exactly the total number of valid list votes cast in that SMD. See below for how we deal with this problem.

C_u The sum of the list votes (at the district level) for all parties in the *Ulivo* cartel.

C_p The sum of the list votes (at the district level) for all parties in the *Polo* cartel.

C_o The sum of the list votes (at the district level) for all parties in neither *Ulivo* nor *Polo* cartels, defined as $N - C_u - C_p$.

Following the general argument in Section 14.2, we make the following assumptions about voting behavior:

1. **Party-based preference:** Each voter has a first preference for one of the political parties contesting the PR element of the election.
2. **PR-list vote:** Each voter's PR-list vote is a sincere revelation of this preference.
3. **SMD vote:** Voters cast their candidate-based ballots in the following manner:
   (a) **Party-loyal voting:** If the voter's first-preference party has a candidate in the SMD, then the voter votes for this candidate. This implies that $P_i \geq L_i \forall i$.[5]
   (b) **Cartel-loyal voting:** If the voter's first-preference party does not have a candidate in the SMD, then a cartel-loyal voter supports the candidate sponsored by the cartel to which the voter's first-preference party belongs. We denote cartel-loyal voters as y_p, y_u, and y_o, for *Polo-*, *Ulivo-*, and *other-cartel-*loyal voters, respectively.
   (c) **Cartel-disloyal voting:** If the voter's first-preference party does not have a candidate in the SMD, then a cartel-disloyal voter supports a candidate other than the one sponsored by the cartel to which his or her first-preference party belongs. We denote by d_{ij} the fraction of the cartel-disloyal, frustrated voters whose most preferred party is from cartel i who switched their SMD vote to a party from cartel j $(i \neq j)$. Hence, of the cartel-disloyal voters who voted for a *Polo* candidate in the PR election, d_{pu} denotes the fraction switching to an *Ulivo* candidate, and d_{po} the fraction switching to an other-cartel candidate. Proportions of other groups of cartel-disloyal voters are denoted in a similar way.

We can thus completely partition the vote in a single-member district as in Table 14.1. In each SMD the total number of votes, N, is partitioned both by the PR-list ballots for cartel parties (C_p, C_u, and C_o) and by the plurality ballots for cartel parties (P_p, P_u, and P_o). According to assumption 3(a), any intersection of (C_i, P_i) in Table 14.1 will contain L_i, since all voters whose preferred party has a candidate will vote loyally for that candidate in the SMD. The intersection (C_i, P_i) will contain the cartel-loyal voters who, not having found a candidate from their most preferred party in the SMD, voted for another party's candidate but from the same cartel as their most-preferred party. By definition, the other cells on this row must be empty. The remainder of the plurality vote P_i will consist of cartel-disloyal voters who, not having found a candidate from their most preferred party in the SMD, will have voted for cartel i candidate instead; their proportions are denoted by d with a double subscript indicating their most preferred party's cartel and the cartel to which they switched their vote.

Given the partition of voter types and our parameterization of the quantities to be estimated, mapped to the partition of observed aggregate data, we now turn to the problem of estimating the quantities y and d.

---

[5] This is true in all cases for the two main cartels, although there are seven marginal exceptions for the residual other-cartel category. Our treatment of the other category below makes this irrelevant, as explained in the next section.

Table 14.1 Composition of SMD vote P and list cartel vote C in a SMD

Cartel list vote	Vote type	Cartel plurality vote		
		P_p	P_u	P_o
C_p	Party-loyal	L_p	0	0
	Cartel-loyal	y_p	0	0
	Cartel-disloyal	0	d_{pu}	d_{po}
C_u	Party-loyal	0	L_u	0
	Cartel-loyal	0	y_u	0
	Cartel-disloyal	d_{up}	0	d_{uo}
C_o	Party-loyal	0	0	L_o
	Cartel-loyal	0	0	y_o
	Cartel-disloyal	d_{op}	d_{ou}	0

A FRAMEWORK FOR ESTIMATING VOTE-SPLITTING IN ITALY

Reexpressing the Estimation Problem

Because we observe the quantity L_i in each district, and because it forms part of of both the row and column totals, we can remove it from the vote partition described in Table 14.1 by simply subtracting it from C_i and P_i. This emphasizes what we have called frustrated voters: those whose most-preferred party had no candidate in the SMD. The new formulation also highlights the two sources of votes received by each cartel i candidate from its assumed core of party-loyal voters y_i. First, each cartel i will lose some frustrated voters (represented by d_{ij} and d_{ik}), who transfer their votes to the other two cartels j and k. Second, each cartel i will also pick up some excess votes (represented by d_{ji} and d_{ki}) from frustrated, cartel-disloyal voters from cartels j and k. Following this, we define the quantities as F_i and E_i as follows:

$$F_p = C_p - L_p, \qquad E_p = P_p - L_p,$$
$$F_u = C_u - L_u, \qquad E_u = P_u - L_u,$$
$$F_o = C_o - L_o, \qquad E_o = P_o - L_o.$$

The F's represent frustrated voters whose most-preferred party has no candidate in the single-member district and who therefore have transferred their vote to another party in the SMD. The E's represent the excess votes received by a plurality candidate over his or her loyal core of voters who cast a list ballot for that candidate's party.

Since the vote total N now reflects the subtraction of L_p, L_u, and L_o, we denote by N^T the total transferred votes, so that $N^T = N - \sum L$. We use this designation to reflect the adjustment of the excess votes for the difference between invalid votes in the two ballots.[6]

---

[6] A common problem in estimating split-ticket voting is that the observed totals of valid votes for different ballot types always differ slightly, mainly because of different rates of invalid ballots. As a remedy we took N and N^T in each district to be the midpoint between the two ballot totals, which we denote N^{T*}. No adjustment was needed for the marginals, since we took the relevant input quantities required for input to EI simply as the proportions of the respective ballot totals before averaging the two ballots. Our tests showed that there was no systematic pattern to the differences between ballots, and that the mean of these differences was statistically indistinguishable from zero.

Table 14.2 Vote transfers in an SMD as a 3 × 3 table

	E_p	E_u	E_o	
F_p	y_p	d_{pu}	d_{po}	17,609
F_u	d_{up}	y_u	d_{uo}	32,269
F_o	d_{op}	d_{ou}	y_o	4,386
	17,075	32,238	4,146	

$$N^F = 54,264 \qquad N^E = 53,459$$
$$N^* = 53,862$$

Note: The shaded region provides the 2 × 3 subtable which we estimate after eliminating the third row by the simplifying assumption.

This reduces the partition of voting patterns for each district to the 3 × 3 matrix shown in Table 14.2. The empirical question in which we are interested now becomes one of estimating the differential levels of cartel-loyal versus cartel-disloyal voting, and in comparing these by cartel. For frustrated voters whose most preferred party was a *Polo* cartel member, for instance, how many voted for the *Ulivo* candidate (represented by d_{pu}) and how many voted for a candidate from neither cartel (represented by d_{po})? Because we can observe only the marginals of this table in voting data, the problem becomes one of making ecological inferences about the unobserved cell quantities.

Reducing the Parameter Space

The problem expressed in the Table 14.2 is one of EI, since it characterizes individual-level voting behavior where only aggregate vote quantities are observed. To estimate the cells at the district level, we use a two-stage application of King's (1997) EI algorithm. Because this method does not work with 3 × 3 tables such as Table 14.3, however, we need an additional assumption.

Simplifying Assumption: Voters preferring a party that is not in either the *Polo* or the *Ulivo* cartel will always be considered expressive, since only *Polo* and *Ulivo* have a chance of winning the election overall. Such voters thus do not have a strategic option that allows them to transfer within a cartel that might win the election. This implies that among

Table 14.3 King's 2 × 3 EI parameters to be estimated

	$Pr(E_p)$	$Pr(E_u)$		$Pr(E_o)$		
$Pr(F_p)$	λ_i^b	$1 - \lambda_i^b$	β_i^b	$1 - \beta_i^b$	$[X_i]$
$Pr(F_u)$	λ_i^w	$1 - \lambda_i^w$	β_i^w	$1 - \beta_i^w$	$[1 - X_i]$
	$[V_i]$		$[T_i]$	$[1 - T_i]$	

Note: $Pr(F_p)$ refers (e.g.) to the proportion of frustrated *Polo* supporters voting for the *Polo* candidate, rather than the whole numbers. The quantities in brackets are in King's (1997: 30) notation: X_i refers to the proportion of frustrated *Polo* voters, T_i is the proportion of cartel (non-other) voters, and V_i is the *Polo* proportion of non-other-cartel voters.

Table 14.4 Quantities to be estimated and transformations required from King's parameterization

$\Pr(y_p) = E(\lambda_i^b)\,E(\beta_i^b)$	Proportion of frustrated *Polo* voters who stayed with a *Polo* candidate
$\Pr(y_u) = E(1 - \lambda_i^w)\,E(\beta_i^w)$	Proportion of frustrated *Ulivo* voters who stayed with a *Ulivo* candidate
$\Pr(d_{up}) = E(\lambda_i^w)\,E(\beta_i^w)$	Proportion of frustrated *Ulivo* voters who voted for a *Polo* candidate
$\Pr(d_{pu}) = E(1 - \lambda_i^b)\,E(\beta_i^b)$	Proportion of frustrated *Polo* voters who voted for a *Ulivo* candidate
$\Pr(d_{uo}) = E(1 - \beta_i^w)$	Proportion of frustrated *Ulivo* voters voting for a candidate from the other cartel
$\Pr(d_{po}) = E(1 - \beta_i^b)$	Proportion of frustrated *Polo* voters voting for a candidate from the other cartel

noncartel voters, cartel loyalty or disloyalty – if it applies at all – is not expected to exhibit any systematic pattern. We therefore assume that d_{op}, d_{ou}, and y_o are equal, and assign them their expected values $(rc)/n$, or $(F_i E_j)/N^T$.

Subtracting the row containing d_{op}, d_{ou}, and y_o from the E marginals yields the 2×3 subtable in the shaded region, with a new table total and new totals for the column quantities once the expected values of the third-row frequencies have been computed and subtracted from the relevant column marginals. These new marginals produce the information for an application of EI to the 2×3 table in a two-stage procedure, estimating the quantities shown in Table 14.3. These four parameters can be estimated by using King's *EI* software[7] and the second-stage EI2 procedure for the nested tables. Furthermore, because the precinct-level quantities (here, the electoral unit of the single-member district) can be simulated from the posterior distribution of the main model estimation, EI and EI2 will yield separate estimates of each quantity in each precinct, with corresponding standard errors indicating the uncertainty of each estimate.[8]

Because the parameters β_i^b, β_i^w, λ_i^b, and λ_i^w do not directly represent the row proportions we are interested in estimating, they must be transformed into our quantities of loyal and disloyal voting. Table 14.4 shows the simple algebraic transformation required to yield the direct split-voting quantities of interest. From each stage of EI, we saved the 1,000 simulations of each precinct's simulated values of the quantities β_i^b, β_i^w, λ_i^b, and λ_i^w, transforming them through multiplication of the simulated quantities saved from the output of the EI software. This then yielded in the case of each transformed quantity a vector of 1,000 transformed simulations whose means were used for the point estimates for the precinct-level estimates of y_p, d_{pu}, d_{po}, d_{up}, y_u, and d_{uo} (each transformed into column proportions).

Aggregation Bias and Covariates

Because there are numerous factors that we believe will affect the distribution of the parameter values, we also included covariates in our estimation of the EI quantities. Aggregation bias, as discussed by King (1997) and Voss (this book, Chapter 3) is a problem that occurs when parameter values in specific precincts differ from the general pattern aggregated to the district level. In the Italian data and in studies of split-ticket voting generally, however, not

[7] Or Benoit and King's *EzI* software. See http://Gking.Harvard.Edu/software.shtml
[8] When discussing King's EI estimation, we use the term "precinct" to refer to our unit of observation, which is the single-member district. In King's (1997) terminology, the *precinct* is the minor unit where aggregate behavior is recorded, and the *district* is the larger unit containing the precincts.

only do we expect precinct-level parameters to vary substantially, but indeed it is precisely this variation and the patterns within it that motivate the attempt to estimate the split voting. When this variation can be mapped systematically to other variables, we can improve the EI estimates considerably by including precinct-level covariates. For these reasons we employ the extended EI model using covariates that we expect to explain systematic variation in split-ticket voting at the precinct level.

Particularly in Italy, previous work has indicated that electoral choices can only be understood at the level where they are exercised (Shin and Agnew, 2001). Although party campaign strategies are broadly conducted at the national level, they are implemented at local level and "are likely to be a response to the immediate settings, conditions, and circumstances in which political parties operate" (Shin, 2001). More generally, many of the explanations for vote splitting relate specifically to the local electoral unit where vote splitting may occur. These include the existence of specific party candidates, the competitiveness of a precinct, or the intensity of campaign in a precinct – we would expect these factors to cause precinct-level parameters to vary. By including precinct-level measures of such influences as covariates, therefore, we can improve the estimates of our quantities of interest by introducing additional information available to us from our knowledge of split-ticket voting and from the specific Italian political context.

The covariates we include in the EI estimation of cartel-loyal and cartel-disloyal voting are the following:

Intercartel competitiveness. This variable represents the closeness of the *Ulivo* and *Polo* cartel list votes (C_u and C_p). It is calculated as the absolute difference of C_u and C_p, divided by the total of list votes ($\sum C$). Lower values indicate greater intercartel competitiveness, with the distribution of votes between cartels being more even; likewise, higher values indicate that one cartel had a greater lead over the other and that the district was less competitive between cartels. Our expectation is that higher levels of competitiveness (indicated by smaller values of this variable) will cause higher levels of cartel-loyal voting, as the district is more intensely divided and the election outcome both more contested and more uncertain.

Intracartel fragmentation. This variable, measured separately for both *Ulivo* and *Polo*, measures the dispersion of the list PR votes among the parties in each cartel. It consists of the ratio of the *effective* number of parties in the cartel to the actual number of parties. The effective number of parties is measured as $1/\sum v_i^2$ each party i in the cartel. When all of the cartel party's votes are equal, the effective number of parties will equal the actual number of parties. The intracartel fragmentation variable thus ranges from a theoretical 0 to 1, with higher values indicating greater intracartel fragmentation. Our expectation (generally following Tsebelis, 1988) is that greater levels of fragmentation increase intracartel rivalry, decreasing cartel cohesion and cooperation and hence cartel-loyal voting. This variable is measured at the level of the single-member district.

Dummy variables. In addition to the competitiveness variables, we also included a number of binary variables to represent qualities specific to each plurality district.

Northern district. When coded as 1, this indicated that the district was in the Northern region.[9]

---

[9] Other regions included Central, South, and Islands. We did not include any of these regions as covariates, because neither our prior expectations nor subsequent testing gave us reason to believe that they should explain differences in cartel-loyal and -disloyal voting.

Table 14.5 Aggregate ecological inference estimates, 1996 Italian election data

Quantity	Point Estimate	S.E.	Lower bound	Upper bound
First-stage EI				
β^b	0.9261	0.0005	0.8878	0.9991
β^w	0.9647	0.0004	0.9010	0.9980
N	465			
Simulations	1,000			
Log likelihood	1522.2528			
Second-stage EI				
λ^b	0.8748	0.0014	0.0885	0.9199
λ^w	0.0468	0.0012	0.0157	0.7052
N	465			
Simulations	1,000			
Log likelihood	1253.0066			

Transformed model quantities of interest

Transformed parameter (proportions)	Aggregate estimate	S.E.	95% confidence interval	
y_u	0.9196	0.0012	0.9171	0.9219
y_p	0.8102	0.0014	0.8075	0.8130
d_{up}	0.0451	0.0012	0.0428	0.0474
d_{pu}	0.1159	0.0013	0.1132	0.1185
d_{uo}	0.0353	0.0004	0.0345	0.0362
d_{po}	0.0739	0.0005	0.0729	0.0749

Note: Estimations include covariates listed in Table 14.8. Transformed quantity estimates are transformed as per Table 14.4, based on 1,000 simulations from the aggregate posterior distribution.

Northern League candidate. A score of 1 on this variable indicated that a candidate of *Lega Nord* competed in the plurality contest (as an "Other," or noncartel, candidate). Such candidacies occurred only in the Northern region.

Communist candidate. A score of 1 on this variable indicated that a candidate of the Refounded Communist Party (*Rif. Com.*) competed in the plurality contest.

Neo-fascist candidate. A score of 1 on this variable indicated that a candidate of *Mov. Soc.* competed in the plurality contest.

Incumbency variables. Coded for each cartel, the *Polo, Ulivo,* and noncartel incumbency variables were scored 1 if a candidate competing in 1996 from the respective cartel had won a plurality contest in the 1994 election.

RESULTS

The results from our estimation of the unobserved quantities of interest appear in Table 14.5. The upper panel of this table displays the aggregate-level EI parameters expressed in

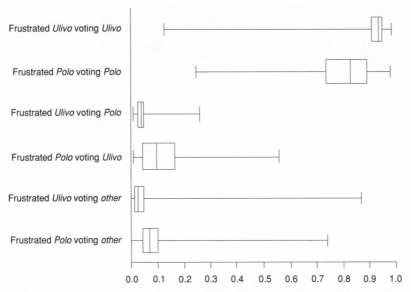

Figure 14.1. Comparing cartel switching and loyalty between *Ulivo* and *Polo* cartels.

the scale of estimation, along with information from the estimation procedure such as the number of cases, simulations, and log likelihood.[10] The lower panel displays the quantities in which we are directly interested, the transformed model quantities of interest (expressed as proportions). The first two quantities we estimate are the degree of cartel loyalty for plurality voters from the *Polo* and *Ulivo* cartels (y_p and y_u respectively). Here we see strong evidence that the *Polo* cartel voters were less cohesive than their *Ulivo* counterparts, with an estimated aggregate proportion of .92 of the frustrated *Ulivo* voters choosing the *Ulivo* candidate in the plurality election, compared to an aggregate proportion of .81 of the frustrated *Polo* voters staying with the *Polo*-sponsored candidate. Because of of our covariates, furthermore, the bounds on these point estimates are very small indeed, yielding very precise aggregate estimates of cartel loyalty as indicated by the 95% confidence intervals.[11]

The aggregate rates of between-cartel defection reveal a similar pattern. The estimate of d_{up}, representing the proportion of frustrated *Ulivo* voters who voted for the *Polo*-sponsored candidate in the plurality elections, was just 0.05. Yet the rate of cross-cartel voting for the frustrated *Polo*-party-preferring voters – represented by d_{pu} – was considerably higher at 0.12. Because these estimates also had very narrow bounds as indicated by the confidence intervals, it can be confidently stated from these results that more than twice as much cross-cartel voting took place among frustrated *Polo* supporters as among frustrated *Ulivo* supporters.

The frustrated *Ulivo* voters also showed greater cohesion in avoiding defections to the noncartel candidates. Our estimates show that at the aggregate level, the proportion of

---

[10] We estimated the model without priors and did not set starting values for the covariates. The model tended to have computational problems in the EI2 stage, requiring us to turn off the multiple imputation feature in the EI software (version 1.5, 5/5/2002) for the EI2 procedure (by setting _EI2_m = −1). The EI manual states that this will result in somewhat smaller standard errors for the simulated parameters, but does not indicate the extent of this effect.

[11] The 95% confidence intervals were computed by taking the middle 95% of the sorted aggregate transformed quantities, computed from the simulations of the aggregate quantities through algebraic transformation as described in the previous section.

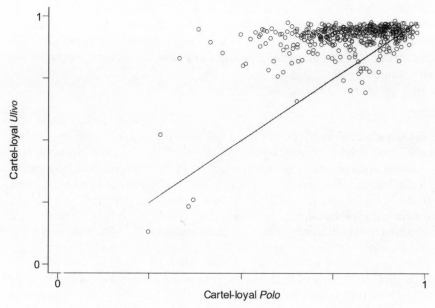

Figure 14.2. Direct comparison of district-level estimates of cartel-loyal voting, *Ulivo* versus *Polo*.

frustrated *Ulivo* supporters voting for a noncartel ("other") candidate was approximately 0.04, compared to an estimated aggregate proportion of 0.07 for *Polo*. Once again, the proportion of frustrated cartel voters defecting to vote for a noncartel candidate was more than twice as great for *Polo* as for *Ulivo*, with the 95% confidence intervals indicating these estimates to be quite precise.

A graphic summary of the district-level results is provided in Figures 14.1 and 14.2. Figure 14.1 depicts all of the estimated precinct quantities in boxplots, pairing the analogous *Ulivo* and *Polo* quantities for comparison. The boxes depict the interquartile range, with the median value represented by the line in the middle of the box. The whiskers represent the minima and maxima of the range of precinct-level point estimates. In Figure 14.1, the top two bars compare the degree of cartel loyalty among frustrated *Ulivo* and *Polo* voters. The results are consistent with the aggregate values reported in Table 14.5. The median for the *Polo* cartel-loyal voters is clearly lower than the corresponding *Ulivo* value, also having a dramatically wider range (measured by the interquartile range shown by the box). The difference between the cross-cartel voters is even more dramatic. Far fewer frustrated *Ulivo* supporters voted for a *Polo* candidate than vice versa. Furthermore, the degree of discipline among frustrated *Polo* voters that did not vote with their cartel was much lower, indicated by the much greater range of the district estimates for the frustrated *Polo*-voting *Ulivo* voters. Finally, the number of frustrated *Ulivo*-voting others was also lower than in typical precinct for *Polo* supporters, with a greater variance as well.

Figure 14.2 compares cartel loyalty directly at the precinct level among *Polo* and *Ulivo* cartel voters. Each small circle in the scatterplot represents a precinct-level estimate of (Y_p, Y_u). As can be seen, in the vast bulk of precincts, the level of cartel loyalty among *Ulivo* voters was much higher, to the upper right of the 45-degree line. For the four districts with much smaller levels of both *Ulivo* and *Polo* cartel loyalty, our examination of these in the data set reveals that there were unusually popular noncartel candidates competing, three of the four coming from a specific region. The fourth candidate was an extremely popular noncartel incumbent, depressing the rates of cartel loyalty on both sides but more so for *Ulivo*. It is precisely these sorts of effects that in the absence of covariates would cause aggregation bias, but that can largely be controlled by introducing independent information about the partisanship and incumbency of specific noncartel candidates, as well some geographically specific information.

Interpretation

Our overall finding is that the *Ulivo* cartel had a higher degree of general voter loyalty than the *Polo* cartel – with *Polo* losing more far more voters to the *Ulivo* cartel than vice versa. This is quite consistent with our knowledge of Italian politics in the 1990s. First and foremost, in 1994 the Italian political scene was dramatically changed by the entry of a new party, *Forza Italia* (FI) and its controversial leader Silvio Berlusconi, a media tycoon who was able to build a party in just a few months and gain spectacular success in the 1994 election. While the strong leadership of Berlusconi was successful in assembling the coalition partners in the *Polo* cartel at the elite level, we may conjecture that his charismatic appeal – being strongly divisive – failed to capture many of the disappointed *Polo* supporters at the *voter* level.

Second, in 1996 the *Polo* cartel built a single nationwide alliance for the first time. In 1994 there had been two electoral alliances: one formed by FI and the Northern League in the north, and one formed by FI and AN in the south. This could also have led to lower cartel loyalty within the *Polo* coalition. On the other hand, the *Ulivo* coalition was composed of more traditional parties and allies who would have been expected to have more capacity of coordinating their voters on a more instrumental choice. In sum, the higher proportion of expressive voters in the *Polo* cartel is very consistent with our initial expectations.

EI Diagnostics

We have discussed our results in general substantive terms, but it is also worthwhile to assess these results by examining some of the characteristics of the data and some intermediate results from the parametric EI procedure. Table 14.6 in the Appendix reports the maximum-likelihood estimates for the covariates from both the EI and EI2 estimations. These values themselves contain a great variety of substantively important information, but we leave the task of interpreting them to future work, having intended primarily to use them to control aggregation bias. But it is to our satisfaction that most are highly statistically significant, indicating that did indeed explain variation in the precinct-level parameter estimates in our data set.

Figures 14.3 and 14.4 show additional information about the data and allow us to assess whether it conforms broadly to the checklist of characteristics recommended for successful application of EI. The left panel of Figure 14.3 graphs X_i against T_i (in this case, the proportion of frustrated *Polo* voters against the proportion of excess noncartel voters), with the size of the circles proportional to the number of frustrated voters in the district. The results show a fairly uniform distribution along X, and a tight clustering along the T dimension, with a single mode, and only two discernable outliers. The right panel shows the tomography plot for the two parameter values β_i^b and β_i^w, with the lines indicating where each parameter must lie according to a well-known deterministic accounting identity. The two ovals represent contour plots for mean posterior contours. For the estimation of β_i^b and β_i^w, there is clear evidence of some nonhomogenous precincts, indicated by the five stray lines, although most tomography lines were tightly clustered in the upper range of the graph. With covariates to control for the nonhomogenous precincts, the tomography plot reveals no pattern substantially violating the assumptions required for estimation using EI.

Table 14.6 Covariate parameter values in scale of estimation, from both EI and EI2 procedures

Covariates	EI Estimation		EI2 Estimation	
	β^b	β^w	λ^b	λ^w
Z^b *Covariates*				
Constant	2.0713	0.2164	2.4320	0.2087
Ulivo competitiveness	−0.7416	0.1308	−0.0887	0.2045
Polo competitiveness	−0.4301	0.2776	−0.0729	0.2046
Ulivo–Polo competitiveness	−0.1598	0.2657	0.0819	0.0139
Northern district (0/1)	−0.0173	0.2219	−0.1612	0.0443
Northern League candidate (0/1)	0.2262	0.0449	0.1294	0.0570
Communist candidate (0/1)	0.3064	0.2955	−0.1266	0.0968
Neo-fascist candidate (0/1)	−0.0212	0.2267	−0.0793	0.0102
Ulivo incumbent (0/1)	−0.0692	0.2260	0.0662	0.2081
Polo incumbent (0/1)	−0.0807	0.1285	−0.0097	0.2037
Other incumbent (0/1)	−0.0906	0.0549	−0.1480	0.2933
Z^w *Covariates*				
Constant	−2.0557	0.1159	2.6610	0.0909
Ulivo competitiveness	−0.0125	0.0345	−0.0902	0.0924
Polo competitiveness	−0.0391	0.1278	−0.0880	0.0531
Ulivo–Polo competitiveness	0.0565	0.0555	0.0690	0.0572
Northern district (0/1)	0.0271	0.2232	−0.1809	0.0365
Northern League candidate (0/1)	−0.0481	0.0196	0.1854	0.0597
Communist candidate (0/1)	0.0989	0.0412	−0.1222	0.1663
Neo-fascist candidate (0/1)	0.0237	0.0583	−0.0096	0.0111
Ulivo incumbent (0/1)	0.0430	0.0460	0.0784	0.1000
Polo incumbent (0/1)	0.0129	0.1505	−0.0115	0.0060
Other incumbent (0/1)	0.0171	0.0465	−0.2050	0.0690
σ^b	−1.8847	0.1161	−2.3770	0.2609
σ^w	−2.9450	0.2701	−2.2720	0.2880
ρ	−0.4115	0.2900	2.0000	0.3930

Figure 14.4 displays the same set of graphic diagnostics for the second-stage estimation of λ_i^b and λ_i^w. Here the patterns are also quite well behaved, with the $X_i - T_i$ graph showing a clear linear pattern (here X_i is a plot of the *estimated* proportion of frustrated *Polo* voters staying with a cartel candidate, with estimates come from the first-stage EI procedure, against the proportion of excess cartel voters represented in EI notation as T_i). Similarly, the mean posterior contours from the tomography plot fall generally around the mode of the intersecting tomography lines. There is nothing in these diagnostics to lead us to suspect that EI would yield unreliable estimates.

DISCUSSION

Our estimation of vote splitting in Italy's mixed-member electoral system provides a clear example of how statistical techniques for ecological inference can be used in multiparty contexts to estimate individual-level parameters when only aggregate data is observed. By proceeding from a very general discussion to modeling the vote-splitting problem in a specific context, and then formulating a specific parameterization for estimating vote splitting, we have illustrated how such modeling is performed and what steps and choices are required to

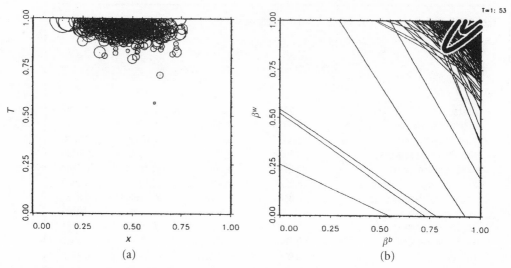

Figure 14.3. Graphs of fit for EI estimation of β^b, β^w.

yield the desired results. The Italian example is somewhat unusual in that its organization into electoral cartels makes possible a significant reduction of the parameter space, something required for the successful application of the EI method used here. But other systems also feature political or institutional arrangements reducing the number of unknowns in split-ticket voting problems to more tractable dimensions. Examples would be the reduction by political brokering to just two candidates of the top-three runoff system in the Hungarian electoral system (Benoit, 2001), or the reduction by institutional means to just two candidates in more restrictive runoff systems, as used in the French and numerous other presidential elections around the world.

More general applications of ecological inference to multiparty voter transition problems will depend on methodological advances in the estimation of $R \times C$ tables (where $R > 2$, $C > 2$). Interesting work on this problem has taken place recently on several fronts, including the use of entropy-maximizing methods (Johnston and Pattie, 2000), information-theoretic

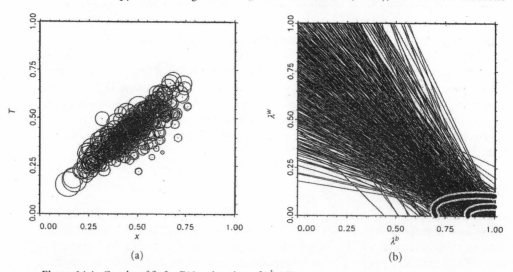

Figure 14.4. Graphs of fit for E12 estimation of λ^b, λ^w.

approaches (Judge, Miller, and Cho, this book, Chapter 7), and parametric extensions of EI using Markov-chain Monte Carlo methods (Rosen, Jiang, King, and Tanner, 2001). These methods, however, remain either difficult to implement practically (e.g., the MCMC method) or largely untested in well-known empirical contexts. Because each additional dimension places greater demands on the data, modeling issues such as distributional assumptions, priors, and covariates assume tremendous importance in the estimation of $R \times C$ ecological inference problems. Greater understanding and experience is needed in the application of $R \times C$ methods – both in a controlled context and in empirical settings where a large amount of contextual information is known in advance by the researcher – before genuine practical advances in split-ticket voting estimation in multiparty contexts can be made.

Our examination here of split-ticket voting in the 1996 Italian elections has also yielded some important substantive findings. First, we have demonstrated that the *Ulivo* cartel was more successful in maintaining voter loyalty and cartel discipline between the list ballot and the relatively recent institution of single-member district voting. Taking "frustrated" to mean those voters whose most-preferred party was by cartel agreement not allowed to field a single-member district candidate, we found that frustrated *Ulivo* supporters were much more likely to vote instrumentally than their frustrated *Polo* counterparts. Frustrated *Polo* supporters were also much more likely to vote for an *Ulivo* candidate than vice versa. These findings were not only firmly in accord with our substantive political knowledge of the Italian case, but also largely confirmed by the election result itself.

Finally, while we did not focus here on the results of the covariate estimations (see Appendix), we also found strong evidence that precinct-level voting varies systematically with a number of precinct-level variables. First, cartel-disloyal voting decreases when competition between cartels is more intense. Second, cartel-disloyal voting increases when competition within a cartel is more intense and when the cartel is more evenly fragmented. Finally, the presence of extreme left Communist candidates tended to drive voters away from the leftist *Ulivo* cartel and increase the level of disloyal voting. Finally, the presence of incumbent candidates, especially noncartel incumbents, tended to attract defectors from other cartels and to increase within-cartel loyalty. We have left a fuller discussion of these results for our future work, but the significance of simply having arrived at these estimates should not be understated.

APPENDIX

Table 14.6 shows the covariate parameter values in scale of estimation.

REFERENCES

Banducci, S., J. Karp, and J. Vowles. 1998. "Vote Splitting under MMP." In J. Vowles et al. (eds.), *Voters' Victory: New Zealand's First Election under Proportional Representation*. Auckland: Auckland University Press.

Beck, Paul Allen. 1997. *Party Politics in America*, 8th ed. New York: Longman.

Benoit, Kenneth. 2001. "Two Steps Forward, One Step Back: Electoral Coordination in the Hungarian Elections of 1998." Manuscript Trinity College.

Benoit, Kenneth, Daniela Giannetti, and Michael Laver. 2002. "'Instrumental' and 'Expressive' Voting in Mixed-Member Electoral Systems: Split-Ticket Voting in Italy." Presented at the Conference on Ecological Inference, Center for Basic Research in the Social Sciences, Harvard University, June 17–18, 2002.

Brennan, Geoffrey and Alan Hamlin. 2000. *Democratic Devices and Desires*. Cambridge: Cambridge University Press.

Brennan, Geoffrey and Loren Lomaski. 1993. *Democracy and Decision*. New York: Cambridge University Press.

Burden, Barry C. and David C. Kimball. 1998. "A New Approach to the Study of Ticket Splitting." *American Political Science Review*, 92: 533–544.

D'Alimonte, Roberto. 1998. Appendix: The Italian elections of 1996. *European Journal of Political Research*, 34: 171–174.

Fiorina, Morris P. 1996. *Divided Government*, 2nd ed. Needham Heights, MA: Allyn and Bacon.

Johnston, Ron and Charles Pattie. 1999. "Constituency Campaign Intensity and Split-Ticket Voting: New Zealand's First Election under MMP." *British Journal of Political Science*, 21: 95–108.

Johnston, Ron and Charles Pattie. 2000. "Ecological Inference and Entropy-Maximizing: An Alternative Procedure for Split-Ticket Voting." *Political Analysis*, 8, 4: 333–345.

King, Gary. 1997. *A Solution to the Ecological Inference Problem*. Princeton: Princeton University Press.

Laver, Michael. 1987. "The Logic of Plurality Voting in Multiparty Systems." In Manfred Holler. (ed.), *The Logic of Multiparty* Systems. Dordrecht: Kluwer Academic Publishers.

Moser, Robert G. 1999. "Electoral Systems and the Number of Parties in Postcommunist States." *World Politics*, 51: 359–384.

Reed, Stephen and Michael F. Thies. 2001. "The Causes of Electoral Reform in Japan." In Shugart and Wattenberg (2001b).

Rosen, Ori, Wenxin Jiang, Gary King, and Martin A. Tanner. 2001. "Bayesian and Frequentist Inference for Ecological Inference: the $R \times C$ Case." *Statistica Neerlandica*, 55, 2: 134–156.

Schuessler, Alexander A. 2000. *A Logic of Expressive Choice*. Princeton: Princeton University Press.

Shin, Michael. 2001. "The Politicization of Place in Italy." *Political Geography*, 20: 331–352.

Shin, Michael E., and John Agnew. 2001. "The Geography of Party Replacement in Italy, 1987–1996." *Political Geography*, 21: 221–242.

Shugart, Matthew S. and Martin P. Wattenberg. 2001a. "Mixed-member Electoral Systems: A Definition and Typology." In Shugart and Wattenberg (2001b).

Shugart, Matthew S. and Martin P. Wattenberg (eds.). 2001b. *Mixed-Member Electoral Systems: The Best of Both Worlds?* Oxford: Oxford University Press.

Strøm, Kaare, Ian Budge, and Michael Laver. 1994. "Constraints on Cabinet Formation in Parliamentary Democracies." *American Journal of Political Science*, 38, 2: 303–335.

Tsebelis, George. 1988. "Nested Games: The Cohesion of the French Coalitions." *British Journal of Political Science*, 18, April: 145–170.

15 A Structured Comparison of the Goodman Regression, the Truncated Normal, and the Binomial–Beta Hierarchical Methods for Ecological Inference*

Rogério Silva de Mattos and Álvaro Veiga

ABSTRACT

This chapter presents an extensive and structured Monte Carlo experiment to compare Goodman regression, King's truncated bivariate normal, and the binomial–beta hierarchical methods for ecological inference. Our purpose was to assess the predictive performance of these methods and the degree to which they match standard properties of statistical prediction theory. The experimental design was based on differences between King's and the binomial–beta hierarchical methods, which are major contributions to the recent EI literature. The results obtained indicate that Goodman regression is the weakest method, the BBH method has good predictive ability but is a biased point predictor, and King's method is the best among the three, doing well in predictive performance as well as in statistical properties. In the concluding section, the methodological relevance of using Monte Carlo experiments to evaluate and compare aggregation-consistent EI methods is highlighted.

15.1 INTRODUCTION

Although the ecological inference problem has challenged social scientists for more than a century, few solution techniques have been proposed in the literature (e.g., Cleave, 1992; Achen and Shively, 1995; King, 1997). Three of these techniques have received much attention in recent years, particularly in political science studies. One is an old approach based on a linear regression model and popularly known as Goodman regression, due to Goodman (1953, 1959). The other two, proposed recently, are a model based on the truncated bivariate normal (TBN) distribution, due to King (1997), and another based on the binomial–beta hierarchical (BBH) distribution, due to King, Rosen, and Tanner (1999; see also Rosen, Jiang, King, and Tanner, 2000). The last was the subject of a review and a proposed reformulation by Mattos and Veiga (2002).

In this chapter, we present an extensive and structured comparison of basic forms of these three EI methods by means of a Monte Carlo experiment. In the recent EI literature, King (1997), Cho (1998), Freedman, Klein, Ostland, and Roberts (1999), and King (2000) used Monte Carlo experiments to examine specific departures from the assumptions of King's TBN method on its estimation performance and as compared to Goodman regression. Anselin and Cho (2002), with similar objectives, developed a more extensive experiment to examine the consequences of spatial effects on predictive performance. Though having some intersections with the latter, our study is different from these others in the number and types of objectives we pursued.

* We acknowledge research support from the *Coordenação de Aperfeioamento de Pessoal de Nível Superior* (CAPES), an agency of the Brazilian Ministry of Education and Culture.

First, we were strictly concerned with *predictive* (not estimation) properties of the EI methods. Second, we studied these properties when the underlying model assumptions are true; this case was not explored enough in the literature, but is relevant to assessing whether EI predictors conform or not with standard properties of statistical prediction theory, namely unbiasedness and minimum mean squared error (in small and large samples). And third, we also explored the predictive performance (ability to fit the disaggregate data) of those methods, but in well-behaved, controlled situations that could inform us better about implications of certain features of the disaggregate data generation process, like the degrees of truncation and asymmetry and of correlation between the quantities of interest. We included the examination of consequences of model construction, such as the incorporation or not of precincts' population sizes and the type of model characteristic used as the vehicle of inference – features that could well produce differences in predictive performance.

As a consequence of these concerns and objectives, our experiment was much more extensive and detailed structured than those of other studies. The results we achieved may be useful to methodologists and practitioners because the experiment has pointed, with much supporting evidence, to strengths, weaknesses, and some new features of the EI methods considered. For instance, King, Rosen, and Tanner (1999; hereafter KRT) argued that the BBH method is generally superior to King's TBN method, but we found that the TBN method is generally better for making point predictions. In addition, under mild degrees of truncation or asymmetry in the disaggregate data, the BBH method displays predictive bias. Our research also led us to consider the role of Monte Carlo experiments for EI methodology in a broader sense, especially its relevance in the evaluation and comparison of EI methods possessing the aggregation consistency property.

In order to run the comparison, we had to resort to a faster device, developed by Mattos and Veiga (2002), to implement the BBH method. Whereas KRT used computer-intensive algorithms of the Markov chain Monte Carlo class that generally take hours to run even on a single data set, the alternative device used in this paper is an instance of the ECM algorithm proposed by Meng and Rubin (1993), which takes minutes of computer time with most data sets. It was of major importance to reduce the computer burden of the Monte Carlo experiment with the inclusion of the BBH method (and three variants of it), once the EI methods had to be applied to nearly 1800 simulated data sets each.

For a proper presentation of our study and its results, we have organized the chapter as follows. We introduce notation and features of the EI problem in Section 15.2. This provides basic elements for the understanding of key aspects of the methods briefly reviewed in the subsequent sections. Goodman regression is presented in Section 15.3, King's TBN method in Section 15.4, and the BBH method in Section 15.5. The type of Monte Carlo experiment we used is considered in Section 15.6. The setting up of the experiment is presented in Section 15.7, and the results of the experiment are graphically presented and discussed in Section 15.8. Concluding comments are presented in Section 15.9. Three appendices present additional details of the experiment design.

15.2 NOTATION AND PROBLEM FEATURES

In this section, we present some notation and basic concepts used throughout the chapter. In the left part of Table 15.1, the variables N_{B_i} and N_{W_i} represent the *unobservable disaggregate frequencies*, which might be, for instance, the numbers of black and white people, respectively, who turn out to vote in the ith sampling unit or precinct. Likewise, the variables N_{T_i},

Table 15.1 Alternative representations of the EI problem

	Frequencies			Proportions		
	Vote	No vote	Total	Vote	No vote	Total
Blacks	N_{B_i}	$n_{X_i} - N_{B_i}$	n_{X_i}	B_i	$1 - B_i$	X_i
Whites	N_{W_i}	$n_i - n_{X_i} - N_{W_i}$	$n_i - n_{X_i}$	W_i	$1 - W_i$	$1 - X_i$
Total	N_{T_i}	$n_i - n_{T_i}$	n_i	T_i	$1 - T_i$	1

n_{X_i}, and n_i represent the *observable aggregate frequencies*,[1] and can be seen as the numbers of people who turn out to vote, who are black, and who are of voting age, respectively, in the ith precinct. Subscript i ranges from 1 to P, where P is the number of precincts or sampling units. The goal of EI consists in predicting values for N_{B_i} and N_{W_i} given knowledge of the values of N_{T_i}, n_{X_i}, and n_i, for $i = 1, \ldots, P$.

The right part of Table 15.1 displays the EI problem in an alternative fashion, with variables represented as proportions and defined as

$$x_i = n_{X_i}/n_i, \tag{15.1}$$

$$T_i = N_{T_i}/n_i, \tag{15.2}$$

$$B_i = N_{B_i}/n_{X_i}, \tag{15.3}$$

$$W_i = N_{W_i}/(n_i - n_{X_i}). \tag{15.4}$$

The EI problem[2] in this case consists in predicting values of B_i and W_i given knowledge of T_i and x_i, for $i = 1, \ldots, P$. The use of proportions instead of frequencies to represent variables in the EI problem and models has been the most common approach followed in the EI literature (see Achen and Shively, 1995; King, 1997). Though both ways of representing the EI problem are considered in this chapter, only the representation in proportions was, ultimately, used in the Monte Carlo experiment.

The use of the term "prediction" we have made above is not casual, because we assume that the target of EI is to recover unobserved values of disaggregate response variables. Some statistically based EI methods proposed in the literature regard the EI problem as an estimation one, as, for instance, do the Goodman regression and the switching regression method of Cho (2001). In these methods, the contents of tables' cells are regarded as constant parameters, either for the whole set of P tables or for some subgroups of them, and the problem of inference is treated as an estimation problem. Instead, we follow in this chapter the perspective that the contents of tables' cells are *unobservable realizations of some sort of random process*, and our goal is to infer the values of these realizations. From a statistical perspective, the appropriate way to follow in such cases is to regard the EI problem as one of prediction.[3]

---

[1] Generally, throughout this chapter, uppercase symbols represent random variables and lowercase symbols observed or known values. Note that the variables n_{X_i} and n_i are written in lowercase because of an assumption usually adopted in statistical EI methods that the row totals are given.

[2] For a direct association with the notation presented in the Introduction to this book, set $B_i = \beta_i^b$ and $W_i = \beta_i^w$.

[3] In statistics, *prediction* refers to guessing the value of a random response variable, and *estimation* refers to guessing the value of a parameter (a fixed constant) of a probability model. An instructive discussion on the distinction between these concepts in classical statistics is available in Spanos (1986: Chapters 12, 14). For the

The EI problem also displays some deterministic information embedded in what is known as the *accounting identity*. For the variables in frequencies of Table 15.1, this identity consists of

$$N_{T_i} = N_{B_i} + N_{W_i}, \tag{15.5}$$

and for the variables in proportions,

$$T_i = B_i x_i + W_i (1 - x_i). \tag{15.6}$$

Whatever our choice of representing the accounting identity, its importance for EI modeling is twofold: First, if predictions for the disaggregate variables generated with a particular EI model respect the accounting identity, then the aggregation of those predictions using Equation 15.5 or 15.6 will necessarily fit the observed values for the aggregate, left hand variables (n_{T_i} or t_i). We call this property *aggregation consistency* and consider it, in principle, as desirable.[4] Second, the accounting identity places lower and upper bounds on the true values taken by N_{B_i} and N_{W_i}, or by B_i and W_i, once the aggregate data have been observed, a feature pointed out first by Duncan and Davis (1953). For instance, it means that $B_i \in [\ell_i^b, u_i^b] \subseteq [0, 1]$ and $W_i \in [\ell_i^w, u_i^w] \subseteq [0, 1]$, where ℓ_i^b, u_i^b, ℓ_i^w, and u_i^w are the Duncan–Davis bounds (for a proof, see King, 1997: 301–303).

Note that if a prediction of the pair (B_i, W_i) produced with a particular EI predictor does not satisfy the accounting identity, then this prediction will not display aggregation consistency. However, it may or may not respect the admissible intervals (implied by the Duncan–Davis bounds). In this case, there are three possibilities:

a. the two intervals are respected;
b. only one interval is respected; or
c. no interval is respected.

Figure 15.1 illustrates the aggregation consistency property and these three possibilities that depart from it. The figure shows, in the plane $B_i \times W_i$, the *unconditional* sample space for the pair (B_i, W_i) represented by the unit square $[0, 1] \times [0, 1]$, and the *conditional* (after a pair (t_i, x_i) is observed) sample space for (B_i, W_i) represented by the negatively sloped line. This line is determined by the accounting identity in Equation 15.6; just rewrite that expression as

$$W_i = \frac{t_i}{1 - x_i} - \frac{x_i}{1 - x_i} B_i \tag{15.7}$$

with T_i replaced by the observed t_i. The projection of the line on the horizontal axis gives $[\ell_i^b, u_i^b]$, and on the vertical axis $[\ell_i^w, u_i^w]$. The true realized pair (b_i, w_i) of disaggregate

case of Bayesian statistics, see, for instance, Gelman, Carlin, Stern, and Rubin (1995: 8–9). Regarding the EI literature, see McCue (2001) for a view that King's (1997) EI method is essentially an application of statistical prediction theory, and Herron and Shotts (2003) for a discussion of the inconsistencies of using King's TBN method in a two-stage EI procedure. The latter authors, however, refer in general to EI outcomes as "estimates" when in a strict sense the word should be "predictions." The distinction between prediction and estimation has potential implications little explored in the recent EI literature, a major one being the fact that only predictive distributions guarantee that EI outcomes will respect the accounting identity and the Duncan–Davis bounds (see McCue, 2001: 107; Mattos and Veiga, 2002). Also, there may be no identification problem in EI when the prediction perspective is taken, so that $2P$ unknowns can be *predicted* from a model *estimated* with only P knowns.

[4] Observe that a prediction which does not satisfy the aggregation consistency property will not satisfy the accounting identity, because these two properties imply one another.

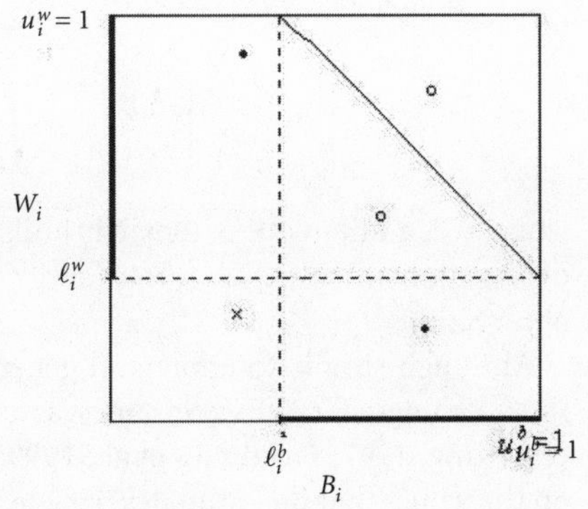

Figure 15.1. Accounting identity and properties of EI predictions.

variables lies somewhere on the line, and predictions that also lie on this line respect the accounting identity. As a consequence, such predictions will display aggregation consistency and respect both intervals. Predictions not lying on the line are inconsistent in aggregation, and the figure illustrates the three situations considered before:

a. predictions like the circles respect both admissible intervals, because they lie somewhere on the inner square $[\ell_i^b, u_i^b] \times [\ell_i^w, u_i^w]$;
b. predictions like the dark points respect only one interval; and
c. predictions like the $\times$ do not respect any interval.

In sum, a desirable property of an EI predictor is that it respects the accounting identity, because the predictions it generates will necessarily display aggregation consistency and respect both admissible intervals. A second best situation would be that the predictions at least respect both intervals, as in case a considered before.[5] As we shall see, among the EI predictors considered here, only the ones derived from King's TBN method and from Mattos and Veigas's version of the BBH method respect the accounting identity.[6]

15.3 GOODMAN REGRESSION

Goodman's (1953, 1959) approach is quite simple: Starting from the accounting identity 15.6, assume that all disaggregate data proportions are fixed across different tables or observations – say, that $B_i = \mu_B$ and $W_i = \mu_W$, where μ_B and μ_W are constants through $i = 1, \ldots, P$. Naturally, the differences between the left and right hand sides of Equation 15.6 should result from purely random effects ε_i, so that we may write Goodman's model as

$$T_i = \mu_B x_i + \mu_W(1 - x_i) + \varepsilon_i. \tag{15.8}$$

This expression is a linear regression model without a constant and with linear coefficients μ_B and μ_W, which, for a given sample of aggregate observations, may be estimated by the method of ordinary least squares. The EI predictions in these cases are generated according

---

[5] In this second best situation, a residual analysis could be possible and model adequacy tests could be developed. See the test statistic proposed by Cho (2001: 250–253). However, the price one pays in using models that allow residuals is that they are not guaranteed to respect the bounds (see Section 15.8.3).

[6] Contrary to what is stated by KRT (p. 64), the EI predictor these authors derived from their version of the BHH model may not satisfy the bounds, because it does not respect the accounting identity. See Section 15.6.2 below, and Mattos and Veiga (2002).

to

$$\begin{bmatrix} \hat{b}_i(t) \\ \hat{w}_i(t) \end{bmatrix} = \begin{bmatrix} \hat{\mu}_B(t) \\ \hat{\mu}_W(t) \end{bmatrix} = (X'X)^{-1} X't, \tag{15.9}$$

where X is a suitable $P \times 2$ matrix built from the information on the (fixed) rows' aggregate observations $x' = [x_1, \ldots, x_P]$, and $t' = [t_1, \ldots, t_P]$ is the vector of columns' aggregate observations.

Although simple to apply and generalize, this EI method is known to have important shortcomings: First, its constancy assumption is barely supported by empirical evidence (e.g. King, 1997; Freedman et al., 1999; Cho, 1998, 2001). Second, no restriction is placed on the values that the estimates $\hat{\mu}_B$ and $\hat{\mu}_W$ may take, what allows them to lie outside of the bounds and to take values that are negative or above 100%. This feature naturally results from the fact that the accounting identity is not respected (for every table).

15.4 KING'S TBN METHOD

King's (1997) EI method was designed to overcome the limitations just mentioned of the Goodman regression. We make here just a short outline of it for the purposes of this chapter. For a full description, see King (1997).

The first feature of King's method is the probability model used to describe the disaggregate DGP. The pair (B_i, W_i) of disaggregate data proportions of Table 15.1 is regarded as a bivariate random vector following a truncated bivariate normal (TBN) distribution, as follows:

$$(B_i, W_i | x_i) \sim \text{TBN}_A(\check{\psi}), \tag{15.10}$$

where $A = [0, 1] \times [0, 1]$ is the domain of truncation and support of the distribution. The vector $\check{\psi}' = [\check{\mu}_B, \check{\mu}_W, \check{\sigma}_B^2, \check{\sigma}_W^2, \check{\rho}]$ contains[7] the parameters (means, variances, and correlation coefficient) of the original, untruncated bivariate normal distribution. Note that x_i ($i = 1, \ldots, P$) is taken as fixed or given (and for simplicity, from now on we follow King, 1997, and omit the conditioning on this variable). It is assumed in Equation 15.10 that (B_i, W_i) is independent of (uncorrelated with) the x_i variable – what is usually called the assumption of *no aggregation bias*.

The second feature of the method is the strict adoption of the accounting identity in Equation 15.6. King took it as an integral part of his model's structure, so that this identity establishes a link between the disaggregate and the aggregate DGPs. Together with an additional assumption of *spatial independence* between the observations, this enabled King to derive the distribution of T_i, say $p(t_i | \check{\psi})$, and the likelihood function based on the aggregate data:

$$L(\check{\psi}) = p(t | \check{\psi}) = \prod_{i=1}^{P} p(t_i | \check{\psi}), \tag{15.11}$$

where t is a vector of observed aggregate proportions, as defined before.

King was also enabled to derive the predictive distributions $p(b_i | t_i, \check{\psi})$ and $p(w_i | t_i, \check{\psi})$, each being a univariate, doubly truncated normal with support in $[\ell_i^b, u_i^b]$ and $[\ell_i^w, u_i^w]$, respectively (King, 1997: Appendix C). We call these *classical predictive distributions*, because,

---

[7] For association with the notation in the Introduction to this book, set $\check{\mu}_B = \mathfrak{B}^b$ and $\check{\mu}_W = \mathfrak{B}^w$.

from a classical statistics perspective, the EI predictions derived with King's TBN method consist of the means of those two distributions with the parameters $\check{\psi}$ evaluated at their maximum likelihood values $\overset{\circ}{\psi}$, as follows:

$$\hat{b}_i(t) = E(B_i | T_i = t_i; \overset{\circ}{\psi}) = \int_{L_i^b}^{U_i^b} b_i \, p(b_i | t_i; \overset{\circ}{\psi}) \, db_i, \qquad (15.12)$$

$$\hat{w}_i(t) = E(W_i | T_i = t_i; \overset{\circ}{\psi}) = \int_{L_i^w}^{U_i^w} w_i \, p(w_i | t_i; \overset{\circ}{\psi}) \, dw_i$$

$$= \frac{t_i}{1 - x_i} - \frac{x_i}{1 - x_i} b_i(t). \qquad (15.13)$$

Note that $\hat{b}_i(\ )$ and $\hat{w}_i(\ )$ are written as functions of the vector t because $\overset{\circ}{\psi} = \overset{\circ}{\psi}(t)$.

Under a Bayesian statistics perspective, a prior distribution $p(\check{\psi})$ for the parameters can be used and the predictive distributions in Equations 15.12 and 15.13 have to be replaced by $p(b_i | t)$ and $p(w_i | t)$, respectively. We call the latter *Bayesian predictive distributions*, and they are obtained by averaging the classical ones over the parameter space to allow for the uncertainty in parameter values. The weighting function used in this averaging is the posterior function $p(\check{\psi} | t) \propto p(\check{\psi}) L(\check{\psi})$.

Though considering these two possibilities of using his model, King at the end adopted a Bayesian approach, which is implemented in his and Benoit's programs EI and EzI (Benoit and King, 1996, 1998). Note that, since King (1997) took the accounting identity as an integral of his EI model, the EI predictions it generates display aggregation consistency and respect the Duncan–Davis bounds, as is clear from Equations 15.12 and 15.13.

15.5 THE BINOMIAL–BETA HIERARCHICAL METHOD

KRT introduced another EI method, based on compounding the binomial and the beta probability distributions into a Bayesian, hierarchical structure. They termed it the binomial–beta hierarchical model for EI, and claimed it is superior to King's TBN method, being capable of recovering a wider spectrum of disaggregate data. Though the reason for this presented by the authors had to do with the flexibility of the BBH model to represent *within precinct multimodality* present in the subjective uncertainty of the analyst, they also used the method to produce point and interval predictions of the disaggregate data via the mean of the marginal posteriors for the binomial probabilities (KRT: 75–77, 84–86).

More recently, Mattos and Veiga (2002) developed a slightly different version of this model that is amenable to a substantially faster implementation, although limited to producing only point and interval predictions. In Section 15.5.1 we briefly describe their version, which is the one we used in the Monte Carlo experiment, and in Section 15.5.2 we highlight its major differences from KRT's version.

15.5.1 Mattos and Veiga's Version

Mattos and Veiga's (2002) version of the BBH method features a hierarchical probability model for the disaggregate DGP, coupled with the accounting identity 15.5.[8] In the first

---

[8] Thus, the model was structured as King (1997) did in the development of the TBN model.

hierarchical stage, the disaggregate data variables N_{B_i} and N_{W_i} at the ith precinct are assumed to follow independent binomial distributions with known counts n_i and n_{X_i}, and binomial probabilities β_i and ω_i. In view of the accounting identity in Equation 15.5, this means that the aggregate data variable follows an *aggregate binomial distribution*. In the second stage, the binomial probabilities β_i and ω_i are assumed to be sampled from beta distributions with parameters (c_b, d_b) and (c_w, d_w), respectively, and these parameters are taken to be constant across all precincts. In the third and last stage, the beta parameters are assumed to follow noninformative priors. The formal description of the BBH model in this case is

$$N_{B_i}|\beta_i \sim \text{Bin}(n_{X_i}, \beta_i), \tag{15.14}$$

$$N_{W_i}|\omega_i \sim \text{Bin}(n_i - n_{X_i}, \omega_i), \tag{15.15}$$

$$N_{T_i}|\beta_i, \omega_i \sim \text{ABin}(n_{X_i}, n_i, \beta_i, \omega_i), \tag{15.16}$$

$$\beta_i|c_b, d_b \sim \text{Beta}(c_b, d_b), \tag{15.17}$$

$$\omega_i|c_w, d_w \sim \text{Beta}(c_w, d_w), \tag{15.18}$$

$$c_b \sim \text{n.i.p.d.}, \tag{15.19}$$

$$d_b \sim \text{n.i.p.d.}, \tag{15.20}$$

$$c_w \sim \text{n.i.p.d.}, \tag{15.21}$$

$$d_w \sim \text{n.i.p.d.} \tag{15.22}$$

for $i = 1, \ldots, P$. Abin(,) in Equation 15.16 stands for the *aggregate binomial distribution*,[9] and n.i.p.d. for the *non informative prior distribution*.[10]

The vector of quantities of interest is given by $\alpha' = [\beta', \omega', h']$, where $\beta' = [\beta_1, \ldots, \beta_P]$, $\omega' = [\omega_1, \ldots, \omega_P]$, and $h' = [c_b, d_b, c_w, d_w]$. Note that the size of the parameter vector α is dependent on the number of observations, as it has $2P + 4$ elements, in contrast with the two EI methods presented before. By assuming independence between sampling units, say, that (N_{B_i}, N_{W_i}) is independent of (N_{B_j}, N_{W_j}), which then implies N_{T_i} is independent of N_{T_j} for $i \neq j$, we can build the aggregate posterior P_A as

$$P_A(\alpha|n_T) \propto \prod_{i=1}^{P} \text{Abin}(n_{T_i}|n_{x_i}, n_i, \beta_i, \omega_i)\text{Beta}(\beta_i|c_b, d_b)\text{Beta}(\omega_i|c_w, d_w). \tag{15.23}$$

In order to implement the full Bayesian method for making inferences at precinct level, we have to determine from Equation 15.23 the marginal bivariate posteriors $p(\beta_i, \omega_i|n_T)$, $i = 1, \ldots, P$, and then the marginal predictive posteriors:

$$p(n_{B_i}|n_T) = \int_0^1 \int_0^1 p(n_{B_i}|n_{T_i}, \beta_i, \omega_i) p(\beta_i, \omega_i|n_T) \, d\beta_i, \, d\omega_i, \tag{15.24}$$

$$p(n_{W_i}|n_T) = \int_0^1 \int_0^1 p(n_{W_i}|n_{T_i}, \beta_i, \omega_i) p(\beta_i, \omega_i|n_T) \, d\beta_i, \, d\omega_i, \tag{15.25}$$

---

[9] The aggregate binomial distribution is obtained from a convolution of independent binomial distributions. See Chapter 1 of this book.

[10] KRT used exponential distributions with high means as priors. In the simulation experiment that we present in this chapter, we used uniform priors defined in [0, 10].

where $n'_T = [n_{T_1}, \ldots, n_{T_P}]$ is the vector of observed aggregate data. In the kernel of the integrands in Equations 15.24 and 15.25, $p(n_{B_i}|n_{T_i}, \beta_i, \omega_i)$ and $p(n_{W_i}|n_{T_i}, \beta_i, \omega_i)$ are each a noncentral hypergeometric density. These predictive posteriors are expected to reflect our uncertainty with regard to the realized but unobserved values of the disaggregate variables N_{B_i} and N_{W_i}.

We can make point predictions of the disaggregate frequencies by computing

$$\hat{n}_{B_i}(n_T) = E(N_{B_i}|N_T = n_T)$$

$$= \sum_{n_{B_i}=n_{B_i}^L}^{n_{B_i}^U} n_{B_i}\, p(n_{B_i}|n_T), \tag{15.26}$$

$$\hat{n}_{W_i}(n_T) = E(N_{W_i}|N_T = n_T)$$

$$= \sum_{n_{W_i}=n_{W_i}^L}^{n_{W_i}^U} n_{W_i}\, p(n_{W_i}|n_T)$$

$$= n_{T_i} - \hat{n}_{B_i}(n_T). \tag{15.27}$$

In the Bayesian setting, these predictions minimize the quadratic loss function. Mattos and Veiga (2002) developed a fast device to implement this method, based on the ECM algorithm (Meng and Rubin, 1993). A limitation of this approach is that it produces only point and interval predictions. We can use the same formulas 15.26 and 15.27 to make predictions for the disaggregate data in proportions, as follows:

$$\hat{b}_i(t) = \frac{\hat{n}_{B_i}(n \odot t)}{n_i}, \tag{15.28}$$

$$\hat{w}_i(t) = \frac{\hat{n}_{W_i}(n \odot t)}{n_i}, \tag{15.29}$$

where $n' = [n_1, \ldots, n_P]$ is the vector of population sizes in the sample of precincts. Here the symbol $\odot$ stands for the elementwise product, such that $n \odot t = n_T$.

Note that this version of the BBH model respects the accounting identity because the derivation of the distribution of the aggregate frequency (see Equation 15.16) made implicit use of Equation 15.5. As a consequence, predictions generated according to Equations 15.28 and 15.29 display aggregation consistency and respect the bounds.

15.5.2 KRT's Version

Both Mattos and Veiga's (2002) and KRT's versions of the BBH model are developed hierarchically in three stages. The central difference between them is in the first stage, in that under KRT's formulation the disaggregate DGP is not considered. The authors model the aggregate DGP directly by assuming N_{T_i} follows a binomial distribution with a given count n_i and an "aggregate" binomial probability $\beta_i x_i + \omega_i(1 - x_i)$. That is to say, under KRT's formulation, we have

$$N_{T_i}|\beta_i, \omega_i \sim \text{Bin}(n_i, \beta_i x_i + \omega_i(1 - x_i)) \tag{15.30}$$

in place of Equations 15.14, 15.15, and 15.16 to represent the first stage of the BBH model.

The only instances in which the binomial distribution in Equation 15.30 is consistent with Mattos and Veiga's assumptions for the disaggregate DGP in Equations 15.14 and 15.15 are when $\beta_i = \omega_i$ or when each disaggregate binomial distribution has probability parameter equal to $\beta_i x_i + \omega_i(1 - x_i)$. In more general settings, the sum $N_{T_i} = N_{B_i} + N_{W_i}$ necessarily follows an aggregate binomial distribution (see Mattos and Veiga, 2002).

Another difference is that, instead of using the predictive posteriors in Equations 15.24 and 15.25, KRT undertook the inferences at precinct level using the marginal posteriors for the binomial probabilities: $p(\beta_i|n_T)$ and $p(\omega_i|n_T)$. The authors used these distributions in full to summarize the uncertainty about the disaggregate data, and obtained them from the joint posterior for the vector α, which we denote here as P_A^*. By considering $p(h) \propto$ constant, this posterior is written

$$P_A^*(\alpha|n_T) \propto \prod_{i=1}^{P} \mathrm{Bin}(n_{T_i}|n_i, \beta_i x_i + \omega_i(1 - x_i))\mathrm{Beta}(\beta_i|c_b, d_b)\mathrm{Beta}(\omega_i|c_w, d_w). \quad (15.31)$$

The determination of $p(\beta_i|n_T)$ and $p(\omega_i|n_T)$ involves complex, multidimensional integrations of Equation 15.31. KRT used powerful Markov chain Monte Carlo algorithms to simulate those marginal posteriors in full. Because of the computer-intensive nature of those algorithms, we used Mattos and Veiga's faster approach to the BBH model to run the experiment described in the next sections.

As a consequence of using the binomial probabilities as the vehicle of inference, this approach fails to respect the accounting identity (see Mattos and Veiga, 2002, for a detailed discussion on this issue). Thus, KRT's version of the BBH model for EI will not in general display aggregation consistency and may not respect the Duncan–Davis bounds.

15.6 MONTE CARLO EXPERIMENTS

The purpose of this chapter is to present a comparison of the three EI methods described earlier by means of a Monte Carlo simulation experiment. The Monte Carlo method is widely used, though in different modalities, for the study of system behavior in a number of research areas (e.g., Naylor, Balintfy, Burdick, and Chu, 1966; Watson and Blackstone, 1989). In statistics, Monte Carlo simulations serve diverse purposes, mostly the approximation of probability distributions and the computation of integrals (expectations). The technique is useful when it is not possible to obtain in analytic form the probability distributions or the functions to be integrated. Its usefulness here also comes from the analytical intractability displayed by the distributions of estimators and predictors, which prevents the analytical study of their statistical properties in small samples and, in certain cases, also in large samples when asymptotic results are not available.

A statistical Monte Carlo experiment consists in general of two stages. In the first, a large number of data sequences, now interpreted as samples of observations, are randomly generated from the probability distribution that characterizes the data generation process, under predetermined assumptions for its parameter values. In the second, the samples are analyzed with the estimation or prediction method being studied, producing numerical estimates or predictions based on each sample, and also, when desired, performance statistics. The latter might be, for instance, the coverage of prediction errors within a particular interval.

If the number of simulated samples is sufficiently large, it is possible to approximate the full probability distributions of the estimators or predictors, and of the statistics of interest, via their empirical distribution function. In certain contexts, an alternative approach which is less demanding on the number of simulated samples can be used, for instance when we are interested only in first and second moments of an estimator or predictor distribution, not in its overall shape. It was an experiment of the latter kind that we developed to compare the EI methods based on the TBN and the BBH distributions. This choice of ours was important in reducing the computer burden imposed by the detailed nature of the experimental design, while allowing us to assess conformity with the standard statistical properties of EI predictors.

We remark that by performing a Monte Carlo experiment we are taking each EI method as a predictor – say, as a rule of predictive inference in the context of repeated sampling. This means that we consider every $\hat{b}_i(T)$ and $\hat{w}_i(T)$ described earlier (see Equations 15.9, 15.12, 15.13, 15.28, and 15.29) as functions of a random (independent[11]) sample $T' = [T_1, \ldots, T_P]$. Thus, the experiment allowed us to explore properties, typical of classical statistics, of the sampling distributions of the predictors considered, even though these predictors were developed under a Bayesian approach. Though we are aware that Bayesian statisticians may contest this way of proceeding as inconsistent with Bayesian inference (see, for instance, O'Hagan, 1994: 82–83), we regard it as a valid, and often necessary, effort to improve our understanding of operating characteristics that underlie EI methods.

Finally, it is well known that Monte Carlo experiments do not replace the analytical study of the distributions and properties of estimators and predictors. When possible, the analytical study can determine precisely the conditions under which those properties are valid and do so at the highest level of generality, that is, considering the whole parameter space. The Monte Carlo study is restricted to pointlike elements of this space and, by evaluating the behavior of estimators and predictors under particular conditions, has more value in providing clues for methodological improvements of them. This restriction forms the basis for the careful design effort required for us to come to substantive conclusions.

15.7 EXPERIMENTAL DESIGN

We structured the Monte Carlo experiment motivated in large part by an interest in improving our understanding of operating features that characterize the TBN and BBH methods, as these are major contributions made in the recent EI literature. We also included in the comparison the Goodman regression, because it has often been taken as a benchmark method in other EI studies based on Monte Carlo experiments (Cho, 1998; Freedman et al., 1999; Anselin and Cho, 2002).

Our development of the experiment was based on the following factors that seem relevant for the evaluation and comparison of the recent EI methods:

a. intrinsic differences between the TBN and the BBH models;
b. potential (standardized) situations of the EI problem.

In this section and the appendices, we detail how we used these factors to design the experiment. Note that we have not used features or assumptions of the Goodman regression to generate or simulate the data used in the experiment. We only assessed this EI method's performance in situations assumed by the recent models.

15.7.1 Differences between the EI models

The TBN and the BBH models are alternative probabilistic models used to describe the disaggregate DGP in EI problems. Though designed to characterize the same type of phenomenon, they display substantive differences that we summarize in Table 15.2.

---

[11] A *random sample* is defined in classical statistics as a set or vector of i.i.d. random variables, and an *independent sample* as a set or vector of independent random variables which are not identically distributed (see, for instance, Spanos, 1986: 216–217). The sample $T' = [T_1, \ldots, T_P]$ lies in the second category according to King's TBN model and both versions of the BBH model, by construction.

Table 15.2 Main differences between the TBN and the BBH models

TBN	BBH
1. The model for the disaggregate DGP is a TBN distribution.	1. The model for the disaggregate DGP is a bivariate BBH distribution.
2. Response variables are proportions.	2. Response variables are frequencies.
3. Admits correlation in the disaggregate DGP.	3. Does not admit correlation in the disaggregate DGP.
4. Observations are weighted in an equal fashion.	4. Observations are weighted differently (but can be given equal weights by means of a data normalization procedure).
5. Unique predictor.	5. Two predictors. • posterior mode of the binomial probabilities; • mean of the predictive posterior density.

From the first three differences, we determined how the various samples or data sequences were simulated. Because of difference 1, the experiment was undertaken in two parts: In the first, the EI methods were compared using samples simulated from a TBN distribution, and in the second the samples were simulated from a bivariate BBH distribution. Our purpose was to evaluate the relative performance of each EI method on data sets generated from different distributions, of which one is the distribution assumed by the corresponding method.[12]

Difference 2 is relevant to technical problems in the comparison of the methods. Since the TBN model assumes the data are proportions, in principle the methods based on them could not be used to analyze frequency data simulated in the second part of the experiment. In the same way, the methods based on the BBH model could not be used to analyze proportion data simulated in the first part of the experiment. Therefore, conversions between frequencies and proportions had to be used, and the technical details are explained in Appendices 1 and 2.

From difference 3, it follows that the TBN model allows the disaggregate proportions B_i and W_i to be correlated. Mattos and Veiga's version of the BBH model, in contrast, does not admit correlation between the corresponding disaggregate variables N_{B_i} and N_{W_i} because they are assumed independent in the disaggregate DGP.

From difference 4, the BBH model admits different weights for the observations in the posterior function 15.29. These weights are determined nonlinearly by the variable n_i, the size of the ith sampling unit. Thus, predictors based on the BBH model use the available information with greater efficiency. On the other hand, it is easy to make both models have the same status using a data normalization procedure that gives all observations the same weight. It is possible then to estimate the BBH model with varying or constant weights across observations, obtaining two different predictors. Both approaches were considered in the experiment for the evaluation of the BBH model, although the more appropriate one, from a rigorous point of view, is the one with varying weights.[13]

In a similar way, difference 5 points to additional alternative ways of using the BBH model, namely, the possibility of working with either of two predictors:

a. the posterior mode for the binomial probabilities, or
b. the mean of the predictive distribution for the disaggregate frequencies.

---

[12] With the exception of the Goodman regression.
[13] This twofold choice in using the BBH model is possible only when the variables of interest of the EI problem are represented as proportions. In the case where these variables are represented as frequencies (as on the left side of Table 15.1), the normalization procedure alters the scale of predictions vis-à-vis the scale of the observed frequencies, inducing artificially large prediction errors.

These two predictors[14] were also considered in the experiment, though only the predictive mean in predictor b is appropriate: first, because it is consistent with the view of the EI problem as a prediction problem, and second, because it respects the accounting identity and thus generates predictions with aggregation consistency and which stay within the admissible intervals for the cells values. That does not happen with predictor a, based on the posterior mode, as discussed before in Section 15.6.

15.7.2 Methods Compared

According to the discussion made at the end of the previous subsection, the BBH model can be used or implemented in four ways:

a. estimation with *raw* data and prediction with the posterior *mode* for the binomial probabilities;
b. estimation with *raw* data and prediction with the *mean* of the predictive distribution for the frequencies;
c. estimation with *normalized* data and prediction with the posterior *mode* for the binomial probabilities;
d. estimation with *normalized* data and prediction with the *mean* of the predictive distribution for the frequencies;

Raw data mean different weights (n_i), while normalized data mean equal weights given to each observation in the likelihood or posterior function. The procedure for rescaling or normalizing the data used in versions c and d is explained in Appendix 1. In a rigorous sense, only procedure b above, which corresponds to Mattos and Veiga's version of the BBH method, is the correct one, and the others should be viewed as variants developed for exploratory purposes only. In sum, the six alternative EI methods below were compared within the experiment:

1. Goodman regression;
2. TBN (King's method);
3. BBHa (version a), or Mattos and Veiga's method;
4. BBHb (version b);
5. BBHc (version c);
6. BBHd (version d).

15.7.3 Potential Situations

We tried to evaluate and compare the six EI methods above in different situations for the EI problem. Each situation considered reflects a particular form of realization of the underlying disaggregate DGP. In the first part of the experiment, the situations were created so that the disaggregate DGP displayed:

1. different degrees of truncation;
2. different degrees of prior correlation;
3. different sample sizes.

For each of these features, we considered three possibilities as presented in Table 15.3.

---

[14] According to Bayesian estimation theory, the posterior *mode* in version a minimizes the expected absolute loss function, while the predictive posterior *mean* in version b minimizes the expected quadratic loss. The latter predictor is directly comparable with the predictor of King's TBN model, which uses the mean of the predictive posterior, and with the predictor of KRT's version of the BBH model, which uses the posterior mean. In the Monte Carlo experiment, we chose to include also the posterior mode in version a because it is a by-product

Table 15.3 Alternative situations considered for simulation

	P		
Type of correlation	Truncation: weak	Intermediate	Strong
Negative	20, 50, 100	20, 50, 100	20, 50, 100
Null	20, 50, 100	20, 50, 100	20, 50, 100
Positive	20, 50, 100	20, 50, 100	20, 50, 100

Each cell in Table 15.3 characterizes a *situation*: a combination of correlation and truncation. We simulated 150 samples per situation, grouped according to three sample sizes: 50 samples with $P = 20$ observations; 50 samples with $P = 50$ observations, and 50 samples with $P = 100$ observations. This represents nine data sets (one per situation) with 150 samples each, for a total of $9 \times 150 = 1,350$ samples simulated from a TBN distribution.

In the second part of the experiment, a similar procedure was adopted to simulate samples from the BBH distribution. However, since this distribution assumes independence between the disaggregate simulated variables, only the line corresponding to the null correlation in Table 15.2 was considered. In place of the idea of truncation, we used the notion of asymmetry, since the BBH distribution is not obtained by truncating another distribution. Thus, we considered just three situations here: weak asymmetry, intermediate asymmetry, and strong asymmetry. Each situation gave rise to the simulation of 150 samples in the same way as the situations of Table 15.3, for a total of $3 \times 150 = 450$ samples simulated from a bivariate BBH distribution.

15.7.4 Data Simulation

The procedures followed to simulate the disaggregate data samples in both parts are described in this section.[15]

SIMULATING THE TBN DATA (FIRST PART)

For each column of Table 15.3, we considered a particular hypothesis for the parameter vector $\breve{\psi}' = [\breve{\mu}_B, \breve{\mu}_W, \breve{\sigma}_B^2, \breve{\sigma}_W^2, \breve{\rho}]$, as follows:

    a. *Weak truncation*: $\breve{\psi}' = [0.5, 0.5, 0.065, 0.065, \breve{\rho}]$
    b. *Strong truncation*: $\breve{\psi}' = [0.1, 0.9, 0.065, 0.065, \breve{\rho}]$
    c. *Intermediate truncation*: $\breve{\psi}' = [0.9, 0.5, 0.065, 0.065, \breve{\rho}]$.

And for each item above (or row of Table 15.3), we considered three alternative hypotheses of correlation:

    d. *Null correlation*: $\breve{\rho} = 0$
    e. *Positive correlation*: $\breve{\rho} = 0.5$
    f. *Negative correlation*: $\breve{\rho} = -0.5$.

---

of the ECM algorithm used to implement Mattos and Veiga's version of the BBH model and thus was readily available for tests and comparisons with the other methods within the experiment.

[15] In Chapter 16 of this book, some of the simulated data sets produced here were also used by Micah Altman, Jeff Gill, and Michael McDonald to examine issues related to numerical properties of EI algorithms.

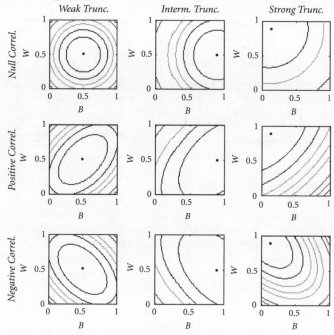

Figure 15.2. Contours of the generating TBN distributions.

Figure 15.2 shows, for each situation, the contours of the generating TBN distribution. As mentioned, these hypotheses set up situations well-behaved for the disaggregate DGP. Note that the mode of the TBN distribution (represented by the dark points) was always positioned inside the unit square, even in the situations of the strong truncation type. In addition, the variances were made small to allow a certain concentration of probability in some regions within the unit square.

We had also to generate the observations for the aggregate variables x_i and T_i. These variables were treated in different ways because x_i is taken as given in the TBN model, while T_i is assumed random. Thus, the variable x_i was generated only once for each sample size according to a uniform distribution defined on $[0, 1]$, but the variable T_i was generated 50 times for each sample size by applying the accounting identity 15.6 over the 50 simulated values of B_i and W_i and the single simulated value of x_i. Further details are presented in Appendix 1.[16]

SIMULATING THE BBH DATA (SECOND PART)

In the second part of the experiment we generated 450 samples from a bivariate binomial–beta distribution. As mentioned before, it is not possible to consider correlation in the disaggregate DGP according to the BBH model assumptions; thus, we only examined

---

[16] As described in Appendix 1, the simulations of the TBN random values were made under all the assumptions of King's TBN model, including those of "no aggregation bias" and "no spatial autocorrelation" in the disaggregate DGP. In general, since the simulated situations are relatively well behaved, this procedure also does not induce violations of those assumptions in the samples, even for the situations with high degree of truncation, correlation between the disaggregate proportions, and small number of observations. This is also the case for the BBH random values simulated in the second part of the experiment.

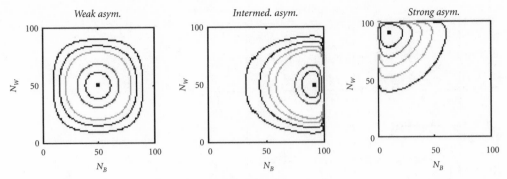

Figure 15.3. Contours of the generating BBH distributions.

differences in the degree of asymmetry. For each degree of asymmetry, we considered a specific hypothesis for the parameter vector $h' = [c_b, d_b, c_w, d_w]$, as follows:

a. *Symmetry*: $h' = [3, 3, 3, 3]$
b. *Strong asymmetry*: $h' = [1.32, 3.9, 3.9, 1.32]$
c. *Intermediate asymmetry*: $h' = [3.9, 1.32, 3, 3]$.

Figure 15.3 presents the contours associated to the generating distributions for the pairs (N_{B_i}, N_{W_i}), according to each of the above situations. These distributions correspond to the product of two binomial–beta distributions, say, $p(n_{B_i}, n_{W_i}) = p(n_{B_i})p(n_{W_i})$, this being the reason why the contours were drawn in the plane $N_{B_i} \times N_{W_i}$. Note that we tried here to recreate similar situations to those of the first part in the case without correlation by positioning the modes of the distributions (dark points) in similar places.

In an analogous fashion to the case of simulations from the TBN distribution, the data simulated from the BBH distribution in the form of frequencies had to be converted in proportions to be analyzed by the TBN method and also by the Goodman regression, where both assume the disaggregate data are in the form of proportions. Details of the procedures followed are described in Appendix 2.

15.7.5 Evaluation and Comparison Indicators

In the two parts of the experiment, the predictive properties of the EI methods were evaluated, and the methods compared, based on their average performance within each group of 50 simulated samples, as described in the previous sections. Four criteria (indicators) were considered, in view of the objectives of the study:

a. 10% coverage interval for the prediction errors (proportion of prediction errors lying within 10% of deviation from the true);
b. predictive bias (or mean of the prediction error);
c. standard deviation of the prediction error;
d. root mean square error of prediction.

The prediction error for the variable B_i is defined as $e_{B_i,m} = \hat{b}_{i,m} - b_{i,m}$, and for variable W_i as $e_{W_i,m} = \hat{w}_{i,m} - w_{i,m}$, where the variable with a hat is the prediction and the one without the hat is the true, simulated value. The index m refers to the mth simulated sequence, and the above statistics were first computed across all observations and then across all simulated sequences. See the formulas used in Appendix 3.

Item a was used for assessment of predictive performance, while items b, c, and d were used for the evaluation of conformity with standard statistical properties.

15.8 RESULTS

The results of the experiment are presented through of a number of graphs displayed in Figures 15.4–15.19. Figures 10.4–10.11 refer to the results for the first part of the experiment, and Figures 10.12–10.19 to the results for the second part.

15.8.1 First Part

We start by observing the predictive performance shown by the 10% coverage intervals (Figures 15.4 and 15.5). The Goodman regression did worse than all other methods in practically all situations. Under weak truncation, a tie is observed in the performance of the TBN method and the four BBH methods, for both variables. Moving to the situations with intermediate and strong truncations, the TBN method improves over the others. The degree of correlation seems not to affect, in general, the relative and absolute performance of any method. When we consider each level of truncation in isolation, differences in the degree of correlation tend to produce small effects.

Considering now the statistical properties, the first aspect to examine is the predictive bias presented by the methods (Figures 15.6 and 15.7). Under weak truncation, all six methods are practically unbiased, displaying bias levels between -0.015 and 0.015 for the small samples of 20 observations, and between -0.05 and 0.05 for the large samples with 100 observations. When we observe the corresponding standard deviations (Figures 15.8 and 15.9), we note

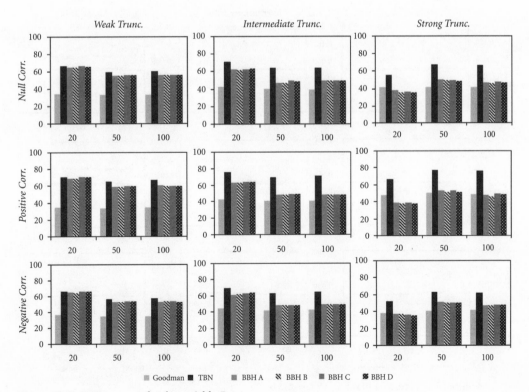

Figure 15.4. 10% coverage for the variable B.

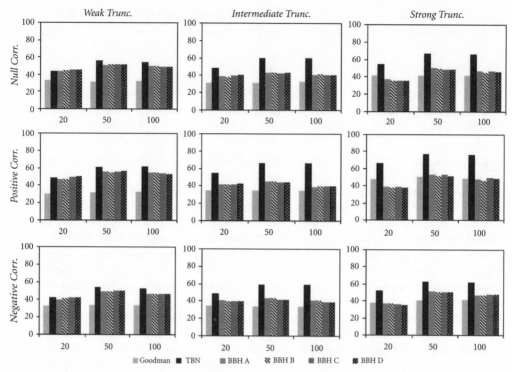

Figure 15.5. 10% coverage for the variable *W*.

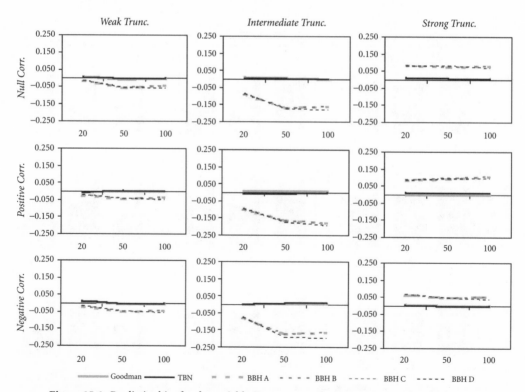

Figure 15.6. Predictive bias for the variable *B*.

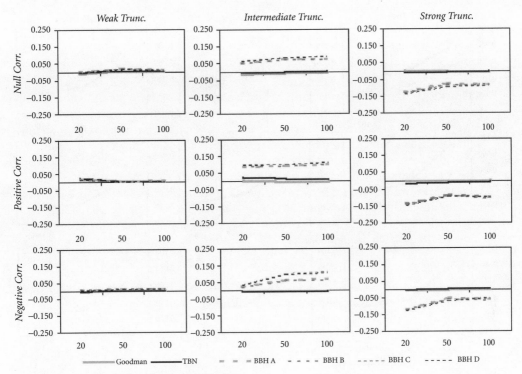

Figure 15.7. Predictive bias for the variable *W*.

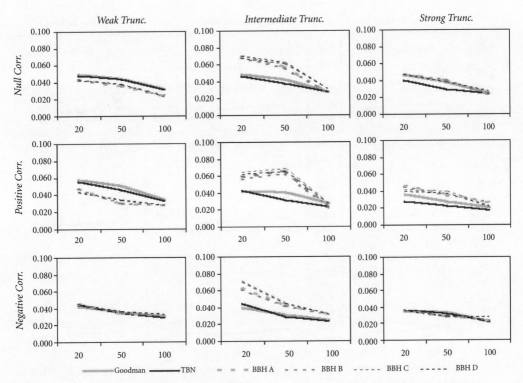

Figure 15.8. Standard deviation for the variable *B*.

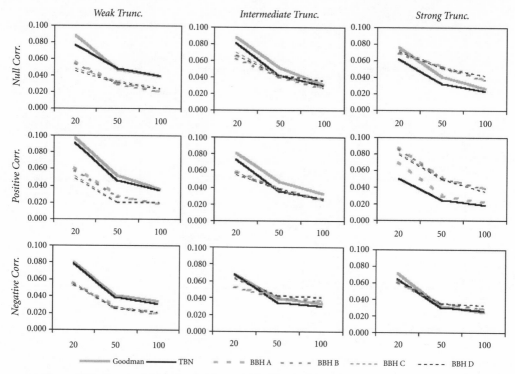

Figure 15.9. Standard deviation for the variable *W*.

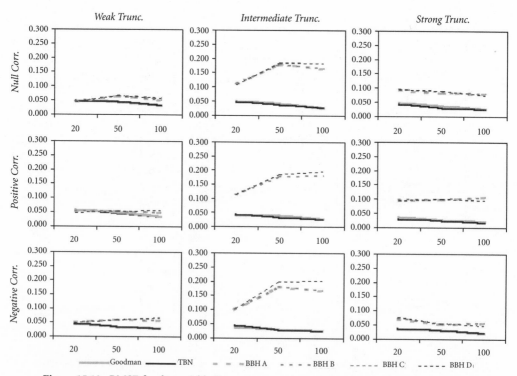

Figure 15.10. RMSE for the variable *B*.

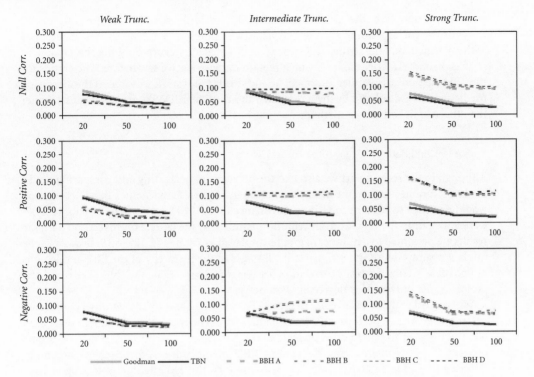

Figure 15.11. RMSE for the variable W.

these bias levels stay well below one standard deviation. However, moving to the situations of intermediate and strong truncation, the methods cluster in two groups: one composed of the Goodman regression and the TBN model, which remain unbiased in all situations; and another composed of all BBH methods, which begin to display predictive biases in a quite similar fashion. The biases of the latter methods do not seem to diminish with the increase in sample size, as we observe from the graphs of Figures 15.6 and 15.7. Though for small samples the biases of the BBH methods are less evident because the standard deviations in these cases are larger, for the larger samples they surpass two standard deviations in all cases of intermediate and strong truncation, for both variables.

Another aspect is the negative correlation between predictive biases for the variables B and W, displayed by each BBH method. For instance, considering the situations with intermediate truncation, for each BBH method its predictive bias for B is negative, while for W it is positive. This also happens in the situations with strong truncation, though in reverse order, with positive biases of each BBH method for B and negative ones for W.

The standard deviations of predictions of the various methods display similar behavior (Figures 15.8 and 15.9) in all situations and for both variables: they diminish gradually with the increase in sample size. Under weak truncation, the standard deviations of the BBH methods are clearly smaller, for the three sample sizes, than the standard deviations of the TBN method and the Goodman regression. When we augment the degree of truncation, there is a tendency to reverse this situation, with the methods presenting standard deviations much closer under strong truncation for both variables. Only in the case of strong truncation with positive correlation, also for both variables, do we note an effective reversal, with the Goodman regression and the BBH methods displaying smaller standard deviations.

The behavior of the RMSE (Figures 15.10 and 15.11) reflects the combined effects of predictive biases and standard deviations. As all methods appeared to be unbiased in the weak truncation case, the graphs of the RMSEs for both variables are quite similar to those of the corresponding standard deviations (Figures 15.8 and 15.9). Yet in the cases with intermediate and strong truncation, such behavior occurs only for the Goodman regression and the TBN method, which remain unbiased as we saw before. The graphs for the BBH methods, also under intermediate and strong truncation, now reflect the increasing predictive biases displayed by these methods, and thus their RMSEs are significantly higher than those of the other two methods.

15.8.2 Second Part

Although in the second part we also had the objective of evaluating and comparing the EI methods, another important motivation of ours was to verify whether the TBN method would continue to present superior performance to the BBH ones when the data samples were drawn from the generating distribution assumed by the latter. For this second part, the results are presented in a number of graphs displayed in Figures 15.12–15.19. Because of the implicit assumption of independence in all stages of the hierarchy of the BBH model, it is not possible to consider prior correlation between the disaggregate variables. The simulated samples differ only in their degree of asymmetry.[17]

With regard to the 10% coverage of errors (Figures 15.12 and 15.13), we observe the same pattern of predictive performance as in the first part. The method of Goodman regression was the worst in the three cases of asymmetry. Under weak asymmetry, a new tie occurs between the TBN method and the various BBH methods for both variables. Moving to the situations of intermediate and strong asymmetry, the TBN method gets progressively better, both in absolute and in relative terms, than the BBH methods. Some absolute decay in performance also happens here for the latter methods when we move from intermediate to strong asymmetry.

The patterns of the first part also repeat for the statistical properties. Under weak asymmetry, the predictive biases are practically null for all methods in both variables (Figures 15.14 and 15.15) and always correspond to less than one standard deviation (Figures 15.16 and 15.17). In the cases of intermediate and strong asymmetry, the Goodman regression and the TBN method remain unbiased, but now there are predictive biases for all the BBH methods. For the latter ones, their predictive biases in these cases are generally around two standard deviations, and in the case of strong asymmetry achieve more than five standard deviations for the samples with 100 observations of the variable B. There is also here a negative correlation between the predictive biases for the variables B and W, either for weak or for strong asymmetry.

The analysis of standard deviations (Figures 15.15 and 15.17) shows once again a similarity in behavior, for all situations and both variables. In the three cases of asymmetry, the standard deviations of all methods decrease along with the increase in sample size. Now, in the cases of weak and intermediate asymmetry, the four BBH methods display for the three sample sizes standard deviations similar to those of the Goodman regression and the TBN model. All methods practically tie in the case of strong asymmetry for both variables.

Finally, the analysis of the RMSE (Figures 15.18 and 15.19) indicates that, in the case of weak asymmetry, the behavior of all the methods reflects the respective behavior of standard deviations, because all are unbiased in this case. Under intermediate and strong asymmetry, the behavior repeats itself only for the Goodman regression and the TBN model, which

---

[17] Remember that, as explained before, the disaggregate data variables generated from the BBH distribution were converted to proportions for uniform comparison of the six methods.

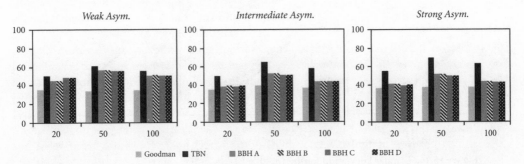

Figure 15.12. 10% coverage for the variable *B*.

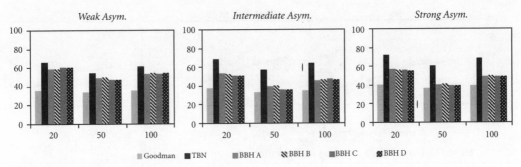

Figure 15.13. 10% coverage for the variable *W*.

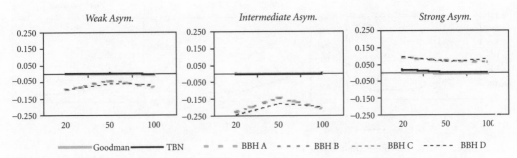

Figure 15.14. Predictive bias for the variable *B*.

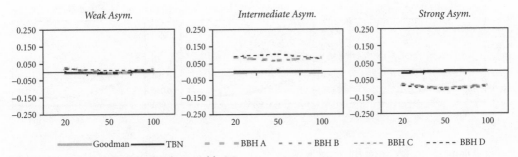

Figure 15.15. Predictive bias for the variable *W*.

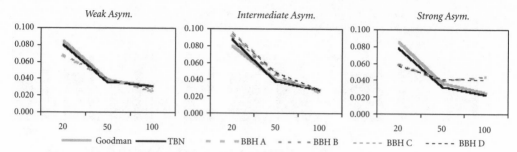

Figure 15.16. Standard deviation for the variable *B*.

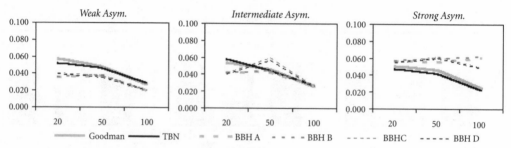

Figure 15.17. Standard deviation for the variable *W*.

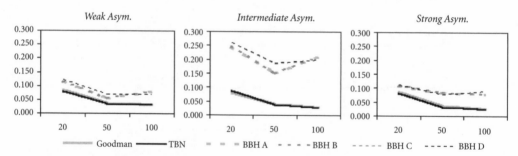

Figure 15.18. RMSE for the variable *B*.

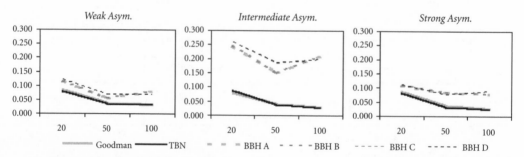

Figure 15.19. RMSE for the variable *W*.

remain unbiased. The graphs for the BBH methods also reflect here the predictive biases they displayed in these cases before.

15.8.3 Discussion

There are three important issues to highlight from the results just presented:

1. The Goodman regression showed the weakest predictive performance of the three methods, though it presented good statistical properties.
2. The BBH methods behaved quite similarly as a group, showing good predictive performance but poor statistical properties (predictive biases) when the degree of truncation or asymmetry in the disaggregate DGP is significant.
3. The TBN method displayed the best overall performance, both in predictive terms and in the statistical properties it presented.

Issue 1 reports a result expected because of the intrinsic limitations of the Goodman regression, long recognized in the literature. We shall however note that the Goodman regression did worst even in the well-behaved situations considered here, which points to the need for researchers to consider the alternative, more recent methods in applications. If we take this together with the best overall performance of King's TBN method in issue 3, additional support was provided by our experiment to the view that the latter is indeed a significant advance over the Goodman regression.

Issue 2 deserves careful consideration. Our experiment was of an exploratory nature, and its central merit lay in helping us to uncover properties of interest that characterize the EI methods studied. However, to go further and unveil reasons for particular features displayed by them, additional research may be necessary. With this in mind, we have two comments on issue 2: First, there is the similar performance of the four BBH methods. It suggests that their differences are of minor importance for explaining their predictive performance in relative terms. The type of weighting (equal or different weights attributed to aggregate observations) and the type of predictor (posterior mode for binomial probabilities or predictive distribution mean) did not appear to be relevant factors.

With regard to the type of weighting, this result was somewhat unexpected, since different sizes of the population across sampling units[18] should, in principle, induce significant differences in predictors' behavior. However, since the considered situations are well behaved, we cannot ignore the fact that practical situations displaying higher variations in sampling unit sizes come to produce significant differences in the performance of the BBH methods, in absolute terms and as compared to the TBN one. The same well-behaved situations used can also explain why the two types of predictors yielded a negligible difference in performance of the BBH methods.

Second, and maybe more important, there is the pattern of predictive bias shown by the BBH methods. Though these methods presented better predictive performance than the Goodman regression, they displayed a significant degree of predictive bias in the situations of intermediate and strong truncation or asymmetry. Because the expressions for generating predictions with this EI method have turned out to be intractable analytically (both for the posterior mode and for the mean of the predictive distribution), it is difficult to establish the true sources of this biased behavior. Note that this pattern of predictive bias of the BBH methods showed up even in the cases where the disaggregate data were generated according to a BBH distribution. In view of the recent debate about EI, this shows the important fact that

---

[18] Sizes varied between 50 and 450 in the experiment.

even when the assumptions fit an EI model, its derived EI predictor can displays undesirable statistical properties. This fact is not new in the general statistical literature, which displays a number of examples of estimators and predictors that fail to display desirable properties even when underlying assumptions for the probability DGP model being studied are true.

A factor which is likely, in our view, to be related to our two comments above and which therefore we consider worthy of further investigations is the BBH model feature that the number of parameters in the first hierarchical stage – the binomial probabilities – increases with the sample size P. Aside from the inherent limitation of the BBH model in incorporating correlation in the disaggregate DGP, that feature is its only difference in methodological construction from King's TBN model. A consequence it brings is the breakdown of results that guarantee consistency and asymptotic normality of the Bayesian posteriors 15.23 and 15.31, and also of the sampling distributions of the two types of BBH predictors considered. More, it limits the "borrowing of strength" process (King, 1997: 95–96) in ecological inferences at the precinct level, because for every new aggregate observation made available, another pair of model parameters needs to be inferred, which makes it difficult for common features of different precincts to be captured by the model. Anyway, further simulation experiments like the one we used here, particularly designed to examine this and other factors, should produce useful results.

To resume with issue 2, the fact that the four BBH methods displayed less than best performance is not to be overemphasized, because the basic motivation of KRT in developing the BBH model was to allow the analyst to catch within-precinct multimodality in marginal posteriors, rather than to provide a new method to generate point predictions. When the goal of an EI analysis is the former, Bayesian hierarchical models and other methods alike may in general be more appropriate than the less flexible, single-peaked approach of King's TBN method.

With regard to issue 3, the best overall performance of the TBN method is associated with its best predictive performance – both when its underlying distributional assumption is true (disaggregate DGP following a TBN distribution) and in the alternative case (disaggregate DGP following a bivariate BBH distribution) – as well as with its good statistical properties in all situations. However, we cannot identify the true sources of this best performance. For instance, it may indicate that the TBN distribution offers more flexibility of functional forms to fit the disaggregate data than the bivariate BBH distribution does. Almost surely, it is not a consequence of the particular ability of the TBN distribution to allow for correlation between proportions in the disaggregate DGP, because in the first part of the experiment it was the degree of truncation, not the degree of correlation, that induced differences of predictive performance between the TBN and the BBH methods. As another possibility, that best performance of the former may result from the pattern of predictive bias of the BBH methods discussed above. One should naturally expect it to induce poor predictive performance of the latter. Here also, the proper addressing of these issues deserves further study.

Another sort of issue, which we consider in brief, regards EI methodology in a broader sense. As is well known, the impossibility of observing the disaggregate data in real EI situations prevents the use of some forms of diagnostic checking to evaluate EI methods. Although King (1997) suggested diagnostic checking procedures to use in such cases, these seem to be of restricted applicability (Cho, 1998; Freedman et al., 1999). Effectively, researchers have dealt with this problem in the recent EI literature by using *test sets of disaggregate data* built from real or simulated data to make *ex ante* evaluations of the EI methods, say, prior to their use in real EI applications. However, some indirect evaluation of an EI method in a real EI analysis would be possible if the method allowed *aggregate residuals*, or differences between the aggregate observations and the fitted aggregate model (say, $T_i - \hat{T}_i \neq 0$ for some or all

$i = 1, \ldots, P$). These residuals could allow us to make residual analysis and to compute associated goodness of fit and test statistics, as used, for instance, in the context of standard linear regression methodology to assess model adequacy and compare different models. But EI methods that allow nonzero residuals, such as for instance Goodman regression and KRT's version of the BBH model, display the drawback of not respecting the accounting identity and thus are also not guaranteed to respect the Duncan–Davis bounds.

On the other hand, EI methods that satisfy the accounting identity display aggregation consistency and, as a consequence, do not produce aggregate residuals (say, $T_i - \hat{T}_i = 0$ for all $i = 1, \ldots, P$). In other words, when using this kind of method we have neither the disaggregate data nor the aggregate residuals for making diagnostic checks in real EI analyses. In these cases, the use of test data sets in evaluations of EI methods is unavoidable, but these sets allow such evaluations only on an *ex ante* basis. We argue here that the kind of experiment we have undertaken appears to be a suitable alternative for working with such test data sets. At least, it should be useful in conjunction with empirical data sets. Indeed, structured Monte Carlo experiments allow us to evaluate and compare EI methods in a controlled fashion and in accordance with the problem in hand, via exploring either the effects of different disaggregate DGPs or those of a number of different features of the same disaggregate DGP on the predictive properties of the EI methods being investigated. Therefore, Monte Carlo experiments should be seriously considered as an integral part of an EI methodology for aggregation-consistent EI methods.

15.9 CONCLUSION

We have presented a Monte Carlo experiment by means of which we compared the Goodman regression, the TBN, and the BBH methods for EI. The experiment was distinguished from similar ones used in other studies by the degree of structure of its design and by its concern with prediction instead of estimation. We made some assessment of the predictive ability of those EI methods by exploring their predictive performance as well as their conformity with standard properties of statistical prediction theory, in small and large samples. In the situations considered, the experiment pointed out as basic results that (1) Goodman regression is a limited method as compared to the more recent ones; (2) the BBH method is generally biased as a point predictor, except in cases where the degree of truncation and asymmetry in the disaggregate data is small; and (3) King's TBN method is the best among the three, doing well in predictive performance and conforming well with the statistical properties.

Based on those results, we also discussed technical issues that deserve further study, in particular the pattern of predictive bias of the BBH method. We also addressed an issue of foremost importance for EI methodology, which is the fact that EI models displaying the aggregation consistency property can only be evaluated and compared by means of test data sets. We stressed the importance in these cases of using simulated data sets produced with controlled simulation experiments of the kind we have undertaken. In addition to allowing some assessment of predictive performance, this is a valuable research tool to evaluate standard statistical properties (when analytic studies are impossible or difficult) using structured, detailed designs developed from underlying assumptions and intrinsic features of the investigated models.

For those methods which do not present the aggregation consistency property, a possibility is open for the development of model adequacy tests that are based on residual analysis and thus can be used in real EI studies. However, as these methods fail to respect the accounting identity, they are not guaranteed to satisfy the Duncan–Davis bounds. It therefore points out to a great challenge for future EI research: that of developing EI methods that satisfy the bounds and at the same time allow residual analysis, with the associated computations of model adequacy tests and goodness-of-fit statistics.

APPENDIX 1. SIMULATING FROM A TBN DISTRIBUTION

In order to simulate an observation point (B_i, W_i) from the truncated bivariate normal distribution, we followed the procedure used by King (1997), which consists in simulating from an untruncated bivariate normal distribution and accepting the point only if it lies in the closed unit square $A = [0, 1] \times [0, 1] \in R^2$. Let $(Z_{B_i}, Z_{W_i}) \sim BN(\breve{\mu}, \breve{\Sigma})$, with $\breve{\mu}$ and $\breve{\Sigma}$ defined as

$$
\breve{\mu} = \begin{bmatrix} \breve{\mu}_B \\ \breve{\mu}_W \end{bmatrix} \qquad \breve{\Sigma} = \begin{bmatrix} \breve{\sigma}_B^2 & \breve{\rho}\breve{\sigma}_B\breve{\sigma}_W \\ \breve{\rho}\breve{\sigma}_B\breve{\sigma}_W & \breve{\sigma}_W^2 \end{bmatrix},
\tag{15.32}
$$

and perform the following steps:

1. Simulate an observation pair $\tilde{z}_i' = (\tilde{z}_{B_i}, \tilde{z}_{W_i})$.
2. Compute $\tilde{v}_i = \breve{\Sigma}^{1/2} \tilde{z}_i + \breve{\mu}$, where $\tilde{v}_i' = (\tilde{b}_i, \tilde{w}_i)$.
3. Apply the rule: If $(\tilde{b}_i, \tilde{w}_i) \in A$, reject the observation; otherwise, accept it.
4. Repeat steps 1–3 until P pairs have been accepted.

To generate 50 samples with $P = 20$, we repeated steps 1–4 a total of 50 times; we did the same for the cases $P = 50$ and $P = 100$.

For the aggregate variables x_i and T_i, $i = 1, \ldots, P$, the procedures adopted were the following:

1. Each x_i was simulated only once from a uniform distribution defined in $(0, 1)$ for each $P = 20, 30$, and 50.
2. Each T_i was computed from the simulated $\tilde{x}_i$'s and $(\tilde{b}_i, \tilde{w}_i)$'s through the accounting identity $\tilde{t}_i = \tilde{b}_i \tilde{x}_i + \tilde{w}_i(1 - \tilde{x}_i)$; thus, 50 sequences of t_i's $(i = 1, \ldots, P)$ were simulated for $P = 20, 30$, and 50.

Conversion to Frequencies

For the data simulated as above to be analyzed by the BBHa and BBHb methods, it was necessary to make a conversion of the simulated proportions B_i, W_i, x_i, and T_i to frequencies, producing corresponding observations for the variables N_{B_i}, N_{W_i}, n_{x_i}, and N_{T_i}. Therefore, it was necessary first to choose values for the variable n_i, that represents the total population of the ith precinct considered by the BBH model. The procedures adopted were the following:

1. Let $\tilde{z}_i$ be a value simulated from a Unif(0, 1). The simulated value for n_i was obtained by making $\tilde{n}_i = a(400\tilde{z}_i + 50)$, where $a(\ )$ represents rounding towards the nearest integer. This was done only once for each value $P = 20, 50$, and 100. Note that we forced each $\tilde{n}_i$ to be simulated between the values 50 and 450, which gives a mean of 250. We kept above the minimum value in order to assure the asymptotic properties and to reduce distortions from the rounding process, and kept below the maximum value to avoid excessive computation time in the E stage of the ECM algorithm (see Mattos and Veiga, 2002).

2. Then compute, in the following order,

$$\tilde{n}_{X_i} = a(\tilde{x}_i \times \tilde{n}_i), \tag{15.33}$$

$$\tilde{n}_{B_i} = a(\tilde{b}_i \times \tilde{n}_{X_i}), \tag{15.34}$$

$$\tilde{n}_{W_i} = a(\tilde{w}_i(\tilde{n}_i - \tilde{n}_{X_i})), \tag{15.35}$$

$$\tilde{n}_{T_i} = \tilde{n}_{B_i} + \tilde{n}_{W_i} \tag{15.36}$$

for $i = 1, \ldots, P$.

Normalization

We must remember that the BBHc and BBHd methods normalize the raw data before estimation. Internally, the program routines used to implement these two methods execute a quite simple procedure: from a common scaling factor F, which can be defined by the user, the associated aggregate frequencies are computed as

$$\tilde{\tilde{n}}_{X_i} = a(F \times \tilde{x}_i), \tag{15.37}$$

$$\tilde{\tilde{n}}_{T_i} = a(F \times \tilde{t}_i) \tag{15.38}$$

and then used in place of the simulated raw data $\tilde{n}_{X_i}$ and $\tilde{n}_{T_i}$. We used $F = 250$ in the simulations.

APPENDIX 2. SIMULATING FROM A BIVARIATE BBH DISTRIBUTION

It was necessary first to simulate the aggregate variables n_i and n_{X_i}, which, because they are treated as given in the BBH model, were simulated only once for each sample size. By the simulation of two random variables Z_i and X_i from a Unif(0, 1), we computed

$$\tilde{n}_i = a(400\tilde{z}_i + 50), \tag{15.39}$$

$$\tilde{n}_{X_i} = a(\tilde{x}_i \times \tilde{n}_i). \tag{15.40}$$

The next step was the simulation of the pairs of disaggregate variables (N_{B_i}, N_{W_i}), $i = 1, \ldots, P$. As the BBH model assumes independence in all stages of the hierarchy, the observations for N_{B_i} were simulated independently from the observations for N_{W_i} to produce the pair (N_{B_i}, N_{W_i}). The procedure adopted followed Tanner (1996), and is as follows:

1. Given the parameters c_b and d_b (see Section 15.8.4), simulate an observation $\tilde{\beta}_i$ from a Beta(c_b, d_b).
2. Then use simulated value $\tilde{\beta}_i$ to simulate an observation N_{B_i} from a Bin($\tilde{n}_{X_i}, \tilde{\beta}_i$).
3. Repeat steps 1–2 until $i = P$.

The result of steps 1–2 is a pair $(\tilde{n}_{B_i}, \tilde{\beta}_i)$, since those steps are the process of generating observations from the joint density $p(n_{B_i}, \beta_i) = p(n_{B_i}|\beta_i) p(\beta_i)$. Note however that, taken individually, N_{B_i} follows the marginal distribution $p(n_{B_i})$, which is a binomial–beta distribution with parameters $\tilde{n}_{X_i}$, c_b, and d_b. The observations simulated for N_{W_i} were obtained independently but in analogous fashion through steps 1–3. The final results were samples of $\tilde{n}_{W_i}$ simulated from a marginal binomial-beta distribution with parameters $\tilde{n}_i - \tilde{n}_{X_i}$, c_w, and d_w. Finally, the other aggregate variable was generated by making $\tilde{n}_{T_i} = \tilde{n}_{B_i} + \tilde{n}_{W_i}$.

Conversion to Proportions

For the four BBH methods, the predictors in a strict sense are frequencies. For instance, $\hat{N}_{B_i}$ is the prediction generated by one of these methods for the true frequency N_{B_i}. For all the methods to be compared in the same way, say, using the same statistics of predictive performance, the predicted frequencies of the BBH methods, as well as the true frequencies simulated from the BBH distribution, were converted to proportions as follows:

$$\tilde{b}_i = \tilde{n}_{B_i}/\tilde{n}_{X_i}, \tag{15.41}$$

$$\hat{\tilde{b}}_i = \hat{\tilde{n}}_{B_i}/\tilde{n}_{X_i}, \tag{15.42}$$

$$\tilde{w}_i = \tilde{n}_{W_i}/(\tilde{n}_i - \tilde{n}_{X_i}), \tag{15.43}$$

$$\hat{\tilde{w}}_i = \hat{\tilde{n}}_{W_i}/(\tilde{n}_i - \tilde{n}_{X_i}). \tag{15.44}$$

Normalization

To normalize the data so that they could be used by the BBHc and BBHd methods, we did the following: (a) for x_i, we simply used their simulated values $\tilde{x}_i$ as described in the beginning of this appendix, and then applied Equation 15.37; (b) for t_i, we computed $\tilde{t}_i = \tilde{n}_{T_i}/\tilde{n}_i$ and then applied Equation 15.38.

APPENDIX 3

Suppose that m indexes the $M = 50$ samples of a situation group and that i indexes the P simulated observations per sample. Define, for the variable B,

$$\tilde{b}_m = \sum_{i=1}^{P} \tilde{b}_{i,m}/P, \tag{15.45}$$

$$\hat{\tilde{b}}_m = \sum_{i=1}^{P} \hat{\tilde{b}}_{i,m}/P, \tag{15.46}$$

$$\bar{\mu}_B = \sum_{m=1}^{M} \tilde{b}_m/M, \tag{15.47}$$

$$\hat{\bar{\mu}}_B = \sum_{m=1}^{M} \hat{\tilde{b}}_m/M, \tag{15.48}$$

where

$\tilde{b}_{i,m}$ = true disaggregate proportion in sample m,
$\hat{\tilde{b}}_{i,m}$ = prediction of the disaggregate proportion in sample m,
$\tilde{b}_m$ = mean of the disaggregate proportions in sample m,
$\hat{\tilde{b}}_m$ = mean of the predictions for disaggregate proportions in sample m,
$\bar{\mu}_B$ = global mean of the true disaggregate proportions,
$\hat{\bar{\mu}}_B$ = global mean of the predictions for the disaggregate proportions.

Furthermore, define the prediction error as $e_{B_i,m} = \hat{b}_{i,m} - b_{i,m}$ and the prediction error mean across observations as $e_{B,m} = \sum_{i=1}^{P} e_{B_i,m}/P = \hat{b}_m - \tilde{b}_m$. The statistics of predictive performance are then obtained by averaging across simulated sequences, as follows:

Prediction bias:

$$e_B = \sum_{m=1}^{M} e_{B,m}/M = \hat{\bar{\mu}}_B - \tilde{\mu}_B. \qquad (15.49)$$

Standard deviation of the prediction error:

$$DP(e_B) = \sqrt{\sum_{m=1}^{M}(e_{B,m} - e_B)^2/M}. \qquad (15.50)$$

Root mean square error:

$$RMSE_B = \sqrt{DP^2(e_B) + e_B^2}. \qquad (15.51)$$

10% coverage interval:

$$CI10_B = \sum_{m=1}^{M} CI10_{B,m}/M$$

$$= \sum_{m=1}^{M}\sum_{i=1}^{P} I(|\hat{\tilde{b}}_{i,m} - \tilde{b}_{i,m}| \le 0.1)/MP, \qquad (15.52)$$

where

$$I(|\hat{\tilde{b}}_{i,m} - \tilde{b}_{i,m}| \le 0.1) = \begin{cases} 1, & |\hat{\tilde{b}}_{i,m} - \tilde{b}_{i,m}| \le 0.1, \\ 0 & \text{otherwise.} \end{cases}$$

For the variable W, the formulas are analogous and can be obtained by replacing B with W and b with w.

REFERENCES

Achen, C. H. and W. P. Shively. 1995. *Cross-Level Inference*. Chicago: University of Chicago Press.

Anselin, L. and W. K. T. Cho. 2002. "Spatial Effects and Ecological Inference," *Political Analysis* 10, 3: 276–297.

Benoit, K. and G. King. 1996. "EzI: An Easy Program for Ecological Inference." Manuscript. http://gking.harvard.edu.

Benoit, K. and G. King. 1998. "EI: A Program for Ecological Inference." Manuscript. http://gking.harvard.edu.

Cho, W. K. T. 1998. "Iff the Assumption Fits...: A Comment on the King Ecological Inference Solution," *Political Analysis*, 7: 143–163.

Cho, W. K. T. 2001. "Latent Groups and Cross-Level Inferences," *Electoral Studies*, 20, 2: 243–263.

Cleave, N. 1992. "Ecological Inference." Ph.D. Dissertation. University of Liverpool.

Duncan, O. D. and B. Davis. 1953. "An Alternative to Ecological Correlation," *American Sociological Review*, 18: 665–666.

Freedman, D. A., S. P. Klein, M. P. Ostland, and M. R. Roberts. 1999. "A Solution to the Ecological Inference Problem. Book Review," *Journal of the American Statistical Association*, 93: 1518–1522.

Gelman, A., J. B. Carlin, H. S. Stern, and D. Rubin. 1995. *Bayesian Data Analysis*. New York: Chapman & Hall/CRC.

Goodman, L. 1953. "Ecological Regression and the Behavior of Individuals," *American Sociological Review*, 18, 663–664.

Goodman, L. 1959. "Some Alternatives to Ecological Correlation," *American Journal of Sociology*, 64, 610–625.

Herron, M. C. and K. W. Shotts 2003. "Using Ecological Inference Point Estimates in Second Stage Linear Regressions," *Political Analysis*, 11, 44–64.

King, G. 1997. *A Solution to the Ecological Inference Problem: Reconstructing Individual Behavior from Aggregate Data*. Princeton: Princeton University Press.

King, G. 2000. "Geography, Statistics, and Ecological Inference. Book Review Forum," *Annals of the Association of American Geographers*, 90, 3: 579–606.

King, G., O. Rosen, and M. A. Tanner. 1999. "Binomial–beta Hierarchical Models for Ecological Inference," *Sociological Methods and Research*, 28, 1: 61–90.

Mattos, R. and A. Veiga. 2002. "The Binomial–Beta Hierarchical Method for Ecological Inference: Methodological Issues and Fast Implementation via the ECM Algorithm." Manuscript. `http://web.polmeth.ufl.edu`.

McCue, K. F. 2001. "The Statistical Foundations of the EI Method," *The American Statistician*, 55, 2: 106–110.

Meng, X. L. and D. B. Rubin. 1993. "Maximum Likelihood Estimation via the ECM Algorithm: A General Framework," *Biometrika*, 80, 267–278.

Naylor, T. H., J. L. Balintfy, D. S. Burdick, and K. Chu. 1966. *Computer Simulation Techniques*. New York: Wiley.

O'Hagan, A. 1994. *Bayesian Inference. Kendall's Advanced Theory of Statistics*. New York: Wiley.

Rosen, O., W. Jiang, G. King, and M. A. Tanner, 2000. "Bayesian and Frequentist Inference for Ecological Inference: The $R \times C$ Case," *Statistica Neerlandica*, to appear.

Spanos, A. 1986. *Statistical Foundations of Econometric Modeling*. Cambridge, U.K.: Cambridge University Press.

Tanner, M. A. 1996. *Tools for Statistical Inference: Methods for the Exploration of Posterior Distributions and Likelihood Functions*, 3rd ed. New York: Springer.

Watson, H. J. and J. H. Blackstone, Jr. 1989. *Computer Simulation*, 2nd ed. New York: Wiley.

16 A Comparison of the Numerical Properties of EI Methods

Micah Altman, Jeff Gill, and Michael P. McDonald

ABSTRACT

The numerical accuracy of commonly used statistical software packages has been evaluated recently by a number of authors. A primary concern among them is that different embedded numerical methods produce vastly different solutions from the same data and model. In previous work we examined the sensitivity of King's EI procedure to implementation versions, computing platforms, random number generators, and optimization options. In this chapter, we extend that work with a comparison of the numerical properties of King's EI with other solutions to the EI problem. We analyze the performance of these separate approaches to the ecological inference problem, using data perturbation and comparative reliability assessment. The data perturbation technique is used to evaluate the pseudostability of these competing techniques across identical data sets. The results that we provide illuminate the trade-offs among correctness, complexity, and numerical sensitivity.

16.1 INTRODUCTION

The numerical accuracy of commonly used statistical software packages has been evaluated recently by a number of concerned authors (McCullough and Vinod, 1999; McCullough 1998, 1999a, 1999b; Altman and McDonald, 2001; Altman, Gill, and McDonald, 2003). The primary concern among these authors is that different embedded numerical methods actually produce vastly different solutions from the same data and model. Clearly this is alarming. Furthermore, there is great variation in the quality and thoroughness of programmers of statistical software and their sensitivity to purely statistical concerns (Knuth, 1997). Specific cases of incorrect analyses due to these problems have recently been documented in published research (Altman and McDonald, 2003), and others are sure to exist.

Methodologists in the social sciences are increasingly sophisticated in their use of statistical software. Elaborate models are now commonly programmed into advanced statistical packages. Such sophistication and power are not free; numerical issues remain important for ensuring high quality results, yet are often ignored. Just as worrisome, many models are becoming increasingly fragile, purely due to the complexity of the specification (Achen, 2003).

Among the most complex model specifications in the social sciences are those proposed as a solution to the *ecological inference problem*, inferences of individual behavior drawn from analysis of aggregate data. As described in the Introduction of this volume, until recently, the gold standard of statistical-based ecological inference solutions was a simple linear regression approach proposed by Goodman (1953). The numerical methods underpinning the regression algorithm are elementary, and although poor implementations of the algorithm still exist in some commercial software, it is generally understood how to implement it in a numerically accurate way. In contrast, recent solutions to the ecological inference problem are much more complex. Achen and Shively (1995), King (1997), and McCue (2001) in response to King, have proposed solutions to the ecological inference problem that purport to produce more accurate (and realistic) estimates of the true individual values, but with a considerable increase in algorithmic complexity.

King's method, in particular, has drawn wide attention. Although much of the attention has been positive, King's solution has been criticized by a number of authors (Tam Cho, 1998; Ferree, 1999; Freedman, Ostland, Roberts, and Klein, 1999; Herron and Shotts, 2003, 2004). Recently, McCue (2001) has argued that King's use of simulation and a constrained maximum likelihood algorithm are unnecessary.[1] McCue's less statistically complex model is still much more elaborate than Goodman's regression, respecting many of the same underlying assumptions as King.

Even though McCue (2001) argues for his proposed method primarily on computational grounds, he offers no direct evidence that his computational alternative for estimating the EI model is more accurate or reliable than the method he is attempting to displace. This is unfortunate but not unusual – in social science, computational issues tend to be mentioned in passing. For example, although the software that King distributes to compute his EI model contains many numerically sophisticated features, King devotes only two out of the nearly three hundred and fifty pages in his book to computational details (see King, 1997, Appendix F).

Whatever the final outcome of the controversy, attention paid to low-level computational details is ultimately productive. And, critiques notwithstanding, since a speedy resolution of the debate over ecological inferences does not seem forthcoming, it is therefore imperative to subject the contending methods to numerical testing.

As scholars in social science work more frequently with sophisticated statistical models, attention to computational details has begun to increase slightly. In this volume, three other authors address computational issues – focusing particularly on computational efficiency: Wakefield (Chapter 1) devotes a section to various strategies for efficiently computing multistage Bayesian approaches to ecological inference; Grofman and Merrill (Chapter 5) devote their attention to "quick and dirty" approaches to computing ecological inference more quickly (although admittedly with less statistical sophistication), and Mattos and Veiga (Chapter 15), as part of investigating the predictive correctness of alternative models, develop a fast alternative to MCMC methods for computing the beta–binomial hierarchical EI model.

Although we focus here on computation, we do not propose faster ways of computing EI models. Instead, we probe the numerical properties of the proposed solutions. In previous work (Altman, Gill, and McDonald, 2003: Chapter 7) we examined the sensitivity of King's EI procedure with respect to implementation versions, computing platforms, random number generators, and optimization options. In this chapter, we extend previous work with a comparison of the numerical properties of King's EI with other leading solutions to the EI problem. We analyze the performance of these separate approaches to "solving" the ecological inference problem through data perturbation and comparative reliability assessment. The data perturbation technique is used to evaluate the pseudostability of these competing techniques across identical data sets. The results that we provide illuminate the tradeoffs among correctness, complexity, and numerical sensitivity.

The chapter proceeds as follows: we describe potential sources of numerical inaccuracies within various proposed solutions, to the ecological inference problem, provide ways to

---

[1] McCue's method has garnered critiques of its own, most notably an exchange between McCue and Lewis (2002) in the letters-to-the-editor section of the *American Statistician*. Lewis defends King's derivation of the conditional probability $P(\beta^b \mid T)$ against McCue's earlier criticism. Nevertheless, it is noteworthy that Lewis does not criticize McCue's computational strategy itself. If Lewis's contested claim regarding the derivation of $P(\beta^b \mid T)$ is correct, King's EI method is bolstered, but McCue's alternative computational strategy is not invalidated.

test for the presence of such inaccuracies (not only in this context but in a broader context as well), perform tests, and describe ways to ameliorate the inaccuracies we identify. The primary purpose is to give an accurate picture of the extent to which numerical issues can affect substantive conclusions in ecological inference models.

16.2 SOURCES OF NUMERICAL INACCURACY IN ECOLOGICAL INFERENCE

Computational problems may affect any statistical program. For ecological inference solutions there are three potential areas of concern where computation may affect estimates of the ecological inference problem: floating point error, the choice of optimization algorithms, and imperfect random number generation. In this section we give a brief overview of these sources of error – for an extensive discussion, see Altman, Gill, and McDonald (2003: Chapter 2).

16.2.1 Floating Point Arithmetic

Most statistical programs, and all of the ecological inference techniques examined here, use floating point arithmetic. Numerical inaccuracies are introduced because statistical programs use a fixed number of bits to store binary numbers and to perform calculations with them. Accuracy is lost when numbers must be rounded to fit the limits of the binary representation, when calculations underflow because the result is too small a number to be represented, or when calculations overflow because the result is too large. When such numerical errors accumulate within complex calculations, the effect can be deadly to statistical computing procedures. Furthermore, different mathematically equivalent formulations of a problem may have quite different numerical implications.

16.2.2 Nonlinear Optimization

Estimating a solution for a regression, such as Goodman's approach, involves a straightforward series of closed-form calculations which may be found in any intermediate-level statistics book. Methods such as King's and McCue's, which rely on maximum likelihood algorithms, require completing a computationally more challenging task – finding the global optimum of a nonlinear function. In particular, King's programs use the Gauss implementation of a constrained maximum likelihood solver, cml, to fit the truncated bivariate normal onto the unit square and estimate the parameters of its solution, while McCue advocates an estimation process using unconstrained optimization, with the Duncan–Davis (1953) bounds built in. Both use forms of nonlinear optimization.

Standard techniques for the optimization of likelihood functions typically involve (1) choosing a set of starting values for the parameters of the model, (2) using the numerically calculated or analytic gradients of the likelihood function, given the current parameter values, to determine a direction for further optimization, (3) taking a step in that direction, and (4) updating the parameters accordingly. Steps 2, 3, and 4 are then repeated until the algorithm has converged to a stationary point, or some other stopping criterion (such as a limit on the number of iterations) is reached. Unless the likelihood surface is well behaved and unimodal, no efficient optimization algorithm is guaranteed to converge to a global optimum.[2] As one eminent set of practitioners in the field wrote, "Finding a global

---

[2] King speculates, but does not prove, that the likelihood mode for the Truncated Bivariate Normal (TBVN) distribution is globally unique (King, 1997: Appendix D). We further discuss techniques for the identification of global optima in Altman, Gill, and McDonald (2003).

extremum is, in general, a very difficult problem" (Press, Teukolsky, Vetterling, and Flannery, 2002: 398). Even in the absence of floating point inaccuracies, standard optimization algorithms generally converge to the closest local optimum. If this local optimum does not coincide with the global optimum, the resulting parameter estimates obtained will be incorrect.

In addition, floating point errors can affect nonlinear optimization, even for unimodal likelihood functions. Data that is ill-conditioned with respect to the EI optimization problem or implementations with numerical inaccuracies may inadvertently induce false optima. This, in turn, can lead to bad parameter estimates.

16.2.3 Pseudorandom Number Generation

Goodman's regression technique uses a deterministic algorithm (least squares) for finding a solution. McCue's method does not require random number generation, but since some maximum likelihood algorithms use randomly chosen starting values (model parameters), McCue's method may rely on random number generation. King's method, in addition, makes explicit use of random number generation, since it relies on Monte Carlo simulation to perform estimates of some of the parameters of interest.[3]

Such reliance on random numbers introduces another potential source of inaccuracy, since the random numbers provided by computer algorithms are never genuinely random. Instead, these numbers are produced by *pseudorandom number generators* (PRNGs), deterministic processes that create a sequence that is statistically similar, in limited respects, to random draws from a uniform distribution. Pseudorandom number generators start with a single *seed* value and generate a repeating sequence with a certain fixed length, or *period* (p). In order for simulation or sampling results to be accurate, a PRNG should satisfy three criteria: long period, independence, and consistency in distribution. In addition, all require a truly random seed to produce independent sequences (Ripley, 1987, 1988; Knuth, 1997; Gentle, 1999).

Random number generation is an important, but understudied, aspect of applied statistical computing, at least on the high end of statistical package evaluation. Some authors have shown the deleterious effects of poorly designed random number generation procedures (Gentle, 1999; Morgan, 1984). And we know from a vast foundational literature that serious problems can be caused by poorly written PRNG algorithms (see Altman, Gill, and McDonald, 2003: Chapters 2 and 5, for a review).

Fortunately, even King's solution, which makes more extensive use of random numbers than any other, is fairly light in that use. Moreover, previous research suggests that the choice of random number generators does not affect it (see Altman, Gill, and McDonald, 2003: Chapter 7).

16.3 ASSESSING THE NUMERICAL ACCURACY OF STATISTICAL ESTIMATES

In this section we define accuracy, stability, and conditioning and discuss how data perturbations can be used to probe for numerical problems.[4]

---

[3] King claims that some of these quantities are not available as closed-form solutions, and thus require simulation to compute.

[4] This section has been condensed and adapted from a much more detailed discussion. For an extensive treatment, including the mathematical details of perturbation effects, see Chapters 2, 3, and 4 of Altman, Gill, and McDonald (2003).

16.3.1 Defining Accuracy and Stability

Broadly defined, a statistical estimate is the mapping:

$$\{data,\ model,\ priors,\ inference\ method\} \Rightarrow \{estimates\},$$

or, symbolically

$$\{\mathbf{X},\ M,\ \pi,\ Im\} \Rightarrow e.$$

If, however, the estimate is too complex to calculate analytically using only "pencil and paper," we have to consider how computation may affect the results. In such a case, if the output from the computer is not necessarily equivalent to e, it can be inaccurate. Moreover, the output may be dependent upon the algorithm chosen to perform the estimation, the parameters given to that algorithm, the accuracy and correctness of the implementation of that algorithm, and implementation-specific parameters.[5]

Including these factors results in a more complex mapping:

$$\{\mathbf{X},\ M,\ \pi,\ Im,\ algorithm,\ algorithm\ parameters,\ implementation,\ implementation\ parameters\} \Rightarrow output.$$

The *accuracy* of the output actually presented to the user is thus the dissimilarity or distance (using a well-behaved measure) between estimates and output[6]:

$$accuracy = Distance = \nabla[e,\ output]. \tag{16.2}$$

Accuracy alone is often not enough to ensure correct inferences, because of the possibility of model misspecification, and the ubiquity of unmodeled measurement error in the data and of rounding error in implementations. Where noise is present in the data or its storage representation, and not explicitly modeled, correct inference requires the output to be *stable*.

Stability is simply the distance of the true estimate from output, in the presence of noise: $stability = \nabla\left(e,\ output'\right)$, where $output'|Y' \equiv Y + \Delta Y$. Note that instability could be due to sensitivity in the algorithm, implementation, or model – regardless, if there is any error in the data from any source, inferences will be incorrect if the output is not stable. (Less formally, a stable algorithm gives, to quote Higham, 2002, "almost the right answer to almost the same problem.")

16.3.2 Measuring Accuracy and Stability

Ideally, we could compute formal bounds on the accuracy and stability of every EI estimate. However, while such bounds are computable for individual computation in matrix algebra and for some simple functions, the complexity of the competing EI models makes analytic bound computation prohibitively difficult.[7]

---

[5] By "algorithm" we intend to encompass choices made in creating output that are not part of the statistical description of the model and that are independent of a particular computer program or language: This includes the choice of mathematical approximations for elements of the model (e.g., the use of Taylor series expansion to approximate a distribution) and the method used to find estimates (e.g., a nonlinear optimization algorithm). "Implementation" is meant to capture all remaining programming details, including bugs, and the implementation of data storage and arithmetic operations (e.g., using floating point double precision).

[6] Since "accurate" is often used loosely in other contexts, it is important to distinguish between computational accuracy, as above, and correct inference. A perfectly accurate computer program can still lead one to incorrect results if the model being estimated is misspecified.

[7] To our knowledge, no one has attempted to derive formal bounds for any procedure close in complexity to King's EI model. Empirical bounding techniques like interval arithmetic might still be applicable, but the resulting bounds are almost always uninformative.

So, what can one do to assess or ensure the accuracy and stability of one's estimation procedure when formal bounds are not known and cannot be determined? There are several general heuristics that can help to draw attention to potential computational problems:

1. **Test benchmark cases.** It is sometimes possible to devote extraordinary effort to computing correct estimates exactly (or to a known level of accuracy) for a particular set of test data and a particular model. This approach is useful, and should be a minimal requirement for any publicly distributed software, wherever feasible. However, it has several significant drawbacks. First, benchmarks are often infeasible for complex models, like EI.[8] Second, most feasible benchmarks are not very realistic. Third, benchmarks can detect some inaccuracies, but cannot prove that the program and algorithm yield accurate results outside of the data tested.

2. **Use independent information to confirm results.** Substantive plausibility, known analytic necessary conditions, and diagnostics (e.g. likelihood profile plots) should be used wherever possible. However, such additional information is rarely sufficient to confirm the accuracy of any given solution.

3. **Use sensitivity analysis.** One popular approach in statistical computation is to replicate the analysis, keeping the data and model the same, but using multiple different algorithms, algorithmic parameters (such as starting values), and implementations (e.g. different PRNGs and/or different optimization software). If results disagree, one should investigate (applying the other techniques) until one has determined the root cause of the difference and understands which set of results should be discarded. A second, complementary, approach is to replicate the analysis while perturbing the input data, and to observe the sensitivity of the estimates to such perturbations. (Sensitivity, or "pseudo-instability" is not a measure of true computational stability, since values for the correct estimates are unknown.) This has the advantage of drawing attention to results that cannot be supported confidently given the current data, model, and algorithm/implementation; and unlike the first method, it is easy to implement.

These approaches cannot be used to prove the accuracy of a particular method, but are useful in drawing attention to potential problems. Further experimentation and analysis may be necessary to determine the specific cause of the problem. For example, if two software packages disagree on the estimates for the same model and data, or if a particular technique exhibits instability across data perturbations, the discrepancy or instability could be a result of several factors:[9]

- **Implementation issues.** Either one or both programs have a bug, perform (some) calculations less accurately, or give results conditioned on different implementation-level parameters (e.g. a difference in a convergence tolerance setting).
- **Algorithmic issues.** One or both programs uses an algorithm with preconditions that are violated by the particular model and data. Each algorithm may afford different levels of approximation error. Or, the results are conditioned on different values for algorithm-specific parameters (e.g. starting values for local optimization algorithms).
- **Data and model issues.** The problem is ill-conditioned. The most general definition of conditioning is *the sensitivity of the model to perturbations of the data* (Higham, 2002:

---

[8] Even when the true precinct-level parameters are known, we cannot use these true values as the correct answers for our benchmarks, since correct application of an ecological inference model does not imply that the estimates equal the true parameters, even if accurately calculated.

[9] Note that the size and form of the noise are not what serve to differentiate numerical problems from model and data problems – even simple uniform noise at the level of machine roundoff can affect analyses, purely because of model and data problems. It is the combination of perturbations and varying implementations that allows one to gain some insight into the sources of sensitivity.

Sections 1.5–1.6). For example, if a scalar function f is twice differentiable, a useful way to define the relative condition number of f is $c(x) = |xf'/f(x)|$. (Note that conditioning is based on the purely mathematical properties of the function. A problem can be ill-conditioned even in the absence of any numerical inaccuracies.) Although ill-conditioning can easily exacerbate any numerical inaccuracies or limitations, social scientists should not assume that all computational inaccuracies are *simply* a matter of conditioning.[10] Moreover, the conditioning of the problem depends on the data, the model, the algorithm, and the form of perturbation. In other words, there is no such thing as data that is well-conditioned with respect to every model. Thus it is an open question how and whether one can actually determine if one's data is ill-conditioned with respect to an ecological inference model, without performing a sensitivity analysis.[11]

Combining the two methods of sensitivity analysis is often useful. By running multiple implementations and/or algorithms on the same sets of perturbed data, one can start to separate competing explanations for any instability. For example, if one implementation is more stable than another, the difference in pseudostability must be a result of the implementation and algorithm, since model and data are kept fixed.

Sensitivity analyses are invaluable because they can often be applied where benchmark tests and independent confirmation are unavailable or inconclusive, and can be applied to the actual data being analyzed. Sensitivity analysis cannot demonstrate that a particular set of results is correct or incorrect, nor can they be used to improve estimates of "correct" values. However, these analyses can serve to draw attention to potential problems in an algorithm, implementation, or model.

16.3.2.1 Using Data Perturbations for Sensitivity Analysis

The definition of stability above suggests an exploratory test for a given model, set of data, and implementation: introduce small random perturbations to the data, on the order of the measurement error of the instruments used to collect it, and recalculate the estimate. This technique is roughly analogous to bootstrapping. However, in bootstrapping the sample selection is randomly perturbed but individual observations are not, whereas in our strategy the sample selection is not perturbed but the individual observations are.

Data perturbations were first described as a sensitivity test by Beaton, Rubin, and Barone (1976, 1977), who developed a stability index based on it. Similar methods have been recommended by Gill, Murray, and Wright (1981), Pregibon (1981), and Cook (1986).[12]

To see how these perturbations affect the estimation process, consider two likelihood functions: a standard form based on the observed data $\ell(\theta, \mathbf{x})$, and an identical specification but with perturbed data $\ell_{\mathbf{p}}(\theta, \mathbf{x_p})$. Here $\mathbf{p}$ denotes an individual perturbation scheme $\mathbf{p} = [p_1, p_2, \ldots, p_n] \in \mathfrak{R}^n$ applied to the data $\mathbf{x} = [x_1, x_2, \ldots, x_n] \in \mathfrak{R}^n$. Thus we can show that comparing the two likelihood functions is analogous to comparing an unweighted

---

[10] In fact, a computation method with a large backward error will yield inaccurate results even where the problem itself is well-conditioned. Here the *backward error* is defined as the minimum $|\Delta x|$ for which our computation of y, $\bar{y}$ satisfies $\bar{y} = f(x + \Delta x)$.

[11] While it might appear tempting to use condition number estimators produced by standard statistical software (such as Matlab) to calculate condition numbers for a particular data set, the results are bound to be misleading, since the formulas used by these estimators are tailored to specific types of problems in linear algebra, such as matrix inversion. These formulae may be completely inappropriate for estimating the conditioning of another type of problem or computation procedure.

[12] Recent work by Parker, Pierce, and Eggert (2000) formalizes a variant of numerical perturbations, which they call "Monte Carlo arithmetic." Essentially, they replicate an analysis while introducing uniformly distributed perturbations (in the form of random rounding) into all values in all calculations.

likelihood function $\ell(\theta, \mathbf{x}) = \sum_i \ell_i(\theta, \mathbf{x}_i)$ with a weighted version $\ell_{\mathbf{p}}(\theta, \mathbf{x}_{\mathbf{p}}) = \sum_i p_i \ell_i(\theta, \mathbf{x}_i)$. Or we could define the unperturbed likelihood function to be one in which there are null perturbations or weights: $\ell_{\mathbf{p}_0}(\theta, \mathbf{x}_{\mathbf{p}_0}) = \sum_i p_{0i} \ell_i(\theta, \mathbf{x}_i)$, where $\mathbf{p}_0$ is simply a vector of 1's. This setup gives us two maximum likelihood vectors to compare: $\hat{\theta}$ and $\hat{\theta}_{\mathbf{p}}$.

In this context, our approach is to evaluate the range of $\hat{\theta}$ produced by multiple samples of $\mathbf{x}_{\mathbf{p}}$ generated by random production of $\mathbf{p}$ disturbances across different data sets $\mathbf{x}$. The idea builds upon the mechanical approach of Cook (1986), who looks for maximizing and minimizing perturbation, and roughly follows a simpler test of logistic regression given by Pregibon (1981).

Although this evaluation methodology does not require that the likelihood function be statistically well-behaved, it does have a natural interpretation for well-behaved maximum likelihood estimations. If the likelihood function for an MLE is well behaved, as King surmises for his model (see 1997: 310–311), then there is a simple mapping between perturbations of data and perturbations of the model. For example, small normally distributed noise added to the data should induce a correspondingly small mean shift in the likelihood curve (St. Laurent and Cook, 1993).

16.3.2.2 Perturbations and Measurement Error

Perturbations can be considered in exactly the same way as measurement error. The effects of measurement error on statistical models is quite well known and may take two forms: zero mean measurement error and nonzero mean measurement error. Nonzero mean measurement error obviously and immediately leads to biased coefficients in the opposite direction to the bias. That is, in a linear model, multiplying some nontrivial $\delta > 1$ in every case of explanatory variable $\mathbf{X}$ implies that larger increases in this variable are required to provide the same effect on the outcome variable, thus reducing the magnitude of the coefficient estimate. Another way of thinking about this is that a one-unit change in $\mathbf{X}$ now has a smaller expected change in $\mathbf{Y}$. This effect also occurs in generalized linear models, where there is the additional complexity of taking into account the implications of the link function.

It is possible to demonstrate that outcome variable measurement error is benign and explanatory variable measurement error is dangerous. Having discussed the modeling problems with measurement error, we would never advise intentionally including it. Instead, the perturbations act like unintended, but completely known, measurement error as a means of testing the behavior of estimators and algorithms. Models that react dramatically to modest levels of measurement error warrant caution.

In summary, perturbation may introduce bias, but if the problem is well-conditioned and the algorithm and implementation accurate, the bias should be small. Moreover, any bias introduced by perturbations should be the same when the same model and perturbed data are used in different implementations. So if two implementations of the same model show marked differences in pseudo-stability with respect to similar perturbation analyses, the root cause is asserted to be computational and not statistical.[13]

16.3.2.3 Some Practical Details of Applying the Perturbation Method

Using the core idea of random perturbation, we can assess whether results are reliable, whether they are consistent with respect to small perturbations in the data, and whether

---

[13] This approach is complementary to the one proposed by Judge, Miller, and Cho (Chapter 7 in this volume). Their approach uses instrumental variables, where available, to reduce the effects of measurement error. Our approach provides a diagnostic of the results' sensitivity to it.

other implementation factors affect the estimates. This methodology complements standard diagnostic plots in two ways. First, one can use the strictly numerical results as an unambiguous check: simply evaluate whether the range of results across input perturbations still fits the original substantive conclusions about the results. Second, this methodology may sometimes reveal numerical problems missed in standard diagnostic plots.

With regard to input perturbation, what is considered "small" for any particular case is a matter of subjective judgment. There is an obvious lower limit: perturbations of the data at the level below the precision of the machine should not be expected to cause meaningful changes in output. The upper limit on perturbations is less clear, but should be bounded by the accuracy of data measurement.

In political science and many other social sciences, measurement error certainly dominates machine precision as a source of input inaccuracy. For example, in macroeconomic data, much of the data is reported as rounded to the 1000's place. Introducing perturbations on the order of the rounding error of these data is tractable.[14]

Sometimes, as in our case, data is bounded, which introduces complications to perturbations. The simplest way of avoiding the bounding problem is to truncate any illegal value generated by perturbations to the constraint, but this introduces mass at the boundary points. To avoid this problem, we use resampling to draw sample perturbations from a set of truncated noise distribution, made symmetric to avoid biasing the data. A consequence of this is that observations closest to the [0,1] constraint are effectively subject to less noise. We report results using the second, more conservative method. As a check, we replicated our results with the first method; our substantive conclusions did not change.[15]

Choosing the number of perturbed data sets to generate is also something of an art. The literature does not specify a particular number of samples that is guaranteed to be sufficient for all cases. Parker (1997) and Parker, Pierce, and Eggert (2000) use as many as 100 and as few as four samples in their Monte Carlo arithmetic analysis. Parker (1997) also shows that (in all but pathological cases) the distribution of the means of coefficients calculated under random rounding are normal, which suggests that 30 to 50 samples should be adequate. Moreover, since the perturbation technique can be replicated indefinitely, one can simply rerun the analysis, increasing the number of samples, until the variance across replications is acceptable for the substantive problem at hand.

Care must be used to distinguish between differences among implementations of a particular algorithm and differences between algorithms used to compute the same quantity of interest. We expect that new versions of software will be made more accurate as implementations are improved and better algorithms found. Software writers have a responsibility not only to make improvements, but also to document the range of acceptable conditions for running their software and the accuracy that may be expected from it. Furthermore, as improvements are made, facilities should be provided to replicate the results from previous versions.[16]

---

[14] The form of the perturbation is usually either uniform noise, as in Beaton et al. (1976, 1977), Gill, Murray, and Wright (1981), and Parker et al. (2000), or normal, as in St. Laurent and Cook (1993). However, the proportional data used as the input to an EI analysis complicates the perturbation. Both types of perturbations can yield proportions outside of the legal [0,1] interval.

[15] In future research, it would be interesting to model the form of the measurement error according to the substantive data-generating process. For example, in a two-party race, it is possible that the primary source of error is miscounting individual ballots, and that each ballot has a small chance of being miscounted. Even if the probability of misclassification were the same for each ballot, the resulting measurement error would not necessarily be mean zero in terms of proportions: In a heavily partisan district, there would be more opportunities to misclassify votes from one party than from the other.

[16] King's EI software provides considerable built-in support for replication, diagnosis of statistical and computational problems, and different computational options. Such support is quite rare, and to be lauded. EI's reliance

16.4 A NUMERICAL COMPARISON OF ECOLOGICAL INFERENCE MODELS

This section provides a comparison of the performance of four methods of ecological inference: Goodman's regression, Achen and Shively's quadratic extension of Goodman's regression, King's solution, and McCue's approach, with regard to both their numerical accuracy
and how "correct" the estimates are – how close the answers they produce come to the truth
(when the true behavior of the social system being modeled is known). Again, note that
perturbing data introduces attenuation bias, so the estimates from perturbed data are not
expected to reproduce the truth. However, estimates far from the truth are an indication of
problems with numerical accuracy or data.

This section makes use of existing implementations of these proposed ecological inference
solutions. King (1997) distributes two software versions of his model: a Gauss program,
which King calls EI, and a standalone DOS version, which he calls EzI. McCue has not
released an official version of his model, but David James (directly provided, 2002) has made
available to us a Stata version that he coded in consultation with McCue, and that he calls
AnEI (for "Analytical EI").[17] Also, the analysis in this section will use implementations of
Goodman's regression routines supplied by both of these authors in their programs. For the
analysis reported here we use version 1.7 of EI running with cml version 2.0 and Gauss
version 4.0.26. For the McCue algorithm we use AnEI 4.0 running in Stata version 7.0.

Interest here is focused on the correctness of four methods in estimating ecological inference parameters, as well as their sensitivity to perturbation. In addition, particular attention
is paid to the often overlooked importance of analyzing performance with different software option settings that the authors provide, or that are a component of the underlying
programming language.

16.4.1 Goodman's Regression

Goodman (1953) proposed a simple linear regression solution to the ecological inference
problem, and simplicity is often a virtue with regard to numerical accuracy. Numerous
studies have shown that implementations of linear regression in most statistical packages
are more accurate than nonlinear models (McCullough and Vinod, 1999; McCullough,
1998, 1999a, 1999b; Altman and McDonald, 2001). Consequently, the expectation is that
Goodman's regression model will show the same robust behavior.

Goodman's regression is implemented by both King's and James's programs. Goodman's
regression serves as a consistency check for the estimation of the more complex models,
as well as a diagnostic for the presence of aggregation bias. In King's EI implementation,
Goodman's regression is estimated by executing a command within Gauss, while in EzI
it is estimated through a command given to the program through the user interface. In the
McCue–James software implementation, Goodman's regression is only estimated if the user
requests it *and* if AnEI successfully finds an ecological inference solution. AnEI sometimes
fails to produce such an estimate, and then the software subsequently relies only on the
Gauss estimates of Goodman's regression for reported results.

In addition, Achen and Shively recommend weighting Goodman's model when the units
of analysis, such as census blocks or voting precincts, are of different population sizes. We

---

on Gauss as a statistical environment sometimes interferes with replication, however, as changes across Gauss
versions cannot be controlled for in EI. Furthermore, although many computational options are provided in
EI, the accuracy of these options is not always well documented.

[17] According to McCue, the James method also corrects an error in McCue's linear estimator, such that the original
estimator can fall outside the interval [0,1].

constructed a weighted Goodman's model in R, using bootstrap replications to compute the standard errors.

16.4.2 Achen and Shively's Quadratic Model

Achen and Shively (1995) extend Goodman's regression using an explicitly modeled quadratic term. They demonstrate that this ameliorates the effects of aggregation bias. This model also permits either β_B or β_W (but not both simultaneously) to vary at the precinct level.

The model starts with the assumption that β_B and β_W are both linear functions of $\mathbf{X}$:

$$\begin{aligned} \beta_{Bi} &= b_1 + b_2\mathbf{X} + \epsilon_{Bi}, \\ \beta_{Wi} &= b_3 + b_4\mathbf{X} + \epsilon_{Wi}. \end{aligned} \tag{16.3}$$

Substituting these equations into the basic Goodman model yields a model which can be estimated through standard linear regression (OLS):

$$T = B_0 + B_1\mathbf{X} + B_2\mathbf{X}^2 + \epsilon,$$

where

$$\begin{aligned} B_0 &= b_3, \\ B_1 &= b_1 - b_3 + b_4, \\ B_2 &= b_2 - b_4. \end{aligned} \tag{16.4}$$

In this framework, Goodman's regression is a special case of the quadratic model when $b_2 = b_4 = 0$. However, the quadratic model requires additional assumptions to make it identified. B_0, B_1, and B_2 are known, while the parameters of interest, b_1, b_2, b_3, and b_4, are unknown. To extract the parameters of interest ($b_1, \ldots, b_4$), Achen and Shively propose the following steps:

1. Make assumptions to enable identification of the model. Achen and Shively assume that the relationships between β_B and β_W are positive, which implies $b_2 \geq 0$ and $b_4 \geq 0$. Under this assumption, they prove that aggregation bias of Goodman's regression is reduced using the following identification rule:

$$\begin{aligned} &\text{when } B_2 > 0, \text{ set } b_4 = 0; \\ &\text{when } B_2 < 0, \text{ set } b_2 = 0; \\ &\text{when } B_2 = 0, \text{ set both equal to zero.} \end{aligned} \tag{16.5}$$

This allows the calculation of the estimated parameters $\hat{b}_1, \ldots, \hat{b}_4$.
2. Estimate the precinct-level parameters $\tilde{\beta}_{Bi}$ and $\tilde{\beta}_{Wi}$, using $\hat{b}_1, \ldots, \hat{b}_4$ and Equation 16.3.
3. Compute the district-level parameters $\tilde{\beta}_B$ and $\tilde{\beta}_W$, using a weighted average of the precincts:

$$\begin{aligned} \tilde{\beta}_B &= \sum \tilde{\beta}_{Bi} N_i \mathbf{X}_i / N_B, \\ \tilde{\beta}_W &= \sum \tilde{\beta}_{Wi} N_i \mathbf{X}_i / N_W, \end{aligned}$$

where

$$N_B = \sum N_i \mathbf{X}_i, \qquad N_W = \sum N_i (1 - \mathbf{X}_i). \tag{16.6}$$

Achen and Shively do not specify a particular method for calculating the standard errors of the estimates. In our analysis, we report bootstrap standard errors for the weighted quadratic and weighted Goodman models.

Achen and Shively's assumption that $b_2 \geq 0$ and $b_4 \geq 0$ is based on empirical knowledge of the situation under study. If external information provides a basis for believing otherwise, the identification rules above should be changed.

Achen and Shively prove that with an uninformative prior, this assumption, plus the identification rules above, yields less expected bias than Goodman's regression. However, it is easy to show that assuming $b_2 \leq 0$ and $b_4 \leq 0$ and reversing the identification rules (e.g., when $B_2 > 0$, set $b_2 = 0$) yields exactly the same expected bias. Unfortunately, the two solutions do not yield (substantively) identical parameter estimates.

Because of this, and because the authors of the analyses which we replicate did not identify priors that would allow us to determine whether $b_2 \leq 0$, we assume an uninformative prior and report results under both sets of assumptions.

16.4.3 King's EI

Our intention is to choose, where possible, the set of options most favorable to running each program accurately. This involves adjusting options away from their defaults both within the EI program and in the Gauss statistical environment.

Our previous research showed the importance of using an accurate cumulative bivariate normal distribution. And, in our analysis, we used the most accurate option that EI provides, as described above. In addition, estimates where the final Hessian would not invert were discarded, as the use of the algorithm by EI alerts the user to take care in making inferences from the estimates. Finally, two options available to Gauss's CML algorithm are employed: a more numerically accurate method of calculating central derivatives, White's (1982) quasi-maximum-likelihood (QML) covariance matrix. (Note also that the documentation accompanying Gauss recommends this method as being more expensive, but uniformly better, than the alternative methods Gauss provides for computing the covariance matrix.)

CML offers a number of options for computing derivatives. The default method is to use forward differences, but the most accurate approach is for the user to supply subroutines to compute analytic derivatives (and Hessians). No analytic derivatives are known to exist for EI's likelihood function, and EI uses the default CML method. However, an intermediate option exists – *central* differences – and it is used here. This is more computationally expensive than the default, but is generally more accurate (see Gill et al., 1981, and Altman, Gill, and McDonald, 2003).

The analysis also uses the cml library's option to calculate QML covariances. White (1981, 1982) observes that when the variance–covariance matrix can be calculated in multiple ways, and the results differ, then it is an indication of serious model misspecification. White's test is related to that of Hausman (1978), but is free from some of its well-noted deficiencies (Kramer and Sonnberger, 1986; Thursby, 1985). The variance–covariance matrix can be calculated from either the expected or the observed Fisher's information matrix (with almost sure convergence, according to White's (1981) information matrix equivalence theorem), so a comparison of the two variance–covariance matrices has the potential to reveal misspecification resulting from computationally introduced problems, provided that the two methods *should* give the same answer in the absence of such problems (e.g., when one is computed with analytical derivatives and the other is computed with forward differences). The procedure defines a vectorized difference of the two matrices: $\nabla = \text{vec}(1/(-\mathbf{H}(\theta|y)) - 1/\mathbf{G}(\theta|y))$, but the test statistic is calculated from a subvector, ∇^*, selected so that its asymptotic covariance C^* is nonsingular: $W = \nabla^* C^* \nabla^*$. White gives the procedures for Wald and Lagrange tests based on the asymptotic χ^2 distribution of W with degrees of freedom equal to the rank of C^*. While this test has found its way into a number of computing packages and is recommended in Gauss, some authors criticize its utility on account of its selection of numerically unstable estimates for the subvector and associated covariance (Fahrmeir and Tutz, 2001; Andrews, 1988).

A second important implementation option is the choice of method for inverting a non-positive-definite Hessian. In these circumstances the program uses specialized methods to find a "close"[18] Hessian that is nonsingular and therefore invertible. The _EI_vc option controls how the EI program attempts a number of methods in sequence, and exits on the execution of the first successful method. As new versions of the program have been developed, new techniques have been devised to handle situations when the Hessian is not strictly positive definite. The sequence of methods applied when the normal method fails has also changed. In early versions of the EI, the first specialized method that the program will attempt is documented as a "wide step procedure" or "quadratic approximation with falloff" (King, 1997: 9). In later versions of EI, the program attempts a generalized inverse Cholesky alternative proposed in a paper by Gill and King (2003) and based on Schnabel and Eskow's (1990) procedure. These methods are not guaranteed to produce meaningful results in all cases; the researcher must exercise caution, since there is a paucity of theoretical and empirical work in favor of any particular method. One should also note that noninvertible Hessians may signal limitations in data or in numerical methods, and that the generalized inverse method used by King is justified in the former case. If the Hessian is noninvertible because, e.g., the likelihood function or derivatives are insufficiently accurate, a more orthodox, and well-studied, approach would be to increase the accuracy of those calculations, rather than trying to correct the Hessian at a later stage. In fact, in some of our replications we discovered that though EI produced noninvertible Hessians using the replication settings, the Hessian was invertible when the analysis was run again using a more accurate version of the cumulative bivariate normal distribution function.

A third implementation option is the choice of the cumulative bivariate normal distribution algorithm, which is an important factor in determining the shape of the likelihood function for the EI method. The shape of the likelihood function determines not only the location of the mode of posterior, but also the Hessian matrix, which is the curvature around this mode as measured by the second derivative of the likelihood function at the modal value. The importance of the Hessian matrix is that it produces, by inversion, the variance–covariance matrix of the coefficient estimate. King recognizes that this process is not always straightforward and provides options for users to choose six different methods of calculating the cumulative bivariate normal distribution with the _Ecdfbvn option, which we refer to as cdfbvn (from "cumulative density function, bivariate normal"). The original default cdfbvn is a fast algorithm, but subject to inaccuracies for small values, while the current default represents a tradeoff between accuracy and speed. King once recommended the use of the current default (King, 1997: 8), but he now provides a more accurate version.[19]

---

[18] Here the definition of "close" is that the diagonal of the Hessian matrix is changed as little as possible in order to obtain a barely invertible matrix form.

[19] The improvements to the cdfbvn function within EI were made following our earlier numerical accuracy investigations of the EI program. When we discussed these results with King, he convinced us that much of this sensitivity could be corrected by increasing the accuracy of the cumulative distribution function for the bivariate normal distribution. We consulted an expert in this area, Professor Allen Genz, who supplied us with

16.4.4 The McCue–James Approach

Ken McCue does not distribute a program to estimate the model he proposes in his 2001 *American Statistician* article, so instead this section uses an implementation of the program written for Stata by David James, who worked in consultation with McCue. McCue's model is similar to King's in that it stipulates a bivariate normal specification, but McCue claims that he can avoid the Bayesian-style simulations required in EI by using Lagrange multipliers to arrive at a generalized least squares problem instead of the more complicated posterior that King uses. The article actually leaves out some of the computational and technical details, but James's implementation seems to produce answers as advertised.

Unfortunately Stata does not allow users the same degree of option control as Gauss, but it does not require as much patience either. There is one option available in Stata's maximum likelihood algorithm that may affect numerical accuracy, the *difficult* option, which is only invoked by user request and is recommended for "difficult" likelihood problems. Stata's documentation of the difficult option is minimal. Similar to King's _EI_vc option, Stata's difficult option appears to allow the invocation of a different method to calculate the Hessian: "difficult states that there may be regions where −**H** is not invertible and that, in those regions, **ml**'s [Stata's maximum likelihood command] may not work well" (Stata Corporation, 1999: 385). More specifically, using difficult causes Stata to switch from Newton–Raphson to steepest descent when the Hessian (temporarily) cannot be inverted (Gould and Sribney, 1999).

In the experiments, however, the use of the difficult option did not improve the correctness or sensitivity of the solutions. In fact, it prevented convergence in a number of cases, without providing any noticeable change in the results of the analysis. Thus, in creating the tables, we used only the default options.

16.4.5 Observations and Evaluations: Sensitivity and Correctness

This section analyzes the correctness and pseudostability of these four methods for solving the ecological inference problem using both simulated and real data. These simulated data is drawn from eighteen variants of the truncated bivariate normal distribution – each with high, low, or moderate degrees or truncation; positive, zero, or negative correlations; and either 20 or 100 observations – as described in detail by Mattos and Vega (this book, Chapter 15).[20]

This real data is drawn from the seven example cases described in King's (1997) book (and above), as supplied in his replication archive. For each of the eighteen simulated and seven replication data sets, 50 replications are created with 1% normally distributed, mean zero error added to X_i and T_i.[21]

---

a quadruple-precision function based on an extension of Drezner and Wesolowsky (1989). After porting this function to Gauss and integrating it into King's program, we tested the areas of previous instability. These were greatly improved, although not eliminated. The more accurate function has now been incorporated into a new version of King's programs as an option. This approach to remove numerical inaccuracies may prove fruitful for sophisticated consumers of statistical software.

[20] Professors Mattos and Veiga provided this data set and nine additional, each with 50 observations each. We appreciate their support and willingness to share their data for this project and others.

[21] The experiment was repeated with an additional set of perturbations in the form of 5% uniformly distributed error with mean zero. Since the results are not substantially different, we prefer to make our points using the more modest perturbations. The number of replications chosen was based on practice in the literature (see above) and computational tractability – the computations for this study required 6 months of computer time at 1000 MIPS. Moreover, three additional replications using other forms of input perturbations (as above) did not yield substantially different results.

In the estimation of the perturbed data sets, the recommended option settings described above are used for each program. For King's `EI`, the recommended settings use QML covariance calculations and the most precise version of `cdfbvn`, and exclude those cases where `EI` finds a noninvertible Hessian. For McCue's `AnEI`, the default option setting proved to be the most useful. Also for Goodman's regression and Achen and Shively's extensions, the standard defaults are employed.[22]

Of interest are two characteristics of these perturbed data: the sensitivity and correctness of the resulting estimates. Sensitivity (or "pseudostability"), described above, refers to the consistency of the estimates across perturbed data sets, where less variation in the results is an indication of less sensitivity to error induced from measurement error or numerical errors found in the algorithm and implementation. Again one should be cautioned that these data perturbations are diagnostic tests, not classical statistical tests. As mentioned above, estimates of perturbed data may be sensitive to other aspects of the model, such as a broad and flat curvature around the MLE solution in the data space (in the multidimensional sense) or data that is ill-conditioned with respect to the estimation. There is no threshold for the degree of statistical significance to attach to the results we observe; however, caution is warranted when small amounts of measurement or numerical error substantially change the inferences drawn from a statistical model. As a rule of thumb, we recommend caution where the confidence intervals reported in the original estimates are much narrower than the simulated confidence intervals generated when the data is slightly perturbed.

Correctness in this context refers to the reproduction of true values: estimates closer to the truth are an indication of an internally valid estimation process. For the real data, all but one of King's examples, **NJ**, are based on aggregate data generated from individual data, so the estimates generated by these models can be compared with the truth. Unfortunately, even a numerically accurate solution is not guaranteed to produce correct answers (answers that match the truth), because the model itself could be misspecified. Furthermore, as discussed above, adding data perturbations introduces attenuation bias into the estimates. For these reasons, one should not expect a particular solution to provide a perfectly correct estimate, although it is important to gain insight into how perturbations affect the correctness of the answer. Particularly, since the same data is tested on all four methods, we should be interested in cases where different estimates are produced using these same data.

First, we present results based on simulated data. Figure 16.1 provides evidence of the comparative sensitivity of the Goodman, Achen–Shively, King, and McCue methods under different conditions: twelve variations of the number of observations, type of correlation, and degree of truncation. Here shorter bars are better, since they indicate sensitivity of the algorithm and software to data perturbations by presenting the standard deviation of the parameter across β^b fifty perturbation of simulated data.

Three major patterns are demonstrated by this analysis:

- In all four solutions, the sensitivity to perturbations decreases, holding other factors constant, as the number of observations in the original data set increases.
- The sensitivity to perturbations decreases with moderate data truncation. For `EI`, the decrease was even greater with strong truncation.

---

[22] Many additional configurations were investigated but are not presented here. For `AnEI`, all parts of the analysis were replicated using the `Stata` difficult option. For `EI`, the replicated analysis used the software defaults. In addition, the reanalyzed `EI` results includes corrected Hessians. Combined with variations of the perturbations (1% normal and 5% uniform, with and without resampling and adjustment for observations near the boundaries), there was an additional examination of 32 variations of Table 16.1. The table presented is based on the most conservative assumptions about noise, and uses the options most favorable to each software package. None of these variations produced results that were substantially different from those in Table 16.1.

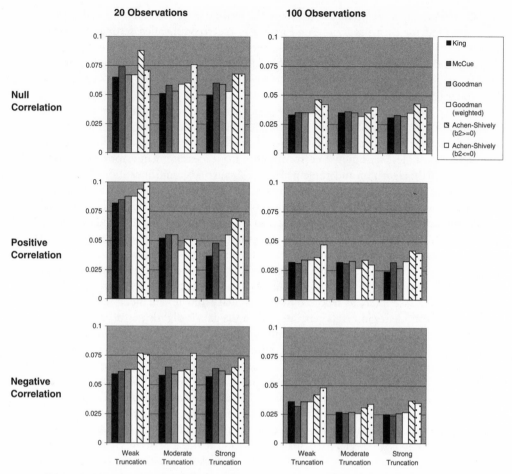

Figure 16.1. Comparing stability across EI solutions: relative stability (shorter is better) of the King, McCue, Goodman, weighted Goodman, and quadratic (Achen–Shively) Goodman methods. The height of the bars shows the standard deviation of the parameter β^b across fifty perturbations, on a scale of $[0, 0.1]$

- The sensitivity is worst, in all methods, when observations are few, truncation is weak, and X and T are positively correlated.

We find it reassuring that these findings follow the natural intuition that increasing the amount of information in the data improves the performance of the methods.

Although King's EI is internally the most complex algorithm, it is typically less sensitive to perturbations than Goodman's regression (and weighted Goodman's), Achen and Shively's quadratic model (and our extension of it), and McCue's simpler alternative when the number of observations is small. In cases with more observations, all four solutions show similar sensitivity to data perturbations, although EI tends to shows the least sensitivity when there is null correlation or when the degree of truncation is strong, AnEI tends to perform slightly better in the presence of negative and positive correlation and weak truncation, and weighted Goodman's shows the least sensitivity when there is moderate truncation.

Table 16.1 Comparison of Ecological Inference Solution Algorithms

King Example		Parameter	Weighted Goodman	Achen & Shively	Achen & Shively $b_2 \leq 0$	Truth
CENS1910	$(n = 50)$	β_i^b	0.5989 (.0023) [0.5936,0.06031]	0.5525 (0.0030) [0.5450,0.5594]	0.6559 (0.0024) [0.6508,0.6611]	0.734
		SE(β_i^b)	0.008567 (0.0021) [0.004276,0.01347]	0.01862 (0.0042) [0.01054,0.03051]	0.01153 (0.0023) [0.007458,0.01656]	–
		β_i^w	0.9663 (0.0019) [0.9625,0.9707]	0.9578 (0.0013) [0.9547,0.9613]	0.9148 (0.0011) [0.9125,0.9173]	0.9339
		SE(β_i^w)	0.004367 (0.0012) [0.002358,0.006656]	0.007552 (0.0018) [0.004352,0.01215]	0.005342 (0.0012) [0.002793,0.008270]	–
FULTON	$(n = 50)$	β_i^b	0.6836 (0.0029) [0.6765,0.6890]	0.5084 (0.0044) [0.4972,0.5156]	0.8051 (0.0041) [0.7974,0.8152]	0.530
		SE(β_i^b)	0.04327 (0.0091) [0.01611,0.06202]	0.07601 (0.018) [0.04335,0.1083]	0.06989 (0.0018) [0.06587,0.07380]	–
		β_i^w	−0.2244 (0.0060) [−0.239,−0.209]	0.1909 (0.010) [0.1732,0.2190]	−0.5089 (0.0093) [−0.5311,−0.4893]	0.06472
		SE(β_i^w)	0.1094 (0.021) [0.04772,0.1538]	0.1829 (0.042) [0.1056,0.2606]	0.1587 (0.0039) [0.1501,0.1675]	–
KYCK88	$(n = 50)$	β_i^b	0.07862 (0.067) [−0.08550,0.2034]	−0.4921 (0.19) [−1.430,−0.3530]	0.3217 (0.64) [−0.4460,2.114]	0.666
		SE(β_i^b)	0.4936 (0.083) [0.2898,0.6524]	0.9837 (0.67) [0.1315,3.90]	4.009 (1.4) [0.4814,6.757]	–
		β_i^w	0.7943 (0.0038) [0.7861,0.8034]	0.8577 (0.013) [0.8482,0.9207]	0.7995 (0.046) [0.6726,0.8521]	0.7533
		SE(β_i^w)	0.02053 (0.0041) [0.01290,0.02907]	0.06585 (0.044) [0.01080,0.2535]	0.2742 (0.096) [0.02979,0.4670]	–

(continued)

Table 16.1 (continued)

King Example		Parameter	Weighted Goodman	Achen & Shively	Achen & Shively $b_2 \leq 0$	Truth
LAVOTE	($n = 50$)	β_i^b	0.6262 (0.00048) [0.6252,0.6272]	0.6238 (0.00064) [0.6223,0.6251]	0.6315 (0.00068) [0.6301,0.6328]	0.6168
		SE(β_i^b)	0.004443 (0.0011) [0.002563,0.007148]	0.004696 (0.0011) [0.002503,0.006999]	0.004321 (0.0011) [0.002437,0.006746]	—
		β_i^w	0.7063 (0.00026) [0.7057,0.7069]	0.7125 (0.00024) [0.7120,0.7131]	0.7097 (0.00032) [0.7090,0.7104]	0.6842
		SE(β_i^w)	0.001717 (0.00038) [0.0008528,0.002666]	0.001971 (0.00055) [0.001133,0.003612]	0.001667 (0.00037) [0.0009344,0.002515]	—
MATPROII	($n = 50$)	β_i^b	0.3399 (0.0075) [0.3261,0.3570]	0.1464 (0.028) [0.08254,0.2243]	0.6860 (0.013) [0.6617,0.7141]	0.5847
		SE(β_i^b)	0.07670 (0.017) [0.04369,0.1134]	0.1827 (0.040) [0.1036,0.2655]	0.08726 (0.023) [0.03971,0.1453]	—
		β_i^w	0.8857 (0.0030) [0.8784,0.8917]	0.9744 (0.0081) [0.9513,0.9935]	0.8212 (0.0035) [0.8144,0.8281]	0.8242
		SE(β_i^w)	0.02579 (0.0055) [0.01319,0.03680]	0.05259 (0.011) [0.02990,0.07649]	0.02916 (0.0075) [0.01487,0.04804]	—
NJ	($n = 50$)	β_i^b	0.03915 (0.0048) [0.02865,0.05020]	−0.05729 (0.0047) [−0.0684,−0.0465]	0.2624 (0.0061) [0.2487,0.2729]	—
		SE(β_i^b)	0.02334 (0.0070) [0.01187,0.03812]	0.02949 (0.0068) [0.01319,0.04178]	0.06979 (0.015) [0.03524,0.1020]	—
		β_i^w	0.3848 (0.00084) [0.3829,0.3867]	0.4324 (0.00095) [0.4305,0.4342]	0.3582 (0.0014) [0.3556,0.3614]	—
		SE(β_i^w)	0.005125 (0.0012) [0.002470,0.008875]	0.006764 (0.0016) [0.003551,0.009718]	0.01405 (0.0031) [0.007209,0.02036]	—
SCSP	($n = 50$)	β_i^b	−0.3889 (0.0075) [−0.4050,−0.3750]	−0.01020 (0.027) [−0.1088,−0.9630]	0.7224 (0.026) [0.6703,0.7936]	0.1313
		SE(β_i^b)	0.03524 (0.0081) [0.01801,0.05568]	0.1884 (0.047) [0.09150,0.2918]	0.2034 (0.048) [0.1268,0.3275]	—
		β_i^w	0.6536 (0.0070) [0.6403,0.6685]	1.247 (0.025) [1.194,1.309]	−0.3582 (0.024) [−0.4240,−0.3100]	0.1732
		SE(β_i^w)	0.03312 (0.0075) [0.01787,0.05187]	0.1732 (0.043) [0.08461,0.2706]	0.1878 (0.044) [0.1166,0.3021]	—

King Example	Parameter	King EI(v1.7) (best settings, invertible Hessians)	McCue-James AnEI default settings	Goodman's Regression	Truth
CENS1910 (obs = 1040)	LL	2405 (12) [2378,2432] $n=50$	2404 (5.8) [2395,2412] $n=7$	—	—
	β_i^b	0.6396 (0.0018) [0.6359,0.6435] $n=50$	0.5742 (0.0022) [0.5708,0.5773] $n=7$	0.6125 (0.0011) [0.6099,0.6146] $n=50$	0.734
	SE(β_i^b)	0.003438 (0.00028) [0.002927,0.003973] $n=50$	0.1179 (0.0012) [0.1161,0.1198] $n=7$	0.006542 (0.000050) [0.006500,0.006600] $n=50$	—
	β_i^w	0.9494 (0.00094) [0.9476,0.9513] $n=50$	0.9502 (0.0013) [0.9485,0.9517] $n=7$	0.9347 (0.00062) [0.9335,0.9360] $n=50$	0.9339
	SE(β_i^w)	0.001426 (0.0012) [0.001200,0.001672] $n=50$	0.04542 (0.00044) [0.04457,0.04577] $n=7$	0.003786 (0.000035) [0.003700,0.003800] $n=50$	—
FULTON (obs = 289)	LL	586.5 (2.4) [582.0,592.9] $n=24$	726.0 (7.1) [712.3,741.7] $n=50$	—	—
	β_i^b	0.5724 (0.0012) [0.5703,0.5763] $n=24$	0.5482 (0.0031) [0.5407,0.5553] $n=50$	0.6725 (0.0024) [0.6674,0.6779] $n=50$	0.5530
	SE(β_i^b)	0.002129 (0.00017) [0.001800,0.002500] $n=24$	0.09725 (0.00096) [0.09463,0.09925] $n=50$	0.01179 (0.00014) [0.01143,0.01200] $n=50$	—
	β_i^w	0.03826 (0.0011) [0.03620,0.04030] $n=24$	0.06366 (0.0069) [0.05127,0.08259] $n=50$	−0.1947 (0.0050) [−0.2061, −0.1841] $n=50$	0.06472
	SE(β_i^w)	0.005033 (0.00042) [0.004300,0.006000] $n=24$	0.05230 (0.0034) [0.04678,0.06572] $n=50$	0.02437 (0.00029) [0.02380,0.02480] $n=50$	—
KYCK88 (obs = 118)	LL	214.0 (1.1) [211.8,216.8] $n=39$	216.5 (2.2) [213.4,219.5] $n=12$	—	—
	β_i^b	0.4152 (0.051) [0.3520,0.6333] $n=39$	0.3752 (0.088) [0.1291,0.4525] $n=12$	−0.4139 (0.045) [−0.5021, −0.2968] $n=50$	0.6660
	SE(β_i^b)	0.09954 (0.023) [0.06210,0.1828] $n=39$	0.1579 (0.023) [0.1381,0.2225] $n=12$	0.2056 (0.0049) [0.1928,0.2147] $n=50$	—
	β_i^w	0.7705 (0.0044) [0.7546,0.7783] $n=39$	0.8209 (0.0042) [0.8163,0.8324] $n=12$	0.8516 (0.0023) [0.8460,0.8552] $n=50$	0.7533
	SE(β_i^w)	0.007079 (0.0016) [0.004500,0.01340] $n=39$	0.1023 (0.0023) [0.09704,0.1055] $n=12$	0.01173 (0.00019) [0.01123,0.01200] $n=50$	—

(continued)

Table 16.1 (*continued*)

King Example	Parameter	King EI(v1.7) (best settings, invertible Hessians)	McCue-James AnEI default settings	Goodman's Regression	Truth
LAVOTE (obs = 3262)	LL	6784 (8.0) [6768,6799] $n = 50$	6913 (10) [6890,6931] $n = 50$	—	—
	β_i^b	0.6252 (0.00051) [0.6241,0.6263] $n = 50$	0.5627 (0.00048) [0.5618,0.5637] $n = 50$	0.6278 (0.00047) [0.6267,0.6288] $n = 50$	0.6168
	SE(β_i^b)	0.001120 (0.000078) [0.001000,0.001300] $n = 50$	0.2182 (0.00028) [0.2175,0.2187] $n = 50$	0.003386 (0.000035) [0.003300,0.003400] $n = 50$	—
	β_i^w	0.7067 (0.00026) [0.7060,0.7072] $n = 50$	0.7089 (0.00023) [0.7084,0.7094] $n = 50$	0.7111 (0.00023) [0.7107,0.7116] $n = 50$	0.6842
	SE(β_i^w)	0.0004020 (0.000025) [0.0003275,0.0005000] $n = 50$	0.07096 (0.00025) [0.07050,0.07163] $n = 50$	0.001794 (0.000024) [0.001700,0.001800] $n = 50$	—
MATPROII (obs = 268)	LL	407.2 (2.6) [399.4,411.2] $n = 41$	415.9 (2.5) [411.2,420.9] $n = 50$	—	—
	β_i^b	0.6143 (0.0068) [0.6006,0.6279] $n = 41$	0.5255 (0.0097) [0.5045,0.5432] $n = 50$	0.5152 (0.0046) [0.5061,0.5249] $n = 50$	0.5847
	SE(β_i^b)	0.03602 (0.0026) [0.02835,0.04000] $n = 41$	0.1947 (0.0030) [0.1891,0.2024] $n = 50$	0.04547 (0.00025) [0.04485,0.04597] $n = 50$	—
	β_i^w	0.8078 (0.0024) [0.8009,0.8139] $n = 41$	0.8565 (0.0032) [0.8508,0.8639] $n = 50$	0.8673 (0.0016) [0.8630,0.8703] $n = 50$	0.8242
	SE(β_i^w)	0.01022 (0.00078) [0.008040,0.01149] $n = 41$	0.1255 (0.0011) [0.1231,0.1277] $n = 50$	0.01787 (0.000097) [0.01760,0.01807] $n = 50$	—

		Col 1	Col 2	Col 3	Col 4
NJ (obs = 268)	LL	1038 (3.3) [1031,1045] n = 50	1097 (6.6) [1081,1111] n = 50	—	—
	β_i^b	0.06136 (0.0027) [0.05636,0.06890] n = 50	0.07508 (0.0035) [0.06686,0.08368] n = 50	0.02267 (0.0033) [0.01285,0.03015] n = 50	—
	SE(β_i^b)	0.006602 (0.00054) [0.005528,0.007718] n = 50	0.02542 (0.0086) [0.01250,0.05127] n = 50	0.02676 (0.00014) [0.02643,0.02707] n = 50	—
	β_i^w	0.3796 (0.001) [0.3778,0.3817] n = 50	0.4003 (0.0006) [0.3989,0.4015] n = 50	0.4150 (0.00065) [0.4139,0.4164] n = 50	—
	SE(β_i^w)	0.001528 (0.00013) [0.001300,0.001772] n = 50	0.07929 (0.0011) [0.07705,0.08105] n = 50	0.004850 (0.000051) [0.004800,0.004900] n = 50	—
SCSP (obs = 3185)	LL	5613 (1.2) [5612,5614] n = 2	5317 (9.5) [5295,5334] n = 50	—	—
	β_i^b	0.05720 (0.0074) [0.05200,0.06240] n = 2	0.1454 (0.00066) [0.1438,0.1469] n = 50	−0.1847 (0.0050) [−0.1942,−0.1722] n = 50	0.1313
	SE(β_i^b)	0.003050 (0.00092) [0.002400,0.003700] n = 2	0.1004 (0.0011) [0.09817,0.1029] n = 50	0.02486 (0.000097) [0.02470,0.02507] n = 50	—
	β_i^w	0.2429 (0.0069) [0.2380,0.2478] n = 2	0.1777 (0.00059) [0.1764,0.1789] n = 50	0.4838 (0.0046) [0.4725,0.4927] n = 50	0.1732
	SE(β_i^w)	0.002800 (0.00085) [0.002200,0.003400] n = 2	0.1693 (0.00087) [0.1672,0.1713] n = 50	0.02276 (0.000088) [0.02260,0.02290] n = 50	—

Counterintuitively, the most basic and simple algorithm, Goodman's regression, is not always the least sensitive to data perturbations. This is because Goodman's regression, unlike the more complex alternatives, is not constrained to fall within the unit interval. Out-of-bounds values cannot be produced by King's or McCue's method, and that explains, in part, the higher degree of sensitivity of Goodman's regression to data perturbations.

Achen and Shively's quadratic model is consistently the most sensitive to perturbations. This may simply be because Achen and Shively's approach is mathematically more sensitive to measurement error. Since **X** appears in the linear form of the regression in two places (and *squared* in the second), the effect of a perturbation to **X** is greater in Achen and Shively's quadratic model than in Goodman's regression, with a only single **X** term. Cheng and Van Ness (1999: Section 6.4) look at this phenomenon in detail in terms of a general polynomial form

$$\eta_i = \beta_0 + \beta_1 \xi + \beta_2 \xi^2 + \cdots + \beta_k \xi^k \qquad (16.7)$$

for $i = 1, \ldots, n$ cases. They find that the resulting regression error term is augmented by a component resulting from the polynomial specification.

We analyze each of the 50 separate perturbed data sets, based on the data provided by King (1997) using Goodman's regression, Achen and Shively's quadratic model, EI, and AnEI. The results are organized by the following cases: for the log likelihood, the coefficients β^w and β^b, and their associated standard errors. In every case where one of the three algorithms produced an estimate, the table lists the mean, standard deviation, and 95% range (2.5% and 97.5% quantiles) based on the observed standard deviation across the 50 runs. In addition, for comparison purposes, we report the "truth," available in all but the **NJ** example.

There are some notable patterns in the results. First, it is clear that some caution is warranted when employing the quadratic model. Generally, the quadratic model was more sensitive to perturbations in these examples (the variance of the estimates across perturbations is larger than for the other models), as it was with the simulated data. In addition, results from the quadratic model were often substantially different when one assumed $b_2 \leq 0$. Moreover, the quadratic model often was much farther from the true estimates than EI and never much closer.

Second, there are some similarities among the results. For one data set, **LAVOTE**, all models produce estimates of β^b and β^w that are close to one another and close to the "truth" (i.e., are less than 7 percentage points – 0.07 – from the latter). In addition, Goodman's regression (unweighted), EI, and AnEI produced mean estimates of β^b and β^w across the perturbed data sets close to one another and close to the "truth" for **NJ**[23] and **MATPROII**. For **CENS1910**, the three methods produced correct estimates for β^w, but all underestimated β^b by at least 10 percentage points (EI coming closest to the "truth"). For all of these examples, the three solutions also appeared to be relatively insensitive to perturbations. However, the standard errors of the estimates for AnEI were sometimes much larger than the other two models.

Third, EI performed quite well (when run with the best options, and after discarding the runs that resulted in noninvertible Hessians). Its estimates were close to the true values more often than any of the competitors', were sometimes much closer to them than the other models', and were never much farther away from them than the others.' In addition, the estimates were, for the most part, quite stable across the perturbations: the range of the

---

[23] For **NJ**, this data is not generated from individual data aggregated to pose on ecological inference problem, so the "truth" is not known for this one example.

perturbed estimates was small, and the standard deviation of the perturbed estimates was almost always considerably smaller than the originally estimated standard deviation.

Finally, there were some notable dissimilarities among the models, and some anomalies. For **FULTON**, **KYCK88**, and **SCSP**, Goodman's regression and its weighted variant produced incorrect estimates outside the $[0:1]$ unit square, and in addition produced more sensitive estimates than in the other four examples. (As King notes, such results suggest aggregation bias.)

Despite the aggregation bias in **FULTON**, the quadratic model, EI, and AnEI estimate β^b close to the "truth." However, the quadratic model produces estimates of β^w relatively far from the "truth." EI has difficulty arriving at a solution, finding an invertible Hessian only 23 of 50 times. AnEI reaches a solution for all 50 perturbed data sets, which were on average close to the "truth."

With **KYCK88**, King observes a ridge in the tomography plot for β^b, indicating that the likelihood surface is flat over a large region around the solution for this parameter. Our perturbation results highlight the lack of information in the data: For all four methods, estimates of β^b have large standard errors, are far from the "truth," and are sensitive to data perturbations. The sensitivity to perturbations for β^b, although large, is not worrisome, because it does not exceed the original confidence intervals: While the estimates are not good, the researcher would not have been misled.

In **KYCK88** EI produces an estimate of β^b that is closer to the "truth" than any other method. For β^w, both EI and AnEI come close to the "truth" – although EI is closer. In addition, EI finds invertible Hessians for 39 of 50 cases, and AnEI converges only 12 times, although the range of the β^b estimates is quite large.

With **SCSP**, Achen and Shively's quadratic model fails, producing estimates outside the legal bounds on using either form of the model. For these coefficients, the quadratic model shows considerably more sensitivity to data perturbations, and much larger standard errors than EI. AnEI produces good parameter estimates, but very large standard errors. EI encounters particular difficulties in inverting the Hessian, resorting to using the generalized inverse or generalized Cholesky method of inverting the Hessian for all but 2 of the 50 runs. (It is important to recall that it seemed more conservative to analyze only the runs where no warnings about Hessians were issued. This approach can lead to few final observations, as is the case here. We reanalyzed the data using the previously excluded 48 runs, but this did not substantially affect our conclusions.) The large number of warnings encountered during the perturbation runs signals that numerical issues have caused problems for EI – in King's original analysis, the results were much closer to the "truth."

16.5 CONCLUSION

Readers of this volume may be overwhelmed by the plethora of solutions proposed and the subsequent critiques of these approaches. We believe this is a sign that the field of ecological inference has moved into a new and dynamic phase of scientific progress. We have tried to exploit this situation by studying herein the various tradeoffs between complexity and accuracy. We noted most basically that when the problem is one of the easy forms, there is little to be lost in selecting between the approaches studied, as they produce similar examples, all close to the truth when it is known. When more challenging problems arise, Goodman's regression often produces invalid results outside the unit square. EI's basic constructs preclude such nonsensical results, but the necessary complexity of the method can lead to slightly more sensitivity in the underlying statistical computations. This is a basic tradeoff: sensitivity versus validity.

Using the recommended, most numerically accurate options may help improve the researcher's accuracy, but this is not a guarantee of success. King's repeated admonishments to users of his EI program should be well heeded. Users should carefully scrutinize all available diagnostic tools available to them, including common sense. To the diagnostic tests incorporated into the EI program, we herein suggest data perturbations as an additional diagnostic test: Numerical and data problems can be revealed by failure to converge across a large proportion of slightly perturbed data sets, or by variances of the estimated coefficients that substantially exceed the originally reported confidence intervals.

These results raise the question: is numerical accuracy for ecological inference related to the statistical problems? Estimated results may be more sensitive when the problem is ill conditioned, so that small changes in the data may result in relatively large changes in the shape of the likelihood function to be estimated. In this situation, data perturbations may provide another diagnostic test for the presence of aggregation bias or for other mismatches between the data and the statistical assumptions of the model. It is not a procedure recommended for initial data exploration, as the amount of time to conduct this suggested test increases linearly with the number of perturbed data sets – but it should be used before publication of results.

REFERENCES

Achen, Christopher H. 2002. "Toward a New Political Methodology: Microfoundations and ART," *Annual Review of Political Science*, 5: 423–50.

Achen, Christopher and Phillips Shively. 1995. *Cross-level Inference*, Chicago: University of Chicago Press.

Altman, Micah, Jeff Gill, and Michael P. McDonald. 2003. *Numerical Issues in Statistical Computing for the Social Scientist*. New York: Wiley.

Altman, Micah and Michael P. McDonald. 2001. "Choosing Reliable Statistical Software," *PS: Political Science and Politics*, XXXIV: 681–687.

Altman, Micah and Michael P. McDonald. 2003. "Replication with Attention to Numerical Accuracy," *Political Analysis*, 11: 302–307.

Andrews, D. W. K. 1988. "Chi-Square Diagnostic Tests for Econometric Models: Theory," *Econometrica* 56: 1419–1453.

Beaton, Albert E., Donald B. Rubin, and John L. Barone. 1976. "The Acceptability of Regression Solutions: Another Look at Computational Accuracy," *Journal of the American Statistical Association*, 71: 158–168.

Beaton, Albert E., Donald B. Rubin, and John L. Barone. 1977. "More on Computational Accuracy in Regression: Comment," *Journal of the American Statistical Association*, 72, 600–601.

Cheng, C., and J. W. Van Ness. 1999. *Statistical Regression with Measurement Error*. London: Arnold.

Cook, R. Dennis. 1986. "Assessment of Local Influence," *Journal of the Royal Statistical Society*, 48: 133–169.

Drezner, Z. and G. O. Wesolowsky. 1989. "On the Computation of the Bivariate Normal Integral," *Journal of Statistical Computation and Simulation*, 35: 101–107.

Duncan, Otis Dudley and Beverly Davis. 1953. "An Alternative to Ecological Correlation," *American Sociological Review*, 18: 665–166.

Fahrmeir, L. and G. Tutz. 2001. *Multivariate Statistical Modelling Based on Generalized Linear Models*, 2nd ed. New York: Springer-Verlag.

Ferree, Karen. 1999. "Iterative Approaches to $R \times C$ Ecological Inference Problems: Where They Can Go Wrong." Presented at Summer Methods Conference, College Station, TX. Available as http://polmeth.wustl.edu/papers/99/ferre99.pdf.

Freedman, D. A., M. Ostland, M. R. Roberts, and S. P. Klein. 1999. "Response to King's Comment," *Journal of the American Statistical Association*, 94: 355–357.

Gentle, J. E. 1999. *Random Number Generation and Monte Carlo Methods*. New York: Springer-Verlag.

Gill, Jeff and Gary King. 2003. "Inverting Hessians" in Altman, Micah, Jeff Gill, and Michael P. McDonald. 2003. Numerical Issues in Statistical Computing for the Social Scientist. New York: Wiley.

Gill, Phillip E., Walter Murray, and Margaret H. Wright. 1981. *Practical Optimization*. San Diego: Academic Press.

Goodman, Leo. 1953. "Ecological Regressions and the Behavior of Individuals," *American Sociological Review*, 18: 663–666.

Gould, W. and W. Sribney. 1999. *Maximum Likelihood Estimation with Stata*. College Station, TX: Stata Press.

Hausman, J. A. 1978. "Specification Tests in Econometrics," *Econometrica*, 46: 1251–1271.

Herron, M. C. and K. W. Shotts. 2004. "Testing for Logical Inconsistency in EI-based Second Stage Regressions," *American Journal of Political Science*, 48: 172–183.

Herron, M. C. and K. W. Shotts. 2003. "Using Ecological Inference Point Estimates As Dependent Variables in Second-Stage Linear Regressions," *Political Analysis*, 11, 1: 44–64. With a response from Adolph and King (pp. 65–76), a reply (pp. 77–86), and a summary by Adolph, King, Herron, and Shotts (pp. 86–94).

Higham, Nicholas J. 2002. *Accuracy and Stability of Numerical Algorithms*, 2nd ed. Philadelphia: SIAM.

King, Gary. 1997. *A Solution to the Ecological Inference Problem*. Princeton: Princeton University Press.

Knuth, Donald E. 1997. *The Art of Computer Programming*, 3rd ed. Reading, MA: Addison-Wesley.

Kramer, W. and H. Sonnberger. 1986. "Computational Pitfalls of the Hausman Test," *Journal of Economic Dynamics and Control*, 10: 163–165.

Lewis, J., followed by a reply by K. McCue, (2002). Comment on "The Statistical Foundations of the EI Method" and Reply (An exchange in the letter's to the editor section.) The American Statistician 56: 255–257.

McCue, Kenneth. 2001. "The Statistical Foundations of the 'EI' Method," *The American Statistician*, 55: 106–111.

McCullough, B. D. 1998. "Assessing the Reliability of Statistical Software: Part I," *The American Statistician*, 53: 149–159.

McCullough, B. D. 1999a. "Econometric Software Reliability: Eviews, LIMDEP, SHAZAM, and TSP," *Journal of Applied Econometrics*, 14: 191–202.

McCullough, B. D. 1999b. "Assessing the Reliability of Statistical Software: Part II," *The American Statistician*, 53: 149–159.

McCullough, B. D. and H. Vinod. 1999. "The Numerical Reliability of Econometric Software," *Journal of Economic Literature*, 37: 633–665.

Morgan, Byron J. T. 1984. *Elements of Simulation*. New York: Chapman & Hall.

Parker, D. Stott. 1997. "Monte Carlo Arithmetic: Exploiting Randomness in Floating-Point Arithmetic." Technical Report CSD-970002. Computer Science Dept., UCLA. http://www.cs.ucla.edu/ stott/mca/.

Parker, D. Stott, Brad Pierce, and Paul R. Eggert. 2000. "Monte Carlo Arithmetic," *Computing in Science and Engineering*, July, 58–68.

Pregibon, D. 1981. "Logistic Regression Diagnostics." *Annals of Statistics*, 9: 705–724.

Press, William H., Saul A. Teukolsky, William T. Vetterling, and Brian P. Flannery. 2002. *Numerical Recipes in C++: The Art of Scientific Computing*, 2nd ed. Cambridge, U.K.: Cambridge University Press.

Ripley, Brian D. 1987. *Stochastic Simulation*. New York: Wiley.

Ripley, Brian D. 1988. "Uses and Abuses of Statistical Simulation," *Mathematical Programming*, 42: 53–68.

Schnabel, Robert B. and Elizabeth Eskow. 1990. "A New Modified Cholesky Factorization," *SIAM Journal of Scientific Statistical Computing*, 11: 1136–1158.

Stata Corporation, 1999. *Stata Statistical Software Release 6.0*. College Station, TX: Stata Corporation.

St. Laurent, R. T. and R. D. Cook. 1993. Leverage, Local Influence and Curvature in Nonlinear Regression. Biometrika 80: 99–106.

Tam Cho, Wendy K. 1998. "Iff the Assumption Fits . . . : A Comment on the King Ecological Inference Model," *Political Analysis*, 7: 143–164.

Thursby, Jerry G. 1985. "The Relationship among the Specification Tests of Hausman, Ramsey, and Chow." *Journal of the American Statistical Association*, 80: 926–928.

White, Halbert. 1981. "Consequences and Detection of Misspecified Nonlinear Regression Models." *Journal of the American Statistical Association*, 76: 419–433.

White, Halbert. 1982. "Maximum Likelihood Estimation of Misspecified Models." *Econometrica*, 50: 1–26.

Index